INTERNATIONAL POLITICAL ECONOMY

PERSPECTIVES ON GLOBAL POWER AND WEALTH

INTERNATIONAL POLITICAL ECONOMY

PERSPECTIVES ON GLOBAL POWER AND WEALTH

SECOND EDITION

Jeffry A. Frieden
University of California, Los Angeles

David A. Lake
University of California, Los Angeles

St. Martin's Press New York

Senior Editor: Don Reisman
Project Management: Barbara Bert / North 7 Atelier Ltd
Copyeditor: Cheryl Kupper
Production Supervisor: Kathy Battiste
Cover Design: Suzanne Bennett

Library of Congress Catalog Card No.: 89-63897

54321

fedcb

For information, write to:
St. Martin's Press, Inc.
175 Fifth Avenue
New York, NY 10010

ISBN: 0-312-03718-X

PREFACE

This second edition of *International Political Economy: Perspectives on Global Power and Wealth* maintains the general structure of the first edition but sharpens the theoretical discussions and updates the readings. As in the first edition, three broad theoretical perspectives are represented, and both the readings and the editorial introductions reflect recent theoretical advances. Most of the substantive articles in the current volume are recent—almost all were originally published after 1985. This means both that they discuss recent events in the world's political economy and that they incorporate recent scholarship The readings were revised and expanded with a fully international audience in mind. Finally, the current-events section has been expanded to encompass a broader range of issues, to meet the interests of a more international audience.

The readings provided here are intended primarily to introduce the study of International Political Economy to those with little or no prior knowledge of the subject. The book is designed for use in courses in International Political Economy, International Relations, and International Economics. The selections present both clear and identifiable theoretical arguments and important substantive material.

Although the thirty-one selections can be used in any order, they are grouped in four parts that reflect some of the more common organizing principles used in International Political Economy courses. Each part begins with an introduction by the editors which provides background information and highlights issues raised in the readings. Each reading is preceded by an abstract summarizing its specific arguments and contributions. The readings have been edited to eliminate extraneous or dated information, and most footnotes have been removed. The introduction defines the study of International Political Economy, summarizes the three major theoretical perspectives on the field, and identifies several current debates. Part I then presents examples of the three perspectives on International Political Economy: Liberalism, Marxism, and Realism. The three readings in this part are intended to suggest the underlying logic and types of arguments used by proponents of each approach. Although they represent their respective schools, they do not necessarily capture the wide range of opinion within each approach.

Part II, which reviews the history of the international economy since the seventeenth century, provides the background and perspective necessary to understand the contemporary international political economy. The selections describe major developments in the history of the modern international economy from a variety of different theoretical viewpoints. The post-1945 international political economy is surveyed in Part III, the longest section of the book. Following an overview of the contemporary era, the readings in Part III are organized into three subsections on production, money and finance, and trade. Finally, Part IV examines current problems in the politics of international economics. The selections in this volume have been used successfully in our respective versions of Political Science 124, International Political Economy, at the University of California, Los Angeles. In our own research, we approach the study of International Political Economy from very different perspectives. Yet we find that this set of readings accommodates our individual approaches to the subject matter while simultaneously covering the major questions of the field. The students of Political Science 124 experimented with several versions of this text as it was being "fine-tuned." David Dollar, of the University of California, Los Angeles, Department of Economics, made helpful suggestions on the editors' introductions, as did Ronald A. Francisco and several anonymous reviewers.

Don Reisman and Heidi Schmidt of St. Martin's Press helped us shepherd the second edition through the publication process. We would also like to acknowledge Mark Brawley, Scott Bruckner, Carlos Juarez, Javier Maldonado, Nora Monk, and Cynthia Tournat, who assisted in the editing of the first and second editions. We also want to thank the following reviewers who supplied us with the useful information to help guide our revisions of this second edition: Robert A. Blecker, Pedro A. Caban, John Conybeare, Richard Flaskamp, Ole R. Holsti, Barry B. Hughes, Victor T. LeVine, Ufo I. Okeke, Bob Mandel, Eduardo M. Ochoa, Sven Steinmo, David Skidmore, Joel P. Wolfe, and Chen-shen J. Yen.

Finally, we want to thank our respective spouses, Anabela Costa and Wendy K. Lake, for their encouragement.

JEFFRY A. FRIEDEN
DAVID A. LAKE

CONTENTS

Introduction

INTERNATIONAL POLITICS AND INTERNATIONAL ECONOMICS

Over the past twenty years, the study of International Political Economy has gone through a remarkable resurgence. Virtually nonexistent before 1970 as a field of study, International Political Economy is now one of the most popular areas of specialization for both undergraduates and graduate students, as well as the source of some of the most innovative and influential work by modern social scientists. The revival of International Political Economy after nearly forty years of dormancy has enriched both social science and public debate, and promises to continue to do both.

International Political Economy is the study of the interplay of economics and politics in the world arena. In the most general sense, the *economy* can be defined as the system of producing, distributing, and using wealth; *politics* is the set of institutions and rules by which social and economic interactions are governed. *Political economy* has a variety of meanings. For some, it refers primarily to the study of the political basis of economic actions, the ways in which government policies affect market operations. For others, the principal preoccupation is the economic basis of political action, the ways in which economic forces mold government policies. The two focuses are in a sense complementary, for politics and markets are in a constant state of mutual interaction.

It should come as no surprise to inhabitants of capitalist societies that markets exist and are governed by certain fundamental laws that operate more or less independently of the will of firms and individuals. Any shopkeeper knows that an attempt to raise the price of a readily available and standardized product—a daily newspaper, for example—above that charged by nearby and competing shopkeepers will very rapidly cause customers to stop buying newspapers at the higher price. Unless the shopkeeper wants to be left with stacks of unsold newspapers, he or she will have to bring the price back into line with "what the market will bear." The shopkeeper will have learned a microcosmic lesson in what economists call the market-clearing equilibrium point, the price at which the number of goods supplied equals the number demanded or the point at which supply and demand curves intersect. At the base of all modern economics is the general assertion that, within certain carefully specified parameters, markets operate in and of themselves to maintain balance between supply and demand. Other things being equal, if the supply of a good increases far beyond the demand for it, the good's price will be driven down until demand rises to meet supply, supply falls to meet demand, and the market-clearing equilibrium is restored. By the same token, if demand exceeds supply, the good's price will rise, thus causing demand to decline and supply to increase until the two are in balance.

If the international and domestic economies functioned like perfectly competitive markets, they would be relatively easy to describe and comprehend. Fortunately or unfortunately, however, the freely functioning market is only a highly stylized or abstract picture that is rarely reproduced in the real world. A variety of factors influence the workings of domestic and international markets in ways that a focus on purely economic forces does not fully capture. Consumer tastes can change—how large is the American market for spats or sarsaparilla today?—as can the technology needed to make products more cheaply, or even to make entirely new goods that displace others (stick shifts for horsewhips, calculators for slide rules). Producers, sellers, or buyers of goods can band together to try to raise or lower prices unilaterally, as OPEC did with petroleum in 1974 and 1979. And governments can act, consciously or inadvertently, to alter patterns of consumption, supply, demand, prices, and virtually all other economic variables.

It is this last fact, political "interference" with economic trends, that is the most visible, and probably the most important, reason to go beyond market-based, purely economic explanations of social behavior. Indeed, many market-oriented economists are continually surprised by the ability of governments—or of powerful groups pressuring governments—to contravene economic tendencies. When OPEC first raised oil prices in December 1973, some market-minded pundits, and even a few naive economists, predicted that such naked manipulation of the forces of supply and demand could last only a matter of months. What has emerged from the past twenty years' experience with oil prices is that they are a function of both market forces and the ability of OPEC's member states to organize concerted intervention in the oil market. Somewhat less dramatic are the everyday operations of local and national governments that affect prices, production, profits, wages, and almost all other aspects of the economy. Wage, price, and rent controls; taxation; incentives and subsidies; tariffs; government spending—all serve to mold modern economies and the functioning of markets themselves. Who could understand the suburbanization of the United States after World War II without taking into account government tax incentives to home-mortgage holders, government-financed highway construction, politically driven patterns of local educational expenditures? How many American (or Japanese or European) farmers would be left if agricultural subsidies were eliminated? How many Americans would have college educations were it not for public universities and government scholarships? Who could explain the proliferation of nonprofit groups in the United States without knowing the tax incentives given to charitable donations?

In these instances, and many more, political pressure groups, politicians, and government bureaucrats have at least as much effect on economic outcomes as do the fundamental laws of the marketplace. Social scientists, especially political scientists, have spent decades trying to understand how these political pressures interact to produce government policy. Many of the results provide as elegant and stylized a view of politics as the economics profession has developed of markets; as in economics, however, social science models of political behavior are little more than didactic devices whose accuracy depends on a wide variety of unpredictable factors, including underlying economic trends. If only a foolish economist would dismiss the possibilities of intergovernmental producers' cartels (such as OPEC) out of hand, only a foolish political scientist would not realize that the economic realities of modern international commodity markets ensure that successful producers' cartels will be few and far between.

It is thus no surprise that political economy is far from new. Indeed, until a century ago, virtually all thinkers concerned with understanding human society wrote about political economy. For individuals as diverse as Adam Smith, John Stuart Mill, and Karl Marx, the economy was eminently political and politics was obviously tied to economic phenomena. Few scholars before 1900 would have taken seriously any attempt to describe and analyze politics and economics separately.

In the last years of the nineteenth century and the first years of the twentieth century, however, professional studies of economics and politics became more and more divorced from one another. Economic investigation began to focus on understanding more fully the operation of specific markets and their interaction; the development of new mathematical techniques permitted the formalization of, for example, laws of supply and demand. By the time of World War I, an economics profession per se was in existence, and its attention focused on understanding the operation of economic activities in and of themselves. At the same time, other scholars were looking increasingly at the political realm in isolation from the economy. The rise of modern representative political institutions, mass political parties, more politically informed populations, and modern bureaucracies all seemed to justify the study of politics as an activity that had a logic of its own.

With the exception of a few isolated individuals and an upsurge of interest during the politically and economically troubled Depression years, the twentieth century saw an increasing separation of the study of economics and politics. Economists developed ever more elaborate and sophisticated models of how economies work; similarly, other social scientists spun out ever more complex theories of political development and activity.

The resurgence of Political Economy since 1970 has had two interrelated sources. The first was dissatisfaction among academics with the gap between abstract models of political and economic behavior on the one hand, and the actual behavior of politics and economies on the other. As theory became more ethereal, it also seemed to become less realistic. Many scholars began to question the intellectual justifications for a strict analytical division between politics and economics. Second, as the stability and prosperity of the first twenty-five postwar years started to disintegrate in the early 1970s, economic issues became politicized, and political systems became increasingly preoccupied with economic affairs. In August 1971, Richard Nixon ended the gold-dollar standard that had formed the basis for postwar monetary relations; two-and-a-half years later, a previously little-known group, the Organization of Petroleum Exporting Countries (OPEC), succeeded in substantially raising the price of oil. In 1974 and 1975, the industrial nations of Western Europe, North America, and Japan fell into the first worldwide economic recession since the 1930s; unemployment and inflation were soon widespread realities and explosive political issues. In the world arena, the underdeveloped countries—most of them recently independent—burst onto center stage as the Third World, demanding a fairer division of global wealth and power. If in the 1950s and 1960s economic growth was taken for granted while politics occupied itself with other matters, in the 1970s and 1980s economic stagnation fed political strife while political conflict exacerbated economic uncertainty.

For both intellectual and practical reasons, then, social scientists began seeking, once more, to understand how politics and economics interact in modern society. As interest in political economy grew, a series of fundamental questions were posed, and a broad variety of contending approaches arose.

To be sure, today's political economists have not simply reproduced the studies of earlier (and perhaps neglected) generations of political economists. The professionalization of both Economics and Political Science led to major advances in both fields, and scholars now understand both economic and political phenomena far better than they did a generation ago. It is on this improved basis that the new political economy is being constructed, albeit with some long-standing issues in mind.

Just as in the real world, where politicians must pay close attention to economic trends and economic actors must keep track of political tendencies, those who would understand the political process must take the economy into account and vice versa. A much richer picture of social processes emerges from an integrated understanding of both political and economic affairs than from the isolated study of politics and economics as separate realms.

This much is by now hardly controversial; it is in application that disagreements arise. Government actions may color economic trends, but government actions themselves may simply reflect the pressures of economic interest groups. Economic interest groups may be central in determining government policy, yet the political system—democratic or totalitarian, two-party or multiparty, parliamentary or presidential—may crucially color the outlooks and influence of economic interests. In the attempt to arrive at an integrated view of how politics and economics interact, we must disentangle economic and political causes and effects. In this effort, different scholars have different approaches, with different implications for the resulting view of the world.

THREE PERSPECTIVES ON INTERNATIONAL POLITICAL ECONOMY

Nearly all studies in International Political Economy can be classified into one of three mutually exclusive perspectives: Liberalism, Marxism, and Realism. Each of the three perspectives has a unique set of simplifying assumptions used to render the world less complex and more readily understandable. Assumptions are assertions accepted as true for purposes of further investigations. The value of an assumption lies in the ability of the theory built upon it to explain observed phenomena. Thus, assumptions are neither true nor false, only useful or not useful.

The assumptions upon which each of these three perspectives is based lead international political economists to view the world in very different ways. Many Liberals regard foreign direct investment in less developed countries, for instance, as a mutually rewarding exchange between entrepreneurs. Many Marxists, on the other hand, see the foreign firm as exploiting the less developed country. Consequently, a first step in studying International Political Economy is to understand the assumptions made by each of the three perspectives.

Liberalism

The Liberal perspective is drawn primarily from the field of economics and can be traced to the writings of Adam Smith (1723-1790) and David Ricardo (1772-1823). Smith and Ricardo were reacting to the pervasive economic controls that existed under mercantilism between the sixteenth and nineteenth centuries. In this period, the domestic and international economies were tightly regulated by governments in order to expand national power and wealth. Smith, Ricardo, and their followers argued that the philosophy underlying this practice was mistaken. Rather, these Liberals asserted that national wealth was best increased by allowing free and unrestricted exchange among individuals in both the domestic and international economies. As their ideas gained adherents in the early nineteenth century, many of the mercantilist trade restrictions were dismantled (see Kindleberger, Reading 4).

Smith and the nineteenth-century Liberals were the economic reformers of their era. In International Political Economy, advocates of free trade and free markets are still referred to as Liberals. In twentieth-century American domestic politics, on the other hand, the term has come to mean just the opposite. In the United States today, "Conservatives" generally support free markets and less government intervention, while "Liberals" advocate greater governmental intervention in the market to stimulate growth and mitigate inequalities. These contradictory uses of the term "Liberal" may seem confusing, but in the readings below and elsewhere, the context usually makes the author's meaning clear.

Three assumptions are central to the Liberal perspective. First, Liberals assume that individuals are the principal actors within the political economy and the proper unit of analysis. While this may seem obvious, as all social activity can ultimately be traced back to individuals, this first assumption gains its importance by comparison with Marxism and Realism, each of which makes alternative assumptions (see below).

Second, Liberals assume that individuals are rational, utility-maximizing actors. Rational action means that individuals make cost-benefit calculations across a wide range of possible options. Actors are utility maximizers, when, given a calculated range of benefits, they choose the option which yields the highest level of subjective satisfaction. This does not imply that individuals actually gain from every utility-maximizing choice. In some circumstances, utility maximization implies that the individual will choose the option that makes him or her least worse off.

Third, Liberals assume that individuals maximize utility by making trade-offs between goods. Consider the trade-off between clothing and jewelry. At high levels of clothing and low levels of jewelry some individuals—depending upon their desires for these two goods—might be willing to trade some of their wearing apparel for more jewelry. Likewise, if an individual possesses a great deal of jewelry but little clothing, he or she might be willing to trade jewelry for apparel. Individuals thus increase their utility, according to Liberals, by exchanging goods with others. Those who desire jewelry more strongly than clothing will trade the latter for the former. Others who prefer clothing over jewelry will trade jewelry for apparel. This process of exchange will occur until each individual, given the existing quantities of jewelry and clothing, is as well off as possible without making someone else worse off. At this point, all individuals in society will have maximized their uniquely defined utilities. Some will possess jewelry but no clothing. Others will possess only clothing. The vast majority of us, on the other hand, will possess varying mixes of both.

The Liberal argument has traditionally been applied primarily to the economy, in which it implies that there is no basis for conflict in the marketplace. Because market exchanges are voluntary, and if there are no impediments to trade among individuals, Liberals reason, everyone can be made as well off as possible given existing stocks of goods and services. All participants in the market, in other words, will be at their highest possible level of utility. Neo-classical economists, who are generally Liberals, believe firmly in the superiority of the market as the allocator of scarce resources.

Liberals therefore believe that the economic role of government should be quite limited. Many forms of government intervention in the economy, they argue, intentionally or unintentionally restrict the market and thereby prevent potentially rewarding trades from occurring.

Liberals do generally support the provision by government of certain "public goods," goods and services that make society better off but that would not be provided by private markets.[1] The government, for example, plays an important role in supplying the conditions necessary for the maintenance of a free and competitive market. Governments must provide for the defense of the country, protect property rights, and prevent unfair collusion or concentration of power within the market. The government should also, according to most Liberals, educate its citizens, build infrastructure, and provide and regulate a common currency. The proper role of government, in other words, is to provide the necessary foundation for the market.

At the level of the international economy, Liberals assert that a fundamental harmony of interests exists between as well as within countries. As Richard Cobden argued in the fight against trade protection in Great Britain during the early nineteenth century, all countries are best off when goods and services move freely across national borders in mutually rewarding exchanges. If universal free trade were to exist, Cobden reasoned, all countries would enjoy the highest level of utility and there would be no economic basis for international conflict and war.

Liberals also believe that governments should manage the international economy in much the same way as they manage their domestic economies. They should establish rules and regulations—often referred to as "international regimes"—to govern exchanges between different national currencies and ensure that no country or domestic group is damaged by "unfair" international competition.

Liberals realize, of course, that governments often do far more than this at both the domestic and international levels, and they have applied their theoretical tools to analyze patterns of government activity. As might be expected, the principal Liberal approach—known generally as "public choice" or "rational choice"—thinks of the political arena as a marketplace. Politicians compete among each other for the privilege of holding office; individuals and groups compete among each other to get support for their preferred policies from office-holders—with votes, campaign contributions, and lobbying. This view, closely related to long-standing theories of interest-group pluralism, sees government action as the result of competition among politicians, and among their constituents.

Marxism

Marxism originated with the writings of Karl Marx, a nineteenth-century political economist and perhaps capitalism's severest critic. Just as Liberalism emerged in reaction to mercantilism, Marxism was a response to the spread of Liberalism in the nineteenth century. Where for Liberals the market allows individuals to maximize their utility, Marx saw capitalism and the market creating extremes of wealth for capitalists and poverty for workers. While everyone may have been better off than before, the capitalists were clearly expanding their wealth more rapidly than all others. Marx rejected the assertion that exchange between individuals necessarily maximizes the welfare of the whole society. Accordingly, Marx perceived capitalism as an inherently conflictual system that both should and will be inevitably overthrown and replaced by socialism.

Marxism makes three essential assumptions. First, Marxists believe that classes are the dominant actors in the political economy and are the appropriate unit of analysis. Marxists identify two economically determined aggregations of individuals, or classes, as central: capital, or the owners of the means of production, and labor, or workers.

Second, Marxists assume that classes act in their material economic interests. Just as Liberals assume that individuals act rationally to maximize their utility, Marxists assume that each class acts to maximize the economic well-being of the class as a whole.

Third, Marxists assume that the basis of the capitalist economy is the exploitation of labor by capital. Marx's analysis began with the labor theory of value, which holds that the value of any product is determined by the amount of past and present labor used to produce it. Marx believed that under capitalism the value of any product could be broken down into three components: constant capital, or past labor as embodied in plant and equipment or the raw materials necessary to produce the good; variable capital, the wages paid to present labor to produce the item; and surplus value—defined as profits, rents, and interest—which was expropriated by or paid to the capitalist. The capitalists' expropriation of surplus value, according to Marx, denies labor the full return for its efforts.

This third assumption leads Marxists to see the political economy as necessarily conflictual, because the relationship between capitalists and workers is essentially antagonistic. Surplus value is not the capitalist's "reward" for investment, but something that is taken away from labor. Because the means of production are controlled by a minority within society—the capitalists—labor does not receive its full return; conflict between the classes will thus occur because of this exploitation. For Marx, the relationship between capital and labor is zero-sum; any gain for the capitalist must come at the expense of labor, and vice versa.

Starting with these three assumptions, Marx constructed a sophisticated theory of capitalist crisis. Such crisis would, Marx believed, ultimately lead to the overthrow of capitalism by labor and the erection of a socialist society in which the means of production would be owned jointly by all members of society and no surplus value would be expropriated.

While Marx wrote primarily about domestic political economy, or the dynamics and form of economic change within a single country, Lenin extended Marx's ideas to the international political economy to explain imperialism and war (see selections from *Imperialism,* Reading 6). Imperialism, Lenin argued, was endemic to modern capitalism. As capitalism decayed in the most developed nations, these nations would attempt to solve their problems by exporting capital abroad. As this capital required protection from both local and foreign challengers, governments would colonize regions to safeguard the interests of their foreign investors. When the area available for colonization began to shrink, capitalist countries would compete for control over these areas and intracapitalist wars would eventually occur.

Today, Marxists who study the international political economy are primarily concerned with two sets of analytical and practical issues. The first concerns the fate of labor in a world of increasingly internationalized capital. With the growth of multinational corporations and the rise of globally integrated financial markets, the greater international mobility of capital appears to have weakened the economic and political power of labor. If workers in a particular country demand higher wages or improved health and safety measures, for example, the multinational capitalist can simply shift production to another country where labor is more compliant. As a result, many Marxists fear that labor's ability to negotiate with capital for a more equitable division of surplus value has been significantly undermined. Understanding how and in what ways labor has been weakened and how workers should respond to the increased mobility of capital is thus an important research agenda.

Second, Marxists are concerned with the poverty and continued underdevelopment of the Third World. Some Marxists argue that development is blocked by domestic ruling classes who pursue their own narrow interests at the expense of national economic progress (see Pastor, Reading 20). "Dependency" theorists, on the other hand, extend Marx's class-analytic framework to the level of the international economy. According to these Marxists, the global system is stratified into an area of autonomous self-sustaining growth, the "core" or First World, and a region of attenuated inhibited growth, the "periphery" or Third World. International capitalism, in this view, extracts surplus value from the periphery and concentrates it in the core, just as capitalists exploit workers within a single country. The principal questions here focus on the mechanisms of exploitation—whether they be multinational corporations (Newfarmer, Reading 12; Schatz, Reading 11), international financial markets and organizations (Pastor, Reading 20), or trade (Robinson, Reading 24; Broad and Cavanagh, Reading 26)—and the appropriate strategies for stimulating autonomous growth and development in the periphery.

While Liberals perceive the political economy as inherently harmonious, Marxists believe conflict is endemic. Marxists adopt different assumptions and derive a very different understanding of the world. For Marxists, economics determines politics. The nature of politics and the fundamental cleavages within and between societies, in other words, are rooted in economics.

Realism

Realism has perhaps the longest pedigree of the three principal perspectives in International Political Economy, starting with Thucydides's writings in 400 B.C. and including Niccoló Machiavelli, Thomas Hobbes, and the mercantilists Jean-Baptiste Colbert and Friedrich List. Discredited with the rise of Liberalism in the nineteenth century, Realism reemerged as an important perspective only in the aftermath of the Great Depression of the 1930s as scholars sought to understand the causes of the widespread economic warfare of "beggar-thy-neighbor" policies initiated in 1929. Realists believe that nation-states pursue power and shape the economy to this end. Unlike Liberals and Marxists, Realists perceive politics as determining economics.

Realism is based upon three assumptions. First, Realists assume that nation-states are the dominant actors within the international political economy and the proper unit of analysis. According to Realists, the international system is anarchical, a condition under which nation-states are sovereign, the sole judge of their own behaviors, and subject to no higher authority. If no authority is higher than the nation-state, Realists also believe that all actors are subordinate to the nation-state. While private citizens can interact with their counterparts in other countries, Realists assert that the basis for this interaction is legislated by the nation-state. Thus, where Liberals focus on individuals and Marxists on classes, Realists concentrate on nation-states.

Second, Realists assume that nation-states are power maximizers. Because the international system is based upon anarchy, the use of force or coercion by other nation-states is always a possibility and no other country or higher authority is obligated to come to the aid of a nation-state under attack. Nation-states are thus ultimately dependent upon their own resources for protection. For Realists, then, each nation-state must always be prepared to defend itself to the best of its ability. It must always seek to maximize its power; the failure to do so threatens the very existence of the nation-state and may make it vulnerable to others. Power is a relative concept. If one nation-state (or any other actor) expands its power over another, it can do so only at the expense of the second. Thus, for Realists, politics is a zero-sum game and by necessity conflictual. If one nation-state wins, another must lose.

Third, Realists assume that nation-states are rational actors in the same sense that Liberals assume individuals are rational. Nation-states are assumed to perform cost-benefit analyses and choose the option which yields the greatest value, in this case, the one which maximizes power.

It is the assumption of power maximization that gives Realism its distinctive approach to International Political Economy. While economic considerations may often complement power concerns, the former are—in the Realist view—subordinate to the latter. Liberals and Marxists see individuals and classes, respectively, as always seeking to maximize their economic well-being. Realists, on the other hand, allow for circumstances in which nation-states sacrifice economic gain to weaken their opponents or strengthen themselves in military or diplomatic terms. Thus, trade protection—which might reduce a country's overall income by restricting the market—may be adopted for reasons of national political power.

Given its assumptions, Realist political economy is primarily concerned with how changes in the distribution of international power affect the form and type of international economy. The best known Realist approach to this question is the "theory of hegemonic stability," which holds that an open international economy—that is, one characterized by the free exchange of goods, capital, and services—is most likely to exist when a single dominant or hegemonic power is present to stabilize the system and construct a strong regime (see Krasner, Reading 3, and Lake, Reading 7). For Realists, then, politics underlies economics. In the pursuit of power, nation-states shape the international economy to best serve their desired ends.

Each of these three perspectives adopts different assumptions to simplify reality and render it more explicable. Liberals assume that individuals are the proper unit of analysis, while Marxists and Realists make similar assumptions for classes and nation-states, respectively. The three perspectives also differ on the inevitability of conflict within the political economy. Liberals believe economics and politics are largely autonomous spheres, Marxists maintain that economics determines politics, and Realists argue that politics determines economics.

These three perspectives lead to widely different explanations of specific events and general processes within the international political economy. Their differences have generated numerous debates in the field, many of which are contained in the readings herein. Overlying these perspectives are two additional debates on the relative importance of international and domestic factors, and of social or state forces, in determining economic policy. We now turn to this second set of issues.

ANALYTICAL ISSUES IN INTERNATIONAL POLITICAL ECONOMY

Within International Political Economy, two sets of important analytical issues serve to define many of the debates that divide scholars. To an extent, these debates cut across the three perspectives outlined above; on some issues, there is more agreement between Realists and some Marxists than amongst Realists or Marxists themselves. The first set of problems that divides the discipline has to do with the relationship between the international and domestic political economies; the second set concerns the relationship between the state and social forces.

It should surprise no one that American tariff policy, Japanese international financial goals, and South Korean development strategies are important in the world's political economy. Disagreements arise, however, over how best to explain the sources of the foreign economic policies of individual nations, or of nation-states in general. At one end of the international-domestic spectrum, some scholars believe that national foreign economic policies are essentially determined by the global environment. The actual room for national maneuvering of even the most powerful of states, these scholars believe, is limited by the inherent nature of the international system. At the other end of the spectrum are scholars who see foreign economic policies primarily as the outgrowth of national, domestic-level political and economic processes; for them, the international system exists only as a jumble of independent nation-states, each with its own political and economic peculiarities.

The international-domestic division is at the base of many debates within International Political Economy, as in the world at large. While some argue, for example, that the cause of Third World poverty lies in the unequal global economic order, others blame domestic politics and economics in developing nations. Many see multinational corporations as a powerful independent force in the world—whether for good or for evil—while others see international firms as both tools and products of their home countries.

The distinction between the two approaches can be seen quite clearly, for example, in explanations of trade policy. To take a specific instance, both the United States and many European governments have over the past decade imposed restrictions on the import of Japanese automobiles. The form of control has varied widely: the United States and Japanese governments negotiated "voluntary" export restraints which Japanese producers agreed to abide by, while in some European countries quantitative quotas have been imposed unilaterally. Generally speaking, support for these policies came from European and North American automakers and from the trade unions that represent their employees, both of which were concerned over stiff Japanese competition that was reducing profits and employment. From this, one clear analytical conclusion would be that domestic political and economic pressures—the electoral importance of the regions where auto industries are concentrated, the economic centrality of the sector to the European and North American economies, the political clout of the autoworkers' unions—led to important foreign economic measures, that is, the restriction of Japanese automobile imports. Indeed, many scholars saw the restrictions as confirmation of the primacy of domestic concerns in the making of foreign economic policy.

Yet analysts who search for the causes of national foreign economic policies in the international, rather than the domestic, arena, could also find support in the auto import policies. After all, the policies responded to the rise of Japan as a major manufacturer and exporter of automobiles, a fact which had little to do with the domestic scene in the United States and Europe. Many North American and European industries have lost competitive ground to rapidly growing overseas manufacturers, a process that is complex in origin but clearly one of worldwide proportions. Realists have argued that trade policy is a function of realities inherent in the international system, such as the existence of a leading, hegemonic, economic power and the eventual decline of that power (see Krasner, Reading 3). In this view, the decline of American power set the stage for a proliferation of barriers to trade. On the other hand, the internationally minded scholar might also argue that it is also important to understand why the European and American measures took the relatively mild form they did, simply limiting the Japanese to established (and often very appreciable) shares of the markets. If the measures had been adopted simply to respond to the distress of local auto industries, the logical step would have been to exclude foreign cars from the markets in question. Yet, the position of Europe and the United States in the global economic and political system—and here we could include everything from world finance to international military alliances—dictated that European and North American policymakers not pursue overly hostile policies toward the Japanese.

More generally, scholars have explained long-term changes in trade policy in very different ways. During the period between World War I and World War II, and especially in the 1930s, almost all of the European nations and the United State were highly protectionist. Since World War II, on the other hand, the North American and Western European markets have been opened gradually and continuously to each other and to the rest of the world. Scholars with an international theoretical bent point out that domestic politics in Europe and the United States have not changed enough to explain such a radical shift. The role of the United States and Western Europe in the international political and economic system, however, has indeed been different since World War II than it was during the 1930s: after World War II North American and Western European countries were united in an American-led military and economic alliance against the Soviet Union. Systemic-level analysts, such as proponents of the "theory of hegemonic stability" (see Lake, Reading 7), would argue that the causes of post-war foreign economic policies in North America and Western Europe can be found in the dramatic changes in the international position of these regions—the increase in American power, the decline of Europe, the Soviet challenge, the rise of the Atlantic Alliance.

Domestic-level explanations take the opposite tack. For them, the postwar system was itself largely a creation of the United States and the major Western European powers. To cite the modern international political economy as a source of American or British foreign economic policy, domestically oriented scholars argue, is to put the cart before the horse, since it was United States and its allies that created the institutions—the Marshall Plan, the Bretton Woods Agreements, the European Community—of today's international political economy. The true roots of the shift in trade policy in North America and Western Europe must therefore be searched for within these nations.

The example of trade policy illustrates that serious scholars can arrive at strikingly different analytical conclusions on the basis of the same information. For some, domestic political and economic pressures caused the adoption of auto import restrictions. For others, trends in the international environment explain the same action.

It should be pointed out that, to a certain extent, the distinction drawn between international and domestic sources of foreign economic policy is an artificial one. Most scholars recognize that both systemic and domestic pressures are important in explaining why governments choose the policies they do. Yet there are fundamental disagreements over the relative weight that should be placed on each set of causes; for some, international sources are primary, for others, domestic causes predominate. And the division cuts across ideological lines: some Marxists, for example, are "systemic-level theorists" and believe that the international capitalist system is the primary cause of national policies, while other Marxists downplay international aspects and focus on the national development of capitalism. Similar divisions exist among Realists and Liberals as well.

The interaction between state and society, or between national governments and the social forces they represent, rule, or ignore serves as a second dividing line within International Political Economy. In the study of the politics of the world economy, questions continually arise about the relative importance of independent government action versus a variety of societal pressures on the policymaking process.

The role of the state is at the center of all Political Science; International Political Economy is no exception. Foreign economic policy is made, of course, by foreign economic policymakers; this much is trivial. But just as scholars debate the relative importance of overseas and domestic determinants of foreign economic policies, so too do they disagree over whether policymakers represent a logic of their own, or reflect domestic lobbies and interest groups. In one vision, the national state is relatively insulated or autonomous from the multitude of social, political, and economic pressures that emanate from society. The most that pluralistic interest groups can produce is a confused cacophony of complaints and demands, while coherent national policy comes from the conscious actions of national leaders and those who occupy positions of political power. The state, in this view, molds society, and foreign economic policy is one part of this larger mold. For the opposing school of thought, policymakers are little more than the reflectors of underlying societal demands. At best, the political system can organize and regularize these demands, but the state is simply a tool in the hands of socioeconomic and political interests. Foreign economic policy, like other state actions, evolves in response to social demands; it is society that molds the state, and not the other way around.

Once again, it should be noted that this simplistic dichotomy hardly describes actual theoretical approaches; nearly all scholars recognize that both state actors and sociopolitical forces are important determinants of foreign economic policies. The disagreements are over relative weights to be assigned to each set of causes. Once more, the state-society division cuts across other theoretical differences: pluralist Liberals and some Marxists assign primacy to social forces, while statist Realists and structural Marxists give pride of place to autonomous state action.

We can illustrate the difference in focus with the previously discussed example of trade policy in North America and Western Europe before and since World War II. Many of those who look first and foremost at state actors would emphasize the dramatic change in the overall foreign policy of these governments after World War II, starting with the Atlantic Alliance to meet the demands of European reconstruction and the Cold War, which required that the American market be opened to foreign goods in order to stimulate the economies of the country's allies. Eventually the European Communities (Common Market) arose as a further effort to cement the Atlantic Alliance against the Soviet Union. In this view, trade liberalization arose out of national-security concerns, understood and articulated by a very small number of individuals in the American and Western European governments, who then went about "selling" the policies to their publics. Other scholars, for whom society is determinant, emphasize the major socioeconomic and political changes that had been gaining force within the industrial capitalist nations after World War I. Corporations were becoming more international, and had come to fear overseas competition less. For important groups, trade protection was counterproductive, because it limited access to the rest of the world economy; freer trade and investment opened broad and profitable new horizons for major economic actors in North America and Western Europe.

A wide variety of theoretical and analytical differences separate scholars interested in International Political Economy. The selections in this reader serve both to provide information on broad trends in the politics of international economic relations and to give an overview of the contending approaches to be found within the discipline.

NOTE

1. More specifically, a public good is one that, in its purest form, is *nonrival in consumption* and *nonexcludable*. The first characteristic means that consumption of the good by one person does not reduce the opportunities for others to consume the good: clean air can be breathed by one without reducing its availability to others. The second characteristic means that nobody can be prevented from consuming the good—those who do not contribute to pollution control are still able to breathe clean air. These two conditions are fully met only rarely, but goods that come close to them are generally considered public goods.

I

CONTENDING PERSPECTIVES ON INTERNATIONAL POLITICAL ECONOMY

Three contending perspectives dominate the study of international political economy: Liberalism, Marxism, and Realism. The Introduction addressed the principal assumptions underlying each of these perspectives. Part I contains three selections, one representing each approach as applied to a specific issue. Cletus C. Coughlin, K. Alec Chrystal, and Geoffrey E. Wood, all neo-classical economists, present the Liberal argument for free trade among nations. Peter Cocks provides a Marxist analysis of how changes in the economic characteristics of modern capitalism gave rise to movements toward the greater integration of Western European nation-states. Finally, Stephen D. Krasner discusses the relationship between the distribution of power and international economic openness and closure, a question at the center of Realist inquiry. Each selection reflects the assumptions, research agenda, and types of arguments developed in its respective school. Understanding how these schools work is, in turn, essential for understanding current issues in the field of international political economy.

1

Protectionist Trade Policies: A Survey of Theory, Evidence, and Rationale

CLETUS C. COUGHLIN,
K. ALEC CHRYSTAL, and
GEOFFREY E. WOOD

In this article, three economists review the Liberal case for free trade in light of new theories and evidence. Beginning with an exposition of the principle of comparative advantage, Coughlin, Chrystal, and Wood examine modern forms of protection, the costs of trade protection in the United States and the world, and contemporary arguments for restricting trade. They conclude that free trade remains the optimal policy for all countries. To explain why countries nonetheless adopt protection, they emphasize the distributional effects of trade policy and the incentives for specific groups to seek governmentally imposed trade restrictions. This article highlights both the classic Liberal arguments in favor of free and unrestricted international commerce and the rapidly expanding public-choice literature.

Protectionist pressures have been mounting worldwide during the 1980s. These pressures are due to various economic problems including the large and persistent balance of trade deficit in the United States; the hard times experienced by several industries, and the slow growth of many foreign countries. Proponents of protectionist trade policies argue that international trade has contributed substantially to these problems and that protectionist trade policies will lead to improved results. Professional economists in the United States, however, generally agree that trade

1 "Protectionist Trade Policies: A Survey of Theory, Evidence, and Rationale" by Cletus C. Coughlin, K. Alec Chrystal, and Geoffrey E. Wood. Federal Reserve Bank of St. Louis.

restrictions such as tariffs and quotas substantially reduce a nation's economic well-being.

This article surveys the theory, evidence and rationale concerning protectionist trade policies. The first section illustrates the gains from free trade using the concept of comparative advantage. Recent developments in international trade theory that emphasize other reasons for gains from trade are also reviewed. The theoretical discussion is followed by an examination of recent empirical studies that demonstrate the large costs of protectionist trade policies. Then, the rationale for restricting trade is presented. The concluding section summarizes the paper's main arguments.

THE GAINS FROM FREE TRADE

The most famous demonstration of the gains from trade appeared in 1817 in David Ricardo's *Principles of Political Economy and Taxation.* We use his example involving trade between England and Portugal to demonstrate how both countries can gain from trade. The two countries produce the same two goods, wine and cloth, and the only production costs are labor costs. The figures below list the amount of labor (e.g., worker-days) required in each country to produce one bottle of wine or one bolt of cloth.

	Wine	Cloth
England	3	7
Portugal	1	5

Since both goods are more costly to produce in England than in Portugal, England is absolutely less efficient at producing both goods than its prospective trading partner. Portugal has an absolute advantage in both wine and cloth. At first glance, this appears to rule out mutual gains from trade; however, as we demonstrate below, absolute advantage is irrelevant in discerning whether trade can benefit both countries.

The ratio of the production costs for the two goods is different in the two countries. In England, a bottle of wine will exchange for 3/7 of a bolt of cloth because the labor content of the wine is 3/7 of that for cloth. In Portugal, a bottle of wine will exchange for 1/5 of a bolt of cloth. Thus, wine is relatively cheaper in Portugal than in England and, conversely, cloth is relatively cheaper in England than in Portugal. The example indicates that Portugal has a comparative advantage in wine production and England has a comparative advantage in cloth production.

The different relative prices provide the basis for both countries to gain from international trade. The gains arise from both exchange and specialization.

The gains from *exchange* can be highlighted in the following manner. If a Portuguese wine producer sells five bottles of wine at home, he receives one bolt of cloth. If he trades in England, he receives more than two bolts of cloth. Hence, he can gain by exporting his wine to England. English cloth-producers are willing to trade in Portugal; for every 3/7 of a bolt of cloth they sell there, they get just over two bottles of wine. The English gain from exporting cloth to (and importing wine from) Portugal, and the Portuguese gain from exporting wine to (and importing cloth from) England. Each country gains by exporting the good in which it has a comparative advantage and by importing the good in which it has a comparative disadvantage.

Gains from *specialization* can be demonstrated in the following manner. Initially, each country is producing some of both goods. Suppose that, as a result of trade, 21 units of labor are shifted from wine to cloth production in England, while, in Portugal, 10 units of labor are shifted from cloth to wine production. This reallocation of labor does not alter the total amount of labor used in the two countries; however, it causes the production changes listed below.

	Bottles of wine	Bolts of cloth
England	- 7	+ 3
Portugal	+ 10	- 2
Net	+ 3	+ 1

The shift of 21 units of labor to the English cloth industry raises cloth production by three bolts, while reducing wine production by seven bottles. In Portugal, the shift of 10 units of labor from cloth to wine raises wine production by 10 bottles, while reducing cloth production by two bolts. This reallocation of labor increases the total production of both goods: wine by three bottles and cloth by one bolt. This increased output will be shared by the two countries. Thus, the consumption of both goods and the wealth of both countries are increased by the specialization brought about by trade based on comparative advantage.

TRADE THEORY SINCE RICARDO

Since 1817, numerous analyses have generated insights concerning the gains from trade. They chiefly examine the consequences of relaxing the assumptions used in the preceding example. For example, labor was the only resource used to produce the two goods in the example above; yet, labor is really only one of many resources used to produce goods. The example also assumed that the costs of producing additional units of the goods are constant. For example, in England, three units of labor are used to produce one bottle of wine regardless of the level of wine production. In reality, unit production costs could either increase or decrease as more is produced. A third assumption was that the goods are produced in perfectly competitive markets. In other words, an individual firm has no effect on the price of the good that it produces. Some industries, however, are dominated by a small number of firms, each of which can affect the market price of the good by altering its production decision. . . .

These theoretical developments generally have strengthened the case for an open trading system. They suggest three sources of gains from trade. First, as the market potentially served by firms expands from a national to a world market, there are gains associated with declining per unit production costs. A second source of gains results from the reduction in the monopoly power of domestic firms. Domestic firms, facing more pressure from foreign competitors, are forced to produce the output demanded by consumers at the lowest possible cost. Third is the gain to consumers from increased product variety and lower prices. Generally speaking, the gains from trade result from the increase in competitive pressures as the domestic economy becomes less insulated from the world economy.

FORMS OF PROTECTIONISM

Protection may be implemented in numerous ways. All forms of protection are intended to improve the position of a domestic relative to foreign producer. This can be done by policies that increase the home market price of the foreign product, decrease the costs of domestic producers or restrict the access of foreign producers to the home market in some other way.

Tariffs

Tariffs, which are simply taxes imposed on goods entering a country from abroad, result in higher prices and have been the most common form of protection for domestic producers. Tariffs have been popular with governments because it appears that the tax is being paid by the foreigner who wishes to sell his goods in the home economy and because the tariff revenue can be used to finance government services or reduce other taxes.

In the 20th century, U.S. tariff rates peaked as a result of the Smoot-Hawley Tariff of 1930. For example, in 1932, tariff revenue as a percentage of total imports was 19.6 percent. An identical calculation for 1985 yields a figure of 3.8 percent. The decline was due primarily to two reasons. First, since many of the tariffs under Smoot-Hawley were set as specific dollar amounts, the rising price level in the United States eroded the effective tariff rate. Second, since World War II, numerous tariff reductions have been negotiated under the General Agreement on Tariffs and Trade.

On the other hand, various other forms of protection, frequently termed non-tariff barriers, have become increasingly important. A few of the more frequently used devices are discussed below.

Quotas

A quota seems like a sensible alternative to a tariff when the intention is to restrict foreign producers' access to the domestic market. Importers typically are limited to a maximum number of products that they can sell in the home market over specific periods. A quota, similar to a tariff, causes prices to increase in the home market. This induces domestic producers to increase production and consumers to reduce consumption. One difference between a tariff and a quota is that the tariff generates revenue for the government, while the quota generates a revenue gain to the owner of import licenses. Consequently, foreign producers might capture some of this revenue.

In recent years, a slightly different version of quotas, called either orderly marketing agreements or voluntary export restraints, has been used. In an orderly marketing agreement, the domestic government asks the foreign government to restrict the quantity of exports of a good to the domestic country. The request can be viewed as a demand, like the U.S.-Japan automobile agreement in the 1980s, because the domestic country makes it clear that more restrictive actions are likely unless the foreign government "voluntarily" complies. In effect, the orderly marketing agreement is a mutually agreed upon quota.

Regulatory Barriers

There are many other ways of restricting foreigners' access to domestic markets. . . . The 1983 *Tariff Schedules of the United States Annotated* consists of 792 pages, plus a 78-page appendix. Over 200 tariff rates pertain to watches and clocks. Simply ascertaining the appropriate tariff classification, which requires legal assistance and can be subject to differences of opinion, is a deterrent.

Product standards are another common regulatory barrier. These standards appear in various forms and are used for many purposes. The standards can be used to service the public interest by ensuring that imported food products are processed according to acceptable sanitary standards and that drugs have been screened before their introduction in the United States. In other cases, the standards, sometimes intentionally, protect domestic producers. An example of unintended restrictions may be the imposition of safety or pollution standards that were not previously being met by foreign cars.

Subsidies

An alternative to restricting the terms under which foreigners can compete in the home market is to subsidize domestic producers. Subsidies may be focused upon an industry in general or upon the export activities of the industry. An example of the former. . . is the combination of credit programs, special tax incentives and direct subsidy payments that benefit the U. S. shipbuilding industry. An example of the latter is the financial assistance to increase exports provided by the U.S. Export-Import Bank through direct loans, loan guarantees and insurance, and discount loans. In either case, production will expand.

An important difference between subsidies and tariffs involves the revenue implications for government. The former involves the government in paying out money, whereas tariffs generate income for the government. The effect on domestic production and welfare, however, can be the same under subsidies as under tariffs and quotas. In all cases, the protected industry is being subsidized by the rest of the economy.

Exchange Controls

All of the above relate directly to the flow of goods. A final class of restrictions works by restricting access to the foreign money required to buy foreign goods. For example, a government that wished to protect its exporting and import competing industries may try to hold its exchange rate artificially low. As a result, foreign goods would appear expensive in the home market while home goods would be cheap overseas. Home producers implicitly are subsidized and home consumers implicitly are taxed. This policy is normally hard to sustain. The central bank, in holding the exchange rate down has to buy foreign exchange with domestic currency. This newly issued domestic currency increases the domestic money stock and eventually causes inflation. Inflationary policies are not normally regarded as a sensible way of protecting domestic industry.

There is another aspect to exchange controls. The justification is that preventing home residents from investing overseas benefits domestic growth as it leads to greater domestic real investment. In reality, it could do exactly the opposite. Restricting access to foreign assets may raise the variance and lower the return to owners of domestic wealth. In the short run, it also may appreciate the domestic exchange rate and, thereby, make domestic producers less competitive.

COSTS OF TRADE PROTECTIONISM

The specific goal of protectionist trade policies is to expand domestic production in the protected industries, benefiting the owners, workers and suppliers of resources to the protected industry. The government imposing protectionist trade policies may also benefit, for example, in the form of tariff revenue.

The expansion of domestic production in protected industries is not costless; it requires additional resources from other industries. Consequently, output in other domestic industries is reduced. These industries also might be made less competitive because of higher prices for imported inputs. Since protectionist policies frequently increase the price of the protected good, domestic consumers are harmed. They lose in two ways. First, their consumption of the protected good is reduced because of the associated rise in its price. Second, they consume less of other goods, as their output declines and prices rise.

The preceding discussion highlights the domestic winners and losers due to protectionist trade policies. Domestic producers of the protected good and the government (if tariffs are imposed) gain; domestic consumers and other domestic producers lose. Foreign interests are also affected by trade restrictions. The protection of domestic producers will harm some foreign producers; oddly enough, other foreign producers may benefit. For example, if quotas are placed on imports, some foreign producers may receive higher prices for their exports to the protected market.

There have been numerous studies of the costs of protectionism. We begin by examining three recent studies of protectionism in the United States, then proceed to studies examining developed and, finally, developing countries.

Costs of Protectionism in the United States

Recent studies by Tarr and Morkre (1984), Hickok (1985) and Hufbauer et al. (1986) estimated the costs of protectionism in the United States. These studies use different estimation procedures, examine different protectionist policies and cover different time periods. Nonetheless, they provide consistent results.

Tarr and Morkre (1984) estimate annual costs to the U.S. economy of $12.7 billion (1983 dollars) from all tariffs and from quotas on automobiles, textiles, steel and sugar. Their cost estimate is a net measure in which the losses of consumers are offset partially by the gains of domestic producers and the U.S. government.

Estimates by Hickok (1985) indicate that trade restrictions on only three goods—clothing, sugar, and automobiles—caused increased consumer expenditures of $14 billion in 1984. Hickok also shows that low-income families are affected more than high-income families. The import restraints on clothing, sugar and automobiles are calculated to be equivalent to a 23 percent income tax surcharge (that is, an additional tax added to the normal income tax) for families with incomes less than $10,000 in 1984 and a 3 percent income tax surcharge for families with incomes exceeding $60,000.

Hufbauer et al (1986) examined 31 cases in which trade volumes exceeded $100 million and the United States imposed protectionist trade restrictions.They generated estimates of the welfare consequences for each major group affected. [Their] figures indicate that annual consumer losses exceed $100 million in all but six of the cases. The largest losses, $27 billion per year, come from protecting the textile and apparel industry. There also are large consumer losses associated with protection in carbon steel ($6.8 billion), automobiles ($5.8 billion) and dairy products ($5.5 billion).

The purpose of protectionism is to protect jobs in specific industries. A useful approach to gain some perspective on consumer losses is to express these losses on a per-job-saved basis. In 18 of the 31 cases, the cost per-job-saved is $100,000 or more per year; the consumer losses per-job-saved in benzenoid chemicals, carbon steel (two separate periods), specialty steel, and bolts, nuts and screws exceeded $500,000 per year.

[This study] also reveals that domestic producers were the primary beneficiaries of protectionist policies; however, there are some noteworthy cases where foreign producers realized relatively large gains. For the U.S.-Japanese voluntary export agreement in automobiles, foreign producers gained 38 percent of what domestic consumers lost, while a similar computation for the latest phase of protection for carbon steel was 29 percent.

Finally, [the study] indicates that the efficiency losses are small in comparison to the total losses borne by consumers. These efficiency losses. . . result from the excess domestic production and the reduction in consumption caused by protectionist trade policies. In large cases such as textiles and apparel, petroleum, dairy products and the maritime industries, these losses equal or exceed $1 billion. It is likely that these estimates understate the actual costs because they do not capture the secondary effects that occur as production and consumption changes in one industry affect other industries. In addition, restrictive trade policies generate additional costs because of bureaucratic enforcement costs and efforts by the private sector to influence these policies for their own gain as well as simply comply with administrative regulations.

Costs of Protectionism Throughout the World

In 1982, the Organization for Economic Cooperation and Development (OECD) began a project to analyze the costs and benefits of protectionist policies in manufacturing in OECD countries. The OECD (1985) highlighted a number of ways that protectionist policies have generated costs far in excess of benefits. Since protectionist policies increase prices, the report concludes that the attainment of sustained noninflationary growth is hindered by such price–increasing effects. Moreover, economic growth is potentially reduced if the uncertainty created by varying trade policies depresses investment.

. . . [The] OECD study stresses the fact that a reduction in imports via trade restrictions does not cause greater employment. A reduction in the value of imports results in a similar reduction in the value of exports. One rationale for this finding is that a reduction in the purchases of foreign goods reduces foreign incomes and, in turn, causes reduced foreign purchases of domestic goods.

While the reduction in imports increases employment in industries that produce products similar to the previously imported goods, the reduction in exports decreases employment in the export industries. In other words, while some jobs are saved, others are lost; however, this economic reality may not be obvious to businessmen, labor union leaders, politicians and others. . . . [The] jobs saved by protectionist legislation are more readily observed than the jobs lost due to protectionist legislation. In other words, the jobs that are protected in, say, the textile industry by U.S. import restrictions on foreign textiles are more readily apparent (and publicized) than the jobs in agriculture and high technology industries that do not materialize because of the import restrictions. These employment effects will net to approximately zero. . . .

ARGUMENTS FOR RESTRICTING TRADE

If protectionism is so costly, why is protectionism so pervasive? This section reviews the major arguments for restricting trade and provides explanations for the existence of protectionist trade policies.

National Defense

The national defense argument says that import barriers are necessary to ensure the capacity to produce crucial goods in a national emergency. While this argument is especially appealing for weapons during a war, there will likely be demands from other industries that deem themselves essential. For example, the footwear industry will demand protection because military personnel need combat boots.

The national defense argument ignores the possibility of purchases from friendly countries during the emergency. The possibilities of storage and depletion raise additional doubts about the general applicability of the argument. If crucial goods can be stored, for example,.the least costly way to prepare for an emergency might be to buy the goods from foreigners at the low world price before an emergency and store them. If the crucial goods are depletable mineral resources, such as oil, then the restriction of oil imports before an emergency will cause a more rapid depletion of domestic reserves. Once again, stockpiling might be a far less costly alternative.

Income Redistribution

Since protectionist trade policies affect the distribution of income, a trade restriction might be defended on the grounds that it favors some disadvantaged group. It is unlikely, however, that trade policy is the best tool for dealing with the perceived evils of income inequality, because of its bluntness and adverse effects on the efficient allocation of resources. Attempting to equalize incomes directly by tax and transfer payments is likely less costly than using trade policy. In addition, as Hickok's (1985) study indicates, trade restrictions on many items increase rather than decrease income inequality.

Optimum Tariff Agreement

The optimum tariff argument applies to situations in which a country has the economic power to alter world prices. This power exists because the country (or a group of countries acting in consort like the Organization of Petroleum Exporting

Countries) is such a large producer or consumer of a good that a change in its production or consumption patterns influences world prices. For example, by imposing a tariff, the country can make foreign goods cheaper. Since a tariff reduces the demand for foreign goods, if the tariff-imposing country has some market power, the world price for the good will fall. The tariff-imposing country will gain because the price per unit of its imports will have decreased.

There are a number of obstacles that preclude the widespread application of this argument. Few countries possess the necessary market power and, when they do, only a small number of goods is covered. Secondly, in a world of shifting supply and demand, calculating the optimum tariff and adjusting the rate to changing situations is difficult. Finally, the possibility of foreign retaliation to an act of economic warfare is likely. Such retaliation could leave both countries worse off than they would have been in a free trade environment.

Balancing the Balance of Trade

Many countries enact protectionist trade policies in the hope of eliminating a balance of trade deficit or increasing a balance of trade surplus. The desire to increase a balance of trade surplus follows from the mercantilist view that larger trade surpluses are beneficial from a national perspective.

This argument is suspect on a number of grounds. First, there is nothing inherently undesirable about a trade deficit or desirable about a surplus. For example, faster economic growth in the United States than in the rest of the world would tend to cause a trade deficit. In this case, the trade deficit is a sign of a healthy economy. Second, protectionist policies that reduce imports will cause exports to decrease by a comparable amount. Hence, an attempt to increase exports permanently relative to imports will fail. It is doubtful that the trade deficit will be reduced even temporarily because import quantities do not decline quickly in response to the higher import prices and the revenues of foreign producers might rise.

Protection of Jobs—Public Choice

The protection of jobs argument is closely related to the balance of trade argument. Since a reduction in imports via trade restrictions will result in a similar reduction in exports, the overall employment effects, as found in the OECD (1985) study and many others, are negligible. While the *overall* effects are negligible, workers (and resource owners) in specific industries are affected differently.

A domestic industry faced with increased imports from its foreign competition is under pressure to reduce production and lower costs. Productive resources must move from this industry to other domestic industries. Workers must change jobs and, in some cases, relocate to other cities. Since this change is forced upon these workers, these workers bear real costs that they are likely to resist. A similar statement can be made about the owners of capital in the affected industry.

Workers and other resource owners will likely resist these changes by lobbying for trade restrictions. The previously cited studies on the costs of protectionism demonstrated that trade restrictions entail substantial real costs as well. These costs likely exceed the adjustment costs because the adjustment costs are one-time costs, while the costs of protectionism continue as long as trade restrictions are maintained.

An obvious question is why politicians supply the protectionist legislation demanded by workers and other resource owners. A branch of economics called public choice, which focuses on the interplay between individual preferences and political outcomes, provides an answer. The public choice literature views the politician as an individual who offers voters a bundle of governmentally supplied goods in order to vote in elections. Many argue that politicians gain by providing protectionist legislation. Even though the national economic costs exceed the benefits, the politician faces different costs and benefits.

Those harmed by a protectionist trade policy for a domestic industry, especially household consumers, will incur a small individual cost that is difficult to identify. For example, a consumer is unlikely to ponder how much extra a shirt costs because of protectionist legislation for the textiles and apparel industry.

Even though the aggregate effect is large, the harm to each consumer may be small. This small cost, of which an individual may not even be aware, and the costs of organizing consumers deter the formation of a lobby against the legislation.

On the other hand, workers and other resource owners are very concerned about protectionist legislation for their industry. Their benefits tend to be large individually and easy to identify. Their voting and campaign contributions assist politicians who support their positions and penalize those who do not. Thus, politicians are likely to respond to their demands for protectionist legislation.

Infant Industries

The preceding argument is couched in terms of protecting a domestic industry. A slightly different argument, the so-called infant industry case, is couched in terms of *promoting* a domestic industry. Suppose an industry, already established in other countries, is being established in a specific country. The country might not be able to realize its comparative advantage in this industry because of the existing cost and other advantages of foreign firms. Initially, owners of the fledgling firm must be willing to suffer losses until the firm develops its market and lowers its production costs to the level of its foreign rivals. In order to assist this entrant, tariff protection can be used to shield the firm from some foreign competition.

After this temporary period of protection, free trade should be restored; however, the removal of tariff protection frequently is resisted. As the industry develops, its political power to thwart opposing legislation also increases.

Another problem with the infant industry argument is that a tariff is not the best way to intervene. A production subsidy is superior to a tariff if the goal is to expand production. A subsidy will do this directly, while a tariff has the undesirable side effect of reducing consumption.

In many cases, intervention might not be appropriate at all. If the infant industry is a good candidate for being competitive internationally, borrowing from the private capital markets can finance the expansion. Investors are willing to absorb losses *temporarily* if the prospects for future profits are sufficiently good.

Spillover Effects

The justification for protecting an industry, infant or otherwise, frequently entails a suggestion that the industry generates spillover benefits for other industries or individuals for which the industry is not compensated. Despite patent laws, one common suggestion is that certain industries are not fully compensated for their research and development expenditures. This argument is frequently directed toward technologically progressive industries where some firms can capture the results of other firms' research and development simply by dismantling a product to see how it works.

The application of this argument, however, engenders a number of problems. Spillovers of knowledge are difficult to measure. Since spillovers are not market transactions, they do not leave an obvious trail to identify their beneficiaries. The lack of market transactions also complicates an assessment of the value of these spillovers. To determine the appropriate subsidy, one must be able to place a dollar value on the spillovers generated by a given research and development expenditure. Actually, the calculation requires much more than the already difficult task of reconstructing the past. It requires complex estimates of the spillovers' future worth as well. Since resources are moved from other industries to the targeted industry, the government must understand the functioning of the entire economy.

Finally, there are political problems. An aggressive application of this argument might lead to retaliation and a mutually destructive trade war. In addition, as interest groups compete for the governmental assistance, there is no guarantee that the right groups will be assisted or that they will use the assistance efficiently.

Strategic Trade Policy

Recently theoretical developments have identified cases in which so-called strategic trade policy is superior to free trade. As we discussed earlier, decreasing unit production costs and market structures that contain monopoly elements are common in industries involved in international trade. Market imperfections immediately suggest the potential benefits of governmental intervention. In the strategic trade policy argument, governmental policy can alter the terms of competition to favor domestic over foreign firms and shift the excess returns in monopolistic markets from foreign to domestic firms.

Krugman (1987) illustrates an example of the argument. Assume that there is only one firm in the United States, Boeing, and one multinational firm in Europe, Airbus, capable of producing a 150-seat passenger aircraft. Assume also that the aircraft is produced only for export, so that the returns to the firm can be identified with the national interest. This export market is profitable for either firm if it is the only producer; however, it is unprofitable for both firms to produce the plane. Finally, assume the following payoffs are associated with the four combinations of production: 1) if both Boeing and Airbus produce the aircraft, each firm loses $5 million; 2) if neither Boeing nor Airbus produces the aircraft, profits are zero; 3) if Boeing produces the aircraft and Airbus does not, Boeing profits by $100 million and Airbus has zero profits; and 4) if Airbus produces the aircraft and Boeing does not, Airbus profits by $100 million and Boeing has zero profits.

Which firm(s) will produce the aircraft? The example does not yield a unique outcome. A unique outcome can be generated if one firm, say Boeing, has a head start and begins production before Airbus. In this case, Boeing will reap profits of $100 million and will have deterred Airbus from entering the market because Airbus will lose $5 million if it enters after Boeing.

Strategic trade policy, however, suggests that judicious governmental intervention can alter the outcome. If the European governments agree to subsidize Airbus' production with $10 million no matter what Boeing does, then Airbus will produce the plane. Production by Airbus will yield more profits than not producing, no matter what Boeing does. At the same time, Boeing will be deterred from producing because it would lose money. Thus, Airbus will capture the entire market and reap profits of $110 million, $100 million of which can be viewed as a transfer of profits from the United States.

The criticisms of a strategic trade policy are similar to the criticisms against protecting a technologically progressive industry that generates spillover benefits. There are major informational problems in applying a strategic trade policy. The government must estimate the potential payoff of each course of action. Economic knowledge about the behavior of industries that have monopoly elements is limited. Firms may behave competitively or cooperatively and may compete by setting prices or output. The behavior of rival governments also must be anticipated. Foreign retaliation must be viewed as likely where substantial profits are at stake. In addition, many interest groups will compete for the governmental assistance. Though only a small number of sectors can be considered potentially strategic, many industries will make a case for assistance.

Reciprocity and the "Level Playing Field"

. . . U.S. trade policy discussions in recent years have frequently stressed the importance of "fair trade." The concept of fair trade, which is technically referred to as reciprocity, means different things to different people.

Under the General Agreement on Tariffs and Trade, negotiations to reduce trade barriers focus upon matching concessions. This form of reciprocity, known as first-difference reciprocity, attempts to reduce trade barriers by requiring a country to provide a tariff reduction of value comparable to one provided by the other country. In this case, reciprocity is defined in terms of matching changes.

Recent U.S. demands, exemplified by the Gephardt amendment to the current trade legislation, reveal an approach that is called full reciprocity. This approach seeks reciprocity in terms of the level of protection bilaterally and over a specific range of goods. Reciprocity requires equal access and this access can be determined by bilateral trade balances. A trade deficit with a trading partner is claimed to be *prima facie* evidence of unequal access. Examples abound. For example, U.S. construction firms have not had a major contract in Japan since 1965, while Japanese construction firms did $1.8 billion worth of business in the United States in 1985 alone. Recent legislation bars Japanese participation in U.S. public works projects until the Japanese offer reciprocal privileges.

As the name suggests, the fundamental argument for fair trade is one of equity. Domestic producers in a free trade country argue that foreign trade barriers are unfair because it places them at a competitive disadvantage. In an extreme version, it is asserted that this unfair competition will virtually eliminate U.S. manufacturing, leaving only jobs that consist primarily of flipping hamburgers at fast food restaurants or. . . rolling rice cakes at Japanese owned sushi bars. While domestic producers *are* relatively disadvantaged, the wisdom of a protectionist response is doubtful. Again, the costs of protectionism exceed substantially the benefits from a national perspective.

In an attempt to reinforce the argument for fair trade, proponents also argue that retaliatory threats, combined with changes in tariffs and non-tariff barriers, allow for the simultaneous protection of domestic industries against unequal competition and induce more open foreign markets. This more flexible approach is viewed as superior to a "one-sided" free trade policy. The suggestion that a fair trade policy produces a trading environment with fewer trade restrictions allows proponents to assert that such a policy serves to promote both equity and efficiency. In other words, not only will domestic and foreign producers in the same industry be treated equally, but the gains associated with a freer trading environment will be realized.

On the other hand, critics of a fair trade policy argue that such a policy is simply disguised protectionism — it simply achieves the goals of specific interest groups at the expense of the nation at large. In many cases, fair traders focus on a specific practice that can be portrayed as protectionist while ignoring the entire package of policies that are affecting a nation's competitive position. In these cases, the foreign country is more likely either not to respond or retaliate by increasing rather than reducing their trade barriers. In the latter case, the escalation of trade barriers causes losses for both nations, which is exactly opposite to the alleged effects of an activist fair trade policy.

Critics of fair trade proposals are especially bothered by the use of bilateral trade deficits as evidence of unfair trade. In a world of many trading countries, the trade between two countries need not be balanced for the trade of each to be in global balance. Differing demands and productive capabilities across countries will cause a specific country to have trade deficits with some countries and surpluses with other countries. These bilateral imbalances are a normal result of countries trading on the basis of comparative advantage. Thus, the focus on the bilateral trade deficit can produce inappropriate conclusions about fairness and, more importantly, policies attempting to eliminate bilateral trade deficits are likely to be very costly because they eliminate the gains from a multilateral trading system.

CONCLUSION

The proliferation of protectionist trade policies in recent years provides an impetus to reconsider their worth. In the world of traditional trade theory, characterized by perfect competition, a definitive recommendation in favor of free trade can be made. The gains from international trade result from a reallocation of production resources toward goods that can be produced less costly at home than abroad and the exchange of some of these goods for goods that can be produced at less cost abroad than at home.

Recent developments in international trade theory have examined the consequences of international trade in markets where there are market imperfections, such as monopoly and technological spillovers. Do these imperfections justify protectionist trade policies? The answer continues to be no. While protectionist trade policies may offset monopoly power overseas or advantageously use domestic monopoly power, trade restrictions tend to reduce the competition faced by domestic producers, protecting domestic producers at the expense of domestic consumers.

The empirical evidence is clear-cut. The costs of protectionist trade policies far exceed the benefits. The losses suffered by consumers exceed the gains reaped by domestic producers and government. Low-income consumers are relatively more adversely affected than high-income consumers. Not only are there inefficiencies associated with excessive domestic production and restricted consumption, but there are costs associated with the enforcement of the protectionist legislation and attempts to influence trade policy.

The primary reason for these costly protectionist policies relies on a public choice argument. The desire to influence trade policy arises from the fact that trade policy changes benefit some groups, while harming others. Consumers are harmed by protectionist legislation; however, ignorance, small individual costs, and the high costs of organizing consumers prevent the consumers from being an effective force. On the other hand, workers and other resource owners in an industry are more likely to be effective politically because of their relative ease of organizing and their individually large and easy-to-identify benefits. Politicians interested in re-election will most likely respond to the demands for protectionist legislation of such an interest group.

The empirical evidence also suggests that the adverse consumer effects of protectionist trade policies are not short-lived. These policies generate lower economic growth rates than the rates associated with free trade policies. In turn, slow growth contributes to additional protectionist pressures.

Interest group pressures from industries experiencing difficulty and the general appeal of a "level playing field" combine to make the reduction of trade barriers especially difficult at the present time in the United States. Nonetheless, national interests will be served best by such an admittedly difficult political course. In light of the current Uruguay Round negotiations under the General Agreement on Tariffs and Trade, as well as numerous bilateral discussions, this fact is especially timely.

REFERENCES

Hickok, Susan. "The Consumer Cost of U.S. Trade Restraints," Federal Reserve Bank of New York *Quarterly Review* (Summer 1985), pp. 1-12.

Hufbauer, Gary Clyde, Diane T. Berliner, and Kimberly Ann Elliott. *Trade Protection in the United States: 31 Case Studies* (Institute for International Economics, 1986).

Krugman, Paul R. "Is Free Trade Passé?" *Journal of Economic Perspectives* (Fall 1987), pp. 131-44.

Organization for Economic Co-Operation and Development (OECD). *Costs and Benefits of Protection* (1985).

Tarr, David G., and Morris E. Morkre. *Aggregate Costs to the United States of Tariffs and Quotas on Imports: General Tariff Cuts and Removal of Quotas on Automobiles, Steel, Sugar, and Textiles,* Bureau of Economics Staff Report to the Federal Trade Commission (December 1984).

World Bank. *World Development Report 1987* (Oxford University Press, 1987).

2

Towards a Marxist Theory Of European Integration

PETER COCKS

The author presents a Marxist interpretation of European political and economic integration. In this view, the purpose of the state is to provide the conditions under which capitalists can thrive. Economically, the state must ensure that capitalists can extract surplus value from workers in the context of expanding markets. Politically, the state must provide legitimacy, that is, acceptance of the capitalist rules of the game by the working class. During the initial stages of capitalism, as the scope of capitalist production and markets grew geographically, states were driven to develop into modern nation-states. Today, as the scope of capitalist production has become much larger and the tasks of the capitalist state have become much more complex, European integration is seen as a way in which capitalists and capitalism overcome their economic and political problems.

The significance of the European Communities (EC) remains obscure. The reason is that orthodox integration literature is fundamentally ahistorical: it fails to give an adequate account of the roots of modern European integration. And however admirable the project might be in itself, we cannot rectify the failure simply by chronicling the admittedly much ignored origins of the EC in the 1950s. For the EC is systematically connected to earlier cases of integration in Europe. Only by understanding the evolution of these integrational forms—from early modern Britain, to nineteenth century Germany, to contemporary Europe—can one begin to make sense of the EC. In brief, one must seek to understand the "present as

---

2 "Towards a Marxist Theory of European Integration" by Peter Cocks. Reprinted from *International Organization*, Vol. 34, No. 1, Peter Cocks, "Towards a Marxist Theory of European Integration," by permission of the MIT Press, Cambridge, MA.

history," a task that few writers on regional integration have yet attempted, and none with any success. . . .

In order to overcome the shortcomings of both orthodox and Marxist writers, we must investigate why particular patterns of integration, the EC among them, emerged in Europe in specific eras. I argue that integration evolved as a policy response to certain problems endemic to the growth of capitalism. I conceive successful political integration in Europe since the sixteenth century as a method of state-building at the national and international level. It has performed two critical state functions: provision of the political infrastructure for the expansion of productive forces in protocapitalist and capitalist societies; and an appropriate means for legitimating the power necessary to maintain the social relations integral to these societies. It is on the basis of these two factors that our analysis must begin. But before we can discuss the process of political integration itself, it is imperative to understand the social and political setting within which it is situated.

CAPITALISM AND THE STATE

Political integration plays a crucial part in the development of the state in capitalist society. In order to make plain this connection, we must first understand the nature of the capitalist social formation and the function of the state within that formation. Though I have compressed the discussion of these two phenomena unmercifully, what remains is nonetheless a somewhat lengthy, but absolutely necessary prologue to the discussion of integration per se. . . .

Expansion provides the dynamic urge of capitalism and is its ultimate necessary condition. Without such growth, capital accumulation cannot take place, and without accumulation there can be no realization of surplus value, which is the capitalist's enduring, overriding objective. Looked at from a slightly different angle, capital accumulation rests on the ability of the bourgeoisie to realize surplus value–that is, not only to produce, but also to sell goods (thus, the crises induced in capitalism by underconsumption and overproduction). These activities are situated within the context of competition between capitals: in order to assure its own survival, each capital must constantly find ways to grow—i.e., to realize surplus value and thus to accumulate capital. In this process some fall by the wayside, some become absorbed by other capitals; hence, Marx's observations on the tendency towards concentration and centralization of capitalist enterprises.

Under the impetus of these imperatives, capitalism becomes a peerless world system in which cores, or metropoles (economically advanced, politically dominant, and ethnically distinct areas) live symbiotically with peripheries, or hinterlands (economically backward, politically weak, and ethnically different from the metropoles). The latter come to depend upon the former for their development, yet, paradoxically, are held back by that very relationship.

What role does the state play in these developments? From the bourgeoisie's point of view, the state ought to provide minimally for three interconnected things: the accumulation of capital; the realization of surplus value for the capitalist class; maintenance of the private ownership of the means of trade and/or production. The creation and preservation of these essential characteristics of capitalism entail certain functions for bourgeois and hybrid bourgeois/aristocratic states—functions which, of course, show a rather wide variety of weights in different historical periods. The functions are: the creation of a secure environment for industry and commerce, complete with legal systems protecting private property, contracts, and the like; the provision of at least an acquiescent labor force; the ensuring of markets both at home and abroad; the construction of an ideological climate favorable to capitalism.

INTEGRATION IN THE DEVELOPMENT OF CAPITALISM

At the risk of doing injustice to its considerable subtleties, I contend that integration in Europe was and is a significant way of realizing the spread of authority (state functions) across larger and larger territorial areas so that the fundamental features of capitalism will remain intact. It arises as a possible policy when political elites see it as a mechanism to establish or reestablish the conditions for economic growth and political legitimation. It is thus the content of the process—integration for what?—that is of critical importance. Political and economic integration are methods of providing the institutional conditions for the expansion of capital, while social integration is the process of legitimating the new institutions. Thus, political integration refers to the building of new organizations that assure over wider jurisdictions, first, a correspondingly enlarged legal system that protects private property and enforces contracts and, second, an adequate supply of labor. Economic integration refers to the construction of economic unions over various geographical areas, usually, as we shall see, demarcated by territorial state, nation-state, and international-regional groupings. Progress towards economic unions, and thus the creation of new possibilities for economic growth, depends on the widening of consumer markets, the creation of conditions for the greater mobility of the factors of production, and the creation of new monetary arrangements. Social integration refers to the degree of ideological support that masses and elites will give to new integrational structures. One can distinguish between utilitarian (instrumental) and affective (emotional) beliefs about integration. The former—espoused first by elites and sometimes, indeed, in advance of the actual emergence of integrational institutions—chronologically precede the latter in the process of integration. In as far as affective beliefs, which are largely the province of the masses, are favorable to new integrational structures, they enhance the legitimation of capitalist social formations.

In sum, integration refers to the geographical spread of state functions in response to the exigencies of capital accumulation and the realization of surplus value, on the one hand, and their associated legitimation problems, on the other. It is, in blunter terms, a method of resolving certain actual or potential crises intrinsic to capitalist development. Let us now examine the concrete historical links between integration and problems confronting the state in proto-capitalist and capitalist societies.

Integration in Early Capitalism

. . . . The politically fragmented and economically stagnant worlds of feudal society were transformed in the fifteenth and sixteenth centuries by policies of internal unification and external expansion pursued by Renaissance and absolutist states. Individual governments were able to participate in the expansion that became a "concern of all Europe" only if they could consolidate their home base. In this respect, given the organizational capacities of the epoch, the smaller states initially had an advantage. . . .

The ideology of political integration, stressing the importance of the expansion of central authority at the expense of the aristocracy and the Roman Catholic Church, found its theoretical justification in the theory of mercantilism and its political analogue, absolutism. Mercantilism made explicit the connection between centralizing power and economic plenty. It emphasized the necessity of breaking down local barriers to trade, the achievement of political unification—processes that might well be described in terms of "internal colonialism"—and the use of colonies as the suppliers of raw materials and the consumers of finished goods produced in the core areas. The whole scheme was cast domestically in the context of government regulation of industry and trade, and internationally in the garb of protectionism and imperialism. And though internal unity and expansion abroad were intimately connected to the primitive accumulation of capital, mercantilism was not always favorable to the early development of the capitalist mode of production. Whether it enhanced or injured that development depended on the outcome of prolonged class struggles, between peasant and landlord, aristocracy and emergent bourgeoisie, capitalist, and artisan.

There were several distinct patterns of unification among the Renaissance and absolutist states, determined by the relative strength of socio-economic classes within the state and by the particular country's relationship to the international system. In some countries absolutist politics decisively blocked the emergence of capitalism. In others, in the face of the great ambivalence of the traditional authorities towards it, proto-capitalism nonetheless maintained its tenuous hold. And in one justly famous case, that of England, centralizing power proved to be sufficiently sympathetic to the new economic forces that political unity and the victory of capitalism went hand-in-hand.

In Europe east of the Elbe, the politically and economically dominant landed aristocracy sought during the sixteenth and seventeenth centuries to wring greater production from their fundamentally agrarian economies. Whether stimulated to do so by the greater demand for grain in the west or by the need to repel the invasions of western European states (Sweden in particular), the end result was the same: the imposition of the second serfdom. Feudalism remained thoroughly entrenched. The absence of real bourgeois threats to the dominance of the landed aristocracy initially made possible absolutist unification. And as the agrarian elite squeezed increased economic surplus from the peasant classes, it reinforced its own supremacy. Having to make no concessions to a wealthy bourgeoisie in order to support its spending on luxuries and war, and having kept the peasants in the thrall of serfdom, such regimes obstructed the growth of social relations from which capitalism could emerge, and condemned eastern Europe in the long-run to economic backwardness.

In contrast to the experience of the east, the countries of western Europe offered much greater potential for the simultaneous development of capitalism and absolutist unification. Despite this promise, in some cases, such as Spain, the heavy hand of absolutism blighted rather strong proto-capitalist tendencies. . . . Yet for all the wealth the Spanish garnered from the New World and the great accretion of political power they achieved in the sixteenth century, by the middle of the seventeenth century, the country was in decay, a victim of stifled bourgeois initiative, unproductive investment, backward education, and the crippling fiscal burden of war. . . .

In France, though state regulation stunted the forces of economic growth, they were not stifled as they were in Spain. The mercantilism of Colbert in the seventeenth century extended governmental control over the country's economy, sometimes suffocating rather than breathing life into it. In addition, he was unsuccessful in eliminating internal tariffs. Without the destruction of these barriers the economic stimulus of a unified market was lost; it was a loss to remain unrepaired until the creation of domestic free trade by the revolutionary regime of 1789-90. But the political omissions and commissions of French officials by no means halted the forward movement of the economy. For French absolutism was reformed rather than reactionary and its administration depended heavily on the ennobled bourgeoisie who, rather than adopting the hostility to bourgeois values characteristic of the hereditary aristocracy, retained their bourgeois mentality.

In England the coeval achievement of political and economic unity was thoroughly interlaced with the triumph of capitalism. On the face of it, internal unification and overseas expansion seemed to complement each other on the same pattern as that of Spain. Yet there was a critical difference from the Spanish and the French, to say nothing of the eastern European, experiences. . . . English unity (I would go so far as to say British unity) was founded on a coalition composed of merchants, on the one hand, and that uniquely British social class, the gentry, on the other. The gentry were an agrarian elite imbued with the rudiments of capitalist mentality and with strong merchant connections—both in domestic and overseas trade—who were the dominant force in English, then, more widely, British politics from the mid-sixteenth to the early eighteenth century. While the monarch could not rule effectively without the financial help of the city-dwelling merchants, the gentry played the decisive role in political integration, for they were willing to support the crown only to the extent that it helped them consolidate their preeminent position in the hinterland. True first for the English gentry, in the course of the sixteenth and seventeenth centuries, it became equally so for their Scottish and Welsh counterparts who, assiduously divorcing themselves from their fellow Celts, were drawn into the English political-economic ambit. Together the gentry and merchants of the three countries decisively repulsed the crown's efforts in the 1640s to establish absolutist unity on the continental European model. The process of integration between England, Scotland, and Wales was thoroughly favorable to the development of capitalism precisely because the asphyxic qualities of the would-be absolutist monarchy were beaten back in the seventeenth century.

This unity, so conducive to the growth of new economic forces, had been forged from a gentry-merchant alliance dating back to Tudor times. The progressive unification of England, Scotland, and Wales provided the framework for the primitive accumulation of capital, the fruits of which reinforced this same alliance. The political and material resources of unified England, hewed from the suppression of centrifugal feudal rivalries, made possible the colonial plunder and exploitation which constituted the overseas sources of primitive accumulation. So too the winning of the domestic sources relied upon reasonably strong central government, eventually extended to Scotland, and the spread of economic integration qua domestic free trade, national credit system, and increased mobility of the factors of production. Thus were made possible the expropriation of the peasantry through the enclosure movement (closely associated with the growth of gentry, market-oriented farming), and the replacement of the artisanate by the putting-out system and, eventually, by factory production under the control of an emerging bourgeoisie.

By the beginning of the eighteenth century the three countries were ruled by a central authority in London, sympathetic to capitalist development. Together these nations comprised an economically integrated territory that was the largest free trade area in Europe. The state here facilitated, at the very least, and enforced, at best, the passage of economic surplus and accumulated capital into the hands of those willing and able to employ it productively. More effective government reduced transactions' costs and eased the task of urban and rural entrepreneurs by cheapening security and information, creating more efficient legal enforcement of contracts, and inducing greater labor mobility.

The changing class conditions necessary to create a genuine capitalist breakthrough occurred between the middle of the sixteenth and the start of eighteenth century in Britain alone. This meant that only there was unification a resolutely pro-capitalist process. And in due course it propelled the country into a dominant position in the nineteenth century. Other countries may have unified, but they did so without benefit of this new class structure. Without it they were condemned to relative backwardness. Some, such as France, eventually created the conditions for the coexistence of political unity and capitalism. Others, such as Spain and eastern Europe, remained mired in their pre-capitalist history. Yet others, like Germany, made a belated but decisive break with the past, both unifying and accelerating quickly into a phase of capitalist industrialization.

Integration in Conditions of Delayed Industrialization

The relationship between integration and capitalism in conditions of delayed industrialization in the nineteenth century presents a rather different picture. By this era, maturing capitalist economies with extensive empires (particularly the British Empire) already existed. This situation put pressure on the governments of the backward economies to take activist roles in the promotion of industrialization and thence to acquire or reacquire political power in the international system. And power that could not be had without the development of industrialization rested partially, but to an important extent, on territorial unification. This was particularly the case in fragmented regions such as Italy and Germany. In such circumstances unification was crucial to the reduction of transaction costs, and hence to the opening up of profitable horizons for the entrepreneur. Traditional ruling classes took a calculated gamble in some, although not all, such backward economies. They calculated that under their tutelage the evolution of capitalism and a unification suited to it would serve to prolong and/or consolidate their political power and social position. The state occupied a significant, even crucial, place in this transitional period, welding old (political) and new (economic) forces into a particular amalgam that constituted revolution from above.

In conditions of economic backwardness, the roles of legitimation and ideology were also readily distinguishable from those under early capitalism. The uneven development of world capitalism was crucial in providing the impetus for national integration in these "backward" cases. . . . Nationalism remained the elemental ideological force in politics and provided the doctrinal basis of unification, joining the rulers and the ruled in a spurious bond of harmony and mutuality of interest. Providing a rationale for the burdens and promises of unification, it became the keystone of the legitimation construct. Nationalism provided a temporary means for substituting "we" for "them" and "us" in the political equation. Needless to say, mercantilist ideas fitted very well with nationalism, although they remained the preserve of the administrative and economic elite. All of the foregoing, albeit in different degrees, characterized the most well-known cases of delayed industrialization in the nineteenth century: Germany, Russia, and Japan. Japan was in a sense the extreme example. Drawn from its traditional ruling classes, its modernizers in the Meiji period systematically destroyed a moribund feudal unity and replaced it with a new unity suited to capitalist growth, while at the same time maintaining an entirely protective stance towards the outside world and preserving the main features of the traditional social structure.

The German case of unification is also instructive. Economic and political integration, especially the operation of the Zollverein, were critical factors in fostering rapid economic development after 1848. The effect on member states was paradoxical. On the one hand, they could not afford to pass up the benefits that the growth of industrial capitalism would bring: increased wealth and power; enlarged government revenue that made the legitimation of existing institutions that much easier. On the other hand, the growth of industrialism was inherently a destabilizing social force. To the ruling elites, the benefits outweighed the costs as long as a depression did not aggravate such social dislocations. But unification, and with it industrial capitalism, brought bust as well as boom. The smaller Zollverein states may have proved capable of coping with political and social instabilities intrinsic to the fast economic growth Germany experienced in the 1850s and 1860s, but confronting the depression of the 1870s was another matter. These states lacked the sheer size and strength to formulate appropriate policy responses to an event whose ramifications were as widespread as the newly integrated national economy would suggest. The legitimation of existing social arrangements now relied on the Reich's countermeasures to these economic reverses.

In the 1870s and 1880s economic issues, though remaining connected with unification and constitutional questions, displaced them as the burning concerns of the day. Bismarck himself—the architect of unity—recognized that the chief threats to the existing order were the socially divisive effects of the depression. He accepted, therefore, the need for ensuring the necessary conditions for that order: primarily, continued prosperity. . . . On the one hand, this entailed the construction of a rudimentary welfare state to achieve the interconnected objectives of reducing class antagonism and subverting the appeals of socialism. On the other, it implied the expansion of markets, preferably via informal imperialism, but by formal colonial ties if the need arose. Together these policies were a task for nothing smaller than the unified German state.

Integration in Mature Capitalist Society

Just as previous forms of integration in Europe mirrored the characteristic problems of earlier epochs, so has twentieth century integration reflected certain facets of capitalism peculiar to the contemporary period. Two aspects that are particularly relevant to integration compel attention here. First, the bourgeoisie has only fairly recently begun really to understand economic fluctuations, and has thus acquired the means of contriving to escape the domination of the business cycle. In particular, the Keynesian revolution provided a basis for controlling the more extreme vagaries of capitalism, so that the bourgeoisie ceased to see themselves as entirely at the mercy of unalterable laws. This did not necessarily mean that they could prevent crises, but rather that they were better able than their predecessors to control the economic system and, as a result, to perpetuate their predominant role within the whole socio-economic formation.

Second, capitalism since the end of the Second World War has been characterized by both increased monopolization and a growing interpenetration of state and economy. Government investment has fuelled economic expansion. Paradoxically such expansion in turn has progressively weakened the authority of the nation-state, since higher rates of economic growth were accompanied by, and causally linked to, growing international economic interdependence.

The imperative of growth forced new developments in the capitalist state, which had to provide the requisite infrastructure for the achievement of profits. Growth was necessary not only for the realization of surplus value, but also for the provision of legitimation: distinct factors in social analysis perhaps, but in real life, indivisible. Yet, as the world capitalist economy became increasingly interdependent, the state's capacity for handling these factors partially passed from its grasp to an international arena over which it had much less authority. (This argument applied, a fortiori, to those countries that had lost or were in the process of losing control over colonial empires.)

The type of strategy used to assert or reassert greater control over realization and legitimation depended on the status of the particular country in the international economy. Free trade policies were apt only as long as one's own country was the dominant economy and made the rules for international economic intercourse. For subordinate capitalist countries, supranationalism—a mercantilist policy writ large—was appropriate.

After the Second World War, several occurrences were crucial in setting the tone for European politics: first, was the war itself, both in terms of destructiveness and of its implications for successful government intervention in the economy; second, were the closely connected events of prewar depression and the breakdown of constitutional politics that had resulted from it, the recrudescence of which statesmen now sought to avoid; third, the perceived threat to European security posed by the Soviet Union; and fourth, the growth of colonial independence movements.

In brief, Western politicians saw themselves faced with the interconnected tasks of creating security (to avoid another intra-European war and to prevent dominance by the USSR) and prosperity. The former was dealt with largely through the establishment of NATO. Security, however, was less important for European integration than prosperity. The pursuit of affluence was the main link between, on the one side, the formation and subsequent progress of the European Communities, and, on the other, the continuing legitimation of capitalist social relations.

Despite their ambivalence to some aspects of it, European politicians and civil servants shared an ideology that was based on belief in the efficacy of possessive individualism, peaceful political change via constitutionalism, and government intervention to achieve social welfare and economic growth. Socioeconomic change that could not be accommodated within such limits effectively was ruled out of the mainstream of political discourse. The postwar years were heralded as the era of the "end of ideology," an epoch in which the major political parties seemed to agree upon the methods of dealing with fundamental issues that had proved so divisive in the 1920s and 1930s. . . . Everyone, it was said, agreed on the main objectives of society; the basic, technical question was how to get there. And that was something that economists, politicians, and civil servants could now decide, away from the heady, fissiparous struggles where ideologies (i.e., differences over the basic objectives of politics) intruded.

The fundament of the "end of ideology" was the permanence of high rates of economic growth, since growing affluence appeared to eradicate discussion of . . .

the appropriate class shares of social resources. Thus, in Europe the issue of who got what in society was removed temporarily from the realm of visible struggle—in effect, depoliticized—though it is clear that the act of such removal was profoundly political in that it served to freeze existing shares of wealth and income. . . . [P]olitical decision-makers' pursuit of increased economic welfare (conceived as essentially a technical, non-political problem) gave great impetus to regional organization. The "end of ideology" laid the ground for the first surge of European integration and was, in turn, reinforced by the greater economic growth that integration brought.

European integration played an integral part in European leaders' aspirations to create what Warren has termed the ideal neo-capitalist political economy. Its main features are: the harmonization of private and public investment spending; controls, including wage controls where necessary, over private consumption; full employment, but, when needed, government policy to reduce disturbances from balance of payments crises and/or unemployment; international coordination of trade and monetary policies; cooptation of the working class into the process of economic planning.

Given the goal of maintaining extant socio-economic systems, political leaders were compelled to make policies within the structural parameters of mature capitalist political economy. This entailed meeting problems on national, regional, and international levels. . . .

European integration was a regional component in the postwar reconstruction of world capitalism. With the establishment of the IBRD and the IMF, the Bretton Woods agreement constituted the broad international framework for western economic revival. But this structure alone was insufficient to ensure the prosperity of Europe, a factor as important to the U.S. as to European elites themselves. Global economic interdependence made the demise of Europe, or its relapse into national mercantilist policies, unthinkable to American policy makers. Hence the construction of the Marshall Plan, the OEEC, and the great American emphasis on the need for European integration.

For European decision makers unification held out several important possibilities. The first, and most important, was its putative capacity to ensure high rates of export-led economic growth. . . . Self-consciously many policy makers may have thought that these factors were simply economic, though as I have been at pains to point out, they were at the same time profoundly political. In European integration, politicians were not trying to create a radically new world; rather, they were trying via new growth-inducing machinery to preserve existing socioeconomic structures.

The second possibility was that European nations together might be able to do what they could not do apart: to forge a counterweight to American hegemony. (The major exception was Britain, whose leaders believed for many years against all the odds that the country would be able to provide by its own efforts the plenty upon which power was based. Having discovered that his was not feasible, Britain ended up by joining the EC.)

The third possibility was that European integration would be a means to perpetuate basically traditional relations with ex-colonies under a new guise. This certainly appeared to be the case with the Yaoundé Conventions (1963, 1969). . . .

The EC presented new opportunities for economic expansion. Decision makers in the member countries believed the Common Market to be a prime cause of the continued high rates of growth after 1958. In this sense, European integration was a nexus between prosperity and domestic political legitimation. But the EC brought other consequences, not necessarily directly intended, which also facilitated the legitimation of existing political institutions.

The establishment of a large common market helped to allay such fears as there were about increasing monopoly at the national level. In the new larger European context national monopolies were forced to compete with other corporations: competition was injected thereby with new life. The other side of the picture, of course, was that the foundation of the EC stimulated yet further growth of national monopolies, aided and abetted by national governments. Corporate mergers were encouraged in order to create firms large enough to compete in this new setting, particularly against American transnational companies which had taken advantage of the EC to invade Europe as never before. The creation of the EC, therefore, provided the means for reconciling the exigencies of the economies of scale with adherence to the ideology of competition.

An important side effect of the creation of larger corporations was to make the work of economic planners easier just when planning was coming to play an increasingly important role in European policy making. Planning was conceived as the technocratic answer to the need for high rates of growth based upon improved competitive positions for one's own firms in the international market. . . . On the employers' side, planning mainly involved monopolistic and oligopolistic industries. Planners did not discourage the yet greater concentration of industry desired by corporate leaders since it made the former's task that much easier. On the employees' side, planning assumed worker cooperation, even if in the end employers and civil servants dominated the outcomes of the process. That cooperation was most easily handled through trade unions, and the bulk of the unionized work force was in the non-competitive sector of the economy. A consequence of this—albeit unequal—partnership was to strengthen the economic position of organized labor in the industries that were the main beneficiaries of the EC. And this tended to reinforce the division between organized and unorganized labor. To the degree that united labor action is necessary to challenge effectively the traditional prerogatives of capital, such a division enhanced social stability, gave greater scope for the state to legitimate its powers, and in the end, ensured the domination of capital.

On the international level, working class solidarity was affected by the difficulties that trade unions had in forming a viable European-wide organization to combat transnational capital. Capital has spread across national boundaries much more easily than have labor organizations. One reason for this is that trade unions cannot become transnational without becoming multinational at the same time; the essence of international unions is that they are run by several different nationalities. By contrast, transnational corporations, precisely the kind of firms whose operations were facilitated by the EC, are managed in the upper echelons overwhelmingly by one nationality. They do not have to deal head-on, as do labor unions, with the whole gamut of ethnic rivalries and suspicions in their own management. . . .

By and large, national governments were willing to support the Common Market, and thus legitimate its institutions, provided that its policies coincided with what national elites thought best for their own interests. Each individual state and its administrators, acting as defenders of the collective capitalist interest (and therefore acting against the interests of some capitalists), judged the EC according to whether in their view it forwarded this interest or not. If national administrators saw that EC policies undermined rather than enhanced the legitimacy of their regimes, they resorted to all sorts of tactics in order to avoid the EC mandate. Since the legitimation of the EC relies primarily on support from national elites and, secondarily, on non-participatory diffuse support at the national level, such evasion bespeaks a considerable problem for the Eurocrats. The latter wish to implement policy effectively, but not at the cost of creating popular disaffection and undermining the authority of national elites. . . . The process of legitimation at the national level is one in which elites are able at least to convince the masses of the rightness of those two pillars of legitimation ideology: possessive individualism and nationalism. The EC's contribution to the former is clear. With respect to the latter, EC decision makers must ensure that their policies do not undermine the sense of nationhood that underlies strong government . . . —a paradox, indeed, for the progenitors and supporters of European integration.

Regional disparities in economic growth and wealth—especially when they are exacerbated by recession or depression—can erode the nationalist pillar of legitimation by reviving previously slumbering ethnic sensibilities. Given that strong national governments are vital for the preservation of the EC and, indeed, of European capitalism itself, it follows that elites would attempt to formulate policies at both national and European levels to ameliorate regional inequalities. Reducing regional economic differences is not antithetical to the capitalist ethos. . . . The means to it, however, are somewhat more controversial, particularly since they involve the transfer of funds from the richer countries (mainly West Germany) to the poorer (Italy, Ireland, and Great Britain).

If we accept the arguments on the limits to economic growth that I have laid out earlier in this article, the kind of affluence that Europeans witnessed in the 1950s and 1960s may simply be unattainable in the foreseeable future. That possibility raises the specter of pressures for the redistribution of wealth, income, and power among social classes, with all the bitter conflict that that implies. Indeed, there are signs of resurgent class struggle in Europe around these and allied issues, such as the ownership and control of industry and the democratization of the work-place. . . . Built to foster growth rather than to settle divisive political issues, the EC can scarcely provide good answers to these questions. Its regional policy is of dubious success, and it is altogether ill-equipped to deal with the job of lessening inequalities between classes. National governments are only marginally better armed to cope with the last-mentioned problem. The stagnation of the EC simply parallels the present inability of the political institutions of capital in general to find plausible answers to their most pressing questions. . . .

SUMMARY AND CONCLUSION

Political integration in the capitalist system is one dimension of the essential role of the state in reproducing the totality of capitalist social relations. One can describe it as a process of state-building, exhibited both at the national and the international level. New political institutions arise which have as their purpose the spread of state functions over progressively larger territorial areas. Political integration, however, is not irreversible. The unification of territorial states, for example, may not be a once-and-for-all business: the process of uneven capitalist development may eventually threaten such political unity.

Social, economic, and political integration evolve at different speeds in capitalist systems. The particular configuration of these three phenomena at a point in time depends at minimum on the specific phase of capitalist development, the technological and administrative state of knowledge, the level of political consciousness of the masses, and the perception and activities of the dominant political and economic classes. . . .

Everywhere in sixteenth and seventeenth century Europe the landed classes held political power. With the demise of feudalism there appeared absolutist states (that were both caused by and caused that demise) espousing the economic tenets of mercantilism. Leaders stressed the creation of territorial states in opposition to the universal claims of the Roman Catholic Church. In these centuries the masses were to all intents and purposes politically irrelevant. Mercantilism and absolutism were ideologies of dominant classes seeking to impress their authority over defined territorial areas. Mercantilism was at once a principle of territorial unification and the creation of a national market.

At the same time, capitalism was growing in the interstices of medieval economy. Whether it would be stifled or not, and for how long, would be a matter of wide-ranging variation. In some places, such as England, unification based on absolutism and mercantilism and wrought under the aegis of a landed class was conducive to the development of capitalism. In other countries, such as Spain, France, and Russia, unification did not have the same effect. Thus, absolutism and mercantilism were not merely "produced" by capitalist economy. In fact, they were often part of anti-capitalist ideologies. The English example tended to be the exception, although a vitally important one, not the rule.

In the eighteenth and nineteenth centuries the morphology of unification began to change. Absolutism, the ideological preserve of the elite, gave way towards the end of the eighteenth century to nationalism, the property of both elites and masses. This new creed provided part of the ideological underpinnings for industrialization, for it created a necessary sense of unity across the potentially disruptive class divisions born of capitalism itself. Mercantilism could live with such a political ideology, and frequently did. Growing disaffection with mercantilist restrictions among merchants and industrialists, however, nurtured the laissez-faire impulse. Political leaders were compelled to adapt their policies and ideologies to the changing international economic structure. Internationalism, qua laissez-faire/laissez-passer, was the response of elites in England, the leading capitalist country. In "backward" countries, such as Germany, reactive nationalism was the response of political leaders to their particular predicament. There, nationalism was both an elite and mass belief conducive to the building of the national unity necessary for capitalism to take off into industrialization. The bourgeoisie espoused nationalism and protectionism, for under the cloak of the latter they could create viable businesses. Aware of the great increases in political power that industrialization had brought to Britain, the traditional leaders joined forces with the bourgeoisie, while maintaining their political dominance.

By the end of the nineteenth century, markets in the major European countries were nationally unified. Moreover, the concept of a nation-state seemed to have some meaning, to the degree that unified territorial states more or less coincided with the geography of national consciousness. Although most major European states were ruled by some kind of coalition of bourgeoisie and landed classes, the former became a stronger and stronger force in politics.

The interests of the bourgeoisie, which after the First World War increasingly dominated European politics, were dealt a heavy blow by the depression of the inter-war years. It was a seminal event, though, not only for the elites but also for the masses, and, more generally, for the future direction of capitalism. Beggar-my-neighbor policies proved to be no way to deal with a slump which, with growing capitalist interdependence, was of patently international dimensions. The virtual breakdown of the European economy and the consequent threat to constitutional politics convinced the dominant political and social classes that the return of widescale depression would be destructive of the society that they embraced. The experience of the 1930s, combined with the new role of the United States as a hegemonic power, provided the impetus for European integration after the Second World War. Again, therefore, it was the dynamic of international capitalism and its related legitimation problems which gave rise to a new form of economic and political unity.

European state officials recognized the importance of regional groupings for economies that had spilled over national frontiers but which were not nearly as strong and competitive as that of the United States. Regional integration was a mechanism for accommodating and reinforcing the expansion of European capital while simultaneously protecting it from the possibly excessive rigors of international competition. Ideologically, supranationalist ideas such as federalism and functionalism provided moral and intellectual justifications at the elite level for European regional organization. Supranationalism coexisted uneasily with nationalism: elites supported the former to the degree that it enhanced the legitimacy of the national state. At the mass level nationalism remained the prevailing ideology, although some rudimentary support for supranationalism was evident quite early in the process of regional integration. In times of crisis both elites and masses tended to retreat into economic and political nationalism.

Although integration under capitalism has always occurred as an elite process, the remainder of the population, as it has become more politicized, has had to be convinced in some manner of the efficacy of integration. The necessity of generating support for new integrational institutions, and thus legitimating the power that flows from them, is at the bottom of integration ideology. It follows that there is a built-in tension in the transition from one level of integration to another, since the politically relevant population must modify at least some of the major, and almost axiomatic, principles by which it has lived hitherto.

As with so much else in European politics, political integration can be understood only in the context of the major transformations of European history. Political integration is a form of political development, qua institution building, that arises as a response to the dual pressures of legitimation and economic expansion as they are manifested in these transitional epochs. My argument is that such legitimation problems themselves derive from capitalist necessities of accumulation of capital and the realization of surplus value. When serious obstacles to economic growth endanger the attainment of these two requisites, political difficulties threaten. To the extent that integration is a means of establishing or restoring the conditions for accumulation and realization, it is likely to emerge as a practical political policy. It is therefore vital both to understand the intersubjective meanings attributed to integration by the participants in the process and to identify the epochal parameters within which they act.

3

State Power and the Structure of International Trade

STEPHEN D. KRASNER

In this essay, Stephen Krasner applies a Realist analysis to the relationship between the interests and power of major states and the trade openness of the international economy. He identifies four principal goals of state action: political power, aggregate national income, economic growth, and social stability. He then combines the goals with different national abilities to pursue them, relating the international distribution of potential economic power to alternative trade regimes. Krasner maintains, most significantly, that the hegemony of a leading power is necessary for the creation and continuance of free trade. He applies his model to six periods. While the argument works well for three of the periods, it works less well for the other three and requires an amendment. Krasner's analysis in this 1976 article is a well-known attempt to use Realist ideas to explain international economic affairs. The theory he propounds, which has been dubbed the "theory of hegemonic stability," has influenced most other Realist and neo-Realist writing on the subject.

INTRODUCTION

In recent years, students of international relations have multinationalized, transnationalized, bureaucratized, and transgovernmentalized the state until it has virtually ceased to exist as an analytic construct. Nowhere is that trend more apparent than in the study of the politics of international economic relations. The basic conven-

---

3 "State Power and the Structure of International Trade" by Stephen D. Krasner. Stephen Krasner, "State Power and the Structure of International Trade," *World Politics*, Vol. 28, No. 3 (April 1976).

tional assumptions have been undermined by assertions that the state is trapped by a transnational society created not by sovereigns, but by nonstate actors. Interdependence is not seen as a reflection of state policies and state choices (the perspective of balance-of-power theory), but as the result of elements beyond the control of any state or a system created by states.

This perspective is at best profoundly misleading. It may explain developments within a particular international economic structure, but it cannot explain the structure itself. That structure has many institutional and behavioral manifestations. The central continuum along which it can be described is openness. International economic structures may range from complete autarky (if all states prevent movements across their borders), to complete openness (if no restrictions exist). In this paper I will present an analysis of one aspect of the international economy—the structure of international trade; that is, the degree of openness for the movement of goods as opposed to capital, labor, technology, or other factors of production. Since the beginning of the nineteenth century, this structure has gone through several changes. These can be explained, albeit imperfectly, by a state-power theory: an approach that begins with the assumption that the structure of international trade is determined by the interests and power of states acting to maximize national goals. The first step in this argument is to relate four basic state interests—aggregate national income, social stability, political power, and economic growth—to the degree of openness for the movement of goods. The relationship between these interests and openness depends upon the potential economic power of any given state. Potential economic power is operationalized in terms of the relative size and level of economic development of the state. The second step in the argument is to relate different distributions of potential power, such as multipolar and hegemonic, to different international trading structures. The most important conclusion of this theoretical analysis is that a hegemonic distribution of potential economic power is likely to result in an open trading structure. That argument is largely, although not completely, substantiated by empirical data. For a fully adequate analysis it is necessary to amend a state-power argument to take account of the impact of past state decisions on domestic social structures as well as on international economic ones. The two major organizers of the structure of trade since the beginning of the nineteenth century, Great Britain and the United States, have both been prevented from making policy amendments in line with state interests by particular societal groups whose power had been enhanced by earlier state policies.

THE CAUSAL ARGUMENT: STATE INTERESTS, STATE POWER, AND INTERNATIONAL TRADING STRUCTURES

Neoclassical trade theory is based upon the assumption that states act to maximize their aggregate economic utility. This leads to the conclusion that maximum global welfare and Pareto optimality are achieved under free trade. While particular countries might better their situations through protectionism, economic theory has generally looked askance at such policies. . . . Neoclassical theory recognizes that trade regulations can . . . be used to correct domestic distortions and to promote infant industries, but these are exceptions or temporary departures from policy conclusions that lead logically to the support of free trade.

State Preferences

Historical experience suggests that policy makers are dense, or that the assumptions of the conventional argument are wrong. Free trade has hardly been the norm. Stupidity is not a very interesting analytic category. An alternative approach to explaining international trading structures is to assume that states seek a broad range of goals. At least four major state interests affected by the structure of international trade can be identified. They are: political power, aggregate national income, economic growth, and social stability. The way in which each of these goals is affected by the degree of openness depends upon the potential economic power of the state as defined by its relative size and level of development.

Let us begin with aggregate national income because it is most straightforward. Given the exceptions noted above, conventional neo-classical theory demonstrates that the greater the degree of openness in the international trading system, the greater the level of aggregate economic income. This conclusion applies to all states regardless of their size or relative level of development. The static economic benefits of openness are, however, generally inversely related to size. Trade gives small states relatively more welfare benefits than it gives large ones. Empirically, small states have higher ratios of trade to national product. They do not have the generous factor endowments or potential for national economies of scale that are enjoyed by larger—particularly continental—states.

The impact of openness on social stability runs in the opposite direction. Greater openness exposes the domestic economy to the exigencies of the world market. That implies a higher level of factor movements than in a closed economy, because domestic production patterns must adjust to changes in international prices. Social instability is thereby increased, since there is friction in moving factors, particularly labor, from one sector to another. The impact will be stronger in small states than in large, and in relatively less developed than in more developed ones. Large states are less involved in the international economy: a smaller percentage of their total factor endowment is affected by the international market at any given level of openness. More developed states are better able to adjust factors: skilled workers can more easily be moved from one kind of production to another than can unskilled laborers or peasants. Hence social stability is, *ceteris paribus,* inversely related to openness, but the deleterious consequences of exposure to the international trading system are mitigated by larger size and greater economic development.

The relationship between political power and the international trading structure can be analyzed in terms of the relative opportunity costs of closure for trading partners. The higher the relative cost of closure, the weaker the political position of the state. Hirschman has argued that this cost can be measured in terms of direct income losses and the adjustment costs of reallocating factors. These will be smaller for large states and for relatively more developed states. Other things being equal, utility costs will be less for large states because they generally have a smaller proportion of their economy engaged in the international economic system. Reallocation costs will be less for more advanced states because their factors are more mobile. Hence a state that is relatively large and more developed will find its political power enhanced by an open system because its opportunity costs of closure are less. The large state can use the threat to alter the system to secure economic or noneconomic objectives. Historically, there is one important exception to this generalization—the oil-exporting states. The level of reserves for some of the states, particularly Saudi Arabia, has reduced the economic opportunity costs of closure to a very low level despite their lack of development.

The relationship between international economic structure and economic growth is elusive. For small states, economic growth has generally been empirically associated with openness. Exposure to the international system makes possible a much more efficient allocation of resources. Openness also probably furthers the rate of growth of large countries with relatively advanced technologies because they do not need to protect infant industries and can take advantage of expanded world markets. In the long term, however, openness for capital and technology, as well as goods, may hamper the growth of large, developed countries by diverting resources from the domestic economy, and by providing potential competitors with the knowledge needed to develop their own industries. Only by maintaining its technological lead and continually developing new industries can even a very large state escape the undesired consequences of an entirely open economic system. For medium-size states, the relationship between international trading structure and growth is impossible to specify definitively, either theoretically or empirically. On the one hand, writers from the mercantilists through the American protectionists and the German historical school, and more recently analysts of *dependencia,* have argued that an entirely open system can undermine a state's effort to develop, and even lead to underdevelopment. On the other hand, adherents of more conventional neoclassical positions have maintained that exposure to international competition spurs economic transformation. The evidence is not yet in. All that can confidently be said is that openness furthers the economic growth of small states and of large ones so long as they maintain their technological edge.

From State Preferences to International Trading Structures

The next step in this argument is to relate particular distributions of potential economic power, defined by the size and level of development of individual states, to the structure of the international trading system, defined in terms of openness.

Let us consider a system composed of a large number of small, highly developed states. Such a system is likely to lead to an open international trading structure. The aggregate income and economic growth of each state are increased by an open system. The social instability produced by exposure to international competition is mitigated by the factor mobility made possible by higher levels of development. There is no loss of political power from openness because the costs of closure are symmetrical for all members of the system.

Now let us consider a system composed of a few very large, but unequally developed states. Such a distribution of potential economic power is likely to lead to a closed structure. Each state could increase its income through a more open system, but the gains would be modest. Openness would create more social instability in the less developed countries. The rate of growth for more backward areas might be frustrated, while that of the more advanced ones would be enhanced. A more open structure would leave the less developed states in a politically more vulnerable position, because their greater factor rigidity would mean a higher relative cost of closure. Because of these disadvantages, large but relatively less developed states are unlikely to accept an open trading structure. More advanced states cannot, unless they are militarily more powerful, force large backward countries to accept openness.

Finally, let us consider a hegemonic system—one in which there is a single state that is much larger and relatively more advanced than its trading partners. The costs and benefits of openness are not symmetrical for all members of the system. The hegemonic state will have a preference for an open structure. Such a structure increases its aggregate national income. It also increases its rate of growth during its ascendancy—that is, when its relative size and technological lead are increasing. Further, an open structure increases its political power, since the opportunity costs of closure are least for a large and developed state. The social instability resulting from exposure to the international system is mitigated by the hegemonic power's relatively low level of involvement in the international economy, and the mobility of its factors.

What of the other members of a hegemonic system? Small states are likely to opt for openness because the advantages in terms of aggregate income and growth are so great, and their political power is bound to be restricted regardless of what they do. The reaction of medium-size states is hard to predict; it depends at least in part on the way in which the hegemonic power utilizes its resources. The potentially dominant state has symbolic, economic, and military capabilities that can be used to entice or compel others to accept an open trading structure.

At the symbolic level, the hegemonic state stands as an example of how economic development can be achieved. Its policies may be emulated, even if they are inappropriate for other states. Where there are very dramatic asymmetries, military power can be used to coerce weaker states into an open structure. Force is not, however, a very efficient means for changing economic policies and it is unlikely to be employed against medium-size states.

CHART 1. Probability of an Open Trading Structure with Different Distributions of Potential Economic Power

LEVEL OF DEVELOPMENT OF STATES	SIZE OF STATES		
	Relatively Equal		Very Unequal
	Small	Large	
Equal	Moderate-High	Low-Moderate	High
Unequal	Moderate	Low	Moderate-High

Most importantly, the hegemonic state can use its economic resources to create an open structure. In terms of positive incentives, it can offer access to its large domestic market and to its relatively cheap exports. In terms of negative ones, it can withhold foreign grants and engage in competition, potentially ruinous for the weaker state, in third-country markets. The size and economic robustness of the hegemonic state also enable it to provide the confidence necessary for a stable international monetary system, and its currency can offer the liquidity needed for an increasingly open system.

In sum, openness is most likely to occur during periods when a hegemonic state is in its ascendancy. Such a state has the interest and the resources to create a structure characterized by lower tariffs, rising trade proportions, and less regionalism. There are other distributions of potential power where openness is likely, such as a system composed of many small, highly developed states. But even here, that potential might not be realized because of the problems of creating confidence in a monetary system where adequate liquidity would have to be provided by a negotiated international reserve asset or a group of national currencies. Finally, it is unlikely that very large states, particularly at unequal levels of development, would accept open trading relations.

These arguments, and the implications of other ideal typical configurations of potential economic power for the openness of trading structures, are summarized in [Chart 1].

THE DEPENDENT VARIABLE: DESCRIBING THE STRUCTURE OF THE INTERNATIONAL TRADING SYSTEM

The structure of international trade has both behavioral and institutional attributes. The degree of openness can be described both by the flow of goods and by the *policies* that are followed by states with respect to trade barriers and international payments. The two are not unrelated, but they do not coincide perfectly.

In common usage, the focus of attention has been upon institutions. Openness is associated with those historical periods in which tariffs were substantially lowered: the third quarter of the nineteenth century and the period since the Second World War.

Tariffs alone, however, are not an adequate indicator of structure. They are hard to operationalize quantitatively. Tariffs do not have to be high to be effective. If cost functions are nearly identical, even low tariffs can prevent trade. Effective tariff rates may be much higher than nominal ones. Non-tariff barriers to trade, which are not easily compared across states, can substitute for duties. An undervalued exchange rate can protect domestic markets from foreign competition. Tariff levels alone cannot describe the structure of international trade.

A second indicator, and one which is behavioral rather than institutional, is trade proportions—the ratios of trade to national income for different states. Like tariff levels, these involve describing the system in terms of an agglomeration of national tendencies. A period in which these ratios are increasing across time for most states can be described as one of increasing openness.

A third indicator is the concentration of trade within regions composed of states at different levels of development. The degree of such regional encapsulation is determined not so much by comparative advantage (because relative factor endowments would allow almost any backward area to trade with almost any developed one), but by political choices or dictates. Large states, attempting to protect themselves from the vagaries of a global system, seek to maximize their interests by creating regional blocs. Openness in the global economic system has in effect meant greater trade among the leading industrial states. Periods of closure are associated with the encapsulation of certain advanced states within regional systems shared with certain less developed areas.

A description of the international trading system involves, then, an exercise that is comparative rather than absolute. A period when tariffs are falling, trade proportions are rising, and regional trading patterns are becoming less extreme will be defined as one in which the structure is becoming more open.

Tariff Levels

The period from the 1820's to 1879 was basically one of decreasing tariff levels in Europe. The trend began in Great Britain in the 1820's, with reductions of duties and other barriers to trade. In 1846 the abolition of the Corn Laws ended agricultural protectionism. France reduced duties on some intermediate goods in the 1 830's, and on coal, iron, and steel in 1852. The *Zollverein* established fairly low tariffs in 1834. Belgium, Portugal, Spain, Piedmont, Norway, Switzerland, and Sweden lowered imposts in the 1850's. The golden age of free trade began in 1860, when Britain and France signed the Cobden-Chevalier Treaty, which virtually eliminated trade barriers. This was followed by a series of bilateral trade agreements between virtually all European states. It is important to note, however, that the United States took little part in the general movement toward lower trade barriers.

The movement toward greater liberality was reversed in the late 1870's. Austria-Hungary increased duties in 1876 and 1878, and Italy also in 1878; but the main breach came in Germany in 1879. France increased tariffs modestly in 1881, sharply in 1892, and raised them still further in 1910. Other countries followed a similar pattern. Only Great Britain, Belgium, the Netherlands, and Switzerland continued to follow free-trade policies through the 1880's. Although Britain did not herself impose duties, she began establishing a system of preferential markets in her overseas Empire in 1898. The United States was basically protectionist throughout the nineteenth century. The high tariffs imposed during the Civil War continued with the exception of a brief period in the 1890's. There were no major duty reductions before 1914.

During the 1920's tariff levels increased further. Western European states protected their agrarian sectors against imports from the Danube region, Australia, Canada, and the United States, where the war had stimulated increased output. Great Britain adopted some colonial preferences in 1919, imposed a small number of tariffs in 1921, and extended some wartime duties. The successor states of the Austro-Hungarian Empire imposed duties to achieve some national self-sufficiency. The British dominions and Latin America protected industries nurtured by wartime demands. In the United States the Fordney-McCumber Tariff Act of 1922 increased protectionism. The October Revolution removed Russia from the Western trading system.

Dramatic closure in terms of tariff levels began with the passage of the Smoot-Hawley Tariff Act in the United States in 1930. Britain raised tariffs in 1931 and definitively abandoned free trade at the Ottawa Conference of 1932, which introduced extensive imperial preferences. Germany and Japan established trading blocs within their own spheres of influence. All other major countries followed protectionist policies.

Significant reductions in protection began after the Second World War; the United States had foreshadowed the movement toward greater liberality with the passage of the Reciprocal Trade Agreements Act in 1934. Since 1945 there have been seven rounds of multilateral tariff reductions. The first, held in 1947 at Geneva, and the Kennedy Round, held during the 1960's, have been the most significant. They have substantially reduced the level of protection.

The present situation is ambiguous. There have recently been some new trade controls. In the United States these include a voluntary import agreement for steel, the imposition of a 10 per cent import surcharge during four months of 1971, and export controls on agricultural products in 1973 and 1974. Italy imposed a deposit requirement on imports during parts of 1974 and 1975. Britain and Japan have engaged in export subsidization. Non-tariff barriers have become more important. On balance, there has been movement toward greater protectionism since the end of the Kennedy Round, but it is not decisive. The outcome of the multilateral negotiations that began in 1975 remains to be seen.

In sum, after 1820 there was a general trend toward lower tariffs (with the notable exception of the United States), which culminated between 1860 and 1879; higher tariffs from 1879 through the interwar years, with dramatic increases in the 1930's; and less protectionism from 1945 through the conclusion of the Kennedy Round in 1967.

Trade Proportions

With the exception of one period, ratios of trade to aggregate economic activity followed the same general pattern as tariff levels. Trade proportions increased from the early part of the nineteenth century to about 1880. Between 1880 and 1900 there was a decrease, sharper if measured in current prices than constant ones, but apparent in both statistical series for most countries. Between 1900 and 1913—and here is the exception from the tariff pattern—there was a marked increase in the ratio of trade to aggregate economic activity. This trend brought trade proportions to levels that have generally not been reattained. During the 1920's and 1930's the importance of trade in national economic activity declined. After the Second World War it increased.

. . . There are considerable differences in the movement of trade proportions among states. They hold more or less constant for the United States; Japan, Denmark, and Norway . . . are unaffected by the general decrease in the ratio of trade to aggregate economic activity that takes place after 1880. The pattern described in the previous paragraph does, however, hold for Great Britain, France, Sweden, Germany, and Italy.

. . . Because of the boom in commodity prices that occurred in the early 1950's, the ratio of trade to gross domestic product was relatively high for larger states during these years, at least in current prices. It then faltered or remained constant until about 1960. From the early 1960's through 1972, trade proportions rose for all major states except Japan. Data for 1973 and 1974 show further increases. For smaller countries the trend was more erratic, with Belgium showing a more or less steady increase, Norway vacillating between 82 and 90 per cent, and Denmark and the Netherlands showing higher figures for the late 1950's than for more recent years. There is then, in current prices, a generally upward trend in trade proportions since 1960, particularly for larger states. This movement is more pronounced if constant prices are used.

Regional Trading Patterns

The final indicator of the degree of openness of the global trading system is regional bloc concentration. There is a natural affinity for some states to trade with others because of geographical propinquity or comparative advantage. In general, however, a system in which there are fewer manifestations of trading within given blocs, particularly among specific groups of more and less developed states, is a more open one. Over time there have been extensive changes in trading patterns between particular areas of the world whose relative factor endowments have remained largely the same.

Richard Chadwick and Karl Deutsch have collected extensive information on international trading patterns since 1890. Their basic datum is the relative acceptance indicator (RA), which measures deviations from a null hypothesis in which trade between a pair of states, or a state and a region, is precisely what would be predicted on the basis of their total share of international trade. When the null hypothesis holds, the RA indicator is equal to zero. Values less than zero indicate less trade than expected, greater than zero more trade than expected. For our purposes the critical issue is whether, over time, trade tends to become more concentrated as shown by movements away from zero, or less as shown by movements toward zero. . . .

There is a general pattern. In three of the four cases, the RA value closest to zero—that is the least regional encapsulation—occurred in 1890, 1913, or 1928; in the fourth case (France and French West Africa), the 1928 value was not bettered until 1964. In every case there was an increase in the RA indicator between 1928 and 1938, reflecting the breakdown of international commerce that is associated with the depression. Surprisingly, the RA indicator was higher for each of the four pairs in 1954 than in 1938, an indication that regional patterns persisted and even became more intense in the postwar period. With the exception of the Soviet Union and Eastern Europe, there was a general trend toward decreasing RA's for the period after 1954. They still, however, show fairly high values even in the late 1960's.

If we put all three indicators—tariff levels, trade proportions, and trade patterns—together, they suggest the following periodization.

Period I (1820-1879): Increasing openness—tariffs are generally lowered; trade proportions increase. Data are not available for trade patterns. However, it is important to note that this is not a universal pattern. The United States is largely unaffected; its tariff levels remain high (and are in fact increased during the early 1860's) and American trade proportions remain almost constant.

Period II (1879-1900): Modest closure—tariffs are increased; trade proportions decline modestly for most states. Data are not available for trade patterns.

Period III (1900-1913): Greater openness—tariff levels remain generally unchanged; trade proportions increase for all major trading states except the United States. Trading patterns become less regional in three out of the four cases for which data are available.

Period IV (1918-1939): Closure—tariff levels are increased in the 1920's and again in the 1930's; trade proportions decline. Trade becomes more regionally encapsulated.

Period V (1945-c. 1970): Great openness—tariffs are lowered; trade proportions increase, particularly after 1960. Regional concentration decreases after 1960. However, these developments are limited to non-Communist areas of the world.

THE INDEPENDENT VARIABLE: DESCRIBING THE DISTRIBUTION OF POTENTIAL ECONOMIC POWER AMONG STATES

Analysts of international relations have an almost pro forma set of variables designed to show the distribution of potential power in the international *political* system. It includes such factors as gross national product, per capita income, geographical position, and size of armed forces. A similar set of indicators can be presented for the international economic system.

Statistics are available over a long time period for per capita income, aggregate size, share of world trade, and share of world investment. They demonstrate that, since the beginning of the nineteenth century, there have been two first-rank economic powers in the world economy—Britain and the United States. The United States passed Britain in aggregate size sometime in the middle of the nineteenth century and, in the 1880's, became the largest producer of manufactures. America's lead was particularly marked in technologically advanced industries turning out sewing machines, harvesters, cash registers, locomotives, steam pumps, telephones, and petroleum. Until the First World War, however, Great Britain had a higher per capita income, a greater share of world trade, and a greater share of world investment than any other state. The peak of British ascendance occurred around 1880, when Britain's relative per capita income, share of world trade, and share of investment flows reached their highest levels. Britain's potential dominance in 1880 and 1900 was particularly striking in the international economic system, where her share of trade and foreign investment was about twice as large as that of any other state.

It was only after the First World War that the United States became relatively larger and more developed in terms of all four indicators. This potential dominance reached new and dramatic heights between 1945 and 1960. Since then, the relative position of the United States has declined, bringing it quite close to West Germany, its nearest rival, in terms of per capita income and share of world trade. The devaluations of the dollar that have taken place since 1972 are reflected in a continuation of this downward trend for income and aggregate size.

The relative potential economic power of Britain and the United States is shown in [Tables I and II].

In sum, Britain was the world's most important trading state from the period after the Napoleonic Wars until 1913. Her relative position rose until about 1880 and fell thereafter. The United States became the largest and most advanced state in economic terms after the First World War, but did not equal the relative share of world trade and investment achieved by Britain in the 1880's until after the Second World War.

TABLE I. Indicators of British Potential Power (Ratio of British value to next highest)

	Per Capita Income	Aggregate Size	Share of World Trade	Share of World Investment*
1860	.91(US)	.74(US)	2.01(FR)	n.a.
1880	1.30(US)	.79(1874-83 US)	2.22(FR)	1.93(FR)
1900	1.05(1899 US)	.58(1899 US)	2.17(1890 GERM)	2.08(FR)
1913	.92(US)	.43(US)	1.20(US)	2.18(1914 FR)
1928	.66(US)	.25(1929 US)	.79(US)	.64(1921-29 US)
1937	.79(US)	.29(US)	.88(US)	.18(1930-38 US)
1950	.56(US)	.19(US)	.69(US)	.13(1951-55 US)
1960	.49(US)	.14(US)	.46(1958 US)	.15(1956-61 US)
1972	.46(US)	.13(US)	.47(1973 US)	n.a.

*Stock 1870-1913; Flow 1928-1950

Years are in parentheses when different from those in first column.

Countries in parentheses are those with the largest values for the particular indicator other than Great Britain.

TESTING THE ARGUMENT

The contention that hegemony leads to a more open trading structure is fairly well, but not perfectly, confirmed by the empirical evidence presented in the preceding sections. The argument explains the periods 1820 to 1879, 1880 to 1900, and 1945 to 1960. It does not fully explain those from 1900 to 1913, 1919 to 1939, or 1960 to the present.

1820-1879. The period from 1820 to 1879 was one of increasing openness in the structure of international trade. It was also one of rising hegemony. Great Britain was the instigator and supporter of the new structure. She began lowering her trade barriers in the 1820's, before any other state. The signing of the Cobden-Chevalier Tariff Treaty with France in 1860 initiated a series of bilateral tariff reductions. It is, however, important to note that the United States was hardly involved in these developments, and that America's ratio of trade to aggregate economic activity did not increase during the nineteenth century.

Britain put to use her internal flexibility and external power in securing a more open structure. At the domestic level, openness was favored by the rising industrialists. The opposition of the agrarian sector was mitigated by its capacity for adjustment: the rate of capital investment and technological innovation was high enough to prevent British agricultural incomes from falling until some thirty years after the abolition of the Corn Laws. Symbolically, the Manchester School led by

TABLE II. Indicators of U.S. Potential Power (Ratio of U.S. value to next highest)

	Per Capita Income	Aggregate Size	Share of World Trade	Share of World Investment Flows
1860	1.10(GB)	1.41(GB)	.36(GB)	Net debtor
1880	.77(GB)	1.23(1883 GB)	.37(GB)	Net debtor
1900	.95(1899 GB)	1.73(1899 GB)	.43(1890 GB)	n.a.
1913	1.09(GB)	2.15(RUS)	.83(GB)	Net debtor
1928	1.51(GB)	3.22(USSR)	1.26(GB)	1.55(1921-29 UK)
1937	1.26(GB)	2.67(USSR)	1.13(GB)	5.53(1930-38 UK)
1950	1.78(GB)	3.15(USSR)	1.44(GB)	7.42(1951-55 UK)
1960	2.05(GB)	2.81(USSR)	2.15(1958 GB)	6.60(1956-61 UK)
1972	1.31(GERM)	n.a.	1.18(1973 GERM)	n.a.

Years are in parentheses when different from those in first column.

Countries in parentheses are those with the largest values for the particular indicator other than the United States.

Cobden and Bright provided the ideological justification for free trade. Its influence was felt throughout Europe where Britain stood as an example to at least some members of the elite.

Britain used her military strength to open many backward areas: British interventions were frequent in Latin America during the nineteenth century, and formal and informal colonial expansion opened the interior of Africa. Most importantly, Britain forced India into the international economic system. British military power was also a factor in concluding the Cobden-Chevalier Treaty, for Louis Napoleon was more concerned with cementing his relations with Britain than he was in the economic consequences of greater openness. Once this pact was signed, however, it became a catalyst for the many other treaties that followed.

Britain also put economic instruments to good use in creating an open system. The abolition of the Corn Laws offered continental grain producers the incentive of continued access to the growing British market. Britain was at the heart of the nineteenth-century international monetary system which functioned exceptionally well, at least for the core of the more developed states and the areas closely associated with them. Exchange rates were stable, and countries did not have to impose trade barriers to rectify cyclical payments difficulties. Both confidence and liquidity were, to a critical degree, provided by Britain. The use of sterling balances as opposed to specie became increasingly widespread, alleviating the liquidity problems presented by the erratic production of gold and silver. Foreign private and central banks increasingly placed their cash reserves in London, and accounts were cleared through changing bank balances rather than gold flows. Great Britain's extremely sophisticated financial institutions, centered in the City of London, provided the short-term financing necessary to facilitate the international flow of goods. Her early and somewhat fortuitous adherence to the gold—as opposed to the silver or bimetallic—standard proved to be an important source of confidence as all countries adopted at least a *de facto* gold standard after 1870 because of the declining relative value of silver. In times of monetary emergency, the confidence placed in the pound because of the strength of the British economy allowed the Bank of England to be a lender of last resort.

Hence, for the first three-quarters of the nineteenth century, British policy favored an open international trading structure, and British power helped to create it. But this was not a global regime. British resources were not sufficient to entice or compel the United States (a country whose economy was larger than Britain's by 1860 and whose technology was developing very rapidly) to abandon its protectionist commercial policy. As a state-power argument suggests, openness was only established within the geographical area where the rising economic hegemony was able to exercise its influence.

1880-1900. The last two decades of the nineteenth century were a period of modest closure which corresponds to a relative decline in British per capita income, size, and share of world trade. The event that precipitated higher tariff levels was the availability of inexpensive grain from the American Midwest, made possible by the construction of continental railways. National responses varied. Britain let her agricultural sector decline, a not unexpected development given her still dominant economic position. Denmark, a small and relatively well-developed state, also refrained from imposing tariffs and transformed its farming sector from agriculture to animal husbandry. Several other small states also followed open policies. Germany, France, Russia, and Italy imposed higher tariffs, however. Britain did not have the military or economic power to forestall these policies. Still, the institutional structure of the international monetary system, with the City of London at its center, did not crumble. The decline in trade proportions was modest despite higher tariffs.

1945-1960. The third period that is neatly explained by the argument that hegemony leads to an open trading structure is the decade and a half after the Second World War, characterized by the ascendancy of the United States. During these years the structure of the international trading system became increasingly open. Tariffs were lowered; trade proportions were restored well above interwar levels. Asymmetrical regional trading patterns did begin to decline, although not until the late 1950's. America's bilateral rival, the Soviet Union, remained—as the theory would predict—encapsulated within its own regional sphere of influence.

Unlike Britain in the nineteenth century, the United States after World War II operated in a bipolar political structure. Free trade was preferred, but departures such as the Common Market and Japanese import restrictions were accepted to make sure that these areas remained within the general American sphere of influence. Domestically the Reciprocal Trade Agreements Act, first passed in 1934, was extended several times after the war. Internationally the United States supported the framework for tariff reductions provided by the General Agreement on Tariffs and Trade. American policy makers used their economic leverage over Great Britain to force an end to the imperial preference system. The monetary system established at Bretton Woods was basically an American creation. In practice, liquidity was provided by the American deficit; confidence by the size of the American economy. Behind the economic veil stood American military protection for other industrialized market economies—an overwhelming incentive for them to accept an open system, particularly one which was in fact relatively beneficial.

The argument about the relationship between hegemony and openness is not as satisfactory for the years 1900 to 1913, 1919 to 1939, and 1960 to the present.

1900-1913. During the years immediately preceding the First World War, the structure of international trade became more open in terms of trade proportions and regional patterns. Britain remained the largest international economic entity, but her relative position continued a decline that had begun two decades earlier. Still, Britain maintained her commitment to free trade and to the financial institutions of the City of London. A state-power argument would suggest some reconsideration of these policies.

Perhaps the simplest explanation for the increase in trade proportions was the burst of loans that flowed out of Europe in the years before the First World War, loans that financed the increasing sale of goods. Germany and France as well as Britain participated in this development. Despite the higher tariff levels imposed after 1879, institutional structures—particularly the monetary system—allowed these capital flows to generate increasing trade flows. Had Britain reconsidered her policies, this might not have been the case.

1919-1939. The United States emerged from the First World War as the world's most powerful economic state. Whether America was large enough to have put an open system in place is a moot question. As Table II indicates, America's share of world trade and investment was only 26 and 55 per cent greater than that of any other state, while comparable figures for Great Britain during the last part of the nineteenth century are 100 per cent. What is apparent, though, is that American policy makers made little effort to open the structure of international trade. The call for an open door was a shibboleth, not a policy. It was really the British who attempted to continue a hegemonic role.

In the area of trade, the U.S. Fordney-McCumber Tariff of 1922 increased protection. That tendency was greatly reinforced by the Smoot-Hawley Tariff of 1930 which touched off a wave of protective legislation. Instead of leading the way to openness, the United States led the way to closure.

In the monetary area, the American government made little effort to alter a situation that was confused and often chaotic. During the first half of the 1920's, exchange rates fluctuated widely among major currencies as countries were forced, by the inflationary pressures of the war, to abandon the gold standard. Convertibility was restored in the mid-twenties at values incompatible with long-term equilibrium. The British pound was overvalued, and the French franc undervalued. Britain was forced off the gold standard in September 1931, accelerating a trend that had begun with Uruguay in April 1929. The United States went off gold in 1933. France's decision to end convertibility in 1936 completed the pattern. During the 1930's the monetary system collapsed.

Constructing a stable monetary order would have been no easy task in the political environment of the 1920's and 1930's. The United States made no effort. It refused to recognize a connection between war debts and reparations, although much of the postwar flow of funds took the form of American loans to Germany, German reparations payments to France and Britain, and French and British war-debt payments to the United States. The great depression was in no small measure touched off by the contraction of American credit in the late 1920's. In the deflationary collapse that followed, the British were too weak to act as a lender of last resort, and the Americans actually undercut efforts to reconstruct the Western economy when, before the London Monetary Conference of 1933, President Roosevelt changed the basic assumptions of the meeting by taking the United States off gold. American concern was wholly with restoring the domestic economy.

That is not to say that American behavior was entirely obstreperous; but cooperation was erratic and often private. The Federal Reserve Bank of New York did try, during the late 1920's, to maintain New York interest rates below those in London to protect the value of the pound. Two Americans, Dawes and Young, lent their names to the renegotiations of German reparations payments, but most of the actual work was carried out by British experts. At the official level, the first manifestation of American leadership was President Hoover's call for a moratorium on war debts and reparations in June 1931; but in 1932 the United States refused to participate in the Lausanne Conference that in effect ended reparations.

It was not until the mid-thirties that the United States asserted any real leadership. The Reciprocal Trade Agreements Act of 1934 led to bilateral treaties with twenty-seven countries before 1945. American concessions covered 64 per cent of dutiable items, and reduced rates by an average of 44 per cent. However, tariffs were so high to begin with that the actual impact of these agreements was limited. There were also some modest steps toward tariff liberalization in Britain and France. In the monetary field, the United States, Britain, and France pledged to maintain exchange-rate stability in the Tripartite Declaration of September 1936. These actions were not adequate to create an open international economic structure. American policy during the interwar period, and particularly before the mid-thirties, fails to accord with the predictions made by a state-power explanation of the behavior of a rising hegemonic power.

1960-present. The final period not adequately dealt with by a state-power explanation is the last decade or so. In recent years, the relative size and level of development of the U.S. economy has fallen. This decline has not, however, been accompanied by a clear turn toward protectionism. The Trade Expansion Act of

1962 was extremely liberal and led to the very successful Kennedy Round of multilateral tariff cuts during the mid-sixties. The protectionist Burke-Hartke Bill did not pass. The 1974 Trade Act does include new protectionist aspects, particularly in its requirements for review of the removal of nontariff barriers by Congress and for stiffer requirements for the imposition of countervailing duties, but it still maintains the mechanism of presidential discretion on tariff cuts that has been the keystone of postwar reductions. While the Voluntary Steel Agreement, the August 1971 economic policy, and restrictions on agricultural exports all show a tendency toward protectionism, there is as yet no evidence of a basic turn away from a commitment to openness.

In terms of behavior in the international trading system, the decade of the 1960's was clearly one of greater openness. Trade proportions increased, and traditional regional trade patterns became weaker. A state-power argument would predict a downturn or at least a faltering in these indicators as American power declined.

In sum, although the general pattern of the structure of international trade conforms with the predictions of a state-power argument—two periods of openness separated by one of closure—corresponding to periods of rising British and American hegemony and an interregnum, the whole pattern is out of phase. British commitment to openness continued long after Britain's position had declined. American commitment to openness did not begin until well after the United States had become the world's leading economic power and has continued during a period of relative American decline. The state-power argument needs to be amended to take these delayed reactions into account.

AMENDING THE ARGUMENT

The structure of the international trading system does not move in lockstep with changes in the distribution of potential power among states. Systems are initiated and ended, not as a state-power theory would predict, by close assessments of the interests of the state at every given moment, but by external events—usually cataclysmic ones. The closure that began in 1879 coincided with the Great Depression of the last part of the nineteenth century. The final dismantling of the nineteenth-century international economic system was not precipitated by a change in British trade or monetary policy, but by the First World War and the Depression. The potato famine of the 1840's prompted abolition of the Corn Laws; and the United States did not assume the mantle of world leadership until the world had been laid bare by six years of total war. Some catalytic external event seems necessary to move states to dramatic policy initiatives in line with state interests.

Once policies have been adopted, they are pursued until a new crisis demonstrates that they are no longer feasible. States become locked in by the impact of prior choices on their domestic political structures. The British decision to opt for openness in 1846 corresponded with state interests. It also strengthened the position of industrial and financial groups over time, because they had the opportunity to operate in an international system that furthered their objectives. That system eventually undermined the position of British farmers, a group that would have supported protectionism if it had survived. Once entrenched, Britain's export industries, and more importantly the City of London, resisted policies of closure. In the interwar years, the British rentier class insisted on restoring the prewar parity of the pound—a decision that placed enormous deflationary pressures on the domestic economy—because they wanted to protect the value of their investments.

Institutions created during periods of rising ascendancy remained in operation when they were no longer appropriate. For instance, the organization of British banking in the nineteenth century separated domestic and foreign operations. The Court of Directors of the Bank of England was dominated by international banking houses. Their decisions about British monetary policy were geared toward the international economy. Under a different institutional arrangement more attention might have been given after 1900 to the need to revitalize the domestic economy. The British state was unable to free itself from the domestic structures that its earlier policy decisions had created, and continued to follow policies appropriate for a rising hegemony long after Britain's star had begun to fall.

Similarly, earlier policies in the United States begat social structures and institutional arrangements that trammeled state policy. After protecting import-competing industries for a century, the United States was unable in the 1920's to opt for more open policies, even though state interests would have been furthered thereby. Institutionally, decisions about tariff reductions were taken primarily in congressional committees, giving virtually any group seeking protection easy access to the decision-making process. When there were conflicts among groups, they were resolved by raising the levels of protection for everyone. It was only after the cataclysm of the depression that the decision-making processes for trade policy were changed. The Presidency, far more insulated from the entreaties of particular societal groups than congressional committees, was then given more power. Furthermore, the American commercial banking system was unable to assume the burden of regulating the international economy during the 1920's. American institutions were geared toward the domestic economy. Only after the Second World War, and in fact not until the late 1950's, did American banks fully develop the complex institutional structures commensurate with the dollar's role in the international monetary system.

Having taken the critical decisions that created an open system after 1945, the American Government is unlikely to change its policy until it confronts some external event that it cannot control, such as a worldwide deflation, drought in the great plains, or the malicious use of petrodollars. In America perhaps more than in any other country "new policies," as E. E. Schattschneider wrote in his brilliant study of the Smoot-Hawley Tariff in 1935, "create new politics,"[1] for in America the state is weak and the society strong. State decisions taken because of state interests reinforce private societal groups that the state is unable to resist in later periods. Multinational corporations have grown and prospered since 1950. International economic policy making has passed from the Congress to the Executive.

Groups favoring closure, such as organized labor, are unlikely to carry the day until some external event demonstrates that existing policies can no longer be implemented.

The structure of international trade changes in fits and starts; it does not flow smoothly with the redistribution of potential state power. Nevertheless, it is the power and the policies of states that create order where there would otherwise be chaos or at best a Lockian state of nature. The existence of various transnational, multinational, transgovernmental, and other nonstate actors that have riveted scholarly attention in recent years can only be understood within the context of a broader structure that ultimately rests upon the power and interests of states, shackled though they may be by the societal consequences of their own past decisions.

NOTE

1. E. E. Schattschneider, *Politics, Pressures and the Tariff: A Study of Free Enterprise in Pressure Politics as Shown in the 1929-1930 Revision of the Tariff* (New York: Prentice-Hall, 1935), p. 288.

II

HISTORICAL PERSPECTIVES

A truly international economy first emerged during the "long sixteenth century," the period from approximately 1480 to 1650. In its earliest form the modern international economy was organized on the basis of mercantilism, a doctrine which asserted that power and wealth were closely interrelated and legitimate goals of national policy. Thus, wealth was necessary for power, and power could be used to obtain wealth. Because power is a relative concept, as one country can gain it only at the expense of another, mercantilist nations perceived themselves to be locked into a zero-sum conflict in the international economy.

Countries pursued a variety of policies during this period intended to expand production and wealth at home while denying similar capabilities to others. Six policies were of nearly universal importance. First, countries sought to prevent gold and silver, a common mercantilist measure of wealth, from being exported. Spain declared the export of gold or silver punishable by death at the beginning of the sixteenth century. Demonstrating the difficulties of enforcing such regulations, France declared the export of coined gold and silver illegal in 1506, 1540, 1548, and 1574. Second, regulations (typically, high tariffs) were adopted to limit imports to necessary raw materials. Importing raw materials was desirable because it lowered prices at home and thereby reduced costs for manufacturers. By limiting imports of manufactured and luxury items, on the other hand, countries sought to stimulate production at home while reducing it abroad. Third, exports of manufactured goods were encouraged for similar reasons. Fourth, just as they sought to encourage imports of raw materials, countries sought to limit the export of these goods, both to lower prices at home and to limit the ability of others to develop manufacturing capabilities of their own. Fifth, exports of technology—including both machinery and skilled artisans—were restricted to inhibit potential foreign competitors. Finally, many countries adopted navigation laws mandating that a certain percentage of their foreign trade had to be carried in native ships. This last trade regulation was intended to stimulate the domestic shipping and shipbuilding industries, both necessary resources for successful war making.

By the early nineteenth century, mercantilist trade restrictions were coming under widespread attack, particularly in Great Britain. Drawing upon the Liberal writings of Adam Smith and David Ricardo, Richard Cobden and other Manchester industrialists led the fight for free trade which culminated in 1846 in the abolition of the "Corn Laws" (restrictions on grain imports), the last major mercantilist impediment to free trade in Britain. Other countries soon followed the United Kingdom's example. Under Britain's hegemonic leadership, a period of European free trade was ushered in which lasted from 1860 to 1879 (see Kindleberger, Reading 4). This trend toward freer trade was reversed in the last quarter of the nineteenth century. The purported causes of this reversal are many, including the decline of British hegemony, the onset of the first "Great Depression" of 1873-1896, and the new wave of industrialization on the continent, which led to protection for domestic manufacturers from British competition (see Gourevitch, Reading 5). For whatever reason—and the debate continues even today—by 1890, nearly all countries except Great Britain had once again imposed significant restrictions on imports.

Coupled with this trend toward increased protection was a new wave of formal colonialism. For reasons discussed by V.I. Lenin (Reading 6), Britain had already begun to expand its holdings of foreign territory during the period of free trade. After 1880, it was joined by Germany and France. In 1860, Great Britain possessed 2.5 million square miles of colonial territory, France held only 0.2 million square miles, and Germany had not yet entered the colonial race. By 1899, Britain's holdings had expanded to 9.3 million square miles, France's to 3.7 million, and Germany's to 1.0 million. This expansion occurred primarily in Africa and the Pacific. In 1876, slightly less than 11 percent of Africa and nearly 57 percent of Polynesia were colonized. By 1900, over 90 percent of Africa and almost 99 percent of Polynesia were controlled by European colonial powers and the United States.

World War I, which many Realists and Marxists believe to have been stimulated by the race for colonies and particularly Germany's aggressive attempt to catch up with Great Britain, destroyed the remaining elements of the *Pax Britannica*. The mantle of leadership, which had previously been borne by Britain, was now divided between the United States and the United Kingdom. Yet, neither country could—or desired to—play the leadership role previously performed by Britain (see Lake, Reading 7).

World War I was indeed a watershed in American international involvement. The terrible devastation caused by the war in Europe served to weaken the traditional world powers, while the war brought the United States a period of unexpected prosperity. The Allies, short of food and weapons, bought furiously from American suppliers; to finance their purchases, they borrowed heavily from American banks and, eventually, once the United States entered the war, from the American Government. As a result, American factories and farms hummed as the war dragged on and industrial production nearly doubled during the war years. Because the war forced the European powers to neglect many of their overseas economic activities, American exporters and investors were also able to move into areas they had never before influenced. When the war began, the United States was a net debtor of the major European nations; by the time it ended, the United States was the world's principal lender, and all of the allies were deeply in debt to American banks and the American government.

Despite the position of political and economic leadership the United States shared with Great Britain after World War I, the country rapidly retreated into its traditional inward orientation. To be sure, many American banks and corporations continued to expand abroad very rapidly in the 1920s, and the United States remained an important world power, but the United States refused to join the League of Nations or any of the other international organizations created in the period. American tariff levels, reduced on the eve of World War I, were once again raised. The reasons for the country's post-World War I "isolationism," as it is often called, are many and controversial. Chief among them were the continued insularity of major segments of the American public, traditionally inward-looking in political and economic matters; the resistance to American power of such European nations as Great Britain and France; and widespread revulsion at the apparently futile deaths that had resulted from involvement in the internecine strife of the Old World.

Whatever the reasons for the isolationism of the 1920s, these tendencies were heightened as the world spiraled downward into depression after 1929. In the Smoot-Hawley Act of 1930, the United States dramatically increased its tariffs, and by 1933 the world was engulfed in a bitter trade and currency conflict. In 1933, desperate to encourage domestic economic recovery, Franklin Roosevelt significantly devalued the dollar, sounding the death knell of what remained of the nineteenth-century international economic order.

During the nearly four centuries summarized here, the international economy underwent several dramatic transformations. From a closed and highly regulated mercantilist system, the international economy evolved toward free trade in the middle of the nineteenth century. After a relatively brief period of openness, the international economy reversed direction and, starting with resurgence of formal imperialism and accelerating after World War I, once again drifted toward closure. This historical survey highlights the uniqueness of the contemporary international political economy, which is the focus of the rest of this reader. It also raises a host of analytic questions, many of which appear elsewhere in the book as well. Particularly important here is the question of what drives change in the international economy. In the readings that follow, Charles Kindleberger focuses on interest groups and ideology, Gourevitch examines interest groups and political structures, Lenin finds the locus of change in the stages of capitalism, and Lake emphasizes changes in the international distribution of power.

4
The Rise of Free Trade in Western Europe

CHARLES P. KINDLEBERGER

Liberal economist Charles P. Kindleberger examines the process by which mercantilist trade restrictions were dismantled and evaluates several of the best known theses concerning the ascendance of free trade in Western Europe. According to Kindleberger, free trade in many instances arose as individual entrepreneurs pressured their government to lift restrictions on international trade and finance so that they could pursue overseas business opportunities. Yet, Kindleberger points out that political activity by entrepreneurs cannot explain the rapid expansion of free trade in Europe after 1850. He suggests that this "second wave" of free trade may have been motivated by ideology rather than economic or political interests. This important article offers a persuasive explanation of how and why the market principle gained dominance within the international economy during the nineteenth century.

I

. . . The beginnings of free trade internationally go back to the eighteenth century. French Physiocratic theory enunciated the slogan *laisser faire, laisser passer* to reduce export prohibitions on agricultural products. Pride of place in practice, however, goes to Tuscany, which permitted free export of the corn of Sienese Maremma in 1737, after the Grand Duke Francis had read Sallustio Bandini's *Economical Discourse*. Beset by famine in 1764, Tuscany gradually opened its mar-

4 "The Rise of Free Trade in Western Europe" by Charles P. Kindleberger. From *The Journal of Economic History*, Vol. 35, No. 1 (1975) The Economic History Association. Reprinted with the permission of Cambridge University Press.

ket to imported grain well before the Vergennes Treaty of 1786 between France and Britain put French Physiocratic doctrine into practice. Grain exports in Tuscany had been restricted under the "policy of supply," or "provisioning," or "abundance," under which the city-states of Italy limited exports from the surrounding countryside in order to assure food to the urban populace. Bandini and Pompeo Neri pointed out the ill effects this had on investment and productivity in agriculture.

The policy of supply was not limited to food. In the eighteenth and early nineteenth century exports were restricted in, among others, wool and coal (Britain), ashes, rags, sand for glass and firewood (Germany), ship timbers (Austria), rose madder (the Netherlands), and silk cocoons (Italy). The restrictions on exports of ashes and timber from Germany had conservation overtones. The industrial revolution in Britain led further to prohibitions on export of machinery and on emigration of artisans, partly to increase the supply for local use, but also to prevent the diffusion of technology on the Continent. We return to this below.

What was left in the policy of supply after the Napoleonic War quickly ran down. Prohibition of export of raw silk was withdrawn in Piedmont, Lombardy and Venetia in the 1830's, freedom to export coal from Britain enacted in the 1840's. Details of the relaxation of restrictions are recorded for Baden as part of the movement to occupational freedom. The guild system gradually collapsed under the weight of increasing complexity of regulations by firms seeking exceptions for themselves and objecting to exceptions for others. A number of prohibitions and export taxes lasted to the 1850's—as industrial consumers held out against producers, or in some cases, like rags, the collectors of waste products. Reduction of the export tax on rags in Piedmont in 1851 produced a long drawn-out struggle between Cavour and the industry which had to close up thirteen plants when the tax was reduced. To Cavour salvation of the industry lay in machinery and the substitution of other materials, not in restricting export through Leghorn and Messina to Britain and North America.

Elimination of export taxes and prohibitions in nineteenth-century Europe raises doubt about the universal validity of the theory of the tariff as a collective good, imposed by a concentrated interest at the expense of the diffuse. The interest of groups producing inputs for other industries are normally more deeply affected than those of the consuming industries, but it is hardly possible that the consuming is always less concentrated than the producing industry.

II

The question of export duties sought by domestic manufacturers on their raw materials, and of import duties on outputs demanded by producers for the domestic market was settled in the Netherlands in the eighteenth century in favor of mercantile interests. These were divided into the First Hand, merchants, shipowners and bankers; the Second Hand, which carried on the work of sorting and packing in staple markets, and wholesaling on the Continent; and the Third Hand, concerned with distribution in the hinterland. Dutch staple trade was based partly on mercantile skills and partly on the pivotal location of Amsterdam, Rotterdam, and other staple towns dedicated to trade in particular commodities, largely perishable, non-standardized and best suited to short voyages. The First Hand dominated Dutch social and political life and opposed all tariffs on export or import goods, above a minimum for revenue, in order to maximize trade and minimize formalities. From 1815 to 1830 when Holland and Belgium were united as the Low Countries, the clash between the Dutch First Hand and Belgian producers in search of import protection from British manufactures was continuous and heated.

The First Hand objected to taxes for revenue on coffee, tea, tobacco, rice, sugar, and so on, and urged their replacement by excises on flour, meat, horses and servants. Tariffs for revenue must be held down to prevent smuggling and to sustain turnover. The safe maximum was given variously as three percent, five percent, and on transit even as one-half percent. Transit in bond, and transit with duty-cum-drawback were thought too cumbersome. The Dutch made a mistake in failing to emulate London which in 1803 adopted a convenient entrepôt dock with bonding. Loss of colonies and of overseas connections in the Napoleonic Wars made it impossible from early in the period to compete with Britain in trade. Equally threatening was Hamburg which supplied British and colonial goods to Central Europe in transit for one-half percent revenue duty maximum, many products free, and all so after 1839. More serious, however, was the rise of direct selling as transport efficiency increased. Early signs of direct selling can be detected at the end of the seventeenth century when Venice and Genoa lost their role as intermediary in traffic between Italy and the West. By the first half of the nineteenth century, they were abundant. "By the improved intercourse of our time (1840), the seller is brought more immediately into contact with the producer." Twenty years earlier, the Belgian members of a Dutch Belgian fiscal commission argued that "there was no hope of restoring Holland's general trade. Owing to the spread of civilization, all European countries could now provide for themselves in direct trading."[1]

It is a mistake to think of merchants as all alike. As indicated, First, Second and Third Hands of the Netherlands had different functions, status and power. In Germany, republican merchants of Hamburg differed sharply from those of the Imperial city, Frankfurt, and held out fifty years longer against the Zollverein. Within Frankfurt there were two groups, the English-goods party associated with the bankers, and the majority, which triumphed in 1836, interested in transit, forwarding, retail and domestic trade within the Zollverein. In Britain a brilliant picture had been drawn of a pragmatic free trader, John Gladstone, father of William, opposed to timber preferences for Canada, enemy of the East India Company monopoly on trade with China and India, but supportive of imperial preference in cotton and sugar, and approving of the Corn Laws on the ground of support for the aristocracy he hoped his children could enter via politics. The doctrinaire free traders of Britain were the cotton manufacturers like Gladstone's friend, Kirman Finlay, who regarded shipowners and corn growers as the two great monopolists.

The doctrinaire free trade of the Dutch merchants led to economic sclerosis, or economic sickness. Hamburg stayed in trade and finance and did not move into industry. In Britain, merchants were ignorant of industry, but were saved by the coming of the railroad and limited liability which provided an outlet for their surplus as direct trading squeezed profits from stapling. The economic point is simple: free trade may stimulate, but again it may lead to fossilization.

III

The movement toward freer trade in Britain began gross in the eighteenth century, net only after the Napoleonic Wars. In the initial stages, there was little problem for a man like Wedgewood advocating free trade for exports of manufactures under the Treaty of Vergennes with France, but prohibitions on the export of machinery and emigrations of artisans. Even in the 1820's and 1830's, a number of the political economists—Torrens, Baring, Peel, Nassau Senior—favored repeal of the Corn Laws but opposed export of machinery. The nineteenth century is seen by Brebner not as a steady march to *laisser-faire* but as a counterpoint between Smithian *laisser-faire* in trade matters and, after the Reform Bill, Benthamic intervention of 1832 which produced the Factory, Mines, Ten Hours and similar acts from 1833 to 1847.

First came the revenue aspect, which was critical to the movement to freer trade under Huskisson in the 1820's, Peel in the 1840's, and Gladstone in the 1850's. Huskisson and Gladstone used the argument that the bulk of revenue was produced by taxes on a few items—largely colonial products such as tea, coffee, sugar, tobacco, and wine and spirits—and that others produced too little revenue to be worth the trouble. Many were redundant (for example, import duties on products which Britain exported). Others were so high as to be prohibitory or encouraged smuggling and reduced revenue. When Peel was converted to free trade, it was necessary to reintroduce the income tax before he could proceed with repeal of 605 duties between 1841 and 1846, and reductions in 1035 others. The title of Sir Henry Parnell's treatise on freer trade (1830) was *Financial Reform*.

But Huskisson was a free trader, if a cautious one. He spoke of benefits to be derived from the removal of "vexatious restraints and meddling interference in the concerns of internal industry and foreign commerce."[2] Especially he thought that imports stimulated efficiency in import-competing industry. In 1824 the prohibition on silk imports had been converted to a duty of thirty percent regarded as the upper limit of discouragement to smuggling. In a speech on March 24, 1826, said by Canning to be the finest he had heard in the House of Commons, Huskisson observed that Macclesfield and Spitalfield had reorganized the industry under the spur of enlarged imports, and expanded the scale of output. Both Michel Chevalier and Count Cavour referred to this positive and dynamic response to increased imports in England.

Restrictions on export of machinery and emigration of artisans went back, as indicated, to the industrial revolution. Prohibition of export of stocking frames was enacted as early as 1696. Beginning in 1774 there was a succession of restrictions on tools and utensils for the cotton and linen trades and on the emigration of skilled artisans. The basis was partly the policy of supply, partly naked maintenance of monopoly. Freedom had been granted to the emigration of workmen in 1824. After the depression of the late 1830's, pressure for removal of the prohibition came from all machinery manufacturers. Following further investigation by a Select Committee of Parliament, the export prohibition was withdrawn.

The main arguments against prohibition of the export of machinery and emigration of artisans were three: they were ineffective, unnecessary, and harmful. Ineffectuality was attested to by much detail in the Select Committee reports on the efficiency of smuggling. Machinery for which licenses could not be obtained could be dispatched illegally in one of a number of ways—by another port, hidden in cotton bales, in baggage or mixed with permitted machinery and in a matter of hours. Guaranteed and insured shipments could be arranged in London or Paris for premia up to thirty percent.

That prohibition was unnecessary was justified first by the inability of foreigners, even with English machinery and English workmen, to rival English manufacturers. Britain has minerals, railways, canals, rivers, better division of labor, "trained workmen habituated to all industrious employments."[3] "Even when the Belgians employed English machines and skilled workers, they failed to import the English spirit of enterprise, and secured only disappointing results."[4] In 1825, the Select Committee concluded it was safe to export machinery, since seven-year-old machinery in Manchester was already obsolete.

In the third place it was dangerous. Restriction on emigration of artisans failed to prevent their departure, but did inhibit their return. Restriction of machinery, moreover, raised the price abroad through the cost of smuggling, and stimulated production on the Continent. Improvement in the terms of trade through restriction of exports (but failure to cut them off altogether) was deleterious for its protective effect abroad.

Greater coherence of the Manchester cotton spinners over the machinery makers spread over Manchester, Birmingham and London may account for the delay from 1825 to 1841 in freeing up machinery, and support Pincus' theory on the need of concentrated interests. But the argument of consistency was telling. In 1800 the Manchester manufacturers of cloth had demanded a law forbidding export of yarn, but did not obtain it. The 1841 Second Report concluded that machinery making should be put on the same footing as other departments of British industry. It is noted that Nottingham manufacturers approved free trade but claim an exception in regard to machinery used in their own manufacture. Babbage observed that machinery makers are more intelligent than their users, to whose imagined benefits their interests are sacrificed, and referred to the "impolicy of interfering between two classes."[5] In the end, the Manchester Chamber of Commerce became troubled by the inconsistency and divided; the issue of prohibition of machinery was subsumed into the general attack on the Corn Laws. In the 1840's moreover, the sentiment spread that Britain should become the Workshop of the World, which implied the production of heavy goods as well as cotton cloth and yarn.

Rivers of ink have been spilled on the repeal of the Corn Laws, and the present paper can do little but summarize the issues and indicate a position. The questions relate to the Stolper-Samuelson distribution argument, combined with the Reform Bill of 1832 and the shift of political power from the landed aristocracy to the bourgeois; incidence of the Corn Laws and of their repeal, within both farming and manufacturing sectors; the potential for a dynamic response of farming to lower prices from competition; and the relation of repeal to economic development on the Continent, and especially whether industrialization could be halted by expanded and assured outlets for agricultural produce, a point of view characterized by Gallagher and Robinson as "free-trade imperialism." A number of lesser issues may be touched upon incidentally: interaction between the Corn Laws and the Zollverein, and its tariff changes in the 1840's; the question of whether repeal of the Corn Laws, and of the Navigation Acts would have been very long delayed had it not been for potato famine in Ireland and on the Continent; and the question of whether the term "free-trade imperialism" is better reserved for Joseph Chamberlain's Empire preference of fifty years later.

In the normal view, the Reform Bill of 1832 shifted power from the land and country to the factory and city, from the aristocratic class to the bourgeois, and inexorably led to changes in trade policies which had favored farming and hurt manufacturing. One can argue that repeal of the Corn Laws represented something less than that and that the Reform Bill was not critical. The movement to free trade had begun earlier in the Huskisson reforms; speeches in Parliament were broadly the same in 1825 when it was dominated by landed aristocrats as in the 1830's and 1840's. Numbers had changed with continued manufacturing expansion, but nothing much more. Or one can reject the class explanation, as Polanyi does, and see something much more ideological. "Not until the 1830's did economic liberalism burst forth as a crusading passion." The liberal creed involved faith in man's secular salvation through a self-regulating market, held with fanaticism and evangelical fervor. French Physiocrats were trying to correct only one inequity, to break out of the policy of supply and permit export of grain. British political economists of the 1830's and 1840's, who won over Tories like Sir Robert Peel and Lord Russell, and ended up in 1846 with many landlords agreeable to repeal of the Corn Laws, represented an ideology. "Mere class interests cannot offer a satisfactory explanation for any long-run social process."[6]

Under a two-sector model, free trade comes when the abundant factor acquires political power and moves to eliminate restrictions imposed in the interest of the scarce factor which has lost power. In reality factors of production are not monolithic. Some confusion in the debate attached to the incidence of the tax on imported corn within both farming and manufacturing. The Anti-Corn Law League of Cobden and Bright regarded it as a tax on food, taking as much as twenty percent of the earnings of a hand-loom weaver. Cobden denied the "fallacy" that wages rose and fell with price of bread. Benefits, moreover, went to the landlord and not to the farmer or farm-laborer, as rents on the short leases in practice rose with the price of corn. There are passages in Cobden which suggest that hurt of the Corn Laws fell upon the manufacturing and commercial classes rather than labor but the speeches run mainly in terms of a higher standard of living for the laborer who would spend his "surplus of earnings on meat, vegetables, butter, milk and cheese," rather than on wheaten loaves. The Chartists were interested not in repeal, but in other amenities for the workers. Peel's conversion waited on his conclusion that wages did not vary with the price of provision, and that repeal would benefit the wage earner rather than line the pockets of the manufacturer.

In any event, with Gladstone's reductions in duties on meat, eggs and dairy products, with High Farming, and an end to the movement off the farm and out of handwork into the factory real wages did rise in the 1850's, but so did profits on manufacturing. As so often in economic debates between two alternatives, history provides the answer which economists abhor, both. Nor did repeal bring a reduction in incomes to landlords—at least not for thirty years—as the farm response to repeal, and to high prices of food produced by the potato famine, was more High Farming.

Cobden may have only been scoring debating points rather than speaking from conviction when on a number of occasions he argued that the repeal would stimulate landlords "to employ their capital and their intelligence as other classes are forced to do in other pursuits" rather than "in sluggish indolence," and to double the quantity of grain, or butter, or cheese, which the land is capable of providing, with "longer leases, draining, extending the length of fields, knocking down hedgerows, clearing away trees which now shield the corn" and to provide more agricultural employment by activity to "grub up hedges, grub up thorns, drain, ditch." Sir James Caird insisted that High Farming was the answer to the repeal of the Corn Laws and many shared his view. The fact is, moreover, that the 1850's were the Golden Age of British farming, with rapid technical progress through the decade though it slowed thereafter. Repeal of the Corn Laws may not have stimulated increased efficiency in agriculture, but they did not set it back immediately, and only after the 1870's did increases in productivity run down.

The political economists in the Board of Trade—Bowring, Jacob, MacGregor—sought free trade as a means of slowing down the development of manufacturing on the Continent. They regarded the Zollverein as a reply to the imposition of the Corn Laws, and thought that with its repeal Europe, but especially the Zollverein under the leadership of Prussia, could be diverted to invest more heavily in agriculture and to retard the march to manufacturing. There were inconsistencies between this position and other facts they adduced: Bowring recognized that Germany had advantages over Great Britain for the development of manufacturing, and that Swiss spinning had made progress without protection. The 1818 Prussian tariff which formed the basis for that of the Zollverein was the lowest in Europe when it was enacted—though the levying of tariffs on cloth and yarn by weight gave high effective rates of protection despite low nominal duties to the cheaper constructions and counts. Jacob noted that the export supply elasticity of Prussian grain must be low, given poor transport. "To export machinery, we must import corn,"[7] but imports of corn were intended to prevent the development of manufacturers abroad, whereas the export of machinery assisted it. The rise and progress of German manufacturing was attributed to restrictions on the admission of German agricultural products and wood, imposed by France and England, but also to "the natural advantages of the several states for manufacturing industry, the genius and laborious character and the necessities of the German people, and . . . especially the unexampled duration of peace, and internal tranquility which all Germany enjoyed."[8]

The clearest statements are those of John Bowring. In a letter of August 28, 1839 to Lord Palmerston he asserted that the manufacturing interest in the Zollverein "is greatly strengthened and will become stronger from year to year unless counteracted by a system of concessions, conditional upon the gradual lowering of tariffs. The present state of things will not be tenable. The tariffs will be elevated under the growing demands and increasing power of the manufacturing states, or they will be lowered by calling into action, and bringing over to an alliance, the agricultural and commercial interests."[9] In his testimony before the Select Committee on Import Duties in 1840 he went further: "I believe we have created an unnecessary rivalry by our vicious legislation; that many of these countries never would have been dreamed of being manufacturers."

On this showing, the repeal of the Corn Laws was motivated by "free trade imperialism," the desire to gain a monopoly of trade with the world in manufactured goods. Zollverein in the 1830's merely indicated the need for haste. Torrens and James Deacon Hume, among others, had been pushing for importing corn to expand exports in the 1820's, before Zollverein was a threat.

Reciprocity had been a part of British commercial policy in the Treaty of Vergennes in 1786, in treaties reducing the impact of the Navigation Laws in the 1820's and 1830's. The French were suspicious, fearing that they had been outtraded in 1786. They evaded Huskisson's negotiations in 1828. But reciprocity was unnecessary, given David Hume's law. Unilateral reduction of import duties increased exports. Restored into the British diplomatic armory in 1860, reciprocity later became heresy in the eyes of political economists, and of the manufacturing interest as well.

The view that ascribes repeal of the Corn Laws to free-trade imperialism, however, fails adequately to take account of the ideology of the political economists, who believed in buying in the cheapest market and selling in the dearest, or of the short-run nature of the interests of the Manchester merchants themselves. It was evident after the 1840's that industrialization on the Continent could not be stopped, and likely that it could not be slowed down. The Navigation Acts were too complex; they had best be eliminated. The Corn Laws were doomed, even before the Irish potato famine, though that hastened the end of both Corn Laws and Navigation Acts, along with its demonstration of the limitation of market solutions under some circumstances.

"A good cause seldom triumphs unless someone's interest is bound up with it."[10] Free trade is the hypocrisy of the export interest, the clever device of the climber who kicks the ladder away when he has attained the summit of greatness. But in the English case it was more a view of the world at peace, with cosmopolitan interests served as well as national.

It is difficult in this to find clearcut support for any of the theories of tariff formation set forth earlier. Free trade as an export-interest collective good, sought in a representative democracy by concentrated interests to escape the free rider would seem to require a simple and direct connection between the removal of the tariff and the increase in rents. In the repeal of the Corn Laws, and the earlier tariff reductions of Huskisson and Peel, the connection was roundabout—through Hume's law, which meant that increased imports would lead to increased prices or quantities (or both) exported on the one hand, and/or through reduced wages, or higher real incomes from lower food prices on the other. Each chain of reasoning had several links.

Johnson's view that free trade is adopted by countries with improving competitiveness is contradictory to the free-trade-imperialism explanation, that free trade is adopted in an effort to undermine foreign gains in manufacturing when competitiveness has begun to decline. The former might better account in timing for Adam Smith's advocacy of free trade seventy years earlier—though that had large elements of French Physiocratic thought—or apply to the 1820's when British productivity was still improving, before the Continent had started to catch up. In turn, free-trade imperialism is a better explanation for the 1830's than for the end of the 1840's, since by 1846 it was already too late to slow, much less to halt, the advance of manufacturing on the Continent.

Vested interests competing for rents in a representative democracy, thrusting manufacturers seeking to expand markets, or faltering innovators, trying as a last resort to force exports on shrinking markets—rather like the stage of foreign direct investment in Vernon's product cycle when diffusion of technology has been accomplished—none of these explanations seems free of difficulties as compared with an ideological explanation based on the intellectual triumph of the political economists, their doctrines modified to incorporate consistency. The argument took many forms: static, dynamic, with implicit reliance on one incidence or another, direct or indirect in its use of Hume's law. But the Manchester School, based on the political economists, represented a rapidly rising ideology of freedom for industry to buy in the cheapest and sell in the dearest market. It overwhelmed the Tories when it did not convert them. Britain in the nineteenth century, and only to a slightly lesser extent the Continent, were characterized by a "strong, widely-shared conviction that the teachings of contemporary orthodox economists, including Free Traders, were scientifically exact, universally applicable, and demanded assent."[11] In the implicit debate between Thurman Arnold who regarded economic theorists (and lawyers) as high priests who rationalize and sprinkle holy water on contemporary practice, and Keynes who thought of practical men as responding unconsciously to the preaching of dead theorists, the British movement to free trade is a vote, aided by the potato famine, for the view of Keynes.

IV

France after 1815 was a high-tariff country which conformed to the Pincus model for a representative democracy with tariffs, for various interests, except that (a) there were tariffs for all, and (b) it was not a democracy. The Physiocratic doctrine of *laisser-faire* for agricultural exports had been discredited in its reciprocal form by the disaster wreaked by imports up to 1789 under the Treaty of Vergennes. The Continental system, moreover, provided strong protection to hothouse industries which was continued in the tariff of 1816, and elaborated in 1820 and 1822. To the principles of Turgot, that there should be freedom of grain trade inside France but no imports except in period of drought, were added two more: protection of the consumer by regulating the right of export of wheat—a step back from Physiocratic doctrine—and protecting the rights of producers by import tariffs. In introducing the tariff of 1822 for manufactures, Saint-Cricq defended prohibitions, attacked the view that an industry which could not survive with a duty of twenty percent should perish, saying that the government intended to protect all branches together: "agriculture, industry, internal commerce, colonial production, navigation, foreign commerce finally, both of land and of sea."[12]

It was not long, however, before pressures for lower duties manifested themselves. Industries complained of the burden of the tariff on their purchases of inputs, and especially of the excess protection accorded to iron. It was calculated that protection against English iron cost industrial consumers fifty million francs a year and had increased the price of wood—used for charcoal, and owned by the many noble *maîtres de forges*—by thirty percent on the average and in some places fifty percent. Commissions of inquiry in 1828 and 1834 recommended modifications in duties, especially to enlarge supplies which local industry was not in a position to provide, and to convert prohibitions into tariffs. A tumult of conflict broke out in the Chamber among the export interests of the ports, the textile interests of Alsace and Normandy, the *maîtres de forges* and the consumers of iron, with no regard, says the protectionist Gouraud, for the national interest. The Chambers were then dissolved by the cabinet, and tariffs adjusted downward, in coal, iron, copper, nitrates, machinery, horses. Reductions of the 1830's were followed in the peaks of business by similar pressure for reductions in prosperous phases of the cycle of the 1840's and 1850's.

A troubling question that involved conflicting interests in this period was presented by sugar, for which it was impossible to find a solution agreeable at the same time to colonial planters, shipowners, port refiners, consumers and the treasury. Colonial supply was high cost and a 55 francs per 100 kilograms duty on foreign supplies was needed to keep the sugar ports content. This, however, made it economical to expand beet-sugar production, begun during the Continental blockade, and the sugar ports turned to taxing this domestic production, less heavily at first, but with full equality in 1843. By this time it was too late, and with the freeing of the slaves in 1848, French colonial sugar production no longer counted.

The free-trade movement in France had its support in Bordeaux, the wine-exporting region; Lyon, interested in silk; and Paris, producer of so-called Paris articles for sale abroad (cabinet ware, perfumes, imitation jewelry, toys, and so on). Later Norman agricultural interests in the export of butter and eggs to London teamed up with Bordeaux in wine to resist the attempts by textile interests to enlist agriculture in favor of higher tariffs.

Intellectual support to free trade led by Bastiat from Bordeaux, and with Michel

Chevalier as its most prestigious member, is dismissed by Lévy-Leboyer as unimportant. Nonetheless, Chevalier had an important part in the negotiation of the treaty, and in persuading Napoleon III to impose it on France in the face of the united opposition of the Chamber of Deputies. Some attention to his thought is required.

The prime interest of the *Société d'Economie Politique* and of Chevalier was growth. His two-year visit to the United States in 1833-1835 impressed him with the contribution of transport to economic growth and contributed to his 1838 major work on *The Material Interests of France in Roads, Canals and Railroads.* American protectionist doctrine of Henry Carey seems not to have affected him. Polytechnician, graduate of the *Ecole des Mines,* Chevalier's first interest in freer trade came from a project to establish woolen production in the Midi, and to obtain cheaper wool. Much of his later reasoning was in terms of the penalty to industry from expensive materials: Charging 35 francs for a quintal of iron worth 20 imposes on industry "the labor of Sisyphus and the work of Penelope."[13] His major argument, at the *Collège de France,* and in his *Examen du Système Commercial,* cited the success of Spitalfield and Macclesfield when Huskisson permitted competition of imports; and the experience of the manufacturers of cotton and woolen textiles in Saxony who were worried by the enactment of Zollverein but sufficiently stimulated by import competition so that in two or three years their industry was flourishing. The letter of Napoleon III to Fould talks in specifics of the need to abolish all duties on raw materials essential to industry to encourage production, and to reduce by stages the duties on goods which are consumed on a large scale. In the more general introduction it states that "lack of competition causes industry to stagnate," echoing the Chevalier view. Chevalier himself was one of the judges of the Universal Exposition of 1855 in Paris and noted that France received so many prizes that no one dared confess to being a protectionist.

There were economic purposes behind the Anglo-French treaty, as evidenced by the proposal in France in 1851 for tariffs of twenty percent, ten percent and a duty-free on wholly manufactured goods, semi-finished manufactures and raw materials; by actual reductions in duties on coal, iron and steel in 1852 as the railroad boom picked up; and by the legislative proposal designed by Napoleon III in 1855, but not put forward until after the Crimean War, to admit 241 items duty free, reduce tariffs on 19 others, remove all prohibitions and set a top limit of thirty percent. This last was turned down by the Chamber and Napoleon promised not to submit a new tariff proposal before 1861.

Economic interests were involved, and the theories of great men like Cobden and Chevalier. However, there was more: Napoleon III was starting to engage in foreign adventure. He wanted to rid Italy of Austrian rule by use of arms. The British opposed his military measures, despite their recent use of force in Crimea. The treaty was used to hold British neutrality, as much as or more than to stimulate growth in France. Moreover, it did not need to be submitted to the Chamber. Under the Constitution of 1851, the Emperor had the sole power to make treaties, and such treaties encompassed those dealing with trade.

The move was successful both politically and economically. With the help of the

French armies, Italy was unified under the leadership of Piedmont, and French growth never faltered under the impetus of increased imports. French industries met competition successfully and checked the growth of imports after two years. While its effects are intermingled with those of the spread of the French railroad network, it "helped to bring about the full development of the industrial revolution in France."

Further, it added impetus to the free-trade movement in Europe. This was under way in the early 1850's, following repeal of the Corn Laws. The Swiss constitution of 1848 had called for a tariff for revenue only and protective duties were reduced progressively from 1851 to 1855. The Netherlands removed a tariff on ship imports and a prohibition against nationalization of foreign ships. Belgium plugged gap after gap in its protective system in the early 1850's, only to turn around at the end of the decade and adopt free trade down the line. Piedmont, as we shall see, and Spain, Portugal, Norway and Sweden (after 1857) undertook to dismantle their protective and prohibitive restrictions. With the Anglo-French treaty the trickle became a flood. France, Germany, Italy and Britain engaged in negotiating reciprocal trade treaties with the most-favored nation clause.

Following French defeat at Sedan in 1870 and the abdication of Louis Napoleon, the Third Republic brought in the protectionist Thiers. The Cobden treaty was denounced in 1872. Reversal of policy waited upon the repeal of the Le Chapelier law of 1791, taken in the heat of the French revolution against associations, which forbade economic interests from organizing. Dunham claims that a country with leadership would have accepted a moderate tariff in 1875, but that the free traders had neither organization nor conviction, that is, too many free riders.

The French movement to free trade was taken against the weight of the separate interests, in the absence of strong export interests, with an admixture of economic theory of a dynamic kind, and imposed from above. The motivation of that imposition was partly economic, partly, perhaps even mainly, political. Moreover, it had a bandwagon effect in spreading freer trade.

In the French case, the leadership overwhelmed the concentrated economic interests. That leadership earned its surplus to use Frohlich, Oppenheimer and Young's expression, in a coin different than economic, that is, in freedom to maneuver in foreign policy. It may be possible to subsume increases in leadership surplus in this form into an "economic theory of national decision-making" with costs to vested interests accepted in exchange for political benefits to a national leader, ruling by an imposed constitution, the legitimacy of which is not questioned. The effort seems tortured.

V

As mentioned earlier, the Prussian tariff of 1818 was regarded when it was enacted as the lowest in Europe. But the duties on coarse yarns and textiles were effectively high, since the tariff was levied by weight. Jacob in 1819 noted that the "system of the Prussian government has always been of manufacturing at home everything consumed within the Kingdom; of buying from others, nothing that can be dispensed with," adding "As scarcely any competition exists, but with their own countrymen, there is little inducement to adopt the inventions of other countries, or to exercise their facilities in perfecting their fabrics; none of these have kept pace...."[14] Baden, on joining the Zollverein which adopted the Prussian tariff for the totality, believed itself to be raising its tariff level when it joined. What Baden did, however, was to acquire enforcement: its long border had previously been effectively open.

The Prussian tariff dominated that of the Zollverein, organized in the years from 1828 to 1833, primarily because Prussia took a very liberal view of tariff revenues. Most goods by sea entered the German states via Prussia, directly or by way of the Netherlands, but the text of the Zollverein treaty of 1833 provided that the revenues from the duties after deduction of expenses would be divided among the contracting states according to population. Prussia thus received 55 percent, Bavaria 17 percent, Saxony 6.36 percent, Wurtemberg 5.5 percent, and so on, and was said in 1848 to have sacrificed about two million thalers a year, exclusive of the fiscal loss sustained by smuggling along the Rhine and Lake Constance. This can be regarded as a side-payment made by the beneficiary of income-distribution under Pareto-optimal conditions to gain its policy, or as the disproportionate share of overhead costs of the collective good saddled on the party that most wanted it.

Despite adjustments made in Prussian customs duties between 1819 and 1833, the tariff remained low by British standards. Junker grain growers were hopeful of importing British manufactures in order to sell Britain more grain. Junker bureaucrats, brought up on Adam Smith and free trade by instinct, were fearful that highly protective rates would reduce the revenue yield.

Outside of Prussia plus Hamburg and Frankfort and the other grain-growing states of Mecklenburg, Pomerania, and so on, there was interest in higher tariffs, but apart from the Rhineland, little in the way of organized interests. Von Delbrück comments that Prussia and Pomerania had free trade interests and shipping interests, but that outside the Rhineland, which had organized Chambers of Commerce under the French occupation, there were few bureaucrats, or organs with views on questions of trade and industry. Nor did the Prussian government see a need to develop them.

Saxony was sufficiently protected by its interior location so as not to feel threatened by low tariffs, which, as mentioned, were not really low on coarse cloths. On joining the Zollverein, Baden was concerned over raising its tariff, and worried lest it be cut off from its traditional trading areas of Switzerland and Alsace. It fought with the Zollverein authorities over exemptions for imported capital equipment, but gradually evolved into a source of pressure, with Bavaria and Wurtemberg, for higher tariffs on cotton yarns and iron. Fischer points out the request for lifting the duty on cotton yarns from two talers per centner to five was resisted by the weavers of Prussia (the Rhineland) and Silesia.

Cotton yarns and iron were the critical items. Shortly after the formation of Zollverein, a trend toward protection was seen to be under way. The Leipsig consul reported a new duty on iron to the Board of Trade in February 1837 and observed that the switch from imports of cotton cloth to imports of yarn pointed in the direction of ultimate exclusion of both. Bowring's letter of August 1839 noted that the manufacturing interest was growing stronger, that the existing position was untenable, and that tariffs would be raised under the growing demands and increasing power of the manufacturing states, or would be lowered by an alliance between the agricultural and commercial interests.

Open agitation for protection began two and one-half years after the formation of the Zollverein when the South pushed for duties on cotton yarns. Linen yarns and cloth went on the agenda in 1839 and iron, protection for which was sought by Silesian and west German ironwork owners, beginning in 1842. But these groups lacked decisive power. The Prussian landed nobility covered their position by citing the interests of the consumers, and Prince Smith, the expatriate leader of the doctrinaire free traders, in turn tried to identify free trade and low tariffs with the international free-trade movement rather than with the export interests of the Junkers. The tariff on iron was raised in 1844, those on cotton yarns and linen yarns in 1846. Von Delbruck presents in detail the background of the latter increases, starting with the bureaucratic investigations into linen, cotton, wool, and soda, with their negative recommendation, continuing through the negotiations, in which Prussia was ranged against any increase and all the others in favor, and concluding that the Prussian plenipotentiary to the Zollverein conference was right in not vetoing the increases, as he could have done, operating on the theory that a compromise was more important than the rationally correct measure of this or that tariff. The head of the Prussian Handelsamt was not satisfied with the outcome of the conference but had to accept it.

From 1846 on, the direction of Zollverein tariffs was downward, aided first by the repeal of the Corn Laws and secondly by the Cobden-Chevalier treaty. With the increases of the 1840's and English reductions, the Zollverein tariff from one of the lowest in Europe had become relatively high. Von Delbruck was one of the doctrinaire free traders in the Prussian civil service and notes that in 1863 he had been trying for a reduction on the tariff in pig iron for seven years, since the tariff reform of 1856, which reordered but did not lower duty schedules. He also wanted a reduction in the tariff on cotton cloth; duties on woolens were no longer needed. The opportunity came with the announcement of the Anglo-French treaty. He noted that Austria had gone from prohibitions to tariffs, that the Netherlands had reformed its tariffs with a five percent maximum on industrial production, and that the levels of Italian duties were lower than those in Germany. "Could we stay away from this movement? We could not."[15]

Bismarck was no barrier to the Junker bureaucracy. His view about tariff negotiations was expressed in 1879 in the question: "Who got the better of the bargain?" Trade treaties, he believed, were nothing in themselves but an expression of friendship. His economic conscience at this time, he said later, was in the hands of others. Moreover, he had two political ends which a trade treaty with France might serve: to gain her friendship in the Danish question, and to isolate Austria which was bidding for a role in the German Confederation. Austrian tariffs were high. The lower the levels of the Zollverein the more difficulty she would have in joining it and bidding against Prussia for influence. The Zollverein followed the 1863 treaty with France with a series of others.

Exports of grain from Prussia, Pomerania, and Mecklenberg to London as a percentage of total English imports hit a peak in 1862 at the time of the Civil War and proceeded down thereafter as American supplies took over. The free-trade movement nonetheless continued. Only hesitation prevented a move to complete free trade at the peak of the boom in 1873. There is debate whether the crash later in the year triggered off the return to protection in 1879 or not. Victory in 1871 had enlarged competition in iron and cotton textiles by including Alsace and Lorraine in the new German Empire. Radical free traders and large farmers achieved the reduction in duties on raw iron in 1873 and passed legislative provision for their complete removal in 1877. But Lambi notes that *Gewerbefreiheit* (freedom of occupation) had caused dissatisfaction and in some versions subsumed free trade. By 1875 the iron interests are organizing to resist the scheduled elimination of iron duties in 1877.

The difference between the 1873 depression which led to tariffs, and the 1857 crisis which did not, lay in (a) the fact that the interests were not cohesive in the earlier period and (b) that Britain did not keep on lowering duties in the later period as it had in the first. On the first score the Verein Deutscher Eisen- und Stahl Industrielle was formed in 1873 after vertical integration of steel back to iron mining had removed the opposition between the producers and consumers of iron. This much supports the view of the effectiveness of concentrated interests achieving their tariff goals when scattered interests will not—though again it has nothing to do with representative democracy. On the other hand, the free traders also organized; in 1868 the Kongress Nord-Deutscher Landwirte was organized, and in 1871 it was broadened to cover all Germany. In 1872, a Deutsche Landwirtschaftsrat was formed. Many of these organizations and the once free-trade Congress of German Economists were subverted and converted to protection after 1875, but a new Union for the Promotion of Free Trade was formed in September 1876. German economic interests as a whole became organized, and the struggle was among interests concentrated on both sides.

Abandonment of the opposition of the landed interests is perhaps critical. Consumers of iron in machinery, they opposed tariffs on iron up to 1875, but with the decline in the price of grain and the threat of imports, their opposition collapsed. It might have been possible to support tariffs for grain and free trade for iron, but inconsistency is open to attack. After von Delbruck's resignation or discharge in April 1876, Bismarck forged the alliance of bread and iron. As widely recounted, he had strong domestic political motives for higher tariffs on this occasion, as contrasted with his international political gains from lower tariffs up to 1875.

In general, however, the German case conforms to the Stolper-Samuelson explanation: the abundant factor wants free trade; when it becomes relatively scarce, through a gain in manufacturing at home and an expansion of agriculture abroad, it shifts to wanting tariffs. Doctrine was largely on the side of free trade. List's advocacy of national economy had little or no political force. His ultimate goal was always free trade, and his early proposal of ten percent duties on colonial goods, fifteen percent on Continental and fifty percent on British was more anti-British than national. In the 1840's he was regarded in Germany, or at least by the Prussians, as a polemicist whose views were offered for sale. Bismarck is often regarded as the arch-villain of the 1879 reversal of Zollverein low tariffs, but it is hard to see that his role was a major one. . . .

VI

My first conclusion reached from this survey was that free trade in Europe in the period from 1820 to 1875 had many different causes. Whereas after 1879, various countries reacted quite differently to the single stimulus of the fall in the price of wheat—England liquidating its agriculture, France and Germany imposing tariffs, though for different political and sociological reasons, Italy emigrating (in violation of the assumptions of classical economics), and Denmark transforming from producing grain for export to importing it as an input in the production of dairy products, bacon and eggs—before that the countries of Europe all responded to different stimuli in the same way. Free trade was part of a general response to the breakdown of the manor and guild system. This was especially true of the removal of restrictions on exports and export taxes, which limited freedom of producers. As more and conflicting interests came into contention, the task of sorting them out became too complex for government (as shown in *Gewerbeförderung* in Baden, and the refinement of the Navigation Laws in England), and it became desirable to sweep them all away.

Part of the stimulus came from the direct self-interest of particular dominant groups, illustrated particularly by the First Hand in the Netherlands. In Britain, free trade emerged as a doctrine from the political economists, with a variety of rationalizations to sustain it in particular applications: anti-monopoly, increases to real wages, higher profits, increased allocative efficiency, increased productivity through innovation required by import competition. In France, the lead in the direction of free trade came less from the export interests than from industrial interests using imported materials and equipment as inputs, though the drive to free trade after 1846 required the overcoming of the weight of the vested interests by strong governmental leadership, motivated by political gain in international politics. The German case was more straightforward: free trade was in the interest of the exporting grain and timber-producing classes, who were politically dominant in Prussia and who partly bought off and partly overwhelmed the rest of the country. The Italian case seems to be one in which doctrines developed abroad which were dominant in England and in a minority position in France, were imported by strong political leadership and imposed on a relatively disorganized political body.

Second thoughts raise questions. The movement to free trade in the 1850's in the Netherlands, Belgium, Spain, Portugal, Denmark, Norway and Sweden, along with the countries discussed in detail, suggests the possibility that Europe as a whole was motivated by ideological considerations rather than economic interests. That Louis

Napoleon and Bismarck would use trade treaties to gain ends in foreign policy suggests that free trade was valued for itself, and that moves toward it would earn approval. Viewed in one perspective, the countries of Europe in this period should not be considered as independent economies whose reactions to various phenomena can properly be compared, but rather as a single entity which moved to free trade for ideological or perhaps better doctrinal reasons. Manchester and the English political economists persuaded Britain which persuaded Europe, by precept and example. Economic theories of representative democracy, or constitutional monarchy, or even absolute monarchy may explain some cases of tariff changes. They are little help in Western Europe between the Napoleonic Wars and the Great Depression.

NOTES

1. H. R. C. Wright, *Free Trade and Protection in the Netherlands, 1816-1830: A Study of the First Benelux* (Cambridge: Cambridge University Press, 1955) p. 124.

2. *William Huskisson, (The Speeches of the Right Honorable)* (London: John Murray, 1832), 11, p. 328.

3. Report of the Select Committee on the Laws Relating to the Export of Tools and Machinery, 30 June 1825, in *Parliamentary Papers, Reports of Committee, (*1825), Vol . V, p. 12.

4. H. R. C. Wright, *Free Trade and Protection*, p. 130.

5. Charles Babbage, *The Economy of Machinery and Manufactures* (London: Charles Knight, 4th ed., 1835), p. 364.

6. Karl Polanyi, *The Great Transformation* (New York: Farrar & Rinehart, 1944), p. 152-53.

7. Testimony of Thomas Ashton, in *First Report of the Select Committee*, para. 235.

8. John MacGregor, *Germany, Her Resources, Government, Union of Customs and Power under Frederick William IV* (London: Whittaker and Co., 1948), p. 68.

9. John Bowring, "Report on the Prussian Commercial Union 1840," *Parliamentary Papers*, 1840, Volume XXI, p. 287.

10. Mill, cited by Bernard Semmel, *The Rise of Free Trade Imperialism: Classical Political Economy, The Empire of Free Trade and Imperialism, 1750-1850* (Cambridge: Cambridge University Press, 1970), p. 207.

11. Kenneth Fielden, "The Rise and Fall of Free Trade," in C. J. Bartlett, ed., *Britain Pre-eminent: Studies in British World Influence in the Nineteenth Century* (London: Macmillan, 1969), p. 78.

12. Charles Gouraud, *Histoire de la politique commerciale de la France et son influence sur le progre's de la richesse publique depuis le moyen age jusqu'à nos jours*, 1, 11 (Paris: Auguste Durand, 1854), p. 208.

13. Michel Chevalier, *Cours d'economie politique, Fait au Collège de France*, 1, 11, 111 (2nd ed., Paris: No publisher stated, 1855), p. 538.

14. William Jacob, *A View of the Agriculture, Manufactures, Statistics and Society in the State of Germany and Parts of Holland and France* (London: John Murray, 1820), pp. 201-12.

15. Rudolph von Delbrück, *Lebenserinnerungen, I* (Leipsig: Duncker u. Humblot, 1905), p. 200.

5

International Trade, Domestic Coalitions, and Liberty: Comparative Responses to the Crisis of 1873-1896

PETER ALEXIS GOUREVITCH

Peter Gourevitch examines the impact of the Great Depression of 1873-1896 upon the trade policies and political coalitions of four countries, during which Germany and France adopted high tariffs on both agricultural and industrial products, Great Britain maintained its historic policy of free trade, and the United States protected industry but not agriculture. In attempting to explain this pattern of response, Gourevitch compares four alternative hypotheses: economic interests, largely the public choice approach of Liberal political economy; political systems; international systems, drawn from the Realist perspective; and economic ideology. Economic interests supplemented by a concern with political systems, he concludes, provides the most persuasive account of these four cases. Not only does Gourevitch give a detailed and informative history of the trade policies of the four great economic powers of the late nineteenth century, but he explicitly compares and contrasts two of the three perspectives in International Political Economy.

5 "International Trade, Domestic Coalitions, and Liberty: Comparative Responses to the Crisis of 1873-1896" by Peter Alexis Gourevitch. Reprinted from *The Journal of Interdisciplinary History*, VIII (1977), 281-313, with the permission of the editors of *The Journal of Interdisciplinary History* and the MIT Press, Cambridge, MA.

For social scientists who enjoy comparisons, happiness is finding a force or event which affects a number of societies at the same time. Like test-tube solutions that respond differently to the same reagent, these societies reveal their characters in divergent responses to the same stimulus. One such phenomenon is the present world-wide inflation/depression. An earlier one was the Great Depression of 1873-1896. Technological breakthroughs in agriculture (the reaper, sower, fertilizers, drainage tiles, and new forms of wheat) and in transportation (continental rail networks, refrigeration, and motorized shipping) transformed international markets for food, causing world prices to fall. Since conditions favored extensive grain growing, the plains nations of the world (the United States, Canada, Australia, Argentina, and Russia) became the low cost producers. The agricultural populations of Western and Central Europe found themselves abruptly uncompetitive.

In industry as well, 1873 marks a break. At first the sharp slump of that year looked like an ordinary business-cycle downturn, like the one in 1857. Instead, prices continued to drop for over two decades, while output continued to rise. New industries—steel, chemicals, electrical equipment, and shipbuilding—sprang up, but the return on capital declined. As in agriculture, international competition became intense. Businessmen everywhere felt the crisis, and most of them wanted remedies.

The clamour for action was universal. The responses differed: vertical integration, cartels, government contracts, and economic protection. The most visible response was tariffs. . . .

Although the economic stimuli were uniform, the political systems forced to cope with them differed considerably. Some systems were new or relatively precarious: Republican France, Imperial Germany, Monarchical Italy, Reconstruction America, Newly-Formed Canada, Recently Autonomous Australia. Only Britain could be called stable. Thirty years later when most of these political systems had grown stronger, most of the countries had high tariffs. The importance of the relation between the nature of the political system and protection has been most forcefully argued by Gershenkron in *Bread and Democracy in Germany*. The coalition of iron and rye built around high tariffs contributed to a belligerent foreign policy and helped to shore up the authoritarian Imperial Constitution of 1871. High tariffs, then, contributed to both world wars and to fascism, not a minor consequence. It was once a commonly held motion that free trade and democracy, protection and authoritarianism, went together. . . .

These basic facts about tariff levels and political forms have been discussed by many authors. What is less clear, and not thoroughly explored in the literature, is the best way to understand these outcomes. As with most complex problems, there is no shortage of possible explanations: interest groups, class conflict, institutions, foreign policy, ideology. Are these explanations all necessary though, or equally important? This essay seeks to probe these alternative explanations. It is speculative; it does not offer new information or definitive answers to old questions. Rather, it takes a type of debate about which social scientists are increasingly conscious (the comparison of different explanations of a given phenomenon) and extends it to an old problem that has significant bearing on current issues in political economy—the interaction of international trade and domestic politics. The paper examines closely the formation of tariff policy in late nineteenth-century Germany, France, Britain, and the United States, and then considers the impact of the tariff policy quarrel on the character of each political system.

EXPLAINING TARIFF LEVELS

Explanations for late nineteenth-century tariff levels may be classified under four headings, according to the type of variable to which primacy is given.

1. Economic Explanations Tariff levels derive from the interests of economic groups able to translate calculations of economic benefit into public policy. Types of economic explanations differ in their conceptualization of groups (classes vs. sectors vs. companies) and of the strategies groups pursue (maximizing income, satisficing, stability, and class hegemony).

2. Political System Explanations The "statement of the groups" does not state everything. The ability of economic actors to realize policy goals is affected by political structures and the individuals who staff them. Groups differ in their access to power, the costs they must bear in influencing decisions, prestige, and other elements of political power.

3 . International System Explanations Tariff levels derive from a country's position in the international state system. Considerations of military security, independence, stability, or glory shape trade policy. Agriculture may be protected, for example, in order to guarantee supplies of food and soldiers, rather than to provide profit to farmers (as explanation 1 would suggest).

4. Economic Ideology Explanations Tariff levels derive from intellectual orientations about proper economic and trade policies. National traditions may favor autarchy or market principles; faddishness or emulation may induce policy makers to follow the lead given by successful countries. Such intellectual orientations may have originated in calculations of self-interest (explanation 1), or in broader political concerns (explanation 2) or in understandings of international politics (explanation 3), but they may outlive the conditions that spawned them.

These explanations are by no means mutually exclusive. The German case could be construed as compatible with all four: Junkers and heavy industry fought falling prices, competition, and political reformism; Bismarck helped organize the iron and rye coalition; foreign policy concerns over supply sources and hostile great powers helped to create it; and the nationalist school of German economic thought provided fertile ground for protectionist arguments. But were all four factors really essential to produce high tariffs in Germany? Given the principle that a simple explanation is better than a complex one, we may legitimately try to determine at what point we have said enough to explain the result. Other points may be interesting, perhaps crucial for other outcomes, but redundant for this one. It would also be useful to find explanations that fit the largest possible number of cases.

Economic explanation offers us a good port of entry. It requires that we investigate the impact of high and low tariffs, both for agricultural and industrial products, on the economic situation of each major group in each country. We can then turn to the types of evidence—structures, interstate relations, and ideas—required by the other modes of reasoning. Having worked these out for each country, it will then be possible to attempt an evaluation of all four arguments.

GERMANY

Economic Explanations What attitude toward industrial and agricultural tariffs would we predict for each of the major economic groups in German society, if each acted according to its economic interests? A simple model of German society contains the following groups: small peasants; Junkers (or estate owners); manufacturers in heavy, basic industries (iron, coal, steel); manufacturers of finished goods; workers in each type of industry; shopkeepers and artisans; shippers; bankers; and professionals (lawyers, doctors). What were the interests of each in relation to the new market conditions after 1873?

Agriculture, notes Gerschenkron, could respond to the sharp drop in grain prices in two ways: modernization or protection. Modernization meant applying the logic of comparative advantage to agriculture. Domestic grain production would be abandoned. Cheap foreign grain would become an input for the domestic production of higher quality foodstuffs such as dairy products and meat. With rising incomes, the urban and industrial sectors would provide the market for this type of produce. Protection, conversely, meant maintaining domestic grain production. This would retard modernization, maintain a large agricultural population, and prolong national self-sufficiency in food.

Each policy implied a different organization for farming. Under late nineteenth-century conditions, dairy products, meats, and vegetables were best produced by high quality labor, working in small units, managed by owners, or long-term leaseholders. They were produced least well on estates by landless laborers working for a squirearchy. Thus, modernization would be easier where small units or production already predominated, as in Denmark, which is Gerschenkron's model of a modernizing response to the crisis of 1873. The Danish state helped by organizing cooperatives, providing technology, and loaning capital.

In Germany, however, landholding patterns varied considerably. In the region of vast estates east of the Elbe, modernization would have required drastic restructuring of the Junkers' control of the land. It would have eroded their hold over the laborers, their dominance of local life, and their position in German society. The poor quality of Prussian soil hindered modernization of any kind; in any case it would have cost money. Conversely, western and southern Germany contained primarily small- and medium-sized farms more suited to modernization.

Gerschenkron thinks that the Danish solution would have been best for everyone, but especially for these smaller farmers. Following his reasoning, we can impute divergent interests to these two groups. For the Junkers, protection of agriculture was a dire necessity. For the small farmers, modernization optimized their welfare in the long run, but in the short run protection would keep them going; their interests, therefore, can be construed as ambivalent.

What were the interests of agriculture concerning industrial tariffs? Presumably the agricultural population sought to pay the lowest possible prices for the industrial goods that it consumed, and would be opposed to high industrial tariffs. Farmers selling high quality produce to the industrial sector prospered, however, when that sector prospered, since additional income was spent disproportionately on meat and eggs. Modernizing producers might therefore be receptive to tariff and other economic policies which helped industry. For grain, conversely, demand was less elastic. Whatever the state of the industrial economy, the Junkers would be able to sell their output provided that foreign sources were prevented from undercutting them. Thus, we would expect the Junkers to be the most resolutely against high industrial tariffs, while the smaller farmers would again have a less clearcut interest.

Neither were the interests of the industrial sector homogenous. Makers of basic materials such as iron and steel wanted the producers of manufactured products such as stoves, pots and pans, shovels, rakes, to buy supplies at home rather than from cheaper sources abroad. Conversely the finished goods manufacturers wanted cheap materials; their ideal policy would have been low tariffs on all goods except the ones that they made.

In theory, both types of industries were already well past the "infant industry" stage and would have benefited from low tariffs and international specialization. Indeed, German industry competed very effectively against British and American products during this period, penetrating Latin America, Africa, Asia, and even the United States and United Kingdom home markets. Low tariffs might not have meant lower incomes for industry, but rather a shift among companies and a change in the mix of items produced.

Nevertheless tariffs still offered certain advantages even to the strong. They reduced risk in industries requiring massive investments like steel; they assured economies of scale, which supported price wars or dumping in foreign markets; and to the extent that cartels and mergers suppressed domestic production, they allowed monopoly profits. Finally, iron and steel manufacturers everywhere faced softening demand due to the declining rate of railroad building, not wholly offset by shipbuilding. As we shall see, steelmen were in the vanguard of protectionist movements everywhere including Britain (their only failure).

All industrialists (except those who sold farm equipment) had an interest in low agricultural tariffs. Cheap food helped to keep wages down and to conserve purchasing power for manufactured goods.

The interests of the industrial work force were pulled in conflicting directions by

TABLE 1. Interests of Different Groups in Relation to Industrial and Agricultural Tariffs (Germany)

INDUSTRIAL TARIFFS	AGRICULTURAL TARIFFS: HIGH	AGRICULTURAL TARIFFS: LOW
HIGH	The outcome: high tariffs SMALL	Heavy industry Workers in heavy industry FARMERS
LOW	Junkers	Workers in finished manufacturing Finished manufacturers

the divergent claims of consumer preoccupations and producer concerns. As consumers, workers found any duties onerous, especially those on food. But as producers, they shared an interest with their employers in having their particular products protected, or in advancing the interests of the industrial sector as a whole.

Shippers and their employees had an interest in high levels of imports and exports and hence in low tariffs of all kinds. Bankers and those employed in finance had varied interests according to the ties each had with particular sectors of the economy. As consumers, professionals and shopkeepers, along with labor, had a general interest in keeping cost down, although special links (counsel to a steel company or greengrocer in a steel town) might align them to a high tariff industry.

This pattern of group interests may be represented diagrammatically. Table 1 shows each group's position in relation to four policy combinations, pairing high and low tariffs for industry and agriculture. The group's intensity of interest can be conveyed by its placement in relation to the axis: closeness to the origin suggests ambiguity in the group's interest; distance from the intersection suggests clarity and intensity of interest.

Notice that no group wanted the actual policy outcome in Germany—high tariffs in both sectors. To become policy, the law of 1879 and its successors required trade-offs among members of different sectors. This is not really surprising. Logrolling is expected of interest groups. Explanation 1 would therefore find the coalition of iron and rye quite normal.

Nevertheless, a different outcome—low tariffs on both types of goods—also would have been compatible with an economic interest group explanation. Logrolling could also have linked up those parts of industry and agriculture that had a plausible interest in low tariffs: finished goods manufacturers, shippers and dock-workers, labor, professionals, shopkeepers, consumers, and farmers of the West and South. This coalition may even have been a majority of the electorate, and at certain moments managed to impose its policy preferences. Under Chancellor Georg von Caprivi (1890-1894), reciprocal trade treaties were negotiated and tariffs lowered. Why did this coalition lose over the long run? Clearly because it was weaker, but of what did this weakness consist?

Political Explanations One answer looks to aspects of the political system which favored protectionist forces at the expense of free traders: institutions (weighted voting, bureaucracy); personalities who intervened on one side or another; the press of other issues (socialism, taxation, constitutional reform, democratization); and interest group organization.

In all these domains, the protectionists had real advantages. The Junkers especially enjoyed a privileged position in the German system. They staffed or influenced the army, the bureaucracy, the judiciary, the educational system, and the Court. The three class voting system in Prussia, and the allocation of seats, helped overrepresent them and propertied interests in general.

In the late 1870s, Bismarck and the emperor switched to the protectionists' side. Their motives were primarily political. They sought to strengthen the basic foundations of the conservative system (autonomy of the military and the executive from parliamentary pressure, a conservative foreign policy; dominance of conservative social forces at home; and preservation of the Junkers). For a long time, industry and bourgeois elements had fought over many of these issues. Unification had helped to reconcile the army and the middle classes, but many among the latter still demanded a more liberal constitution and economic reforms opposed by the Junkers. In the 1870s Bismarck used the Kulturkampf to prevent a revisionist alliance of Liberals, Catholics, and Federalists. In the long run, this was an unsatisfactory arrangement because it made the government dependent on unreliable political liberals and alienated the essentially conservative Catholics.

Tariffs offered a way to overcome these contradictions and forge a new, conservative alliance. Industrialists gave up their antagonism toward the Junkers, and any lingering constitutionalist demands, in exchange for tariffs, anti-Socialist laws, and incorporation into the governing majority. Catholics gave way on constitutional revision in exchange for tariffs and the end of the Kulterkampf (expendable because protection would now carry out its political function). The Junkers accepted industry and paid higher prices for industrial goods, but maintained a variety of privileges, and their estates. Peasants obtained a solution to their immediate distress, less desirable over the long run than modernization credits, but effective nonetheless. Tariff revenues eased conflicts over tax reform. The military obtained armaments for which the iron and steel manufacturers received the contracts. The coalition excluded everyone who challenged the economic order and/or the constitutional settlement of 1871. The passage of the first broad protectionist measure in 1879 has aptly been called the "second founding" of the Empire.

Control of the Executive allowed Bismarck to orchestrate these complex trade-offs. Each of the coalition partners had to be persuaded to pay the price, especially that of high tariffs on the goods of the other sector. Control of foreign policy offered instruments for maintaining the bargain once it had been struck. . . . The Chancellor used imperialism, nationalism, and overseas crises to obscure internal divisions, and particularly, to blunt middle-class criticism. Nationalism and the vision of Germany surrounded by enemies, or at least harsh competitors, reinforced arguments on behalf of the need for self-sufficiency in food and industrial production and for a powerful military machine. . . .

The protectionists also appear to have organized more effectively than the free-traders. In the aftermath of 1848, industry had been a junior partner, concerned with the elimination of obstacles to a domestic German free market (such as guild regulations and internal tariffs). Its demands for protection against British imports were ignored. . . .The boom of the 1860s greatly increased the relative importance of the industrialists. After 1873, managers of heavy industry, mines and some of the banks formed new associations and worked to convert old ones: in 1874 the Association of German Steel Producers was founded; in 1876, the majority of the Chambers of Commerce swung away from free trade, and other associations began to fall apart over the issue. These protectionist producers' groups were clear in purpose, small in number, and intense in interest. Such groups generally have an easier time working out means of common action than do more general and diffuse ones. Banks and the state provided coordination among firms and access to other powerful groups in German society.

The most significant of these powerful groups—the Junkers—became available as coalition allies after the sharp drop in wheat prices which began in 1875. Traditionally staunch defenders of free trade, the Junkers switched very quickly to protection. They organized rapidly, adapting with remarkable ease, as Gerschenkron notes, to the *ère des foules*. Associations such as the Union of Agriculturalists and the Conservative Party sought to define and represent the collective interest of the whole agricultural sector, large and small, east and west. Exploiting their great prestige and superior resources, the Junkers imposed their definition of that interest—protection as a means of preserving the status quo on the land. To legitimate this program, the Junker-led movements developed many of the themes later contained in Nazi propaganda: moral superiority of agriculture; organic unity of those who work the land; anti-Semitism; and distrust of cities, factories, workers, and capitalists. . . .

The alternative (Low/Low) coalition operated under several political handicaps. It comprised heterogeneous components, hence a diffuse range of interests. In economic terms, the coalition embraced producers and consumers, manufacturers and shippers, owners and workers, and city dwellers and peasants. Little in day to day life brought these elements together, or otherwise facilitated the awareness and pursuit of common goals; much kept them apart—property rights, working conditions, credit, and taxation. The low tariff groups also differed on other issues such as religion, federalism, democratization of the Constitution, and constitutional control of the Army and Executive. Unlike the High/High alliance, the low tariff coalition had to overcome its diversity without help from the Executive. Only during the four years of Caprivi was the chancellor's office sympathetic to low tariff politics, and Caprivi was very isolated from the court, the kaiser, the army, and the bureaucracy.

Despite these weaknesses, the low tariff alliance was not without its successes. It did well in the first elections after the "refounding" (1881), a defeat for Bismarck which . . . drove him further toward social imperialism. From 1890, Caprivi directed a series of reciprocal trade negotiations leading to tariff reductions. Caprivi's ministry suggests the character of the programmatic glue needed to keep a low tariff coalition together: at home, a little more egalitarianism and constitutionalism (the end of the antisocialist laws); in foreign policy, a little more internationalism—no lack of interest in empire or prestige, but a greater willingness to insert Germany into an international division of labor.

International System Explanations A third type of explanation for tariff levels looks at each country's position in the international system. Tariff policy has consequences not only for profit and loss for the economy as a whole or for particular industries, but for other national concerns, such as security, independence, and glory. International specialization means interdependence. Food supplies, raw materials, manufactured products, markets become vulnerable. Britain, according to this argument, could rely on imports because of her navy. If Germany did the same, would she not expose her lifeline to that navy? If the German agricultural sector shrank, would she not lose a supply of soldiers with which to protect herself from foreign threats? On the other hand, were there such threats? Was the danger of the Franco-British-Russian alliance an immutable constituent fact of the international order, or a response to German aggressiveness? This brings us back to the Kehr-Wehler emphasis on the importance of domestic interests in shaping foreign policy. There were different ways to interpret the implications of the international system for German interests: one view, seeing the world as hostile, justified protection; the other, seeing the world as benevolent, led to free trade. To the extent that the international system was ambiguous, we cannot explain the choice between these competing foreign policies by reference to the international system alone.

A variant of international system explanations focuses on the structure of bargaining among many actors in the network of reciprocal trade negotiations. Maintenance of low tariffs by one country required a similar willingness by others. One could argue that Germany was driven to high tariffs by the protectionist behavior of other countries. A careful study of the timing of reciprocal trade treaties in this period is required to demonstrate this point, a type of study I have been unable to find. The evidence suggests that at least in Germany, the shift from Caprivi's low tariff policy to Bernhard Bulow's solidarity bloc (protection, naval-building, nationalism, antisocialism) did not come about because of changes in the behavior of foreign governments. Rather, the old Bismarckian coalition of heavy industry, army, Junkers, nationalists, and conservatives mobilized itself to prevent further erosion of its domestic position.

Economic Ideology A fourth explanation for the success of the protectionist alliance looks to economic ideology. The German nationalist school, associated with Friedrich List, favored state intervention in economic matters to promote national power and welfare. Free trade and laissez-faire doctrines were less entrenched than they were in Britain. According to this explanation, when faced with sharp competition from other countries, German interests found it easier to switch positions toward protection than did their British counterparts. This interpretation is plausible. The free trade policies of the 1850s and 1860s were doubtless more shallowly rooted in Germany and the tradition of state interventionism was stronger.

All four explanations, indeed, are compatible with the German experience: economic circumstances provided powerful inducements for major groups to support high tariff; political structures and key politicians favored the protectionist coalition; international forces seemed to make its success a matter of national security; and German economic traditions helped justify it. Are all these factors really necessary to explain the protectionist victory, or is this causal overkill? I shall reserve judgement until we have looked at more examples.

FRANCE

The French case offers us a very different political system producing a very similar policy result. As with Germany, the causes may explain more than necessary. The High/High outcome (Table 1) is certainly what we would expect to find looking at the interests of key economic actors. French industry, despite striking gains under the Second Empire and the Cobden-Chevalier Treaty, was certainly less efficient than that of other "late starters" (Germany and the United States). Hence manufacturers in heavy industry, in highly capitalized ones, or in particularly vulnerable ones like textiles had an intense interest in protection. Shippers and successful exporters opposed it.

Agriculture, as in Germany, had diverse interests. France had no precise equivalent to the Junkers; even on the biggest farms the soil was better, the labor force freer, and the owners less likely to be exclusively dependent on the land for income. Nonetheless, whether large or small, all producing units heavily involved in the market were hard hit by the drop in prices. The large proportion of quasi-subsistence farmers, hardly in the market economy, were less affected. The prevalence of small holdings made modernization easier than in Prussia, but still costly. For most of the agriculture sector, the path of least resistance was to maintain past practice behind high tariff walls.

As we would expect, most French producer groups became increasingly protectionist as prices dropped. In the early 1870s Adolphe Thiers tried to raise tariffs largely for revenue purposes but failed. New associations demanded tariff revision. In 1881, the National Assembly passed the first general tariff measure, which protected industry more than agriculture. In the same year American meat products were barred as unhealthy. Sugar received help in 1884, grains and meats in the tariffs of 1885 and 1887. Finally, broad coverage was given to both agriculture and industry in the famous Méline Tariff of 1892. Thereafter, tariffs drifted upwards, culminating in the very high tariff of 1910.

This policy response fits the logic of the political system explanation as well. Universal suffrage in a society of small property owners favored the protection of units of production rather than consumer interests. Conflict over nontariff issues, although severe, did not prevent protectionists from finding each other. Republican, Royalist, Clerical, and anti-Clerical protectionists broke away from their free-trade homologues to vote the Méline Tariff. Méline and others even hoped to reform the party system by using economic and social questions to drive out the religious and constitutional ones. This effort failed but cross-party majorities continued to coalesce every time the question of protection arose and high tariffs helped reconcile many conservatives to the Republic.

In France, protection is the result we would expect from the international system explanation: international political rivalries imposed concern for a domestic food supply and a rural reservoir of soldiers. As for the economic ideology explanation, ideological traditions abound with arguments in favor of state intervention. The Cobden-Chevalier Treaty had been negotiated at the top. The process of approving it generated no mass commitment to free trade as had the lengthy public battle over the repeal of the Corn Laws in Britain. The tariffs of the 1880s restored the *status quo ante*.

Two things stand out in the comparison of France with Germany. First, France had no equivalent to Bismarck, or to the state mechanism which supported him . The compromise between industry and agriculture was organized without any help from the top. Interest groups and politicians operating through elections and the party system came together and worked things out. Neither the party system, nor the constitution, nor outstanding personalities can be shown to have favored one coalition over another.

Second, it is mildly surprising that this alliance took so long to come about—perhaps the consequence of having no Bismarck. It appears that industry took the lead in fighting for protection, and scored the first success. Why was agriculture left out of the Tariff of 1881 (while in Germany it was an integral part of the Tariff of 1879), when it represented such a large number of people? Why did it take another eleven years to get a general bill? Part of the answer may lie in the proportion of people outside the market economy; the rest may lie in the absence of leaders with a commanding structural position working to effect a particular policy. In any case, the Republic eventually secured a general bill, at about the same time that the United States was also raising tariffs.

GREAT BRITAIN

Britain is the only highly industrialized country which failed to raise tariffs on either industrial or agricultural products in this period. Explanation 1 appears to deal with this result quite easily. British industry, having developed first, enjoyed a great competitive advantage over its rivals and did not need tariffs. International specialization worked to Britain's advantage. The world provided her with cheap food, she supplied industrial products in exchange and made additional money financing and organizing the exchange. Farmers could make a living by modernizing and integrating their units into this industrial order. Such had been the logic behind the repeal of the Corn Laws in 1846.

Upon closer inspection, British policy during the Great Depression seems less sensible from a materialist viewpoint. Conditions had changed since 1846. After 1873, industry started to suffer at the hands of its new competitors, especially American and German ones. Other countries began to substitute their own products for British goods, compete with Britain in overseas markets, penetrate the British domestic market, and erect tariff barriers against British goods. Britain was beginning that languorous industrial decline which has continued uninterrupted to the present day.

In other countries, industrial producers, especially in heavy industry, led agitation for protection in response to the dilemma of the price slump. Although some British counterparts did organize a Fair Trade league which sought protection within the context of the Empire (the policy adopted after World War I), most industrialists stayed with free trade.

If this outcome is to be consistent with explanation 1, it is necessary to look for forces which blunted the apparent thrust of international market forces. British producers' acceptance of low tariffs was not irrational if other ways of sustaining income existed. In industry, there were several. Despite Canadian and Australian tariff barriers, the rest of the Empire sustained a stable demand for British goods; so did British overseas investment, commercial ties, and prestige. International banking and shipping provided important sources of revenue which helped to conceal the decline in sales. Bankers and shippers also constituted a massive lobby in favor of an open international economy. To some degree, then, British industry was shielded from perceiving the full extent of the deterioration of her competitive position.

In agriculture, the demand for protection was also weak. This cannot be explained simply by reference to 1846. Initially the repeal of the Corn Laws affected farming rather little. Although repeal helped prevent sharp price increases following bad harvests, there was simply not enough grain produced in the world (nor enough shipping capacity to bring it to Europe) to provoke a major agricultural crisis. The real turning point came in the 1870s, when falling prices were compounded by bad weather. Why, at this moment, did the English landowning aristocracy fail to join its Junker or French counterpart in demanding protection? The aristocrats, after all, held a privileged position in the political system; they remained significantly overrepresented in the composition of the political class, especially in the leadership of Parliament; they had wealth and great prestige.

As with industry, certain characteristics of British agriculture served to shield landowners from the full impact of low grain prices. First, the advanced state of British industrial development had already altered the structure of incentives in agriculture. Many landowners had made the change from growing grain to selling high quality foodstuffs. These farmers, especially dairymen and meat producers, identified their interests with the health of the industrial sector, and were unresponsive to grain growers' efforts to organize agriculture for protection.

Second, since British landowners derived their income from a much wider range of sources than did the Junkers the decline of farming did not imply as profound a social or economic disaster for them. They had invested in mining, manufacturing, and trading and had intermarried with the rising industrial bourgeoisie. Interpenetration of wealth provided the material basis for their identification with industry. This might explain some Tories' willingness to abandon protection in 1846, and accept that verdict even in the 1870s.

If repeal of the Corn Laws did not immediately affect the British economy it did profoundly influence politics and British economic thought in ways, following the logic of explanations 2 and 4, that are relevant for explaining policy in the 1870s. The attack on the Corn Laws mobilized the Anti-Corn Law League (which received some help from another mass movement, the Chartists). Over a twenty year period, the League linked the demand for cheap food to a broader critique of landed interest and privilege. Its victory, and the defection of Peel and the Tory leadership, had great symbolic meaning. Repeal affirmed that the British future would be an industrial one, in which the two forms of wealth would fuse on terms laid down for agriculture by industry. By the mid-1850s even the backwoods Tory rump led by Disraeli had accepted this; a decade later he made it the basis for the Conservative revival. To most of the ever larger electorate, free trade, cheap food, and the reformed political system were inextricably linked. Protection implied an attack on all the gains realized since 1832. Free trade meant freedom and prosperity. These identifications inhibited the realization that British economic health might no longer be served by keeping her economy open to international economic forces.

Finally, British policy fits what one would expect from analysis of the international system (explanation 3). Empire and navy certainly made it easier to contemplate dependence on overseas sources of food. It is significant that protection could be legitimated in the long run only as part of empire. People would do for imperialism what they would not do to help one industry or another. Chamberlain's passage from free trade to protection via empire foreshadows the entire country's actions after World War I.

UNITED STATES

Of the four countries examined here, only the United States combined low-cost agriculture and dynamic industry within the same political system. The policy outcome of high industrial tariffs and low agricultural ones fits the logic of explanation 1. Endowed with efficient agriculture, the United States had no need to protect it; given the long shadow of the British giant, industry did need protection. But despite its efficiency (or rather because of it) American agriculture did have severe problems in this period. On a number of points, it came into intense conflict with industry. By and large industry had its way.

Monetary policy The increasing value of money appreciated the value of debt owed to Eastern bankers. Expanding farm production constantly drove prices downward, so that a larger amount of produce was needed to pay off an ever increasing debt. Cheap money schemes were repeatedly defeated.

Transportation Where no competition among alternative modes of transport or companies existed, farmers were highly vulnerable to rate manipulation. Regulation eventually was introduced, but whether because of the farmers' efforts or the desire of railroad men and other industrialists to prevent ruinous competition—as part of their "search for order"—is not clear. Insurance and fees also helped redistribute income from one sector to the other.

Tariffs The protection of industrial goods required farmers to sell in a free world market and buy in a protected one.

Taxation Before income and corporate taxes, the revenue burden was most severe for the landowner. Industry blocked an income tax until 1913.

Market instability Highly variable crop yields contributed to erratic prices, which could have been controlled by storage facilities, government price stabilization boards, and price supports. This did not happen until after World War I.

Monopoly pricing practices Differential pricing (such as Pittsburgh Plus, whereby goods were priced according to the location of the head office rather than the factory) worked like an internal tariff, pumping money from the country into the Northeast. The antitrust acts addressed some of these problems, but left many untouched.

Patronage and pork-barrel Some agrarian areas, especially the South, fared badly in the distribution of Federal largesse.

In the process of political and industrial development, defeat of the agricultural sector appears inevitable. Whatever the indicator (share of GNP, percentage of the work force, control of the land) farmers decline; whether peasants, landless laborers, family farmers, kulaks, or estate owners, they fuel industrialization by providing foreign exchange, food, and manpower. In the end they disappear.

This can happen, however, at varying rates: very slowly, as appears to be the case in China today, slowly as in France, quickly as in Britain. In the United States, I would argue, the defeat of agriculture as a *sector* was swift and thorough. This may sound strange in light of the stupendous agricultural output today. Some landowners were successful. They shifted from broad attacks on the system to interest group lobbying for certain types of members. The mass of the agricultural population, however, lost most of its policy battles and left the land.

One might have expected America to develop not like Germany, . . . but like France: with controlled, slower industrial growth, speed sacrificed to balance, and the preservation of a large rural population. For it to have happened the mass of small farmers would have to have found allies willing to battle the Eastern banking and industrial combine which dominated American policy-making. To understand their failure it is useful to analyze the structure of incentives among potential alliance partners as was done for the European countries. If we take farmers' grievances on the policy issues noted above (such as money and rates) as the functional equivalent of tariffs, the politics of coalition formation in the United States become comparable to the equivalent process in Europe.

Again two alliances were competing for the allegiance of the same groups. The protectionist core consisted of heavy industry, banks, and textiles. These employers persuaded workers that their interests derived from their roles as producers in the industrial sector, not as consumers. To farmers selling in urban markets, the protectionists made the familiar case for keeping industry strong.

The alternative coalition, constructed around hostility toward heavy industry and banks, appealed to workers and farmers as consumers, to farmers as debtors and victims of industrial manipulation, to the immigrant poor and factory hands against the tribulations of the industrial system, to farmers as manipulated debtors, and to shippers and manufacturers of finished products on behalf of lower costs. Broadly this was a Jackson-type coalition confronting the Whig interest—the little man versus the man of property. Lower tariffs and more industrial regulation (of hours, rates, and working conditions) were its policies.

The progressive, low tariff alliance was not weak. Agriculture employed by far the largest percentage of the workforce. Federalism should have given it considerable leverage: the whole South, the Midwest, and the trans-Mississippi West. True, parts of the Midwest were industrializing, but then much of the Northeast remained agricultural. Nonetheless the alliance failed: the explanation turns on an understanding of the critical realignment election of 1896. The defeat of populism marked the end of two decades of intense party competition, the beginning of forty years of Republican hegemony and the turning point for agriculture as a sector. It will be heuristically useful to work backwards from the conjuncture of 1896 to the broader forces which produced that contest.

The battle of 1896 was shaped by the character and strategy of William Jennings Bryan, the standard bearer of the low tariff alliance. Bryan has had a bad historical press because his populism had overtones of bigotry, anti-intellectualism, archaicism, and religious fundamentalism. Politically these attributes were flaws because they made it harder to attract badly needed allies to the farmers' cause. Bryan's style, symbols, and program were meaningful to the trans-Mississippi and Southern farmers who fueled Populism, but incomprehensible to city dwellers, immigrants, and Catholics, to say nothing of free-trade oriented businessmen. In the drive for the Democratic nomination and during the subsequent campaign, Bryan put silver in the forefront. Yet free coinage was but a piece of the populist economic analysis and not the part with the strongest appeal for nonfarmers (nor even the most important element to farmers themselves). The city dweller's grievances against the industrial economy were more complex. Deflation actually improved his real wages, while cheap money threatened to raise prices. In the search for allies other criticisms of the industrial order could have been developed but Bryan failed to prevent silver from overwhelming them.

Even within the agrarian sector, the concentration on silver and the fervid quality of the campaign worried the more prosperous farmers. By the 1890s, American agriculture was considerably differentiated. In the trans-Mississippi region, conditions were primitive; farmers were vulnerable, marginal producers: they grew a single crop for the market, had little capital, and no reserves. For different reasons, Southern agriculture was also marginal. In the Northeast and the Midwest farming had become much more diversified; it was less dependent on grain, more highly capitalized, and benefited from greater competition among railroads, alternative shipping routes, and direct access to urban markets. These farmers related to the industrial sector, rather like the dairymen in Britain, or the Danes. Bryan frightened these farmers as he frightened workers and immigrants. The qualities which made him attractive to one group antagonized others. Like Sen. Barry Goldwater and Sen. George McGovern, he was able to win the nomination, but in a manner which guaranteed defeat. Bryan's campaign caused potential allies to define their interests in ways which seemed incompatible with those of the agricultural sector. It drove farmers away rather than attracting them. Workers saw Bryan not as an ally against their bosses but as a threat to the industrial sector of the economy of which they were a part. To immigrants, he was a nativist xenophobe. Well-to-do Midwestern farmers, Southern Whigs, and Northeast shippers all saw him as a threat to property.

The Republicans, on the other hand, were very shrewd. Not only did they have large campaign funds, but, as Williams argues, James G. Blaine, Benjamin Harrison, and William McKinley understood that industrial interests required allies the support of which they must actively recruit. Like Bismarck, these Republican leaders worked to make minimal concessions in order to split the opposition. In the German coalition the terms of trade were social security for the workers, tariffs for the farmers and the manufacturers, guns and boats for the military. In America, McKinley, et al., outmanoeuvred President Grover Cleveland and the Gold Democrats on the money issue; when Cleveland repealed the Silver Purchase Act, some of the Republicans helped pass the Sherman Silver Purchase Act. The Republican leaders then went after the farmers. Minimizing the importance of monetary issues, they proposed an alternative solution in the form of overseas markets: selling surpluses to the Chinese or the Latin Americans, negotiating the lowering of tariff levels, and policing the meat industry to meet the health regulations Europeans had imposed in order to keep out American imports. To the working class, the Republicans argued that Bryan and the agrarians would cost them jobs and boost prices. Social security was never mentioned— McKinley paid less than Bismarck.

In 1896, the Republican candidate was tactically shrewd and the Democratic one was not. It might have been the other way around. Imagine a charismatic Democrat from Ohio, with a Catholic mother, traditionally friendly to workers, known for his understanding of farmers' problems, the historical equivalent of Senator Robert Kennedy in the latter's ability to appeal simultaneously to urban ethnics, machine politicians, blacks, and suburban liberals. Unlikely but not impossible: had he existed, such a candidate would still have labored under severe handicaps. The difference between Bryan and McKinley was more than a matter of personality or accident. The forces which made Bryan the standard bearer were built into the structure of American politics. First, McKinley's success in constructing a coalition derives from features inherent in industrial society. As in Germany, producers' groups had a structural advantage. Bringing the farmers, workers, and consumers together was difficult everywhere in the industrial world during that period. In America, ethnic, geographic, and religious differences made it even harder.

Second, the industrialists controlled both political parties. Whatever happened at the local level, the national Democratic party lay in the firm grip of Southern conservatives and Northern businessmen. Prior to 1896, they wrote their ideas into the party platforms and nominated their man at every convention. The Gold Democrats were not a choice but an echo.... A Bryan-type crusade was structurally necessary. Action out of the ordinary was required to wrest the electoral machine away from the Gold Democrats. But the requirements of that success also sowed seeds for the failure of November, 1896.

Why, in turn, did the industrialists control the parties? The Civil War is crucial. At its inception, the Republican party was an amalgam of entrepreneurs, farmers, lawyers, and professionals who believed in opportunity, hard work, and self-help; these were people from medium-sized towns, medium-sized enterprises, medium-sized farms. These people disliked the South not because they wished to help the black race or even eliminate slavery, but because the South and slavery symbolized the very opposite of "Free Soil, Free Labor, Free Men". By accelerating the pace of industrialization, the Civil War altered the internal balance of the Party, tipping control to the industrialists. By mobilizing national emotions against the South, the Civil War fused North and West together, locking the voter into the Republican Party. Men who had been antibusiness and Jacksonian prior to 1860 were now members of a coalition dominated by business.

In the South, the Old Whigs, in desperate need of capital, fearful of social change, and contemptuous of the old Jacksonians looked to the northern industrialists for help in rebuilding their lands and restoring conservative rule. What would have been more natural then to have joined their northern allies in the Republican party? In the end, the hostility of the Radical Republicans made this impossible, and instead the Old Whigs went into the Democratic Party where they eventually helped sustain the Gold Democrats and battled with the Populists for control of the Democratic organization in the South.

There were, then, in the American system certain structural obstacles to a low-tariff coalition. What of economic ideology (explanation 4) and the international system (explanation 3)? Free trade in the United States never had the ideological force it had in the United Kingdom. Infant industries and competition with the major industrial power provided the base for a protectionist tradition, as farming and distrust of the state provided a base for free trade. Tariffs had always been an important source of revenue for the Federal government. It is interesting that the "Free Soil, Labor and Men" coalition did not add Free Trade to its program.

Trade bore some relation to foreign policy. . . . Nonetheless, it is hard to see that the international political system determined tariff policy. The United States had no need to worry about foreign control of resources or food supply. In any case the foreign policy of the low tariff coalition was not very different from the foreign policy of the high tariff coalition.

In conclusion, four countries have been subjected to a set of questions in an attempt to find evidence relevant to differing explanations of tariff levels in the late nineteenth century. In each country, we find a large bloc of economic interest groups gaining significant economic advantages from the policy decision adopted concerning tariffs. Hence, the economic explanation has both simplicity and power. But is it enough? It does have two weaknesses. First, it presupposes a certain obviousness about the direction of economic pressures upon groups. Yet, as the argumentation above has sought to show, other economic calculations would also have been rational for those groups. Had farmers supported protection in Britain or opposed it in Germany and France, we could also offer a plausible economic interpretation for their behavior. The same is true for industrialists: had they accepted the opposite policy, we could find ways in which they benefited from doing so. We require an explanation, therefore, for the choice between two economic logics. One possibility is to look at the urgency of economic need. For protectionists the incentive for high tariffs was intense and obvious. For free traders, the advantages of their policy preference, and the costs of their opponents' victory, were more ambiguous. Those who wanted their goals the most, won.

Second, the economic explanation fails to flesh out the political steps involved in translating a potential alliance of interest into policy. Logrolling does take some organization, especially in arranging side payments among the partners. The iron-rye bargain seems so natural that we forget the depth of animosity between the partners in the period preceding it. To get their way, economic groups had to translate their economic power into political currency.

The political structures explanation appears to take care of this problem. Certain institutions and particular individuals helped to organize the winning coalition and facilitate its victory. Looking at each victory separately, these structures and personalities bulk large in the story. Yet viewed comparatively, their importance washes out. Bismarck, the Junkers, the authoritarian constitution, the character of the German civil service, the special connections among the state, banking, and industry—these conspicuous features of the German case have no equivalents elsewhere. Méline was no Bismarck and the system gave him no particular leverage. Mobilization against socialism did not occur in the United States, or even in Britain and France. Yet the pattern of policy outcomes in these countries was the same, suggesting that those aspects of the political system which were *idiosyncratic* to each country (such as Bismarck and regime type) are not crucial in explaining the result. In this sense the political explanation does not add to the economic one.

Nonetheless, some aspects of the relation between economic groups and the political system are *uniform* among the countries examined here and do help explain the outcome. There is a striking similarity in the identity of victors and losers from country to country: producers over consumers, heavy industrialists over finished manufacturers, big farmers over small, and property owners over laborers. In each case, a coalition of producers' interests defined by large scale basic industry and substantial landowners defeated its opponent. It is probable, therefore, that different types of groups from country to country are systematically not equal in political resources. Rather, heavy industrialists and landowners are stronger than peasants, workers, shopkeepers, and consumers. They have superior resources, access to power, and compactness. They would have had these advantages even if the regimes had differed considerably from their historical profiles. Thus a republicanized or democratized Germany would doubtless have had high tariffs (although it might have taken longer for this to come about, as it did in France). A monarchist France (Bourbon, Orleanist, or Bonapartist) would certainly have had the same high tariffs as Republican France. An authoritarian Britain could only have come about through repression of the industrialists by landowners, so it is possible a shift in regime might have meant higher tariffs; more likely, the industrialists would have broken through as they did in Germany. Certainly Republican Britain would have had the same tariff policy. In the United States, it is possible (although doubtful) that without the critical election of 1896, or with a different party system altogether, the alternation between protectionist Republicans and low tariff Democrats might have continued.

Two coalitions faced each other. Each contained a variety of groups. Compared to the losers, the winners comprised: (1) groups for which the benefits of their policy goal were intense and urgent, rather than diffuse; (2) groups occupying strategic positions in the economy; and (3) groups with structurally superior positions in each political system. The uniformity of the winners' economic characteristics, regardless of regime type, suggests that to the extent that the political advantages derive from economic ones, the political explanation is not needed. The translation of economic advantage into policy does require action, organization, and politics; to that extent, and to varying degrees, the economic explanation by itself is insufficient. It is strongest in Germany, where the rapidity of the switch from free trade to protection is breathtaking, and in France where economic slowness made the nation especially vulnerable to competition. It works least well for Britain where the policy's advantages to the industrialists seem the least clear, and for the United States, where the weakness of agriculture is not explicable without the Civil War. Note that nowhere do industrialists fail to obtain their preferences.

In this discussion, we have called the actors groups, not classes, for two reasons. First, the language of class often makes it difficult to clarify the conflicts of interest (e.g., heavy industry vs. manufacture) which exist within classes, and to explain which conception of class interest prevails. Second, class analysis is complex. Since interest group reasoning claims less, and works, there is no point in going further.

The international system and economic ideology explanations appear the least useful. Each is certainly compatible with the various outcomes, but has drawbacks. First, adding them violates the principle of parsimony. If one accepts the power of the particular economic-political explanation stated above, the other two explanations become redundant. Second, even if one is not attracted by parsimony, reference to the international system does not escape the difficulty inherent in any "unitary actor" mode of reasoning: why does a particular conception of the national interest predominate? In the German case, the low tariff coalition did not share Bismarck's and Bulow's conception of how Germany should relate to the world. Thus the international system explanation must revert to some investigation of domestic politics.

Finally, the economic ideology explanation seems the weakest. Whatever its strength in accounting for the Free Trade Movement of the 1850s and 1860s, this explanation cannot deal with the rapid switch to protection in the 1870s. A national culture argument cannot really explain why two different policies are followed within a very short span of time. The flight away from Free Trade by Junkers, manufacturers, farmers, and so on was clearly provoked by the price drop. For the United Kingdom, conversely, the continuity of policy makes the cultural argument more appropriate. Belief in free trade may have blunted the receptivity of British interest groups toward a protectionist solution of their problems. The need for the economic ideology explanation here depends on one's evaluation of the structure of economic incentives facing industry: to whatever extent empire, and other advantages of having been first, eased the full impact of the depression, ideology was superfluous. To whatever extent industry suffered but avoided protection, ideology was significant.

6

Selections from *Imperialism: The Highest Stage of Capitalism*

V. I. LENIN

In his 1916 pamphlet, V. I. Lenin offers both an analysis of the world's predicament at the time and a call for future action. He outlines the development of "monopoly capitalism" and the domination of the world's leading countries by finance capital. In order to escape declining rates of profit at home, according to Lenin, capitalists invest abroad with the support of their governments. As more and more land is seized by imperial powers, economic and military competition between the capitalist nation-states escalates. Lenin compares his view of this new phase of capitalism to other interpretations. He goes on to describe the characteristics of monopoly capitalism and the process of imperialism inherent within it. In doing so, Lenin provides an important account of imperialism in the late nineteenth century.

THE EXPORT OF CAPITAL

Under the old type of capitalism, when free competition prevailed, the export of *goods* was the most typical feature. Under modern capitalism, when monopolies prevail, the export of *capital* has become the typical feature.

Capitalism is commodity production at the highest stage of development, when labour power itself becomes a commodity. The growth of internal exchange, and particularly of international exchange, is a special feature of capitalism. The uneven and spasmodic character of the development of individual enterprises, of individual branches of industry and individual countries, is inevitable under the capitalist system. England became a capitalist country before any other, and in the middle of

---

the nineteenth century, having adopted free trade, claimed to be the "workshop of the world," the great purveyor of manufactured goods to all other countries, which in exchange were to keep her supplied with raw materials. In the last quarter of the nineteenth century, *this* monopoly was already undermined. Other countries, protecting themselves by tariff walls, had developed into independent capitalist countries. On the threshold of the twentieth century, we see a new type of monopoly coming into existence. First, there are monopolist capitalist combines in all advanced capitalist countries; secondly, a few rich countries, in which the accumulation of capital reaches gigantic proportions, occupy a monopolist position. An enormous "superfluity of capital" has accumulated in the advanced countries.

It goes without saying that if capitalism could develop agriculture, which today lags far behind industry everywhere, if it could raise the standard of living of the masses, who are everywhere still poverty stricken and underfed, in spite of the amazing advance in technical knowledge, there could be no talk of a superfluity of capital. This "argument" the petty-bourgeois critics of capitalism advance on every occasion. But if capitalism did these things it would not be capitalism; for uneven development and wretched conditions of the masses are the fundamental and inevitable conditions and premises of this mode of production. As long as capitalism remains what it is, surplus capital will never be utilized for the purpose of raising the standard of living of the masses in a given country, for this would mean a decline in profits for the capitalists; it will be used for the purpose of increasing those profits by exporting capital abroad to the backward countries. In these backward countries, profits usually are high, for capital is scarce, the price of land is relatively low, wages are low, raw materials are cheap. The possibility of exporting capital is created by the entry of numerous backward countries into international capitalist intercourse; main railways have either been built or are being built there; the elementary conditions for industrial development have been created, etc. The necessity of exporting capital arises from the fact that in a few countries capitalism has become "over-ripe" and (owing to the backward state of agriculture and the impoverished state of the masses) capital cannot find "profitable" investment.

Here are approximate figures showing the amount of capital invested abroad by the three principal countries:

Capital Invested Abroad (In billions of francs)

Year	Great Britain	France	Germany
1862	3.6	-	-
1872	15.0	10 (1869)	-
1882	22.0	15 (1880)	?
1893	42.0	20 (1890)	?
1902	62.0	27-37	12.5
1914	75-100	60	44.0

This table shows that the export of capital reached formidable dimensions only in the beginning of the twentieth century. Before the war the capital invested abroad by the three principal countries amounted to between 175 and 200 billion francs. At the modest rate of 5 per cent, this sum brought in from 8 to 10 billions a year. This provided a solid basis for imperialist oppression and the exploitation of most of the countries and nations of the world; a solid basis for the capitalist parasitism of a handful of wealthy states!

How is this capital invested abroad distributed among the various countries? *Where* does it go? Only an approximate answer can be given to this question, but sufficient to throw light on certain general relations and ties of modern imperialism.

Approximate Distribution of Foreign Capital (about 1910)
(In billions of marks)

Continent	Great Britain	France	Germany	Total
Europe	4	23	18	45
America	37	4	10	51
Asia, Africa, Australia	29	8	7	44
Total	70	35	35	140

The principal spheres of investment of British capital are the British colonies, which are very large also in America (for example, Canada), as well as in Asia, etc. In this case, enormous exports of capital are bound up with the possession of enormous colonies, of the importance of which for imperialism we shall speak later. In regard to France, the situation is quite different. French capital exports are invested mainly in Europe, particularly in Russia (at least ten billion francs). This is mainly *loan* capital, in the form of government loans and not investments in industrial undertakings. Unlike British colonial imperialism, French imperialism might be termed usury imperialism. In regard to Germany, we have a third type; the German colonies are inconsiderable, and German capital invested abroad is divided fairly evenly between Europe and America.

The export of capital greatly affects and accelerates the development of capitalism in those countries to which it is exported. While, therefore, the export of capital may tend to a certain extent to arrest development in the countries exporting capital, it can only do so by expanding and deepening the further development of capitalism throughout the world. The countries which export capital are nearly always able to obtain "advantages," the character of which throws light on the peculiarities of the epoch of finance capital and monopoly. The following passage, for instance, occurred in the Berlin review, *Die Bank*, for October 1913:

> "A comedy worthy of the pen of Aristophanes is being played just now on the international money market. Numerous foreign countries from Spain to the Balkan states, from Russia to the Argentine, Brazil and China, are openly or secretly approaching the big money markets demanding loans, some of which are very urgent. The money market is not at the moment very bright and the political outlook is not yet promising. But not a single money market dares to refuse a loan for fear that its neighbor might grant it and so secure some small reciprocal service. In these international transactions the creditor nearly always manages to get some special advantages: an advantage of a commercial-political nature, a coaling station, a contract to construct a harbour, a fat concession, or an order for guns."

Finance capital has created the epoch of monopolies, and monopolies introduce everywhere monopolist methods: the utilization of "connections" for profitable transactions takes the place of competition on the open market. The most usual thing is to stipulate that part of the loan that is granted shall be spent on purchases in the country of issue, particularly on orders for war materials, or for ships, etc. In the course of the last two decades (1890-1910), France often resorted to this method. The export of capital abroad thus becomes a means for encouraging the export of commodities. In these circumstances transactions between particularly big firms assume a form "bordering on corruption," as Schilder "delicately" puts it. Krupp in Germany, Schneider in France, Armstrong in England, are instances of firms having close connections with powerful banks and governments whose "share" must not be forgotten when arranging a loan.

France granted loans to Russia in 1905 and by the commercial treaty of September 16, 1905, she "squeezed" concessions out of her to run till 1917. She did the same thing when the Franco-Japanese commercial treaty was concluded on August 19, 1911. The tariff war between Austria and Serbia, which lasted with a seven months' interval, from 1906 to 1911, was partly caused by competition between Austria and France for supplying Serbia with war material. In January 1912, Paul Deschanel stated in the Chamber of Deputies that from 1908 to 1911 French firms had supplied war material to Serbia to the value of 45,000,000 francs.

A report from the Austro-Hungarian Consul at Sao-Paulo (Brazil) states:

> "The construction of the Brazilian railways is being carried out chiefly by French, Belgian, British and German capital. In the financial operations connected with the construction of these railways the countries involved also stipulate for orders for the necessary railway material."

Thus, finance capital, almost literally, one might say, spreads its net over all countries of the world. Banks founded in the colonies, or their branches, play an important part in these operations. German imperialists look with envy on the "old" colonizing nations which in this respect are "well established." In 1904, Great Britain had 50 colonial banks with 2,279 branches (in 1910 there were 72 banks with

5,449 branches); France had 20 with 136 branches; Holland, 16 with 68 branches, and Germany had a "mere" 13 with 70 branches.

The American capitalists, in their turn, are jealous of the English and German: "In South America," they complained in 1915, "five German banks had forty branches and five English banks had seventy. . . . During the last twenty-five years, Great Britain and Germany have invested in the Argentine, Brazil and Uruguay about four billion dollars, which places under their control 46 per cent of the total trade of these three countries."

The capital exporting countries have divided the world among themselves in the figurative sense of the term. But finance capital has also led to the *actual* division of the world.

IMPERIALISM AS A SPECIAL STAGE OF CAPITALISM

We must now try to sum up and put together what has been said above on the subject of imperialism. Imperialism emerged as the development and direct continuation of the fundamental attributes of capitalism in general. But capitalism only became capitalist imperialism at a definite and very high stage of its development, when certain of its fundamental attributes began to be transformed into their opposites, when the features of the period of transition from capitalism to a higher social and economic system began to take shape and reveal themselves all along the line. The fundamental economic factor in this process is the substitution of capitalist monopolies for capitalist free competition. Free competition is the fundamental attribute of capitalism and of commodity production generally. Monopoly is exactly the opposite of free competition; but we have seen the latter being transformed into monopoly before our very eyes, creating large-scale industry and eliminating small industry, replacing large-scale industry by still larger-scale industry, finally leading to such a concentration of production and capital that monopoly has been and is the result: cartels, syndicates and trusts, and merging with them, the capital of a dozen or so banks manipulating thousands of millions. At the same time monopoly, which has grown out of free competition, does not abolish the latter, but exists alongside it and hovers over it, as it were, and, as a result, gives rise to a number of very acute antagonisms, friction and conflicts. Monopoly is the transition from capitalism to a higher system.

If it were necessary to give the briefest possible definition of imperialism we should have to say that imperialism is the monopoly stage of capitalism. Such a definition would include what is most important, for, on the one hand, finance capital is the bank capital of the few big monopolist banks, merged with the capital of the monopolist combines of manufacturers; and, on the other hand, the division of the world is the transition from a colonial policy which has extended without hindrance to territories unoccupied by any capitalist power, to a colonial policy of the monopolistic possession of the territories of the world which have been completely divided up.

But very brief definitions, although convenient, for they sum up the main points, are nevertheless inadequate, because very important features of the phenomenon that has to be defined have to be especially deduced. And so, without forgetting the conditional and relative value of all definitions, which can never include all the concatenations of a phenomenon in its complete development, we must give a definition of imperialism that will embrace the following five essential features:

1. The concentration of production and capital developed to such a stage that it creates monopolies which play a decisive role in economic life.
2. The merging of bank capital with industrial capital, and the creation, on the basis of "finance capital," of a financial oligarchy.
3. The export of capital, which has become extremely important, as distinguished from the export of commodities.
4. The formation of international capitalist monopolies which share the world among themselves.
5. The territorial division of the whole world among the greatest capitalist powers is completed.

Imperialism is capitalism in that stage of development in which the domination of monopolies and finance capital has established itself; in which the export of capital has acquired pronounced importance; in which the division of the world among the international trusts has begun; in which the partition of all the territories of the globe among the great capitalist powers has been completed.

We shall see later that imperialism can and must be defined differently if consideration is to be given, not only to the basic, purely economic factors—to which the above definition is limited—but also to the historical place of this stage of capitalism in relation to capitalism in general, or to the relations between imperialism and the two main tendencies in the working class movement. The point to be noted just now is that imperialism, as interpreted above, undoubtedly represents a special stage in the development of capitalism. In order to enable the reader to obtain as well grounded an idea of imperialism as possible, we deliberately quoted largely from *bourgeois* economists who are obliged to admit the particularly indisputable facts regarding modern capitalist economy. With the same object in view, we have produced detailed statistics which reveal the extent to which bank capital, etc., has developed, showing how the transformation of quantity into quality, of developed capitalism into imperialism, has expressed itself. Needless to say, all the boundaries in nature and in society are conditional and changeable, and, consequently, it would be absurd to discuss the exact year or the decade in which imperialism "definitely" became established. . . .

We notice three areas of highly developed capitalism, that is, with a high development of means of transport, of trade and of industry. These are the Central European, the British and the American areas. Among these are three states which dominate the world: Germany, Great Britain, the United States. Imperialist rivalry and the struggle between these countries have become very keen because Germany has only a restricted area and few colonies (the creation of "central Europe" is still a matter for the future; it is being born in the midst of desperate struggles). For the moment the distinctive feature of Europe is political disintegration. In the British and American areas, on the other hand, political concentration is very highly developed, but there is a tremendous disparity between the immense colonies of the one and the insignificant colonies of the other. In the colonies, capitalism is only beginning to develop. The struggle for South America is becoming more and more acute.

There are two areas where capitalism is not strongly developed: Russia and Eastern Asia. In the former the density of population is very small, in the latter it is very high; in the former political concentration is very high; in the latter it does not exist. The partition of China is only beginning, and the struggle between Japan, U.S.A., etc., in connection therewith is steadily gaining in intensity. . . .

Finance capital and the trusts are aggravating instead of diminishing the differences in the rate of development of the various parts of world economy. When the relation of forces is changed, how else, *under capitalism,* can the solution for contradictions be found, except by resorting to *violence?*

Railway statistics provide remarkably exact data on the different rates of development of capitalism and finance capital in the world economy. . . .

. . . The development of railways has been more rapid in the colonies and in the independent or semi-independent states of Asia and America. Here, as we know, the finance capital of the four or five biggest capitalist states reigns undisputed. Two hundred thousand kilometres of new railways in the colonies and in the other countries of Asia and America represent more than 40,000,000,000 marks in capital, newly invested under particularly advantageous conditions, with special guarantees of a good return and with profitable orders for steel works, etc., etc.

Capitalism is growing with the greatest rapidity in the colonies and in trans-oceanic countries. Among the latter, *new* imperialist powers are emerging *(e.g.,* Japan). The struggle of world imperialism is becoming aggravated. The tribute levied by finance capital on the most profitable colonial and trans-oceanic enterprises is increasing. In sharing out this booty, an exceptionally large part goes to countries which, as far as the development of productive forces is concerned, do not always stand at the top of the list. . . .

About 80 percent of the total existing railways are concentrated in the hands of the five great powers. But the concentration of the *ownership* of these railways, that of finance capital, is much greater still: French and English millionaires, for example, own an enormous amount of stocks and bonds in American, Russian and other railways.

Thanks to her colonies, Great Britain has increased "her" length of railways by 100,000 kilometres, four times as much as Germany. And yet it is well known that the development of productive forces in Germany, and especially the development of the coal and iron industries, has been much more rapid during this period than in England—not to mention France and Russia. In 1892, Germany produced 4,900,000 tons of pig iron, and Great Britain produced 6,800,000 tons; in 1912, Germany produced 17,600,000 tons and Great Britain, 9,000,000 tons. Germany, therefore, had an overwhelming superiority over England in this respect!

We ask, is there *under capitalism* any means of remedying the disparity between the development of productive forces and the accumulation of capital on the one side, and the division of colonies and "spheres of influence" by finance capital on the other side—other than by resorting to war?

THE PLACE OF IMPERIALISM IN HISTORY

We have seen that the economic quintessence of imperialism is monopoly capitalism. This very fact determines its place in history, for monopoly that grew up on the basis of free competition, and out of free competition, is the transition from the capitalist system to a higher social economic order. We must take special note of the four principal forms of monopoly, or the four principal manifestations of monopoly capitalism, which are characteristic of the period under review.

1. Monopoly arose out of the concentration of production at a very advanced stage of development. This refers to the monopolist capitalist combines: cartels, syndicates and trusts. We have seen the important role these play in modern economic life. At the beginning of the twentieth century, monopolies acquired complete supremacy in the advanced countries. And although the first steps towards the formation of the combines were first taken by countries enjoying the protection of high tariffs (Germany, America), England, with her system of free trade, was not far behind in revealing the same phenomenon, namely, the birth of monopoly out of the concentration of production.
2. Monopolies have accelerated the capture of the most important sources of raw materials, especially for the coal and iron industry, which is the basic and most highly trustified industry in capitalist society. The monopoly of the most important sources of raw materials has enormously increased the power of big capital, and has sharpened the antagonism between trustified and non-trustified industry.
3. Monopoly has sprung from the banks. The banks have developed from modest intermediary enterprises into the monopolists of finance capital. Some three or five of the biggest banks in each of the foremost capitalist countries have achieved the "personal union" of industrial and bank capital, and have concentrated in their hands the power to dispose of thousands upon thousands of millions which form the greater part of the capital and revenue of entire countries. A financial oligarchy, which throws a close net of relations of dependence over all the economic and

political institutions of contemporary bourgeois society without exception—such is the most striking manifestation of this monopoly.

4. Monopoly has grown out of colonial policy. To the numerous "old" motives of colonial policy, finance capital has added the struggle for the sources of raw materials, for the export of capital, for "spheres of influence," *i.e.*, for spheres of good business, concessions, monopolist profits, and so on; in fine, for economic territory in general. When the colonies of the European powers in Africa comprised only one-tenth of that territory (as was the case in 1876), colonial policy was able to develop by methods other than those of monopoly—by the "free grabbing" of territories, so to speak. But when nine-tenths of Africa had been seized (approximately in 1900), when the whole world had been shared out, there was inevitably ushered in a period of colonial monopoly and, consequently, a period of intense struggle for the partition and the repartition of the world.

The extent to which monopolist capital has intensified all the contradictions of capitalism is generally known. It is sufficient to mention the high cost of living and the power of the trusts. This intensification of contradictions constitutes the most powerful driving force of the transitional period of history, which began at the time of the definite victory of world finance capital.

Monopolies, oligarchy, the striving for domination instead of the striving for liberty, the exploitation of an increasing number of small or weak nations by an extremely small group of the richest or most powerful nations—all these have given birth to those distinctive features of imperialism which compel us to define it as parasitic or decaying capitalism. More and more there emerges, as one of the tendencies of imperialism, the creation of the "bondholding" *(rentier)* state, the usurer state, in which the bourgeoisie lives on the proceeds of capital exports and by "clipping coupons." It would be a mistake to believe that this tendency to decay precludes the possibility of the rapid growth of capitalism. It does not. In the epoch of imperialism, certain branches of industry, certain strata of the bourgeoisie and certain countries betray, to a greater or less degree, one or other of these tendencies. On the whole capitalism is growing far more rapidly than before, but it is not only that this growth is becoming more and more uneven; this unevenness manifests itself also, in particular, in the decay of the countries which are richest in capital (such as England).

In regard to the rapidity of Germany's economic development, Riesser, the author of the book on the great German banks, states:

> "The progress of the preceding period (1848-70), which had not been exactly slow, stood in about the same ratio to the rapidity with which the whole of Germany's national economy and with it German banking progressed during this period (1870-1905), as the mail coach of the Holy Roman Empire of the German nation stood to the speed of the present-day automobile . . . which in whizzing past, it must be said, often endangers not only innocent pedestrians in its path, but also the occupants of the car."

In its turn, this finance capital which has grown so rapidly is not unwilling (precisely because it has grown so quickly) to pass on to a more "tranquil" possession of colonies which have to be captured—and not only by peaceful methods—from richer nations. In the United States, economic development in the last decades has been even more rapid than in Germany, and *for this very reason* the parasitic character of modern American capitalism has stood out with particular prominence. On the other hand, a comparison of, say, the republican American bourgeoisie with the monarchist Japanese or German bourgeoisie shows that the most pronounced political differences become insignificant during the imperialist period—not because they are unimportant in general, but because throughout it is a case of a bourgeoisie with definite traits of parasitism.

The receipt of high monopoly profits by the capitalists in one of the numerous branches of industry, in one of numerous countries, etc., makes it economically possible for them to corrupt individual sections of the working class and sometimes a fairly considerable minority, and win them to the side of the capitalists of a given industry or nation against all the others. The intensification of antagonism between imperialist nations for the partition of the world increases this striving. And so there is created that bond between imperialism and opportunism, which revealed itself first and most clearly in England, owing to the fact that certain features of imperialist development were observable there much sooner than in other countries. . . .

From all that has been said in this book on the economic nature of imperialism, it follows that we must define it as capitalism in transition, or, more precisely, as moribund capitalism. It is very instructive in this respect to note that the bourgeois economists, in describing modern capitalism, frequently employ terms like "interlocking," "absence of isolation," etc.; "in accordance with their functions and course of development," banks are "not purely private business enterprises; they are more and more outgrowing the sphere of purely private business regulations." And this very Riesser, who uttered the words just quoted, declares with all seriousness that the "prophecy" of the Marxists concerning "socialization" has not been realized!

What then does this word "interlocking" express? It merely expresses the most striking feature of the process going on before our eyes. It shows that the observer counts the separate trees without seeing the wood. It slavishly copies the superficial, the fortuitous, the chaotic. It reveals the observer as one overwhelmed by the mass of raw material and utterly incapable of appreciating its meaning and importance. Ownership of shares and relations between owners of private property "interlock in a haphazard way." But the underlying factor of this interlocking, its very base, is the changing social relations of production. When a big enterprise assumes gigantic proportions, and, on the basis of exact computation of mass data, organizes according to plan the supply of primary raw materials to the extent of two-thirds, or three-fourths of all that is necessary for tens of millions of people; when these raw materials are transported to the most suitable place of production, sometimes hundreds or thousands of miles away, in a systematic and organized manner; when a single centre directs all the successive stages of work right up to the manufacture of numerous varieties of finished articles; when these products are distributed according to a single plan among tens of hundreds of millions of consumers (as in the case of the distribution of oil in America and Germany by the American "Standard Oil")—then it becomes evident that we have socialization of production, and not mere "interlocking"; that private economic relations and private property relations constitute a shell which is no longer suitable for its contents, a shell which must of necessity begin to decay if its destruction be postponed by artificial means; a shell which may continue in a state of decay for a fairly long period (particularly if the cure of the opportunist abscess is protracted), but which must inevitably be removed. . . .

7

International Economic Structures and American Foreign Economic Policy, 1887-1934

DAVID A. LAKE

David Lake looks at American foreign economic policy before the United States's rise to world leadership. Lake relates changes in the American position in the international economy to particular changes in the nation's tariff. He begins with a discussion of hegemonic stability theory (see also Krasner, Reading 3) and of the international economic structure. He applies a differentiated analysis of changes in the United States international economic position to four periods of American foreign economic policy from 1887 to 1934. Lake argues that when Great Britain was the dominant economic power, the United States could adopt protectionist policies at home while pursuing export expansion abroad. As Britain declined, the United States was forced to reduce its tariffs. With the collapse of the international economy during the Great Depression, American policy swung first toward greater protection and then, after 1934, toward freer trade and world leadership. Lake's analysis in this article builds on the Realist approach to foreign economic policy. For Lake, as for most Realists, national policies are dictated first and foremost by the nation's international environment and only secondarily by the domestic setting.

---

7 "International Economic Structures and American Foreign Economic Policy, 1887-1934" by David A. Lake. *World Politics*, Vol. 35, No. 4 (July 1983).

In the 1890 tariff debate Representative William McKinley stated, "This is a domestic bill; it is not a foreign bill."[1] Many scholars have echoed this view of the tariff and American foreign economic policy. Tom E. Terrill argues that tariff policies in the United States during the late 19th century resulted from the struggle between the Democratic and Republican parties to break the political equipoise of the era. Theodore J. Lowi, drawing upon E. E. Schattschneider, contends that tariff policy before 1934 was primarily shaped by the distributive nature of the issue area. And nearly every account of the passage of the Reciprocal 1 Trade Agreements Act of 1934, which overturned America's century-old commitment to protectionism, attributes an important role to the personal beliefs of Secretary of State Cordell Hull.

Recently, the "theory of hegemonic stability" has been put forth as a systemic-level explanation of international economic regime change. Despite this emergence of a "third image" in international political economy, comparatively little attention has been devoted to the international sources of foreign economic policy in individual countries. This is unfortunate. Not only do state policies provide additional cases to refine and test the theory of hegemonic stability—and this is important because of the limited number of international economic regimes available for study—but the central propositions of the theory of hegemonic stability form the basis for a powerful and parsimonious explanation of foreign economic policy and policy change in individual countries over time.

In this article, I examine the international sources of American foreign economic policy between 1887 and 1934, an era of rapid and dramatic changes. Immediately after the Civil War, the United States had sought to insulate itself from the international economy; it adopted protectionism at home and a *laissez faire* policy toward exports. After 1887, the United States began actively to promote exports through bilateral reciprocity treaties and duty-free raw materials while maintaining the essential structure of protection. Between 1897 and World War I, America's recognition that its policies could and did affect the international economy was primarily reflected in the pursuit of the Open Door abroad. After 1913, the United States undertook a greater leadership role within the international economy. It lowered its tariff wall at home and, at the end of the war, attempted to create and maintain a new and fundamentally liberal international economy based on the Open Door principle. In the late 1920s, the United States briefly abdicated its position of international economic leadership and returned to protectionism via the Smoot-Hawley Tariff Act of 1930, but reversed direction again in the Reciprocal Trade Agreements Act of 1934.

Between 1887 and 1934, the United States evolved from a highly protectionist into an internationally liberal country. In this article, I offer an alternative explanation of this evolution in American foreign economic policy from that contained in the several domestic approaches summarized in the opening paragraph. My central proposition is that American foreign economic policy, and policy change during the period 1887-1934, was shaped in important ways by the international economic structure and the position of the United States within it. The source of American foreign economic policy, in other words, was within the international political economy.

The discussion is divided into two principal sections. First, I review and refine the theory of hegemonic stability, proposing a new category of international actor which better describes the position of the United States within the international economic structure. Second, I examine the theory of hegemonic stability through an analysis of American foreign economic policy between 1887 and 1934. In the conclusion, I discuss the strengths and weaknesses of an explanation of foreign economic policy derived from international economic structures, and summarize the implications of this analysis for the theory of hegemonic stability.

THE THEORY OF HEGEMONIC STABILITY

There are two variants of the theory of hegemonic stability. The first, associated with Charles P. Kindleberger's *The World in Depression 1929-1939*,[2] focuses on the provision of the collective good of international stability, where instability is defined as a condition in which small disruptions (e.g., the stock market crash of 1929) have large consequences (the Great Depression). Assuming that markets are inherently unstable—or nonhomeostatic systems—and tend toward stagnation and fragmentation, Kindleberger argues that the international economy will be stable only if a single leader is willing to assume responsibility for "(a) maintaining a relatively open market for distress goods; (b) providing countercyclical long-term lending; and (c) discounting in a crisis."[3] He has subsequently added two additional responsibilities: (d) "managing, in some degree, the structure of exchange rates," and (e) "providing a degree of coordination of domestic monetary policies."[4]

Leadership, for Kindleberger, is altruistic. A stable international economy is produced only at a net physical cost to the country in exchange for the amorphous "privilege" of leading. The ability of a country to assume responsibility for stabilizing the international economy is primarily determined by its position within the international economic structure, which Kindleberger defines along the single dimension of size: "Small countries have no economic power. At the same time they have no responsibility for the economic system, nor any necessity to exert leadership."[5] Small states, in other words, are "free riders." Middle-sized countries are "big enough to do damage to the system, but not substantial enough to stabilize it. . . ."[6] Since they tend to act as if they were small free riders, middle-sized countries are extremely destabilizing and are the "spoilers" of the system. Only large states have both the capability and responsibility for leading the international economy. "The main lesson of the inter-war years," Kindleberger states, is that, "for the world economy to be stabilized, there has to be a stabilizer, one stabilizer."[7]

The second variant, drawn from the works of Robert Gilpin,[8] differs from the first in three substantive ways: the phenomenon to be explained, the nature of leadership, and the definition of the international economic structure. Gilpin does not address the question of stability directly; rather, he seeks to explain why regimes—or the rules and norms that govern international economic relations—emerge and change. In addressing this question, Gilpin subsumes much of Kindleberger's argument and draws heavily upon the collective goods approach. Despite this intellectual debt, Gilpin moves beyond Kindleberger's conception of altruism and develops an interest-based explanation of leadership. While noting that all countries gain from a liberal regime, Gilpin asserts that the strongest and most advanced countries reap a disproportionate share of the benefits. Britain and the United States, in other words, constructed and maintained liberal international economic regimes at their hegemonic zeniths because the benefits outweighed the costs. When this favorable payoff disappeared, the hegemonic powers stopped leading.

Gilpin defines the position of a country within the international economy along two dimensions: political-military power and efficiency. In Gilpin's conceptualization, political-military power primarily indicates the quantity of influence a state possesses over the international economic regime. Efficiency, on the other hand, largely determines the degree to which a state's interests are associated with a liberal international economic regime. The more efficient the nation, the larger the relative gains from trade, and the greater the country's support for a liberal regime. Within this definition of the international economic structure, Gilpin identifies three categories of international actors: peripheral states, which because of their small size are of little consequence for the regime; "growth nodes," which emerge as challengers to the liberal regime and, presumably, are of relatively low efficiency; and hegemonic leaders, which are extremely large and highly efficient countries. Although "growth nodes" are a more active threat to a liberal international economy than are Kindleberger's "middle-sized" countries, the two sets of categories are essentially similar; I refer to them as free riders, spoilers, and hegemonic leaders.

These three categories of international actors do not exhaust the logical possibilities presented within a two-dimensional conception of the international economic structure. Nor do they adequately describe the position of the United States within the international economy between 1887 and 1934. The theory of hegemonic stability, perhaps due to its focus on the absence or presence of hegemony, has failed to develop the analytic tools necessary to comprehend adequately the interests and policies of all countries within the international economy. To accomplish this task, Gilpin's two dimensions of political-military power and efficiency must be redefined. Political-military power may be a necessary condition for economic hegemony, but the relationship between political-military power and influence over the international economic regime diminishes once the analysis is extended beyond the category of hegemonic leadership. West Germany and Japan, for instance, possess much greater influence over the international economic regime today than their political-military strength would indicate. Relative size, operationalized by issue area, is a more appropriate indicator of international economic influence. Because the following discussion focuses primarily on trade policy, relative size is measured here by a country's proportion of world trade.

Gilpin's second dimension suffers less from a problem of theory than from one of semantics. Strictly defined, efficiency refers to the least wasteful means of production and is specific to time, place, and the available mix of the factors of production. Efficiency has little impact upon the absolute or relative gains from trade. Rather, the concept to which Gilpin appears to be referring is relative productivity—defined as relative output per unit of labor input. . . .

The three categories of nations identified by Gilpin and Kindleberger are defined graphically in Figure 1 within the two dimensions of relative size and relative productivity. . . . An important fourth category of international actor—supporters—has not been examined by either of these authors. Supporters are middle-sized countries of high relative productivity; they are not simply smaller or less effective hegemonic leaders. Supporters cannot unilaterally lead the international economy, nor—unlike a hegemonic leader—are they willing to accept high short-term costs for long-term gains. Rather, supporters seek to balance their short-term costs and benefits, and prefer to bargain for collective movement toward specified goals. Similarly, while hegemonic leaders forsake protectionism at home in order to lead the international economy as a whole toward greater openness, supporters are in most cases unwilling to do so. Even the most productive countries possess internationally uncompetitive industries. If a hegemonic leader were to protect such industries, it would undercut its ability to lead the international economy. Indeed, some measure of self-sacrifice in the short run may be necessary for a hegemonic leader to achieve its goal of constructing a liberal international economy. Supporters, on the other hand, are not subject to the same constraints of leadership; they will protect their least competitive industries whenever possible.

When a hegemonic leader exists within the international economy, supporters will free-ride, protecting industry at home and expanding exports abroad. They assume, in short, that the hegemonic leader will carry the burden of preserving their export markets while they remain free to pursue self-seeking policies at home.

When no hegemonic leader exists and two or more supporters are present in the international economy, their mutual desire to export will constrain protectionism in each other. Supporters, because of their high relative productivity, value export markets more than protection at home, but will sacrifice the latter only if necessary to obtain the former. An international-economic structure of bilateral (or multilateral) supportership is likely, as a result, to contain higher levels of protectionism than a hegemonic structure, but will not experience extremely high levels of protection because the interaction between supporters places limits on protectionism in any single supporter. Bilateral supportership can be a stable system in which protectionism or beggar-thy-neighbor policies are moderated by mutual constraints between supporters, and in which a measure of cooperation and collective interna-

FIGURE 1. Four Categories of International Economic Affairs

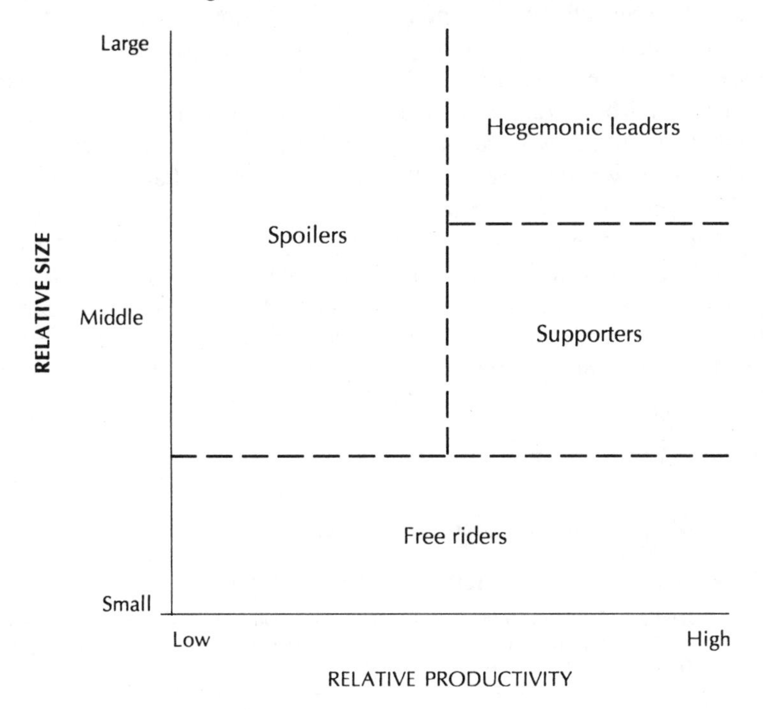

tional leadership exists. Considerable potential for instability does exist, however. Either supporter may try to "cheat" on the other, or either may be unwilling to carry an equitable share of the leadership burden.

International economic structures with only one supporter, by contrast, are highly unstable. When no hegemonic leader exists and only a single supporter is present, there are no constraints on protectionism within the supporter. Although it will continue to value export markets and may attempt to lead the international economy, a single supporter will lack the resources to stabilize the international economy successfully, or to create and maintain a liberal international economic regime. If the supporter believes that it cannot preserve its export markets, the protectionist fires at home will be fueled. The growing flames may precipitate the abdication of whatever leadership role had been held by the supporter.

The foreign economic policy of any individual country is affected both by the international economic structure (defined as the number and category of states within the international economy), and by the state's position within it. The international economic structure from 1870 to 1938 is detailed in Table I and illustrated in Figure 2. Throughout the period, the United States was a supporter. Its share of world trade rose steadily from 8.8 percent in 1870 to a high of 13.9 percent in 1929, only to decline to 11.3 percent in 1938. Its relative productivity was high and rising steadily until 1929; it surpassed the level of productivity of the United Kingdom in the late 1890s. Germany and France were spoilers throughout the period. Germany's proportion of world trade and its relative productivity gradually increased until World War I. After the war, its share of world trade and relative productivity declined to approximately the levels that had obtained in 1870. France's share of world trade eroded throughout the period after having reached a high of 11.4 percent in 1880. Its relative productivity was low and fluctuated before World War I; it was somewhat higher after the war than before, although it was still below the levels attained by the United Kingdom and the United States. The United Kingdom changed from a hegemonic leader into a supporter immediately before World War I, and into a spoiler in the late 1920s. Its share of world trade fell from a high of 24.0 percent in 1870 to a low of 13.3 percent in 1929, while its relative productivity dropped from 1.67 in 1870 to .92 in 1938.

TABLE 1. The International Economic Structure, 1870-1938

	UNITED STATES		UNITED KINGDOM		GERMANY		FRANCE	
	Proportion of World Trade	Relative Productivity[i]	Proportion of World Trade	Relative Productivity[i]	Proportion of World Trade	Relative Productivity[i]	Proportion of World Trade	Relative Productivity[i]
1870	8.8[a]	1.22	24.0[a]	1.63	9.7[a]	.66	10.8[a]	.65
1880	8.8[c]	1.29	19.6[c]	1.50	10.3[b]	.64	11.4[c]	.69
1890	9.7[d]	1.37	18.5[d]	1.45	10.9[d]	.69	10.0[d]	.63
1900	10.2[e]	1.42	17.5[e]	1.30	11.9[e]	.74	8.5[e]	.65
1913	11.1[f]	1.56	14.1[f]	1.15	12.2[f]	.73	7.5[f]	.68
1929	13.9[g]	1.72	13.3[g]	1.04	9.3[g]	.66	6.4[g]	.74
1938	11.3[h]	1.71	14.0[h]	.92	9.0[h]	.69	5.2[h]	.82

[a]Mulhall data, 1870, 1880; see Simon Kuznets, Modern Economic Growth (Yale University Press, 1966), 306.

[b]Mulhall data, 1880,1889, ibid., 306.

[c]League of Nations data, 1876-1880. League of Nations, Industrialization and Foreign Trade (Geneva, 1945), 157-67.

[d]League of Nations data, 1886-1890, in Kuznets, 307.

[e]League of Nations data, 1896-1900, ibid., 307.

[f]League of Nations data, 1911-1913, ibid., 307.

[g]League of Nations, Review of World Trade, 1927-1929.

[h]Ibid., 1936-1938.

[i]Relative Productivity data derived from Angus Maddison, "Long Run Dynamics of Productivity Growth" Banca Nazionale del Lavoro Quarterly Review, No. 128 (March 1979), 43.

FIGURE 2. The International Economic Structure, 1870-1938

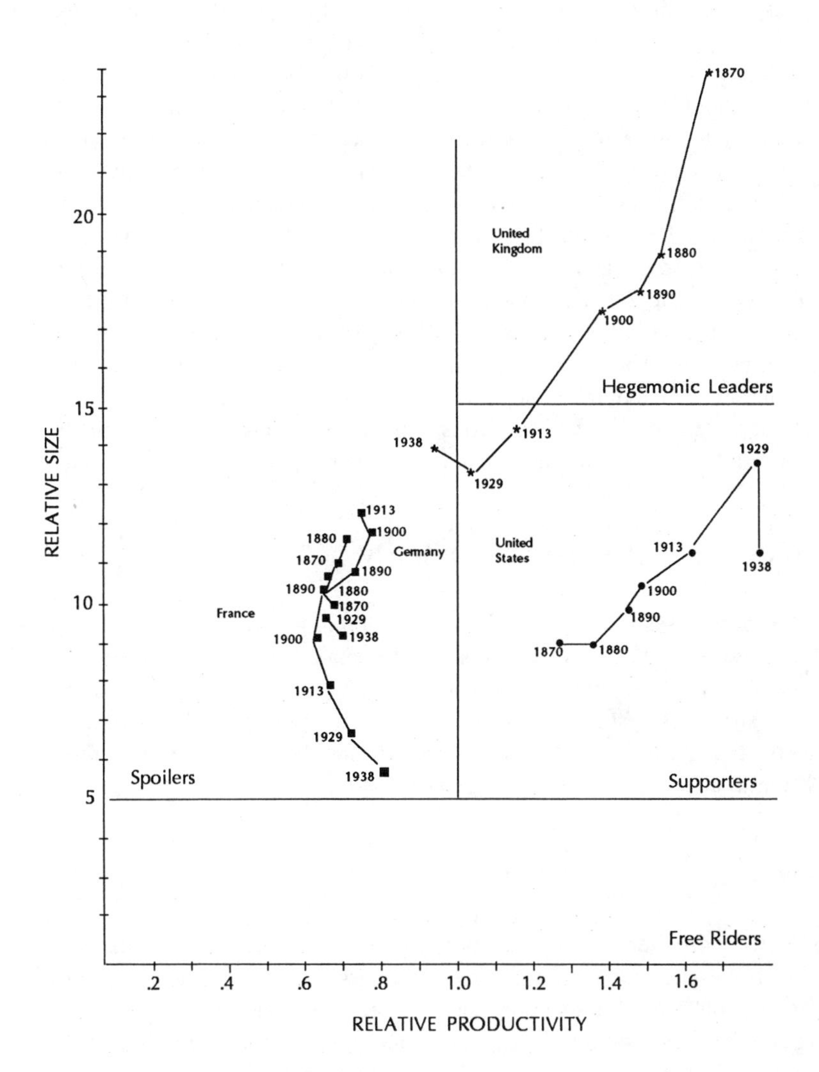

The position of the United Kingdom changed most dramatically between 1870 and 1938, creating three distinct international economic structures. A hegemonic structure under British leadership existed from before 1870 until approximately World War I. Next, a structure of bilateral supportership, in which the United States and the United Kingdom were the key actors, was present from approximately 1913 to the late 1920s. Finally, a structure of unilateral supportership, centering on the United States, existed from 1929 through World War II.

If my basic proposition is correct, these changes in the international economic structure and the position of the United States as a supporter should be reflected in American foreign economic policy and changes in that policy. Specifically, the United States should have attempted to free-ride within the structure of British hegemony. As the British position began to decline, however—and particularly after the United States had surpassed the United Kingdom in productivity—America should have gradually moved toward a more active and liberal policy in the international economy. Once the structure was transformed from hegemony to bilateral supportership, the United States should have adopted more liberal policies and sought to negotiate the rules and norms of a new, more protectionist yet still liberal international economic regime. Finally, both United States policy and the international economy should have entered into a period of instability after the United Kingdom evolved from supporter to spoiler. Within this structure of unilateral supportership, the United States should have remained liberal in its policies only so long as it believed it could maintain or expand its export markets.

AMERICAN FOREIGN ECONOMIC POLICY

There were four phases in American foreign economic policy during the period 1887-1934. The goals of this policy remained the same they had been for over a century: national development and domestic prosperity. What changed were the policies and strategies best suited to the attainment of these goals. We will now examine how the international economic structure, and the position of the United States within it, affected American foreign economic policy.

1887-1897

Prior to 1887, exports were not regarded as a proper sphere of government intervention; the tariff was perceived as a strictly domestic issue. The "American system" of moderately high tariff protection was explicitly enacted to stimulate and encourage the industrialization of the country. The agrarian community—still the largest sector of the economy—was encouraged to accept the American system through promises that an adequate and sufficiently stable home market would be created for its surplus.

While exports gradually became more important to agricultural interests, most manufacturers continued to regard exports as secondary to their main markets and primarily as a means of dumping (in the economic sense) their occasional surpluses. Those Americans who did seek to expand exports systematically did not link foreign expansion and the tariff. Rather, their emphasis was on infrastructural improvements, such as port and canal construction, and railroad development and regulation.

After 1887, under the efforts of David Ames Wells, James G. Blaine, and President Grover Cleveland, the tariff was reconceptualized as an instrument of foreign economic policy whose manipulation could serve to expand American exports. The opening of this new debate was marked by Cleveland's Annual Message to Congress in 1887, which he devoted entirely to the tariff question. While focusing primarily on the high consumer prices and favoritism that resulted from protectionism, Cleveland also sounded the theme of export expansion through cheaper raw materials and lower duties. This latter theme was developed more fully in the debate over the legislatively unsuccessful Mills bill, based on Cleveland's tariff principles, and in the "Great Tariff Debate" in the presidential election of 1888.

Cleveland and other leading Democrats were heavily influenced by the ideas of Wells. A former Republican Commissioner of Revenue, Wells had maintained as early as 1868 that American farmers and manufacturers faced a condition of chronic overproduction. Unless the United States increased its exports, he contended, periodic depressions would result. Wells consistently linked his diagnosis and prescription to tariff policy. In an analysis reminiscent of the British Anti-Corn Law League, Wells argued that high tariffs restricted the market place. Low tariffs, on the other hand, would broaden the market and stimulate exports by easing the exchange of goods and services, and reducing the costs of manufacturing through cheaper raw materials.

Even though Cleveland lost the Great Debate of 1888 at the polls and failed to enact his tariff reform principles in the Wilson-Gorman Tariff of 1894 in the face of protectionist opposition in the Senate (see Table 2 for a comparison of rates of duty) during his second administration, the export expansionists were ultimately victorious. In response to Democratic demands for tariff reduction, the majority of Republicans limited themselves to reciting the litany of protectionist arguments and emphasizing the adequacy of the home market. A minority of Republicans, however, under the leadership of Blaine, began to formulate a new perspective which shared Wells's assumption of overproduction, but maintained the essential structure of protection. Rather than seeking to lower the entire tariff wall, as the Democrats advocated, Blaine sought to expand exports by negotiating tariff reciprocity treaties with other countries. Despite initial opposition from the majority of Republicans, Blaine's conception of reciprocity prevailed in the McKinley Tariff of 1890 and, to a lesser extent, in the Dingley Act of 1897 (see Table 2).

Blaine's success illustrates how far the reconceptualization of the tariff had progressed. By the early 1890s, the leaders of both political parties agreed on the need for export expansion and on the proposition that the tariff could serve as a useful instrument for accomplishing this aim. They disagreed only on the means of expansion: the Democrats favored duty-free raw materials, with the market mechanism determining the level of imports; the Republicans preferred reciprocity, with the government determining which raw materials from which countries would be admitted to the United States.

Despite this desire for export expansion, there was little recognition of the effects United States policy had upon the international economy. To Americans of this period, it appeared that exports could be expanded indefinitely through adjusting the tariff without damaging the principle of protection. For the Cleveland Democrats, duty-free raw materials were a means of increasing the competitiveness of American manufactured exports. For the Republicans, reciprocity based primarily on the admittance of raw materials at a preferential rate of duty was a wedge to pry open additional markets for American exports. The proposition that, in order to sell to the world, a country must buy from the world was not readily accepted outside a small circle of academic economists and "free trade" Democrats. Nor was there any widespread recognition that American exports depended on the continued willingness of other countries—particularly the United Kingdom, America's single largest trading partner—to accept American goods. Rather, existing markets tended to be taken for granted and new markets were perceived to be ripe for picking.

As predicted above, so long as the United Kingdom remained a hegemonic leader, the United States would free-ride even though it was a supporter. America remained protectionist and sought to expand its exports. It contributed little or nothing to the stability of the international economy and actually helped to undermine the existing liberal international economic regime. During this first phase, in short, the United States free-rode on free trade.

1897-1912

By the late 1890s, the country's growing productivity and events in Europe and China forced the United States to recognize the effects of its policies on other nations. Confronted with an American commercial "invasion" spurred by rising relative productivity in the United States, several European statesmen began to advocate protecting their markets against American imports. "The destructive competition with transoceanic countries," Count Agenor Goluchowski, Foreign Minister of Austria-Hungary, stated on November 20, 1897, "requires prompt and thorough counteracting measures if vital interests of the peoples of Europe are not to be gravely compromised.... The European nations must close their ranks in order successfully to defend their existence."[9] Three weeks later, Baron von Thielmann, Secretary of the German Treasury and a former Ambassador to the United States, argued before the Reichstag that the recently passed Dingley Tariff put America in the position of a pike in a carp pool. The carp, he warned, must combine. Though these statements were noted with some alarm in the American press, more ominous, perhaps, was the growing movement in the United Kingdom for an imperial preference system led by Joseph Chamberlain, who had been appointed Colonial

Secretary in 1895. It was unlikely that the highly divided Europeans of the late 19th century would combine into the customs union proposed by Goluchowski and Thielmann, but for Britain to adopt imperial preferences would have been a matter of concern for the United States and was recognized as such.

Events in China, which threatened to disrupt American trade with that country—important more for its promise than for its actual levels—drew a more concrete response from the United States. In March 1898, after several years of increasing Russian, German, and French encroachments on China's territory and sovereignty, Britain approached the United States and inquired "whether they could count on the cooperation of the United States in opposing any such action by Foreign Powers and whether the United States would be prepared to join with Great Britain in opposing such measures should the contingency arise."[10] The United States refused. Britain, in a significant departure from its past policy of free trade and nondiscrimination, then began to move away from the principle of the Open Door, leasing the port of Kowloon and expelling the Chinese Imperial Maritime Customs Service. In September 1899, Secretary of State John Hay issued the now famous Open Door notes.

The Open Door principle had existed long before the United States issued these notes. Lord Balfour, in the parliamentary debates of 1898, referred to it as "that famous phrase that has been quoted and requoted almost *ad nauseam.* [11] In the September notes, the United States invited Russia, Germany, Great Britain, France, and Japan to adhere to three principles: noninterference with the vested interests within the existing spheres of influence in China, the uniform application of Chinese treaty tariffs at all ports, and nondiscrimination regarding railroad and harbor charges. All the powers responded, though some quite vaguely, that they would respect the Open Door to the extent that all other nations did. Hay, in what is generally regarded as a brilliant tactical move, announced that all the powers had agreed to uphold the Open Door in China and that he considered their replies to be "final and definitive."[12] The Open Door notes in themselves had little practical effect. It was clear that the United States would not use more than moral suasion to enforce the principle. Moreover, the notes were almost swallowed up in the march of events in China. The military intervention of the foreign powers (including the United States) to put down the Boxer Rebellion in 1900 soon led to an increase in the authority exerted by foreign governments in China. Yet, the Open Door notes were significant for three reasons. First, as Thomas McCormick writes:

> the promulgation of the [Open Door notes] did pass the scepter of open door champion from Great Britain to the United States. For a half-century the British had successfully used an open door policy to create and maintain their economic supremacy in the Chinese Empire. . . . Now, as Britain's power waned—and with it her commitment to the open door, the United States made a concerted effort to adapt the nineteenth-century policy to the expansive needs of a twentieth-century industrial America."[13]

Second, the Open Door notes demonstrated the important effect that Britain's move away from free trade had in shaping American foreign economic policy after 1898. Third, while they were not recognized as doing so at that time, the Open Door notes repudiated the concept of reciprocity and signaled a new era in which the principle of nondiscrimination, or the Open Door, was to be the cornerstone of American foreign economic policy.

This new commitment to nondiscrimination was reflected in the next Republican tariff bill—the Payne-Aldrich Act of 1909. In this bill, Congress established a system of minimum and maximum tariff rates. The President was given the authority to impose duties 25 percent higher than the minimum rates on goods from any country that discriminated against American exports. During the House debate, Representative Edgar D. Crumpacker of Indiana (R), a member of the House Ways and Means Committee, argued:

> It is a wise provision, and its main virtue is in the retaliatory power it contains to compel foreign countries to accord our exports the same treatment they give to those of other countries. *Our foreign commercial and industrial policy ought to be that of the open door*. We ask only equal consideration at the hands of foreign countries, and that we should insist upon. I have little respect for reciprocity in its narrow sense—in the sense that it is a system of international dickers under which one line of products may secure special advantages in foreign markets in consideration of a grant of special advantages to a particular line of products in return. . . . The broad reciprocity of treating all competitors and all producers exactly alike is the principle that this country ought to encourage as the permanent commercial policy of the civilized world.[14]

Despite this commitment to the liberal principle of the Open Door, the United States remained unwilling to abolish its tariff wall. Pressure on the government for tariff reduction rose throughout the first decade of the 20th century. Active on the issue were, on the one hand, the Progressives, who perceived the tariff as aiding the process of consolidation in American industry, and, on the other, the large and internationally competitive businesses, which defined their interests in broad internationalist terms. President Theodore Roosevelt, who feared that revising the tariff would split his then-dominant Republican party, successfully avoided the issue and bequeathed the problem to this successor. Although William Taft had run on an election platform that advocated tariff reform, he was unable to contain protectionist pressures within his party once he was in office. The Payne-Aldrich Act, which contained the minimum-maximum schedule with the aim of expanding the Open Door, only slightly lowered the average rates of duty from those of the Dingley Act of 1897 (see Table 2). Taft's inability to fulfill his promise of tariff reform engendered a considerable groundswell of resentment. This negative reaction effectively thwarted Taft's ability to utilize the higher maximum schedule so as to secure a further expansion of the Open Door abroad because he feared popular condemnation of a further increase in the tariff.

TABLE 2. Levels of Duty by Tariff Act, 1887-1934*

Tariff Act, Date	Level of Duty on All Imports	Level of Duty on Dutiable Imports	Percentage of All Imports on Free List
McKinley, 1890	23.7	48.4	50.8
Wilson-Gorman, 1894	20.5	41.2	50.0
Dingley, 1897	26.2	47.6	45.1
Payne-Aldrich, 1909	20.0	41.0	51.3
Underwood, 1913	8.8	26.8	67.5
Fordney-McCumber, 1922	13.9	38.2	63.5
Smoot-Hawley, 1930	19.0	55.3	65.5

Source: Statistical Abstract of the United States, selected years.

*Average rates of duty and average percentage of imports on free list for all full years during which the tariff was in effect (e.g., McKinley Tariff Act passed in October 1890; duties calculated on 1891-1893).

As Britain's hegemony waned and the United States' productivity rose, the latter—as predicted by the refined theory of hegemonic stability—adopted more liberal policies within the international economy, but continued to free-ride. The Open Door policy was a significant recognition that the United States depended on export markets and that it could no longer rely entirely upon the United Kingdom to maintain openness abroad. Still, Washington was unwilling to accept the costs of enforcing the Open Door principle in China, or of restricting protection for American industry.

1913-1929

Woodrow Wilson, in accepting the Democratic presidential nomination, stated: "The tariff was once a bulwark; now it is a dam. Foreign trade is reciprocal; we cannot sell unless we also buy."[15] Pledged to tariff reform, Wilson called Congress into special session in order to enact the Underwood Tariff Act of 1913. In a speech before Congress, he declared:

> It is clear to the whole country that the tariff duties must be altered. They must be changed to meet the radical alteration in the conditions of our economic life which the country has witnessed within the last generation. While the whole face and method of our industrial and commercial life were being changed beyond recognition the tariff schedules have remained what they were before the change began or have moved in the direction they were given when no large circumstance of our industrial development was what it is to-day. Our task is to square them with actual facts.[16]

The Underwood Act, when passed, lowered the average rate of duty on all imports into the United States to 8.8 percent and on dutiable imports alone to 26.8 percent (see Table 2). While it abolished the minimum and maximum schedules of the Payne-Aldrich Act, the new tariff constituted a major step by the United States toward supporting a liberal international economy.

During and after World War I, the liberal international economy, to which the United States had just made an important contribution, was threatened by rising economic nationalism in Europe. At the Paris Economic Conference in 1916, France and Britain agreed on a plan to organize trade on a state capitalist basis around exclusive regional trading blocs. This plan was never fully implemented, however, because of American pressure and inter-Ally disagreements. After the war, Britain adopted a moderate form of imperial preference; France enacted a two-tiered tariff in which the highest duties did not apply to countries that discriminated against French goods (as this type of tariff had traditionally been used), but to those that imposed "high" duties on French exports. Both policies contravened America's conception of the Open Door.

The principal instrument in the effort to extend the Open Door abroad was the "bargaining tariff," or the Fordney-McCumber Act of 1922. The concept of a flexible tariff, which was similar to the minimum and maximum provisions of the Payne-Aldrich Act, had gained wider acceptance in the United States after the Paris Economic Conference. In 1916, the National Foreign Trade Council called for the development of an effective bargaining tariff and expressed its willingness to work with the newly created Tariff Commission in writing such a bill. Immediately after the war, however, there was renewed interest in the concept of reciprocity as an instrument for acquiring special trading advantages. The Harding Administration, under the leadership of William S. Culbertson, argued for the Open Door. Culbertson, with the aid of Senator Smoot, was successful: the final version of the bill provided the President with the authority to impose penalty duties against countries that discriminated against American goods. The Fordney-McCumber Act, though it had been passed as a protectionist measure, did not raise tariff levels dramatically. The average tariff on all imports was raised to 13.9 percent while the tariff on dutiable imports was raised to 38.2 percent; both measures were below the average tariffs found in the first two phases discussed earlier.

In 1922, the Harding Administration also decided to abandon the conditional form of the most-favored-nation (MFN) principle and adopt a more liberal unconditional variant. Previously, trade concessions granted by the United States to second-party states had been extended to third-party states only upon the receipt of equivalent concessions. After it adopted the unconditional form of the MFN principle, the United States automatically extended concessions to all nations with which it had an MFN treaty. In conjunction with the flexible tariff provision of the Fordney-McCumber Tariff, this shift in policy illustrates the desire of the United States to play a greater and more liberal role within the international economy.

Constrained by domestic partisanship and a commitment to moderate protectionism, however, the Republicans were unable to wield the tariff as an effective offensive weapon to break down the barriers to discrimination abroad. The Europeans remained recalcitrant. In response to American criticism, they argued that the greatest obstacles to world trade were not their discriminatory tariff schedules, but the relatively high rates all nations faced in the United States. Americans, and especially Secretary of Commerce Herbert Hoover, replied that aggregate imports by the United States continued to rise despite the higher Fordney-McCumber duties and, indeed, that imports were rising faster than exports. Neither side would yield, and little progress was made.

Thus, the United States quest for a worldwide Open Door was not achieved in the 1920s. Even though the Europeans finally agreed at the Geneva International Economic Conference in 1927 that the unconditional MFN principle was the most desirable basis upon which to organize international trade, they continued to evade the Open Door principle in practice.

The United States recognized that its export trade was dependent not only on a liberal international economic regime, but also on a revitalized Europe; it therefore sought to assist in the rebuilding of the war-torn European economy. American decision makers perceived the isolation and embitterment of Germany as the central threat to European stability; once the United States had failed to join the League of Nations, however, few instruments remained by which it could attempt to induce or coerce the Europeans, and particularly France, into reintegrating Germany into the European economic and political orders. As a result, Washington was forced to expand its conception of foreign economic policy beyond the trade policy arena, and to include, for the first time, the issue areas of international finance and investment.

The outstanding war debts provided one of two instruments to influence European policies toward Germany. France, minimizing its responsibility for debts incurred during the war, wanted to extract the largest possible indemnity from Germany. The United States, focusing on Europe's long-term stability, sought a much lighter reparations burden. By denying any linkage between war debts and reparations—in contravention of the European view—the United States sought to limit the size of the final reparations settlement; it refused to yield until its allies agreed to make significant concessions to Germany.

The second major instrument available to American decision makers was the loan control program. The voluntary program adopted by the government in March 1922 stated that no loans by American bankers would be approved for "governments or citizens in countries who have failed to maintain their obligations to the United States."[17] In this way, the loan-control program was intended to apply pressure on the Europeans through the war-debt issue. Subjected to both official and unofficial American pressure and facing increasing financial difficulties, all the relevant European nations became increasingly willing to compromise. Between 1924 and 1926, the London Conference and the Dawes Loan temporarily settled the reparations issue; the Locarno Treaties helped stabilize the European political order by resolving several outstanding points of disagreement between France and Germany; and the Mellon-Berenger Agreement settled the war-debt program (again temporarily). In each of these cases, the final agreement was close to the position advocated by the United States.

In this third phase, the United States emerged as a significant but nonhegemonic leader within the international economy. Washington closely conformed to the policies expected of a supporter in an international economic structure of bilateral supportership as outlined above. Before the war, it made a significant move toward greater liberalism in its foreign economic policies through the Underwood Tariff Act. It also attempted to rebuild a liberal international economy during the 1920s. The United States could not unilaterally lead the international economy; as a result, it sought to bargain with the Europeans in order to meet its objectives. There were significant elements of cooperation with the United Kingdom, particularly in the area of international finance and currency stabilization. On the other hand, considerable criticism and threats of retaliation from the Europeans, and from the United Kingdom in particular, helped to restrain protectionism within the United States. Relatively high U.S. tariffs and the instruments used by the United States—primarily the outstanding war-debt issue and the loan control program—to influence European policies did engender considerable controversy and conflict within the international community. Considering the magnitude of the war's destruction, the international economy was relatively stable during the 1920s even though no clear hegemonic leader was present. But it was not without tension.

1930-1934

The modicum of international stability that existed during the 1920s disappeared by 1929. In the presidential campaign of 1928, the Republicans pledged to relieve farm distress, which had been a problem throughout the 1920s, by raising tariffs on agricultural goods imported into the United States. Congress was called into special session by President Herbert Hoover for this purpose, but the legislative mandate was soon redefined as a general upward revision of the tariff. The domestic advocates of protectionism, who had been restrained during the 1920s, took this opportunity to press for special favors. The Smoot-Hawley Act of 1930, which raised tariffs on all imports to 19.0 percent and on dutiable imports to 55.3 percent (see Table 2), sparked a global increase in protectionism. In the two years that followed, Canada, Switzerland, Austria, France, Germany, Italy, and many other countries also adopted increased protection. The United Kingdom passed the protectionist Abnormal Importations and Horticultural Products Acts in 1931. In 1932, it adopted the Import Duties Act, which imposed a 10 percent *ad valorem* tariff on all imports into the country. And, in the Ottawa Agreements of 1932, the United Kingdom accepted a full-scale imperial preference system as first advocated by Chamberlain in 1895.

The London Economic Conference was organized in 1933 to discuss measures to halt the proliferation of protectionist and beggar-thy-neighbor policies throughout the international economy. While the Conference was in session, President Franklin D. Roosevelt dashed any hopes of success by his "bombshell" message of July 2, in which he deplored the emphasis on currency stabilization and stated that the creation of sound domestic economies should be the Conference's principal concern.

One year later, the wheels of international trade having ground to a halt, President Roosevelt reversed American policy with the passage of the Reciprocal Trade Agreements Act (RTAA). This act gave the President three years to negotiate foreign trade agreements that could reduce American tariffs by as much as 50 percent from the Smoot-Hawley levels. The emphasis on tariff reduction distinguishes the RTAA from all past American trade policies. For the first time, the United States sought to bargain not only for equality of access or for the Open Door, but for lower tariffs in foreign countries. Between 1934 and 1938, America negotiated 18 treaties that lowered duties at home and abroad. Each contained the unconditional MFN clause. These treaties were among the major stimuli of the resurgence of world trade in the late 1930s.

American foreign economic policy after 1930 was in accord with the prediction for a single supporter within the international economy. When the mutual constraints of bilateral supportership were lifted from the United States, protectionism was unleashed. Once retaliation had occurred and world trade was diminished, the United States stood to gain only if it expanded its export markets. This expansion could be accomplished only by lowering tariffs abroad; hence, the RTAA. The United States was not a hegemonic leader in the 1930s, however. It did not act altruistically or accept short-term costs for long-term gains. It continued to behave as predicted for a supporter: it bargained over tangible goods (tariffs) to achieve a specific goal (reductions) with immediate rewards.

CONCLUSIONS

American foreign economic policy between 1887 and 1934 generally conformed with the behavior predicted for a supporter. While the United Kingdom remained a hegemonic leader, the United States attempted to free-ride. Once the British position began to weaken and American productivity had surpassed that of the United Kingdom, the United States began to play a more active and liberal role in the international economy. Within the structure of bilateral supportership, the United States emerged as a leader, restraining protectionism at home, attempting to reestablish the rule of nondiscrimination or the Open Door in the international economy, and seeking to stabilize Europe. Once Britain evolved from a supporter into a spoiler, leaving the United States as the sole supporter within the IES, both American policy and the international economy became unstable. In sum, the international economic structure and the position of the United States within it appear to provide a parsimonious and reasonably powerful explanation of American foreign economic policy and policy change. . . .

The structural theory outlined earlier lacks a conception of process, or an explanation of how the constraints or interests derived from the international economic structure are transformed into decisions or political strategies within particular countries. As a result, the causal link between the systemic-level international economic structure and national-level policy is open to question. Ultimately, structure and process must be integrated in a theory of political economy. In this article, however, I have only attempted to clarify the constraints facing the United States in the period 1887-1934 and to demonstrate the strength and usefulness of a purely structural argument as a first and necessary step toward an integrated theory. . . .

NOTES

1. *Congressional Record,* 51st Cong., 1st sess. (1890), 4250.

2. Charles Kindleberger, *The World in Depression 1929-1939* (Berkeley: University of California Press, 1973).

3. *Ibid.*, 292.

4. Kindleberger, "Dominance and Leadership in the International Economy: Exploitation, Public Goods, and Free Rides," *International Studies Quarterly* 25 (June 1981), 247.

5. *Ibid.*, 249.

6. *Ibid.*, 250.

7. Kindleberger, *The World in Depression,* 305.

8. See Robert Gilpin, *U.S. Power and the Multinational Corporation: The Political Economy of Foreign Direct Investment* (New York: Basic Books, 1975), and "Economic Interdependence and National Security in Historical Perspective," in Klaus Knorr and Frank N. Trager, eds., *Economic Issues and National Security* (Lawrence, Kansas: Regents Press of Kansas, 1977), 1966.

9. Quoted in Charles S. Campbell, Jr., *Special Business Interests and the Open Door Policy* (Hamden, Conn.: Archon Books, 1968), 6.

10. George F. Kennan, *American Diplomacy 1900-1950* (Chicago: University of Chicago Press, 1951), 25-26.

11. *Ibid.*, 25.

12. *Ibid.*, 32.

13. Thomas J . McCormick, *China Market: America's Quest for Informal Empire 1893-1901* (Chicago: Quadrangle Books, 1967), 127.

14. Congressional Record, 61st Cong., 1st sess., 1909, 285; emphasis added.

15. Quoted in William Diamond, "The Economic Thought of Woodrow Wilson, "*Johns Hopkins University Studies in Historical and Political Science,* 61 (No. 4, 1943), 134.

16. H.R. Richardson, *Messages and Papers of the Presidents*, XVIII (New York: Bureau of National Literature), 8251-52.

17. Herbert Feis, *The Diplomacy of the Dollar: First Era l919-1932* (Baltimore: The Johns Hopkins University Press, 1950), 11.

III

THE CONTEMPORARY INTERNATIONAL POLITICAL ECONOMY

A. Overview

The contemporary international political economy is characterized by unprecedented levels of multinational production, cross-border financial flows, and international trade. It is also plagued by increasing political conflict as individuals, groups, classes, and countries clash over the meaning and implications of these economic transactions. The contradiction between increasing economic integration and the wealth that it produces, on the one hand, and the desire for political control and national autonomy, on the other, will define the coming decade.

For over thirty years, the general pattern of relations among non-Communist nations was set by American leadership, and this pattern continues to influence the international political economy today. In the political arena, formal and informal alliances tied virtually every major non-communist nation into an American-led network of mutual support and defense. In the economic arena, a wide-ranging set of international economic organizations—including the International Monetary Fund, the General Agreement on Tariffs and Trade, and the European Common Market—grew up under a protective American umbrella, and often as direct American initiatives. The world economy itself was heavily influenced by the rise of modern multinational corporations and banks, whose contemporary form is largely of United States origin.

American plans for a reordered world economy go back to the mid-1930s. After World War I, the United States retreated into relative economic insularity for reasons explored above (see Historical Perspectives). When the Great Depression hit, American political leaders virtually ignored the possibility of international economic cooperation in their attempts to stabilize the domestic economy. Yet, even as the Roosevelt administration looked inward for recovery, by 1934 new American initiatives were signaling a shift in America's traditional isolation. Roosevelt's Secretary of State, Cordell Hull, was a militant free trader, and in 1934 he convinced Congress to pass the Reciprocal Trade Agreements Act, which allowed the Executive to negotiate tariff reductions with foreign nations. This important step toward trade liberalization and international economic cooperation was deepened as war threatened in Europe and the United States drew closer to Great Britain and France.

The seeds of the new international order, planted in the 1930s, began to grow even as World War II came to an end. The Bretton Woods Agreement reached among the Allied powers in 1944 established a new series of international economic organizations that became the foundation for the postwar American-led system. As the wartime American-Soviet alliance began to shatter, a new economic order emerged in the non-Communist world. At its center were the three pillars of the Bretton Woods system: international monetary cooperation under the auspices of the International Monetary Fund, international trade liberalization negotiated within the General Agreement on Tariffs and Trade, and investment in the developing countries stimulated by the International Bank for Reconstruction and Development (World Bank). All three pillars were essentially designed by the United States and dependent on American support.

As it developed, the postwar capitalist world reflected American foreign policy in many of its details. One principal concern of the United States was to build a bulwark of anti-Soviet allies; this was done with a massive inflow of American aid under the Marshall plan, and the encouragement of Western European cooperation within a new Common Market. At the same time, the United States dramatically lowered its barriers to foreign goods, and American corporations began to invest heavily in foreign nations. Of course, the United States was not acting altruistically; European recovery, trade liberalization, and booming international investment helped bring and ensure great prosperity within the United States as well.

American policies, whatever their motivation, had an undeniable impact on the international political economy. Trade liberalization opened the huge American market to foreign producers. American overseas investment provided capital, technology, and expertise for both Europe and the developing world. American government economic aid—whether direct or channeled through such institutions as the World Bank—helped finance economic growth abroad. In addition, the American military "umbrella" allowed anti-Soviet governments in Europe, Japan, and the developing world to rely on the United States for security and to turn their attentions to encouraging economic growth.

All in all, the non-Communist world's unprecedented access to American markets and American capital provided a major stimulus to world economic growth, not to mention to the profits of American businesses and to general prosperity within the United States. For over twenty-five years after World War II, the capitalist world experienced impressive levels of economic growth and development, all within a general context of international cooperation under American political, economic, and military tutelage.

This period is often referred to as the *Pax Americana* because of its broad similarity to the British-led international economic system that reigned from about 1820 until World War I known as the *Pax Britannica*. In both instances, general political and economic peace prevailed under the leadership of an overwhelming world power—the United Kingdom in one case, the United States in the other.

Just as the *Pax Britannica* eventually ended, however, the *Pax Americana* gradually eroded. By the early 1970s, strains were developing in the postwar system. Between 1971 and 1975, the postwar international monetary system, which had been based on a gold-backed United States dollar, fell apart and was replaced by a new, improvised pattern of floating exchange rates in which the dollar's role was still strong but no longer quite so central. At the same time, pressures for trade protection began to mount from uncompetitive industries in North America and Western Europe, and, although tariff levels remained low, a variety of nontariff barriers to world trade such as import quotas soon proliferated. In the political arena, detente between the United States and the Soviet Union seemed to make the American security umbrella less relevant for the Japanese and Western Europeans; in the less developed countries, North-South conflict appeared more important than East-West strife. In short, as American economic strength declined, the Bretton Woods institutions weakened, and the Cold War thawed during the 1970s, the *Pax Americana* drew to a close.

The United States remains the most important country within the contemporary international political economy, but it is no longer dominant. The era of American hegemony has been replaced by a new multilateral order based upon the joint leadership of Western Europe, Japan, and the United States. Together, these countries have successfully managed—some would say, muddled through—the "oil shocks" of the 1970s, the debt crisis of the early 1980s, and the exchange rate, trade, and financial gyrations of the Reagan era. Despite greater success than many thought possible, multilateral leadership and the liberal international order remain fragile. At the moment, conflicts of interest and economic tensions remain muted, but they could erupt at any time.

As might be expected, the rise and decline of the *Pax Americana* and the emergence of the new multilateral order have led to great scholarly controversy. For some analysts, America's global dominance was a principal determinant of its interests and policies and, in turn, of the liberal international economy. The decline of the United States, in this view, presages the eventual collapse of international openness. For others, the policies of the United States, as well as those of other countries, were affected in more important ways by domestic economic and political pressures. From this perspective, the decline of American hegemony is expected to have little effect on international openness. For still others, the consequences of the liberal order have fundamentally altered the interests of the United States and other countries. The internationalization of production and finance and the rise of economic interdependence have created vested interests in favor of the free flow of goods, services, and capital across national borders.

The remainder of this book is devoted to understanding the contemporary international political economy and its likely future. In the sections that follow, a variety of thematic issues are addressed; in each cluster of issues, alternative theoretical and analytical perspectives compete. The selections thus serve both to illuminate important substantive issues in the modern international political economy and to illustrate divergent theoretical approaches to the analysis of these issues.

B. Production

Productive activity is at the center of any economy. Agriculture, mining, and manufacturing are the bases upon which domestic and international commerce, finance, and other services rest. No society can survive without producing. Production is thus crucial to both domestic and international political economies.

In the international arena, production abroad by large corporations has gained enormously in importance since World War I. However, the establishment of productive facilities in foreign lands is nothing new; the planters who settled the southern portion of the Thirteen Colonies under contract to, and financed by, British merchant companies were engaging in foreign direct investment in plantation agriculture. Before the twentieth century, indeed, foreign investment in primary production—mining and agriculture—was quite common. European and North American investors financed copper mines in Chile and Mexico, tea and rubber plantations in India and Indochina, and gold mines in South Africa and Australia.

Around the turn of the century, and especially after World War I, a relatively novel form of foreign direct investment arose: the establishment of overseas branch factories of manufacturing corporations. In its origin, the phenomenon was largely North American, and it remained so until the 1960s when European and then Japanese manufacturers also began investing in productive facilities abroad. These internationalized industrial firms were called multinational or transnational corporations or enterprises (MNCs, MNEs, TNCs, or TNEs), usually defined as firms with productive facilities in three or more countries. Such corporations have been extraordinarily controversial for both scholars and politicians. There are about sixteen thousand MNCs in the world. Most are relatively small, but the top several hundred are so huge, and so globe-straddling, as to dominate major portions of the world economy. It has in fact been estimated that the 350 largest MNCs in the world, with over twenty-five thousand affiliates, account for 28 percent of the non-Communist world's output. The largest MNCs have annual sales larger than the gross national product of all but a few of the world's nations.[1]

One major analytical task is to explain the very existence of multinational manufacturing corporations. It is, of course, simple to understand why English investors would finance tea plantations in Ceylon—they could hardly have grown tea in Manchester. Yet, in the abstract, there is little logic in Bayer producing aspirin in the United States. If the German aspirin industry is more efficient than the American, Bayer could simply produce the pills in its factories at home and export them to the United States. Why, then, does Ford make cars in England, Volkswagen make cars in the United States, and both companies make cars in Mexico, instead of simply shipping them, respectively, across the Atlantic or the Rio Grande?

For the answer, students of the MNC have examined both economic and political factors. The political spurs to overseas direct investment are straightforward. Many countries maintain trade barriers in order to encourage local industrialization: this makes exporting to these nations difficult, and MNCs choose to "jump trade barriers" and produce inside protected markets. Similar considerations apply where the local government uses such policies as "buy American" regulations, which favor domestic products in government purchases, or where, as in the case of Japanese auto investment in the United States, overseas producers fear the onset of protectionist measures.

Economic factors in the spread of MNCs are many and complex. The simplest explanation is that foreign direct investment moves capital from more developed regions where capital is abundant and cheap to less developed nations where capital is scarce and expensive. This captures some of the story, but leaves much unexplained. Why, for example, does this transfer of capital not take the form of foreign lending rather than the much more complex form of foreign direct investment? And why is most foreign direct investment *among* developed countries with similar endowments of capital rather than between developed and developing nations?

Characteristics of multinational corporations associated with their size have often been put forth as explanations of foreign direct investment. Because MNCs are very large in comparison to local firms in most countries, they can mobilize large amounts of capital more easily than local enterprises. Foreign corporations may then, simply by virtue of their vast wealth, buy up local firms in order to eliminate competitors. In some lines of business, such as large-scale appliances or automobiles, the initial investment necessary to begin production may be prohibitive for local firms, giving MNCs a decisive advantage. Similarly, MNC access to many different currencies from the many markets in which these enterprises operate may give them a competitive advantage over firms doing business in only one nation and currency. And the widespread popularity of consumption patterns formed in North America and Western Europe and then transplanted to other nations—a process which often leads to charges of "cultural imperialism"—may lead local consumers to prefer foreign brand names to local ones: much of the Third World brushes with Colgate and drinks Coke, brands popularized by American literature, cinema, television, and advertising. Although these points may be accurate, however, they do not amount to a systematic explanation of foreign direct investment.

The first step in the search for a more rigorous explanation of foreign direct investment was the "product-cycle theory" developed by Raymond Vernon. Vernon pointed out that products manufactured by MNCs typically follow similar patterns or cycles. The firms begin by introducing new products which they manufacture and sell at home; over time, they expand exports to foreign markets; as the product becomes more widely known, they eventually engage in foreign investment; finally, as production of the good is standardized, they begin exporting back to the home market. This jibes with observations that MNCs tend to operate in oligopolistic markets with products that have a great deal of embodied new technology, and that MNCs tend to have important previous exporting experience.

The product cycle did not answer all the economic questions, however. For most neo-classical economists there was still no explanation of why firms would invest abroad instead of simply exporting from their presumably more congenial home base, or licensing the production technology, trademark, or other distinguishing market advantage to local producers. In the past twenty years, most economists have come to regard the multinational corporation as a special case of the vertically or horizontally integrated corporation. In this view, large companies come to organize certain activities inside the firm rather than through the marketplace because some transactions are difficult to carry out by normal market means. especially where prices are hard to calculate or contracts are hard to enforce. Applied to MNCs, this approach suggests that foreign direct investment takes place because the firms involved have access to unique technologies, managerial skills, or marketing expertise that it is more profitable for them to maintain within the corporate network rather than sell on the open market. In Reading 8, neo-classical economist Richard Caves surveys the modern economic theories of MNCs.

If the origins of MNCs are analytically controversial, their effects are debated with even more ferocity. In the 1950s and 1960s, as American-based corporations expanded rapidly into Western Europe, protests about foreigners buying up the European economies were common. Most Americans regarded these protests as signs of retrograde nationalism, for Americans have traditionally taken MNCs for granted. Few even realize that such firms as Shell, Bayer, Saks Fifth Avenue, Nestle, CBS Records, and Firestone Tires are foreign-owned.

However, as investment in the United States by firms from the rest of the world has grown, a significant body of thought has arisen to argue that this development represents a threat to American control over the US economy. Readings 13 and 14, by Thomas Omestad and Mack Ott respectively, present two contending views on the issue; Omestad is deeply concerned about what he sees as a danger to American sovereignty, while Ott sees little or no risk at all in allowing foreign firms free access to American assets.

Although foreign direct investment is controversial in the developed countries, it is far more contentious in the Third World. Developed nations, after all, have technically advanced regulatory agencies and relatively large economies, while most less developed countries (LDCs) have economies smaller that the largest MNCs, and the regulatory bureaucracies of many LDC governments are no match for MNC executives. In many LDCs, then, the very presence of MNCs is viewed with suspicion. MNCs have been known to interfere in local politics, and the competition huge foreign enterprises present to local businesspeople is often resented. Over the years many LDCs have imposed stringent regulations on foreign direct investors, although most of them continue to believe that on balance MNCs have a beneficial impact on national economic and political development. In the section that follows, the articles by Sayre Schatz and Richard Newfarmer (readings 11 and 12) evaluate the arguments in favor of and opposed to multinational corporations.

The rise of enormous business corporations whose activities span many nations is also a fact of great interest to analysts of world politics. Yet scholars disagree over the independent importance of MNCs. For many, especially those associated with

Realist schools of thought, MNCs are not so much a new, independent political and economic force as they are adjuncts to home or host countries' more general national goals. Nation states continue to have significant bargaining advantages over multinational corporations, especially the ability to deny corporations access to national territory. Realist Stephen Krasner (Reading 10) asserts that even the relatively weak states of the Third World have been successful in forcing MNCs to bend to state interests and goals.

For others, especially those with a Liberal perspective and some Marxists, MNCs have begun to surpass the power of individual nation-states. The concentrated economic power of the MNCs and their ability to move rapidly from nation to nation leaves states nearly powerless to control them. For Liberals, the increased integration of national markets is a major spur to global economic efficiency and governments should refrain from interfering in this process. Along these lines, Walter Wriston, one of America's corporate leaders, argues in Reading 9 that MNCs are remaking the world and that attempts to stand in their way are both futile and misguided.

Multinational corporations will in the view of some lead to a new era in world politics, making national distinctions unimportant. For others, MNCs are simply one more tool in the hands of still-powerful nation-states. Whether the truth lies with one or another view or somewhere in between, there is little doubt that MNCs will remain an important topic in the study of the international political economy, as well as a live issue in domestic and world politics.

NOTE

1. United Nations Centre on Transnational Corporations, *Transnational Corporations in World Development: Third Survey* (New York: UN, 1983), p. 46.

8

The Multinational Enterprise as an Economic Organization

RICHARD E. CAVES

This neo-classical economist provides a survey of economic explanations of the multinational enterprise (MNE). He focuses on how certain circumstances can make it difficult to carry out transactions in the marketplace. These include conditions in which it is hard to measure or establish a "fair" price for an asset, such as a new technology or managerial expertise. In these circumstances, firms, including MNEs, can overcome the problems of market transactions involving such hard-to-price assets by carrying out the transactions internally, within the corporation. This reading presents the predominant economic explanation for the rise and existence of MNEs.

The multinational enterprise (MNE) is defined here as an enterprise that controls and manages production establishments—plants—located in at least two countries. It is simply one subspecies of multiplant firm. We use the term "enterprise" rather than "company" to direct attention to the top level of coordination in the hierarchy of business decisions; a company, itself multinational, may be the controlled subsidiary of another firm. The minimum overseas "plant" needed to make an enterprise multinational is, as we shall see, judgmental. The transition from an overseas sales subsidiary or a technology licensee to a producing subsidiary is not always clear cut, for good economic reasons. What constitutes "control" over a foreign establishment is another judgmental issue. Not infrequently a MNE will hold a minor fraction of the equity of a foreign affiliate, and we shall see that what

---

8 "The Multinational Enterprise as an Economic Organization" by Richard E. Caves. From "The Multinational Enterprise as an Economic Organization" by R.E. Caves in *Multinational Enterprise and Economic Growth.*

fraction of equity a parent holds in its foreign subsidiary is itself an economic decision. Countries differ in regard to the minimum percentage of equity ownership that they count as a "direct investment" abroad, as distinguished from a "portfolio investment," in their international-payments statistics.

The purpose of this study is not to sort the MNEs from the national firms in the world's enterprises. However, the definition does have the valuable function of identifying the MNE as essentially a multi-plant firm. We are back to Coase's classic question of why the boundary between the administrative allocation of resources within the firm and the market allocation of resources between firms falls where it does. In the environment of a market economy, entrepreneurs are free to try their hand at displacing market transactions by increasing the scope of transactions handled administratively within their firms. In the Darwinian tradition we expect that the most profitable pattern of enterprise organization will ultimately prevail: Where more profit results from placing plants under a common administrative control, multiplant enterprises will predominate, and single-plant firms will merge or go out of business. In order to explain the existence and prevalence of MNEs, we require models that predict where the multiplant firm enjoys "transactional" advantages from displacing the arm's-length market and where it does not. In fact, the prevalence of multiplant (multinational) enterprises varies greatly from sector to sector and from country to country, affording a ready opportunity to test any models of the MNE that we develop.

The models of the multiplant firm potentially relevant to explaining the presence of MNEs are quite numerous and rather disparate in their concerns. It proves convenient to divide them into three groups: (1) One type of multiplant firm turns out essentially the same line of goods from its plants in each geographic market. Such firms are common in U.S. domestic industries such as metal containers, bakeries, and brewing. Similarly, many MNEs establish plants in different countries to make the same or similar goods. We refer to these firms as horizontally integrated. (2) Another type of multiplant enterprise produces outputs in some of its plants that serve as inputs to other of its plants. We then describe the firm as vertically integrated. Vertically integrated firms, MNE or domestic, may make physical transfers of intermediate products from one of their plants to another, but that practice is not required by our definition; they need only be producing at adjacent stages of a vertically related set of production processes. (3) The third type of multiplant firm is the diversified company whose plants' outputs are neither vertically nor horizontally related to one another. As an international firm, we refer to it as a diversified MNE.

HORIZONTAL MULTIPLANT ENTERPRISES AND THE MNE

We start by equating the horizontal MNE to a multiplant firm with plants in different countries. Its existence requires, first, that *locational forces* justify spreading the world's production around so that plants are found in different national markets.

Given this dispersion of production, there must be some *transactional advantage to* placing the plants (some plants, at least) under common administrative control. This is the abstract, static approach that provides the most general and most satisfying avenue to explaining the multinational company. . . . We assume at first that plant A was located in southeast England because that was the lowest-cost way to serve the market it in fact serves. We also assume that this locational choice was not essentially influenced by whether the plant was built by an MNE, bought by an MNE, or not owned by an MNE at all. The static approach also puts aside the vital question of why a company grows into MNE status—something we can explain much better once the static model is in hand.

The transactional approach asserts, quite simply, that horizontal MNEs will exist only if the plants they control and operate attain lower costs or higher revenue productivity than if the plants function under separate managements. Why should this net-revenue advantage arise? Some of the reasons have to do with minimizing costs of production and closely associated logistical activities of the firm. The more analytically interesting reasons—and, we shall see, surely the more important ones empirically—concern the complementary nonproduction activities of the firm.

Intangible Assets

The concept that has proved most fruitful for explaining the nonproduction bases for the MNE is that of intangible assets belonging to the firm. Successful firms in most industries possess one or more types of intangible assets. An asset may represent technology—knowledge about how to produce a cheaper or better product at given input prices, or how to produce a given product at a lower cost than competing firms. This intangible asset might take the specific form of a patented process or design, or it might simply rest on know-how shared among employees of the firm. Or the intangible might take the form of a marketing asset. The firm may possess special skills in styling or promoting its product that make it such that the buyer can distinguish it from those of competitors. Such an asset has a revenue productivity for the firm because it signifies the willingness of some buyers to pay more for that firm's product than for an otherwise comparable variety of the same good that lacks this particular touch. Assets of this type are closely akin to product differentiation, a market condition in which the distinctive features of various sellers' outputs cause each competing firm to face its own downward-sloping demand curve. Once again, the intangible asset may take the form of a specific property—a registered trademark or brand—or it may rest in marketing and selling skills shared among the firm's employees. Finally, the distinctiveness of the firm's marketing-oriented assets may rest with the firm's ability to come up with frequent innovations; its intangible asset then may be a patented novelty, or simply some new combination of attributes that its rivals cannot quickly or effectively imitate.

An intangible asset yields a rent to the time and makes the firm appear successful. But why should that cause it to be multiplant and multinational? The answer lies in the problems of market failure associated with arm's-length transactions in intangible assets. These failures deter a successful one-plant firm from selling or renting its intangible assets to other single-plant firms and thereby foster the existence of multiplant (and multinational) firms. Intangible assets are subject to a daunting list of infirmities for being put to efficient use by conventional markets:

1. They are, at least to some degree, *public goods*. Once a piece of knowledge has been developed and applied at a certain location, it can be put to work elsewhere at little extra cost and without reducing the "amount" of the idea available at the original site. From society's point of view, the marginal conditions for efficient allocation of resources then require that the price of the intangible asset be equal to its marginal cost, zero or approximately zero. But no one gets rich selling his bright ideas for zero. Therefore, intangible assets tend to be underprovided or to be priced inefficiently (at a net price exceeding their marginal cost) or both.
2. Transactions in intangibles suffer from *impactedness* combined with *opportunism*. This problem is best explained by examples: I have a piece of knowledge that I know will be valuable to you. I try to convince you of this value by describing its general nature and character. But 1 do not reveal the details, because then the cat would be out of the bag, and you would be free to use the knowledge without paying for it. But you therefore decline to pay me as much as the knowledge would in fact be worth to you, because you suspect that I am opportunistic and overstate my claims. With these conditions present, I cannot collect in an arm's-length transaction the full net-revenue productivity of my knowledge. I will underinvest in the knowledge, or I may try to earn the most I can from what knowledge I do acquire by putting it to work myself.
3. An element amplifying the problem of impactedness is *uncertainty*. If the knowledge were the recipe for a truly superb chocolate cake, I could bring about an efficient arm's-length transaction by letting you taste the cake and guaranteeing that (once you have bought the recipe and executed it properly) yours will taste just as good. Conversely, if neither of us can predict accurately how well the knowledge will perform when you use it, and if we are both risk averse, too small a volume of transactions will take place in the intangible knowledge.

Consider what these propositions imply for the MNE: There are seven soap factories in seven countries—each an independent firm One discovers a way to make its product especially attractive to buyers at little added cost, and its rivals, by assumption, cannot imitate the innovation simply by copying it. The innovator could license its discovery to the other six firms, but would (for reasons set forth earlier) probably be able to collect less than the full net-revenue productivity. It could expand its output and export to the other six markets, but that would incur excessive transportation costs if the plants were all efficiently located at the start (as we assume). The most profitable solution for the seven plants (firms) jointly is to band together into one MNE in order to share the intangible asset. This analysis generates the empirical prediction that we should find a greater incidence of MNEs in industries where intangible assets are important. Tests of the proposition will be reviewed later. . . .

Scale Economies and Cost Minimization

The theory of multiplant operation—has also indicated a number of economies more directly relating to the firm's production activities, and these could apply to the MNE if they do not stop at the national boundary. There may be transactional economies in the procurement of raw materials that go beyond the input needs of the single plant. Economies may arise in the transportation network for outbound shipments of finished goods that extend beyond the single plant's output. Localized demand fluctuations may call for pooling plants' capacities so that several plants' outputs can be flexibly shipped wherever the peak demand is occurring. If the industry's output consists of a line of goods, it may be efficient for each plant to specialize in some items rather than for each to turn out the whole array. It is an empirical question how fully these economies are available to a multiplant firm operating across national boundaries, because they depend on the free movement of goods (inputs or outputs) among plants or the common use of managerial resources. But the hypothesis is there to be tested.

Empirical Evidence

These hypotheses about horizontal MNEs have received rather extensive statistical testing. The usual strategy of research involves correlating the prevalence of MNEs in an industry with structural traits of that industry: If attribute x promotes the formation of MNEs, and successful firms in industry A have a lot of x, then MNEs should be prevalent in industry A. One can analyze the shares of sales held by foreign subsidiaries in a national market such as Canada or the United Kingdom to determine whether or not high shares occur in industries marked by the traits that should give rise to MNEs. One can perform the same exercise by examining interindustry differences in the relative sizes of foreign assets held by companies based in the various manufacturing industries of the United States or Sweden. One can compare the activities of national companies to those of MNEs. Let us summarize the conclusions that have emerged from these studies.

The presence of intangible assets as an encouragement to foreign investment has been affirmed in many studies. Although intangible assets by their nature resist any direct measurement, their prevalence is revealed by the outlays that companies make for the purpose of producing them. As indicators of these assets, economists have seized on the outlays for advertising and research and development (R&D) undertaken by firms classified to an industry. That the share of the foreign-subsidiary assets in the total assets of U.S. corporations increases significantly with the importance of advertising and R&D outlays in the industry has been confirmed statistically in many studies. . . . [T]he influence of advertising appears most strongly in the food and chemicals sectors (the latter includes pharmaceuticals, soaps and detergents, and some other consumer goods), whereas the influence of the industry's research intensity appears strongest in the machinery sectors. This pattern closely matches one's sense of the apparent importance of different sorts of intangible assets in those industries. . . .

Other statistical investigations have dealt with inflows of foreign investment to countries such as Canada and the United Kingdom. Once again, R&D and advertising levels, especially when measured in the United States—the principal source country for the foreign investors—are significantly related to the shares of the local market held by the subsidiaries. . . .

Although horizontal manufacturing investments have held the attention of researchers, horizontal MNEs have expanded vigorously in banking and other services as well. The descriptive literature indicates that the intangible-assets hypothesis again makes a good showing—especially when expanded to take in an ongoing selling contractual relationship between the service enterprise and the nonfinancial MNE with which it does business. A bank, advertising agency, or accounting firm acquires a good deal of specific knowledge about its client's business, and the two firms may sustain an ongoing relation based on trust that lowers the cost of contracting and the risks of opportunistic behavior. If the service firm has such a quasi-contractual relation with a parent MNE, it enjoys a transactional advantage for supplying the same service to the MNE's foreign subsidiaries. But the service must be supplied locally, and so the service firm goes multinational to follow its customers.

Much casual evidence reveals this intangible asset of a quasi-contractual customer relation behind service industries' foreign investments. The banking sector's case is particularly well documented. Grubel affirmed the transactional model but also pointed to two other factors. Some banks may acquire particular product-differentiating skills analogous to those found in some goods-producing industries; although these cut little ice in most banking markets, they may explain banks' foreign investments in less-developed countries. Also, national banking markets often appear somewhat noncompetitive because of cartelization or regulation or both, and foreign banks are well-equipped potential entrants. The Eurocurrency markets can be largely explained on this basis. The traits of foreign banks' operations in the United States affirm these propositions. Their assets include proportionally more commercial and industrial loans than those of their domestic competitors, reflecting the primacy of business with their foreign-MNE customers. As they age, they develop other business from this base—drumming up other loan and deposit customers, undertaking large interbank transactions to balance their foreign parents' dollar positions.

Dynamics of the MNE

The transactional approach to the MNE has the advantage that it can explain the dynamic course of development of the firm over time, as well as the prevalence of

MNEs at a given time—the approach we have explored thus far. If the MNE can sometimes seize an advantage to displace a market and reduce transactions costs, the firm itself faces costs of securing information and arranging transactions that shape its behavior. Here we shall set forth some propositions that arise from this fact. . . .

The dynamic transactional approach first makes an elementary point about why MNEs are not ubiquitous. Each person is normally a citizen of some particular country and brings to his business a general knowledge of the legal and social system, the "ways of doing things," peculiar to that nation. The business firm, unless already a mature MNE, has a clear-cut national base and identity, with its internal planning and decision making carried out in the context of that nation's legal and cultural framework. When the entrepreneurial unit extends itself to found or acquire subsidiaries in foreign lands, it must incur a fixed transactions cost of learning how things are done abroad. If it sends home-office personnel to run and develop the subsidiary, they will (for a time, at least) be less effective than at home for this reason. Foreign nationals can be hired to run the shop, but then a similar fixed cost must be incurred to teach them the firm's way of doing things. Either choice leaves the potential MNE facing a virtual disadvantage in the foreign market with respect to its local competitors, who are steeped in their social and cultural milieu and need incur no such fixed transactions cost. The transactional advantages of the MNE are necessary to get it over this intrinsic transactional disadvantage.

The transactional approach also implies that intangible assets are developed by firms in some national market. These assets influence a series of investment decisions taken over time by successful firms, including decisions to begin and expand foreign investments. The approach helps to predict how these decisions will be made. First, the firm that comes to possess some rent yielding skill or intangible asset cannot overnight undertake all the profitable projects it can find utilizing that asset. Various constraints limit the firm's growth, because there is a limit to how rapidly it can expand its management cadre and its equity-capital base. The firm ponders various strategies for using its distinctive assets so as to maximize the expected present value of its future profits. Suppose that its decisive advantage over (at least some of) its rivals becomes clear when it is a single-nation firm holding 10 percent of its national market. For its next big investment, does it expand into foreign markets, or does it go for another 10 percent of the domestic market? The answer could go either way, but information costs do create a bias toward continuing domestic expansion. This is "more of the same" and does not require the firm to incur new information and search costs associated with going abroad.

If fortune continues to smile on the firm and its share of the domestic market grows, the marginal returns to additional expansion there eventually decline. Given the elasticity of the market demand curve, the higher our expanding firm's market share, the lower the demand elasticity that it perceives. Also, its increasing market share comes at the cost of dislodging stronger and stronger competitors. Expanding to serve overseas markets becomes more and more attractive.

Once investments abroad rise to the top of the list of profitable investments for the firm, the choice of destination should be affected by information costs as they vary among foreign destinations. The first overseas investment is likely to be made in the national market where the entrepreneur faces the least disadvantage of language and culture.

The empirical evidence on patterns of expansion by multinational firms strongly supports these propositions. Horst compared firms within industries to see what traits discriminate between those that go abroad and those not yet holding MNE status. The only significant difference he found was in the size (market share) they had already attained in the domestic market. This result supports the hypothesis that the successful firm runs out its successes in the domestic market before incurring the transactions costs of going abroad. Another strong pattern of evidence bears on the countries that firms pick for their first ventures abroad. For example, U.S. firms tend strongly to make Canada the first stop. Evidence . . . shows that each source country's MNEs pick their debut foreign markets so as to minimize the information and transactions costs associated with foreign investment. The new MNE can easily accommodate to the familiar environment while it is learning the ropes—acquiring knowledge that reduces the cost (or risk) of future expansions into more alien terrain. And its intangible assets provide it with some offsetting advantages at the earliest stages. It can work its plant at designed capacity sooner than a comparable independent firm, and a product innovation borrowed from its parent involves fewer shakedown difficulties for the subsidiary.

VERTICALLY INTEGRATED MNES

It is now an easy step to identify the vertically integrated MNE as simply a species of vertically integrated firm whose production units lie in different nations. Our quest for models to explain the vertically integrated multinational immediately turns to the economic analysis of vertically integrated firms. Again, we suppose that production units are placed around the world according to conventional locational pressures—the bauxite mine where the bauxite is, the smelter that converts alumina into aluminum near a source of low-cost electric power. The question is, why do they come under common administrative control?

Until recent years the economic theory of vertical integration contained only a small and unsatisfying inventory of models. Some dealt with the physical integration of production processes: If you make structural shapes out of the metal ingot before it cools, you need not incur the cost of reheating it. Such gains from physical integration explain why sequential processes ale grouped in a single plant, but they hardly explain the common ownership of far-flung plants. The other group of traditional models proposed that vertical integration might be preferable to a stalemate between a monopolistic seller and a monopsonistic buyer. The deduction is reasonable enough, but it hardly explains vertical integration in the many markets that do not represent bilateral monopoly (even if they are less than purely competitive).

Transactional Explanations of Vertical Integration

The great source of enrichment to the theory of vertical integration has been a transactional approach of the same genus we employed to explain horizontal MNEs. Vertical integration occurs, the argument goes, because the parties prefer it to the contracting costs and uncertainties that would mar the alternative state of arm's-length transactions. The vertically integrated firm internalizes a market for an intermediate product, just as the horizontal MNE internalizes markets for intangible assets. Suppose that there were universal pure competition in each intermediate-product market, with large numbers of buyers and sellers, the product homogeneous (or its qualities readily evaluated by the parties), information about prices and availability in easy access to all parties in the market. Neither seller nor buyer would then have any reason (other than personal esteem) to maintain a long-term relation with any particular transactor on the other side of the market. When these assumptions no longer hold, however, both buyers and sellers acquire a variety of motives to make long-term alliances. To retain our emphasis on transactions costs, suppose that parties in the market incur a substantial fixed cost if they shift from one transactions partner to another. Each seller's product may be somewhat different, and the buyer incurs significant costs of testing or adapting to new varieties, or merely learning the requirements and organizational routines of new partners. The buyer and seller have an incentive to enter into some kind of long-term arrangement.

If buyers and sellers are still numerous, however, why should these switching costs impair the operation of a competitive market? The disappointed transactions partner can always switch in the long run. Why does that consideration not keep everyone honest? The answer is that under plausible assumptions it can pay to be opportunistic and try to improve one's deal with an ongoing transactions partner. If everyone knows this, there is an incentive to enter into long-term contracts with terms fully specified in advance so as to avoid any uncertainty and entrapment.

But that effort bumps into another problem with arm's-length vertical relations. Suppose the parties sit down to work out a contract that specifies how each will behave under all possible contingencies and provides policing and enforcement mechanisms that avert the problem of opportunism. Well and good, but the bargaining sessions may be prolonged indeed. The alternative to the uncertainty about how one will fare in an ongoing bargain is the high cost of negotiating in advance a contract that will anticipate every uncertainty and close every loophole. Careful definition of the agreement in advance bargaining saves on the costs of monitoring the agreement and haggling over unexpected developments after it is signed, of course, but only at the expense of greater negotiation costs. There is, as usual, no free lunch.

Internalizing the market through vertical integration at that point becomes an attractive option. Although internal coordination of a vertically related MNE is not without its costs and strains on managerial capacity, it does allow adapting to the flow of events without concern for who benefits more.

To summarize this somewhat complex argument, intermediate-product markets can be organized in a spectrum of ways stretching from anonymous spot market transactions through a variety of long-term contractual arrangements at arm's length to vertical integration. Switching costs and durable, specific assets discourage spot transactions and favor one of the other modes. If, in addition the costs of negotiating and monitoring arm's-length contracts are high, the choice falls on vertical integration. These are the empirical predictions of the "transactions" approach to vertical integration.

One other aspect of the theory of vertical integration holds promise for explaining MNEs of this type. Vertical integration can occur because of failings in markets for information, as analyzed earlier in the context of intangible assets. A processing firm must plan its capacity on some assumption about the future price and availability of its key raw material. The producers of that raw material have the cheapest access (and perhaps exclusive access) to that information. But they may have an incentive not to reveal it accurately to the prospective customer; the more capacity those customers can be induced to build, the higher the price they are likely to bid in the future for any given quantity of the raw material. Therefore, vertical integration may occur in order to get around impacted information coupled with opportunism.

Empirical Evidence

The available literature testing these hypotheses has included far fewer statistical studies than has the literature concerned with horizontal MNEs. . . .

A great deal of information exists on individual extractive industries in which MNEs operate on a worldwide basis, and this case-study evidence merits a glance in lieu of more systematic findings. For example, Stuckey found the international aluminum industry to contain not only MNEs integrated from the mining of bauxite through the fabrication of aluminum projects but also a network of long-term contracts and joint ventures. All of these indicate a general unwillingness of market participants to settle for spot transactions in bauxite (the raw ore) and alumina (output of the first processing stage). Stuckey likewise did not assign much importance to the small number of market participants worldwide. Rather, the problem is that switching costs are extremely high. That is, alumina refining facilities need to be located physically close to bauxite mines (to minimize transportation costs), and they are constructed to deal with the properties of specific ores. Likewise, for technical and transportation-cost reasons, aluminum smelters are somewhat tied to particular sources of alumina. Therefore, arm's-length markets tend to be poisoned by the problems of small numbers and switching costs. And the very large specific and durable investments in facilities also invoke the problems of long-term contracts that were identified earlier. . . .

A good deal of evidence on vertical integration also appears in the vast and contentious literature on the oil industry. The more ambitious investigations of vertical integration have addressed the U.S. segment of the industry, but there appears to be no central difference between the forces traditionally affecting vertical integration in national and international oil companies. These studies give considerable emphasis to the risks faced by any nonintegrated firm in petroleum extraction or refining. Refineries normally operate at capacity and require a constant flow of crude-oil input. Storing large inventories of input is quite costly, and so backward integration that reduces uncertainly about crude supplies can save the refiner a large investment in storage capacity. It also reduces risks in times of "shortages" and "rationing," when constraints somewhere in the integrated system (crude-oil supplies are only the most familiar constraint) can leave the unintegrated firm out in the cold. . . .

Finally, country-based studies of the foreign-investment process have also underlined vertical MNEs as the outcome of failed arm's-length market transactions. Japanese companies have tended to become involved with extractive foreign investments only after the experience of having arm's-length suppliers renege on long-term contracts, and they have also experimented with low-interest loans to independent foreign suppliers as a way to establish commitment.

Vertical Integration: Other Manifestations

The identification of vertically integrated foreign investment with extractive activities is traditional and no doubt faithful to the pattern accounting for the bulk of MNE assets. However, it gives too narrow an impression of the role of vertically subdivided transactions in MNEs.

First of all, it neglects a form of backward integration that depends not on natural resources but on subdividing production processes and placing abroad those that are both labor-intensive and footloose. For example, semiconductors may be produced by capital-intensive processes and assembled into electronic equipment by similarly mechanized processes both undertaken in the United States. But, in between, wires must be soldered to the semiconductors by means of a labor-intensive technology. Because shipping costs for the devices are low relative to their value, it pays to carry out the labor-intensive stage in a low-wage country. The relationship of the enterprises performing these functions in the United States and abroad must obviously be a close one, involving either detailed contractual arrangements or common ownership. This subdivision of production processes should occur through foreign investment to an extent that depends again on the transactional bases for vertical integration. Some theoretical models have suggested that this type of vertical dis-integration proceeds as an industry enlarges, permitting real gains from an expanded division of labor as more and more separable processes are carried out by firms specializing in them. The model probably is applicable to the type of foreign investment just described. The gains from an expanded division of labor. . . may depend on the geographical dispersion of production processes to specialized establishments and may have little to do with the form of transactions between the specialized establishments (spot, contract, or vertical MNE relationships).

Writers on the rapid expansion of offshore procurement and the associated international trade always refer to the role of foreign investment in transplanting the necessary know-how and managerial coordination. Jarrett has explored statistically both the structural determinants of this type of trade and the role of MNEs in carrying it out. His data pertain to imports under a provision of the U.S. tariff whereby components exported from the United States for additional fabrication abroad can be reimported with duty paid only on the value added abroad; his statistical analysis addresses both the total value of imports of such articles and the value added abroad. Furthermore, the analysis explains how these activities vary both among U.S. industries and among countries taking part in this trade. His results confirm the expected properties of the industries that make use of vertically disintegrated production: Their outputs have high value per unit of weight, possess reasonably mature technology (so are out of the experimental stage), are produced in the United States under conditions giving rise to high labor costs, and are easily subject to decentralized production. Among overseas countries, U.S. offshore procurement favors those not too far distant (transportation costs) and with low wages and favorable working conditions. With these factors controlled, there is a positive relation of the component flows to the extent of U.S. foreign investment, both among industries and among foreign countries.

A considerable amount of vertical integration is also involved in the "horizontal" foreign investments described earlier in this chapter, and we shall see that the behavior of horizontal MNEs cannot be fully understood without recognizing the complementary vertical aspects of their domestic and foreign operations. Often the foreign subsidiary does not just produce the parent's good for the local market; it processes semifinished units of that good, or it packages or assembles them according to local specifications. Pharmaceuticals, for example, are prepared in the locally desired formulations using basic preparations imported from the parent. The subsidiary organizes a distribution system in the host-country market, distributing partly its own production, but with its line of goods filled out with imports from its parent or other affiliates. Or the subsidiary integrates forward to provide local servicing facilities of information and customer service. These activities are bound up with the development and maintenance of the enterprise's goodwill asset, as described earlier, through a commitment of resources to the local market. The firm can thereby assure local customers, who are likely to incur fixed investments of their own in shifting their purchases to the MNE, that the company's presence is not transitory; because the MNE has sunk some costs locally, it will continue even in the face of some adverse disturbances. This consideration helps explain foreign investment in some producer-goods industries for which the intangible-assets hypothesis otherwise seems rather dubious. All of these activities represent types of forward integration by the MNE, whether into final-stage processing of its goods or into ancillary services.

The evidence of this confluence of vertical and horizontal foreign investments mainly takes the form of casual descriptions rather than systematic data. . . . It is implied by the available data on the extent of intracorporate trade among MNE affiliates—flows that would be incompatible with purely horizontal forms of intracorporate relationships. We can, for example, turn to data on imports of finished goods by Dutch subsidiaries from their U.S. parents. These were high as percentages of the affiliates' total sales in just those sectors where imports might complement local production for filling out a sales line—chemicals (24.9 percent), electrical equipment (35.4 percent), and transportation equipment (65.5 percent). The prevalence of intracorporate trade in engineering industries also suggests the importance of components shipments.

Recently, some statistical evidence has appeared on U.S. exports and imports passing between corporate affiliates that sheds light on this mixture of vertical and horizontal foreign investment. Lall analyzed the factors determining the extent of U.S. MNEs' exports to their affiliates (normalized either by their total exports or by their affiliates' total production). He could not discriminate between two hypotheses, although he concluded that they jointly have significant force: (1) that trade is internalized where highly innovative and specialized goods are involved and (2) that trade is internalized where the ultimate sales to final buyers must be attended by extensive customer engineering and after-sales services. Jarret confirmed these hypotheses with respect to the importance in U.S. imports of the interaffiliate component, which in his data includes exports by foreign MNEs to their manufacturing and marketing subsidiaries in the United States as well as imports by U.S. MNEs from their overseas affiliates. Jarrett also found evidence that interaffiliate trade in manufactures reflects several conventional forms of vertical integration: More of it occurs in industries populated (in the United States) by large plants and companies, capable of meeting the scale-economy problems that arise in the international dis-integration of production, and in industries that carry out extensive multiplant operations in the United States. . . .

PORTFOLIO DIVERSIFICATION AND THE DIVERSIFIED MNE

The formal purpose of this section is to complete the roster of international multiplant firms by accounting for those whose international plants have neither a horizontal nor a vertical relationship. An obvious explanation of this type of MNE (though not the only one, it turns out) lies in the goal of spreading business risks. Going multinational in any form brings some diversification gains to the enterprise, and these reach their maximum when the firm diversifies across "product space" as well as geographical space.

The hypothesis that companies act to avoid risks may seem obvious, but it requires some explanation. The risk-averse investor generally must choose between investments involving greater risks and higher expected returns and those involving lesser risks and lower expected returns (somebody else has already seized any high-return low-risk options). Because foreign investment itself usually is supposed to be a risky activity, the risk-averse business would be expected to avoid it. However, that conjecture neglects the process of diversification. Pool the cash-flow streams from two risky projects, and the uncertainty of the combined stream is almost always less than the uncertainty of either stream separately. the reduction demands only that the expected returns of the two projects be imperfectly correlated: Among various possible states of nature, *A* and *B* do not always have their ups and downs at the same time. *A* has the greatest diversification value for *B* if *A*'s ups coincide with *B's* downs and vice versa, but some diversification is achieved whenever they are not perfectly correlated. As an explanation of MNEs, this analysis suggests quite simply that the risk-averse corporation may find that plants operated in different countries offer good prospects for diversification . . .

Now we can assess diversification as a motive for the MNE. Within national economies, many shocks affect all firms rather similarly—recessions, major changes in government policy. Between countries, such disturbances are more nearly uncorrelated, creating opportunities for international diversification. Also, changes in exchange rates and terms of trade tend to favor business profits in one country while worsening them elsewhere. Statistical evidence confirms that MNEs enjoy diversification gains: The larger the share of foreign operations in total sales, the lower the variability of the firm's rate of return on equity capital. . . . .

None of this evidence, it should be stressed, directly affirms the hypothesis that diversified foreign investment has a premium value for risk spreading. However, risk spreading is not inconsistent with any of the positive influences on diversified foreign investment that have been uncovered. And those influences account for only a small proportion of the observed diversified foreign investment, leaving plenty of room for risk spreading, and other influences yet unidentified.

SUMMARY

The existence of the MNE is best explained by identifying it as a multiplant firm that sprawls across national boundaries, then applying the transactional approach to explain why decentralized plants should fall under common ownership and control rather than simply trade with each other (and with other agents) on the open market. This approach is readily applied to the horizontal MNE (its national branches produce largely the same products), because the economies of multiplant operation can be identified with use of the firm's intangible assets, which suffer many infirmities for trade at arm's length. This hypothesis receives strong support in statistical studies, which also identify an influence of other "excess capacities" in the firm, such as managerial skills.

A second major type of MNE is the vertically integrated firm, and several economic models of vertical integration stand ready to explain its existence. Once again, the transactional approach holds a good deal of power, because vertical MNEs in the natural-resources sector seem to respond to the difficulties of working out arm's-length contracts in small-numbers situations where each party has a durable and specific investment at stake. Evading problems of impacted information also seems to explain some vertical foreign investment. The approach also works well to explain the rapid growth of offshore procurement by firms in industrial countries, which involves carrying out labor-intensive stages of production at low-wage foreign locations. Although some procurement occurs through arm's-length contracts rather than foreign investment, the foreign-investment proportion is clearly large. Finally, numerous vertical transactions flow between the members of apparently horizontal MNEs as the foreign subsidiary undertakes final fabrication, fills out its line with imports from its corporate affiliates, or provides ancillary services that complement these imports.

Diversified foreign investments, which have grown rapidly in recent decades, suggest the use of foreign investment as a means of spreading risks to the firm. Foreign investment, whether diversified from the parent's domestic product line or not, does apparently offer some diversification value. Diversified foreign investments can be explained in part by the parent's efforts to utilize its diverse R&D discoveries, and certain other influences as well. But the evidence at hand does not specifically tie diversified foreign investment to the corporate motive of spreading risks through diversification among both products and national markets.

9

Agents of Change Are Rarely Welcome

WALTER B. WRISTON

In this essay, Walter Wriston, former chairman and chief executive officer of Citibank, aggressively defends the multinational corporation (MNC) as a source of prosperity and positive change in the world economy. Every society, he argues, has been torn between two cultures: mercantilism, in which politics dominates business and impedes economic growth, and laissez-faire, or Liberalism, which holds that business is politically neutral and economically efficient. The current debate over the MNC, he suggests, is merely the extension of this cultural tension to the international arena. The opponents of MNCs, in his view, are retrograde forces, while the MNC itself is progressive, promising to make the most efficient possible use of the world's resources and raise the material well-being of the greatest number of people, regardless of which country they happen to be citizens of. Until the World War II, mercantilism reigned within the international economy, and it remains a powerful force today. Yet, Wriston concludes, MNCs have been making inroads upon the mercantilist world, improving welfare and winning supporters through the benefits they provide.

. . . The great global corporations of the world are now the principal agents for the peaceful transfer of technology and ideas from one part of the world to the other.

---

9 "Agents of Change Are Rarely Welcome" by Walter B. Wriston. From *Risk and Other Four-Letter Words* by Walter B. Wriston. Copyright © 1986 by Walter B. Wriston. Reprinted by permission of Harper & Row, Publishers, Inc.

Since no country has a monopoly on industrial and agricultural skills, this transfer of men, money, and ideas is necessary if we are to raise the world's living standards, but the perceptions of the needs of mankind are not uniform in the public and private sectors. As a general rule, the politicians have been engaged in fragmenting the world, while the multinational corporations have been viewing the planet as a single marketplace, and drawing peoples together in the process. The clash of these perceptions has understandably created a great deal of intellectual friction, which has been manifest in great outpourings of scholarly and not so scholarly attempts to clarify the issues between the public and the private sectors. We have witnessed lengthy debates about such weighty details as whether we should call a company multinational, transnational, international, supernational, or perhaps some other term in some other language. None of this rhetoric has been really useful. It is the kind of clarification that consists of filling in the background with so many details that the foreground sinks out of sight.

What has tended to be pushed from sight is the real nature of the choice confronting us. The arguments that use the world corporations as their focus are only a proxy for the real issue. The struggle for control of the future is not between national companies versus international, nor European companies versus American or Japanese, nor even the fashionable theme of the developed countries versus the developing, most recently styled as a north-south confrontation. The debate is really the continuation and intensification of the battle between two historic ideas concerning economic and social behavior.

One idea, associated with terms like "free trade" and "free enterprise" and "laissez-faire," holds that business is politically neutral, existing only to satisfy the economic desires of the world's people. The other, older idea holds that business is—or should be—the chosen instrument of the state; or, what amounts to the same thing, that the state should be the chosen instrument of business.

In order to draw any useful conclusions about the place of the world corporation in this dispute, it is necessary to set multinational enterprise in historical perspective. It is then possible to comprehend why our world corporations are so profoundly upsetting to so many people in and out of governments around the world.

Each of us in every country is the child of individual experience. The difficulty in communicating our value systems to one another is further complicated by the fact that the cultural histories of others do not have high priority in our national universities. In a word, we tend to be ignorant of other societies.

Despite the enormous advances in communication and the remarkable technology for instant transfer of visual images via satellite, we are still surprised and amazed when people in different parts of the world espouse value systems radically at variance with our own. It astonishes many Americans to find that some of the ideas of Colbert, the finance minister of Louis XIV, still appear to dominate a certain section of European thinking about trade and investment. The highly restrictive purchasing regulations in effect in many European countries stem from Colbert's dictum:

> All purchases must be made in France, rather than in foreign countries, even if the goods should be a little poorer and a little more expensive, because if the money does not go out of the realm, the advantage to the state is double.

In my own country, some of our Buy American laws were passed, unwittingly, under the influence of Colbert's dead hand.

To a European or to a Japanese, it is elemental that foreign trade is a country's lifeblood. Trade generates the revenue that sustains their governments. Foreign trade should inevitably be part of foreign policy. It comes as a shock to Americans, however, to discover that foreign ambassadors to the United States are helping to sell airplane engines, machine tools, or whatever their nationals need help in selling. At the same time, it is equally incomprehensible to Europeans, to Japanese, to Latin Americans, and to Africans that the United States Government takes a basically adversarial position toward business. Activities of American companies in foreign lands have long been regarded with great suspicion here at home. To Americans, foreign trade has until recently been a peripheral activity engaged in only in the event that the domestic market did not absorb our entire production. All these attitudes are deeply rooted in history and so will change only slowly. One consequence is the inherent unpopularity of the multinational corporation.

There are other, deeper roots for this hostility, however, which date back to medieval times. The first merchants, traders and moneylenders were motivated largely by profit considerations. Feudal barons, on the other hand, looked to military power for survival and expansion. As competition between feudal rulers increased, the merchants and traders began to associate themselves with the sovereign authorities to gain commercial advantage. In return for commercial favors, they financed the wars of competing sovereigns. Merchants bankrolled the Crusades. In return they got monopoly powers to trade in large areas of the known world. The fusion of the tradesman and the royal sovereign in the sixteenth and seventeenth centuries eventually became known as mercantilism, and all external business was conducted by the chosen instruments of the state. It is not surprising, therefore, that developing countries now believe that the navy always follows the traders; if, indeed, it does not precede them. In the mercantilist world, commerce and industry were viewed as what present-day mathematicians call a zero-sum game; profit for one side inevitably meant equal loss for the other. The reality that buyer and seller could both profit from the same transaction defied mercantilist logic. The truth that business is not a poker game which transfers a static pot of money from one player to another, that instead the game creates wealth for all players, was perceived only over many years, with painful slowness.

In the mercantilist world, nations vied for overseas territories in order to control their markets. Many countries set up monopolistic trading corporations to manage trade and supply all commodities to the colonists, whether natives or settlers. There were the Dutch East India Company, the English East India Company, the French

East India Company, the Hudson Bay Company and the Virginia Company. Since these companies made a profit, mercantilist dogma made it clear that exploitation of the colonists must be involved. Therefore, this practice of picking a commercial enterprise as a chosen instrument served to intensify the hostility against both the monopolistic companies and the metropolitan country that chartered them. In the American case, enmity generated by this commercial device was one of the precipitating causes of our Revolution . . . .

On the other side of the world, trade as exploitation also left its imprint. The Meiji restoration, dating from 1868, marked the beginning of the modern Japanese state. But even that enlightened restoration was based broadly on the concept that Japan could not withstand hated foreign encroachments unless its society was totally reorganized as an industrial power with great military strength. Japanese hatred of foreigners was not new; it dated back two centuries to the edict of 1636, which closed Japan to all foreigners, particularly Christians. That edict also forbade Japanese ships from sailing to foreign countries, prohibited Japanese from going abroad on penalty of death, and prescribed death to any Japanese who had lived abroad and tried to return to his homeland. While much of this changed following the Meiji restoration, the concept of strong, centralized power endured.

While many peoples of the world were building centralized government structures, America's economic and political impulses developed along contrary lines. Colonial experience led Americans to be opposed to centralization of economic power in chartered companies and to centralization of political power. The separation of powers, written into our Constitution as a guarantee of political freedom, also affected economic thought. The proof of this hostility to the centralization of power is evident from the fact that our basic antitrust law bears the name of a senator whose credentials as a conservative were impeccable.

Moreover, the existence of the frontier tended for many years to influence our thinking. It was not a totally alien frontier, such as existed in the older settled parts of the world, but was merely the edge of untapped resources and an enormous land mass. Our huge continent furnished an outlet for all our goods and services. The development of those seemingly illimitable resources demanded both practical and technical innovation. Because of this heritage, many Americans even today fail to understand that America is only a subsection of the world market, and that our value system is not shared by many others. Thus the Japanese and the Europeans are hard put to comprehend what often seems the strange behavior of Americans. The arrogance of the U.S. Government's desire to export its complicated antitrust concepts around the world is properly viewed by our friends abroad with both amazement and hostility. Governments in Japan and in Europe regard their business establishments as great national assets which furnish the revenue to support increasing standards of living for their people, and for the world's people as well. It is difficult for them to understand, let alone credit, the often inherently hostile position taken by the U.S. Government toward American business.

In this country, we are acutely conscious of the mercantilist tradition in Europe and the enormous concentration of power in the zaibatsu complexes of Japan. Many former colonial countries see the chartered monopolies of the imperial nations as the forerunners of today's world corporations. To them, our global corporations seem to be thinly disguised, government- directed chosen instruments dedicated to the pursuit of governmental foreign policy under the guise of a commercial establishment. Bitter experience with government-chartered monopolies throughout history did little to create in many of the developing countries a welcome environment for the new worldwide economic structures that began to grow during the great postwar international expansion. Even today, the Sunday supplements love to hint darkly that the modern world corporation is really an instrument of today's nation-state. The suspicion of a modern mercantilism hangs in the air. The days of gunboat diplomacy are indeed gone. We have now come full circle in the western world to what appears to many as the successor to the chosen instrument of imperialism. Thus the world corporation is questioned, not only by the host governments but in many cases by their own governments, wherever the head office may be located, despite the enormous success of these firms in supplying the world's needs.

Part of this attack stems from the clash of historic value systems. As new philosophers, thinkers, and traders appeared on the world stage at the time of the Industrial Revolution, the idea began to dawn that man by his own efforts could improve his lot in the world. Economic growth and improvement and the betterment of social conditions seemed attainable dreams. The enunciation of the principles of free trade and the doctrines of comparative advantage by Smith, Ricardo, and others can be seen as a decisive break with the mercantilist tradition. What flowed from these new ideas was a concept of dynamic economic growth, as opposed to the old notion that profit to one was loss to the other—the zero-sum game. With this new concept came a recognition of the growing interdependence of economic units. The new emerging entrepreneurial class showed an aversion to war, and began to develop more of an adversary relationship with government. In short, the hostility was mutual.

It was against this background of changing values that the prototype world corporations first began to appear in the latter half of the nineteenth century. As far back as 1865, Germany's Friedrich Bayer built a plant in Albany, New York; the next year, Sweden's Alfred Nobel established a factory in Hamburg; and the year after that, the U.S.'s Isaac Merrit Singer opened his first overseas plant in Glasgow.

In widest historical perspective, then, commercial and political history exhibited an interplay between two basically competing value systems. The first stems from the medieval age and developed through the mercantilism of the sixteenth and seventeenth centuries into nineteenth-century imperialism, then twentieth-century totalitarianism. This was accompanied by the tradition of business as the chosen instrument of government policy. The second value system arose from the earliest merchant and financier classes of the precapitalistic era and grew through the Industrial Revolution. The entrepreneurial tradition of the capitalist, independent of government, is the basis from which grew the adversary relationship between business and the state.

Of course, as in all living things, neither system developed in a pure form. Through the period of the Second World War, there is no question that the mercantilist-imperialist tradition was dominant, though the entrepreneurial tradition, when it gained preeminence from time to time and from place to place, was responsible for much of the progress in general welfare that took place among the world's peoples.

Viewed against this background, the modern world corporation is the extension to global proportions of the business tradition that grew out of capitalism and the Industrial Revolution. It is now learning how to operate in the global marketplace. The motivating factors which drive the world corporations today are basically the same as those which drove earlier entrepreneurs. Like their predecessors, the world corporations are a new expression of the entrepreneurial thrust that thrives on the free exchange of goods, services, factors of production, technology, capital, and ideas.

Since time has proved that it is more effective to attack the carrier of an alien idea than the idea itself, the agents of change come under sustained, intensified attack. All these criticisms overlook a fundamental point. In the tough, competitive global marketplace, it does not matter where a multinational corporation's headquarters are located. Any global company, whether based in the United States, Europe, Japan, or somewhere else, will sooner or later have to operate under the same economic and political rules that govern its international competitors. In order to stay in business, any company is compelled to get its materials for production from wherever they are available most cheaply, conduct its processing activities wherever they are most efficient, and market its goods wherever there is a demand. And all of this has to be done in compliance with a bewildering variety of laws and value systems which have been constructed by our nation-states.

It is precisely this economic necessity that makes the multinational enterprise the best instrument for assuring the most efficient, most thrifty use of the world's resources. In an era when many people express concern that those resources might be squandered, the need to make them go as far as possible and to avoid waste is an economic and human necessity. Yet efficient use of the world's resources does not generate much applause for the world corporations.

The neomercantilistic ideas have never died and still furnish ammunition for critics of multinationals, both at home and abroad. These familiar themes are articulated by some in developing countries who accuse multinational companies of milking the economies of their host countries by taking more out of them than they put in. At the same time that these charges are leveled at the world's corporations abroad, labor leaders at home aver that multinationals are exporting capital, technology, and jobs that might otherwise be used to build a domestic economy.

It is a two-front war. If the international managers prove to a host country that they are creating more wealth for it than they are taking out, this very evidence will be used against them at home. If they prove to the labor unions at home that, on balance, they are creating more jobs at home than they export, or prove to their governments that the repatriated foreign earnings are good for the home country's balance of payments, that evidence fuels the arguments of their foreign critics.

Because of their intellectual training, many of the critics are quite sincere in believing that international managers are lying when they say that everybody profits from their operations, home and host countries alike. The fundamental fact, however, is that the payrolls and jobs of the multinationals exceed profits by a factor of twenty to one. That is a hard fact. It can be ignored, as can anything by the partisan, but it cannot be argued with.

The concept of global wealth creation, however, places a great strain on even the most liberal of modern nation-states. Each ruling government is primarily concerned with optimizing conditions within its own boundaries. All countries participate to some degree in international specialization, contributing to the world economy what they can do best and most profitably. But every country at some point subordinates its possible economic advantages to considerations of military security, domestic stability, the protection of home industries or economic groups, or even national pride. Many of the developing countries, struggling to feed and educate their people, deem it more prestigious to build a steel mill than a fertilizer plant or public schools.

National governments often assert their dominance over business enterprises not only in pursuit of competitive advantage abroad but also in furtherance of domestic political policies. No county permits completely free enterprise, but controls in today's world tend to come from one of two diametrically opposed political extremes, with the freer countries positioned somewhere in the middle of the spectrum.

One type of government tends to organize its economy to favor public ownership of enterprise. It adopts policies of income redistribution, regulates consumption, maximizes central planning and government allocation of resources. At the authoritarian extreme of this system are countries like the People's Republic of China, the U.S.S.R., the nations of Eastern Europe, North Korea, Vietnam, Cambodia, and the socialist countries of Africa. The fruits of this system are written plain in the current record. The medium-term economic consequences of such policies always involve depressed internal growth rates and can lead to extreme economic degeneration, as we saw in Nasser's Egypt, Sukarno's Indonesia, and Allende's Chile.

At the other end of the political spectrum, another group of countries pursue policies that favor private business ownership, deliberately depresses current consumption in favor of capital accumulation, permits market mechanisms rather than fiat to allocate resources, tightly controls labor unions, and generally practices social regimentation. These states tend to take a positive view of the world economy and favor policies that foster global interdependence. They usually also experience relatively strong growth rates. But very often these societies produce a serious maldistribution of income that may ultimately create an explosive social situation. If the situation deteriorates, it is not unusual to see what is euphemistically called a strong military group take over the government.

All the other national economies are strung out somewhere along the spectrum between those extremes. The most comfortable location is somewhere as close as possible to the middle, but it takes an effort to stay there. Every economic crisis creates pressure on governments to flirt with one extreme or the other, sometimes with both at the same time. There is always the temptation to solve short-term problems by exchanging them for long-term instability.

In the long run, both types of controlled economies are unstable. The progressive ruination of the economy in the one case and the social regimentation and inequitable income distribution in the other cause internal pressures for radical change. When internal pressures become irresistible, the regimes in charge may either give ground gradually or be quickly replaced. The transfers of leadership from Sukarno to Suharto in Indonesia, Nasser to Sadat in Egypt, Allende to Pinochet in Chile, and Spinola to Soares in Portugal are examples of how rapidly events occur.

No matter where a government is positioned on the political spectrum, often the public and private sectors are in conflict. This natural interplay has generated a great deal of nonsense about the relative power of multinationals and governments. The facts are clear and simple.

A multinational corporation, no matter how large, is essentially helpless in the hands of a nation-state, no matter how small. Despite overwhelming evidence of this truism, disbelief abounds. The Group of Eminent Persons appointed by the United Nations Economic and Social Council in 1972, at the instigation of the then-Communist government of Chile, investigated the relative powers of multinational companies and the sovereign states. It is not now, nor ever has been, a contest. I can give you one example from New York City, where I live right next door to the United Nations headquarters.

New York, as you may know, is a hard place to park an automobile. Members of missions assigned to the UN enjoy diplomatic immunity. They can, if they choose, ignore the No Parking signs, which many of them do, to the constant irritation of less privileged New Yorkers. If I park my car in my neighborhood, the Police Department tows it away. The head of every global company is in the same fix.

There you see the true difference between sovereignty and the lack of it. If the example I chose seems a little simplistic, it is no more so than books with titles like *Sovereignty at Bay*. Or for that matter, some of the reports that were turned out by the Group of Eminent Persons who parked their cars with impunity outside my apartment house in clear defiance of local laws.

As a last resort, all any multinational company can do in its relations with a sovereign state is to make an appeal to reason. If that fails, capital, both human and material, will leave for countries where it is more welcome. Since men and money in the long run go where they are wanted and stay where they are well treated, capital can be attracted but not driven.

In the long run, it all comes down to this: the future of a global company in any one area will be determined by the degree to which a particular government is willing and able to put the material well-being of its citizens ahead of outmoded political, protectionist, or other local narrow interests. Everything discussed thus far will be resolved almost automatically when our nation-states make up their minds concerning that basic question.

The reality of a global marketplace has been the driving force pushing us along the path of developing a rational world economy. Progress that has been made owes almost nothing to political imagination. It has been the managers of the multinational corporations who have seen the world whole and moved to supply mankind's needs as efficiently as politics would allow. The thousands of jobs and products that have helped raise the living standards of mankind have made this economic process highly visible to millions of people. Far too many of the world's people have now seen what the global shopping center holds in store for them. They will not easily accept having the doors slammed shut by nationalism.

The development of the truly multinational organization has produced a group of managers of many nationalities who really believe in one world. They know that there can be no truly profitable markets where poverty is the rule of life. They are a group that recognizes no distinction because of color or sex, since they understand with the clarity born of experience that talent is the commodity in shortest supply in the world. They are managers who are against the partitioning of the world, not only on a political or theoretical basis but on the pragmatic ground that the planet has become too small, that our fates have become too interwoven one with another for us to engage in the old nationalistic games which have so long diluted the talent, misused the resources, and dissipated the energy of mankind.

They realize that the engine that drives the growth of nations gives humanity the wherewithal to deal with the wretchedness of the human condition. They have learned that the multinational corporation can function amid diverse value systems, though like all instruments of progress it must move in a resisting medium.

Woodrow Wilson proclaimed a league of free nations—but the League of Nations did not survive. Wendell Willkie argued, correctly, that we have one world, a fact that the astronauts vividly proved. Nevertheless, the politicians of the world will not act. The political problems of the United Nations are a stark manifestation. The divisiveness of the European Economic Community is further evidence. Despite all our advances, the world is still socially fragmented and the incompatibility of the world's value systems has always been and still remains a cause of potential conflict. History is replete with the tragedies wrought by the efforts of one society to impose its concepts upon others.

Agents of change involve new ideas and values. They have never been welcome in any society. This is especially true when the carrier of new or strange values is, or is thought to be, alien to the society that is affected. Often the most effective way to resist change is by identifying the carrier of the new values as foreign. The word for "foreigner," from the Golden Age of Greece right up to the Middle Ages, was "barbarian." Anyone who spoke a foreign language, dressed differently, adhered to different customs and mores, was automatically considered a barbarian. "Stranger" and "foreigner" have thus from time immemorial been pejorative terms, and often synonymous with "enemy."

It should not surprise us, therefore, that the world corporation is sometimes unwelcome even though it is the carrier of technology, which is the best hope of closing the gap between the very rich and the very poor. It is often unwelcome because it is perhaps the most effective instrument by which value systems are transferred from one part of the world to another.

Mere physical change, manifested by a new factory, a new building, or a piece of complex machinery generally does not arouse the passions of the populace. But when the change moves into the realm of ideas, a wholly different and more massive impact upon society follows. If, for example, a world corporation introduces the idea of upward mobility based only on merit and not on status, this may well offend an establishment fighting to preserve its privileges.

The nature of the value systems that are carried by world corporations, as agents of change, runs the gamut from simple improvements, like better lighting in manufacturing plants, to renovating whole neighborhoods. For example, Park Avenue in New York City north of Grand Central Station used to be lined on both sides with old apartment houses. It was not until a British-based multinational corporation, Unilever, saw the potential of putting a modern office building in this area that a whole new development was sparked in my city, and opened in time new opportunities elsewhere. Today, a certain portion of the pensions received by retired employees of the British Post Office come from rents on the Merchandise Mart in Chicago, which they own.

Old ideas die hard; yesterday's liberals, who feel that central, national control is the answer to everything, are still in control of many intellectual circles. They all labor under an old illusion, which John Gardner once put as follows: "Those who seek to bring societies down always dream that after the blood bath *they* will be calling the tune." That outworn doctrine of the controlled economy—a relic of mercantilism—is becoming more and more a manifestation of the persistence of illusion over reality.

10
Multinational Corporations

STEPHEN D. KRASNER

From a Realist perspective, Krasner argues that less developed countries have inherent advantages over private corporations, including multinational corporations (MNCs). Such states, even small developing states, have legal sovereignty over their territories and can deny foreign corporations access. Over time, this structural characteristic of states in the international system has allowed LDC governments to extract ever larger concessions from MNCs.

INTRODUCTION

In the period since the conclusion of the Second World War multinational corporations have become major actors in the world economy. During the 1960s, direct foreign investment from the thirteen OECD countries grew approximately one and a half times as quickly as the average growth rate. By the mid-1970s goods imported by American multinationals into the United States from their majority-owned affiliates accounted for about 30 percent of U.S. trade. On a global basis, intracorporate trade was estimated at 25 percent of all trade (excluding the centrally planned economies). Multinationals command a dominant position in many of the leading technology industries. They have become a primary vehicle for the transfer of technology across national boundaries. They are an important source of transnational capital flows.

---

10 "Multinational Corporations" by Stephen D. Krasner. From Stephen Krasner. *Structural Conflict: The Third World Against Global Liberalism.* Reprinted by permission of the University of California Press.

Despite their importance, however, the degree of general North-South conflict (as opposed to disputes of specific countries) over multinationals has not been as intense as it has been over other issues. Commodity agreements, trade, official capital flows including the behavior of the IMF and World Bank, and the Law of the Sea have all engendered more intense debate. Through the early 1980s the various international arrangements related to multinationals have taken the form of international codes or guidelines rather than definitive agreements or the creation of separate international institutions.

The somewhat moderated level of conflict concerning multinationals rests on the fact that the prevailing regime governing their behavior incorporates some of the major preferences of developing countries because of the significance of juridical sovereignty. All actors recognize that national states have the right to control economic behavior that takes place within their borders. A multinational cannot function without the sanction of the state. The notion of sovereignty at bay, so fashionable in the early 1970s, was never an accurate characterization. Despite their international and domestic weaknesses, Third World states have been able to use their juridical sovereignty, the constitutive principle of the present international system, to establish national principles and rules related to multinational corporations.

The specific character and effectiveness of national regulation have depended on the relative bargaining power of the host country on the one hand and the corporation on the other. The state's leverage has been derived, in the first instance, from its power to grant access to its territory. In addition, every state in the contemporary international system has at least formal control over a panoply of policy instruments that can be applied to economic actors. The extent to which a state can actually impose controls depends on its ability to provide itself with capital, technology, and market access. A state that must rely entirely on multinationals for these services cannot drive a very hard bargain. The extent to which developing countries control such resources has varied over time and across sectors. There has been a general intertemporal improvement in the bargaining power of host-country governments. Their power has been most extensive in the area of raw materials where they have been able to assert formal and effective control over most fuel and mineral exploitation. In the area of manufactures, LDC leverage is less impressive.

In addition to national regulation, LDCs have supported new international rules of the game. The postwar liberal regime for multinational corporations (MNCs) emphasized national treatment, just and adequate compensation, and the right of companies to appeal to their home countries. The Third World has pressed for agreements that would legitimate the right to discriminate between national and multinational corporations, curtail the right of MNCs to alienate their property, and leave the determination of compensation and the resolution of any disputes to legal institutions in host countries. Industrialized states have advocated voluntary codes, whereas the Third World has preferred, but not insisted on, mandatory agreements.

New international principles and norms could enhance national bargaining power. New rules could coordinate the behavior of developing states making it more difficult for a multinational corporation to play one country off against another. They could change the expectations of corporate officials regarding treatment in Third World countries. Developing host countries would be less susceptible to pressure from the home countries of multinationals if they could claim that their national regulations conformed to international arrangements, even voluntary codes. The various oversight and enforcement mechanisms associated with codes of conduct could provide additional information about the practices of both other states and multinational corporations.

In sum, national juridical sovereignty provides all states with the ability to block the entrance of multinationals but not to compel multinationals to invest or to prevent their exit. Given that a corporation chooses to invest, the primary determinant of the division of gains is the extent to which the host country can command capital, technical skills, and knowledge of the market. New international rules of the game can enhance the bargaining power of Third World host countries by encouraging uniform treatment of multinationals, reducing the ability of corporations to play off one country against another, limiting the interventions that might be made by industrialized states on behalf of their companies, and providing additional information on MNCs.

THE PATTERN OF DIRECT FOREIGN INVESTMENT

Multinational corporations are not a new phenomenon. Many major industrial and raw-material enterprises were established on a global level by the end of the nineteenth century. However, there has been a dramatic growth in transnational corporate activity since the 1950s. The net direct investment outflow from industrial market-economy countries rose from $3.3 billion in 1965, to $4.6 billion in 1970, to $13.0 billion in 1981. The stock of direct investment abroad for the developed market-economy countries increased from $105.3 billion at the end of 1967 to $287.2 billion at the end of 1976.

Most of this investment has taken place among advanced industrialized countries, not between these countries and the Third World. The share of direct foreign investment (DFI) going to the Third World fell from 31 percent in 1967 to 26 percent in 1974, but rose again in the late 1970s. Despite the global economic slowdown during the latter period, the flow of investments to the developing world increased, rising from an average annual rate of $2.6 billion in 1967-1969, to $3.7 billion in 1970-1972, $6.0 billion in 1973-1975, $10.0 billion in 1976-1978, to $12.8 billion in 1979-1981.

Foreign investment in the Third World is concentrated in more advanced or resource-rich LDCs. At the end of 1977 nearly 57 percent of direct foreign investment in the Third World was in thirty-four countries that had per capita gross national products in excess of $1.000, 18 percent in twenty-three countries with per capita GNPs between $750 and $1.000, and 7 percent in countries with per capita

GNPs of less than $200. In 1975, DFI was equal to about 9.5 percent of GNP for LDCs with incomes above $500 per capita (excluding tax havens and OPEC countries), 6.8 percent for those with incomes between $200 and $499, and 3.3 percent for those with incomes under $200.

NATIONAL REGULATIONS

Developing countries are involved in a mixed-motive game with multinationals. There is an inherent tension between the corporation's desire to integrate its activities on a global basis and the host country's desire to integrate an affiliate with its national economy. Maximizing corporate profit does not necessarily maximize national economic objectives. Conflict can develop over a wide range of issues. Host-country governments generally prefer that vertical links be established among operations within their national boundaries; MNCs may prefer to locate upstream and downstream facilities in other countries. The technology possessed by multinationals has usually been developed in industrialized countries. LDCs may prefer technology more suited to their local environment. Multinationals have been accused of introducing inappropriate products to developing countries, products that may be tolerable in wealthier countries but involve a misallocation of resources in poorer ones. Similarly, multinationals have been accused of generating tastes and preferences that reflect standards in rich countries but are inappropriate for poor ones. Fundamental decisions about corporate activity are taken by executives in advanced countries whose behavior cannot be directly controlled by host-country officials. Because they can affect economic performance, tastes, and the direction of development, MNCs pose a threat to the functional control a state can exercise within its own territorial boundaries.

These are not new problems. Conflicts with host countries are an inherent attribute of multinational corporate activity, especially in smaller and less developed countries. States have used a wide range of measures to control multinationals. For instance, since the nineteenth century, Finland has coped with multinationals by closely monitoring them, denying national treatment, excluding them from key economic sectors, promoting state-owned enterprises, and insisting on Finnish participation on boards of directors. In the contemporary world virtually all countries prohibit foreign investment in some sectors, such as defense and communications. Governments have promulgated rules regarding the establishment of affiliates, repatriation of profits, debt financing, transfer payments, employment of nationals, disclosure of information, and tax rates.

One of the best-known Third World efforts to cope with MNCs has been formulated by the members of the Andean Common Market—Bolivia, Chile, Colombia, Ecuador, Peru, and Venezuela. (Chile withdrew in 1976.) The Foreign Investment Code of the Andean Pact provides for a coordinated investment strategy designed to rationalize production and prevent competitive bidding among its members. Technology transfer must meet legally stipulated criteria, which are enforced by an administrative body. Multinationals are compelled to share ownership with local actors. After three years, at least 15 percent of a firm must be locally owned. Depending on the member country, foreign corporations must phase out their holdings over a period ranging from fifteen to twenty-two years. Corporations that do not act in accordance with these provisions are denied the benefits of the community's customs-duty liberalization, and local capital markets.

Host countries have maintained that it is appropriate to renegotiate contracts and concessions despite the insistence of corporations that such agreements are binding. LDCs, in particular, have argued that multinationals often received excessively favorable treatment during the colonial era; that changes in general economic conditions are a legitimate reason for altering agreements; and that corporations often possess unfair advantages during initial contacts because of their superior knowledge and organization. Host countries have argued that they have the unilateral right to establish grounds for nationalization, and the appropriate compensation should nationalization occur.

Formal rules and regulations, however, are one thing, effective control another. Juridical sovereignty provides a necessary but not sufficient condition for limiting the ability of multinationals to freely alienate property. The relative bargaining power of host countries and multinationals has varied across countries, time, and economic sectors as a function of the ability to command capital, technology, and market knowledge. The bargaining power of host countries has tended to increase over time. The number of multinational corporations has grown, giving host countries a wider range of choice. On a global basis there has been a decline in the concentration of firms in a number of major industries since the 1950s.

Multinationals have become more geographically diverse, with the U.S. share of DFI from the thirteen OECD countries declining from a peak of 60 percent for the period 1961-1967 to about 30 percent for the period 1971-1979. Japanese and European corporations have been more responsive to some controls favored by Third World countries, especially those related to joint ownership. There has also been a long-term increase in the availability of information to Third World states. It has become commonplace, for instance, to publish mining contracts, giving policymakers in one country solid information on arrangements that have been made in others. If nationals with the appropriate training are not available, the services of foreign experts can be procured.

Holding particular industry characteristics constant, larger and more developed Third World countries have greater bargaining leverage. A consumer products manufacturing corporation will accept more controls to secure access to a country with a large market. Larger and wealthier developing countries, which have more capital of their own and greater access to international capital markets, can place greater controls on multinationals. Such controls can facilitate the transfer of technology and managerial skills. A number of developing countries have used international borrowing to establish state-owned corporations that have supplanted or challenged multinationals, a kind of jujitsu turning of the world capitalist system against itself. Countries that are more advanced also have greater indigenous technological skill. Controls are most extensive in the more advanced Latin American countries, which have large markets and a well-trained managerial corps.

Finally, the degree of host-country control has varied across industries. Manufacturing industries with advanced and dynamic technologies have been more difficult to control. In such sectors multinationals offer a bundle of services that cannot be obtained elsewhere. Formal LDC participation may not make much difference because nationals lack the technical expertise to monitor corporate decisions effectively. Developing countries have had their greatest success in the raw-materials area where technical skill and market knowledge have been more accessible.

The increased capabilities of developing countries, especially in the larger states and in the raw materials sector, is reflected in major changes in practices related to multinationals. Ownership patterns have altered even in manufacturing. . . .

Nationalizations increased substantially during the period 1970-1976 as opposed to the 1960s. Aside from nationalization, there has also been an increased tendency to renegotiate contracts. . . .None of these actions guarantees total and effective control, which is contingent on adequate managerial and technical capabilities. But the increase in the level of host-country intervention has been significant.

It is in the area of raw materials that changes have been most dramatic, reflecting the increased bargaining power of host countries. When multinationals first became involved in the international exploitation of minerals and petroleum they enjoyed enormous advantages. Host countries had little capital, virtually no technological skills, and limited knowledge of the market. They were not inclined to bargain vigorously because even initial payments could be a bonanza for hard-pressed treasuries. Direct or indirect colonial control limited possibilities for contract revisions.

Before World War II, concessions that gave one company, or a small consortium of companies, control over large tracts of territory (sometimes over a whole country) were the modal form of arrangement. There were no provisions for relinquishment if particular areas were not developed. Concessions were granted for time periods ranging from fifty to one hundred years. Host countries received modest royalties based on the amount, not the price or profit, of extracted materials. The corporations insisted that concessions had the same character as contracts between private parties and that they were inviolable except in selected circumstances. Thus, oil development in Saudi Arabia was at first controlled by Standard Oil of California and Texaco; in Kuwait by Gulf and British Petroleum; in Iran by British Petroleum (until 1951); in Iraq by a consortium composed of Exxon, Mobil, British Petroleum, Shell, and the Compagnie Francaise des Petroles (CFP). Kennecott and Anaconda accounted for almost all of Chile's copper production, Anglo-American and Roan Selection Trust (controlled by American Metal Climax) for almost all of Zambia's.

The concession regime was swept away during the 1960s and 1970s as bargaining power shifted to host countries. Once discoveries were actually developed and large capital expenditures committed, it became more difficult for corporations to threaten to exit. Additional capital could be generated more easily by host countries whose nationals also acquired greater technical expertise and market knowledge. Almost all major foreign corporations working under old concession agreements were nationalized. New arrangements in the raw materials area have been much more favorable to host countries (perhaps too favorable). . . .

There has been, moreover, a significant shift in actual control. In 1970, transnational corporations owned 94 percent of worldwide crude oil production, in 1979 they owned 45 percent. In 1973, the seven major oil corporations lifted 70 percent of OPEC oil; in 1978, 55 percent, in 1980 less than 33 percent. Oil-exporting states, not corporations, now have the major impact on production levels and prices. Throughout the 1970s they unilaterally changed contractual arrangements. It is not necessary to exaggerate the effectiveness of OPEC as a true cartel to assert that the regime for oil has fundamentally changed since 1970.

A multiplicity of institutional forms has replaced the old concession regime. While investments in raw materials by American and British firms that previously dominated these sectors have fallen, firms from other countries, especially Japan, have increased their activity. Service contracts, production sharing, and technical assistance have become the dominant kinds of arrangements. Contracts have imposed time limits for multinationals to begin operations. They have set minimum levels of production. They have obligated firms to increase local processing. They have imposed criteria for purchases from local suppliers. . . .

In this discussion I do not mean to imply that developing countries can assert full and effective control even with regard to raw materials. Nor are multinationals anxious to place themselves in a vulnerable position. The largest new investors have been Japanese companies. They have abjured full ownership, but they have devised other ways to exercise control. Japan has itself pursued a conscious policy of diversifying sources of supply. Some exporting states are very dependent on Japanese markets. Japanese corporations have retained the most profitable stages of production for themselves while locating less profitable and highly polluting activities in producing countries. Control of transportation and logistics has also helped to enhance the power of Japanese multinationals. The ability of host countries to influence multinationals is nevertheless much greater than it was in the 1960s.

The success developing countries have had in changing the rules of the game has had economic costs. Corporations have become increasingly reluctant to make substantial new raw-material investments in the Third World. Very few such commitments were made during the 1970s. The proportion of exploration expenditures in the mining industry devoted to developing areas fell from 35 percent for the period 1961-1965, to 30 percent for 1966-1970, to 14 percent for 1971-1975. During the 1970s, 68 percent of all seismic prospecting for petroleum and 91 percent of exploratory drilling took place in developed countries. Confronted with the possible loss of large fixed-capital commitments, corporations have increasingly devoted their efforts to the United States, Canada, Australia, and South Africa, which offer less economic promise, because they have been heavily surveyed in the past, but more political stability. . . .

In sum, there have been substantial changes in the rules of the game for direct foreign investment. These changes have been most marked in the area of raw materials, and the proximate cause is the increased bargaining power of host-country governments. In specific terms, this bargaining power involves greater information about, and control over, capital, technology, and markets. The ability to impose these enhanced capabilities ultimately rests, however, on the principle of sovereignty, which accords the state the right to deny access to its territory and to regulate economic activity taking place within its boundaries. The increasingly effective assertion of control by national authorities has led to a change in international attitudes. International corporations and industrialized-country governments have come to accept, tacitly if not always explicitly, the legitimacy of greater national control of multinational corporate activity. Sovereignty is not at bay. However, these new rules of the game have made corporations very wary of putting large amounts of capital at risk in the Third World. . . .

CONCLUSION

Multinational corporations have become major actors in the international economic arena. Their success, however, is contingent on securing access to the territory of more than one state. The fundamental attributes of sovereignty provide even very weak governments with the ability to block such access. Thus, despite the asymmetry of economic power that can exist between corporations and states, host-country governments do have effective leverage. . . .

Developing countries have altered principles, norms, rules, and decision-making procedures related to direct foreign investment. National regulations are increasing. The sanctity of contracts can no longer be adequately defended. The proposition that under the old regime MNCs possessed unfair bargaining power has been widely accepted. Particularly in raw-material exploitation there has been a fundamental shift in effective control in favor of host countries. Multinationals have been compelled to alter their behavior. Simply by being sovereign states, by utilizing the constitutive principle of the international system, developing countries have been able to change the rules of the game for direct foreign investment.

11

Assertive Pragmatism and the Multinational Enterprise

SAYRE P. SCHATZ

In the continuing debate over the net benefits of multinational enterprises (MNEs) to developing countries, Sayre Schatz stakes out a middle ground between the extremes of the Liberal "acceptance" and the Marxist "rejection" approaches. Through assertive pragmatism, Schatz argues, developing countries can and have benefited from multinational investment. Based upon a fundamental skepticism about the general and definitive statements contained in the alternative perspectives, pragmatists focus on the ability of host governments to extract concessions from MNEs. Over time, Schatz suggests, the bargaining leverage of the developing countries has improved, stimulating a process of "self-fulfilling aspiration growth." As a result, he concludes, developing countries have benefited in absolute terms from multinational investment, and both acceptors and rejecters have begun to move toward a more pragmatic position.

Given the sheer volume of writing on multinational enterprises (MNEs), the wide range of opinion on most facets of the subject, and the passion with which contending positions are asserted, one feels a need for a guide through the embattled, and changing, terrain. This chapter proposes a simple conceptual framework, focusing on the impact of MNEs on developing host countries; it submits a

11 "Assertive Pragmatism and the Multinational Corporation" by Sayre P. Schatz. Reprinted from *World Development*, Vol. 9, No. 1, Sayre P. Schatz, "Assertive Pragmatism and the Multinational Enterprise." © 1981, Pergamon Press plc.

brief for one of the approaches delineated in that framework; and it suggests that a process of convergence toward such an approach is under way.

Despite the considerable oversimplification involved, it is useful to distinguish three main approaches to MNEs. Of course, any taxonomy of an extensive and often highly sophisticated literature, even a more highly differentiated one than that presented here, inevitably involves oversimplification: there is considerable diversity within each of the three categories; moreover, the classification is not exhaustive because some writings do not fit well into any of the categories. Still, we can usefully distinguish the acceptance,rejection, and pragmatic approaches to MNEs. This paper will present only a single prototypical position for each approach, not suggesting that it is fully representative of all who may follow that approach.

The three approaches lie along a continuum, without clear-cut demarcations between them. The *acceptance approach* conceives of MNE expansion as economically rational, with benefits considerably outweighing costs for the host as well as the home country; considers host-government pressures on MNEs generally harmful on balance; and thus advocates a minimal or restricted role for government. Towards the left end of the continuum, the *rejection approach* sees MNE activities as essentially baleful, with harm to host countries overshadowing benefits. Rejectors believe that host-government efforts to tip the balance toward the beneficial either cannot succeed or entail costs (in terms of expending scarce government capabilities) that exceed the benefits. They therefore propose that government should either reject MNEs entirely or allow them a marginal role, one in which they accord with and accommodate to host-country policies (which should be directed toward fundamental restructuring of the nation's economy). Between these two is the *pragmatic approach,* which views MNE operations as mixed in effect; which believes that feasible government pressures on the MNEs can produce a worthwhile improvement in the benefit-cost mix; and which therefore advocates intelligent bargaining by host countries. A particular form of pragmatism, which we call assertive pragmatism, will be specified in this paper.

1. THE ACCEPTANCE APPROACH

A considerable spectrum of writers follows the acceptance approach, ranging from strong partisans who can see, hear, or speak no evil of MNEs to social scientists of the highest caliber and sophistication. The approach has been persuasively articulated by Raymond Vernon, conceivably the world's leading authority on MNEs, and because of his preeminent status, the prototypical acceptance position presented here is based upon Vernon's argument, although other writers are also referred to. Vernon's position can be presented in the form of six propositions[1]:

1. The pervasive frictions between the world's nation-states and the MNEs are based upon a fundamental conflict between economics and politics. Technological progress and the economic processes that flow there from

produce enormous economic benefits. However, these processes also heighten world economic interdependence, thereby reducing national autonomy. This occurs just when national governments, committed to promoting welfare and development in an historically new way, fiercely desire to *increase their* autonomy and sense of control. Governments thus experience the fundamental economic-political conflict as an excruciating ambivalence: a simultaneous heightening of both their desire for the economic benefits of interdependence and their aversion to its political constraints.

2. The MNE is a major manifestation and embodiment of the economic forces promoting global economic integration and human welfare. World-scale specialization promoted by MNE expansion raises the gross world product and allows higher living standards for all. The giant enterprises have the resources required for costly research and development activities and can spread the costs over their worldwide operations. They can finance huge productive investments that would otherwise be neglected. They increase employment and income in the host countries, raise the levels of worker skills and managerial and entrepreneurial capability, create linkage effects, and promote economic development in many other ways.
3. In contrast, the political forces of nationalism are impeditive and costly. Host-country governments may make demands that impede or prevent useful investment. Within the host-government bureaucracy, unreasoning hostility toward foreign investors may slow down the many processes relating to MNE operations and thereby raise costs. Governments may impose unreasonable and even conflicting requirements. For example, Mexico has required foreign-owned automobile producers not only to produce components domestically, but also to export them to other markets. If such requirements were generalized they would be impossible for the MNEs to meet.
4. Most political criticisms of MNEs, particularly those emanating from developing countries, are emotional and irrational. They arise from frustrations that are not validly attributable to MNEs, and "the imperviousness of the debate to facts" arises from the impotent anger generated by these frustrations. The MNEs have the misfortune to serve as "unwitting and unwilling lightning rods" for this anger. . . .
5. This is not to say that there are no real conflicts between governments and MNEs. There are many: governments want the capacity to control capital movements but MNEs are capable of avoiding controls; governments want foreign exchange stability but the MNEs "have the potential for contributing substantially to the instability of currencies"; governments want the power to tax as they wish, but "the consequences of unilateral [tax] action by any major country can be quite substantial"; in general, "[t]he capacity of any government to undertake a specified task in support of a public policy . . . has been reduced."

   Government's desire for firmer powers is understandable, but even on most of these real issues the criticisms of multinationals are misguided. The various governments are often pursuing conflicting national interests in a zero-sum game; the gain of one country is offset by the loss of another. Such interactions, furthermore, threaten the spread of beggar-thy-neighbor policies which would sharply diminish the welfare of all.

6. Finally, as a practical matter, government action specifically aimed at MNEs should be quite limited. This follows partially from a pessimistic view of the realities of state intervention. Some public measures would clearly be worth undertaking if it were possible to implement them. For example,because of the multinationality of MNEs, government action even on affairs normally considered domestic might have international repercussions; on such matters it would be worthwhile to secure international agreement aimed at avoiding unilateral actions inadvertently harmful to other states,and at achieving multilateral actions where coordination is desirable. However, given the domestic sensitivity of the issues,which are subject to fierce political struggles within each country, useful international agreement has been virtually unobtainable. In point of fact, the measures which are actually being implemented tend to do more harm than good. Thus what *should* be and *can* be done is minimal and what *is* being done tends to be harmful.

2. THE REJECTION APPROACH

The rejection approach is based typically on Marxian theory or on quasi-Marxian dependence theory, although the Rejectors include other writers as well. The formulation presented in the next paragraph is my own but is based on Marxian theory.

The tensions associated with the spread of MNEs can be seen in this formulation as manifestations on a global scale of the basic Marxian contradiction of capitalism: between the social or interdependent nature of the productive system itself and the private nature and purpose of the control of that system. (Production involves a highly interdependent meshing of a country's many different productive undertakings; it is carried on by a complex *system* of thoroughly interrelated enterprises. But the productive operations are *governed* by separate companies, seeking their own individual, not necessarily coordinated and often conflicting, profit-related goals.) This *social-private contradiction* results in poorly coordinated decisions, coordination being achieved only through the *ex post* action of the market ("anarchy of production"), and in decisions based on the criterion of private gain that are often in conflict with the criterion of the public good (e.g, divergences between private profitability and social benefit). The growth of the MNEs represents an extension of the basic Marxist contradiction in a wider arena. The interdependence of the productive system becomes more fully international while the means and purpose of control remain relatively narrow. Thus the MNE is just one more instrument, though a relatively new and important one, of an exploitative, anachronistic economic system.

The social-private contradiction inherent in MNE expansion produces or at least reinforces and extends a characteristic structuring of the world economy: one that may be called hierarchical-geographical as well as imperialistic. The growth of MNEs tends to "produce a hierarchical division of labor between geographical regions.... [It tends to] centralize high-level decision-making occupations in a few key cities in the advanced countries, surrounded by a number of regional subcapitals, and confine the rest of the world to lower levels of activity and income.... [T]he existing pattern of inequality and dependency . . . [is] perpetuated. . . . [T]he basic relationship between different countries . . . [is] one of superior and subordinate. This hierarchical division of the world arises from the private, profit-oriented character of the MNEs and not from the basic nature of the productive forces. It must be stressed that the dependency relationship . . . should not be attributed to technology. The new technology . . . implies greater interdependence but not necessarily a hierarchical structure."[2] Under a different form of control, an entirely different, more rational, more humane world economic structure could emerge.

The rejection approach focuses on the harmful effects for the developing countries of MNE expansion: imperialism and dependence, exploitative transfer pricing, the formation or reinforcement of a baleful set of class relations, an outflow of dividends, interest, royalties, and fees exceeding the inflow of capital, which is viewed as a drainage of capital, and many other negative consequences. Conversely, the approach gives short shrift to host-country benefits generated by the MNEs. Such benefits are seen as accruing primarily to a narrow ruling class or set of elites, including perhaps a small "labor aristocracy" employed by the MNEs, with little or nothing trickling down to the mass of the population.

Thus, the only appropriate and ethical stance is either to reject the MNEs more or less entirely or to allow them a marginal role, completely subordinate to the government economic development orientation, while government devotes its limited capabilities to the fundamental task of reconstructing the nation's political economy, probably on a socialist basis.

3. THE PRAGMATIC APPROACH

(a) Assertive Pragmatism Delineated

Lying between the acceptance and rejection approaches, the pragmatic approach declares the mixed nature of the MNE impact on developing host countries, and in direct contrast with the other approaches' rejections of active government involvement with MNEs, the pragmatic approach favors active host-government bargaining with and regulation of MNEs in order to improve the cost-benefit mix. This approach is in consonance with the strategy employed by most developing countries and with the thought of many social scientists, and represents, I suggest, a position towards which Acceptors and Rejectors are tending to converge (more on this later). This article distinguishes between the pragmatic approach in its most general form and a particular expression of the approach which may be called *assertive pragmatism*. The rationales for both general and assertive pragmatism presented here are the writer's own and would surely not be acceptable to all other pragmatists. For expositional convenience, however, we will speak of *the* pragmatic or *the* assertive pragmatic approach.

Our rationale for pragmatism in general is based upon a social science *uncertainty principle* which simply states that social science is capable of providing only uncertain answers at best. The important issues, particularly in developing countries, are engulfed by uncertainty. Existing theory is inadequate and the real-world situation is immersed in all manner of unknowns.

Uncertainty engulfs attempts at overall appraisal of any major development. Evaluating the costs and benefits of any historical process requires an assessment of the alternatives foregone, and such counter-factual hypotheses are unavoidably highly speculative. Implicit differences in conceptions of the alternatives foregone largely account for the seemingly evidence-resistant nature of many of the grand arguments over the impact of the MNEs. Given these implicit differences, the antagonists commonly talk past one another. Even specifying the actual process is a formidable undertaking. One is hard put simply to identify the vast multiplicity of important economic, political, sociological, and other effects of any major development, let alone to measure them.

It follows from the uncertainty principle that it is more concretely useful to eschew grand historical appraisals in favor of narrower evaluative tasks. The focus most congenial to the pragmatic approach is on the inquiry: in the existing real-world situation, by what means can welfare—of some particular group or class, or of some country or group of countries or of the world—be enhanced. This paper's focus is on the welfare of the "third world" peoples.

It also follows that one should be skeptical of putative, large, long-term gains from a proposed set of measures. The Pragmatist places less credence in such predicted benefits, i.e., attaches a greater discount for risk, than the more convinced analysts who pay little heed to the possibility that they may be wrong, and he or she gives greater weight than they do to definite immediate benefits. The Pragmatist also tends to place a higher premium on measures which are reversible and a greater discount on policies which entail substantial social pain.

The approach is not necessarily conservative. Proposals promising definite, near-term benefits are often opposed because of fears of indirect, long-term harm. The Pragmatist, with her or his greater skepticism about roundabout, long-term effects, is more likely to favor such proposals than the Acceptor who deplores unwarranted interference with the market mechanism or the Rejector who fears diversion of popular energies from the basic task of fundamental social restructuring. Nor is the approach linked only to minor changes. While it does tend to favor piecemeal decisions, allowing evidence and experience to accumulate before proceeding further, even profound social changes can be achieved on a step-by-step basis.

Turning specifically to assertive pragmatism, our rationale is based also on a second conception—an extension of the already discussed Marxian concept of the social-private conflict. This extension departs from the original Marxian vision; even if one considers the Marxian concept a highly useful insight, one need not believe that Marx's horizon was unlimited. Marx did not foresee the unfolding of that conflict.

It can be argued that capitalism's viability has been extended in the face of the social-private conflict by the superimposition of a degree of social management upon the private control of the productive system. This social management took the form of state intervention to deal with system-threatening problems; the state undertook economy-stabilizing fiscal and monetary policy, more effective regulation of the banks, unemployment insurance, social security, and all the other functions that characterize the modern mixed economic system. The social stewardship of the socially interdependent productive system curbed the most ominous domestic malfunctions of the capitalist economies.

We have already suggested that the expansion of the MNEs can be seen within the Marxist paradigm as an extension of the social-private conflict on a global scale. Productive interdependence becomes more thoroughly international, but the means of state control remain national. Once again the means of control are more parochial than the productive system they attempt to harness.

This extension of the Marxian conception depicts a problem but it also directs attention to a possible means of coping with the problem. It suggests the possibility of developing still broader means of control, i.e., some form of governmental action of transnational scope.

Intellectual symmetry suggests parallelism: just as national manifestations of the social-private conflict are dealt with on a national governmental level, so the global manifestations should be handled on a world governmental level. But such an orientation would be visionary. It is more realistic to discuss moves toward more cosmopolitan means of control through increasing the effectiveness and scope of international agencies and international agreements, and more important, through the implementation by individual governments of complementary policies.

Our extension of the Marxian social-private contradiction implies that the web of interdependence in the national and international political economy is loosely enough interwoven so that separate elements can be altered in a way that would improve the functioning of the system. In contrast, systemic interrelations are considered (perhaps implicitly) much more tightly interwoven by Acceptors and Rejectors. For the Acceptor, government interference with the market mechanism is likely to have broad consequences of a negative character that will outweigh apparent improvements. For the Rejector, the system will compensate to preserve the privileges of the ruling class, so that improvement can only be minimal at best while energies are diverted from replacing the system itself. Related to the pragmatic conceptions of loosely woven interdependence and improvability is the associated judgment that despite all their shortcomings governments can be a vehicle for achieving potential improvements.

Assertive pragmatism—with its skepticism about soul-satisfying ideological scenarios, its preference for more certain short-run benefits and distrust of putative long-run benefits, its predisposition toward active use of government—is essentially a mindset, a predisposition on how to proceed. Assertive Pragmatists may differ in many ways: in their degree of assertiveness (for a particular level of bargaining strength), in their preferences for capitalism or socialism, in their conceptions of the balance of benefits and dysbenefits generated by MNE activities, etc. Similarly, assertive pragmatic stances may be adopted by countries with different class structures, different bargaining positions, and other major differences. The approach adumbrates a general position, but it nevertheless leaves wide scope for disagreement, doubt, and indecision.

Let us wind up our definition of assertive pragmatism by returning briefly to Rejector criticisms: that the Pragmatist, even if assertive is willing to settle for relatively small gains; that the benefits that occupy the Pragmatist accrue primarily to a narrow ruling class or set of elites; and that the harm done by MNEs—in aggravating dependence, forming and solidifying exploitative class relations, directing economic growth along capitalist rather than socialist lines—is monumental.

The Assertive Pragmatist does not dismiss Rejector criticisms of the MNE lightly and agrees that a serious case can be made that the impact of the MNE may on balance be injurious. Nevertheless, the Pragmatist (or this one at any rate) justifies his or her position by pointing out that the benefits that do "trickle down" are often too lightly dismissed—such dismissal is only for the affluent—and by reiterating both his uncertainty-based skepticism about trading off these benefits for speculative benefits of a broader nature and also his observation that the capitalist state *has* proved capable of ameliorating fundamental problems. The Pragmatist considers the rejection approach doctrinaire. He also finds that the rejection approach exhibits a curious ahistorical strand that contrasts sharply with the broadly historical character of Marxist and dependency theory. The major problems of any period are typically characterized as inherent in capitalism and ineradicable except through socialism. If in fact the problem is alleviated, attention is then refocused single-mindedly on the new problems that inevitable emerge out of the modified conditions. The improvements are ignored; the error in calling the previous problem immutable is forgotten; and the new problems are again considered ineradicable.

For example, Marxists maintained that foreign investment ineluctably thrust the less developed economies into a primary producing role in the world division of labor. When in fact the MNEs began investing in the industrial subsidiaries in poor countries, neither the industrial progress made nor the error in the previous pronouncements were seriously noted. Instead attention shifted tothe problems generated by these subsidiaries—enterprises which used inappropriate technology and employed a small labor aristocracy to produce inappropriate products for a small elite, thereby increasing unemployment, restricting local demand and thus local production, preventing the emergence of a local capital goods industry producing simpler capital goods, aggravating technological dependence,generating excessive payments to the MNEs, etc. Thus, say some Marxists, industrial growth under MNE auspices "may properly be characterized as 'perverse growth'; that is, growth which undermines, rather than enhances,the potentialities of the economy for long-term growth."[3]

(b) Assertive Pragmatism Implemented

Many international organizations and programs for dealing with MNEs exist or have been proposed. The United Nations has set up a Center on Transnational

Corporations. Other UN bodies, such as UNIDO, FAO, UNCTAD, and others try to assist the developing countries in their relations with the MNEs. International agreements or codes helpful to less developed countries on patents and on the transfer of technology are negotiated. There are proposals for a GATT type of agreement of MNEs. Broad groupings such as the Group of 77 and narrower ones such as the Andean Pact have concerned themselves with MNE-developing country relations, and many other varied schemes for international cooperation have been proposed.

These international bodies and programs provide media for exchange of views and knowledge, for systematic collection and dissemination of information, for undertaking studies, for coordination of policies and reduction of competition between host countries, and for the establishment of informal contacts likely to facilitate cooperation between governments. International organizations might also assist developing nations in negotiations or other dealings with MNEs by providing foreign expertise and training for indigenous personnel.

More important than international bodies and programs, however, are the actions of the individual host countries.

Not long ago, the less developed countries had little confidence in their ability to assert themselves in the international economy. As a former Nigerian minister of economic development lamented, Nigerians must accept "that we shall continue to be under the control of the imperialists and capitalists who have taken the lead in this world in economic development."[4] To a substantial extent, the sense of weakness expressed in this statement was justified.

For one thing, there are significant internal differences within most of the developing countries concerning MNEs. The dominant classes have been in a position to benefit substantially from them, through positions, directorships, bribes, business linkages, and in other ways. The potential personal gains influence their perceptions of the national interest, often to the detriment of the majority. The "labor aristocracy" with good jobs in the large foreign firms, also has a direct stake in the MNEs. Even public-interest motivated government agencies might be partisans of an MNE. For example, the Western Nigeria Development Corporation successfully opposed the establishment of a competing cement company in Western Nigeria in order to protect the monopolistic profitability of the existing multinational subsidiary in which it had a 39 percent holding.

Furthermore, the MNEs constitute formidable bargaining adversaries. Even in extractive industries, where the developing countries are relatively strong in negotiations, MNE negotiating strength generally has been impressive. This is particularly true in the least developed countries, where MNE control of essential technology and market access may be firmer than elsewhere.

In manufacturing for export, "third world" bargaining power with the MNEs is especially weak. The MNEs have firm control of the relevant technologies and of most marketing outlets, particularly if the developing nation is producing a component of some kind. Moreover, the MNEs have the political clout necessary to combat high developed country trade barriers against manufactured imports from less developed countries. Competition to attract MNE export manufacturing subsidiaries further weakens the bargaining position of the developing countries.

When their leverage was slight, the developing countries naturally concluded poor bargains with the MNEs—a problem that was intensified by their very feelings of weakness, for outcome is partially a function of the assurance of the negotiators. Whatever the issue, whether a simple division of economic gain or a broad societal matter, the developing countries were able to capture only a small part of the distance between the minimums they would accept and the maximums the MNEs might concede.

In fact, developing countries have not infrequently incurred direct economic *losses* in their dealings with MNEs. A profitable foreign investment can quite easily reduce national income. The likelihood of a net national loss rises if the host country offers investment incentives such as tariff protection (which imposes a transfer from domestic consumers to the foreign investors). Further, when developing economy bargaining weakness was compounded by foreign swindling or sharp practices and/or by domestic political venality, many joint investment deals have been made which turned out to be complete fiascoes for the host nations. Moreover, some technological change, for example the introduction of labor-saving technology in a labor surplus economy, may also lower host-country welfare. One major study found that almost 40 percent of the MNE manufacturing projects examined in developing economies had negative effects on host-country social income.

If a developing country tried to make tough demands in the era of generally soft bargaining, they were usually unsuccessful. The MNEs could adopt an unyielding stance and if necessary could usually turn to other potential hosts, while the recalcitrants were likely to be left empty-handed.

Gradually, however, developing-country bargaining power has been strengthened, partially by the very process of MNE expansion that was encouraged by developing-country weakness. A variety of factors have been involved.

Once the capital has actually been sunk into a project, the negotiating potency of the host country is sharply increased, particularly if significant amounts of capital are involved. In successful ventures the very profitability of the enterprise makes the MNE more amenable to pressures. The MNE commitment to its overseas ventures also tends to be heightened by organizational changes institutionalizing this commitment and by increasing reliance on foreign markets. Growing familiarity in the host country with the operations of an established subsidiary tends to dispel the air of impenetrable mystery and expertise and increases host-country confidence. The proliferation of multinationals and increasing competition among them has been an important source of host-country stiffening, for these developments have made available multiple sources of capital, technology, other know-how, and even market access, including sources other than those provided by direct investment. Local capability for carrying out operations that were once the exclusive purview of foreign investors has also increased. Developing country ability to win better terms has also been enhanced by the various forms of international cooperation discussed earlier.

These elements of strength are reinforced by a process which we will call *self-fulfilling aspiration growth.* As already indicated, a feeling of bargaining weakness tends to exacerbate that weakness. But as the negotiating position of the developing countries improves they are encouraged to toughen their demands. At some point, a "critical mass" (or average level) of toughness is reached, by which we mean a "mass" or level which institutes the spiral process of self-fulfilling aspiration growth.

The spiral works this way. The increasing demands and aspirations of the developing nations, emerging in a bargaining situation in which these nations have won relatively little, tend to be effective in winning better terms. Encouraged by this, their aspirations and negotiating demands rise. So long as the settlements actually reached fall far short of the maximums that the MNEs would be willing to concede, the heightening of aspirations and demands continues to be successful. A self-reinforcing spiral gets under way: rising aspirations and so on. This is the process of self-fulfilling aspiration growth.

Possible gains are multidimensional, and countries with different goals will presumably seek somewhat different sets of gains. Those more favored by leftist countries, such as income equalization and significant reductions in unemployment, are probably more difficult to bargain for than the more commonly sought gains, such as increases in national income or in government revenue.

The spiral is not an endless one, of course. As the settlements between the developing countries and the MNEs move further from the developing countries' minimums toward the maximums the MNEs are willing to concede, MNE resistance increases and tends to slow down or halt the process. The developing countries find that wresting further concessions from the MNEs incurs increasing costs, particularly in the form of curtailing investment with its infusion of capital, technology, other know-how, and market access, so that after some point the marginal costs of further demands may exceed the marginal benefits.

Experience confirms that the developing countries have been benefiting from tougher bargaining with MNEs, as the thesis of self-fulfilling aspiration growth suggests.

Developing countries have been securing a more favorable distribution of direct economic gains. Many investments have yielded (and prospective investments have promised) considerable quasi-rent to the MNEs, i.e., a return beyond that needed to induce the investor to continue operations or to undertake further investment. It is clear in retrospect that there had been a substantial rent element in earnings related to minerals and petroleum, an element that the developing economies subsequently found that they could tap for themselves. And "there is growing evidence of the existence of 'quasi-rent' . . . in the earnings of transnational manufacturing enterprises in less developed countries as well."[5] The developing countries have been able to raise their share of such income through higher taxes, royalties, participation in ownership, and the like without serious consequences for themselves.

The developing nations have also pressured MNEs into actions which generate further domestic development. They have prodded domestic subsidiaries into creating local linkages. Although many such firms are disposed to secure from their own worldwide corporate family as many of their intermediate inputs as possible, under pressure they have "seemed to be accepting the desirability—or, at any rate, the inevitability of maintaining close ties with the surrounding economies."[6]

The less developed nations have prevailed upon reluctant MNEs to establish domestically operations they would have preferred to carry out elsewhere. They have also promoted deliberate adoption of appropriate technology. They have sometimes spurred foreign investors into a continuing entrepreneurial role. Under pressure many foreign-owned manufacturing subsidiaries "have moved on to other activities: from simple manufacturing processes toward complex ones; from easy marketing in the local economy to difficult marketing abroad."[7]

Developing countries have had relatively longstanding policies of accelerating indigenization of labor and management through informal insistence and formal government action. Indigenization of ownership, i.e., divestiture, has also been pushed, for example, in the Zambian copper mines (with neither of the two nationalized MNEs raising any objections in principle despite previous government denials of nationalization intent), and in Nigeria through its Indigenization Decree.

Local MNE subsidiaries have even been prevailed upon to support broad international political objectives of the host country, sometimes at considerable cost to the subsidiary. For example, Sklar relates how the Zambian copper mining subsidiaries of Anglo-American Corporation and AMAX "cooperated fully and loyally" in Zambia's costly efforts to free itself of logistical dependence upon white minority-ruled Rhodesia.

The MNEs have generally accepted all the prodding and pressuring. They have come to expect continually escalating demands when they are successful, and this is built into their initial investment calculations and decisions. In fact, in favorable circumstances, a "determined and stable public sector . . . can get foreign investors to accept 'unacceptable' conditions while obtaining a rising flow of" foreign investment.[8]

By now it is clear that developing countries have achieved absolute gains and that MNEs have continued to thrive in a milieu of government pressures on and bargaining with MNEs. This of course does not disprove the cases made by the Acceptors or Rejectors, but it has tended to persuade many to moderate their views. "There is no longer the sharp separation between those who think that what is good for General Motors is good for humanity and those who see in the multinational corporations the devil incorporated."[9] The basic orientations remain quite vigorous but there has been some degree of convergence toward the pragmatic approach. Many Acceptors have come to see possible "third world" gains in a somewhat wider range of host-government measures concerning MNEs, and many Rejectors have come to recognize a wider range of actual or potential host-country benefits from MNE activities. In the distribution of positions, the "standard deviation" around the pragmatic position in the center has decreased.

NOTES

1. We have distilled these six propositions from his latest book: Raymond Vernon, *Storm over the Multinationals: The Real Issues* (Cambridge: Harvard University Press, 1977).

2. Stephen Hymer, "The Multinational Corporation and the Law of Uneven Development," in Jagdish Bhagwati (ed.), *Economics and World Order from the 1970s to the 1990s* (New York: Macmillan, 1971), pp. 114 and 124-127.

3. Giovanni Arrighi and John S. Saul, "Socialism and Economic Development in Tropical Africa," *Journal of Modern African Studies* 6, 2 (1968), p. 150.

4. Quoted in Sayre P. Schatz, *Nigerian Capitalism* (Berkeley and Los Angeles: University of California Press, 1977), p. 261.

5. Gerald K. Helleiner, "Transnational Enterprise, Manufactured Exports and Employment in Less Developed Countries, "*Economic and Political Weekly* 11, 5-7 (1976), p. 641, also 644.

6. Raymond Vernon, *Sovereignty at Bay*, (New York: Basic Books, 1971), p. 54.

7. Vernon, *Sovereignty at Bay*, p. 106.

8. Carlos F. Diaz Alejandro, "Direct Foreign Investment in Latin America," in Charles P. Kindleberger (ed.), *The International Corporation* (Cambridge: MIT Press, 1970), p. 324.

9. Paul Streeten, "Multinationals Revisited," *Finance and Development* 16, 2 (1979), p. 39.

12
Multinationals and Marketplace Magic in the 1980s

RICHARD S. NEWFARMER

This article, reflecting structuralist, or dependency, critiques of the international economic order, strongly questions the alleged benefits of multinational enterprises (MNEs) for developing countries. Newfarmer argues that the oligopolistic nature of MNEs may impose economic costs on host countries and that the goals of the MNEs may conflict with the developmental goals of the host. He therefore expects continued government attempts to control MNE activity.

On October 15, 1981, President Ronald Reagan unveiled his program for developing countries. It revolves around three themes closely related to multinational corporations: (1) Reliance on markets to stimulate growth and development; (2) reliance on the private sector to lead development; and (3) minimizing government "interference" in the market. The president put the matter succinctly: "The societies which achieved the most spectacular, broad-based economic progress in the shortest period of time are (those that) . . . believe in the magic of the marketplace."

Certainly a principal actor in the Reagan program is the multinational corporation. By reducing the official development assistance efforts, his program implicitly places a heavy burden on their corporate shoulders. But will unfettered markets and MNCs produce the most rapid and broadly shared development? In addressing this question, this paper first looks at international markets, including the flows of

12 Multinationals and Marketplace Magic in the 1980s" by Richard S. Newfarmer. From C. P. Kindleberger and D. B. Audretsch, Eds. *The Multinational Corporation in the 1980s*.

foreign direct investment to developing countries and then the more complex question of the distribution of gains from multinational investment. Second, it examines the effects of multinational investment on the pattern of development. The discussion suggests that powerful economic and political forces usually trigger government intervention in MNC activities and the administration program will probably be received coolly in most developing countries. Since intervention usually results in bargaining between host government and MNCs, a final section speculates on MNC-host government relations. . . .

I. INTERNATIONAL MARKETS AND GROWTH OF DEVELOPING COUNTRIES

President Reagan stated his position with eloquence in the Philadelphia speech: "Free people," he said, "build free markets that ignite dynamic development for everyone." But it is not always clear that market-led development always does benefit everyone—at least with the sense of equity and fairness implicit in orthodox trade theory. The issue of the distribution of gains from MNC-related trade and investment between host country and home country as well as the internal distributional effects have been the subject of heated political and academic controversy during much of the 1960s and 1970s. Two lines of argument suggest that the international markets in which MNCs operate will not produce growth as rapidly as some more preferable mixture of host-government intervention and market functioning.

The first line of argument focuses on the workings of international capital and technology markets, and points out that the flows in these markets are highly uneven. That is, foreign direct and indirect investment goes to the richest of poor nations and not to the nations which need it most. . . . Eighty seven percent of investment is concentrated in 14 of 132 developing countries—almost all of them oil exporters or wealthy semi-industrialized countries. This is a fair indication that technological transfers associated either with MNCs or sold independently are also quite concentrated.

The poorest 36 countries experienced economic growth rates of 1.6% during the 1960-1979 period, well below those of both the semi-industrialized countries (3.8%) and developed countries (4.0%). Moreover, World Bank projections show that the current account deficits of oil-importing countries will be between $70 and $85 billion over the next five years, of which $40 to $50 billion may be financed through private lending or direct investment. The shortfall must be financed largely through concessional aid. A policy which relies solely on private international capital and technology markets to produce growth in the poor countries will certainly accentuate the pain of their structural adjustment and not ameliorate poverty for much of the 1980s. . . .

Even if markets' capital and technology were perfectly competitive, laissez faire policies would undoubtedly produce similar flows. This is because the distribution of world wealth generates patterns of effective demand that create the most profitable business opportunities in the wealthy countries. Greater wealth means larger markets, greater opportunities for specialization, and economies of scale in production. To the problem which income distribution poses for free-market development, one must add another market failure: the positive externalities associated with higher levels of production and wealth. Income distribution and market failures indicate that free-market policies will probably not produce sufficiently rapid growth in the poorest countries to narrow the gaps in per capita income separating rich and poor countries in the coming decades.

A second line of argument is more complex and requires greater elaboration, for it lies at the root of many MNC-host government conflicts as well as the ill-fated North-South dialogue during the 1970s. The argument is that international markets are systematically biased against developing countries in their distribution of gains from trade and investment. These biases are traceable in part to the very existence of nation-states, which put restrictions on the movement of products and factors, and to the failure of markets to be competitive. This is not to say that trade and investment do not produce economic gains for buying and selling countries. At issue is the distribution of gains between developing and developed countries. . . .

The contention is that imperfect international markets associated with MNC investment bias the distribution of gains against developing countries, ultimately requiring some government intervention for maximum growth

Most economists in both the North and South give some credence to the fundamentally oligopolistic character of the MNCs. . . . This view starts with the insight that the MNC brings not only capital or technology to developing countries, but a *package* of tangible and intangible assets. The package is unique to each firm and thus not readily imitated by would-be competitors, especially domestic firms whose superior knowledge of the local business environment would in other instances give them a competitive edge. MNC control of this unique bundle therefore gives them a monopolistic advantage in all markets and, together with their ability to raise barriers to entry to further protect their advantage, creates a market with a limited number of sellers—oligopoly.

Oligopoly may in certain circumstances be associated with increases in global welfare, such as when it leads to economies of scale, economies of internalization, or increases in innovation. On the other hand, individual countries are not concerned about global welfare, but national welfare, and desire to accumulate benefits locally. From the perspective of developing countries, oligopoly raises the possibility that the costs of obtaining the package of MNC-provided assets is higher than would occur under workably competitive conditions—or if the package were de-bundled and the assets bought separately.

Even viewed more narrowly from the vantage of the product cycle—thought of as "cycles of monopoly" rather than as markets ineluctably working toward greater competition . . . successive waves of MNC market power may put developing countries at a distinct disadvantage in unregulated market transactions. This is because developing countries more often sell their products or factors in competitive markets in their dealings with developed countries or MNCs, while MNCs presumably sell in oligopolistic markets.

Impacts on Market Structure

There is in fact considerable evidence that MNCs operate in oligopolistic markets. For example, Fajnzylber and Martinez Tarrago found that in Mexico, MNCs sold 61% of their total sales in markets where the leading four plants accounted for 50% or greater of the market and less than 10% in markets where the four leaders held less than 25%; by comparison, Mexican firms sold only 29% in the highly concentrated markets and 33% in the low-concentration industries. More sophisticated econometric studies have found a strong correlation between concentration and various indicators of foreign participation. These facts, together with studies showing strong correlations between market structures internationally, suggest that foreign direct investment is the bridge that links concentrated market structures in various countries—except perhaps where the state intervenes to proscribe multinational investments as in Japan.

These indicators of oligopoly—four-firm concentration ratios and the like—miss another important deviation from workable competition, market power attributable to conglomerate organization. A conglomerate is a firm which operates in several product and geographic markets. Almost by definition then, MNCs are large multi-market firms and have at their disposal discretionary power unavailable to single-market firms. This includes the ability to cross-subsidize growth in one market with profits from another, to manipulate transfer prices on in-house product and factor flows between markets, to allocate production among alternative countries, and engage in international price discrimination. Differences in relative size of MNCs and their domestic competitors also create asymmetry in competition. This power may or may not be used in ways which correspond to the dictates of workably competitive markets. . . .

Underlying this association between MNCs and oligopoly is a blend of behavioral and technological causes. Technologies of many modern MNC products play a dual role. Patented technology forms part of the unique package of assets that is the monopolistic advantage of MNCs in the market, and thus accords MNCs an absolute cost advantage over potential competitors. Also, production technologies generate economies of scale which create a scale barrier to entry and limit the number of producers a market can efficiently support. Economies stemming from the internalization of international flows of information may also act as a scale barrier. . . .

But technology and economics of internalization are far from the sole source of MNCs' monopolistic advantage. Company behavior in advertising, acquisitions, and restrictive business practices are probably as important as technology in creating concentrated domestic market structures. Advertising (discussed further below) has been shown to have a positive association with concentration in econometric studies of Brazil, Malaysia, Mexico, the Philippines and other countries. UNCTAD's several studies on restrictive business practices serve to illustrate the importance of interlocking directorates, cross-subsidization, local cartels,and foreclosure of supplies. Unlike patent or scale barriers associated with technology or information transfers, these sources of monopolistic advantage do not usually carry the social benefits that might otherwise offset their effects on market structure. In most cases, their net effect is to restrict competition and raise prices to consumers with little or no efficiency gains.

Another behavioral determinant of domestic market structure stems from the fact that domestic oligopolies dominated by subsidiaries are linked to a larger global network of rivalry. As a newly studied phenomenon, "international oligopoly" merits detailed consideration.

International Oligopoly?

As foreign investment has grown, MNCs in the same industry find themselves in competition with ever more frequency with the same rivals in several national markets. . . . That is, there may be only a few large companies in an industry so that one firm may look out across the international market and recognize its strategic interdependence with a firm based in another industrialized country, eventually facilitating collusive or parallel actions in markets around the world.

One can imagine several kinds of international oligopolistic behavior, including the formation of cartels, spheres of influence, and joint ventures to share markets, as well as oligopolistic reaction in investment strategies; one can also imagine local market effects stemming from international business practices. Let me recount briefly Shepherd's analysis of the history of the international cigarette industry to show how a few of these forms have direct consequences for market structure and performance in developing countries.

In the 1880s, mechanization provided the initial dynamism for consolidation and concentration in the United States. James Duke formed the powerful American Tobacco Company (ATC) and introduced "demand creation" marketing. He turned to foreign investment when it appeared in the 1890s that a wave of quasi-moralistic anti-cigarette publicity and the flood of machine-made cigarettes had led to stagnation in the US market. ATC tried to penetrate the British market where 10-15 small domestic firms competed. These firms, fearing the powerful ATC, banded together to form the Imperial Tobacco Co. (ITC). The resulting struggle among equals eventually ended in truce when in 1903 ATC and ITC decided to establish a world cartel to limit their competition and share markets in the world. They allocated to each other their home territories and established a joint venture to control markets in the third world, called British American Tobacco (BAT). This cartel lasted until US antitrust authorities required its dissolution in 1911. The divestiture arrangement severed management ties among the three companies,though it left some minority equity holdings in place.

But the story of international oligopoly in cigarettes hardly ended there. American producers continued to produce primarily for the US market, comprising perhaps one-half of the world demand. ITC continued to produce in England and some European markets, and BAT continued to have free rein in the developing world. With minor deviations, these "spheres of influence" evolved and lasted with surprising durability until the mid-1960s. Then, the Surgeon General's Report in 1964 and subsequent consumer awareness in the United States that cigarettes were linked to cancer and other diseases caused a dramatic fall in the growth for US producers. They could only react by diversifying within the United States and by investing in foreign markets. This precipitated a wave of foreign investment that impinged on traditional BAT territory. Thus, in sharp contrast to BAT, over 90% of the 150 overseas affiliates of US cigarette manufacturers were established after 1965. Yet the point is that for nearly seven decades some loose form of international oligopolistic behavior determined the number and source of producers in the major cigarette markets of the developing world. . . .

Market Structure and Profitability

A final link in the argument from imperfect international markets to uneven distribution of gains is profitability. Two questions about profitability are relevant: If our concern for the determinants of structure is sound, then structure should be a determinant of profitability. Second, MNCs should be related to higher profitability.

Although widely studied in the industrialized countries, the market structure-profits relationship is only now becoming a concern for development economists. The 15 studies that exist for developing countries are of varied sophistication and use disparate data sets, but they have surprisingly consistent results: Nearly all show a fairly strong positive relationship between imperfect market structures—market concentration, product differentiation, relative market share, and to a lesser extent barriers to entry—and profitability.

The evidence comparing the profitability of MNCs to local firms is mixed. The econometric studies find either no difference or the MNCs in fact report lower profits. Concentration and other market imperfections may thus be the prime factor determining profits, not "foreignness" per se. It is also possible that foreign firms are in fact more profitable but that transfer pricing reduces downward profits reported in the host country.

This evidence is by no means conclusive in proving the assertion that the international system is biased in favor of home countries in the distribution of the gains from MNC-related trade and investment in favor of developing countries. One always wishes for more reliable data, more widely accepted assumptions, and fewer exogenous influences. But the evidence is persuasive that (a) foreign investment is strongly and persistently linked to domestic oligopoly in the host country, and (b) that domestic oligopoly generates high profits for those fortunate enough to operate in these markets. The evidence is sufficiently strong, in my opinion, to throw the burden of proof on those in the administration and in academia who hold that this distribution of gains from MNC-related trade and investment is fundamentally "fair".

Ironically, domestic market structure is a variable that host governments are in a position to influence—through domestic antitrust policy, tariff policy and other industrial policies. This raises the critical question of the role of the state, addressed in detail below. The point to be made here, however, is that any policy of letting "free markets work" will probably produce uneven growth among countries and relegate to developing countries a smaller share of the gains from MNC-related trade and investment than would occur in the presence of government bargaining or de-packaging of MNC assets.

II. MNCS AND THE PATH OF DEVELOPMENT

The consequences of a policy that relies on MNCs as a prime mover of growth extend beyond the consideration of the international distribution of gains. One of the most important consequences to analyze is their dynamic effects on the nature of growth itself—which products are produced, which technologies are employed, and how industries are to fit themselves into an increasingly interdependent global system. MNCs, of course, are not the sole actors in the growth process. But a policy which accords MNCs a central role must recognize their influence in forging the path of development.

The way economies grow, as distinct from the growth rate itself, has an impact on economic sovereignty and national income distribution. From the perspective of a host country, the path that will permit the greatest flexibility and control in dealing with the constraints imposed upon internal growth by the international economy is to be preferred, ceteris paribus, over alternatives. These constraints include the effects of cyclical fluctuations in demand for host country exports associated with growth or recession in the industrialized world, as well as the perennial foreign exchange shortages and technology deficiencies stemming from the process of late-starting industrialization itself. The long-term distributional effects of the way an economy grows are also important from a host-country perspective. The evolution of factor shares over time will depend on changes in relative factor quantities, changes in demand, the elasticity of substitution between factors,and the factor bias in technical change. Government policy and institutional factors, such as the distribution of land or political power, are no less important in affecting income distribution. It is of more than passing interest to planners in host governments how MNCs affect these relationships and with them the path of development.

One approach to the obviously difficult measurement problems in addressing this issue is to study how MNCs "grow differently" from domestic firms in an industry. Holding industry constant (and therefore government policy to the extent it is nondiscriminatory among ownership groups), this comparison can often place differences in behavior in stark relief and we can see how the differences in firm behavior affect development. Let us consider five aspects of firm behavior: advertising, technological appropriateness, technological dependence, trade propensities, and transfer prices. All have implications for economic sovereignty and income distribution.

Advertising

There are several reasons to suspect that MNCs may be associated with increasing levels of advertising. The promotion of certain products over others ultimately influences consumer choices and the mix of products available locally. First, an important monopolistic advantage of many MNCs is their differentiated products coupled with their superior marketing skills. These skills are usually employed to mount substantial advertising campaigns. Second, an element of differentiation in many consumer goods is constant change of model and product design, regardless of the actual usefulness of the change. Sometimes these costs are quite expensive, as in the auto industry. MNCs are the unquestioned leaders in this process as they ride the crest of the product-cycle wave, another element of their monopolistic advantage. Third, many of the new products are designed in the first instance for the mass markets of the home country, markets where wealth and consumer awareness are much higher, and where poverty is far less widespread, leading to questions about the appropriateness of products for poor countries.

Evidence on the issue of advertising is of three types. The first links MNCs to the parallel rise of the multinational advertising agencies. Both are seen as promoting the technology of inefficient consumption. These studies are not particularly helpful in isolating the role of MNCs from domestic actors, who after all use the same foreign advertising agencies. Second, some anecdotal and econometric evidence does seem to indicate that MNCs change promotional norms within an industry. For example, MNCs sponsored 75-80% of radio and newspaper ads in Swahili and English in Kenya and were responsible for 45% of all advertising placed. Econometric findings for Brazil, Mexico, Malaysia, and the Philippines show that the level of foreign ownership was positively correlated with the level of industry advertising, though one study for a more limited sample in Colombia found no difference.

The third variety of evidence is case studies, and is perhaps the most persuasive because it charts the dynamic relation between increases in foreign ownership and changes in promotional norms and product quality. American firms entering Argentina's cigarette industry were responsible for a quadrupling of the advertising expenditures to sales in the three years after their entry in 1966. Other cases are also reported in Mexico's food industry and in pharmaceuticals for Argentina.

The much-discussed case of infant formula offers the clearest case of the link between the growth of multinationals, changes in promotional norms,and the link to inappropriate products. Nestlé's activities in much of the Third World drew attention because the company used saleswomen dressed in white coats to promote sales of infant formula in rural areas. It became popular in several communities to switch from breast-feeding to formula, even at the increased cost to poor consumers. An adverse side consequence in many areas, however, was an increase in infant mortality and malnutrition because mothers mixed the formula with polluted water; they were not able to sterilize their feeding implements; or they cut down the amount of milk powder in the formula mixture to save money. This illustrates the more general point that consumer ignorance is much higher in developing countries, consumer protection laws much weaker, and so the net distorting effects of MNC advertising in "consumption technology" may be greater.

While the evidence is not conclusive, the development implications of increases in advertising associated with foreign investment are extremely important. First, advertising appears to increase industrial concentration in developing countries, with attendant consequences for income distribution and economic efficiency. Second,advertising appears to influence profitability, as discussed above, channeling more resources for investment in the differentiated consumer goods industries—industries that tend to produce goods serving the relatively wealthy. Third, advertising does appear to direct consumer choice towards the advertised products and therefore shift consumption patterns to mirror those in the North, shaping the "ideology of consumption". Advertising levels in developing countries are now comparable to those in the developed countries. . . .

Product choice has a strong impact on the path of development because it influences which industries are established and, to the extent that elasticities of substitution between labor and capital are less than one, which technologies are employed. This has direct implications for distribution and economic sovereignty.

Technological Appropriateness

Because MNCs create technology in an environment where capital is cheap relative to labor, it has been argued that their technology is probably more capital-intensive than is appropriate to developing countries. The transfer of their technology on the heels of their products, the argument runs, creates a bias in growth towards a capital-intensive technology with its adverse effects on employment and income distribution. Despite the large number of studies on the relative labor intensity of multinationals and domestic firms, there are to date few definitive results. . . .

One reason why this question is so difficult to resolve is that technological change is bound up closely with changes in products. Cutting in at any point in time for measurement probably misses imitation effects among ownership groups when a new product or technology is introduced, diluting any statistical results. Also, controlling for product mix and quality is extremely difficult in cross-sectional studies. The most promising area of further research is that of case studies linking the introduction of new products and advertising with changes in technology and market structure.

In conclusion, it should be noted that variation in capital-labor ratios is far more sensitive to industry that to ownership group, suggesting the policy instrument of greatest importance is the selection of which industries are to be established,and only secondarily who produces within any given industry.

Technological Dependence

Technological dependence refers to the continuing inability of a developing country to generate the knowledge, inventions, and innovations necessary to propel self-sustaining growth. If a country does not produce its own technology in at least some industries, it is argued, it will suffer slower growth and more disadvantageous terms of trade in the long run. As the product-cycle model suggests, technological prowess is often the secret to large shares in fast-growing export markets and to some degree of market power,and hence high prices. Developing countries have long recognized that the inability to produce local technology can hamper economic growth. . . . Technological dependence may mean slower or "distorted" growth and reduced economic sovereignty.

Magee, for one, sees MNCs as behaving differently in their approach to local knowledge creation. MNCs create "information" with the hope of appropriating some portion of the prospective monopoly rent associated with the application of the patented information in production and marketing. Since patent protection is imperfect, MNCs are predicted to develop technology for markets where barriers to entry may be expected to supplement patent protection. It follows from Magee's argument that MNCs will transfer technology to developing countries within those institutional frameworks that maximize "appropriable" rents (most desirable the wholly owned subsidiary) and when business conditions make such a transfer the most profitable (usually in response to tariffs, government demands, or threats to the local markets formerly served by exports). It also follows that MNCs will generally prefer to tightly control research and development activities, the source of new information, in the home country. Centralization of the R&D activities of the global company conflicts directly with the interests of developing countries in domestic technological "parity" and independence. . . .

Perhaps the most persuasive case of seeing MNCs as the institutionalization of technological dependence comes from the experience of Japan, which did not permit the establishment of MNC subsidiaries. After World War II, the Japanese continued their policy of not permitting foreign direct investment but of spending liberally for imported licensed technology. Their purchases of technology from abroad were considerable, yet at the same time they spent more than four times that amount on domestic R&D. Within the relatively short period of two decades they transformed themselves into aggressive world leaders in many industries. It is arguable that this would not have occurred had US and European MNCs been allowed to control technology-intensive industries in Japanese manufacturing.

Trade

MNCs' international trade behavior appears to be different as well. With import substitution industrialization, MNCs may initiate local production through the assembly of imported components and then gradually shift to local inputs as supplier industries develop and relative costs shift in favor of local purchase. However, MNCs may lag domestic firms in the process of domestic integration for several reasons: Local inputs may entail risks in quality and supply; parents profit on the export of parts to captive subsidiaries; costs may be different due to economies of scale; exports to subsidiaries from the parent facilitate the accumulation of profits abroad through transfer pricing; and exports from the home country please home governments worried about trade deficits and employment. Domestic firms have different interests in nearly all of these areas. On the other hand, if wide cost differences between local and foreign inputs persist, local producers may join foreign producers in opposing domestic vertical integration.

These dynamics do appear to lead to higher import propensities for foreign subsidiaries than for domestic firms, even among firms in the same industry. Although some studies have shown no difference, the majority point to higher import propensities.

One might expect that any elevated import propensity for MNCs would in some measure be offset by higher export propensities. MNCs have marketing channels in place, know foreign markets better than domestic competitors, and may be better able to take advantage of inter-country difference in costs of production. On the other hand, it could be that with production facilities already in place in several markets, parents would discourage subsidiary exports on the ground that such exports would be competitive with existing operations.

A review of the several studies of relative export performance supports only weak generalizations. Several show that domestic firms perform somewhat better. An exception is when the government has taken carrot-and-stick measures to create incentives for MNCs to export. . . . Another important variable influencing MNC exports from developing countries is the degree of competition experienced in the home country. The aggressive Japanese entrance to the US electronics industry, for example, led American firms to respond by setting up "export platforms" in several developing countries to take advantage of lower labor costs. These situations illustrate the importance of MNC links to the home market in determining firm behavior in the developing country.

Transfer Pricing

Since the sale of a good or a service from one affiliate to another is not subject to the discipline of the market, the appropriate authority in the corporate hierarchy is free to set prices at the most advantageous level for maximizing corporate profits, subject to effective constraints imposed by governments. Intra-firm trade of MNCs accounts for a significant share of manufactured imports and exports of most developing countries. There are several reasons why MNCs might find it advantageous to manipulate transfer prices by over pricing imports to host countries or underpricing exports: to avoid controls on profit repatriation, on royalties payments and on local prices (because inflated import prices show up as higher costs), or to circumvent local tax rules, tariffs, exchange rate controls. The incentives are usually present to use transfer prices against developing countries because taxes in developing countries are often higher, import duties on intermediate goods lower, currencies are less stable, and controls on profit remittances more stringent. The recent precipitous cuts in US corporate taxes under the Reagan administration have probably widened the tax rate differences.

Since Vaitsos' seminal study that found that overpricing of intra-firm exports to affiliates amounted to more than 15% of the world prices in four Colombian industries, a few other studies have indicated that MNCs do indeed take advantage of the mechanism. Robbins and Stobaugh developed an optimization model of MNCs operating under different tax regimes and found that manipulating transfer prices could increase global profits as much as 15%. Their interviews of several companies found that managers of large MNCs were not taking full advantage of transfer prices, though medium-size companies tended to be more aggressive in seeking out transfer pricing profits. More recently the Greek government, for example, found that foreign subsidiaries on average paid 20% higher than the world market price in their sample of metallurgical imports and 25.7% for chemical imports. . . .

This cursory review of five important dimensions of MNC behavior suggests that there is a strong reason to believe that MNCs alter the character of growth in ways that do not always promote broadly shared development. It is entirely possible that their effects on changing the aggregate pattern of demand through advertising, combined with their effects in biasing the factor-intensity of technologies and in shaping market structures that accompany the new products, aggravate income inequities. These tendencies probably more than offset any tendencies in the opposite direction that come through the addition of capital to domestic stocks and hence lower returns to capital relative to labor. Similarly, there is reason to believe that the trade effects do not contribute to greater economic sovereignty or to structures of trade likely to produce the greatest gains in development.

All this is not to say that MNCs do not have a contribution to make to development. To the contrary, often they represent the most immediately available combination of valuable resources. Rather, the conclusion to be drawn from this discussion is that there is much legitimate and well-founded concern about the influence of MNCs on market-led development, and, from the host government's perspective, much to be gained from bargaining vigorously with MNCs.

For that reason, host governments will in all likelihood continue to pressure MNCs for a greater share of the gains from their activities and for changes in their behavior. A US policy that asks host governments to reduce their regulatory role vis-à-vis MNCs thus flies in the face of some powerful political-economic forces.

III. MNCS AND THE STATE: A NEW ERA OF PEACEFUL COEXISTENCE?

. . . . A strong argument can be made for the idea that the era of nationalism and MNC-host government conflict is passed. Some authors have suggested that bargaining power in the bilateral negotiations between states and MNCs has swung irreversibly in favor of host governments, producing a new, more equitable distribution of gains—and with it a new stability. Indeed, several studies of the natural resource industries show that after the huge fixed costs of investments in resource installations are sunk, the host government can in effect "hold the company hostage." Bargains made at entry become obsolete as power shifts from the companies to the state.

At the same time, the technical expertise within the governments to negotiate beneficial contracts has strengthened the governments' bargaining hand. Governments have learned to play off one oligopolist against another. Governments in the Caribbean succeeded in getting Kaiser to break the united opposition of the larger aluminum companies to government participation in their bauxite operations. The Brazilians were able to set up an aircraft industry by creating a state enterprise and buying licenses from Piper, the weaker competitor of Cessna. Cessna had dominated the Brazilian market but it refused government demands to take on domestic partners and begin local production with international technology.

Also, the explosion of international liquidity as petrodollars were recycled through the Eurodollar markets has given host governments an alternative to MNC-provided capital. Between 1970 and 1980, foreign direct investment fell from 34% of nonconcessional flows going to developing countries to 27%, while private bank and bond lending rose from 30% to 36%. In the short period between 1978 and 1980, the claims of American banks on Third World nations rose from $78 billion to $137 billion. It is argued that this has strengthened the hand of host governments in dealing with MNCs.

MNCs, for their part, have demonstrated a new flexibility in their dealings with host governments. This has given rise to unprecedented arrangements in technology transfer and ownership arrangements. One indication of this is the trend toward joint ventures. It is probable that the increase in joint ventures is largely attributable to post-1973 increases in Japanese foreign investment in natural resources in partnership with governments. Joint ventures in manufacturing, undoubtedly more common than a decade ago, are still by and large majority-controlled, with stock dispersed on incipient local capital markets or in the hands of weak joint-venture partners. Nonetheless, the importance of joint ventures should not be overlooked because in the industrialized countries these have historically provided a stepping-stone to full domestic control later. The same could be said for other 'new forms' of multinational activity, such as management contracts and engineering and services.

Yet it would be a mistake to infer from these changes a new era of peaceful coexistence in MNC-host country relations. The thrust of the analysis in the first part of this paper suggests that governments will continue to apply pressure to MNCs to increase their share of the gains from multinational investment, to overcome foreign exchange and technology constraints,and, perhaps with less urgency, to spread the benefits of development. Measures taken range from regulating firm conduct, such as in the transfer of patented technology and requiring exports as a condition for importing, to squeezing MNCs out of industries by systematically favoring domestic or state enterprises over foreign subsidiaries.

To be sure, the parameters of bargaining are considerably narrower than in the 1960s from the viewpoint of both host countries and MNCs. Host countries are more appreciative of the full costs of nationalization and less disposed to rapid expropriation. Companies, for their part, realize that a piece of the market is better than none at all; it may even be embarrassing when a hard-line stance by one oligopolist is broken with a concession of a competitor, who then enjoys the more limited fruits of the bargain; and collusive stances vis-à-vis an aggressive government are arguably more difficult to forge in an international (as opposed to an American) oligopoly. The massive expansion of private international debt has undoubtedly reinforced this parameter on the company side. The international banks, many of which have intimate ties with industrial companies, have a vested interest in the overall macroeconomic success of the developing country. They cannot simply shut down a plant and pull out in a dispute over a single investment or policy; rather they must rely on negotiated outcomes or risk losing an entire portfolio. But the underlying drive within the narrower bargaining parameters continues to be for developing countries to change the structure of their economies, compelling most host countries to pressure the MNCs.

In this view, the primary reason that MNC-host conflicts have abated in the late 1970s is the weakened (not strengthened) position of many states brought about by the abrupt price increases in oil. Developing countries which coped with the oil-induced problems of structural adjustment by borrowing recycled petrodollars were soon dealt a second blow—abrupt increases in world interest rates. These two events have turned terms of trade sharply against oil-importing developing countries, and their current-account deficits moved deeply into the red. Thus, even though commercial bank lending increased in relative share of capital inflows into these countries, foreign investment inflows are no less important for their contribution to capital-account balances. (In fact, with the abrupt rise and instability in international interest rates, governments may well prefer equity over debt as a source of capital.) Any government action to undermine the position of foreign investors during this period jeopardizes this thin stream of inflows.

These events weakened major nationalistic initiatives to change ownership and other relationships with MNCs in Latin America and elsewhere. Brazil, the largest single recipient of foreign inflows among developing countries and one of the most sophisticated regulators of multinational investment, slowed its attempts to leverage industries out of MNC control. The Andean Pact abandoned its Article 24 agreement requiring a fade-out of foreign investment for a mixture of reasons: Chile's withdrawal from the pact after the military coup in 1973, the impact of the foreign exchange shortage induced by the deterioration in terms of trade, and finally the political difficulty of implementing the accords in multiple countries. The change in governments in Peru after 1975 in the face of severe economic recession, together with the change in Chilean policy and the subsequent defeat of Manley in Jamaica, gave rise to the feeling that, among their other "mistakes," the nationalistic regimes in these countries had pressed their bargaining position vis-à-vis the companies too far. Their experience argued for subtlety in negotiation.

Besides the weakening of states attributable to the international economy, the very spread of MNCs in manufacturing has also had an impact upon the internal politics of the state in a way that places new constraints on the "political will" to bargain, and thus requires technocrats use greater finesse in future bargaining. Contrary to the case in raw-materials production, MNCs in manufacturing have far greater linkages to local interest groups—MNCs employ a larger labor force (per unit of capital) than most raw-materials ventures, they usually create a larger network of white-collar employees,and they usually have at least a few domestic competitors who share broad class interests (though not without conflict at the margin). These social groups have much deeper roots in civil society than do elites traditionally associated with raw materials. This makes "foreigners" much less obvious targets of nationalistic forces on the one hand, and on the other, accords them some influence in policymakers' circles. . . .

Also contrary to the raw-materials case, a continual flow of new products and technology emanates from the home country so that the subsidiaries' continued growth and prosperity is contingent to some degree upon its links to the parent. This works to strengthen the hand of multinational manufacturers of differentiated products over time. . . .

A final change in business organization in the 1970s also places a new parameter on the political will of the state: Many advanced developing countries have sired their own multinationals, giving their governments a new stake in an open international commercial system. This tendency is rapidly growing but small in relative importance and so is not yet strong enough to dampen the overall impulse of host governments to bargain.

These two socioeconomic dynamics—a drive for host governments to change the structure of their economies in the face of market pressures to the contrary and narrowing bargaining parameters—will undoubtedly play themselves out differently in each country. Given the narrow parameters of bargaining in manufacturing, government strategies will probably be more subtle, more piecemeal, and slower than the over conflicts of the past that sometimes ended in nationalization of the toppling of a regime—or both. . . .

One element . . . may figure prominently in MNCs-host country relations and is wholly unpredictable: the politics supporting the regimes in advanced developing countries. The current path of development continues to leave large numbers of people isolated from the benefits of development. Unemployment, malnutrition, and low productivity continue to characterize large segments of the population, even in advanced developing countries. To be sure, these groups are not wholly unaffected by growth; the better off among them are not infrequently able to climb above some line of absolute poverty during their lifetimes. Nonetheless, concepts of social justice and human rights to the basic necessities of life often precede the economic model's capacity to deliver them, sowing the seeds of political change. This is especially true of the urban poor, who are most susceptible to the new aspirations for consumption introduced by advertising and most vulnerable to downturns in growth rates. These politics may interact with slow real growth in many developing countries . . . to produce a volatile mixture of political instability. In some countries, these politics will certainly reshape the parameters of negotiation between the state and multinational companies in the coming years.

13

Selling Off America

THOMAS OMESTAD

Thomas Omestad argues forcefully that the current laissez-faire policy of the United States towards foreign direct investment within its borders threatens to weaken America's international economic strength and political power. Since the early 1980s, Omestad finds, the United States has experienced a rapidly rising influx of foreign investment, largely driven by the macroeconomic policies of the Reagan administration. Because the United States is more open to foreign investment than other countries, he argues, this influx unfairly and inappropriately increases America's economic and political dependence on others. Moreover, Omestad maintains, foreign investment has not created a significant number of new jobs in the United States. Realist in its concern for America's international power and position, this article contrasts sharply with the views of Mack Ott (Reading 14).

Foreigners with fistfuls of devalued dollars now comb America for banks, businesses, factories, land, and securities. This shopping spree began in the 1970s, but its growing strength is a principal legacy of Reaganomics. As long as America consumes more than it produces, the imbalance must be made up with foreign money that purchases IOUs and equity. In the 1980s America began trading ownership of assets (and the future incomes they provide) for the privilege of living beyond its means. The result is a continuing erosion of control over decision making and technologies that are crucial to the creation of national wealth and power.

How long Americans will sustain this grand financial experiment is an open question. Anxieties that foreigners, particularly Japanese, are buying up America have coalesced into an emotional political issue, as seen in the 1988 presidential

---

13 "Selling Off America" by Thomas Omestad. Reprinted with permission from *Foreign Policy (76* Fall 1989).

campaign. The anti-investment appeal reflects a serious weakening of public support for traditional U.S. policy toward foreign funds. A 1988 opinion survey taken for *The International Economy* revealed that 74 per cent of Americans believe foreign investment has lessened U.S. economic independence, 78 per cent favor a law restricting foreign ownership of businesses and real estate, and 89 per cent want foreign investors to register with the government. The gulf between current policy and public attitudes means that the Bush administration will come under intensifying pressure to consider controls on foreign ownership, particularly as foreign takeovers continue or even accelerate in the 1990s.

The debate on foreign investment may not bring out the best in the American people. Politicizing foreign investment appeals to the insular, nativist streak in U.S. politics. Foreign purchases offer highly visible signs of America's declining position in the world economy and of the increasing penetration of its economic and political system by foreign interests. When the British purchase Pillsbury, the Japanese buy CBS Records, the West Germans take control of A&P, and the Canadians amass Manhattan skyscrapers, public resentment stirs.

For Canadians and West Europeans, this growing public concern seems premature. Their own unease did not develop until American penetration had reached far greater levels. In the late 1960s and 1970s, distress over extensive American control of key Canadian industries prompted more than 200,000 people to join Independent Canada Associations. But by that time foreign ownership of Canada's manufacturing and energy industries had climbed above 50 per cent. The Canadian government's response was to create a screening agency for foreign acquisitions. In Western Europe, after U.S. investment reached high levels in a number of major industries, the best-selling 1967 book, *The American Challenge,* galvanized public concern about American economic power. French author Jean-Jacques Servan-Schreiber warned darkly that "fifteen years from now the world's third greatest industrial power, just after the United States and Russia, may not be Europe, but American industry in Europe."

Today, it is America's turn to exploit the opportunities and meet the challenges of foreign economic power. The public dialogue on foreign investment is all too easily dominated by those with isolationist instincts on one side and those with vested interests on the other. Needed is a dispassionate debate, but a debate nonetheless. The issues themselves are too important to be dismissed as xenophobic or narrowly nationalistic, as the Reagan and Bush administrations have sought to do.

While the overall degree of foreign ownership in the American economy does not seem excessive at this point, its rate of growth is cause for concern. America's new vulnerability stems above all from the self-inflicted wounds of U.S. macroeconomic policies. Yet it also follows decades of allowing other countries asymmetrically broad access to U.S. companies, especially to high-technology concerns. The foreign investment wave therefore calls for a reassessment of policy in order to ensure that U.S. interests are being preserved, that acquisitions in industries critical to national defense and civilian high-technology are scrutinized, and that the country proceeds along a path of economic interdependence rather than mere dependence.

TRADITIONAL POLICY

Throughout its history the United States has taken an essentially laissez faire approach to foreign investment on the premise that free capital flows maximize economic efficiency. "A world with strong foreign investment flows is the opposite of a zero-sum game," President Ronald Reagan stated in September 1983. "We believe there are only winners, no losers, and all participants gain from it." U.S. international investment policy rests on the principle of national treatment: With few exceptions, the same laws govern investment from foreign and domestic sources. Foreign acquisitions are not routinely screened. The policy reflects both a free-market philosophy and the significant profits American companies have reaped by establishing operations abroad, particularly after World War II in capital-hungry Europe, Japan, and Latin America. Through the 1950s and 1960s foreign investment was largely one-way; for every dollar foreigners invested in the United States, Americans plunked down four or five overseas.

By the early 1970s production by the overseas units of U.S. companies had surpassed total exports from the United States itself. Some American multinational corporations deployed more than half of their total assets abroad and drew more than half of their earnings from those holdings. This outward investment sacrificed manufacturing jobs at home, but it allowed American companies as a whole to hold onto a nearly constant share of world exports from the late 1960s on.

For U.S. policymakers the principle of free capital movement served larger geopolitical purposes. As economist Robert Gilpin pointed out in *The Political Economy of International Relations (1987)*, "Foreign direct investment has been considered a major instrument through which the United States could maintain its relative position in world markets, and the overseas expansion of multinational corporations has been regarded as a means to maintain America's dominant world economic position in other expanding economies." Open investment was part of the broader U.S.-led effort to liberalize and expand international economic activity through the creation of the General Agreement on Tariffs and Trade (GATT), the International Monetary Fund, and the Organization for Economic Cooperation and Development (OECD). U.S. overseas investments and trade relationships were credited with fostering the economic recovery of Western Europe and Japan and strengthening the anticommunist military alliances.

Since the early 1970s, however, the pattern of foreign investment among industrial countries has shifted significantly. The growth of U.S. overseas investment has slowed, and, with economic recovery achieved, investors in Japan and Western Europe have looked to America and elsewhere for commercial opportunities. Financial deregulation and vastly improved communications technologies have allowed investors to move decisively into foreign securities markets. Meanwhile, multinational corporations have come to view overseas investment as part of a larger strategy. Gaining market shares abroad has become synonymous with staying competitive globally, maximizing long-run returns, and hedging against protectionism. That has been especially true of the world's biggest consumer market, the United States.

By investing in America, foreigners advance a number of goals: They place their capital in a political and legal safe haven, exploit economies of scale, secure distribution networks and improve product-related services, gain access to a skilled workforce and research and development efforts, and circumvent protectionist barriers. The final reason grew especially important during the Reagan years as the value of U.S. imports subject to protectionist restraint doubled to 24 per cent.

Constraining Japanese imports has had the paradoxical effect of creating new competitors at home. Restraints on imported cars, semiconductors, and televisions, for example, have spurred the establishment of Japanese assembly plants in the United States.

During the Reagan years foreign investment was also driven by an improvident macroeconomic policy. Reagan entered office with the dual ideological mission of building up U.S. military power and cutting tax rates. Borrowing to cover the new military expenditures drained some three-quarters of America's chronically meager savings. Interest rates rose as government and private sources competed for funds. Foreign investors, attracted to higher rates of return than were available elsewhere, flocked to America, initially plowing their funds into securities, especially government debt. As foreigners bought up dollars with which to invest in America, the dollar's value increased. But the price of U.S. exports also rose, crippling some U.S. industries and pushing more production abroad. America's international investment fortunes were soon reversed; by 1985 the United States had become a net debtor for the first time since World War 1. The mounting imbalance led to monetary coordination among the top industrial countries that since 1985 has sharply devalued the dollar and improved U.S. trade performance. However, the currency's drop undercut the value of dollar-denominated securities at the same time it made hard assets exceedingly cheap for foreign concerns. Thus began a grand debt-for-equity swap that has been dubbed the "fire sale" of America.

Though growing rapidly, foreign investment in the United States is often overstated. Today, foreigners own 4-5 per cent of total U.S. assets. Foreign interests employ around 3 million Americans—3.5 per cent of the labor force. At the end of 1988, according to Commerce Department data, foreigners had $1.79 trillion invested in the United States, while Americans held $1.25 trillion in investments abroad. Thus the United States was a net debtor of $533 billion. (This figure is actually overstated because investments are tabulated according to their book value—the price paid when the asset was acquired. U.S. overseas investments tend to be older than foreign investments here, so their book value falls below current market value to a greater degree than do foreign holdings in America.) Of foreigners' total investment in America in 1988, $329 billion, or just 18 per cent, was direct investment, which the Commerce Department defines as the book value of enterprises in which a foreigner owns at least 10 per cent of the voting securities. All other holdings—such as U.S. Treasury and private bonds and smaller equity stakes—are considered portfolio investments. Portfolio holdings are passive in that they do not confer actual control as foreign direct investment (FDI) usually does. Portfolio investment, however, is more volatile because of its high liquidity and sensitivity to interest rate differences.

FDI in the United States has been advancing briskly since the early 1970s. In 1971 it stood at $14 billion, in 1980 $83 billion, and by the end of 1988 $329 billion, a 23-fold jump since 1971 and almost a quadrupling under Reagan. In 1988 FDI grew 21 per cent. Meanwhile, American direct investment abroad has grown more slowly. U.S. FDI rose from $83 billion in 1971 to $215 billion in 1980 and to $327 billion in 1988. In 1988 it grew only 6 per cent. America's worsening financial position suggests that foreign investment here will be outpacing U.S. investment abroad for some time to come.

The top direct investors are first the British and then the Japanese, the latter group advancing quickly during 1988 to displace the Netherlands as the second largest. Canada and West Germany trail in fourth and fifth place.

Much of the public concern over foreign investment stems from its concentration in particular sectors and localities. About 20 per cent of total banking assets in America are held by foreign banks; foreigners control 12 per cent of the U.S. manufacturing base, though slightly less than I per cent of its agricultural land. Foreign interests own 25-30 per cent of chemical industry assets and about half of the consumer electronics and cement industries. They are making strong inroads in insurance, publishing, machine tools, semiconductors, and wholesale trade.

Foreigners are also buying heavily into America's major cities: In Los Angeles, they own an estimated 46 per cent of the prime commercial real estate, in Houston 39 per cent, and in the nation's capital 33 per cent. The state of Hawaii received more than one quarter of all Japanese real estate investment in the United States from 1985 to 1987, and home prices in Honolulu soared.

AUTONOMY FOREGONE

The most pervasive concern about foreign investment is that it will reduce America's economic and political autonomy. Foreign held debt and foreign ownership imply dependence and vulnerability. With ownership goes control over economic decisions and influence over political ones. Senator Frank Murkowski (R-Alaska) summed up this view bluntly in the December 30, 1985, *New York Times:* "Once they own your assets, they own you."

While foreigners through their investments gain a direct stake in the health of the U.S. economy, they also can pose a unique problem: Their ultimate political loyalties and interests lie elsewhere. For this reason, all countries at least partially shelter their political systems from foreign influence, even when the system is as grounded in the values of openness and pluralism as is America's.

From a historical standpoint, Washington has good reason for concern about the leverage foreigners have on it. This is particularly apparent when the investors are government-controlled, such as the central banks in Europe and Japan that have amassed huge holdings of U.S. government securities in recent years. Economic pressure is a prime tool of foreign-policy influence, which is exerted even against close allies if necessary. In 1956 the United States demonstrated its alarm at the British-French invasion of Egypt's Suez canal by withholding badly needed oil supplies from Britain and France and by refusing to help halt a damaging run on the pound. After the 1973 oil embargo Saudi Arabian holdings of U.S. dollars and government securities emerged as a potential "money weapon" against U.S. foreign policy. The Treasury Department refused to reveal the amount of Saudi holdings to Congress for fear that the Saudis would sell them off and trigger a plunge of the dollar.

America's heavy reliance on foreign capital in the 1980s has greatly accelerated the decline of its global economic power. By 1986 nearly two-thirds of America's net investment in plant, equipment, and housing was being supplied by foreigners. Indeed, without foreign capital, interest rates during 1983-84 might have been five percentage points higher than they were. Foreigners in recent years have financed more than half of the federal budget deficit, and they now hold about 10 per cent of the national debt.

In May 1987 foreign investors showed their clout by balking for two days at the purchase of 30-year Treasury securities; the Treasury quickly cut the price to draw them back into the market. The dumping of Treasury securities by Japanese fund managers, who panicked at the announcement of a poor U.S. trade performance, helped set off the October 1987 stock market crash. And rumors during the 1988 presidential campaign held that Bush was benefiting from an implicit agreement with Bonn and Tokyo to prop up the dollar through election day. Whether or not such an understanding existed, the rumors were a sign of the potential for foreign influence over U.S. economic policy and electoral outcomes.

Dependence on foreign money forced the Reagan administration to replace the previously neutral posture toward foreign investment with an unrestrained welcome. Although couched in terms of free-market economics, the public welcome masked administration fears that foreign funds might flow elsewhere, triggering a hard landing for the economy, the Reagan revolution, and Republican presidential hopes. Thus in 1984 the administration pushed through Congress the repeal of the 30 per cent withholding tax on earnings from foreign-held government and corporate securities. The following year the Treasury allowed publicity-shy foreigners to buy U.S. government bonds anonymously. And Reagan threatened to veto the 1988 trade bill until a proposal for more public disclosure of foreign holdings was removed.

To protect and enhance the value of their investments, foreign interests have stepped up their lobbying and campaign-related activities. Lobbyists and lawyers representing foreign interests are now frequent visitors to Capitol Hill, federal agencies, state legislatures, and city halls. Foreign interests have banded together to form several new lobbying groups, the most influential being the Washington-based Association for Foreign Investment in America led by the prominent former cabinet officer Elliot Richardson.

Foreign interests pressured Florida, California, and other states to repeal their unitary taxes, which are assessed on a company's worldwide sales of goods produced in a state rather than only on the sales made within the state. Sony of America executives threatened to scrap plans to build factories in both California and Florida if their unitary taxes were not lifted. Florida agreed after the governor called a special legislative session during Christmas week 1984. In California foreign interests funneled contributions into the campaign coffers of state legislators. They stressed the state's investment potential and threatened to transfer operations to nonunitary tax states. British Prime Minister Margaret Thatcher asked Reagan to wade back into California politics on the side of repeal; Reagan later announced his support of federal legislation to outlaw the unitary tax nationwide. The legislature in Sacramento eventually scrapped the tax, losing an estimated $300 million in revenue in 1986 alone.

Congress has also faced skillful foreign lobbying efforts. In 1987-88 Toshiba Corporation and its U.S. subsidiary, Toshiba America, orchestrated a grassroots campaign in excess of $9 million that succeeded in easing sanctions intended to punish Toshiba for its sale of high-technology military equipment to the Soviet Union. Toshiba's message to lawmakers was simple: A ban on sales would cost the jobs of thousands of constituents. Toshiba America's lobbyists coordinated protests by companies using its components or selling Toshiba products under their own labels. Ironically, because Toshiba America is considered a U.S. corporation, its lobbyists were not required to register as foreign agents. Another fierce lobbying drive took place in 1988 when foreign investors weighed in against the so-called Bryant amendment, named for Texas Democratic Representative John Bryant, which would have required disclosure of large foreign holdings. Many foreign investors said that they would take their money elsewhere if the amendment were adopted.

The Japanese have been the most active politically. According to Pat Choate, an economist studying foreign political influence in America, 152 Japanese companies and government agencies hired 113 firms for representation in Washington in 1988, three times as many as the British. For this the Japanese paid more than $100 million—"more than the combined budgets of the U.S. Chamber of Commerce, the National Association of Manufacturers, The Business Roundtable, the Committee for Economic Development and the American Business Conference—the five most influential business organizations in Washington," Choate reported in the June 19, 1988, *Washington Post*. Washington lobbying was only part of the elaborate Japanese public relations activities. Japanese corporate philanthropy in America came to $140 million in 1988, while research contracts with universities reached $30 million. Other support goes to museums, think tanks, and public television stations. Clearly, the Japanese have excelled at the American art of winning friends and influencing people.

Foreign investors have also used a major legal loophole to directly influence federal and state campaigns. The Federal Election Campaign Act of 1974 specifically forbids foreign nationals from making contributions to political campaigns. But the Federal Election Commission, in a series of divided opinions, has interpreted the law to permit U.S. subsidiaries owned by foreign firms to donate campaign funds through political action committees (PACs). This interpretation has defeated the congressional intent of barring foreigners from U.S. elections. Foreign-company PACs reportedly contributed more than $1.1 million toward the 1986 election and at least $2 million toward the 1988 election. About 100 foreign-company PACs are now in operation.

Foreign acquisitions raise concerns of another kind when they take place in the defense industry. Thus in 1976 President Gerald Ford set up the Committee on Foreign Investment in the United States (CFIUS), a Treasury-led interagency body that meets on an ad hoc basis to review such investments for their national security implications. Until new legislation was passed recently, the president would have had to declare a national emergency to block such an acquisition. There seemed to be little need, however, because no president has ever found the need formally to bar a sale through CFIUS.

Growing foreign ownership in the U.S. defense industry is one facet of a broader erosion of the defense industrial base. According to a tally of sales reported in the journal *Mergers and Acquisitions*, II companies in military-related industries were sold to foreigners in 1983, while 37 such takeovers, some hostile, occurred in just the first half of 1988.

Defense Department officials have felt that certain purchases could increase the chances of espionage or of other transfers of military technology to adversaries. Thus the Pentagon has sought to safeguard defense activities by obtaining private assurances that research and development and production remain in the United States. The government can demand that foreigners divest themselves of units involved in especially sensitive operations or order the U.S. units to operate as blind trusts, allowing foreign owners to collect the profits but keeping them out of management. It can also continue to limit foreign acquisitions of defense contractors to allied countries. Finally, the Pentagon can deny contracts and security clearances to a foreign-owned firm it considers a risk. Still, Pentagon monitors of foreign investment are handicapped by a troubling lack of timely information about takeovers. The Defense Department often discovers the sale of a defense firm only after the fact, and it does not systematically track ownership trends among its contractors and subcontractors. Consequently, no one really knows the true extent of foreign ownership of defense-related firms.

Anxieties about relying on foreign-owned defense firms came to a head in 1987 when the Japanese electronics giant Fujitsu made a $200-$225 million bid for Fairchild Semiconductor Corporation. Ironically, Fairchild was already owned by a French firm, Schlumberger Ltd., and was supplying $100 million in advanced circuitry annually for U.S. defense efforts. Well-publicized Pentagon criticisms of the sale led Fujitsu to withdraw its bid before CFIUS could issue a recommendation.

Fairchild, the financial loser, was later sold for $120 million to a U.S. firm, National Semiconductor Corp.

Driven by such security concerns, Congress inserted in the 1988 trade bill a provision authored by Senator James Exon (D-Nebraska) and Representative James Florio (D-New Jersey) that allows the president to block foreign acquisitions if they appear to endanger national security, Reagan called the provision unnecessary but did not veto it. The first test of the Exon-Florio amendment came in February 1989 when President George Bush decided against blocking the sale of the Monsanto Company's semiconductor subsidiary to a West German chemical group. The Monsanto firm was the last major U.S. manufacturer of silicon wafers, a vital component of advanced semiconductors. Although CFIUS deliberated on the deal's implications for the defense industry, it proved difficult to justify blocking the sale to a close ally, particularly after the purchaser, Huels A.G., privately committed to keep Monsanto's research and development in the United States.

RESTRICTIONS ABROAD

Political support for foreign investment has been shaken by the long-time imposition of tougher limits on foreign ownership by other countries. The United States places fewer restrictions on foreign investment than any other industrial power. While the Reagan administration publicly prodded trading partners to lower their trade barriers, it exerted little pressure in the investment field. The Bush administration will find itself pressed by Congress to seek treatment for American overseas investment roughly equivalent to treatment of investment here.

Foreign acquisitions in America are blocked in only a few areas related to national security as specified by OECD guidelines. Foreigners may not invest in nuclear energy, control oil pipelines, own U.S.-flag vessels, buy more than 25 per cent of a U.S. airline, or hold a broadcasting license. Thirty states limit foreign purchases of land, particularly farmland. Foreign investors need to register with the federal government only for purchases of farmland. Abroad, a trend toward liberalization of investment regulations is underway, but most countries continue to put up stiffer barriers than the United States. . . .

The Reagan administration quietly sought to lower . . . barriers to U.S. investment by placing foreign investment into an expanded GATT. But progress has been slow. Several Third World countries have opposed the idea out of fear that it would diminish sovereign control of their economies.

Reagan administration officials maintained that a more assertive approach aimed at achieving reciprocity would invite retaliation abroad. They also argued that it would violate the principle of national treatment and undercut efforts to get other countries to liberalize investment regulations. Still, the political pressure for a level playing field in investment led the Reagan and now Bush administrations to consider reciprocity, if only rhetorically, as a policy goal. This pressure will intensify with the approach of Western Europe's internally free market in 1992. The

EC is likely to add another (supranational) layer of review for large foreign acquisitions in Europe. And it is gravitating toward a strategy of capturing the value-added production of high-technology companies that want to do business in the EC. Tough new local content rules on the import of integrated circuits for semiconductors, for example, will probably force U.S. computer chip makers to shift advanced production from America to Europe.

JOBS AND TECHNOLOGY

Proponents routinely contend that foreign investment will help spark the reindustrialization of the American economy. Foreign investors are said to be creating millions of jobs. Lured by this prospect, states and cities entice them with hundreds of millions of dollars annually in incentive packages—tax write-offs, financing, and new infrastructure—that often lead to expensive bidding wars. But the common wisdom that foreign investment is an important source of new jobs may simply be wrong, according to a surprising new analysis of employment data. Economists Norman Glickman and Douglas Woodward, in their 1989 book *The New Competitors: How Foreign Investors Are Changing the U.S. Economy,* analyzed the employment effects of foreign direct investment from new plants and expansions on one hand and cutbacks on the other. They concluded that foreign investment in the United States actually reduced total employment between 1982 and 1986 by 55,900 jobs. If the recession years of 1982 and 1983 are excluded, foreigners created only a net 55,500 jobs, barely 1 per cent of all employment growth over the 1984-86 period. Thus foreign investment is hardly the engine of job growth that is claimed. From a national standpoint, states and cities may be wasting money and unfairly favoring new foreign-owned manufacturers with subsidies.

How is this conclusion possible given the rapid growth of foreign investment? The vast share of FDI represents purchases of existing assets; in 1986, for example, 81 per cent of the value of FDI and 97 per cent of all employment added to foreign payrolls came through mergers and acquisitions. These transactions transfer control of assets and do not necessarily create jobs. Indeed, mergers and acquisitions often lead to corporate restructuring that results in job losses as the new owners move to ease the burden of takeover debt. After the takeovers of Allied Giant and Federated Department Stores by Canadian corporate raider Robert Campeau, for example, more than 10,000 workers were laid off and a number of retail chains were sold. On the other hand, new foreign owners can rescue failing companies, saving jobs that might otherwise be lost. The number of foreign acquisitions that fall into this category is unknown, but one was Japanese Bridgestone's purchase of Firestone Tire and Rubber. Bridgestone appears to have arrested Firestone's downward slide by introducing quality and cost-saving measures and by soothing union-management tensions.

Even more important, foreign investors, chiefly the Japanese, are strategically picking off American competitors. In 1987 the Japanese bought an incredible 20 times as many U.S. high-tech firms as Americans bought in Japan. Japanese multinational corporations have concentrated their U.S. investments in basic industries and in the high-tech and service sectors, and they often bring along their suppliers. Japanese firms, more than European and Canadian ones, have been prone to keep top management, high value-added production, and research and development operations at home, often preferring to build "screwdriver" assembly plants that pay lower wages. "Time after time, the Japanese reserve for themselves the part of the value-added chain that pays the highest wages and offers the greatest opportunity for controlling the next generation of production and product technology," economists Robert Reich and Eric Mankin wrote in the March-April 1986 *Harvard Business Review*.

Most Japanese multinationals have not transferred technology or allowed local control to the degree that American and West European corporations have for decades. Japanese firms have launched many joint ventures in computers, biotechnology, and other high-tech areas with the apparent aim of transporting advanced research to Japan. As a result, American companies lose development and manufacturing experience and are drained of their research findings. As it stands now, some become mere marketers and distributors for Japanese-made products, exacerbating America's deindustrialization. A survey of companies operating in the U.S. automobile, computer and semiconductor industries—where Japanese firms dominate among foreign competitors—taken by Glickman and other researchers found that the proportion of American workers involved in research and development for foreign firms is less than half (3.1 per cent) of that for domestically owned firms (6.6 per cent). In short, some foreign acquisitions weaken the economy's capacity to generate wealth and translate new technologies into commercial applications.

Particularly worrisome is the growing reliance of American high-tech start-up companies on foreign partners for cash and manufacturing expertise. The quid pro quo is usually a transfer of new technologies to the foreign investors, creating future industrial competitors. One case is that of Japan's Kubota, a tractor company that is now making mini-supercomputers after investing in five Silicon Valley firms. The design, chips, and software all came from cash-hungry American firms in which Kubota staked money in exchange for minority shares and the transfer of technology. For a $75 million investment, Kubota is gaining the expertise to make a computer entirely on its own in a few years. Another example is the cash investment by Taiwan's Microtek International in Mouse Systems Corporation, a troubled U.S. maker of optical scanning equipment. Microtek used the deal to secure a source of technology and rights to buy all of Mouse. These cases illustrate a dangerous trend: U.S. companies, acting on short-term needs, are selling off the very technologies that have given them (and the economy) long-term competitive advantages.

In lower-tech areas, American manufacturers are benefiting from joint ventures through an infusion of Japanese management and manufacturing techniques, though others are facing painful competition on their home turf. U.S. automobile and auto parts manufacturers, for example, are being squeezed by Japanese competitors. The United Auto Workers estimated that 200,000 jobs might be lost by 1990 because U.S.-based Japanese manufacturers use labor more efficiently than American firms and import more parts.

However, the competition also motivates American producers to improve efficiency, quality control, and coordination between parts suppliers and assemblers; some U.S. firms are adopting the more demanding Japanese methods, such as just-in-time inventory purchases. At a General Motors-Toyota joint venture in Fremont, California, Japanese manufacturing know-how and management has turned around a failed operation. General Motors says the cars produced there are its best and most efficient. Similar improvements have been reported through joint ventures in the steel industry. From a national policy standpoint, however, the key test will be whether General Motors and other U.S. joint-venture participants can transfer new technology and production expertise to their other operations.

The surge in foreign investment warrants a fresh look at U.S. policy. But the aim of that reassessment must not be a general constriction of the influx of money. Given America's overreliance on foreign funds, that could prompt a recession or provoke even greater restrictions abroad. Yet the emerging public reaction to foreign ownership cannot be assuaged merely by touting the principle of open investment, which most countries thwart in practice, or by preaching the benefits of foreign investment, which are usually overstated. Policymakers need to reassure the public that long-term U.S. interests are being protected amid growing overseas ownership.

The underlying tenet of America's international investment policy must be to end its macroeconomic addiction to foreign money. Accepting the benefits of integration into the world economy does not mean endorsing a fiscal policy that unnecessarily increases U.S. dependence on foreign investors. This policy is unsustainable economically and politically; it also raises the cost of capital and diverts foreign and domestic savings to consumption rather than to the investment that will raise future living standards. It is, in short, no way for an economic superpower to run its affairs. . . .

Refining U.S. investment policy should not degenerate into an attempt to wall off the world economy. Rather, the goal should be to advance American interests within the framework of increasing interdependence. The point is not to blame foreign firms for assertively pursuing their own interests but to recognize that fact and adapt U.S. policy accordingly. The laissez faire attitude that continues to guide policy needs to be shelved in favor of a more pragmatic orientation—one that recognizes the problems, as well as the benefits, of foreign investment.

14

Is America Being Sold Out?

MACK OTT

This liberal economist asserts that the alleged threat of foreign investment to the United States is a myth, thus challenging the view of analysts such as Omestad (Reading 13). Ott argues that investment is mutually beneficial: both the lender or investor (foreigners) and the borrower or host (the United States) gain from the transaction. Thus, he says, foreign investment represents a net gain to the United States, not a threat.

The last time the U.S. current account balance was in surplus was in 1981. During the seven years 1982-88, U.S. deficits averaged over $100 billion. Capital inflows from foreign investors have reduced the U.S. foreign investment position steadily from a net U.S. claim of $141.1 billion at the end of 1981 to net foreign claims on the United States of $368.2 billion at the end of 1987.

Much of the commentary on this reversal has presumed the loss of U.S. economic sovereignty, declining opportunities for American labor, and a reduction in the U.S. standard of living. In rebutting these concerns, analysts have generally concentrated on selected aspects of the phenomenon. For example, recent articles have focused on the relative pace of foreign direct investment, in particular, Japanese direct investment, while others have singled out the benefits of capital inflows for both American investors and labor.

This article takes a broader perspective to review the full range of concerns about foreign investment, both from a logical and an empirical vantage. The public concerns about the flow of foreign investment and its anxiety about the implications of the U.S. net international debtor status are each addressed. We begin with an overview of recent public opinion polls about foreign investment in the United States, and then consider the data on foreign investment. The potential for a foreign

---

14 "Is America Being Sold Out?" by Mack Ott. Federal Reserve Bank of St. Louis.

takeover of the U.S. economy and the pattern of foreign investment in the United States relative of U.S. investment abroad are examined.

FOREIGN INVESTMENT IN THE UNITED STATES IN THE 1980s

In assessing the implications of foreign investment in the United States during the 1980s, it is useful to examine three dimensions of the foreign capital inflows. First is the *perception* of foreign investment as reported by the media and recorded in public opinion polls. Since perceptions are often as important as facts, it is appropriate to begin with them. If there were no perceived threat, it is unlikely that any policy actions would be considered; certainly, the threat of foreign ownership of U.S. assets would not be an issue in the public forum. Second is the *pattern* of foreign investment. The concern seems to be chiefly that foreigners will obtain control of certain U.S. industries vital to national security, industries traditionally dominated by U.S. firms, or high-technology industries. Third is the reported *magnitude* of foreign investment. If the magnitude of such investment is negligible, there cannot be much threat to U.S. overall interests. If the magnitude is substantial, the inflow of foreign capital must be evaluated on its merits.

The Perception of Foreign Investment in the United States

Opinion polls unambiguously reveal that the American public is concerned about increased foreign ownership of U.S. firms and real estate. A poll by the Roper Organization in March 1988 found that 84 percent of the respondents thought that foreign companies buying more companies and real estate in America is not "a good idea for the U.S." In the same poll, by a 49 percent to 45 percent plurality, respondents disapproved of new jobs for Americans in foreign-owned plants, and at least 72 percent thought that foreign companies' investments should be restricted. In May 1988, a CBS News/New York Times survey found that 51 percent of a national sample agreed that the "increase in foreign investment poses a threat to American economic independence." Similar findings were reported by other polling firms.

.... In a survey for the Washington Post-ABC News Poll in mid-February 1989, "Forty-five percent said Japanese citizens should not be allowed to buy property in the United States, and eight of 10 said there should be a limit on how many U.S. companies the Japanese should be allowed to buy."

The Pattern of Foreign Investment in the United States in the 1980s

There has been pronounced opposition to direct investment in the United States by foreigners, especially the Japanese. Direct investment is defined as a 10 percent or greater ownership share in a firm. Foreign direct investment in American firms has been the focus of the greatest unease. Such investment can take place either through stock purchases or the creation of new enterprises in the United States by foreigners, with or without U.S. partners. . . .

. . . . [S]ince the advent of floating exchange rates in the early 1970s, foreign direct investment in the United States has grown faster than U.S. direct investment abroad—an annual growth rate of 18.7 percent vs. 7.6 percent. Consequently, the relative size of foreign direct investment has risen—from about 22 percent of U.S. foreign direct investment in 1975 to about 85 percent in 1987. Of the $41.5 billion of direct U.S. investment by foreigners in 1987, nearly half, $19.1 billion, was in U.S. manufacturing.

The Magnitude of Foreign Investment in the United States in the 1980s

. . . . [S]ince 1975, foreign assets in the United States have increased much faster than U.S. assets abroad. This pattern of faster foreign asset growth is even more pronounced if the comparison is made from 1981, the last year of an American trade surplus, to 1987. From a net claim on foreigners of $141.1 billion, the United States has become the world's largest debtor, with estimated net liabilities to foreigners of $368.2 billion. During this interval, foreign assets increased by 165 percent compared with 62 percent for U.S. assets abroad.

The disparity in accumulation is even greater for assets held by private investors, that is, total foreign investment less U.S. securities held by foreign governments and central banks. Over the seven years 1981-87, private foreign investment in the United States more than tripled, from $398 billion to $1253 billion. The bulk of these capital inflows have gone into foreign holdings of U.S. securities—corporate stocks and bonds and government notes and bonds—and liabilities of U.S. banks—deposits by foreigners. Together, these two asset categories account for about three-fourths of the increase in private foreign investment in the United States, $643 billion of the $855 billion total.

The size of the foreign claims raises another issue, the cost of servicing the net foreign indebtedness. Peter Drucker has called this "the looming transfer crisis". . . .

Starkly put, Drucker believes that the accumulation of U.S. assets by foreigners will force the United States to repudiate its debts, either directly, indirectly by inflation or by reducing the nominal value of the dollar. . . . Such a policy would be injurious not only to foreign investors but to U.S. interests as well. To see why, consider why foreigners invest in the United States and how U.S. labor and investors each benefit from such investment.

WHY DO FOREIGNERS INVEST IN THE UNITED STATES?

There are three reasons for foreign investment in the United States or for U.S. investment abroad: greater profit, lower risk and the trade deficit. The first, greater profit, is the fundamental reason, as it is for any other investment choice. The investor chooses one asset over another because it has a higher risk-adjusted rate of return. Both critics of foreign investment . . . and defenders of unimpeded capital flows . . . are agreed: Foreign investment is motivated primarily by profit. . . .

The second motivation for foreign investment is to reduce the risks of wealth loss due to unforeseen exchange rate changes. This proposition is simply an extension of the risk reduction principle of portfolio diversification to international alternatives. Portfolio diversification—spreading wealth across several assets rather than a single security—reduces losses due to unforeseen events.

Similarly, exchange rate risk can be hedged by holding several assets denominated in different currencies rather that all in a single currency. The investor's wealth is insured against rising or falling by the full amount of any unforeseen exchange rate change. A corollary of this is that multinational firms can reduce the unforeseen variability of their production costs and market sales by producing and selling in several countries rather than in a single one.

The third reason for foreign investment is that it accompanies trade deficits. Foreign investment induced by higher yields or portfolio diversification occurs whether or not international trade is in balance; however, trade deficits imply that net foreign investment *must* occur in the amount by which trade is in deficit. Yet it would be incorrect to infer from this accounting identity that trade deficits cause foreign capital inflows. In other words, foreign investment is not undertaken simply to finance the trade deficit; indeed, it may well be that the capital inflows cause trade deficits. . . .

Thus, capital flows appear to be generated by investors' self-interested profit-seeking. There is broad agreement that, whatever other effects international capital flows may have on domestic economies, foreign investment makes investors and sellers of assets wealthier than they would be if their investment and sales were restricted to domestic assets and buyers. Nonetheless, this leaves open the issue of how labor is affected by international capital flows.

BENEFITS TO DOMESTIC LABOR OF FOREIGN INVESTMENT

Labor and the owners of capital share the value added in production created by transforming raw materials into output. Capital is just a generic term for the tools, buildings, land patents, copyrights, trademarks and goodwill that labor uses to convert one set of goods—raw materials—into another—finished output. The value of each factor of production in a market economy is its opportunity cost, that is, what the raw materials, labor or capital could produce in their most profitable alternative application.

In most cases, labor and capital are complementary, so that an increase in the quantity of one raises the productivity, hence, the value of the services, of the other. For example, providing an auto mechanic or a carpenter with more tools increases the amount or quality of work they can accomplish; this increase in productivity leads to a rise in their wages, or, at the same wages, to an increase in the number of them employed.

Consequently, to the extent that foreign investment is an increment of capital that would otherwise not be available for labor to use, the foreign capital must unambiguously be beneficial to labor. Equally true, the availability of foreign capital lowers the cost of capital to owners; this makes additions to plant and equipment cheaper, makes possible some investment projects that otherwise would not occur and raises the value of firms. Thus, even if the foreign capital does not directly affect the ownership of the firm, it benefits labor and asset owners by lowering interest rates, the cost of capital.

This discussion can be summarized in five postulates about the expected gains and losses from the addition of foreign capital:

(1) Labor gains as the incremental capital raises the productivity of labor, increasing the amount of labor that can be employed or the wages of those who are employed;
(ii) Owners of firms—the shareholders—benefit by the lower interest rates implied by higher asset prices;
(iii) Consumers gain as a result of the lower prices of goods implied by the increased labor productivity;
(iv) The profitability of financial intermediaries may decline since the value of their services in bringing borrowers and lenders together is inversely related to the supply of capital. Moreover, the entry of foreign financial intermediaries makes the industry more competitive, which also tends to reduce the rate return;
(v) Savers may lose interest income as a result of lowered interest rates due to the greater capital availability. This loss is offset, to some extent, as they receive capital gains on their existing fixed-rate portfolio holdings for the same reason as in (ii).

Since foreign investment raises the amount of capital available, labor productivity rises as does the absolute income of labor. Labor is better off with more capital than with less, and the nationality of the investor is a matter of indifference to labor.

THE MYTHICAL THREAT OF WITHDRAWAL OF FOREIGN CAPITAL

In early 1989, the U.S. economy continues its longest peacetime expansion on record, so the dangers of foreign investment are posed as the potential calamity of an abrupt foreign withdrawal. . . .

This scenario entails the confluence of four events: a decline in the dollar's exchange value; a cyclical decline in U.S. interest rates; a withdrawal and subsequent re-entry of foreign investment; and a banking crisis induced by the foreign withdrawal. Thus, to evaluate the dangers posed by foreign ownership of U.S. assets, one must investigate not just the likelihood of each of these events but their joint likelihood, including whether they are mutually consistent.

Decline of the Dollar

From its peak in February 1985, the exchange value of the dollar averaged against the principal industrial currencies has fallen more than 40 percent. . . . Yet, there has been no sign of a widespread flight from dollar assets. Even the record stock-market crash of October 1987, when the dollar's exchange value was at its nadir, did not suffice to trigger a massive withdrawal of foreign capital.

Cyclical Decline of U.S. Interest Rates

Generally, differences in interest rates in one currency vs. another are just sufficient to offset the anticipated depreciation of the higher-interest currency vs. the lower-interest currency as reflected in their forward exchange rate. While interest rates do decline in recessions, the benefit to an investor from selling U.S. assets and shifting to another currency at such times is limited by the likely state of other economies. The world's major economies are so economically integrated that periods of recession in the U.S. economy are generally also periods of recession in the other economies in which attractive substitute investments would be available. Consequently, to the extent that both interest rates and asset prices were to fall in the U.S. economy, the same pattern is likely to have occurred in the rest of the industrial economies as well, so a shift from U.S. to foreign assets would accrue no profit. If other economies' asset prices and interest rates had not fallen with those in the United States, then the depreciation of the dollar's exchange rate would obviate the benefit of such a withdrawal.

Withdrawal and Subsequent Re-entry of Foreign Investment

Investors withdrawing their funds from U.S. assets must do it in two steps—first selling the asset and then using the cash (dollar) proceeds to buy another asset, either another U.S. asset or a foreign currency. An investor selling an asset from a portfolio is, by that action, buying something else—a stock, a bond, a piece of real estate, a quantity of money denominated in some currency. When the dollar proceeds are exchanged for foreign currency, some other investors will acquire the original asset and the U.S. dollars. In the spirit of the scenario, if only domestic U.S. investors are buying the U.S. assets from the prior foreign owners, both a U.S. capital outflow and a sharply declining dollar exchange rate will occur. The capital outflow can only occur if the United States has a trade surplus. In reality, massive withdrawals of foreign capital cannot occur in the short run. Prices and exchange rates adjust first; international payments flows adjust with a substantial lag. Nonetheless, if this unlikely abrupt swing from trade deficit to surplus were to occur because of the foreigners' panic sales, the assets would end up in U.S. investors' hands at considerably lower prices. If foreigners repurchased them shortly thereafter, the result would be increased prices and an appreciation of the exchange value of the dollar with the resulting profit accruing to domestic owners.

Banking Crisis

Here the scenario presumes that foreigners, having sold their portfolios, then convert their dollar deposits to nondollar currencies. To do so, they must buy these currencies from others who, in turn, end up holding dollar deposits. This would put downward pressure on the dollar's exchange rate and would be associated with a capital outflow from the United States. Such substantial withdrawals—even if they replaced dollar for dollar in aggregate—would increase the uncertainty entailed in asset-liability management decisions at *individual* depository institutions.

In particular, this uncertainty would complicate the matching of the duration of assets and deposit liabilities. The likely response of depository institutions to these portfolio shifts would be an increase in their demand for reserves, reflected in a rise of the federal funds rate. Yet, the stress of an abrupt rise in deposit turnover—whether or not it is associated with a net outflow of funds from depository institutions—does not necessarily imply a banking crisis. Such an implication would require that the Federal Reserve take no action to accommodate an abrupt shift in the public's portfolio preferences. The Fed can and has accommodated such increases in the public's demand for liquidity and the rise in depository institutions' demand for reserves.

Overview of the Foreign Withdrawal Myth

In summary, the scenario is extremely unlikely to occur. It is internally inconsistent and depends on inept U.S. monetary policy actions and irrational investment behavior by both domestic and foreign investor. Since interest rates are linked through integrated international capital markets, the presumed low U.S. interest rates and a depreciating dollar are inconsistent. Investors, U.S. resident and foreign, are unlikely to believe that the U.S. monetary authorities would be passive in the event of a U.S. banking crisis. They could profit by buying U.S. assets at prices temporarily depressed by any general foreign withdrawal and subsequently selling them back to other chagrined but wiser foreign investors. In short, rational expectations and the profit motive induce competitive behavior which nullifies the threat of widespread foreign capital withdrawal, the same profit motive that induced the foreign investment in the first place.

HAS FOREIGN DIRECT INVESTMENT CHALLENGED CONTROL OF DOMESTIC U.S. INDUSTRIES?

Misperceptions about the distribution of foreign ownership pervade discussions about foreign investment in the United States. First . . . most foreign investment is concentrated in portfolio and bank deposits. In 1987, foreigners held only about 17 percent of their U.S. assets in direct investment; if official assets are excluded, the share of direct investment rises to about 21 percent. In contrast, U.S. direct investment abroad is about 26 percent of the total or 27 percent of private investment. . . . U.S. direct investment abroad exceeds foreign direct investment in the United States. Moreover, the excess of U.S. direct investment widened in 1987 to $47 billion from $39.2 billion at the end of 1986.

The acceleration of U.S. foreign direct investment beginning with 1985 is obvious. . . . U.S. foreign direct investment fell from 1981 to 1982 and was stagnant until 1985; during this period, foreign direct investment in the United States accelerated. Since 1985, however, U.S. investment abroad has outpaced foreign direct investment in the United States. While there is a lively debate about why this resurgence of U.S. direct investment has occurred, most analysts argue that it reflects the tax reforms of 1986. . . .

The second misperception about foreign direct investment in the United States is the apparent belief that the Japanese are the principal foreign direct investors. This notion is incorrect. . . . Japanese direct investment in the United States ranks a distant third behind that of the British and the Dutch. In fact, the European Community holds about three-fifths of the foreign direct investment in the United States—$157.7 billion of the $261.9 billion in 1987—nearly five times the Japanese stake. . . .

The third misperception is that foreign direct investment is concentrated in the manufacturing sector. . . . [T]he share of U.S. direct investment by foreigners in manufacturing is just over one-third, 35 percent, slightly less than the 41 percent share of U.S. direct investment abroad in manufacturing. In terms of country shares, the Japanese have less than one-sixth of their U.S. direct investment in manufacturing. The top four areas of direct investment show substantial similarity. In descending order, manufacturing, trade, petroleum and finance are the largest foreign direct investment areas in the United States, while manufacturing, petroleum, finance and wholesale are the largest U.S. direct investment areas abroad. . . .

IS THERE ANY CREDIBLE DANGER FROM FOREIGN CAPITAL?

Any credible threat from foreign investment must ultimately depend on the share of foreign ownership of the stock of U.S. assets. That is, a small proportional share of U.S. capital held by foreigners is sufficient to preclude the possibility that foreign investment in the United States is deleterious. In this section, we show that the foreign share of U.S. capital, current and prospective, is too small to support the critics' concern.

The Minuscule Share of Foreign Ownership of U.S. Capital

The market value and the composition of the U.S. reproducible fixed net capital stock [has grown from] 1973, when its market value was $3.6 trillion . . . to $12.2 trillion at the end of 1987. During the period of large U.S. current account deficits beginning in 1982, its annual increase has averaged more than $0.5 trillion—that is, more than five times the average capital inflow—an annual growth rate of about 5.5 percent. Its composition in 1987 was $4.1 trillion of producers' plant and equipment, $2.4 trillion of government capital, $4.0 trillion of residential capital and $1.7 trillion of consumer durable goods such as automobiles, household furnishings and equipment. For purposes of this analysis, we will consider the share of the net U.S. reproducible tangible capital stock (less consumer durables) that the net foreign investment could command as collateral.

.... Considered as a potential claim collateralized by the U.S. capital stock, the estimated foreign holding of U.S. claims at year-end 1987, $1.54 trillion, was about 12.5 percent of the U.S. reproducible capital stock and 14.6 percent of the nonconsumer capital stock. Considered as a claim on the producer capital stock, $4.1 trillion, it amounted to 37.4 percent claim. Subtracting estimated U.S. assets abroad at year-end 1987, $1.17 trillion, from the foreign claims yields net foreign assets in the United States, $0.37 trillion, so that the percentage foreign claim on the net U.S. reproducible nonconsumer capital stock at the end of 1987 was 3.5 percent.

In summary, the net current share of U.S. assets owned by foreigners is implausibly low to substantiate any potential cornering of U.S. asset markets. Even so, this leaves open the question of whether the trend of increasing foreign ownership poses any such likelihood.

Sustained Capital Inflows Are Insufficient to Threaten U.S. Economic Sovereignty

The U.S. Commerce Department estimates that the U.S. international investment position became a net foreign claim in 1985 for the first time since 1914,-$110.7 billion.... Reflecting the U.S. trade deficits during the 1980s, the foreign claim has grown at an average of over $80 billion per year since 1981. Since becoming a net claim, the foreign percentage claim has risen to 3.5 percent of this U.S. wealth measure.

Even if the capital inflows persisted indefinitely at their 1988 level of about $120 billion, this need not result in an eventual foreign control of the U.S. economy in the sense of majority foreign ownership of U.S. nonconsumer assets. This is because the U.S. capital stock also is growing. If either the inflation of replacement prices of physical capital or real capital accumulation is fast enough, the share of foreign capital could rise for a period of years and then decline. The maximum the foreign share would attain and the time at which it would top out vary with the assumed rates of capital stock growth and the rate of capital price appreciation.

The U.S. capital stock grows each year by the amount by which gross investment in new building, roads, housing and industrial plant and equipment exceeds the scrappage and depreciation of the existing stock. The market value of this stock also rises with inflation. . . . [T]he estimated market value of the U.S. nonconsumer capital stock grew from $7.9 trillion at the end of 1981 to $10.5 trillion at the end of 1987. Over this period, the implicit annual rate of inflation of capital stock replacement cost has averaged about 2.3 percent, and the annual growth of the real net stock (at 1982 prices) has averaged about 2.2 percent. The sum of these two effects in the 1980s has implied a nominal capital stock growth rate of 4.5 percent. Combining these recent trends, we can determine the long-term consequences of a continued capital inflow.

. . . [U]nder these assumptions, which are most favorable to the threat scenario, the foreign share actually would rise to a maximum of 14.4 percent in the year 2015 and then decline. Since the assumed sustained capital inflow is probably larger than most analysts would assume, this is a worst-case scenario. For example, under growth and inflation rates averaged over the full floating-rate era, 1973-87, the constant $120 billion capital inflow would generate a peak share of 10.2 percent in 2004. Finally, if the capital inflow declines over the near future as it has since 1987, then the foreign share would peak in 1997 at about 7.3 per cent.

Consequently, the growth of the foreign share of U.S. capital, while large by 20th century experience, does not approach the share necessary to corner the market. Even when expressed as a claim on a subset of U.S. wealth—excluding consumer durable goods, land, and human capital—and presuming an investment pattern which foreign investment has not exhibited, the share of foreign investment does not present a credible takeover threat to the American economy. . . .

CONCLUSION

The joint implication from analysis of the three aspects of foreign investment in the United States—the effect on labor and investors, the threat of withdrawal, and the relative size of the foreign claim—is that the capital inflows are beneficient. The capital inflows benefit labor and management, entrepreneurs and investors alike. Workers benefit from the greater abundance of tools; the increased capital raises labor's productivity and increases its employment or wages. Management benefits from the greater capital availability and lower interest rates; the capital inflows facilitate long-range planning, and the rise in labor productivity enhances management productivity as well. Entrepreneurs benefit from the lower interest rates due to a greater abundance of capital; this increases the range of profitable projects and new firm startups. And investors benefit since a more capital-abundant economy is a richer economy, regardless of who owns the capital.

The United States has imported capital throughout the 1980s, but far from signaling an economy in decline, such investment by foreigners is a measure of the economy's vigor. . . . Clearly, foreign investment in the United States does not signify the selling out of America.

C. Money and Finance

The international economy, like domestic economies, requires a common monetary standard to function smoothly. For individuals and firms to buy and sell and to save and invest, they need some generally acceptable and predictable *unit of account* against which other goods can be measured, a *medium of exchange* with which transactions can be carried out, and a *store of value* in which wealth can be held. National currencies serve this purpose within countries: Americans buy, sell, save, and invest in dollars, for example. In international trade and payments, a variety of common measures are possible. In practice, the two purest cases are a commodity standard and an international currency standard. With a commodity standard, economic actors use a widely traded commodity, such as gold or pork bellies, against which to measure other goods. The classical gold standard was an example. With an international currency standard, they might arrive at some fictitious unit in which goods could be priced. The present-day Special Drawing Rights, which are a sort of "paper gold" issued by the International Monetary Fund and equal to a mix of national currencies, is an example of this arrangement. Because agreement on a fictitious international currency is difficult, such national currencies as the dollar or the pound sterling have often been used as the basis for international payments.

If the international monetary system provides the measures needed to conduct world trade and payments, the international financial system provides the means by which actual trade and payments are carried out. For many hundreds of years, financial institutions, especially banks, have financed trade among clients in different nations, sold and bought foreign currencies, transferred money from one country to another, and lent capital for overseas investment. If, as is often said, the international monetary system is "the great wheel" that allows goods to move in international trade, the international financial system is the grease that allows the wheel to turn.

In the modern era, since 1820 or so, there have been essentially four well-functioning international monetary systems in the non-Communist world; each with corresponding international financial characteristics. From about 1820 until World War I, the world was on or near the classical gold standard, in which many major national currencies were tied to gold at a legally fixed rate. In principle, as Benjamin J. Cohen explains in Reading 15, the gold standard was self-regulating. Should any national currency (and economy) get out of balance, it would be forced back into equilibrium by the very operation of the system. In practice, the pre-World-War-I system was actually a gold-sterling standard. The British pound sterling, backed by a strong government and the world's leading financial center, was "as good as gold," and most international trade and payments were carried out in sterling. The world financial system in the century before World War I was indeed dominated by British banks, which financed much of world trade and channeled enormous amounts of investment capital to rapidly developing countries such as the United States, Australia, Argentina, and South Africa. As time wore on, the financial institutions of other European powers, especially France and Germany, also began to expand abroad. The result was a highly integrated system of international monetary and financial interactions under the *Pax Britannica.*

Even before World War I, strains and rivalries were beginning to test the system. Once the war started in 1914, international trade and payments collapsed: of all the world's major financial markets, only New York stayed open for the duration of the conflict. Indeed, by the time World War I ended, the center of international finance had shifted from London to New York, and Wall Street remained the world's principal lender until the Great Depression of the 1930s.

As might be expected, given the reduced economic might of Great Britain, the prewar gold-sterling standard could not be rebuilt. Yet neither was the United States, beset by the isolationist-internationalist conflict at home, willing to simply replace Great Britain at the apex of the world monetary system. What emerged was the so-called "gold-exchange standard," where most countries went back to tying their currencies to gold, but no one national currency came to dominate the others. Dollars, sterling, and french francs were all widely used in world trade and payments, yet, given the lack of lasting international monetary cooperation in the period, the arrangement was quite unstable and short-lived. Normal international economic conditions were only restored by 1924, and within a few years the depression brought the system crashing down. With the collapse of the gold-exchange standard and the onset of the Depression and World War II, the international monetary and financial systems remained in disarray until after 1945.

As World War II came to an end, the Allied powers led by the United States began reconstructing an international monetary system. This Bretton Woods system was based, in the monetary sphere, on an American dollar tied to gold at the rate of $35 an ounce; other Western currencies were in turn tied to the dollar. This was a modified version of the pre-1914 gold standard, with the dollar at its center rather than sterling. As in the *Pax Britannica,* massive flows of capital from the leading nation—Great Britain in the first instance, the United States in the second—were crucial to the proper functioning of the mechanism. Whereas in the British case these capital flows were primarily private loans, from 1945 to 1965 they were essentially government or multilateral loans and foreign direct investment. Only after 1965 did private international finance become significant. Then, however, it rapidly grew to historically unprecedented proportions and developed new and different characteristics.

Even as the new international financial system, generally known as the Euromarket, was gathering steam, the Bretton Woods monetary system was beginning to weaken. It was, as Benjamin J. Cohen points out, more and more difficult to maintain the dollar's price of $35 an ounce. As pressure built on the dollar and attempts at reform stagnated, the Nixon administration finally decided that the system was unsustainable. In August 1971, President Richard Nixon "closed the gold window," ending the dollar's free convertibility into gold. The dollar was soon devalued. By 1975, the gold-dollar standard had been replaced by a floating-rate system.

Under the current system of floating exchange rates, the value of most currencies is set more or less freely by private traders in world currency markets. Thus, the values of the dollar, the deutsche mark, the franc, and so on, fluctuate on international currency markets. This has led to frequent and rapid changes in the relative prices of major currencies, as well as to frequent complaints about the unplanned nature of the new system. Because of the central role of the U.S. dollar even in today's floating-rate system, changes in American economic policy can drive the U.S. dollar up and down dramatically in ways that have important effects on the economy of the United States and that of the rest of the world.

In the 1970s, as American inflation rates rose, the dollar's value relative to other major currencies dropped. In 1979, however, American monetary policy began to concentrate on fighting inflation. The result was a worldwide rise in interest rates, followed rapidly by a deep recession, a reduction in inflation, and a dramatic rise in the dollar's value. Although inflation was brought down, the strong dollar wreaked havoc with the ability of many American industries to compete internationally. The American trade deficit grew to well above $100 billion, even as the United States government financed large portions of its growing budget deficit by borrowing from foreigners. In the mid-1980s the dollar dropped back down to its lowest levels in nearly forty years, while large American trade and budget deficits continued to be financed by foreigners. Through it all, there was dissatisfaction in many quarters with the underlying uncertainty about international trade and monetary trends. Today currencies fluctuate widely, many of the world's major nations are experiencing unprecedented trade surpluses or deficits, and capital flows across borders in enormous quantities.

Monetary uncertainty has led some nations to seek security in cooperative regional agreements. For example, most of the members of the European Community are linked by the exchange rate mechanism of the European Monetary System within which the different national currencies are essentially fixed against each other but move up and down together against the dollar, the yen, and other non-European monies. Some countries and observers support the development of a new international money, of which Special Drawing Rights might be a precursor; others desire a return to the gold standard.

Many scholars, too, have expressed dissatisfaction with floating rates. In Reading 16, David Calleo argues from a generally Realist perspective that both under Bretton Woods and since the advent of floating rates, the United States has used and misused the international monetary system for its own narrow purposes, ignoring the legitimate concerns of other nations. Liberal economist Norman Fieleke responds (Reading 17) to concerns like those of Calleo and others, concluding that floating rates work reasonably well. Wherever the truth may lie, no real replacement to the floating-rate system has emerged, and it is likely to remain in place for the foreseeable future.

In international finance, the period since 1965 has been extraordinarily eventful. The Euromarket grew to several trillion dollars, and banking became one of the great growth industries in the world economy. Jeff Frieden's article (Reading 18) discusses the political implications of international capital movements, both on nations and on groups and sectors within nations.

The political implications of international financial activities came to the fore in the 1980s in the context of the gravest debt crisis since the Depression of the 1930s. After 1981, dozens of less developed countries, which owe hundreds of billions of dollars to private banks and Western governments, were unable to maintain payments on their debts and were forced to reschedule their obligations. The debt crisis led to economic and political instability in many major debtor nations and to fears of an international banking crisis that would have had serious repercussions for the industrial nations. Although international financial instability was largely avoided, many of the major LDC debtors remain mired in dismal economic conditions.

The causes and consequences of the LDC debt crisis have been hotly debated. Some believe that the principal blame must be borne by the debtor nations themselves because they borrowed money to excess and used it unwisely. In Reading 19, neo-classical economist Robert Aliber argues that the Latin American debt crisis was a predictable result of misguided national policies. Marxist Manuel Pastor (Reading 20) looks instead at structural characteristics of both the international capitalist economy and the capitalist political economies of the Latin American borrowers, where he sees a system biased in favor of global and national capitalists and against workers.

Postwar monetary and financial affairs have given rise to academic and political polemics. Developing countries especially have argued that the existing systems of international monetary relations and international banking work to their detriment, and have proposed sweeping reforms. Most developed nations believe that, imperfect as current arrangements may be, they are the best available and that reform schemes are simply unrealistic.

Among scholars, international monetary and financial relations raise important analytical issues. As in other arenas, the very rapid development of globe-straddling international financial markets has led some to believe that the rise of supranational banks has eroded the power of national states. In this view, international monetary relations essentially serve to enrich increasingly global international banks and their allies in such international institutions as the International Monetary Fund. Other analysts believe that national governments are still the primary determinants of international monetary and financial trends. The specific policies of major states toward their own banks and their own currencies are, in this view, set in line with national interests; banks and currency movements are instruments of national policy and not the other way around. The tension between a monetary and financial system that is in a sense beyond the reach of individual states on the one hand and currencies and banks that clearly have home countries on the other hand gives rise to a fundamental tension in world politics and in the study of the international political economy.

15
A Brief History of International Monetary Relations

BENJAMIN J. COHEN

Benjamin J. Cohen describes the evolution of the international monetary system over the past century. He shows how the system has evolved away from a gold standard toward the use of national currencies, not backed by precious metals, for international trade and payments. As Cohen indicates, the national goals of independent states have often conflicted with the more general international goal of a stable, workable means of international payments. The two most successful experiences in overcoming the contradiction between national desires and global cooperation have been, Cohen argues, in the periods before World War I and after World War II, in which Great Britain and the United States, respectively, served as bankers to the world. In these eras, one nation managed and enforced international monetary relations in ways that conformed both to the hegemon's national goals and to the maintenance of international monetary stability—which is not to say that the resultant order was benevolent to all concerned, as Cohen points out. In any case, just as the decline of British political and economic power undermined the classical gold standard, so too has the United States' relative decline since 1970 led to a reshuffling of existing international monetary arrangements.

15 "A Brief History of International Monetary Relations" by Benjamin J. Cohen. From *Organizing the World's Money,* by Benjamin J. Cohen.

THE CLASSICAL GOLD STANDARD

. . . It is impossible to specify a precise date when the international monetary order began. The origins of international monetary relations, like those of money itself, are shrouded in the obscurity of prehistory. We know that there were well-defined monetary areas in many parts of the ancient world. But it is only with the rise of the Roman Empire that we begin to find documentary evidence of a very explicit international monetary order. The Roman monetary order, which was based initially on the gold coinage of Julius Caesar and later on the gold solidus (bezant, nomisma) for Byzantium, lasted some twelve centuries in all. Though confronted from the seventh century on with competition from a silver bloc centered on the newly emergent Muslim dinar, the Roman system did not break down completely until the sacking of Constantinople in 1203. The next five centuries were characterized by fluctuating exchange rates and a succession of dominant moneys—the "dollars of the Middle Ages," one source has called them[1]—including in later years the Florentine fiorino, the Venetian ducato, the Spanish reale, and the Dutch florin. After the beginning of the Industrial Revolution, it was the British pound sterling that rose to a position of preeminence in world monetary affairs.

As its name implies, the pound sterling was originally based on silver. In fact, however, England began practicing a loose sort of bimetallism—gold coins circulating alongside silver ones—even as early as the fourteenth century. (Gold coinage was first introduced into England in 1344, during the reign of Edward III.) Gresham's Law was coined during the reign of Queen Elizabeth I. Sir Isaac Newton, as Master of the Mint, tried to cope with the problem of bad money driving out good by calculating the value of the gold guinea (named after the region in West Africa where gold was mined) in terms of silver shillings. And in 1817 gold was formally declared legal tender in England alongside silver. From the time of the Napoleonic Wars, the United Kingdom moved rapidly from bimetallism to a single-money system. In 1798 the free coinage of silver was suspended and a £25 limit set on the legal-tender power of silver coins. In 1816 silver's legal-tender powers were further limited to £2. And after 1819 silver could no longer be used to redeem circulating bank notes: paper could be redeemed in gold coin only. From that date onward, the pound was effectively based on gold alone. The British were on a full gold standard.

Other countries, however, resisted the gold standard for several decades more. Most European nations, as well as the United States, remained legally bimetallic for at least another half century; most others, especially in Asia, formally retained silver standards. It was only in the 1870s that the movement toward a full-fledged international gold standard picked up momentum and it is from this decade that the modern history of international monetary relations is customarily dated. In 1871 the new German empire adopted the gold mark as its monetary unit, discontinuing the free coinage and unlimited legal-tender powers of silver. In 1873 a parallel decision followed in the United States (the "Crime of '73"), and by 1878 silver had been demonetized in France and virtually every other European country as well. During this decade, the classical gold standard was born. During succeeding decades, it spread to encompass virtually all of the world's independent countries, as well as all of the various colonial empires of Europe.

The classical gold standard was a comparatively brief episode in world history, ending with the outbreak of World War I in 1914. It was defined by two key features. A country was considered to be "on" the gold standard if (1) its central bank pledged to buy and sell gold (and only gold) freely at a fixed price in terms of the home currency and (2) its private residents could export or import gold freely. Together these two features defined a pure fixed-exchange-rate mechanism of balance-of-payments adjustment. Fixed exchange rates were established by the ratios of the prices at which central banks pledged to buy and sell gold for local currency. Free export and import of gold in turn established the means for reconciling any differences between the demand and supply of a currency at its fixed exchange rate. Deficits, requiring net payments to foreigners, were expected to result in outflows of gold, as residents converted local currency at the central bank in order to meet transactions obligations abroad. Conversely, surpluses, were expected to result in gold inflows. Adjustment was supposed to work through the impact of such gold flows on domestic economic conditions in each country.

The mechanism of liquidity creation under the classical gold standard was very nearly a pure commodity standard—and that commodity, of course, was gold. Silver lost its role as an important reserve asset during the decade of demonetization in the 1870s. And national currencies did not even begin to enter into monetary reserves in significant quantities until after 1900. The most widely held national currency before World War I was the pound; its principal rivals were the French franc and the German mark. But even as late as 1914, the ratio of world foreign-exchange reserves to world gold reserves remained very low. The monetary standard even then was still essentially a pure commodity standard .

After World War I, observers tended to look back on the classical gold standard with a sense of nostalgia and regret—a sort of Proustian *Recherche du temps perdu*. As compared with the course of events after 1918, the pre-1914 monetary order appeared, in retrospect, to have been enormously successful in reconciling the tension between economic and political values. During its four decades of existence, world trade and payments grew at record rates, promoting technical efficiency and economic welfare; yet, looking back, it seemed that problems of balance-of-payments adjustment and conflicts of policy between nations had been remarkably rare. The gold standard seemed to have succeeded to a unique degree in accommodating and balancing the efficiency and consistency objectives. For many, it had literally been a "Golden Age" of monetary relations.

The image of a Golden Age, however, was a myth, based on at least two serious misconceptions of how the gold standard had actually operated in practice. One misconception concerned the process of balance-of-payments adjustment, the other involved the role of national monetary policies. The process of balance-of-payments adjustment was said to have depended primarily on changes of domestic price levels. The model was that of the so-called "price-specie-flow" mechanism: outflows of gold (specie) shrinking the money supply at home and deflating the level of domestic prices, inflows expanding the money supply and inflating domestic prices. National monetary policies, although reinforcing the adjustment process, were said to have been actually concerned exclusively with defense of the convertibility of local currencies into gold. Central banks were said to have responded to gold flows more or less mechanically and passively, with a minimum of discretionary action or judgment. They simply played the "rules of the game," allowing gold flows to have their full impact on domestic money supplies and price levels. Combined, these misconceptions produced a myth of an impersonal, fully automatic, and politically symmetrical international monetary order dependent simply on a combination of domestic price flexibility and natural constraints on the production of gold to ensure optimality of both the adjustment process and reserve supply.

More recent historical research has revealed just how misleading this myth of the Golden Age really was. Regarding the role of monetary policy, for example, Arthur Bloomfield has convincingly demonstrated that central banks before 1914 were rarely quite as mechanical or passive as observers later believed. In fact, central banks exercised a great deal of discretion in reacting to inward or outward flows of gold. The rules of the game could be interpreted in either a negative or a positive sense. In the negative sense, central banks could simply refrain from any actions designed to counteract the influence of gold flows on domestic money supplies; in the positive sense, central banks might have been expected to magnify the domestic monetary influence of gold flows according to their deposit-reserve ratios. Bloomfield has shown that under the classical gold standard, central banks hardly ever adhered to the rules in the positive sense, and sometimes even departed from them in the negative sense. Of course, this was still an era of predominantly laissez-faire attitudes in government economic policy. Yet, even then, central banks were neither entirely unaware of, nor indifferent to, the effects of gold flows on domestic prices, incomes, or public confidence. To counteract such effects when it suited them, monetary authorities developed a variety of techniques for evading the rules of the game—including manipulation of the margins around exchange rates (technically, the "gold points"), direct intervention in the foreign-exchange market, and loans between central banks. Monetary policies in this period were never really either fully passive or simply automatic.

Similarly, regarding the process of balance-of-payments adjustment, Robert Triffin has convincingly demonstrated that domestic price levels rarely played as much of a role before 1914 as observers later believed. In fact, the process of adjustment depended at least as much on changes of domestic income and employment as on price changes. But most of all, the process depended on capital movements. The role of international capital movements in adjusting to payments disequilibria was far more important than any role that the terms of trade may have played. . . .

However, capital movements were not something that all countries could avail themselves of with equal facility. Triffin drew a distinction between countries that were capital exporters and those that were capital importers. Capital-exporting countries usually could avoid the consequences of balance-of-payments deficits—domestic deflation or a possible threat to the gold convertibility of the local currency—simply by slowing down investment abroad. The customary instrument in this regard was the central-bank discount rate (in England, Bank rate); that is, the rate at which the central bank discounted collateral when lending to commercial banks. A rise of the discount rate, cutting back cash reserves of banks, could normally be relied upon to reduce the rate of capital outflow and improve the balance of payments. Borrowing countries, on the other hand, were far less able to control the rate of their capital imports, these being primarily determined by credit conditions in the capital-exporting countries. The Golden Age, therefore, was really limited only to the "core" of advanced nations of Europe and the so-called "regions of recent settlement" (including North America, Australia, South Africa, and Argentina). Elsewhere, the gold standard was far less successful in preserving payments stability or avoiding policy conflict. . . .

Thus, not only was the gold standard neither impersonal nor fully automatic; it was also not politically symmetrical. In fact, the pre-1914 monetary order was arranged in a distinctly hierarchical fashion, with the countries of the periphery at the bottom, the core countries above, and at the peak—Britain. Great Britain dominated international monetary relations in the nineteenth century as no state has since, with the exception of the United States immediately after World War II. Britain was the supreme industrial power of the day, the biggest exporter of manufactured goods, the largest overseas investor. London was by far the most important world financial center, sterling by far the most widely used of the world's currencies for both current- and capital-account transactions. It is sometimes claimed that the gold standard was in reality a sterling-exchange standard. In one sense this appellation is misleading, insofar as most monetary reserves before 1914 (as mentioned above) were still held in gold, not sterling, and insofar as governments continued to be concerned with maintaining the gold value of their currencies, not the sterling value. Yet in another sense the facts cannot be denied: the classical gold standard *was* a sterling standard—a hegemonic regime—in the sense that Britain not only dominated the international monetary order, establishing and maintaining the prevailing rules of the game, but also gave monetary relations whatever degree of inherent stability they possessed.

This stability was ensured through a trio of roles which at that time only Britain had the economic and financial resources to play: (1) maintaining a relatively open market for the exports of countries in balance-of-payment difficulties; (2) providing contracyclical foreign long-term lending; and (3) acting as lender of last resort in times of exchange crisis. These were not roles that the British deliberately sought or even particularly welcomed. As far as the Bank of England was concerned its monetary policies were dictated solely by the need to protect its narrow reserves and the gold convertibility of the pound. It did not regard itself as responsible for global monetary stabilization or as money manager of the world. Yet this is precisely the responsibility that was thrust upon it in practice—acquired, like the British Empire itself, more or less absentmindedly. The widespread international use of sterling and the close links between the larger financial markets in London and smaller national financial markets elsewhere inevitably endowed Britain with the power to guide the world's monetary policy. Changes of policy by the Bank of England inevitably imposed a certain discipline and coordination on monetary conditions in other countries. . . .

It is important to recall, however, that the stability ensured by British monetary management was confined largely to the core of advanced nations in Europe and the regions of recent settlement—countries that were themselves capital exporters or, when necessary, were capable of availing themselves of the lending facilities of London or other financial centers. The less-developed countries of the periphery were, as emphasized, far less able to control the rate of their foreign capital imports; moreover, they suffered from Britain's related power to avoid the continuing cost of adjustment by manipulating its international terms of trade. . . . As Fred Hirsch has argued, Britain "'managed' the system partly at the expense of its weakest members."[2] Over time, this was bound to become a source of serious policy conflict in the monetary order.

In fact, it may be argued that behind the deceptive facade of the Golden Age, the classical gold standard actually bore within itself the seeds of its own destruction. Not only did the order require the continued acquiescence of periphery countries in order to preserve a semblance of stability in the core; it also depended on the continued hegemony of Great Britain in the world's economic affairs. But as many economic historians have noted, this dominance was already beginning to fade, even as early as the turn of the century. From the decade of the 1870s onward, British industrialists were faced with a mounting wave of competition in world export markets, first from Germany and the United States, and later from France, Russia, and Japan. From the 1890s onward, London was faced with growing competition from newly emergent financial centers like Paris, Berlin, and later New York; the pound found itself rivalled *inter alia* by the franc, the mark, and eventually the dollar. As a result of these developments, the British gradually lost a good part of their power to manage the international monetary order. Thus, when it was brought down by the outbreak of World War I, the classical gold standard had already become a rather fragile thing. It is perhaps too much to argue, as does one economic historian, that "the tree felled by the crisis was already rotten."[3] But signs of decay there most certainly were.

THE INTERWAR PERIOD

When World War I broke out, all of the belligerent nations—and soon most others as well—took action to protect their gold reserves by suspending currency convertibility and embargoing gold exports. The classical gold standard was dead. Private individuals could no longer redeem paper currency in gold, nor could they sell it abroad. But they could still sell one paper currency for another (exchange control not being invented until the 1930s) at whatever price the exchange market would bear. The fixed exchange-rate mechanism of the gold standard, therefore, was succeeded by its absolute opposite: a pure floating exchange-rate regime. In the ensuing years, as currency values varied considerably under the impact of wartime uncertainties, the international monetary order could not even come near to realizing its potential for joint gain.

Accordingly, once the war was over and peace arrangements taken care of, governments quickly turned their attention to the problem of world monetary reform. Lulled by the myth of the Golden Age, they saw their task as a comparatively simple one: to restore the classical gold standard (or a close approximation thereof). The major conundrum seemed to be an evident shortage of gold, owing to the extreme price inflations that had occurred in almost all countries during and immediately after the war. These had sharply reduced the purchasing power of the world's monetary gold stock, which was still valued at its old prewar parities. One plausible solution might have been an equally sharp multilateral devaluation of currencies in terms of gold, in order to restore the commodity value of gold reserves. But that was ruled out by most countries on the grounds that a return to "normal" (and to the Golden Age) must include a return to prewar rates of exchange. Yet at the same time, governments understandably wanted to avoid a scramble for gold that would have pushed up the metal's commodity value through competitive deflations of domestic prices. Some other solution had to be found.

The "solution" finally agreed upon was to *economize* on the use of gold. An international economic conference in 1922 (the Genoa Conference) recommended worldwide adoption of a gold-exchange standard in order to "centralize and coordinate the demand for gold, and so avoid those wide fluctuations in the purchasing power of gold which might otherwise result from the simultaneous and competitive efforts of a number of countries to secure metallic reserves."[4] (Central banks were urged to substitute foreign-exchange balances for gold in their reserves as a "means of economizing the use of gold."[5] Gold holdings were to be systematically concentrated in the major financial centers (e.g., London); outside the centers, countries were to maintain their exchange rates by buying and selling "gold exchange" (i.e., currencies convertible into gold, such as sterling) instead of gold itself. The monetary order was thus to combine a pure fixed exchange-rate mechanism of balance-of-payments adjustment modeled on the classical gold standard, with a new mixed commodity-currency standard to cope with the shortage of gold.

The gold-exchange standard came into formal existence early in 1925, when Britain reestablished the gold convertibility of the pound and eliminated restrictions on gold exports. Within a year nearly forty other nations had joined in the experiment, either de jure or de facto, and most other independent governments joined not much later. But the experiment did not last long. In 1931, following a wave of bank failures on the European continent, the British were forced by a run on their reserves to suspend convertibility once again, and in the chaos that ensued the international monetary order broke up into congeries of competing and hostile currency blocs. The largest of these was the sterling bloc, comprising Britain, its overseas dependencies and dominions (except Canada, which had closer financial ties with the United States), and a variety of independent states with traditionally close trading and banking connections with Britain. This bloc was a shrunken remnant of the world that the British had dominated and in effect managed prior to 1914. Members were identified by two main characteristics: they pegged their currencies to sterling, even after convertibility was suspended; and they continued to hold most of their reserves in the form of sterling balances in London. A second bloc after 1931 was informally grouped around the United States (the dollar area), and a third around France (the "gold bloc"). In addition, there was a large group of miscellaneous countries (including, especially, Germany and the states of Eastern Europe) that abandoned convertibility altogether in favor of starkly autarkic trade and financial policies.

The decade of the 1930s, the decade of the Great Depression, was a period of open economic warfare—a prelude to the military hostilities that were to follow after 1939. Never had the conflictual element in international monetary relations been laid quite so bare. It was truly a free-for-all regime. With public confidence shattered, exchange rates tended to fluctuate widely, and governments consciously engaged in competitive depreciations of their currencies in attempting to cope with their critical payments and unemployment problems. As in the years during and immediately after World War I, the monetary order failed to come even near to realizing its potential for joint gain. In 1936 a semblance of cooperation was restored by the Tripartite Agreement among Britain, France, and the United States for mutual currency stabilization. But this was only the barest minimum that might have been done to restore consistency to international monetary relations. Genuine monetary reconstruction had to wait until after World War II.

Why did the interwar experiment fail? Why did the attempt to return to the Golden Age end so disastrously? Mainly because the Golden Age *was* a myth, a myth based on misconceptions and a fundamental misunderstanding of how much the world economy had really changed. Governments failed to read the signs of decay in the prewar era; more importantly, they failed to realize how anachronistic a restored gold standard would be in the new circumstances of the postwar era. Conditions in the 1920s simply did not lend themselves to the adoption of an impersonal and fully automatic monetary order. In reality, the experiment was doomed from the start.

In the first place, governments were in the process of abandoning their inherited attitudes of laissez-faire in general economic policy. Social and political conditions had changed. A Bolshevik revolution had succeeded in Russia; elsewhere, socialism was almost universally on the rise. Governments could no longer afford to tolerate a certain amount of price or income deflation or inflation simply for the sake of maintaining convertibility of their currencies at a fixed price. Domestic stability now had to take precedence if politicians were to hold onto their jobs. If before World War I central banks rarely adhered to the gold-standard rules of the game in the positive sense, after the war they rarely adhered to them even in the negative sense. Instead, a variety of new instruments were devised to counteract and neutralize the domestic monetary influence of external payments disequilibria, just the opposite of what was needed to make a restored gold standard work. . . .

In the second place, prices and wages were becoming increasingly rigid, at least in a downward direction, under the impact of rising trade unionism and expanding social welfare legislation. Domestic price flexibility was a key requirement for a restored gold standard. Without it (and with exchange rates fixed), a disproportionate share of the adjustment process had to consist of changes of domestic incomes, output and employment. It was precisely in order to avoid such impacts, of course, that governments were becoming increasingly interventionist in economic affairs. But the consequences of such interventionism inevitably included a complete short-circuiting of the external adjustment mechanism that the same governments were laboring so hard to rebuild.

A third problem was the distorted structure of exchange rates established under the new gold-exchange standard. In insisting upon a return to convertibility at their prewar parities, governments were taking insufficient note of the fact that price relationships between national economies had been dramatically altered since 1914. Inconvertibility and floating exchange rates had broken the links between national price movements, and domestic inflation rates had varied enormously. When convertibility was finally reestablished after 1925, many governments found themselves with currencies that were overvalued and undervalued by quite significant amounts. Yet they were prevented from doing much about it by the straitjacket of fixed exchange rates. The pound, for example, restored to convertibility at its old prewar parity of $4.86, was overvalued by at least 10 percent; but since subsequent changes of the parity were ruled out by the gold-standard rules of the game, it was not surprising that the British balance of payments stayed under almost continuous strain until 1931, and British unemployment rates remained uncomfortably high. The French, on the other hand, who were an exception to the general rule in returning to gold (de facto in 1926, de jure in 1928) at just one-fifth of their prewar parity, undervalued the franc by perhaps as much as 25 percent. The result in this case was an almost immediate drainage of funds from London to Paris, adding to Britain's woes and, in the end, contributing importantly to the final collapse of the ill-fated experiment in 1931.

A fourth problem was the war's legacy of international indebtedness, which imposed a severe strain on monetary relations throughout the 1920s. The United States was the net creditor in a complicated network of obligations arising from wartime interallied loans and postwar German reparations; the biggest debtor, of course, was defeated Germany. As it turned out, most countries simply did not have the capacity to generate the net current-account surpluses necessary to effect their obligated transfers on capital account. In large measure, therefore, they had to rely instead on private capital outflows from the United States (much of which went to Germany) in a vast circular flow of funds. The Germans paid their reparations essentially with funds borrowed from America; Germany's creditors then used the same funds or other American loans to pay off their debts in the United States. How precarious all of this was became clear in 1929, when the stock-market crash and ensuing Great Depression abruptly cut off virtually all U.S. investment overseas. It is no accident that within two years reparations and interallied debt payments were abruptly cut off as well.

Finally, there was the problem of divided responsibility in the monetary order. If what ensured the apparent stability of the classical gold standard before 1914 was a single dominant center capable of acting as money manager of the world, what ultimately brought down its successor in 1931 was the emergence of competitive financial centers effectively rendering Britain's traditional hegemonic role impossible. Rivals to London had begun emerging even before World War I. During the 1920s this process continued, as Paris reasserted itself as a financial center and New York suddenly appeared on the scene. Still losing ground industrially and now saddled with an overvalued currency as well, Britain was no longer capable of playing the trio of roles that had provided the prewar monetary order with its semblance of stability. Unfortunately, neither were the French capable of shouldering such heavy responsibilities—they lacked the requisite economic and financial resources—and the Americans, who did have the resources, were as yet unwilling to do so. As a result, the system drifted without a leader. As Charles Kindleberger has written: "The United States was uncertain of its international role. . . . The one country capable of leadership was bemused by domestic concerns and stood aside. . . . The instability [came] from the growing weakness of one driver, and the lack of sufficient interest in the other."[6]

Could the two drivers, together with France, possibly have managed the monetary order cooperatively? Perhaps so. But this would have called for greater mutual trust and forebearance than any of the three seemed capable of at the time. Britain was still trying to lead, albeit from weakness, and the United States had not yet learned how to lead from strength. The French, meanwhile, resented both Anglo-Saxon powers, and all three were competing actively for short-term money flows—and even for gold itself. (After 1928, for example, the Bank of France added to the pressures on the British by suddenly opting to convert its sizable accumulation of sterling balances into gold.) The result of this lack of coordination was a continual problem of large-scale transfers of private funds ("hot money" movements) from one financial center to another— the confidence problem. "This shifting of balances from one market to another [was] inevitable in a gold standard system without a single dominating center."[7] In the end, it was such a shifting of balances out of London in 1931 that finally brought the system down. In fact, it was not until 1936, with the Tripartite Agreement, that the three powers eventually got around to acknowledging formally their mutual responsibility for the monetary order. By that time, however, it was too late.

THE BRETTON WOODS SYSTEM

World War II brought exchange control everywhere and ended much of what remained of the element of cooperation in international monetary relations. But almost immediately, planning began for postwar monetary reconstruction. Discussions centered in the Treasuries of Britain and the United States, and culminated in the creation of the International Monetary Fund at a conference of 44 allied nations at Bretton Woods, New Hampshire, in 1944. The charter of the IMF was intended to be the written constitution of the postwar monetary order—what later became known as the Bretton Woods system. The Bretton Woods system lasted only twenty-seven years, however, and died in August 1971.

The Origins of the Bretton Woods System

The Bretton Woods system originated as a compromise between rival plans for monetary reconstruction developed on the one hand by Harry Dexter White of the U.S. Treasury, and on the other hand by Lord Keynes of Britain. In 1944 the differences between these two plans seemed enormous. Today their differences appear rather less impressive than their similarities. Indeed, what is really striking, a third of a century later, is how much common ground there really was among all the participating governments at Bretton Woods. All agreed that the interwar experience had taught them several valuable lessons; all were determined to avoid repeating what they perceived to be the errors of the past. Their consensus of judgment was reflected directly in the contents of the IMF's Articles of Agreement.

Four points in particular stand out. First, it was generally agreed that the interwar period had demonstrated (to use the words of one authoritative source) "the proved disadvantages of freely fluctuating exchanges." [8] The floating rates of the 1930s were seen as having discouraged trade and investment and encouraged destabilizing speculation and competitive depreciations. Nations were loath to return to the free-for-all regime of the Depression years. But at the same time, they were also unwilling to return to the exchange-rate rigidity of the 1920s. The experience of those years was seen as having demonstrated the equal undesirability of the opposite extreme of permanently fixed rates. These, it was agreed, could "be equally harmful. The general interest may call for an occasional revision of currency values." [9] Accordingly, the negotiators at Bretton Woods were determined to find some compromise between the two extremes—one that would gain the advantages of both fixed and flexible rates without suffering from their disadvantages.

What they came up with has since been labeled the "pegged-rate" or "adjustable-peg" regime. Members were obligated to declare a par value (a "peg") for their currencies and to intervene in the exchange market to limit fluctuations within maximum margins (a "band") one percent above or below parity; but they also retained the right, whenever necessary and in accordance with agreed procedures, to alter their par values to correct a "fundamental disequilibrium" in their balance of payments. What constituted a fundamental disequilibrium? Although key to the whole operation of the Bretton Woods adjustment mechanism, this notion was never spelled out in any detail anywhere in the Articles of Agreement. The omission was to come back to haunt members of the Fund in later years.

Second, all governments generally agreed that if exchange rates were not to be freely fluctuating, countries would need to be assured of an adequate supply of official monetary reserves. An adjustable-peg regime "presupposes a large volume of such reserves for each single country as well as in the aggregate."[10] The experience of the interwar period—the gold shortage of the 1920s as well as the breakdown of fixed rates in the 1930s—was thought to have demonstrated the dangers of inadequate reserve volume. Accordingly, a second order of business at Bretton Woods was to ensure a supplementary source of reserve supply. Negotiators agreed that what they needed was some "procedure under which international liquidity would be supplied in the form of pre-arranged borrowing facilities."[11]

What they came up with, in this instance, was the IMF system of subscriptions and quotas. In essence, the Fund was to be nothing more than a pool of national currencies and gold subscribed by each country.

Members were assigned quotas, according to a rather complicated formula intended roughly to reflect each country's relative importance in the world economy, and were obligated to pay into the Fund a subscription of equal amount. The subscription was to be paid 25 percent in gold or currency convertible into gold (effectively the U.S. dollar, which was the only currency still convertible directly into gold) and 75 percent in the member's own currency. Each member was then entitled, when short of reserves, to "purchase" (i.e., borrow) amounts of foreign exchange from the Fund in return for equivalent amounts of its own currency. Maximum purchases were set equal to the member's 25-percent gold subscription (its "gold tranche"), plus four additional amounts each equal to 25 percent of its quota (its "credit tranches"), up to the point where the Fund's holdings of the member's currency equaled 200 percent of its quota. (If any of the Fund's holdings of the member's initial 75 percent subscription of its own currency was borrowed by other countries, the member's borrowing capacity was correspondingly increased: this was its "super-gold tranche.") The member's "net reserve position" in the Fund equaled its gold tranche (plus super-gold tranche, if any) less any borrowings by the country from the Fund. Net reserve positions were to provide the supplementary liquidity that was generally considered necessary to make the adjustable-peg regime work.

A third point on which all governments at Bretton Woods agreed was that it was necessary to avoid a recurrence of the kind of economic warfare that had characterized the decade of the 1930s. Some "code of action" was needed to "guide international exchange adjustments," some framework of rules to ensure that countries would remove their existing exchange controls and return to a system of multilateral payments based on currency convertibility. At Bretton Woods such a code was written into the obligations of Fund members. Governments were generally forbidden to engage in discriminatory currency practices or exchange-control regulation, although two exceptions were permitted. First, convertibility obligations were extended to current international transactions only. Governments were to refrain from regulating purchases and sales of foreign exchange for the purpose of current-account transactions. But they were not obligated to refrain from regulation of capital-account transactions; indeed, they were formally encouraged to make use of capital controls to maintain equilibrium in the face of "those disequilibrating short-term capital movements which caused so much trouble during the 'thirties."[12] And second, convertibility obligations could be deferred if a member so chose during a postwar "transitional period." Members deferring their convertibility obligations were known as Article XIV countries; members accepting them had so-called Article VIII status. One of the functions assigned to the IMF was to oversee this code of action on currency convertibility.

Finally, governments agreed that there was a need for an institutional forum for international consultation and cooperation on monetary matters. The world could not be allowed to return to the divided responsibility of the interwar years. "International monetary relations especially in the years before the Tripartite Agreement of 1936 suffered greatly from the absence of an established machinery or procedure of consultation."[13] In the postwar era, the Fund itself would provide such a forum. Of all the achievements of Bretton Woods, this was potentially the most significant. Never before had international monetary cooperation been attempted on a permanent institutional basis. Judged against the anarchy of the 1930s, this could be considered a breakthrough of historic proportions. For the first time ever, governments were formally committing themselves to the principle of collective responsibility for management of the international monetary order.

These four points together defined the Bretton Woods system—a monetary order combining an essentially unchanged gold-exchange standard, supplemented only by a centralized pool of gold and national currencies, with an entirely new pegged-rate mechanism of balance-of-payments adjustment. The Fund itself was expected to perform three important functions: regulatory (administering the rules affecting exchange rates and currency convertibility), financial (supplying supplementary liquidity), and consultative (providing a forum for the cooperative management of monetary relations). The negotiators at Bretton Woods did not think it necessary to alter in any fundamental way the mixed commodity-currency standard that had been inherited from the interwar years. Indeed, it does not even seem to have occurred to them that there might be any inherent defect in the structure of a gold-exchange standard. The problem in the 1920s, they felt, had not been the gold-exchange standard itself but the division of responsibility—in short, a problem of management. "The nucleus of the gold exchange system consisted of more than one country; and this was a special source of weakness. With adequate cooperation between the centre countries, it need not have been serious."[14] In the Bretton Woods system the IMF was to provide the necessary machinery for multilateral cooperation. The management problem would thus be solved and consistency in monetary relations ensured.

Implicit in this attitude was a remarkable optimism regarding prospects for monetary stability in the postwar era. Underlying the choice of the pegged-rate adjustment mechanism, for instance, seemed to be a clear expectation that beyond the postwar transitional period (itself expected to be brief) payments imbalances would not be excessive. The adjustment mechanism was manifestly biased in principle against frequent changes of exchange rates, presumably because of the experience of the 1930s; governments had to demonstrate the existence of a fundamental disequilibrium before they could alter their par values. At the same time, no government was prepared to sacrifice domestic stability for the sake of external equilibrium. Yet nations were left with few other instruments, other than capital controls, to deal with disturbances to the balance of payments. This suggests that the negotiators at Bretton Woods felt that the major threat to stability was likely to come from private speculation rather than from more fundamental price or income developments. It also suggests that they were confident that most disequilibria would be of a stochastic rather than nonstochastic nature. Underlying the IMF's financial function seemed to be a clear expectation that its centralized pool of liquidity would be sufficient to cope with most financing problems as they emerged.

As matters turned out, this optimism proved entirely unjustified. Monetary relations immediately after the war were anything but stable, and the transitional period anything but brief. Only the United States, Canada, and a small handful of other countries (mainly in Central America) were able to pledge themselves to the obligations of Article VIII right away. Most others were simply too devastated by war—their export capacities damaged, their import needs enormous, their monetary reserves exhausted—to commit their currencies to convertibility. Payments problems, especially in Europe and Japan, could hardly be described as stochastic; the Fund's initial pool of liquidity was anything but sufficient. After a short burst of activity during its first two years, mainly to the benefit of European nations, the Fund's lending operations shrank to an extremely small scale. (In 1950 the Fund made no new loans at all, and large-scale operations did not begin again until 1956.) The burden instead was shifted to one country, the only country after the war immediately capable of shouldering the responsibility for global monetary stabilization—namely, the United States.

Fortunately, this time, for reasons of its own (see below), the United States was willing. As dominant then as Britain had been in the nineteenth century, America rapidly assumed the same trio of managerial roles—in effect, taking over as money manager of the world. A relatively open market was maintained for the exports of foreign goods. A relatively generous flow of long-term loans and grants was initiated first through the Marshall Plan and other related aid programs, then through the reopened New York capital market. And a relatively liberal lending policy was eventually established for the provision of short-term funds in times of exchange crisis as well. Since monetary reserves were everywhere in such short supply—and since the IMF's pool of liquidity was manifestly inadequate—the United States itself became the residual source of global liquidity growth through its balance-of-payments deficits. At the war's end, America owned almost three-quarters of the world's existing monetary gold; and prospects for new gold production were obviously limited by the physical constraints of nature. The rest of the world, therefore, was more than willing to economize on this scarce gold supply by accumulating dollars instead. The dollar thus was enshrined not only as principal "vehicle currency" for international trade and investment but also as principal reserve asset for central banks. In the early postwar years, America's deficits became the universal solvent to keep the machinery of Bretton Woods running. It may be misleading, as I have indicated, to call the classical gold standard a sterling-exchange (though not, I have suggested, to call it a hegemony); it is not at all misleading to call the postwar monetary standard a dollar-exchange standard. Indeed, the Bretton Woods system became synonymous with a hegemonic monetary order centered on the dollar. Though multilateral in formal design, in actual practice (like the classical gold standard before it) the Bretton Woods system was highly centralized.

In effect, what the United States did was to abjure any payments target of its own in favor of taking responsibility for operation of the monetary order itself. Other countries set independent balance-of-payments targets; America's external financial policy was essentially one of "benign neglect." Consistency in monetary relations was ensured not by multilateral cooperation but by America's willingness to play a passive role in the adjustment process, as the *n*th country, in effect: "other countries from time to time changed the par value of their currencies against the dollar and gold, but the value of the dollar itself remained fixed in relation to gold and therefore to other currencies collectively."[15] The growth of the world's liquidity supply was largely determined, consequently, by the magnitude of America's deficits—modified only to the extent that these deficits were settled in gold, rather than dollars, reflecting the asset preferences of surplus countries.

Like the British in the nineteenth century, the Americans did not deliberately seek the responsibility of global monetary management . (In the interwar period they had evaded it.) On the other hand, unlike the British, once the Americans found themselves with it, they soon came to welcome it, for reasons that were a mixture of altruism and self-interest . Being money manager for the world fit in neatly with America's newfound leadership role in the Western Alliance. The cold war had begun, and isolationism was a thing of the past. The United States perceived a need to promote the economic recovery of potential allies in Europe and Japan, as well as to maintain a sizable and potent military establishment overseas. All of this cost money: the privilege of liability-financing deficits meant that America was effectively freed from balance-of-payments constraints to spend as freely as it thought necessary to promote objectives believed to be in the national interest. The United States could issue the world's principal vehicle and reserve currency in amounts presumed to be consistent with its own policy priorities—and not necessarily with those of foreign dollar holders. Foreign dollar holders conceded this policy autonomy to America because it also directly contributed to their own economic rehabilitation. America accepted the necessity, for example, of preferential trade and payments arrangements in Europe, despite their inherent and obvious discrimination against U.S. export sales; likewise, America accepted the necessity of granting Japanese exporters access to the U.S. internal market at a time when other markets still remained largely closed to goods labeled "Made in Japan." In effect, as I have argued elsewhere, an implicit bargain was struck.[16] America's allies acquiesced in a hegemonic system that accorded the United States special privileges to act abroad unilaterally to promote U.S. interests. The United States, in turn, condoned its allies' use of the system to promote their own economic prosperity, even if this happened to come largely at the expense of the United States. . . .

The History of the Bretton Woods System

The subsequent history of the Bretton Woods system may be read as the history of this implicit bargain. The breakdown of the system in 1971 may be read as the bargain's final collapse. . . .

The chronology of Bretton Woods can be divided into two periods: the period of the "dollar shortage," lasting roughly until 1958; and the period of the "dollar glut," covering the remaining dozen years or so. The period of the dollar shortage was the heyday of America's dominance of international monetary relations. The term "dollar shortage," universally used at the time, was simply a shorthand expression of the fact that only the United States was capable of shouldering the responsibility for global monetary stabilization; only the United States could help other governments avoid a mutually destructive scramble for gold by promoting an outflow of dollar balances instead. As David Calleo has written: "Circumstances dictated dollar hegemony."[17] Dollar deficits began in 1950, following a round of devaluations of European currencies, at American insistence, in 1949. (Dollar surpluses prior to 1950 were financed largely by grants and long-term loans from the United States.) In ensuing years, deficits in the U.S. balance of payments (as conventionally measured) averaged approximately $1.5 billion a year. But for these deficits, other governments would have been compelled by their reserve shortages to resort to competitive exchange depreciations or domestic deflations; they would certainly not have been able to make as much progress as they did toward dismantling wartime exchange controls and trade restrictions. Persistent dollar deficits thus actually served to avoid monetary instability or policy conflict before 1953. Not since the Golden Age before World War I, in fact, had the monetary order been so successful in reconciling the tension between economic and political values. The period to 1958 has rightly been called one of' "beneficial disequilibrium."

After 1958, however, America's persistent deficits began to take on a different coloration. Following a brief surplus in 1957, owing to an increase of oil exports to Europe caused by the closing of the Suez Canal, the U.S. balance of payments plunged to a $3.5 billion deficit in 1958 and to even larger deficits in 1959 and 1960. This was the turning point. Instead of talking about a dollar shortage, observers began to talk about a dollar glut; consistency in monetary relations no longer appeared quite so assured. In 1958, Europe's currencies returned to convertibility. In subsequent years the former eagerness of European governments to obtain dollar reserves was transformed into what seemed an equally fervent desire to avoid excess dollar accumulations. Before 1958, less than 10 percent of America's deficits had been financed by calls on the gold stock in Fort Knox (the rest being liability-financed). During the next decade, almost two-thirds of America's cumulative deficit was transferred in the form of gold. Almost all of this went to governments on the continent of Europe.

It was clear that the structure of Bretton Woods was coming under increasing strain. Defects were becoming evident both in the mechanism of liquidity-creation and in the mechanism of payments adjustment.

Credit for first drawing attention to the defects in the liquidity creation mechanism of Bretton Woods is usually given to Robert Triffin for his influential book *Gold and the Dollar Crisis*.[18] The negotiators at Bretton Woods, Triffin argued, had been too complacent about the gold-exchange standard. The problem was not simply one of management. Rather, it was one of structure—an inherent defect in the very concept of a gold-exchange standard. A gold-exchange standard is built on the illusion of convertibility of its fiduciary element into gold at a fixed price. The Bretton Woods system, though, was relying on deficits in the U.S. balance of payments to avert a world liquidity shortage. Already, America's "overhang" of overseas liabilities to private and official foreigners was growing larger than its gold stock at home. The progressive deterioration of the U.S. net reserve position, therefore, was bound in time to undermine global confidence in the dollar's continued convertibility. In effect, governments were caught on the horns of a dilemma. To forestall speculation against the dollar, U.S. deficits would have to cease. But this would confront governments with the liquidity problem. To forestall the liquidity problem, U.S. deficits would have to continue. But this would confront governments with the confidence problem. Governments could not have their cake and eat it too.

Not that governments were unwilling to try. On the contrary, during the early 1960s a variety of ad hoc measures were initiated in an effort to contain speculative pressures that were mounting against the dollar. These included a network of reciprocal short-term credit facilities ("swaps") between the Federal Reserve and other central banks, as well as enlargement of the potential lending authority of the IMF (through the "General Arrangements to Borrow"). Both were intended to facilitate recycling of funds in the event of speculative currency shifts by private investors. They also included creation of a "gold pool" of the major financial powers to stabilize the price of gold in private markets. Later, in 1968, the gold pool was replaced by a two-tier gold-price system—one price for the private market, determined by supply and demand, and another price for central banks, to remain at the previous fixed level of $35 per ounce. These several measures were moderately successful in helping governments cope with the threat of private speculation against the dollar—the private confidence problem. The official confidence problem, however, remained as acute a danger as ever.

Meanwhile, in the mid-1960s, negotiations were begun whose aim was to establish a substitute source of liquidity growth, in order to reduce reliance on dollar deficits in the future. These negotiations were conducted among ten industrial countries—the so-called Group of Ten (G-10)—compromising Belgium, Canada, France, Germany, Italy, Japan, the Netherlands, Sweden, the United Kingdom, and the United States. What came out of the G-10 negotiations was the agreement to create Special Drawing Rights, an entirely new type of world fiduciary reserve asset. The SDR agreement was confirmed by the full membership of the International Monetary Fund in 1968 and activated in 1969. Between 1970 and 1972 some 9.5 billion SDR units were allocated to members of the Fund. Governments were confident that with SDRs "in place," any future threat of world liquidity shortage could be successfully averted. On the other hand, they were totally unprepared for the opposite threat—a reserve surfeit—which in fact is what eventually emerged.

Any number of authors could be credited for drawing attention to the defects in the payments adjustment mechanism of Bretton Woods. Virtually from the time the Charter was first negotiated, observers began pointing to the ambiguity surrounding the notion of fundamental disequilibrium. How could governments be expected to alter their par values if they could not tell when a fundamental disequilibrium existed? And if they were inhibited from altering their par values, then how would international payments equilibrium be maintained? I have already noted that the adjustment mechanism was biased in principle against frequent changes of exchange rates. In practice during the postwar period it became biased even against infrequent changes of exchange rates. At least among the advanced industrial nations, the world seemed to have returned to the rigidities of the 1920s. Governments went to enormous lengths to avoid the "defeat" of an altered par value. (A particularly sad example of this was the long struggle of the British government to avoid devaluation of the pound—a struggle that ended when sterling was devalued by 14.3 percent in 1967.) The resulting stickiness of the adjustment process not only aggravated fears of a potential world liquidity shortage. It also created irresistible incentives for speculative currency shifts by private individuals and institutions, greatly adding to the confidence problem as well.

Speculative currency shifts were facilitated at the time by the growing integration of money and capital markets in all of the advanced industrial nations. Large-scale capital movements had not originally been envisaged by the negotiators at Bretton Woods; as I have indicated, governments actually were encouraged to *control* capital movements for the purpose of maintaining payments equilibrium. In reality, however, capital movements turned out to be promoted rather than retarded by the design of the Bretton Woods system—in particular, by the integrative power of the par-value regime, and by the return to currency convertibility in Europe in 1958. (Japan did not pledge itself to Article VIII of the IMF Charter until 1964.) After 1958, capital mobility accelerated *pari passu* with the growth of the Eurocurrency market—that well-known market for currencies deposited in banks located outside of the country of issue. From its origin in the mid-1950s, the Eurocurrency market rapidly expanded into a broad, full-fledged international financial market; subject to just a minimum of governmental guidance, supervision, and regulation, it became during the 1960s the principal vehicle for private speculation against official exchange parities. Increasingly, governments found it difficult to "defend" unadjusted par values in the face of the high degree of international capital mobility that had been generated.

The most serious adjustment problem during this period was, of course, the dollar glut—more accurately, the persistent payments imbalance between the United States and the surplus countries of Europe and Japan. On each side, complaints were heard about the policies of the other. America felt that its erstwhile European and Japanese allies could do more to eliminate the international payments disequilibrium by inflating or revaluing their currencies; the Europeans and Japanese argued that it was the responsibility of the United States to take the first steps to reduce its persistent deficit. Each felt discriminated against by the other. The surplus countries felt that America's privilege of liability-financing deficits, growing out of the dollar's reserve-currency role, created an asymmetry in the monetary order favorable to the United States. None of them, after all, had such a degree of policy autonomy. America, on the other hand, felt that the use of the dollar by other governments as their principal intervention medium to support par values—the intervention-currency role of the dollar—created an asymmetry in the monetary order more favorable to Europe and Japan. Many sources argued that the dollar was overvalued. Yet how could its value in terms of foreign currencies be changed unilaterally unless all other countries agreed to intervene appropriately in the exchange market? The United States felt it had no effective control over its own exchange rate (no exchange-rate autonomy) and therefore did not feel it could easily devalue to rid itself of its deficit.

In fact the debate over asymmetries masked a deeper political conflict. The postwar bargain was coming unstuck. In the United States, concern was growing about the competitive threat from the European Common Market and Japan to American commercial interests. The period of postwar recovery was over: Europe and Japan had become reinvigorated giants, not only willing but able to compete aggressively with America in markets at home and abroad. The cost of subordinating U.S. economic interests to the presumed political advantage of now strengthened allies was becoming ever more intolerable. Conversely, concern was growing in Europe and Japan about America's use of its privilege of liability-financing to pursue policies abroad which many considered abhorrent (one example was the U.S. involvement in Vietnam), the "exorbitant privilege," as Charles de Gaulle called it. The Europeans and Japanese had just one major weapon they could use to restrict America's policy autonomy—their right to demand conversion of accumulated dollar balances into gold. Robert Mundell has written that "the sole function of gold convertibility in the Bretton Woods arrangement was to discipline the U.S."[19] But by the mid-1960s this was a discipline that most major financial powers were growing somewhat reluctant to use. America's overhang of liabilities was by now far larger than its gold stock. A concerted conversion campaign could have threatened to topple the whole of the Bretton Woods edifice. Governments—with one major exception—did not consider it in their interest to exacerbate the official confidence problem and provoke a systemic crisis. The one major exception was France, which in 1965, in a move strikingly reminiscent of its behavior toward sterling after 1928, began a rapid conversion of its outstanding dollar balances into gold, explicitly for the purpose of exerting pressure on the United States. France alone, however, was unable to change America's policies significantly.

At bottom, the Bretton Woods system rested on one simple assumption—that economic policy in the United States would be stabilizing. Like Britain in the nineteenth century, America had the power to guide the world's monetary policy. The absence of an effective external discipline on U.S. policy autonomy could not threaten the system so long as this assumption held. And indeed, before 1965, the assumption did seem quite justified. America clearly had the best long-term record of price stability of any industrial country; even for some time after 1958 the United States could not justly be accused of "exporting" inflation, however much some governments were complaining about a dollar glut. After 1965, however, the situation reversed itself, as a direct consequence of the escalation of hostilities in Vietnam. America's economy began to overheat, and inflation began to gain momentum. The Bretton Woods system was tailor-made to promote the transmission of this inflation abroad. With exchange rates pegged, tradable-goods price increases in the largest of all trading nations were immediately radiated outward to the rest of the world economy. And with governments committed to defending their pegged rates by buying the surfeit of dollars in the exchange market, a huge reserve base was created for monetary expansion in these other countries as well. Now the United States could justifiably be accused of exporting inflation overseas.

The gathering world inflation after 1965 exposed all of the latent defects of Bretton Woods. American policy was no longer stabilizing, yet other governments were reluctant to use the one power of discipline they had. (Indeed, after the creation of the two-tier gold-price system in 1968, the U.S. government made it quite plain that if a serious depletion of its gold stock were threatened, it would be prepared to close the window and refuse further sales.) The adjustment mechanism was incapable of coping with the widening deficit in the U.S. balance of payments (which soared to $9.8 billion in 1970 and an incredible $29.8 billion in 1971), and the confidence problem was worsening as private speculators were encouraged to bet on devaluation of the dollar or revaluations of the currencies of Europe and Japan. Ultimately, it was the United States that brought the drama to its denouement. Concerned about the rapidly deteriorating U.S. trade balance, as well as about rising protectionist sentiment in the Congress, President Richard Nixon was determined to force the Europeans and Japanese to accept an adjustment of international exchange-rate relationships that would correct the overvaluation of the dollar. Feeling that he lacked effective control over the dollar exchange rate under the prevailing rules of the game, the President decided that the rules themselves would have to be changed. Thus, on August 15, 1971, the convertibility of the dollar into gold was suspended, in effect freeing the dollar to find its own level in the exchange market. With that decision, the Bretton Woods system passed into history.

NOTES

1. Carlo M. Cipolla, *Money, Prices, and Civilization in the Mediterranean World: Fifth to Seventeenth Century* (Princeton: Princeton University Press, 1956), chap. 2.

2. Fred Hirsch, *Money International* (London: Penguin, 1967), p. 28.

3. Marcello de Cecco, *Money and Empire: The International Gold Standard, 1890-1914* (Oxford: Basil Blackwell, 1974), p. 128.

4. Currency Resolution of the Genoa Conference, as quoted in League of Nations, *International Currency Experience* (1944), p. 28.

5. Ibid. As another economy measure, central banks were also urged to withdraw gold coins from circulation.

6. Charles P. Kindleberger, *The World in Depression* (Berkeley: UC Press, 1973), pp. 298-301 .

7. W. A. Brown, *The International Gold Standard Reinterpreted* (New York: NBER, 1944), 2: 769.

8. League of Nations, *International Currency Experience* p. 211.

9. Ibid.

10. Ibid., p. 214.

11. Ibid., p. 218.

12. Ibid., p. 220.

13. Ibid., pp. 22–227.

14. Ibid., p. 46.

15. Marina v. N. Whitman, "The Current and Future Role of the Dollar: How Much Symmetry?" *Brookings Papers on Economic Activity*, no. 3 (1974): 542.

16. Benjamin J. Cohen, "The Revolution in Atlantic Economic Relations: A Bargain Comes Unstuck," in Wolfram Hanrieder, ed. *The United States and Western Europe: Political, Economic and Strategic Perspectives* (Cambridge, Mass.: Winthrop, 1974), pp. 113-120.

17. David P. Calleo, "American Foreign Policy and American European Studies: An Imperial Bias?", in Hanrieder, *United States and Western Europe*, p. 62.

18. Robert Triffin, *Gold and the Dollar Crisis* (New Haven: Yale University Press, 1960). The book first appeared in the form of two long journal articles in 1959.

19. Robert A. Mundell, "Optimum Currency Areas, "*Economic Notes* 3 (September-December 1975): 36.

16

The Atlantic Alliance and the World Economy

DAVID P. CALLEO

This reading traces the evolution of international monetary relations since World War II. In Calleo's largely Realist view, U.S. geopolitical dominance led to its dominance of the international monetary system, and especially to its ability to force foreigners to bear the costs of American fiscal and monetary laxness. Predatory American policies and the privileged position of the dollar allowed the United States to export many of its economic problems. However, the decline of U.S. hegemony has made it increasingly difficult for it to go on exploiting the rest of the world.

Since the 1960s, the problems of America's extended geopolitical posture have found a ready parallel in the strains of its international economic position. The similarity is hardly surprising. The Atlantic military alliance and the global economic system are complementary parts of the same *Pax Americana* and often affect each other directly. Cycles in America's military spending have had major consequences for the world economy. The Truman and Kennedy-Johnson rearmaments, for example, each culminated with a worldwide inflationary boom, exacerbated by a war. Particular policies in one sphere often have a close parallel in the other. Kennedy's flexible-response strategy, which called for greater American control over European defense, had its parallel in his economic Grand Design, which pressed for greater transatlantic economic integration. Similarly, de Gaulle

---

16 "The Atlantic Alliance and the World Economy" by David P. Calleo. From *Beyond American Hegemony*, by David P. Calleo. Copyright © 1987 by The Twentieth Century Fund. Reprinted by permission of Basic Books, Inc., Publishers, New York.

paired his anti-hegemonic policies in NATO with an attack on the dollar's role in the international monetary system. Curbing the dollar, the general hoped, would help keep American military power and geopolitical ambition within the limits he preferred. Success and failure in one sphere reverberate into the other. In the early days of the alliance, economic ties and military solidarity reinforced each other; in recent years, politico-military divergences and economic quarrels have compounded one another. But the alliance's economic stresses, perhaps even more than its political and military differences, have a cumulative as well as cyclical character.

At the heart of Europe's economic grievances lies the belief that the Americans have been manipulating the world economy for two decades in order to compensate for their own internal disorder. To Europeans, America's economy seems in a perpetual disequilibrium, the effects of which are regularly exported to the rest of the world. By the later 1970s, some knowledgeable European observers, not at all unfriendly to the alliance, were counting the effects of this exported disequilibrium a greater threat to Western solidarity than the Soviet Union itself. What is the nature of this American imbalance?

In economics, as in diplomacy and morals, equilibrium is a highly abstract concept. Indicators to measure it are correspondingly elusive. Internationally, a persistent balance-of-payments deficit seems the most obvious sign of fundamental disequilibrium. A country with a basic deficit, that is, a deficit on goods, services, and long-term investment, is, in effect, taking more from the world outside than it earns from it. To finance its deficit, such a country must use its own reserves or else attract foreign capital. When the country is no longer able to do either, impending bankruptcy forces a change in habits. It will no longer be able to take from abroad more than it provides.

In an ever-changing world, there can never be equilibrium all around. Not everyone can be in surplus or deficit at once, and nearly every country oscillates around equilibrium, according to the interaction of its own cycles, policies, and general stage of development with world conditions. A surplus or a deficit sets in motion a chain of reactions that leads toward its opposite. The United States, however, has managed to run a chronic basic balance-of-payments deficit since the end of World War II These deficits, originally welcomed in the interests of European and Japanese recovery, have continued unabated for nearly four decades—quite a remarkable record. No other developed country could have behaved in this fashion for as long. Only America's unique position in the postwar system has made such a perpetual imbalance possible. Thanks to its position, the United States has been able, directly or indirectly, to pass much of the burden of financing its deficits to the rest of the world economy. American policy, moreover, has grown utterly dependent on this international solution. Without it, the United States would have to change drastically its postwar mix of foreign and domestic policies.

While this American dependence on manipulating the international economy has existed at least since the 1960s, the method of doing so has changed significantly. Broadly speaking, American manipulation has employed three formulas: the Bretton Woods formula that lasted through the 1960s, the Nixon formula of the 1970s, and the Reagan formula of the 1980s. All three have depended on the dollar's position in the international monetary system. . . . Here, a brief history may help illustrate how the economic formulas have worked.

The postwar monetary arrangements codified at the famous conference at Bretton Woods in 1944 were not fully in effect until European currencies became convertible in 1958. Technically, the system was a gold-exchange standard, similar to the system that followed World War I, except that an International Monetary Fund was to manage the arrangements, in particular to provide credit and discipline for those countries experiencing a temporary deficit. The guiding rules were free convertibility of national currencies and stable, if occasionally adjustable, exchange rates. The dollar was the *numeraire*. Every other currency had a fixed value in relation to the dollar, a value that its government was supposed to defend and that could be changed only by agreement in the IMF. The dollar, in sum, was freely convertible both into other currencies and into a fixed amount of gold. The dollar was thus the fixed point against which other monies were measured. As seemed only natural under the circumstances, the dollar was the principal reserve currency held and used by foreign central banks to cover their external debts. It was also the principal currency for private international transactions and reserves. With such arrangements, the stability of the world monetary system was uniquely dependent on the stability of the dollar and, hence, on the economic conditions and policies of the United States.

It was presumably the duty of the United States to manage its economy so that the dollar kept a steady value. Since the United States had accumulated most of the world's gold, it also seemed rather important to provide enough dollars to finance the rest of the world's postwar recovery and steady growth thereafter. Politicians and economists regularly warned of a dollar gap that would throttle both.

As it happened, the American economy proved not at all reluctant to provide the liquidity the world demanded. United States balance-of-payments deficits have persisted since 1945. Initially, this flow had a salutary effect on the world economy. Marshall Plan aid helped Europe to rebuild. In the 1950s, continuing U.S. military and economic aid, heavy American private investment, and the growing American appetite for imports and tourism all helped stimulate and stabilize world prosperity and development.

By the Kennedy-Johnson era of the 1960s, the American outflow began to seem excessive. The Bretton Woods system, based as it was on stable exchange rates and free convertibility, presumably never envisaged that any one country could run a balance-of-payments deficit regularly from one decade to the next. Technical and political factors made it possible for the United States to do so. The dollar's reserve-currency status meant that foreign countries were legally able to accumulate the exported dollars in their central banks. Since the United States was also their military protector, the allies felt constrained not to refuse.

For Europeans, the French in particular, the situation grew into a major grievance against the Americans. The accumulating dollar balances in the central banks of Europe and Japan were seen as little better than forced loans, sometimes to finance activities that many Europeans opposed, like the Vietnam War, or that even seemed directly inimical to their own interests, like the heavy influx of U.S. corporations. In short, the United States was seen to be abusing its position as a reserve-currency country.

The abuse seemed not only politically unjust but also economically damaging. According to de Gaulle's favorite economist, Jacques Rueff, American payments deficits were a relentless source of world inflation. Thanks to the dollar's role in the gold-exchange standard, the gold standard's mechanisms of adjustment failed in the case of American deficits.

In the end, the world's currency markets did bring down the Bretton Woods system. Since it was a gold-exchange rather than a pure dollar standard, the dollars were supposed to be convertible into a fixed amount of gold and into foreign currencies at a fixed rate of exchange. As the American balance-of-payments deficit continued year after year, central banks increasingly demanded repayment, and American gold and foreign currency reserves dwindled in relation to American foreign obligations. Private holdings of expatriate dollars accumulated in an immense offshore or Eurodollar capital market. Speculation against the dollar grew more possible and more logical. Kennedy and Johnson both tried to control capital flows and to convince other countries to help defend the dollar's parity, and Johnson used heavy political pressure. But such efforts could not control the private currency market; in the end, the policies adopted were unable to save the dollar's fixed exchange rate. By 1971, Nixon had to float the dollar and then formally devalue it. As the dollar continued to fall, a further devaluation followed in 1973. Still the dollar could not be stabilized, and it continued to float downward through most of the 1970s. The United States could no longer sustain its hegemonic obligation to maintain a stable value for the dollar. A de facto floating-rate system had begun, not formally ratified until the Jamaica agreements of 1976. By then, Bretton Woods was clearly dead, and the United States was well into a new formula for spreading its disequilibrium to the world.

The Kennedy and Johnson administrations had not wanted events to evolve this way. Both had desperately tried to reverse the dollar's growing weakness. Why had they failed?

The immediate cause seemed obvious enough. Neither administration had succeeded in controlling America's persistent balance-of-payments deficit. The United States, it was clear, was suffering from a basic payments disequilibrium vis-a-vis the world economy as a whole. Instead of the permanent dollar gap that had once been feared, there developed an apparently permanent dollar glut.

The causes were never firmly grasped, mainly because the most sensible explanation pointed to conclusions that were universally unwelcome. Two explanatory schools developed among policymakers. The first, popular in the 1960s, focused on particular items from the so-called basic balance of payments. This balance tried to measure only flows from the "real economy"—goods, services, and long-term investments—and thus ignored short-term capital flows. Such measurements invariably indicated that whereas American trade in goods and services was always in surplus, combined outflows for overseas U.S. military forces, aid, long-term corporate investment, and tourism regularly turned the balance into a deficit. The payments deficit thus seemed essentially political. It was an imperial balance-of-payments deficit. Overseas government spending and even corporate investments could be counted the expenses of running a *Pax Americana.* The hegemon's overseas costs were not being met by its overseas income. Now that the European and Japanese allies had manifestly recovered, the obvious solution seemed some form of burden-sharing, as well as an end to any remaining discrimination against American products.

A second explanation for the weakening dollar came from monetarist economists, American and European. From their perspective, any analysis based on singling out particular items in the basic payments balance was economically illiterate. Instead, they argued, overall monetary conditions determined payments balances. When a country had more expansive monetary conditions than the norm in the international system, its excess money tended to flow out as a payments deficit. The increasing internationalization of business, of capital markets in particular, lent weight to monetarist analysis. The dollar was actually brought down, for example, not by the inability to finance the relatively small basic balance-of-payments deficits, but by great waves of speculation in the currency markets. These waves were financed from the enormous pool of dollars available in the Eurodollar capital market. Speculative movements of this sort had nothing directly to do with the American basic balance of payments but were movements of short-term capital, or "hot money," responding to international monetary conditions. They therefore required a monetary explanation.

According to the monetarist model, the United States ran a payments deficit because its monetary conditions were relatively abundant compared to the norm for other countries in the international system as a whole. To diminish the deficit, the U.S. money supply would have to diminish comparatively. While a money supply is an elusive concept whose measurement is difficult within one economy, let alone comparatively, the monetarist model nevertheless has always had great logical force. In effect, it held the United States to be more inflationary than the international norm. The payments deficit meant, logically, that the United States was creating money excessively in comparison to the growth of money elsewhere. But the dollar's international role ensured that America's domestic price inflation did not necessarily reach a rate higher than in the rest of the world. Instead, the United States could export at least part of its surplus money supply. Instead of pushing up prices at home, that part flowed outward as a balance-of-payments deficit, swelling the money supplies of other countries and promoting price inflation abroad.

Why, however, was American monetary policy so expansive—too expansive, in the end, to be compatible with a stable dollar? American monetarists tended to suggest incompetence at the Federal Reserve, or the Fed's lack of institutional and political support. More fundamentally, they blamed neo-Keynesian growth policies that kept the economy stimulated beyond what they called its natural level of unemployment. Foreign monetarist critics, the French particularly, also saw the United States overstretched in its overseas ambitions, as well as tempted into overextension by an international monetary system that permitted the dollar too much leeway. In strict economic logic, American overextension could not be attributed to either external or internal policies and aims, but rather to their combination. Somehow, America's combined goals were too great for its available resources.

Relating an external disequilibrium to excessive political goals requires looking beyond the balance-of-payments deficit to the country's overall macroeconomic conditions and, in particular, to the role of government in shaping those conditions. The government not only tries to shape monetary conditions but is itself a very large consumer. In other words, alongside monetary policy there is fiscal policy. And aside from a perennial payments deficit, a perennial fiscal deficit seems an obvious symptom of overstretching and general disequilibrium. Starting in 1961, an unbroken string of federal fiscal deficits ran through the boom years of the 1960s until 1969, resumed without interruption through the 1970s, and is certainly fated to continue at least through the 1980s. Each decade, moreover, seemed to bring a quantum jump to the size of the average deficit.

It seems scarcely accidental that this string of fiscal deficits first grew up in tandem with the Kennedy-Johnson cycle of rearmament, combined as it was with their equally ambitious program to develop America's human resources. Nor was it accidental that the dollar's external difficulties first grew serious as the rearmament cycle and the Great Society began to gather momentum.

Kennedy and Johnson were able to win domestic support for their ambitious goals because, while reasserting NSC-68's military posture, they also adopted its congenial neo-Keynesian fiscal principles. The unbalanced fiscal policy of the 1960s could not, of course, be blamed on military and space spending alone. The upgraded domestic program proved even more costly. Logically, it was the combination that fueled the great increases in federal spending. The fiscal deficit, moreover, could not be blamed only on increased spending. The proportion of federal taxes to the gross domestic product had also dropped. Thus, according to the analyst's vantage point and policy preferences, deficits could be blamed on military or civilian spending, insufficient taxes, or, indeed, insufficient overall growth of the economy.

In any event, peacetime fiscal deficits were scarcely novel. Since Roosevelt's time, successive administrations had regarded Keynesian counter-cyclical deficits as inevitable and beneficial during a recession. Eisenhower had countenanced record deficits during the recessions of the 1950s. The Kennedy administration, however, greatly expanded the range of economic conditions in which deficits were regarded as legitimate. The neo-Keynesian arguments justifying full-employment budgets were officially adopted and promoted. Fiscal deficits were thereby justified whenever the economy was working at anything less than full capacity. If sufficiently appealing new expenditures could not be found, taxes were to be cut. Kennedy proposed the first full-employment tax cut in 1963, and Congress passed it in 1964, soon after Johnson came into office. The shift in doctrine and practice marked a new phase of American fiscal policy; deficits grew more severe in relation to their general economic context.

Fiscal deficits, of course, need not result in inflation, unless monetary policy also expands to finance or accommodate the deficit. Instead of loosening money and credit in the face of a deficit, central banks can hold steady. Under such conditions, the government bids in the capital market against private borrowers for the extra credit it needs. The government's deficits are then financed by real savings rather than by newly created money. The consequence is not inflation, but high real interest rates that may crowd out investments from the market and dampen economic growth. High interest rates may also encourage a higher level of domestic saving, or an inflow of foreign savings. In any event, so long as monetary policy remains firm, no inflation need follow. Any such sustained tight monetary policy, familiar by the 1980s, was, however, nearly unthinkable in the political and economic conditions of the Kennedy administration. When, for example, the Federal Reserve did begin tightening monetary conditions in 1966, both Congress and the Johnson administration vociferously objected.

Monetary stability was not high on the agenda of the 1960s. Kennedy arrived in office with an ambitious set of domestic and foreign programs. He realized that the resources for these programs could be found only in a period of rapid growth. His gradual conversion to neo-Keynesian growth policies followed. Kennedy was already convinced that the United States had been asleep in the Eisenhower era, its economy stunted, he believed, by a pusillanimous conservatism. As a result of America's slow growth, its industry was losing competitiveness, long-needed domestic programs were blocked, racial conflict was threatening, military superiority had been allowed to decline, and development in the Third World had been left to languish.

A full-employment fiscal policy, the neo-Keynesians promised, could easily achieve the growth needed to reverse this decline. More inflation might result, but, as the Phillips Curve indicated, moderate inflation could be traded for more rapid growth and higher employment. Tight monetary policy, however, would frustrate such a growth policy. Sustained monetary stringency thus seemed intellectually and politically unacceptable, even after high employment was actually reached and the Vietnam War was adding substantially to the federal deficit. As a result, both Kennedy and Johnson opposed using tight money to save the dollar. Its defense was left instead to various ad hoc policies, such as temporary capital controls or taxes designed to insulate domestic monetary conditions from the world capital market.

The first major reversal came in 1968. The progress of American inflation had seemed so alarming that Johnson and Congress finally accepted a tax increase. Fiscal 1969 is, consequently, the only year after 1960 when the federal government did not run a deficit. Meanwhile, the Federal Reserve finally nerved itself to sustain tight money. With fiscal and monetary tightening thus abruptly combined, inflation turned to stagflation. As Richard Nixon came to power in January 1969, the country was heading into its most serious recession since the Second World War.

Recession did help to bolster the dollar. But tight money, higher taxes, and severe recession were unpopular with the voting public, and the 1970 congressional elections registered a sharp defeat for the Republicans. Nixon and the Federal Reserve had already begun to foster a reflation. By the spring of 1971, the dollar was again in crisis. Pressure built up until, on August 15, Nixon officially suspended the dollar's convertibility. Nixon also imposed a substantial surcharge on imports and froze domestic wages and prices. By December of 1971, America's "affluent allies" had formally accepted a dollar devaluation. Bretton Woods might thereby be resurrected, they hoped, and the new dollar parity defended successfully.

The administration followed a different policy. Seconded by the Federal Reserve, Nixon pushed a vigorous economic expansion through his successful bid for reelection in 1972. Victory was celebrated by dismantling not only wage and price controls, but also the capital controls left over from the Johnson administration. As Nixon's boom continued, the dollar's new parity began slipping. The administration had no serious intent to defend it. A second official devaluation followed in 1973. Bretton Woods had clearly broken down. With floating rates the United States had found a new formula for financing its disequilibrium.

The new Nixon formula proved highly successful both in relieving the more egregious problems of the old Bretton Woods system and in permitting the United States to continue to run regular balance-of-payments and fiscal deficits. Under fixed exchange rates, America's habitual inflation had become a twin disability. It had pushed prices of domestically produced goods higher in relation to foreign goods, and it had encouraged American capital to go abroad rather than to invest in modernizing production at home. By the late 1960s, the American trade balance was turning sharply negative for the first time since the nineteenth century. Protectionist pressure from domestic-based industries and their labor unions was growing unmanageable. At the same time, internationally oriented business—multinational corporations and banks—chafed at the capital controls made necessary by the U.S. defense of the inflated dollar's parity.

A floating dollar pleased both groups. With the dollar depreciating substantially and repeatedly, domestically produced goods grew more competitive. Exports in certain key industries, like capital goods, enjoyed remarkable rejuvenation. Pressure for protection subsided. Floating also permitted an end to capital controls, which made managing multinational enterprises easier and effectively fused the domestic and international capital markets. American banks profited greatly as their international earnings grew rapidly and began to equal their domestic business.

Nixon's success was not entirely fortuitous or unplanned. The transformation to floating had been anticipated with an elaborate rationale. By the later 1960s, declining American trade had provoked great disquiet in thoughtful industrial and academic circles. Europe and Japan seemed to be surpassing the United States in industrial competitiveness. Out of this anxiety came a systematic American case against its rich allies, the counterpart to Europe's complaints about America's exported inflation.

This case rested on the assumptions that America's declining competitive position should be blamed on an overvalued dollar, and that the overvalued dollar, in turn, should be blamed on the Bretton Woods monetary arrangements. In this view, a weakening dollar was entirely predictable and not America's fault. It had come about because early in the postwar era the United States had generously permitted its war-devastated competitors to peg their currencies at an undervalued level. Several had managed to devalue their currencies still further. After their recovery, they refused to make the obvious adjustment. The Bretton Woods rules imposed no sanctions to force the rich allies to revalue but made it theoretically impossible for the dollar to devalue. Under such circumstances, American analysts concluded, the United States had no obligation to defend the dollar's distorted exchange rate. Instead, these experts argued, the United States should adopt an attitude of benign neglect. If the needed parity changes could not be negotiated voluntarily, the market, left to its own devices, would eventually bring currencies into a more reasonable relationship. If Bretton Woods collapsed, the fault would lie with America's rich allies, who had proved too irresponsible to share the burden of managing a fixed-rate system.

Benign neglect carried overtones of a broader political case. American analysts began to see the United States being exploited by its own allies. Europeans and Japanese were not only mercantilist chiselers, squeezing commercial advantage by refusing to adjust an outmoded monetary system, but also free riders enjoying cheap military security at America's expense. Nixon's secretary of the treasury, John Connally, pointedly observed how America's basic balance-of-payments deficit tended to approximate, year after year, the exchange costs of American troops stationed overseas, mostly in Western Europe. As an economic explanation for the payments deficit it may have been shaky, but its political logic was all too clear. Taken in a larger framework, moreover, Connally's economic point was more than plausible. Thanks to its protector's role, the United States did carry a much heavier military burden than those rich allies who were also America's major economic competitors. That extra military burden could not easily be ignored in explaining America's fiscal imbalance, its relatively expansive monetary climate, and the dollar's consequent chronic weakness. In effect, item-by-item explanations for the payments deficit, which tended to focus on America's imperial costs, and monetarist explanations, which emphasized inflation, could easily be merged. Together they provide a comprehensive and convincing, if unwelcome, rationale for the dollar's weakness. Imperial costs, combined with the nascent welfare state, promoted an unbalanced fiscal policy and a too-expansive monetary policy: hence, the weak dollar.

The same explanation, however, also makes clear why floating rates were unlikely, in themselves, to cure the dollar's instability. For if the comprehensive imperial monetarist analysis is correct, the dollar's problem was not merely a historical maladjustment of parity, brought on by European and Japanese recovery, but rather a fundamental and continuing American disequilibrium, brought on by the cost of America's combined foreign and domestic objectives. So long as the United States could not find the resources to finance those objectives without inflationary fiscal and monetary policies, American monetary conditions were likely to remain looser than those in Europe or Japan. As a result, no once-and-for-all adjustment of the dollar's parity could, in itself, cure America's disequilibrium—or the dollar's weakness, which was its consequence. With floating rates, repeated depreciation would be the dollar's normal state, interrupted by exceptional periods of domestic monetary and fiscal stringency but resuming whenever the economy returned to expansion, as in 1971. In short, Nixon's formula—domestic expansion and floating rates— meant not merely one or two belated adjustments of a distorted parity, but repeated depreciation and perpetual instability.

The Nixon administration would doubtless have preferred a more genuine cure for America's disequilibrium. Even while trying to promote a boom for 1972, the administration also sought to cut government spending, arms spending in particular. Nixon and Kissinger's elaborate diplomacy of detente and surrogates was designed, among other things, to find a way to back off safely from the budgetary costs of the Kennedy-Johnson rearmament. But while U.S. military expenditures did fall in the wake of Vietnam, the rapid growth of domestic social services more than offset that decline. Johnson's Great Society had developed momentum of its own. Consequently, the Nixon administration managed only a change in the mix of military and civilian expenditures rather than a drop in the overall total.

What is more, Nixon's foreign policy almost ensured that his reductions in military spending would prove only temporary. Cuts in military means were not accompanied by any genuine reduction in broad geopolitical commitments. As a result, the American military grew more and more overstretched, a situation greatly aggravated by the switch to a volunteer army in 1973. This lack of equipoise between commitments and forces was bound to prove unstable, despite the apparent success of Soviet-American detente. Once detente faltered, a strong rebound in military spending was predictable. But even while detente flourished, no administration was able to achieve fiscal equilibrium, thanks to the sharp growth in civilian expenditures. The Ford and Carter administrations continued to witness a depreciating dollar.

The Nixon formula of expansion and depreciation was far more popular at home than abroad. With the collapse of the Bretton Woods formula, it was simply a new way of passing to the world economy the consequences of America's own domestic disequilibrium. For Europeans and Japanese, the Nixon solution posed a serious dilemma between unemployment and inflation. As the dollar fell, their products would grow increasingly less competitive. This, they reasoned, would mean higher unemployment and lower investment in their export industries—a sector far more vital to them than to the United States. If, to avoid these trends, they supported the dollar in currency markets (dirty floating), or otherwise kept pace with American monetary expansion, they risked an inflation that would also undermine their competitiveness and upset their social order.

As the years passed, the unfavorable consequences of the Nixon formula began to be felt strongly at home as well as abroad. Renouncing the obligation to defend the dollar's parity did more than pass on the effects of American inflation; it removed a major barrier against further price augmentation. As inflation mounted precipitously after 1971, the consequences, exacerbated by volatile shifts in Federal Reserve policy, eventually produced a severe recession in 1974. A return to the Nixon formula of reflation and depreciation in the Ford-Carter period brought on even greater inflation in the later 1970s and a still more severe recession in 1980.

As the cyclical oscillations grew worse at home, their effects worsened abroad. The year 1973 saw record price inflation worldwide, much of it exported by an ebulliently expansive American economy. Global inflation naturally had unsettling effects on world commodity prices. Food prices skyrocketed throughout the year, and by the year's end, OPEC was able to engineer an astonishing fourfold increase in oil prices. Much of the subsequent monetary disorder of the 1970s has been blamed on these food and oil shocks. In retrospect, however, such shocks seem not merely exogenous events but also reflections of long- and short-term world economic and political conditions, which American economic policy did much to determine and often to magnify.

The oil price shock, for example, is often blamed for the severe recession of 1974. But in the United States that recession was under way months before the effects of the higher oil prices could be felt. It was a highly exaggerated cyclical downturn reflecting, above all, the reaction to the inflationary excesses of Nixon's election boom. It was made worse by the sharp rise in oil prices, but not caused by it. Once the oil shock had occurred, moreover, America's inflationary policy persisted in magnifying its unsettling consequences. Logically, the vastly increased oil prices implied a secular shift in the terms of trade between oil and manufactures. In one stroke, the oil prices, which had declined relative to industrial prices since the end of World War II, recaptured their lost ground. Since Western Europe and Japan imported most of their oil, to regain external equilibrium they had either to earn more from exports or to use less oil. Logically, government policies in such a situation would strive to conserve energy, dampen domestic demand, and promote exports. Nearly all advanced industrial countries, except the United States, followed such a course.

America's exceptionalism was not so apparent while the recession lasted. By the election year of 1976, however, the Ford administration had succeeded in reflating the economy, while it had still failed to push through any effective program to conserve energy. Instead, domestic American subsidies and controls continued to keep domestic American fuel prices well below world levels. The obvious consequences followed: U.S. energy imports soared and the trade and current-account balances recorded unprecedented deficits. The same conditions continued through the Carter administration. In effect, the United States greatly delayed adjusting its real economy to higher oil prices.

Profligacy with energy resources, combined with comparatively inflationary macroeconomic policy, weakened the dollar still further, particularly since Europe and Japan, trying to adjust their real economies, continued to restrain domestic demand in order to promote exports. As in the Nixon years, a repeatedly depreciating dollar proved to have many advantages. American exports remained competitive abroad despite inflating prices at home. And since world oil was traded in dollars, inflation and a depreciating dollar meant, if oil prices were not raised to compensate, a lower real price for oil—particularly for holders of strong currencies, but also for Americans. After their initial sharp price increase, OPEC countries dared not raise their prices to keep up fully with American inflation and the falling dollar. World recession and energy conservation had glutted the oil market. The United States, with its enhanced hegemonic role in the Middle East, seemed in a strong position to lean on its Saudi and Iranian clients. In short, Nixon's solution to the weak dollar, perpetual dollar depreciation, became also the American solution to the oil crisis.

America's exported inflation also had profound effects on international finance. The huge and unrepentant balance-of-payments deficits channeled a flood of dollars to the oil-rich states. In many instances, their economies could not absorb it. Since no alternative international currency was in sight, and the large holders could not dump their dollars without enormous loss, the surplus dollars continued to accumulate in the Eurodollar market.

The oil shock produced not only a new flood of surplus capital, but also an eager crowd of borrowers. Even countries taking strong measures to adjust to the new oil prices often needed heavy borrowing to finance the transition. For many other countries, particularly in the Third World, adjusting their real economies meant scrapping long-range industrial plans or accepting an intolerable drop in living standards. Like the Americans, they refused to adjust. Unable to print internationally acceptable money themselves, they found bankers eager to lend them surplus dollars. In a climate of general and accelerating inflation, borrowing seemed simpler than facing severely disruptive changes in their economies. Although international agencies tried to manage this financial recycling, private commercial banks were less officious and hence more inviting to borrowers and lenders alike. As the United States gradually ended capital controls and banking regulations, overseas and domestic capital markets grew increasingly integrated. Large American banks, no longer blocked by controls, accumulated an increasing share of the swelling international debt. Thanks to the ardent enterprise of the banks, borrowing was easy and seemed painless. Credit seemed unlimited, and the general level of world debt grew to hitherto astonishing heights. With the exception of the underpopulated OPEC states and a few rich industrial states, nearly every nation ran deficits and lived by borrowing. As in the 1920s, most of these international loans were short-term. With such practices widespread, and with banks competing eagerly for paper profits, the world's financial structure grew more and more fragile.

On the surface, the United States appeared to be doing well in the mid to late 1970s, certainly better than the Europeans. The Nixon solution had permitted Ford's reflation in 1976, despite the recession in the rest of the world. The boom lasted through most of the Carter administration. With a depreciating dollar, domestic inflation did not automatically make domestically produced American products less competitive. American protectionism receded. With no concern for defending the dollar, the painful implications of the energy crisis could be ignored. With capital controls ended, American banks could reap huge profits from the great expansion of credit in the United States and the urgent need for it elsewhere.

The principal losers from this policy were the OPEC countries, who saw their stunning 1973 price increase erode considerably within a few short years. Next came the Europeans and Japanese, who were seriously trying to adjust their real economies. Their competitiveness was menaced by the dollar's depreciation, and their stability by American monetary expansion. From their perspective, the floating monetary arrangements constituted as great an abuse of hegemonic privilege as the decayed Bretton Woods system of the 1960s. The United States was able to get away with so generous a policy of credit creation because of the dollar's special role in the international economy. In economic terms the Nixon solution constituted a use of "money illusion" on a world scale. In relations with both Europe and the oil producers, the illusion was reinforced by power. Rather than exercising their hegemony to guide and stabilize the monetary system, the Americans were exploiting it.

Economically and politically, the Europeans could find no easy way out of their Nixon-imposed dilemma. Floating had not meant that the dollar would give up its preponderant role in the international economy. The dollar was still the world's principal reserve currency, even if many European countries were holding an increasing proportion of their reserves in gold. The dollar was also the main currency for international transactions. Most raw materials were traded in dollars. The United States remained the world's largest economy, intimately tied to others through trade and capital flows. To replace the dollar would require some new international money with a political backing sufficient to make it credible. A new international currency was difficult to envision, except in the long run, and then probably only after some destabilizing catastrophe. Neither the Germans nor the Japanese wanted their currencies to have a greater international role, with all the attendant dangers for domestic stability. Collectively, the Europeans may have had the economic resources, but they lacked sufficient political will and common interest to support a common currency. Attempts at even a limited European Monetary Union were notably unsuccessful until the end of the 1970s.

Behind the technical role that the dollar played in the world economy lay the geopolitical hegemony of the United States. To challenge the dollar's role would have required the major European powers to unite for an economic confrontation with the United States, possibly involving capital controls and trade barriers—a course not easily compatible with their posture as American protectorates. The disaffection engendered by being placed in such a dilemma was part of a growing general awareness that their American protector, also a tough commercial and industrial rival, was increasingly inclined to take shortcuts in securing its own economic interests—even, if necessary, at the expense of the international system it claimed to be guiding.

From an American perspective, U.S. economic policy could easily be justified as merely forcing the free-riding Europeans and Japanese to pay indirectly some of the cost of their own security. No administration was willing to contemplate returning to the orthodoxy of Bretton Woods and fixed exchange rates, a framework that had seemed to guarantee America's domestic decline to the profit of those allies whom it was defending. In economic policy as in security policy, the United States had grown determined to exercise its hegemonic role in a fashion that augmented rather than reduced its own national welfare. Economically as well as militarily, America's diplomatic primacy would increasingly substitute for the abundant force that had once flowed from within.

The Carter administration, having lived off the Nixon legacy, was fated to cope with its bankruptcy. Carter came into office inheriting Ford's reflation of 1976. The consequent boom fitted the Nixon formula. Responding to the combination of domestic stimulation and unrestricted oil imports, the economy expanded, the trade balance deteriorated, and the dollar began a new round of rapid depreciation. The administration nevertheless stimulated the boom further. As was to be expected, debate over transatlantic economic policy grew increasingly polemical. Each side had its characteristic arguments. When the Europeans complained of American inflation and mercantilist exchange-rate policy, the United States was ready with its "locomotive theory" of world recovery. Strong economies, according to the Carter administration, were supposed to pursue expansive policies to offset the oil shock, to permit poorer countries to sell exports, and, in general, to pull the world out of its slump.

By 1979, the days of the Nixon solution appeared numbered. Europeans had revived their project for a European Monetary System and had finally begun to create a European currency bloc. A mechanism was coming in place to permit Europe, in *extremis,* to cut loose from the dollar. The European Community was thus in a better position to bargain. Meanwhile, reactions against inflation in the capital and currency markets began to force a change in American economic policy. By 1979, foreign and domestic reactions came to a climax. An accelerated deterioration of the dollar, combined with a spectacular rise in gold prices, brought money markets to near panic. America's domestic bond market seemed close to collapse as soaring interest rates anticipated runaway inflation. OPEC, worried by declining revenues and deeply shaken by the Iranian revolution, imposed the first major real price increase since 1973. This conjuncture of events in currency, gold, oil, and capital markets constituted an international and domestic revolt against the Nixon economic formula. Europeans, Arabs, and domestic holders of capital reacted together against a policy of deliberate inflation and depreciation.

The collapse of the Nixon formula in the economic sphere paralleled the degeneration of the Nixon-Kissinger formulas in the diplomatic and military spheres. Nixon's dollar policy and detente policy faltered together. Both had been designed to continue America's traditional world role with strained resources. By 1979, the Soviet invasion of Afghanistan had brutally punctured any remaining hope that detente could counterbalance Soviet power in the Third World. It had also steadily grown apparent that arms-control negotiations could not succeed, by themselves, in maintaining American nuclear superiority. Americans could not sustain by negotiation a strategic position they were unwilling to back up with arms. Enthusiasm for SALT II gave way to fears about a window of vulnerability. As the military balance seemed to decline, European fears of decoupling revived, with fresh demands for American nuclear missiles and a populist rebirth of European neutralism. As strategic parity made European conventional defense more significant, and the United States began to plan new forces for the Third World, quarrels over burden sharing intensified. Meanwhile, the policy of relying on surrogates contributed to the humiliations of the Iranian debacle. The Carter Doctrine pronounced a formal American commitment to defend the Persian Gulf, and the United States found itself more entangled than ever in the Middle East.

With this accumulation of defeats and apprehensions, the United States clearly lacked the military strength to sustain its geopolitical role. As Iran demonstrated, a vulnerable United States had become the target of widespread resentment without the means to compel respect.

If the Carter administration cannot be said to have handled these inherited breakdowns with conspicuous skill, it nevertheless did set the path for a new cycle of American policy. By the middle of Carter's term, a mood of confrontation was replacing detente; military budget cutting and hegemony on the cheap were giving way to a Kennedy-style rearmament. But Carter's rearmament cycle was inaugurated under very different economic circumstances. Kennedy had had the great advantage of succeeding the thrifty Eisenhower; Carter followed Nixon and Ford. Both had imitated Eisenhower's parsimonious military policies, but rising domestic expenses had robbed them of Eisenhower's fiscal success. Thus, both the Nixon and Ford administrations, despite their conservative rhetoric, had continued and intensified the neo-Keynesian macroeconomic policies of Kennedy and Johnson. By the end of the 1970s, both the American political system and the world in general were in revolt against the inflation that followed. In short, while one political mood was bent on rearmament, another was ripe for disinflation. The result was worsening schizophrenia in American policy.

Reconciling rearmament with economic restraint posed a political and intellectual challenge of great complexity. The Carter administration tried fitfully to prune its fiscal budget into balance but was soon defeated by military needs. Truman had met a similar challenge through new taxes plus wage and price controls. Carter faced a wave of public opinion demanding not only an end to inflation but also lower taxes and more liberal markets. Under such circumstances, tight monetary policy emerged as the only solution. If the central bank refused to expand credit, fiscal deficits would have to be financed from real savings, at the expense of private borrowers. Rearmament would then mean not inflation but a credit squeeze. The formula had long been used in the Federal Republic of Germany, which had managed for half a decade to combine substantial fiscal deficits with low inflation.

When Carter appointed Paul Volcker as chairman of the Federal Reserve in 1979, American monetary policy resolutely took on its thankless task. Money in America grew tighter than ever before in living memory. For the United States and the world, the coming cyclical downturn developed into the major recession of 1980-82, more severe even than the Nixon-Ford recession of 1974-75. At the same time, the world's ramshackle financial structure faced an international debt crisis more serious than anything experienced since World War II. In short, rearmament, stringent monetary policy, and a deep recession were Carter's legacy to the 1980s.

While the incoming Reagan administration embraced rearmament and tight money, it found a formula to escape from recession. This Reagan formula, like the Bretton Woods and Nixon formulas, relied heavily on manipulating the international economy.

The history of the Reagan administration provides a striking demonstration of the persistent dilemma of postwar American conservatism. On the one hand, the administration strongly supported maintaining America's world role. Many of its prominent members and backers had vociferously warned against declining American military strength and had been notably unimpressed by detente diplomacy. True to his convictions, Reagan pushed through a military budget designed to restore American power. At the same time, the Reaganite platform also opposed heavy government spending, high taxes, inflation, wage and price controls, and big government generally. The administration was particularly determined to cut taxes in order to reverse the bracket creep that kept biting into middle-class wealth. It pushed through the largest tax cut in postwar history. Combining these defense and tax policies led predictably to very large fiscal deficits, an anomalous outcome for a conservative administration ostensibly opposed to big government and inflation.

Like most governments with irreconcilable goals, the Reagan administration sought refuge in political and economic fantasy. Fiscal balance, it kept saying, could be reached by cutting the government's civilian expenditures. But though dismantling the welfare state was a goal with rhetorical appeal among conservatives, budget cuts large enough to right the fiscal balance would mean major reductions in Social Security and Medicare, proposals that would alienate a sizable segment of Reagan's conservative constituency. The president refused even to contemplate such cuts.

Fiscal balance through efficiency was another Reagan bromide. While studies showed how "business methods" could save billions, the administration was notably unsuccessful in translating these familiar observations into actual practice. Indeed, the rapid increase in the size of the arms budget made efficiencies in the egregiously wasteful military sector more elusive than ever. The administration also had a more novel version of efficiency. It proceeded to discard a good deal of environmental and safety regulation and to dismantle much of the accompanying inspection system. It also deregulated a large part of the banking and transportation industries, a policy already under way in the Carter administration. But whatever their intrinsic merits, these initiatives clearly could not generate the revenues or savings needed to plug Reagan's enormous fiscal gap.

The manifest unreality of its budget-cutting proposals suggested that the administration had put its real faith elsewhere. Like the Kennedy administration when it was bent on rearmament, the Reagan administration ended up embracing the NSC-68 fiscal formula. In other words, spending would create its own resources. Since Truman's time, the formula had evolved from spending more without raising taxes to spending more while cutting taxes. The full-employment tax cut, passed in 1964, had been a major step toward the inflation that followed. The Reagan growth model merely decorated the old neo-Keynesian fiscal formula with supply-side rhetoric to make it acceptable to conservatives. Rather than promoting growth through a redistribution of income to poorer consumers, the Reagan model counted on high profits to vigorous entrepreneurs and provident rentiers.

By the time Reagan came to power, however, there was one major difference in the macroeconomic climate. The traditional easy monetary policy had come to an end. The market, the public, and even the economists had grown fed up with inflation. Volcker's monetary policy enjoyed powerful support within Reagan's conservative coalition. Under the circumstances, the administration found itself committed to a tight monetary policy at the same time as its fiscal policy required lower taxes and higher defense spending.

Logically, so bizarre a combination appeared to be self-defeating. Tight money would throttle inflation, but large fiscal deficits combined with tight money would also abort recovery. Certainly that was Volcker's oft-stated view, but despite his misgivings, the Fed went on performing its appointed role. The credit squeeze of 1979-80 brought, not unexpectedly, a dramatic rise in real interest rates and triggered the worst recession since the end of World War II. By 1982, price inflation had dropped sharply while unemployment had risen to 11 percent. Recovery would follow, the Fed hoped, because recession would reduce the demand for money and real interest rates would fall. Continuing monetary stringency, reassuring investors, would sweat the "inflation premium" out of lending rates. Low interest rates, plus low inflation, would help the cyclical recovery grow into a genuine boom, based more on a capital investment for growth, the Fed hoped, than on inflated neo-Keynesian consumer demand.

The Fed's scenario was difficult to reconcile with the administration's huge fiscal deficits. The administration, in any event, had its own scenario. Supply-side tax cuts, deregulation, and, ultimately, tax reform would spark the recovery. The consequent entrepreneurship, investment, and saving would generate the resources needed to eliminate the fiscal deficit.

Events took a different course altogether. By 1982, despite deep recession and a dramatic fall in price inflation, real interest rates refused to come down. As Volcker himself never tired of observing, the reason was not obscure: the government's huge fiscal deficit was the principal culprit. Financing the deficit preempted market funds and kept alive inflationary expectations. As monetary tightness and the deep recession persisted, many analysts began to fear a major depression, possibly set off by a general collapse of the international banking system. Much of the domestic credit industry was also shaky, in particular the huge savings and loan sector.

Faced with these dangers, the Federal Reserve, having tried vainly to get the administration and Congress to bring the fiscal deficit under control, finally returned to easy money. From roughly the middle of 1982 through much of 1984, the money supply increased sharply, in several quarters at a rate apparently exceeding even the pre-inflationary binges of the early and mid-1970s. There followed the Reagan recovery of 1983, a familiar neo-Keynesian consumer boom. Domestic production expanded rapidly, and, for a time, high public and private consumption was matched by a major investment boom. But while credit was abundant, real interest rates still continued at record high levels, as many investors apparently feared history was repeating itself and that a major inflation would follow, particularly with 1984 a presidential election year. From this view, Reagan's boom looked to be merely a somewhat eccentric version of the ever more inflated business cycles common since the mid-1960s.

Even before the end of 1983, the Federal Reserve, alarmed by the bounding speed of the recovery, was thought once more to be trying to restrict credit. With the government's huge financing needs, many analysts, including Volcker and many of Reagan's own economic advisers, feared their monetary tightening would bring sharp increases in the already record real interest rates. An abrupt end to the Reagan recovery was the probable consequence.

Had the United States been a closed national economy, high interest rates would almost certainly have throttled the recovery. But while investment, which grew rapidly in late 1983, had slackened by the middle of 1984, personal consumption and government spending continued to rise strongly. As the boom continued and the U.S. economy moved toward full employment, America's inflated demand was met increasingly by goods imported from abroad. This helped stifle price inflation but also led to unprecedentedly large and rapidly growing trade and current-account deficits. Once more the world economy came to the rescue of America. Throughout the period, American monetary conditions were characterized by a very large net inflow of international capital. Thanks to the capital inflow, the record current-account deficit was financed without difficulty. Indeed, the dollar kept rising.

Why, with its multiple deficits, had the United States become such a magnet for foreign capital? Analysts credited the unusual pairing of Volcker and Reagan policies. Volcker's apparently steadfast monetarism seemed to promise a continuing strong dollar and a low inflation rate. Imports, in fact, kept domestic prices down. Meanwhile, Reagan's huge government deficits kept real interest rates up and resulted in very high levels of return for investors. The capital influx, as it financed the swelling current-account deficit, also pushed up the dollar's exchange rate. By 1983, the floating dollar had regained and surpassed all that it had lost since 1971. For foreign holders, returns from the dollar's high interest rates were topped by profits from the dollar's appreciation. Meanwhile, the Fed's 1982-83 reflation had sparked a stock market boom, itself a major magnet for foreign capital.

The dollar was also thought to benefit from Reagan's psychological reflation of the American image. Investors seemed to accept the administration's view that its boom was the just reward of its virtue. As the administration's supporters explained its success, America had put itself firmly in the hands of a vigorous conservative government, highly appreciative of the beneficent consequences of entrepreneurship, profit, and deregulation. No wonder the country was booming! Reagan's macroeconomic policy had found a magic formula to stem inflation while stimulating growth. Europe, enmeshed in socialism, welfarism, and highly restrictive market practices, was said to be still following traditional deflationary policies to restrain inflation. Unlike Reagan's America, it had not learned to stimulate and liberate its entrepreneurs. Consequently, while America was booming, European growth remained sluggish and unemployment was at its postwar record. Many commentators recorded a severe bout of Europessimism about the old continent's long-range economic prospects and its general socio-economic climate.

For European governments, the contrast to Reagan's ebullient America was both painful and exasperating. America, they believed, was flourishing not from the vaunted economic merits of Reagan's outlandish policy but because that policy constituted a new and highly successful formula for exploiting the rest of the world. After the Bretton Woods and Nixon formulas had come the Reagan formula. With the mammoth net capital inflow to the United States, the languishing world economy was supplying the savings needed to finance America's boom. Thanks to that inflow, America's long-awaited credit squeeze had failed to develop, despite tight money and the huge fiscal deficit. Meanwhile, the unfolding of Reagan's macroeconomic formula, which led to the dollar's unnatural strength, stymied Europe's own efforts at reflation, most notably in France, where the newly elected socialist government was attempting its own neo-Keynesian boom. Depreciating European currencies, while helping to make European exports more competitive, also greatly raised prices for Europe's imported raw materials, generally factored in dollars. Analysts were speaking of Europe's "third oil shock." Further depreciation of European currencies against the dollar threatened to rekindle inflation. In short, from a European perspective, American prosperity was being achieved at Europe's expense. American monetary and fiscal policies were sucking capital from Europe, and the consequences were blighting Europe's domestic prosperity. Europe's monetary interdependence with America was, as usual, leading to highly unsatisfactory results.

Reagan's macroeconomic policy also seemed increasingly dangerous for the world economy in general. Monetary and trade problems aggravated each other. Reagan's policies almost inevitably fed protectionism on both sides of the Atlantic. American manufacturing firms and their workers were increasingly devastated by the effects of an overvalued dollar on their competitiveness. They naturally pressed for limits on competing imports. Europe, with its prolonged recession and high unemployment, grew more and more allergic to competition from Japan or the newly industrialized countries. The dollar's record real interest rates greatly increased carrying charges for the world's debtors—most notably Third World and Eastern European countries that had borrowed heavily and short-term from commercial banks during the Nixonian period of abundant liquidity. The Reagan policy made their interest burden much heavier and dramatically revalued their capital costs.

Their trade opportunities threatened in Europe and America, many Third World debtors already were finding it difficult, despite record exports, to earn the extra dollars needed to finance the greatly augmented carrying charges on their debts. Several major borrowers required rescheduling and several leading American banks were overstretched. Fear of defaults and a general banking crisis threatened to dry up credit still further. The main central banks, the IMF, and the World Bank all grew more and more entangled in what seemed a haphazard, hectic, and perilous series of rescues. Debtors tended to blame not their own imprudence but the fickleness of American monetary conditions that made long-range development planning nearly impossible. Above all, they blamed American fiscal policy, whose deficit financing would apparently require a large part of the world's available savings for the foreseeable future. To many it seemed highly unnatural, not to say obscene, that the world's richest country should also be its biggest borrower.

Along with its moral and political deficiencies, Reagan's prosperity seemed both fragile in the near term and damaging in the long term. With America's borrowing needs so high, and its savings rate traditionally so low, Reagan's prosperity had come to depend on a perpetual net influx of foreign savings. But so long as it lasted, the consequent strong dollar was having predictably disastrous effects on the international competitiveness of the U.S. real economy. By the end of 1984, U.S. trade and current-account deficits were already on a scale scarcely imaginable a few years earlier. . . .

The basic similarity of the three postwar monetary formulas is worth noting. The Kennedy-Bretton Woods formula was, in effect, a way to borrow money by running balance-of-payments deficits. These became, de facto, inconvertible obligations to foreign central banks and overseas capital markets. The Nixon or floating formula allowed the dollar outflow and external indebtedness to continue, even though exchange-rate depreciation was repeatedly reducing its value. In both the Kennedy and Nixon formulas, the inflationary money supply was first created by monetary policy at home, then exported abroad through balance-of-payments deficits. Finally, the Reagan formula used America's swelling fiscal debt as a magnet to attract the exported dollars back home. America's present borrowing was financed by its past borrowing. Meanwhile, the basic balance-of-payments deficit or external disequilibrium of the real economy, remained at record levels. . . .

Predicting the long-range consequences is hardly easy. Until the 1980s, Europe's economic difficulties, however troublesome, were contained without seriously affecting the high level of general prosperity. By the mid-1980s, the continuing record unemployment, even after an upturn, was pointing to a grimmer future and more adventuresome politics. In the 1930s, fierce international competition and high unemployment led to radical domestic politics, protectionist blocs, and widespread cartelization. In the economic circumstances of the 1980s, the prospect of similar consequences naturally comes to mind. Protectionist sentiment is already rampant, if not yet triumphant, and predictions of a gradual transatlantic economic estrangement are easily supported. Broad trade patterns are shifting from the trans-Atlantic axis—European-American trade has declined relatively for twenty years. The Common Market itself is already the world's largest trading bloc—reaching out to the Middle East, Africa, Eastern Europe, and the Soviet Union. America's Pacific trade is already greater than its European trade, and it is still growing rapidly. Much of America's trade with Europe, moreover, is agricultural, while Europeans have troublesome agricultural surpluses of their own.

Against these centrifugal trends, however, are the undoubted countertrends toward international integration. Production is certainly more global in its organization than before World War II. Given existing investments, habits, and expectations, attempts at a serious reversal would meet fierce resistance, not easily overcome without some catastrophic financial breakdown. Just such a breakdown occurred, of course, in the 1930s. The economic dislocations since the 1970s have clearly made states more mercantilist—more assertive in promoting and protecting national industries. International trade and investment have thus grown highly political. So far, this has seemed to work mostly to America's advantage. But the advantage is likely to prove transitory and superficial. The American hegemony we have been describing is more a form of exploitation to compensate for weakness than a real supremacy—more buccaneering than domination. The long-term trend, after all, has been a steady weakening of the United States's economic competitiveness, despite its capacity to manipulate the world monetary system.

In the long run, neither America, Europe, nor Japan seems likely to have the economic weight and political power to dominate the world economy that appears to be developing. In its economic sphere, as in its political and military spheres, the world system will grow increasingly plural—with a proliferation of important actors, including states determined to safeguard their national prosperity. Taken altogether, these conditions and trends point, if anything, toward a new age of cartels—a web of agreements that permits competition but limits the damage. Some such organized competition would be the most rational and humane outcome and perhaps the only way to preserve the fabric of an open world economy in the face of so many destabilizing changes.

Perfecting the arrangements for an organized plural system will necessarily require a great deal of time and mutual forbearance. Prospects for a nontraumatic transformation will be very different if the old system simply collapses. It is therefore extremely foolish to underestimate the risks inherent in this present period of malaise and redirection. As a politico-economic system, the *Pax Americana* is showing severe strain in its economic sphere. For America's international as well as its domestic interests, squaring macroeconomic policy with hegemonic responsibility for maintaining world monetary stability seems an increasingly urgent priority. Without this long-delayed overhaul of American macroeconomic policy, Europe will either have to accept an increasingly damaging instability or be driven to cut itself off from the thrashings of the American monetary machine. To be sure, an indefinite passive resignation is one possible European response, but probably not the most likely. It seems to be in no one's interest to find out.

What chance is there for the United States to achieve an external equilibrium? In theory, every administration since Eisenhower's would have liked to bring the American economy and the world economy into balance. Powerful forces have nevertheless continued to work against equilibrium, and America's balance-of-payments deficits have relentlessly continued to grow. One of the most obvious obstacles has been America's long-standing fiscal deficit. By Reagan's time, that internal disequilibrium was self-evidently linked to external disequilibrium and both were threatening to escape rational political control entirely. Prominent among the reasons for the fiscal imbalance were, on the one hand, the enormous expense of the Carter-Reagan rearmament and, on the other, the overriding popular pressure that led Reagan to a major tax cut. The coexistence of these contrary policies was not merely fortuitous. It was only one more demonstration of how America's postwar geopolitical role has grown out of harmony with the internal dynamics of its domestic political economy. All hegemonic world powers have probably felt the same tension. Most have ultimately been undone by it. . . .

17

The International Monetary System: Out of Order?

NORMAN S. FIELEKE

In this essay, Norman Fieleke offers a spirited defense of the current composite international monetary system. After reviewing the problems of liquidity, confidence, and adjustment in the par value monetary system created at Bretton Woods in 1944, Fieleke demonstrates how the present system has dealt with these problems through greater exchange-rate flexibility. He then suggests that exchange-rate volatility has not substantially inhibited international trade, that speculation has not been a major problem or source of instability, and that suppressing exchange-rate flexibility would not necessarily solve the underlying macroeconomic imbalances which cause prolonged exchange-rate misalignment. Focusing only on the technical, or economic issues of international monetary management, Fieleke perceives the present system as working relatively well. In his words, although it lacks the purity of the "thoroughbred," it possesses the hardiness and adaptability of the "mongrel."

... At this writing, the world is free from both widespread inflation and widespread recession, but many analysts nonetheless believe that the international monetary system is sorely in need of repair. Exchange rates between national currencies are alleged to fluctuate excessively, and for long periods around the wrong levels. More fundamentally, the system is said to lack an effective mechanism for coordinating national macroeconomic policies so as to prevent the emergence of major imbalances in international payments.

And just what is the international monetary system? It is the set of mechanisms by which payments are made across national boundaries, and by which imbalances in these payments—such as the 1986 U.S. current account deficit—are either financed or adjusted. A key distinction between the international monetary system and the typical national system is that the national system utilizes only one currency, while in the current international system national currencies are exchanged for one another in the foreign exchange markets. Within each nation, the quantity of the national currency—and more generally of domestic money—is regulated by the central bank or other national monetary authority; but at the international level, no supreme central bank presides over these national banks. Any disturbance affecting any currency in the world is registered in the international system, if only by a change in the foreign exchange value of that currency.

THE PAR VALUE SYSTEM

As recently as the early 1970s, the world employed an international monetary system that had been designed partly to avoid the major shortcomings now attributed to the current system. In particular, exchange-rate fluctuations in the earlier system were generally constrained to narrow bands, and significant exchange-rate changes were allowed only after much evidence had accumulated as to their suitability. Why, then, was this system relinquished? An examination of the reasons will prove helpful in appraising the present system and proposals for its reform.

The earlier system was codified in the original Articles of Agreement of the International Monetary Fund, an international agreement negotiated in 1944 at Bretton Woods, New Hampshire. The Bretton Woods agreement called for essentially fixed rates of exchange between national currencies, on the assumption that fixed exchange rates would foster international commerce and international cooperation. In order to maintain fixed exchange rates in the foreign exchange markets, most governments specified "par values" for their currencies in terms of the U.S. dollar; they then bought or sold their currencies in exchange for dollars whenever necessary to prevent the dollar values of their currencies from deviating from the par values by more than 1 percent. With the values of other currencies thereby fixed in terms of the dollar, it was unnecessary for the United States to fix the value of the dollar in terms of other currencies. Instead, the obligation assumed by the United States was to fix the value of the dollar in terms of gold for purposes of transactions with foreign monetary authorities. The United States was to supply gold in exchange for dollars presented by these authorities—or to supply dollars in exchange for gold—at the official price of gold, originally set at $35 per ounce.

To make the par value system work, each government held a stock of international reserves—usually gold or dollars. A government could draw upon these reserves (or upon loans from the International Monetary Fund or other sources) to purchase its currency whenever necessary to stop a decline in the foreign exchange value of its currency. This outflow of reserves constituted a deficit in the country's overall balance of payments. If the currency subsequently tended to rise in value, the government would then reacquire reserves that it had previously paid out, and the country would realize a balance-of-payments surplus to offset the earlier deficit. Of course, such deficits and surpluses would not have been realized, and reserves would not have been necessary, if governments had not chosen to fix the values of their currencies in the foreign exchange markets. Instead, foreign exchange rates would have fluctuated freely.

The par value system worked reasonably well for more than two decades. By 1973, however, it had been abandoned, the victim of three related problems: liquidity, confidence, and adjustment.

THE PROBLEMS OF LIQUIDITY, CONFIDENCE, AND ADJUSTMENT

The problem of liquidity in the par value system was the problem of providing the appropriate amount of international reserves. Reserves were to be used to finance temporary deficits in international payments; such deficits could be expected to grow in size as the volume of international transactions increased, so that it was necessary for the volume of international reserves (liquidity) to grow over time. If reserves had not grown, countries would have found that they had less leeway to incur deficits in the short run while waiting for longer run corrective measures to take effect. In this case, governments probably would have resorted to harsh restrictions over international transactions in an attempt to prevent balance-of-payments deficits. On the other hand, if international reserves grew too rapidly, as they sometimes did in the system's later years, inflation was likely to result.

Under the par value system, nearly all of the growth in international reserves took the form of increases in the amounts of key currencies (especially the dollar) that were held by national monetary authorities, because these authorities as a group could not acquire enough gold from private suppliers at the fixed official price to meet their perceived need for international reserves. In fact, instead of purchasing gold, some central banks began sizable sales after 1965 in order to prevent the market price from rising much above the official price of $35 an ounce. In 1968, the participating central banks stopped these sales of gold to private parties and allowed the market price to fluctuate freely, although they maintained the official price at $35 per ounce for dealings among themselves.

Partly because of the lack of growth in their gold reserves, other countries were pleased for a number of years to run a balance-of-payments surplus with the United States, a surplus that added to their holdings of reserves in dollar form. Reserve growth in this form, however, proved to be unsatisfactory, largely because it led to a loss of confidence in the dollar. As foreign central banks purchased the dollar in order to support its price in the foreign exchanges, foreign official claims on the

United States rose to more than $20 billion in 1970, while U.S. gold and other reserves amounted to only about $14 billion. The threat of a run on the bank led the Nixon administration, on 15 August 1971, to formally suspend its willingness to convert foreign official dollar balances into gold or other reserve assets.

This example dramatically illustrates the problem of confidence, which was the problem of avoiding a flight from one reserve asset, such as the dollar, into another reserve asset, such as gold. One obvious way to preclude such a flight would have been to have only one reserve asset. Another partial remedy would have been to stop fixing the price at which one reserve asset could be exchanged for another in dealings between central banks, instead using the market price for such dealings. The difficulty with price-fixing was that flights from one reserve asset into another were encouraged when the market price tended to diverge appreciably from the price fixed for official dealings. For example, after the market price of gold rose well above the official price in 1968, gold was no longer used in international payments. Somehow it went against a central banker's principles to transfer his gold to another central banker at a price far below the market price; instead, dollar balances were used.

The third major problem to arise under the par value system was the problem of adjusting, or eliminating, imbalances in international payments. The foremost illustration was the seeming inability of the United States to eradicate the deficit in its balance of payments. Indeed, the nation was running a huge deficit in the first half of 1971, just before the gold convertibility of the dollar was terminated.

Payments imbalances could have been reduced through timely exchange-rate changes, but exchange-rate change found little favor under the rules of the par value system, and even less favor under the body of custom that grew up beside those rules. The rules also discouraged the use of comprehensive government controls over international transactions. Since exchange-rate changes and controls were discouraged, the only respectable way for a government to eliminate a balance-of-payments surplus or deficit was to alter its monetary or fiscal policy. But governments generally preferred to use these policy tools to pursue full employment or to fight inflation, rather than to correct international imbalances. Therefore, the system was without an adequate balance-of-payments adjustment mechanism.

As a consequence, a number of governments gave up their attempts to fix exchange rates. The reason is nicely illustrated by the experience of the West German central bank in early 1973. To limit increases in the value of the deutsche mark in the foreign exchange market, the West German central bank found itself selling large volumes of marks in exchange for U.S. dollars. The resulting increases in the stock of marks outstanding tended to boost inflation in West Germany at a time when the West German central bank was already very concerned about rising prices. After purchasing a daily record $2.6 billion on March 1, the central bank relinquished its efforts to control the foreign exchange value of the mark and began to focus instead on restraining inflationary pressures. Within a few months, the mark had risen sharply in value against the dollar.

A number of other countries experienced the same dilemma as West Germany, and by the spring of 1973 exchange-rate variation had clearly become a primary means of balance-of-payments adjustment. Now, if a currency were allowed to float perfectly freely in the foreign exchange market, the country whose currency it was would realize no overall balance-of-payments deficit or surplus whatsoever. The country would neither use reserves (incur a deficit) to prop up the price of its currency nor acquire reserves (accrue a surplus) in return for sales of its currency undertaken to suppress the price—although offsetting deficits and surpluses could, of course, still occur in the various *components* of the overall balance of payments (such as merchandise trade, securities purchases, and so on). In fact, no government did permit its currency to float perfectly freely, but the variation allowed in 1973 was still very large and plainly signaled the demise of the par value system.

A COMPOSITE SYSTEM

It was several years before the widespread practice of floating exchange rates received formal international sanction. In January 1976, a committee representing the 128 member countries of the IMF (International Monetary Fund) gave its blessing to proposals that would amend the IMF Articles of Agreement, both to legitimize the new exchange-rate flexibility and to make other fundamental changes. On 1 April 1978, these amendments entered into force.

While the current international monetary system differs from the par value system in several respects, by far the most important is the greater degree of exchange-rate flexibility. On the other hand, no government has gone to the extreme of allowing its currency to float freely; all continue to intervene in the foreign exchange markets, some more vigorously than others, in order to influence exchange rates for their currencies. In fact, at the end of 1986 the governments of 100 countries were fixing exchange rates for their currencies within fairly narrow, clearly specified ranges. Thirty-three of these governments were pegging the exchange rates of their currencies against the U.S. dollar, fourteen were pegging against the French franc, and fifty-three (including the members of the European Monetary System) were pegging against some currency, or group of currencies, other than the dollar or the franc. Fifty other governments, including most of the major industrial countries, were not fixing exchange rates for their currencies within any specified range, although they were prepared to intervene to influence those rates. Therefore, while exchange rates are much more flexible than under the par value system, substantial official intervention still occurs in the foreign exchange markets, and many governments still fix the rates of exchange for their currencies over fairly extended periods of time.

The 1978 amendments to the IMF Articles of Agreement sanction these diverse exchange-rate practices. Might such diversity breed disorder? For example, suppose that the U.S. government became persuaded that the U.S. dollar should have a higher foreign exchange value, especially in deutsche marks, while the West German government held the opposite view. Would the West German authorities sell dollars for marks, while the U.S. authorities made offsetting sales of marks for dollars? The customary communication between central banks makes it very unlikely that such conflicting market intervention would occur merely by accident. However, if a frank and fundamental disagreement developed, how would the issue be resolved?

The amended Articles of Agreement do not offer a detailed formula for resolving such disputes, but they do include some general principles of good behavior that IMF members are expected to observe with respect to exchange rates. Specifically, each member agrees to cooperate to assure "orderly" exchange arrangements, especially by promoting orderly underlying economic and financial conditions and by refraining from exchange-rate manipulation designed either to prevent balance-of-payments adjustment or to gain unfair competitive advantage in international trade. Moreover, the IMF is charged with overseeing the adherence of its members to this code of good behavior and with spelling out the code in more detail. Accordingly, the IMF has added to the code the following principles:

> A member should intervene in the exchange market if necessary to counter disorderly conditions which may be characterized inter alia by disruptive short-term movements in the exchange value of its currency.
>
> Members should take into account in their intervention policies the interests of other members including those of the countries in whose currencies they intervene.[1]

The IMF has also adopted some guidelines to assist it in judging whether its members are adhering to the foregoing code. These "principles of surveillance over exchange rate policies" call for the IMF to be wary of the following developments:

(i) protracted large-scale intervention in one direction in the exchange market;

(ii) an unsustainable level of official or quasi-official borrowing, or excessive and prolonged short-term official or quasi-official lending, for balance of payments purposes;

(iii) (a) the introduction, substantial intensification, or prolonged maintenance, for balance of payments purposes, of restrictions on, or incentives for, current transactions or payments, or

(b) the introduction or substantial modification for balance of payments purposes of restrictions on, or incentives for, the inflow or outflow of capital;

(iv) the pursuit, for balance of payments purposes, of monetary and other domestic financial policies that provide abnormal encouragement or discouragement to capital flows; and

(v) behavior of the exchange rate that appears to be unrelated to underlying economic and financial conditions including factors affecting competitiveness and long-term capital movements.[2]

If the IMF suspects a member country of violating the code of exchange-rate behavior, consultations are held with that member. In principle, a serious offender could be denied the right to borrow from the IMF and could eventually be expelled from the organization.

Thus, to bring about balance-of-payments adjustments, the current international monetary system relies much more heavily than its predecessor on exchange-rate change, although this reliance is not without rules. How does the current system deal with the other problems of liquidity and confidence, which also troubled the par value system?

With respect to liquidity, the stock of international reserves (measurable liquidity) was ample—perhaps too ample—when the par value system broke down. Moreover, governments do not require reserves to support the exchange values of their currencies if exchange rates are permitted to vary freely, and considerable variation is now allowed. It should also be noted that a government deemed creditworthy can always borrow dollars or other foreign exchange if its stock of owned reserves runs low.

The system does make specific provision for the creation of additional reserves if needed. The method is one that was introduced in 1969 and first employed in the twilight years of the par value system. The reserves created by this technique are known as special drawing rights (SDRs). SDRs are issued by the IMF upon the instruction of its member countries and are allocated among these countries in proportion to their financial contributions, or quotas, in the IMF. Although SDRs are nothing more than bookkeeping entries, participating governments have agreed to accept them as means of payment in settling international accounts. The value of an SDR in terms of currency is defined as the value of a "basket," which contained at the end of 1986, U.S. $.42 and specified quantities of four other currencies widely used in international commerce. A total of 21.4 billion SDRs were allocated in the course of two separate issuances, the first during the years 1970-72, the second during 1979-81.

If a government draws upon its allocation of SDRs to make international payments, it must pay net interest to the IMF on the SDRs so expended. The IMF, in turn, pays net interest to the governments that receive SDR transfers in addition to their original IMF allocations. Such interest payments serve a useful function. In their absence, governments generally would have an incentive to use SDRs, allocated to them at no cost, in order to pay for goods obtained from other countries. SDRs that paid no interest would find no willing holders. At this writing, the interest rate on the SDR is equal to a weighted average of the interest rates on prime domestic money market instruments in the five countries whose currencies are included in the SDR's valuation basket.

As noted in the previous section, one way of precluding a confidence problem, or a flight from one reserve asset into another, would be to have only one reserve asset. The 1978 amendments to the Articles of Agreement do include the objective of "making the special drawing right the principal reserve asset in the international monetary system,"[3] but very little progress has been made toward this objective. Of total international reserves as reported by the IMF, SDRs accounted for only 4.4

percent at the end of 1986. By far the largest reserve component continues to be countries' holdings of other countries' currencies, or of short-term assets denominated in those currencies. These foreign exchange holdings accounted for about four-fifths of all international reserves in 1986. Country holdings of reserve positions in the IMF and of gold account for the remainder of international reserves.

Even though the SDR has not been installed as the principal reserve asset, progress has been made in solving the confidence problem. The fact is that the confidence problem stemmed not merely from the existence of more than one reserve asset but also from the effort to fix the price at which these assets were exchanged for each other. Flights from one reserve asset into another were encouraged when the market price tended to diverge appreciably from the officially fixed price, as happened with gold in 1968. This source of the confidence problem was eliminated when such price-fixing was abandoned, leaving central banks free to transfer all reserve assets among themselves for settlement of debts at market-related prices.

From this account, it is clear that the current international monetary system differs significantly from the par value system, but retains various features of that system. Most prominent among the retained features is that many exchange rates are still more or less fixed. Thus, the system is not at all "pure," but is a hybrid, or composite—combining the characteristics of both fixed and flexible exchange rates.

The variegated nature of the system, especially its permissiveness with respect to exchange-rate arrangements, has led to the allegation that it is in fact no system at all, but a nonsystem that invites chaos in international monetary affairs. More specifically, exchange rates are said to be much too volatile and to depart for long periods from their appropriate, or equilibrium, levels. Such criticisms merit careful consideration.

EXCHANGE-RATE VOLATILITY AND RISK

At the time the composite system was adopted, most economists expected it to put an end to the turmoil that had afflicted international financial markets under the par value system, especially during its latter years. No longer would a government feel obliged to intervene to defend an exchange rate that was under massive attack in the market, in a surrounding air of crisis and with the eventual sharp change in the exchange rate as the government yielded to market forces (as the West German central bank did in March of 1973). Now that exchange rates could respond promptly to market influences, they would typically change gradually as the underlying economic "fundamentals" changed, replacing the practice of less frequent, more abrupt changes. Sharp fluctuations from temporary disturbances would be prevented by stabilizing speculators, who would recognize the temporary nature of the disturbances, and who would buy or sell a currency before it fell or rose very much in order later to turn a profit as the currency returned to its longer run equilibrium level.

In the event, these expectations were not fulfilled. Rather than diminishing, exchange-rate variability has been much greater under the composite system than under its predecessor. Nor has there been a trend toward reduced variability as experience has accumulated.

Exchange-rate variation can be measured in various ways. Since any currency exchanges for many other currencies, it is helpful to have an index that summarizes the changing value of a country's currency in terms of other currencies. For this purpose, the changes in value of a currency against other currencies are customarily weighted by the importance of those changes to the international trade of the country for which the index is being constructed. Such an index is said to measure change in the "nominal effective exchange rate."

This nominal index can be adjusted for differences between the rate of inflation in the country whose currency is being indexed and the trade-weighted average of inflation rates abroad. When so adjusted, the index is known as the real effective exchange rate and is commonly used as a measure of changing competitiveness. For example, a marked decline in a country's nominal effective exchange rate (that is, in the average foreign exchange price of the country's currency) would translate—unless offset by a ruse in the country's inflation rate relative to inflation abroad—into lower prices for the country's goods relative to prices of foreign goods; the decline in the real exchange rate would indicate this increased competitiveness. On the other hand, if the decline in the country's nominal effective rate were accompanied by an offsetting rise in the country's relative inflation rate, the real exchange rate would remain constant, indicating no change in the country's overall price competitiveness.

Whether measured in nominal or in real terms, effective exchange rates for the seven major noncommunist industrial countries have displayed much greater variability since the collapse of the par value system. . . . The weighted average of monthly changes in nominal effective exchange rates for these countries was 1.18 percent over the ten years 1974-83, nearly six times as great as the 0.2 percent experienced during the ten years 1961-70. In terms of real effective exchange rates, month-to-month variation was about three times greater in the later period than in the earlier one. Roughly the same increases in variability are discovered if quarter-to-quarter rather than month-to-month changes are examined.

Volatility is not feared for its own sake. Rather, the concern is that increases in volatility raise the risk and cost of international transactions, thereby discouraging international trade and investment. Suppose that greater variability makes it more difficult to forecast the course of an exchange rate. In that case, traders and investors will be less certain of the value in their domestic currency of any foreign currency amounts that they might agree today to pay or receive in the future in order to carry out pending international transactions. They will be more reluctant to commit to such transactions on the same terms as before unless the greater risk they face can somehow be shifted to some other party.

In fact, much of the risk can be shifted. One widely employed mechanism for shifting or neutralizing foreign exchange risk is the forward exchange market. By way of illustration, suppose that a U.S. importer signs a contract to purchase merchandise from West Germany and to pay in deutsche marks when the merchandise is delivered three months hence. Because the rate of exchange between dollars and marks may change over the coming months, the importer cannot be sure what the merchandise will cost in terms of dollars if he waits three months to buy the needed marks. One way he can avoid this uncertainty is to buy marks for future delivery in the forward exchange market. More specifically, his bank will agree to deliver, three months from now, the marks he will then require and will tell him today the rate of exchange (or dollar price) that he will have to pay. By entering this contract, that is, by purchasing "forward cover," the importer can eliminate any uncertainty about the dollar price of the imported merchandise.

Such risk-shifting is not costless, but the costs are relatively small. Banks do not charge commissions for accommodating their customers in the forward exchange market, but profit from selling a currency at a higher price than they pay for it. Typically, this margin between a bank's quoted buying and selling prices is kept very low by intense competition, unless the transaction is quite small. For sizable transactions in the most widely traded currencies, the margin, or cost to a customer, is commonly well below one-tenth of one percent.

In addition to the forward exchange market, other devices are available for neutralizing or hedging against foreign exchange risk. As a practical matter, however, it is not possible for a business firm to avoid all such risk, if only because the firm cannot specify the precise timing of its future receipts and payments in foreign exchange. Thus, in spite of the availability of a variety of hedging techniques, some of which entail very low costs, the international trader or investor will bear some exchange risk, directly or indirectly. Since exchange risk is associated with exchange-rate variability, the question remains whether international commerce has been suppressed by the heightened exchange-rate variability under the current monetary system. No definitive answer has been provided. Various empirical studies, using differing approaches and sets of data, have yielded differing results.

Even if the recent exchange-rate variability were clearly associated with reduced trade, it would not necessarily follow that the pegging of exchange rates would expand trade. For example, exchange rates have sometimes been fixed with the aid of controls such as import restrictions designed to limit an overall balance-of-payments deficit, and such controls may hinder trade more than exchange-rate variability does. More generally, if exchange-rate variability were suppressed, the underlying causal economic forces would produce disturbances elsewhere in the economic system—unless those causal forces arose out of the flexible exchange-rate regime itself. The mere diversion of disturbances from exchange rates to other economic variables would offer little promise of reducing the overall degree of uncertainty. Such a diversion might indeed raise the level of international trade, but at the expense of other economic activity.

THE ROLE OF SPECULATION

The key issue, then, is whether exchange-rate flexibility itself generates forces that make for exchange-rate variability. In particular, if allowed the opportunity, do speculators operate so as to destabilize an exchange rate? For many years, one school of thought has answered this question in the affirmative. The classic example is a 1944 study done for the League of Nations:

> Any considerable or continuous movement of the exchange rate is liable to generate anticipations of a further movement in the same direction, thus giving rise to speculative capital transfers of a disequilibrating kind. . . . Self-aggravating movements of this kind . . . are apt to intensify any initial disequilibrium and to produce what may be called "explosive" conditions of instability.[4]

The classic rebuttal was offered by Milton Friedman in 1953:

> People who argue that speculation is generally destabilizing seldom realize that this is largely equivalent to saying that speculators lose money, since speculation can be destabilizing in general only if speculators on the average sell when the currency is low in price and buy when it is high.[5]

But speculators as a group may indeed lose money from time to time. Moreover, theorists have constructed examples in which speculators could make a profit even if their activity was destabilizing speculation, such as the Dutch tulip mania that drove the price of a single bulb higher than that of a house during the 1630s. Thus, the actual importance of destabilizing speculation cannot be settled by armchair theorizing, but must be submitted to empirical investigation. Such investigation is worthwhile not only because exchange-rate variability can raise the cost and risk of international trade, but because speculation that holds an exchange rate far from its longer run equilibrium levels may lead investors and traders to make the wrong business decisions.

Unfortunately, it has been next to impossible to prove either the presence or the absence of destabilizing speculation in the foreign exchange markets. To measure the impact of speculation, one needs to separate out the other influences on exchange rates, and no econometric model has been constructed that is up to this formidable task. In the absence of a satisfactory econometric model, analysts have resorted to comparing the volatility of foreign exchange rates to that of prices in other financial markets. If volatility in the foreign exchange markets is no greater than in the stock or the bond markets, perhaps it should be viewed as normal and even innocuous, unless one suspects that all such markets are cursed with destabilizing speculation. Comparing the volatility in these markets seems appropriate, since bonds, stocks, and foreign exchange are all financial assets whose prices will be affected by any news that changes expectations about the economic rewards from holding them.

From the comparisons that have been made, the conclusion to be drawn is that foreign exchange rates have generally been less volatile than prices in other financial markets. One study for the years 1973-83 shows that stock market price indexes in a number of noncommunist industrial countries typically displayed two or three times the variability found in the exchange rates for these countries' currencies against the dollar. For bonds, the difference is not so great, but exchange rates still generally exhibited less variation.

While encouraging, such evidence is indirect and inconclusive. More direct evidence is needed on whether speculators play a stabilizing or destabilizing role in the foreign exchange markets. For example, it would be helpful to know if speculators generally make profits, since their activity cannot be stabilizing if they suffer losses.

Unfortunately, profit data are not available, but some data have been collected on the speculative positions taken by U.S. firms in various foreign currencies. . . .

The holders of such foreign currency positions may experience dollar profits or losses depending on what happens to the dollar prices of the foreign currencies held. But the positions taken by the banks as a group seem generally to have been very small. What should be considered small is, of course, open to debate. One way of judging is to compare the banks' position in a currency with their total involvement in that currency, where involvement is defined as total assets and liabilities in the currency plus contracts to buy and sell the currency. . . . The position taken by banks never exceeded four-tenths of one percent of the banks' total involvement in foreign currency, for the currencies and dates shown. Another way of judging the size of the banks' positions is to compare them with the positions taken by nonbank firms. The banks' positions seem very small by this standard as well.

In fact, the positions taken by U.S. banks have been so small that it is hard to see how those positions could have exerted much influence on the course of exchange rates, either to stabilize or to destabilize. Since the banks, especially the major ones, are probably as knowledgeable about the foreign exchange markets as any other group of participants, it seems that they should be able to perform the profitable and socially beneficial role of stabilizing speculators. The fact that their aggregate foreign exchange positions have been so small may, therefore, be cause for concern.

By contrast, the positions taken by nonbank firms usually were much larger, both in absolute amount and in relation to their total involvement in foreign currency. Nonbank positions sometimes amounted to more than 10 percent of involvement, especially in the Canadian dollar.

Apart from the size of the positions, are they likely to have been profitable? A very tentative answer can be obtained by comparing the positions taken in the various currencies with the subsequent behavior of the exchange rates for those currencies. Such a comparison using data for the late 1970s suggests that speculation was not generally profitable, either for U.S. banks as a group or for the nonbank firms. (On the other hand, it also seems likely that neither the banks nor the nonbanks were losing large sums of money.) This outcome is mildly discouraging, for it suggests that the socially useful function of stabilizing speculation was not being performed. Still, it remains to be shown that exchange-rate flexibility has itself generated substantial destabilizing speculation.

EXCHANGE-RATE MISALIGNMENT

Critics of the new monetary system level another charge against it: exchange rates not only vary excessively, but also remain for long periods much higher or lower than warranted by underlying structural economic conditions. That is to say, exchange rates have displayed severe misalignments, or prolonged and marked departures from their appropriate, long-run equilibrium levels. This charge is leveled at the behavior of the real effective exchange rate.

Of course, in order to support the allegation that exchange rates have been misaligned, a method is needed for computing the correct, or long-run equilibrium, rates. Three methods are commonly employed. The first assumes that the long-run equilibrium rate is some average or stable point within any observed, long-run, market-determined movement; the second assumes that the long-run equilibrium is approximately equal to the "purchasing-power parity" rate; and the third identifies the long-run equilibrium with the rate that would yield overall balance in international payments under "normal" circumstances.

As an illustration of the first method, the real effective exchange rate of the U.K. pound fell by 20 percent between 1975 and 1976 and then rose by nearly 75 percent between 1976 and 1981. Critics would say the upward movement implied the mistakenness, or at least the nonessentiality, of the preceding downward movement, and that during the entire period the rate should have hovered somewhere between the extremes that were observed.

The purchasing-power parity method assumes that the real exchange rate should remain virtually unchanged from its level during the most recent period of international equilibrium. In other words, any significant and lasting change in a nominal exchange rate should be merely for the purpose of offsetting a difference in national inflation rates. The nominal rate change would then ensure that the purchasing power of a currency over foreign goods changes by the same degree as its purchasing power over domestic goods. Thus, if prices in Brazil doubled—starting from a period of balance-of-payments equilibrium—while prices elsewhere remained unchanged on average, a unit of Brazil's currency should come to exchange for only half as much foreign currency (and foreign goods) as previously, with no change in the real, or inflation-adjusted, exchange rate.

Adherents of this second method have much cause for dissatisfaction with the current monetary system, for real exchange rate have commonly remained far from the levels associated with earlier equilibriums in international payments. For example, 1980-82 was arguably a period of near-equilibrium for the U.S. balance of payments, yet during both 1984 and 1985 the real effective exchange value of the U.S. dollar averaged more than 20 percent above its value for 1980-82.

The third method involves more sophisticated analysis than the other two. The first step is to make a projection of the net financial lending or borrowing to be experienced by a country in its international transactions over a long period, including both the upswings and downswings of any business cycles. An estimate is then made of the real exchange rate that would bring about a surplus (or deficit) on the country's current account transactions sufficient to offset this projected net capital outflow (or inflow); this is the estimated equilibrium real exchange rate. It is assumed that the country follows policies designed to maintain reasonable balance in its domestic economy and refrains from major controls aimed at influencing its net capital or current account transactions with the rest of the world. The equilibrium exchange rate estimated in this fashion will have to change from time to time in response to change in underlying fundamentals, such as resource discoveries, or growth in domestic productivity relative to foreign productivity; however, the required exchange-rate changes are asserted to be calculable, and either gradual or infrequent.

One proponent of this method has used it to estimate misalignments displayed by the real effective exchange rates of five major industrial-country currencies in the last quarter of 1984. His study suggests that the Japanese yen was then valued 19 percent too low in the foreign exchange markets, and that the dollar was valued 39 percent too high, with smaller errors for the other three currencies. Moreover, according to this study such misalignments have been very tenacious.

A misaligned exchange rate is alleged to impose economic costs. As suggested by the third method of computing the long-run equilibrium rate, a country with a misaligned rate is thought to lend or borrow more or less than it should, accumulating current account surpluses or deficits that are too big or too small. In other words, misalignments are said to promote international resource transfers that are uneconomic—resulting in efficiency losses—since a misalignment presumably constitutes an inappropriate price competitiveness for one country's goods vis-a-vis the goods of other countries. Thus, a country whose competitive prowess is heightened by a misaligned exchange rate will export more and import less than at the long-run equilibrium rate; it will devote too much of its resources to export industries and import-competing industries, and not enough to industries making goods that are not internationally traded.

One seldom hears a citizenry complain that the exchange rate has made their country too competitive. The protests arise from the other side, from countries concerned that a misalignment has damaged their export and import-competing industries. Thus, another cost of misalignment could be the fomentation of protectionism, with its pernicious barriers to international trade.

The emergence of a misalignment can require that resources shift *within* countries—between industries producing internationally traded goods and those producing nontraded goods. Therefore, another cost is associated with misalignments: the cost of transferring resources from one industry to another. These costs can be appreciable, since labor often cannot transfer without physically moving and retraining; some labor, like most machines, is simply not transferable and becomes unemployed for the long term.

Of the three methods summarized here for computing the long-run equilibrium exchange rate, neither the first nor the second requires much reflection. The first method is basically one of blind resistance to abrupt exchange-rate change, since it prescribes opposition to such change without troubling to inquire into the underlying causal forces. In other words, it simply assumes away the possibility of abrupt change in underlying economic structure. Similarly, the purchasing-power parity method envisions change in the nominal exchange rate to offset inflation differentials, but allows for no change in the real exchange rate; this method denies the possibility of any change in underlying economic structure, even in the long run.

By contrast, the third method calls for explicit examination of structural change and focuses on the behavior of factors such as productivity trends, resource availability, and the long-run propensities to save in different nations. The method allows for the possibility of abrupt as well as gradual change in these structural factors. But the presumption is that abrupt change will be the exception, so that the method will seldom prescribe an abrupt change in the real exchange rate. An objection to the method is that calculating a long-run equilibrium exchange rate can be very difficult and lends itself to significant error.

A central difficulty with all these methods is their assumption that significant economic costs are inflicted by any large and prolonged deviation of a real exchange rate from its longer run equilibrium level. On the contrary, "misalignments" may be the most appropriate, or least costly, response to much nonstructural, nonenduring change in international economic conditions. If so, close adherence to the long-run equilibrium would constitute the true misalignment. Many prices, especially in financial markets, do not continuously hover around their long-run average levels, but vary in response to business cycles and other temporary influences. Such variation is commonly accepted as "normal," even as desirable. In all these markets, including the foreign exchange markets, the suppression of price change would not usually eliminate the underlying causal forces, but would divert them into other modes of expression. In particular, a nation that was serious about combating an emerging "misalignment" of its exchange rate would almost certainly have to enlist its macroeconomic policy (especially monetary policy) for the task. The costs of using macroeconomic policy to influence exchange rates, rather than to influence domestic employment or inflation, were perceived to be so great under the par value system as to lead to its demise. Thus, the basic problem with the "misalignment" doctrine is its failure to specify a clearly less costly and more acceptable method than "misalignments" for dealing with the economic causes responsible.

THE ISSUE OF DISCIPLINE

Another major criticism of the current international monetary system is that it fails to prevent national macroeconomic policy blunders, which are often responsible for major imbalances in international payments. Now, flexibility of exchange rates does militate against sizable overall imbalances, or against gains and losses of international reserves, such as nations commonly experienced under the par value system. But the new system has not prevented the occurrence of sizable, albeit offsetting, imbalances in major components of a country's overall balance of payments. Of most concern has been the large and persistent "current account" deficit of the United States (on transactions in merchandise and related items), financed by an equal net inflow of capital from abroad, or by a U.S. "capital account" surplus. Other nations, especially Japan and West Germany, have experienced correspondingly large current account surpluses with capital account deficits, particularly in transactions with the United States.

Moreover, sizable, medium-term swings in exchange rates have accompanied such imbalances. As the capital inflow into the United States swelled between 1981 and 1985—partly in response to attractive returns on investments there—demand by investors for the U.S. dollar helped to push up its real effective foreign exchange value by nearly 25 percent. In turn, the rise in the dollar's foreign exchange price rendered U.S. goods less competitive internationally, thereby magnifying the current account deficit, which in 1985 amounted to almost $118 billion.

One cause of these imbalances was the sharp rise in the U.S. federal budget deficit, a development that led the United States to borrow more from abroad; by contrast, Japan and West Germany pursued somewhat more restrained fiscal policies that fostered increases in their foreign lending. Had there been a disciplining or coordinating mechanism that deterred these three countries from following such divergent fiscal policies, the worrisome payments imbalances and exchange-rate swings could presumably have been avoided, or at least substantially mitigated. The current international monetary system provides no effective mechanism of this sort. . . .

Here, the analysis is limited to the question of whether exchange-rate arrangements might be modified so as to foster coordination and restrain excesses in national macroeconomic policies. An affirmative answer is given by the advocates of "target zones," a proposal examined in the next section.

TARGET ZONES

A target zone would be a fairly wide range within which governments would seek to constrain the movement of an exchange rate. The zone would be established by estimating the real equilibrium exchange rate and then adding a margin of, say, 10 percent on either side to reflect the uncertainty surrounding the estimate as well as the degree of willingness to allow temporary fluctuations. To confine the exchange rate within the zone, governments would intervene to influence the rate directly with purchases or sales of foreign exchange. But the commitment to limit exchange-rate variations would be much weaker than under the par value system. Not only would the target zone be much wider than the narrow bands prescribed for fluctuations under the par value system, but exchange rates might be allowed to stray temporarily beyond the zone. Moreover, the zone would be changed much more readily than the old par values, in response to change in the longer run equilibrium exchange rate.

All countries that wished to do so could establish target zones for their currencies, but advocates consider it especially important that the largest industrial countries enter into the scheme. After all, one purpose is to prevent national policy mistakes that disrupt the world economy, and such weighty mistakes cannot emanate from a small nation. One check against national policy excesses would be the need for participating countries to agree on the target zones for exchange rates between their currencies. In the course of these negotiations, macroeconomic policies would be discussed because of their considerable influence on exchange rates, and governments would have the opportunity to object to policy courses that seemed inappropriate. At least in principle, all policies could be harmonized for the greater good. A further discipline would be the presumption that government policies, especially monetary policies, would be maintained on a course consistent with confining exchange rates within the target zones. While the zones could be violated, and would be revised from time to time, they would, it is argued, provide a formal arrangement through which national governments would be exposed to peer pressure and review as they formulated and executed their macroeconomic policies.

Target zones are a halfway house between the par value system and the free-floating exchange rates to be found within the present system. Establishing such zones would represent a step back in the direction of the par value system, with the goal of capturing some of the discipline, coordination, and exchange-rate stability promised by that system. The record is clear, however, that governments became unwilling to submit to the discipline of the par value system—unwilling, in particular, to devote monetary policy to the function of regulating exchange rates rather than to the functions of regulating domestic employment and price levels. Moreover, given the high uncertainty about the effects of macroeconomic policy changes, intensified coordination could well worsen rather than improve the performance of the world economy. In these circumstances, it would be surprising if target zones evoked the commitment that their adherents seek.

REGULATION OF INTERNATIONAL LIQUIDITY

As already noted, governments do not require international reserves if they permit exchange rates to float freely. But the freedom allowed to exchange rates is far from complete in the present system, and it has sometimes been alleged that the supply of international reserve assets was inadequate.

This criticism is difficult to evaluate because of the difficulty in evaluating the appropriate level of reserves. It was hard to estimate the optimum level of reserves under the par value system, and it is even harder for a system with no general and explicitly targeted limits on exchange-rate fluctuations. What can be said is that governments desiring additional reserves can borrow foreign exchange, or purchase it with their own currencies, and that governments wanting to reduce their reserves can sell some of their holdings. Moreover, governments receive market rates of interest on such additions to reserves—since those reserves are invested—and they pay market or near-market rates for borrowed reserves. Thus, the stock of international reserves is regulated by individual government decisions, based on market interest rates without centralized control.

Of course, a problem can arise for an individual government that wants to forestall a depreciation of its currency but lacks both the reserves to support its currency and the creditworthiness to borrow at going market interest rates. To prevent depreciation, this government must impose foreign exchange controls, such as restrictions on domestic purchases of foreign currency, or it must alter its monetary or fiscal policy. With the eruption of the international debt crisis in 1982, such difficult choices were faced by a number of less developed countries that were unwilling to tolerate rapid and continuous depreciations.

The dilemma of these less developed countries has stimulated proposals for a new issue of SDRs. Receipt of newly created SDRs would give these countries some relief, but the international debt problem has been too sizable to be materially eased by any SDR issuance that creditor countries would have been willing to consider. At bottom, the debt problem requires more fundamental measures for its solution; at this writing, no new SDRs are in the offing.

A BRIEF APOLOGY FOR THE COMPOSITE SYSTEM

Preceding sections have offered defenses of the current international monetary system against some specific charges. Here, a few more general points are made on behalf of the system.

As already noted, some analysts think that the current international monetary arrangements should not be dignified with the label, "system." Thus, the designation, "nonsystem," is sometimes used to characterize the diverse set of exchange-rate practices that sprang up, without any previously agreed blueprint, to replace the carefully designed par value system when it disintegrated in the early 1970s.

To be sure, the present composite system more nearly resembles a mongrel than a thoroughbred. Lacking the thoroughbred's planned breeding and uniformity, it boasts the mongrel's hardiness and adaptability. The latter traits were at a premium in the years following the demise of the par value system, as the world economy struggled through two oil shocks, an international debt crisis, and marked divergencies between macroeconomic policies in different nations. In the face of these severe disturbances, the composite system allowed international trade to increase more rapidly than world output, with relatively few restrictions on international payments. Given the circumstances, no other international monetary system that has been tried would have worked as well.

Aside from these pragmatic observations, economic theory offers more formal justification for countries to opt for varying degrees of exchange-rate flexibility, in accordance with their differing circumstances. Theory suggests that exchange-rate variability will be more acceptable to a large country engaging in relatively little international trade than to a small country that is heavily dependent on international commerce. More precisely, the degree of flexibility that a country chooses should be based on a number of considerations, including the nature of the economic disturbances that affect the country, the resource allocation effects of exchange-rate changes, and the efficacy of monetary and fiscal policy under differing degrees of exchange-rate flexibility. These factors vary not only from country to country but from time to time for any one country so that a country might well opt for more flexibility at one time than another.

Thus, both experience and theory can be invoked on behalf of the composite system. It is desirable that countries have considerable freedom to tailor their exchange-rate practices to their own economic and political structures and philosophies—a freedom that was lacking under the rules of Bretton Woods. Far from tearing apart the fabric of international commerce, the diversity of the current system may serve to knit it more closely, as long as generally accepted norms of behavior are observed.

NOTES

1. As quoted by Andrew Crockett and Morris Goldstein, *Strengthening the International Monetary System: Exchange Rates, Surveillance, and Objective Indicators,* Occasional Paper No. 50 (Washington, D.C.: International Monetary Fund, 1987), p. 80.

2. Ibid., pp. 80-81.

3. International Monetary Fund, *Articles of Agreement of the International Monetary Fund* (Washington, D.C.: IMF, 1985, Article VIII, Section 7.

4. League of Nations, *International Currency Experience* (Geneva: League of Nations, 1944), pp. 211-12.

5. Milton Friedman, "The Case for Flexible Exchange Rates," in Milton Friedman, *Essays in Positive Economics* (Chicago: University of Chicago Press, 1953), p. 175.

18

Capital Politics: Creditors and the International Political Economy

JEFFRY A. FRIEDEN

This essay analyzes the relationship between international investment interests and foreign economic policy. The first step and level of analysis, drawn loosely from the Realist perspective, looks at nation-states as the relevant actors, and claims that a country's international investment position tends to affect its international economic preferences in ways that are easily understood and anticipated. The international asset positions of a country o ften have a predictable impact on its policies toward international monetary relations, cross-border investment, and trade. The second step and level of analysis, Marxist in orientation through its focus on class fractions, looks inside national societies at the international asset positions of various domestic groups. It argues that sectors with varying interests related to their international investment positions contend for influence over national policy. The economic circumstances of each sector lead to sectoral policy preferences with predictable implications for domestic bargaining over foreign economic policy. The general argument is applied briefly to a number of modern creditor countries and sectors, most prominently the United States after World War II. Thus, the framework developed by Frieden bridges the Realist and Marxist perspectives.

18 "Capital Politics: Creditors and the International Political Economy" by Jeffry A. Frieden, From *Journal of Public Policy*, Vol. 8, No. 3/4 (July-December 1988). Reprinted by permission of Cambridge University Press.

International monetary and financial relations are at the center of today's international political economy. Currency values, short- and long-term capital movements, debtor-creditor relations, and related issues are crucial to the private sector, to intergovernmental relations, and to private-public sector interaction around the world. A fundamental analytical and practical question for those concerned about the future of the world economy is indeed the extent to which growing international financial ties will lead toward more cooperation among national policy makers, and among nationally-based businesses, or more conflict among them.

The future of international financial relations, and especially the degree of conflict involved in them, is a function of both economic and political considerations. The scholarly literature on the economics of international capital movements grows daily in both quantity and quality. However, this large economic literature is not matched by a comparable body of work on the political factors involved in international money and finance; a *political economy* approach to the topic is only in its infancy. Just as informed academic and general discussion of international trade conflict and cooperation relies on an integration of economic and political considerations, so too must political economy be brought to bear on the study of international finance to improve the level of debate and the effectiveness of policy.

This essay suggests that the starting point for a political economy of international finance should be the relationship between international investment interests and the foreign economic policy preferences they imply. The argument proceeds in two steps, at different levels of analysis. The first step and level of analysis looks at nation-states as the relevant actors, and claims that a country's international investment position tends to affect its international economic preferences in ways that are easily understood and anticipated. Countries' international asset positions often have a predictable impact on their policies toward international monetary relations, cross-border investment, and trade. The second step and level of analysis looks inside national societies at the international asset positions of various domestic groups. It argues that sectors with varying interests related to their international investment positions contend for influence over national policy. The economic circumstances of each sector lead to sectoral policy preferences with predictable implications for domestic bargaining over foreign economic policy.

The general argument is applied briefly to a number of modern creditor countries and sectors, most prominently the United States after World War Two. The United States was a country rich in capital, and its international economic policies reflected the attempt to ensure as high a return as possible to American capital. At a more disaggregated level of analysis, the varied interests of leading sectors of the U.S. economy, with international economic policy preferences that flow from their domestic and international asset positions, provides the basis for an understanding of domestic debates over U.S. foreign economic policy.

The argument and the examples are preliminary and illustrative. The purpose of the essay is only to present the rudiments of a framework for analyzing the domestic and international political economy of international finance, and to show that the framework fits a stylized review of the evidence. As such, the essay reflects the embryonic nature of attempts to develop a political economy of international finance.

INTERNATIONAL FINANCE AND THE INTERNATIONAL POLITICAL ECONOMY

There are powerful reasons to study the political economy of international capital movements. Economic theory shows that factor movements are substitutes for international trade, and may even perform similar functions more rapidly. If a labor-rich country maximizes its welfare by exporting labor-intensive goods, it does so even more directly by exporting labor and importing capital; the converse holds for a capital-rich country. Trade is only a means to an end, maximizing profits on capital, and exports are only one way of earning profits on foreign activities; it makes as much sense to focus on the end as on the means.

Indeed, international capital markets are today the pivot around which the world economy rotates. The offshore financial markets hold well over a trillion dollars net of inter-bank claims, and hundreds of billions of dollars more are invested abroad in traditional portfolio and direct forms. International capital movements dwarf international trade in sheer size; by rough estimate, more money flows into and out of the United States in a day than goods in a month. In 1984, even according to the inadequate figures available, American overseas investment income was $87.6 billion on overseas private assets of $795 billion. In the same year, merchandise exports were $220 billion; assuming a generous five percent profit margin on overseas sales, this implied that foreign investment earned American businesses eight times as much as did foreign trade. International economic transactions of this size deserve close attention by scholars, especially since the study of the politics of international investment has a long and instructive history.

Another reason to focus systematically on international monetary and financial relations is that there is substantial evidence that these relations themselves help explain developments in other realms of the international political economy. The most obvious example is the effect of real exchange rates on trade: a significant rise in the real exchange rate often leads to protectionist sentiment from traded goods producers whose competitive position is eroded by the currency's appreciation, while a real depreciation tends to dampen protectionist pressure by improving the competitive position of local producers. . . .

Perhaps most obviously, international financial and monetary flows and policy deserve attention from political scientists because they are poorly understood. Trade policy is traditionally a legislative affair, at least in large part, and is thus quite amenable to examination: regional and sectoral interests, trade-offs, and coalitions can be tracked easily. International monetary and financial policies, on the other hand, are almost everywhere centralized in the Treasury and the Central Bank, often in deep secrecy. Yet we know how important foreign economic policy decisions in the monetary and financial arenas can be, from Britain's return to gold in 1925 and America's interwar debts and reparations debates to the 1971 Nixon shocks and the debt crisis of the 1980s.

Many issues in the political economy of international capital movements deserve study. These include the effect of political variables on such economic developments as cross-border capital movements themselves. Our purpose here is more modest: to discuss the origins of government policies directly or indirectly concerning the international movement of capital, especially international monetary policy, the protection of overseas investment, and trade policy.

In analyzing the political economy of international finance, we can draw on two divergent strands within political science. The first, generally associated with what is called the systemic approach to International Relations, ignores domestic politics, focuses on the interaction of national states that it assumes to be unitary, and explores how at the level of the international system this inter-state interaction affects the making of foreign economic policy. The second, generally associated with interest-group or class-analytical approaches, focuses explicitly on bargaining among domestic socio-economic and political groups, and investigates how this domestic political interaction affects the making of foreign economic policy.

Systemic studies of international relations contribute two insights to the analysis of the politics of international economics. The first is that the international economic order generally reflects the preferences of the most important states in the system. This bit of common sense is not so trivial as it might seem; its insistence on *states* as the basic ordering principle of the international system highlights the incompleteness of international economic approaches that look only at market forces. The second insight is that, like all atomistic actors, states face difficulties in coordinating their interaction, even when such coordination would be to their mutual benefit. The point here is that inter-state behavior is subject to the same strategic considerations as interaction among firms or individuals. These two insights have been applied, most prominently and with mixed success, to such issues as the construction of an open international trading system by 'hegemonic' powers—the United Kingdom in the 19th century and the United States after World War Two.

However, systemic International Relations has not been very successful at going beyond these observations to more systematic analyses of the international political economy. The problem is simple: the two insights mentioned above can only be brought to bear for real analysis if the preferences of the actors (states) can be specified. Scholarship in the systemic tradition regards states as rational units interacting strategically in the international system, but the units have nothing to be rational *for*, no utility function to maximize. Indeed, the strategic interaction of states in the international economic policy arena cannot be understood without a clear picture of the states' prior preferences: a state that wants to be integrated into the international economy will behave very differently in trade negotiations than one that prefers economic autarky. Some have tried to evade the problem by assuming that states maximize their power or prospects for survival and building up from there, but since national power or survival are goals consonant with a myriad of economic policies, the preferences imputed on this basis are *ad hoc*.

One way to avoid this problem is to focus on specific issue-areas in which national economic preferences appear self-evident. There are many studies on the strategic interaction of debtor nations and creditor banks in which, quite plausibly, both debtors and creditors are assumed to be purely economic utility maximizers: debtors trade off the benefits of unilateral reductions in debt service against the costs of creditor retaliation, while creditors do the opposite, all in the context of implicit or explicit bargaining toward an equilibrium outcome. Yet this method has not been generalized to other issue-area, and it is rarely extended to inter-state interaction in more than one issue-area.

The first cut proposed here to analyze the political economy of international finance is systemic, and focuses on the ways in which nation-states interact in bargaining over global monetary, financial, and trade relations. In line with the systemic focus on unitary state action, we ignore domestic politics, derive the interests and preferences of nation-states from their international investment positions, then discuss their behavior as they bargain with other nation-states over international financial, monetary, and trade issues.

Even the most cursory knowledge of the politics of international financial relations is enough to make clear how unrealistic is the fundamental assumption of the systemic approach, that domestic politics do not affect foreign economic policymaking. Different domestic groups have varied, sometimes diametrically opposed, interests in relation to the international economy, and they fight for their interests in the domestic political arena.

The domestic-level alternative to systemic International Relations, then, seeks to specify how national economic preferences are derived from bargaining among individuals, firms, and sectors within the nation-state, each of which has preferences derived from its position in society. The analytical bases for this method, which has firm roots in modern political economy, are of course far more developed than systemic interpretations of the international economy. Nevertheless, even at the level of generality of interest to scholars of International Relations the task is extraordinarily complex, since it requires a level of disaggregation sufficient to capture the specifics of various individuals, firms and sectors, and then a reaggregation that is able to assign accurate weights to the relevant actors. This is a daunting task in so detailed and variegated a field as international trade, since goods differ so enormously; it is only slightly less daunting in international financial matters.

Our second cut is thus to examine the effect of the different international economic situations of various groups within national societies on the making of national policies related to international investment. Socio-economic groups with overseas assets are expected to have different interests from those without, and are expected to exert political pressure on policymakers to protect their international interests. These pressures will be brought to bear in issue areas directly related to international investment, such as international monetary and financial policies, as well as in issue areas that affect returns on international investment indirectly, such as trade policy.

The remainder of this paper is an attempt to develop and apply these intersecting approaches. First we examine how the international investment position of a nation-state as a discrete unit might be expected to affect its interests and actions in bargaining over international monetary policy, cross-border capital movements, and international trade. Then we explore how the international investment positions of various groups *within* each nation-state might be expected to affect the groups' positions in domestic political bargaining over national foreign economic policies on international monetary, investment, and trade issues. For tractability we look only at countries with net external assets, creditors. This restriction in the scope of the analysis is artificial and limiting, since the existence of creditors implies the existence of debtors, and they can be expected to interact in important ways. However, the discussion of creditor interests and actions is complex enough for a preliminary essay.

'NATIONAL' CREDITOR INTERESTS AND THE POLITICAL ECONOMY OF INTERNATIONAL FINANCE

In the process of economic growth and development, countries pass through a series of states in their capital accounts. It is intuitively obvious that, inasmuch as economic development involves capital accumulation, the less developed a country is the more poorly endowed with capital it will be, and the more likely the relative capital scarcity will lead to capital imports. There are of course a number of reasons why the process might take the form, not of capital imports, but of an entirely domestically-driven increase in the country's capital stock and capital-to-labor ratio. Nonetheless, a few not particularly strong assumptions are enough to ensure that almost any model will reflect the empirical observation that relatively poor countries tend to import capital, while relatively rich ones tend to export it.

This secular trend can of course be interrupted by shorter-term fluctuations, for example when a wealthy country borrows heavily abroad (the United States in the Reagan years, Weimar Germany) or when a poor country invests abroad (Argentina and Venezuela in the early 1980s). We ignore the fluctuations and focus on the trend. We also begin our analysis not at the beginning, but at the point at which a country ceases to be a debtor and becomes a creditor.

Creditor countries share certain attributes, but it is useful to distinguish between new lenders and mature creditors. The fundamental distinction between the two is the degree to which overseas assets have been accumulated; a specific indicator might be the relationship between new overseas investments and earnings on existing overseas assets.

When a country begins to export capital, its earnings on overseas assets are substantially less than its new overseas loans and investments. Put another way, a *new lender* pays for most capital exports out of the country's trade surplus. After many years of overseas investment, however, the country's existing stock of foreign assets is large enough that repatriated earnings approach or even surpass new capital exports. Earnings from financial and other services directly related to the country's international financial status (insurance and foreign exchange trading, for example) can be added to this. At the point at which the country is, so to speak, living off its existing overseas assets and international financial sector, it is a *mature creditor* or, in less flattering terms, a rentier state.

A country rich in capital and interested in protecting its overseas investments has a number of interests in international monetary and financial relations. In the global arena, a capital-exporter wants to ensure that capital can move across borders smoothly and without undue interference. This implies a need for formal or informal, bilateral or multilateral, arrangements to facilitate cross-border capital flows. One concern is the adjuducation and enforcement of property rights across borders, which can include everything from gunboat diplomacy to investment treaties. Another concern is relatively predictable currency values, whether in the form of the gold standard, the Bretton Woods system, or well-developed forward markets. Creditor countries thus take the lead in maintaining a market for their currency as an international reserve asset, developing international contract law and a mechanism to enforce it, and other such features of financial and monetary stability.

An important aspect of creditor-country status is the financial-center function, by which the country becomes a reliable place for economic agents from other countries to carry out international financial transactions. A financial center's currency must be easily convertible into other currencies and generally trusted, and its financial markets must be strong and reasonably protected from the whims of politicians.

Creditor countries also have important interests in international trade policy. In general, they should be concerned to make their own markets more accessible to their debtors. After all, unless the capital-receiving countries are able, directly or indirectly, to earn the currency of the capital-sending country, creditors will be unable to repatriate their profits. For foreign investing nations, indeed, it is more important that *their own* market be open than that other markets be open; their capital exports can jump trade barriers, but unless foreigners can earn the creditor's currency capital exports can never pay off.

From the standpoint of a major creditor country, such as Great Britain in the nineteenth century and the United States after World War Two, the principal concern is to promote long-term capital movements and short-term exchange stability. World-wide trade liberalization may be of less importance in itself. For a creditor that wishes to enjoy the earnings its foreign assets, after all, it is *one's own* receptiveness to imports that matters most, for service payments and profit remittances depend on the capital importers' ability to earn or purchase the currency of the lender or investor. Similarly, as the Articles of Agreement of the International Monetary Fund make explicit, short-term currency stability may require trade protection rather than liberalization.

New lenders and mature creditors share a common interest in the security of property outside their borders and international monetary and financial stability, but their positions lead to somewhat different trading consideration. New lenders actively accumulate overseas assets, financing this accumulation out of their trade surplus, while mature creditors consume the returns on already-accumulated assets, so that a trade deficit is a necessary concomitant of receiving the fruits of their previous capital exports. New creditors thus have a stronger interest in securing export markets, and less need to open their own markets, than do mature creditors, while mature creditors have a stronger incentive for inward trade liberalization, and a less powerful one for commercial openness on the part of others.

The brief description of creditor-country interests fits the relevant evidence quite well. Holland in its heyday, Britain before World War One, and the United States since World War Two, are indeed quite adequately described as creditor countries with predictable creditor preferences. In all instances, the countries in question engaged in large outflows of long-term capital, a general commitment to help stabilize the international monetary system, and a reduction in barriers to imports. The central economic aspects of such creditor policies thus gave the rest of the world access to the creditor's capital, medium of exchange, and markets. As other nations joined the ranks of the creditors, especially Germany in the 1960s and Japan in the 1970s, their policies also began to reflect traditional creditor concerns.

Holland's domination of European trade in the seventeenth and early eighteenth centuries eventually permitted the Dutch to invest enormous fortunes abroad. The Dutch became the world's most militant partisans of free trade and investment, invented modern international contract law, and acted as Europe's principal center for international finance and related services for many years. In their quest for lucrative outlets for their capital, Dutch investors looked especially to Europe's most dynamic economy, England. Dutch investors purchased huge quantities of English government securities, as well as shares in developing British private enterprises. By the 1770s well over 40 percent of the English national debt was owed to Dutchmen, and wealthy Amsterdam financiers like the Barings and Ricardos were themselves migrating to London. Throughout, the Dutch maintained their classical creditor commitments.

In the oft-cited British case, massive foreign investments shifted Britain's economic weight from the domestic market toward the foreign sector, and from industry toward finance. By 1914 over one-quarter of Britain's national wealth was invested overseas, and the steady flow of finance out of England made the country the greatest creditor and most important international financial center the world had ever seen. The central role of the United Kingdom in enforcing property rights abroad, stabilizing the international gold standard, and liberalizing its trade relations, are all well-known.

The United States after World War Two similarly pursued policies expected of a country extraordinarily rich in capital. Every effort was made to smooth the flow of capital and goods, and to rebuild an environment in which normal patterns of international investment and trade might resume. The ability of the United States to construct a stable and lasting international investment position depended on the reliability of a number of American commitments. First, U.S. goods markets were generally open to the country's real or potential debtors. Second, the market for U.S. dollars was open and predictable, so that savers and investors at home and abroad would be willing to engage in foreign-currency operations; this also required some form of international monetary cooperation. Third, U.S. capital markets were free enough from major government manipulation to overcome investors' and borrowers' fears of political risk. All over the world, investment was spurred by American capital, demand enhanced by American imports, and international payments made predictable by the gold-backed U.S. dollar.

The pattern of international cooperation among creditor countries on issues of mutual interest can also be examined with the tools discussed here. For example, there would appear to be a strong correlation between creditor status and interest in international monetary cooperation. To take two examples, the important Tripartite Monetary Agreement of 1936 eventually came to include all major creditors (the United States, Great Britain, France, the Netherlands, Switzerland, and Belgium), but never attracted the attention of such debtor countries as Germany and Italy. By the same token, as Japan's overseas investments have expanded, its willingness to take an active role in international monetary matters has grown. Past experience with other creditors would indicate that, although the evolution of Japanese policy has been too slow for the tastes of most American policy-makers, it will continue and accelerate as the country accumulates foreign assets.

In another arena, since all creditors share an interest in cross-border property rights, this function has often been carried out in concert. Before World War One, strategic interaction among countries with clear creditor interests in securing foreign investments was of great importance. Multilateral financial control committees to protect the rights of creditors in shaky underdeveloped countries were common. In Serbia, Greece, Tunis, Persia, Egypt, Morocco, and elsewhere committees of private financiers and government officials of the capital-exporting nations were established. In the most limited sense they were charged with ensuring continued debt service, but this task soon involved them in running major portions of the debtors' economies. The best-known example is that of the multinational Ottoman Public Debt Administration, which eventually came to manage a wide variety of the Empire's modern business activities, and to control about one-quarter of Ottoman government revenues.

In the 1920s, during a financial expansion led by the United States and joined by Great Britain, monetary and financial cooperation among creditors was primarily managed by the largest private and central banks of the leading lenders, along with the Economic and Financial Committee of the League of Nations. The Dawes and Young plans to stabilize German finances were emphatically multilateral. The Young Plan indeed gave rise to the Bank for International Settlements (BIS), a formal institution designed to facilitate cooperation among major financial centers.

Since World War Two, multilateral creditor cooperation has evolved along the lines begun in the inter-war period. The IMF-World Bank system has raised the multilateral principles inherent in the BIS to much higher levels, and has come to provide and supervise an extraordinary degree of creditor coordination.

The distinction between new lenders and mature creditors is also useful. It helps explain some of the trade-policy differences among creditor countries, such as why pre-World War One Great Britain was so much more willing to keep its markets open than France or Germany. It also helps explain some of the pattern of evolution in the behavior of creditor nations, such as the gradual shift from moderate neo-mercantilism toward free-trade observed as new lenders become mature creditors. Thus, Great Britain in the mid-19th century, the United States in the 1940s, Western Europe since 1960, and Japan in the last decade reflect the transition from aggressive export promotion and moderate to high controls on imports to a reduction in import barriers.

None of this is to imply that there are not problems of competition and coordination among creditor countries. Nor is it to discount the large variations found even where creditor preferences and policies are similar. For example, one creditor's enforcement of property rights in an underdeveloped area makes it possible for other creditors to free-ride on this enforcement; the first creditor might in this circumstance find attractive to privatize the benefits of enforcement by annexing the underdeveloped area. The approach simply allows the analyst to think more systematically about inter-state relations in such circumstances, in an attempt to understand the conditions in which creditor countries are able to arrive at a cooperative solution (the Ottoman Public Dept Administration) or are driven toward conflict (the late nineteenth-century rush for annexation). Similar exercises could be carried out in the analysis of international monetary cooperation and conflict in the interwar period, or of macroeconomic policy coordination today—all of them attempts to understand how creditor countries with similar preferences can interact in ways that lead to cooperation, conflict, or a combination thereof.

SECTORAL CREDITOR INTERESTS AND THE POLITICAL ECONOMY OF INTERNATIONAL FINANCE

Instead of looking more deeply into the strategic interaction of nation-states with creditor interests, we now turn to a less aggregate level of analysis. It is in fact undeniable that a great deal of the interaction among creditor countries, and between creditor and debtor countries, is driven by domestic rather than international politics. There is, for example, copious evidence that in both the British and American cases much of the impetus for their 'hegemonic' international economic policies came from major domestic economic sectors whose interests may not have been identical with those of the nation as a whole. The powerful financial institutions of the City of London are widely regarded as having had a major impact on British international economic policy from the early nineteenth century up to the present; analogous groups, especially American-based international banks and corporations and their employees, have probably played a similar role in the United States.

To speak of *countries* that are rich in capital can indeed be misleading; the capital does not normally belong to 'the country' but to economic agents in it. In other words, a capital-rich country is one that has more individuals and firms with a great deal of capital than a capital-poor country. This does not imply that *all* firms and individuals in the country are capital-rich, for the accumulation of capital take place very unevenly. The most accurate inference would be that, in a capital-rich country, the economic agents well-endowed with capital outweigh those that are poor in capital but, presumably, well-endowed with other factors.

A policy that can be deduced to be in the interests of a creditor country is not necessarily in the interests of everyone in that country. There are of course many examples of conflict among particular groups over national economic policies, in creditors as in all nations. The protection of overseas property rights may benefit overseas investors a great deal, and peasants very little, but the costs may fall primarily on peasants drafted and sent abroad to do the protecting.

Our previous discussion of creditor-country interests is thus quite incomplete. We cannot simply assume that because some local firms and investors have overseas assets, policy will reflect the interests of those with overseas assets. Even where we have reason to believe that overseas asset-holders will dominate foreign economic policy, such as where most firms with strong preferences about policy are overseas investors, there is always the possibility that the political process will be dominated by economic actors with interests different from or opposed to those of creditors. A more detailed analysis of creditor-country preferences requires us to consider the conflicting interests of those *within* creditor countries. In what follows we discuss some characteristic sectoral interests in creditor countries.

We can distinguish two very broad groups of sectoral interests. First are those whose assets are internationally diversified, and who can thus take advantage of both domestic and overseas investment opportunities. This includes most prominently the creditors themselves, those with existing assets abroad. We define this group to include also those involved in the financial-center functions of a creditor country, whose principal function is to service those with foreign investments. This group should also include producers whose domestic output is competitive on world markets but who have not engaged in overseas investment: those that could invest abroad, but at present have no need to. The second group is make up of import-competing sectors and/or those whose assets are not internationally diversified. This encompasses uncompetitive producers, whose domestic output cannot compete with imports and who have not invested abroad, for whatever reason. It also consists of producers of non-traded goods and services, indifferent to international economic conditions. The categorization is schematic but useful; we can demonstrate its utility by discussing how the different sectors respond to several important policy issues in creditor countries.

Government protection of overseas assets is of interest primarily to those who are real or potential holders of such assets. The rest of the economy bears the costs of such protection—insurance, military intervention, membership in consortia—but receives few of the benefits. A similar calculation holds for international financial and monetary cooperation in general; if such cooperation has costs for the country as a whole, those who receive few benefits will oppose it. This can be brought to bear in the analysis of domestic opposition to colonialism, or to multilateral organizations.

Monetary and fiscal policy, which primarily affect international economic policy through the exchange rate, also give rise to different sectoral interests. Overseas investors and competitive producers (and, if they are organized, consumers of imported products) are expected to exert what might alternately be call deflationary, internationalist, or 'monetarist' pressures. Their competitive and/or international asset position is such that, other things equal, they are profitable with a strong exchange rate. Where a strong currency makes their domestic production less competitive, these investors can respond simply by transferring production overseas. Unless information and currency futures markets are perfect, which they rarely are, investors with international portfolios also have an interest in currency stability and predictability, which domestic inflation endangers. They thus fight against fiscally expansionary policies, and for monetary restraint.

On the other hand, uncompetitive, domestically-bound, and non-tradables producers exert pressures that might alternately be called inflationary, weak-currency, nationalist, or 'fiscalist.' They can only gain from a fiscal stimulus and monetary looseness. A strong currency makes uncompetitive producers even less competitive; depreciation improves their position. By the same token, in most circumstances domestic fiscal stimulation increases demand for domestically produced non-traded goods and services (including goods protected by trade barriers). These groups are thus in the forefront of opposition to monetary stringency and fiscal orthodoxy.

Trade policy is another area of potential conflict. Creditors, along with exporters, have a general interest in inward commercial openness, to avoid retaliation against exports, to allow for profit and interest repatriation and, in the case of multinational firms, for intra-firm trade. For reasons discussed above, creditors in a new lender are less concerned about home-country free trade than creditors in a rentier state. Competitive producers similarly support inward liberalization, for straightforward trade-bargaining reasons. Uncompetitive producers are protectionist; the non-tradable sector is indifferent.

Examples of these sectoral developments recur in the history of creditor states. The Dutch experience is legendary. Even as the country's industries became increasingly unable to compete with foreign manufacturers (especially those protected by British mercantilism), the country's powerful foreign-investment, financial, shipping, and trading interests were able to maintain free trade. . . .

A similar dynamic was at work in Great Britain even at the height of its international creditor status. Industrially-based protectionists, especially supporters of Imperial Preferences, grew steadily stronger after 1880 but were only able to triumph politically, and then only temporarily, in the interwar years. Here, as in

Holland, the outcome was not so much national decline as a change in the *domestic* balance of economic and political power as the nation's role in the world was redefined from that of a new lender to a mature creditor. As British investors built up huge international holdings British industry became increasingly uncompetitive, and sectoral conflicts over monetary and exchange-rate policy were particularly striking. To take one famous example, London's City was a primary pressure group for, and a major beneficiary of, Britain's return to gold in 1925 at an overvalued parity. Sterling overvaluation maintained the value of Britain's overseas investments, and helped keep sterling and the City at the center of international finance. Sterling overvaluation also drove Britain's already weak traditional industries into a recession that only ended when it was superseded by the Depression.

A sketch of crucial episodes in domestic conflict over the foreign economic policy of the United States since World War I demonstrates a similar sectoral dynamic. In the 1920s the relatively new creditor sectors that arose during and after the Great War pressed for American membership in the League of Nations and other multilateral organizations, international financial and monetary cooperation, and trade liberalization. Creditors and the financial services sector, led by the New York banks, were allied with America's highly competitive industrial producers, who were already beginning to expand their overseas direct investments. Their opponents were to be found in the uncompetitive heartland industries and non-traded sectors, the bulwark of Taft Republicanism and isolationism. Although creditor and exporting sectors pressed consistently for the United States to revise its traditional protectionism and lack of involvement in international economic negotiations, they were continually defeated in a Congress fundamentally opposed to 'internationalism,' in economic as in other affairs. It was not until the late 1930s and 1940s that the tides of American politics began to shift toward a less isolationist international economic posture.

In the aftermath of World War Two, with most foreign competition wiped out and economic nationalism discredited, American policy moved in a more traditional creditor direction. Nonetheless, domestic political battles over foreign economic policy continued, on different fronts. 'Fiscalist' forces, represented by Henry Morgenthau's Treasury Department, and by the Keynesians more generally, did battle with a powerful strong-currency lobby, based once more in the financial sector. With much of their international and domestic influence eroded by the global and domestic financial disasters of the 1930s, international financial interests were on relatively weak grounds until international trade and payments revived. Thus, while much of American policy accorded with creditor interests, the New York bankers did initially lose the battle to make the International Monetary Fund a tool of financial orthodoxy and to base international monetary relations on a gold-backed dollar.

Over the course of the late 1940s and early 1950s, however, as the U.S. and world economies returned to normalcy, 'monetarist' groups reasserted themselves. The Treasury Accord of 1951 reestablished traditional Federal Reserve control over monetary policy. Under orthodox American leadership, the IMF evolved into a paragon of financial rectitude. The crucial question was that of the conditions under which member nations would be allowed to borrow from the Fund, and in successive decisions in 1952, 1955, and 1956, the IMF established rigorous standards upon which borrowing was to depend. By the late 1950s the Fund was often making its loans contingent upon such strict quantitative economic conditions as government spending ceilings and credit supply limits. In addition, international monetary relations as they evolved in the 1950s and 1960s looked far more like the key-currency approach of the New York bankers—with the dollar 'as good as gold' and used as an international payments medium—than they did like the wartime plans of American and British Treasury officials.

This framework can also be brought to bear on the political economy of recent US international economic policy. One set of sectors is internationally integrated and/or competitive; another is uncompetitive and/or internationally insulated. In the American context the position of military contractors is especially important within the latter group, because of the widespread acceptance of relatively high levels of military spending in the United States—which can be regarded for our purposes as a fiscal stimulus to goods producers sheltered from international competition. Whether one sees this military spending as motivated primarily by real security concerns, by an ideologically acceptable military Keynesianism, or by the inordinate power of military contractors, the fact is that a degree of economic nationalism in pursuit of military preparedness has long been politically acceptable in the United States.

When private international capital movements began to accelerate after Europe's 1958 return to convertibility, the tension in the United States between deflationary and inflationary, monetarist and fiscalist, groups was a central problem. The position of the country's creditor sectors was endangered by the erosion of international confidence in the dollar, itself a result of the American government's domestic and international fiscal laxity. Rather than capitulate completely to deflationary pressures—for a more stringent monetary policy, for budgetary restraint, for a compression of domestic consumption—the Kennedy and Johnson administrations attempted to shield the domestic economy from trends in the country's capital account. The outflow of American capital was worsening the country's payments balance, thus exacerbating the deflationary pressures on domestic economic policy, but policymakers attempted to avoid domestic deflation without reducing the overseas activities of American firms. This attempt took a number of forms, leading up to the imposition of capital controls that permitted, perhaps even encouraged, American banks and corporations to engage in offshore funding of their overseas investments. The capital controls, which lasted until 1974, only postponed and may ultimately have magnified the conflict.

The Nixon administration also faced conflicting sectoral pressures as it continued to try to square the circle of American international economic policy. Creditor groups encouraged the government to restrain spending enough to strengthen the dollar, and failing that supported a revision of the Bretton Woods system on a cooperative multilateral basis. Meanwhile, domestically based and uncompetitive sectors were under increasing pressure, and support grew for government policies to stimulate the economy, provide trade protection, and devalue the dollar. Much of this sentiment was expressed in Congress, where protectionist sentiment increased rapidly, and through Treasury Secretary John Connally, who was quite sympathetic to domestic business. In August 1971 Nixon appeared to give in to pressures for a revision of traditional American foreign economic policies, much to the chagrin of internationalists around the world.

Conflict continued through the 1970s and into the 1980s. The early Carter administration stimulated the economy, but the result was a serious loss of confidence in the dollar by international investors. The dollar depreciation aided the competitive position of domestically based producers, but seriously worried those whose international investment interests were threatened by inflation and currency instability. In late 1978, as the dollar dropped vertiginously, Carter moved to defend the currency, with little success until in 1979 Paul Volcker and the Federal Reserve moved resolutely to deflate the economy and strengthen the currency. At the same time, the Administration began to exercise some fiscal restraint, but most of the adjustment burden was borne by monetary policy, an arena dominated by the Federal Reserve, which generally reflects the concerns of those who are committed to the international economy and to an anti-inflationary posture.

The conflict between monetarists and fiscalists, deflation and inflation, internationalism and nationalism, accelerated in the Reagan administration. Three varied sets of interests reflected in the Republican Party and the administration can be pointed to. One was based in non-traded sectors, especially trade, real estate, and military contractors from the 'Sunbelt' area. These groups were clear influences in favor of fiscal expansion, although the non- traded nature of their activities made them hostile or indifferent to trade protection. A second broad grouping was declining industrial sectors in the Midwest and Northeast—these inflationary *and* protectionist. Of course, traditional internationalist and creditor groups maintained their fundamental opposition to both fiscal stimulation and economic nationalism.

The Reagan administration's policies, and its frequent internal disagreements, reflected the disparate pressures on it. Anti-inflationary internationalist creditor sectors dominated monetary policy, including policies to manage international financial and monetary matters. However, reflationary non-traded or uncompetitive sectors had substantial influence on the fiscal side, and had some trade-policy successes as well. One outcome of the pulling and hauling between fiscal and monetary policies was a massive capital inflow as foreigners fund Federal deficits. By 1986 the United States was a net debtor; although American investors still have enormous overseas interests, the US government has built up huge debts to the international capital markets. The effect of these contradictory American policies has become the central issue in the world economy. The story is still being played out, but there is no doubt that in the future, as in the past decade, the conflict between sectors with contending international financial interests will play a crucial role in American economic policy.

Tension similar to that found in the United States since World War Two has characterized debates over economic policy in most of the rest of the OECD. As international markets have become more and more integrated, the general trend has been for national policy to reflect more and more the interests of internationally diversified investors. Yet policy-makers have also tried to meet some demands for protection from international competition by more insular and immobile economic actors. In virtually all countries, groups with important international economic ties have dominated, while groups for whom the rest of the world was a threat rather than an opportunity have fought for protection. Here too, domestic bargaining continues; perhaps the most striking topic of debate is the future of the European Community as 1992 approaches.

PRUDENTIAL DISCLAIMERS AND OBSERVATIONS

The framework presented here does not pretend to be a full-blown theory of the laws of motion of the international political economy. There are many issues that the approach does not address, and many questions it does not answer.

As mentioned at the outset, the initial causes of national-level creditor status are not clearly explained. It is especially important to be able to separate the secular or 'natural' evolution of a national economy and sectors within it, from developments that are simply driven by government policy. It would hardly be justified to regard Great Britain in 1914, with a century of international investment experience, as equivalent to a country that became a net creditor solely for perverse policy reasons—as some Third World borrowers with overvalued currencies did after 1980. The same might be said about the United States today: it clearly is not a 'natural' net debtor. In this regard a distinction between short–and long-term, and between public- and private-sector, capital movements may be useful.

In much the same way, it is hardly satisfactory simply to assert that some sectors are 'natural' overseas investors while others are not. Government action, from tax policy through colonialism, can change the incentives to overseas investment in important ways. Long-term prediction on the basis of the framework presented here required a stronger prior notion of what kinds of economic agents are more likely to engage in foreign investment.

In other words, the causal arrows implicit in this analysis are not unambiguous. National or sectoral creditor status may itself be the result of prior conditions that are not examined in the model, such as resource endowments, culturally determined savings propensities, or strategic considerations. Nor does the framework presented here provide determinant predictions of the *outcomes* of the sectoral clashes it forecasts. It claims only that the pattern of sectoral conflict, and the policy preferences of the various sectors, will be as set forth above; it says little about the institutional, political, strategic, and other factors that might influence the success of the various sectoral coalitions. These are important points for the extension of this analysis, and for more systematic tests of it.

Despite its preliminary nature, the discussion in this paper demonstrates that only the careful analysis of the roots of national economic preferences can allow International Relations scholars to analyse international monetary and financial interaction in fruitful ways. The implications of the paper are, further, that national economic interests cannot be derived from the system; while a first cut can be extrapolated from national factor endowments, a far more accurate picture requires a sectoral approach. Throughout, we have used the international investment positions of countries and sectors to explain national policies toward both global monetary and financial relations and such related arenas as international trade.

This paper analyzes the implications of national and sectoral international asset positions for national and sectoral economic interests and interaction. By way of example, it argues that creditor countries have certain identifiable international economic interests, and exhibit certain predictable behavior in line with these interests. Illustrations are drawn from a variety of historical and contemporary cases.

National-level phenomena are not sufficient to explain national economic interests, however, for domestic politics impinges strongly on the making of foreign economic policy. For this reason, the article develops a sectoral approach that distinguishes among domestic socio-economic actors with different international portfolios. It identifies the interests, and the expected behavior, of sectors within nations in domestic bargaining over foreign economic policy; illustrations are drawn from historical and contemporary cases. The analytical framework and empirical evidence presented here are meant primarily to suggest ways in which further research and analysis can be pursued in order to understand better the interplay of politics and economics in the international movement of capital.

19
The Debt Cycle in Latin America

ROBERT Z. ALIBER

Aliber surveys the effects on Latin America of the expansion and subsequent contraction of international finance in the 1970s and 1980s. In his view, the debt crisis of 1981 was firmly rooted in international market forces as, first, lenders increased the availability of foreign finance with "petrodollar recycling" in the 1970s and, second, borrowers used the net capital inflow to pay for increased consumption and imports. The net effect of these international financial flows was to increase national income in the Latin American borrowers in the 1970s and, inevitably, to reduce it in the 1980s. Although the debt crisis itself was largely "unavoidable," its timing and magnitude were determined by macroeconomic developments, and specifically high U.S. interest rates and the global recession. While Manual Pastor (Reading 20) criticizes the role of the International Monetary Fund's stabilization programs, Aliber explicitly exempts the organization from responsibility for the austerity programs currently found in Latin America.

Changes in the volume of new loans issued by the developing countries in Latin America have had a significant impact on the foreign exchange value of their currencies, and on most of their domestic macroeconomic variables. During the 1972-82 decade, the annual increase in external debt of many of these countries exceeded the interest payments on this debt. The result was a net cash inflow derived

---

19 "The Debt Cycle in Latin America" by Robert Z. Aliber. This article first appeared in the Winter 1985-86 issue of the *Journal of Interamerican Studies and World Affairs*, Volume 27, No. 4 as part of a special issue entitled "Interamerican Economic Relations: The New Development View," guest edited by Markos J. Mamalakis.

from the sale of new loans abroad. Consequently, at the time, no real economic cost was associated with this increase in external debt. After 1982 this situation changed.The annual increase in external debt diminished to the point where it was less than the scheduled interest payments. At that point Latin American borrowers began to experience a net cash outflow on their debt account. Thus, in order to generate the foreign exchange needed to pay even part of these scheduled interest charges, the economy had to undergo a costly adjustment process.

The *first section* of this paper will discuss (a) the impact these changes in volume of net external loans had on the exchange rate, and (b) the impact exerted by domestic economic variables on borrower economies during the 1972-82 decade. The *second section* will evaluate some of the different explanations that have been given regarding the cause of the debt crisis. The *third section* will explore ramifications of the adjustment process that took place as a result of this change from a net cash inflow to a net cash outflow on the debt account, and the impact these exerted on the borrowing countries.

The assumption of this article is that the financial markets in the industrial countries are partially integrated with those in the Latin American countries. These countries borrow abroad as an alternative to borrowing at home. The volume of external loans changes according to the willingness of foreign lenders to buy the loans; in this sense, the number of loans being made at any time are a function of lender decisions to grant or ration credit. Borrowers seek to sell more loans abroad when they anticipate that the low interest costs more than compensate for any loss incurred, either due to an increase in the domestic price of foreign exchange or as a reasonable recompense for assuming the exchange risk. Whether they can then sell more loans abroad depends entirely upon demand.

External debt of developing countries frequently is tied to increases in the price of energy, as set by the Organization of Petroleum Exporting Countries (OPEC) beginning in 1973-74. From that time the surpluses generated by the OPEC countries became linked to the deficits of the (energy-importing) developing countries in a recycling process initiated and supervised by the major international banks. Two relationships evolved. On the demand side, oil-importing countries paid higher prices for their petroleum imports, for which some preferred to borrow the additional foreign exchange needed rather than to make economic adjustments at home, either by reducing imports or by increasing exports. On the supply side, OPEC members decided to deposit a substantial portion of their newly-acquired cash surpluses with the major international banks. In turn, the latter used these deposits as loans to developing countries. Two observations confirm the accuracy of this thesis. On an annual basis, external loans of oil-importing developing countries increased at a greater rate than their oil-import bills. This does not apply to oil-exporting countries (such as Mexico, Venezuela, Ecuador, Peru, and others), whose oil-export earnings increased along with their external indebtedness. Obviously the oil-import bills of these countries did not increase. The common factor explaining the increase in external loans of both oil-importing and oil-exporting countries is that international lenders were relaxing their credit-rationing standards.

I. A MODEL OF DOMESTIC ADJUSTMENTS TO EXTERNAL DEBT FLOWS

Changes in the size and direction of net cash flows on the debt account, like changes in the volume of commodity exports, affect the foreign exchange value of a country's currency. During a period in which cash inflow from new loans exceeds both interest-payments plus principal-repayments on its outstanding loans, a country's currency should appreciate in real terms. (An analogous situation would be the sharp increase in foreign demand for US securities due to their high interest rates, which resulted in an increase in the foreign exchange value of the US dollar.)

The change in the value of a country's foreign exchange is a function of the change in the difference between the net foreign exchange obtained from sale of new loans and the cash payments for interest-and-principal on outstanding loans. If the cash inflow from the sale of new loans is *increasing* relative to the cash outflow on outstanding loans, the borrowing country's currency should appreciate in real, price-level adjusted, terms. Conversely, if the cash inflow from the sale of new loans is *decreasing*, relative to cash payments on outstanding loans, the borrowing country's currency should depreciate. If cash inflow from the sale of new loans is the same as the cash payments on outstanding loans, then the value of the borrowers' foreign exchange should remain unchanged, for the scheduled interest payments are fully capitalized, and the rate of growth of the external debt is equal to the rate of interest.

Net cash flows associated with a given volume of new loans may change either because the interest rate on the outstanding loans changes, or, perhaps, because the amount of principal repayment changes. Changes of this nature may be offset by other changes in the volume of new loan sales, so that the net cash inflow associated with new loan sales remains the same. The assumption made in the following paragraphs is that volume of new loans is independent of other factors, including autonomous changes in the trade balance, such as those associated with changes in the price of oil.

Corresponding to changes in the net cash inflow on the debt account may be that the country's trade balance will change in an offsetting way, on the assumption that proceeds from the sale of loans do not lead either to equivalent or greater changes in foreign exchange reserves, or to capital flight. Real appreciation of its currency can occur, changing the trade balance of the borrowing country when issuers of new loans take their loan proceeds to the foreign exchange market to acquire the domestic currency. Thus, an increase in net new loans means that both the country's trade deficit and its current account deficit should increase. An increase in the net export of loans displaces the net export of commodities. Commodity imports increase at the same time that commodity exports decline.

Real appreciation of the currency of the developing country borrower, and the increase in its trade and current account deficit, should work to reduce its rate of inflation. Two factors explain the decrease in inflation. For any given money supply, or an given rate of growth of the money supply, domestic price levels fall (or at least increase more slowly), as the supply of available goods increases in response to the increased trade deficit. Moreover, the decline in the domestic-currency-price of imports may lead to a decline in the rate of inflation since domestic producers will face increased competition from imports.

Interest rates within the borrowing country will also go down as a result of the increase in net cash inflow; the larger trade deficit means that the amount of foreign savings available to borrowers in the developing country increases. One explanation for the decline in domestic interest rates is that external borrowing becomes a substitute for domestic borrowing. A second explanation is that domestic saving increases as income increases (see following paragraph); and a third is that a reduced rate of inflation should be associated with a reduced premium on inflation in terms of nominal interest rates.

Increased net debt sales are often associated with an increase in the role of the government sector because the ability of the government, and of government agencies, to borrow abroad is greater than that of private firms, since lenders consider government to be more credit worthy. For one thing, government and its agencies are less likely to go bankrupt than are private firms because government can obtain any domestic currency needed through its access to the central bank. For another, the size of the government sector is apt to increase along with the volume of new debt sales.

Increased net debt sales abroad are also associated with an increase in the national income of the borrowing country, partly because a decrease in the nominal interest rates is associated with an increase in investment spending by private firms at home. In addition, increased government borrowing abroad is likely to be associated with increased government spending, hence domestic income and employment are also likely to go up. As an increased supply of foreign goods becomes available, spending on domestic goods is likely to increase too. Domestic spending and foreign spending complement each other. The implicit assumption is that sufficient domestic unemployed and underemployed resources are available to satisfy the increased demand for domestic goods. Thus an increased inflow of cash, from the sale of loans abroad, is likely to be associated with an increase in the rate of growth of national income whenever unemployed and underemployed resources exist in the borrowing country. Equity values (or stock prices) go up in tandem with the net cash inflow into the borrowing country. One reason for this is the decline in interest rates. A second is that an increase in spending and income will lead to an increase in corporate profits. These two factors dominate the impact on corporate profits of the real appreciation of the domestic currency, reflecting the fact that corporate profits go down as domestic costs go up, relative to the level of world prices. The explanation is that most sales of firms in developing countries are made to the domestic market, which is protected from import competition. However, to the extent that some firms do export or are in substantial competition with imports, the effective real appreciation will lead to a lower level of corporate profit. The impact on the firm's equity value depends on the extent to which the lower interest rate exerts its influence on their profits.

The increase in long-term external debt of Latin American countries amounted to $197 billion between 1972 and 1982, going from $37 billion in 1972 to $234 billion in 1982; the growth rate exceeded 18% a year. In addition, the short-term external debt of these countries increased, probably at an even more rapid rate. One large component of the funds realized from the sale of loans consisted of paying the interest on these outstanding loans: $37 billion, compounded at the prevailing interest rate, amounted to $108 billion. Front-end fees connected with the issue of new loans also absorbed some of the foreign exchange. Latin America's foreign reserves increased by $30 billion. In the 1972-82 decade, payments abroad for imports of goods and services surpassed earnings from exports of goods and services by $15-20 billion, when compared to the previous 1962-72 decade, or by $1.5-2 billion a year. Most of this represented an increase in payments for imports of commodities relative to exports of same. The big difference between the increase in the external debt (in 1972-82) and the change in the balance of trade (from 1962-72 to 1972-82) provides a first guess as to the level of capital outflow, variously estimated to have been from $100-150 billion.

II. THE SOURCE OF THE EXTERNAL DEBT CRISIS

Once the developing country external debt had increased at rates from 20-30% for a decade, and the levels of external debt had begun to approach 40-50% (or more) of the national income, an external debt crisis became inevitable. The external debt of the borrowers could not continue to increase at rates substantially above the rate of growth of their national income indefinitely. As long as the debt increased more rapidly than income, the ratio of debt to income rose. As long as the debt's rate of growth was greater than its interest rate, the borrowers incurred no current cost by issuing more new debt abroad, since the foreign exchange obtained from the sale of new debt was more than sufficient to pay the interest on the outstanding debt.

When lenders became convinced that the ratio of debt to income could not continue to increase at this rate, their credit rationing would become more severe, the rate at which the debt grew would slow down, and the borrowers would find themselves increasingly less able to promote new loans with which to pay the interest on the loans outstanding. At some stage, it was inevitable that the borrowers would need to make the adjustment from a position of net cash inflow on the debt account to one of net cash outflow. The degree of adjustment would vary according to borrower willingness to pay interest on a scheduled basis, and according to lender willingness to buy new loans from the borrowers, albeit at a reduced rate; Paradoxically, the greater the demonstrated willingness to pay all of the interest on a scheduled basis,the less likely the borrower might be obliged to do so because the mere act of demonstration might persuade the lenders to buy new loans—in this way the scheduled interest payments could be capitalized into an ever-growing amount of external debt.

Both the timing of the external debt crisis and its severity were affected by (a) the increase in nominal interest rates on securities denominated in the US dollar and (b) by the world recession. Higher nominal interest rates meant larger interest payments by the borrowers on the floating interest rate component of their external debt, while the recession meant their export earnings declined. The external debt crisis is particularly associated with the surge in interest rates on this debt, which reduced the net cash inflow associated with a given volume of debt sales. The greatest impact came from reduced net cash inflows produced by the diminished ability to sell new loans. Lenders rationed credit more severely. Lender willingness to buy new loans from Mexico deteriorated as the world recession became more severe and oil prices declined which led, in turn, to lender pessimism regarding Mexico's ability to service its debt. In the absence of cash coming in from the sale of new loans, Mexico could not pay the interest on its outstanding loans. Lenders reacted to the Mexican cash crisis by displaying increased reluctance to buy any new loans from other developing countries as well.

Traditionally borrowing has two purposes. One is to facilitate higher levels of growth by enabling the borrowers to acquire assets whose anticipated returns are greater than the interest rate on the borrowed funds. The second is to facilitate adjustment to external shocks, and especially to cyclical declines in income. The irony is that the borrowers used so much of their available credit lines in the effort to enhance income that their credit lines were exhausted soon after the combination of tight money and world recession had reduced their net export earnings.

III. DOMESTIC ADJUSTMENTS TO THE EXTERNAL DEBT CRISIS

As the cash inflows associated with new debt declined, many relationships noted in the first section became reversed. As a result, the currencies of these countries depreciated in real terms, or much more rapidly than might be inferred from the differentials in national inflation rates. Because the borrowers needed to generate trade surpluses in order to obtain the foreign exchange required to pay at least part of the interest on outstanding loans, real depreciation was extensive, due to both the inelastic demand for exports within the developing countries, and to the inelastic supply of goods for export.

One consequence of the very sharp, real depreciation of borrower currencies was to produce significant upward cost-push pressures on price levels from the higher local-currency price of imports. Moreover, the reduced availability of goods also forced up domestic price levels, so that the price level increase, for the same rate of growth of the domestic money supplies, went up so long as trade deficits were declining. In some countries, the combination of reduction in the trade deficit with increased domestic borrowing led to a surge in the inflation rate, as a result of rapid domestic monetary expansion.

These sharp, real depreciations squeezed both the public and private borrowers, since the domestic-currency equivalents of the scheduled payments of interest and principal on the outstanding loans were significantly higher. In some cases, the domestic-currency equivalent may have increased by a factor of 5 or 6. Both public and private borrowers needed to raise domestic receipts relative to payments to obtain the increased local-currency equivalent of their debt service payments abroad. The surge in the domestic-currency equivalent of interest and principal payments meant that the borrowers were bankrupt in many cases, or that they would have gone bankrupt if the external debt had not been effectively nationalized.

The inability to sell new loans abroad squeezed many borrowers who formerly had relied extensively on such sales for debt finance. Many of these borrowers sought to raise more funds at home as a substitute for funds they could not raise abroad. The result was that domestic interest rates increased sharply in many countries. Governments, especially, were able to use domestic finance as a substitute for external finance, because payments of interest and principal were partially, or fully , indexed to inflation rates. Thus, governments could raise the real returns on these domestic debt issues to the levels needed to sell the debt.

Increase in the real interest rate resulted in private borrowers being squeezed because the interest cost of funds was greater than any return on investment that companies might earn. Nevertheless, many such borrowers were still able to secure additional funds because lenders were reluctant to force private firms out of business. However, many private firms shrunk in size.

The squeeze on public and private borrowers meant that both income and employment declined in the developing countries. Foreign exchange earnings were needed to service debt.

All these adjustments became inevitable once the ability of the borrowers to sell new loans declined, and once lenders lost confidence in borrower willingness to make the adjustments necessary to pay interest on a scheduled basis. The increase in the price levels, and the real depreciation in borrower currencies,were unavoidable, even in the absence of the IMF (International Monetary Fund) programs. The decline in income, and the squeeze on both public and private borrowers, were unavoidable once the ability to sell new loans had declined because credit rationing became more severe as well. IMF programs may have exacerbated the decline in income and employment owing to the Fund's insistence on reducing the inflation rate. At the same time, IMF programs may have lessened the squeeze on the private sector because of the Fund's efforts to reduce fiscal deficits as a share of national income.

20

Latin America, the Debt Crisis, and the International Monetary Fund

MANUEL PASTOR, Jr.

This Marxist interpretation of the Latin American debt crisis differs significantly from that of Liberal economist Robert Aliber (Reading 19). Pastor focuses on long-term, or "structural," characteristics of Latin American interaction with the world economy, and on the economic and political power of domestic and international capitalists. He argues that both the borrowing boom of the 1970s and the debt crisis of the 1980s were the result of features inherent to the international capitalist system. He also asserts that since the debt crisis, the IMF has become an enforcer of domestic financial discipline in Latin America on behalf of capitalists. In Pastor's view, while IMF programs may be in the interest of foreign and Latin American capitalists, they have depressed Latin American growth and harmed the Latin American poor.

Since 1982, the International Monetary Fund (IMF, or Fund) has played a major role in managing the international and intranational conflicts caused by the nearly half trillion dollars of Latin American debt. Throughout the decade, Fund missions have shuttled from country to country, recommending austerity programs that open the door to debt rescheduling. Under IMF direction, debt service has generally been maintained and a depression-scale financial calamity has been avoided. At the same

---

20 "Latin America, the Debt Crisis, and the International Monetary Fund" by Manuel Pastor, Jr., *Latin American Perspectives*, Vol. 16, Issue 60, pp. 790-110.

time, Latin American growth rates and living standards have fallen dramatically, provoking anger and resentment at the Fund and its policies.

As a result, identification with the IMF has become a political liability and rejection of Fund policy has become more frequent.... Indeed, the popular attitude in Latin America toward the Fund is perhaps best summarized by a cartoon from a Mexican daily. In it, a working-class Mexican is hanging from a scaffold while a well-dressed man with a briefcase is reaching into the dying man's pocket to take the last of his money. On the briefcase is stamped "IMF."

What is the IMF and what are they doing in Latin America? In this article I examine the role of the IMF in managing the Latin America debt crisis. I begin with a brief review of various explanations of the causes of the crisis, suggesting various inadequacies in both the Fund's orthodox approach and the approach of its mainstream liberal critics. I briefly discuss some elements of a left analysis of the crisis. Next I examine the entrance of the Fund into the crisis and suggest that the Fund's ability to enforce its vision of appropriate policy was dramatically enhanced in the capital-scarce world of the 1980s. Coordinating private capital flows and steering macroeconomic policy in almost every country in Latin America, the IMF has acted almost as a global capitalist planner.

How has the Fund performed in this role? In the final section I examine the performance of Latin America in the recent era of IMF direction. After criticizing both the Fund's analysis of the crisis and the policies it recommended to resolve the problems, I note that Latin America remains mired in a crisis of stagnant growth, high debt ratios, and regressive income redistribution. In light of this poor performance, I conclude, the IMF may be politically exhausted as a vehicle for crisis resolution and economic restructuring: at the same time, there are important reasons—from the perspective of core bankers and peripheral elites—why the Fund may continue to exercise an important role in the crisis.

THE DEBT CRISIS: COMPETING VIEWS

. . . Latin American current account deficits and net external borrowing grew steadily from 1977 until 1982.... [T]he merchandise trade balance was roughly in balance in this time period; the largest regional deficits in this category occurred in 1974 and 1975 (-7.3 and -9.4 billion U.S. dollars, respectively. Indeed, between 1974-1975 and 1979-1980, the trade deficit as a percentage of the current account deficit fell from over 50 percent to under 10 percent. On the other hand, interest payments were rising dramatically, partly because of debt-financing of previous deficits. This, in turn, led to increasing debt and an even higher structural level of interest payments.

What explains the secular increase in deficits and debt in the pre-1982 period? The IMF and orthodox economists have generally blamed domestic policy, particularly fiscal expansion and exchange rate overvaluation; why so many countries simultaneously mismanaged themselves is an anomaly left unexplained by IMF theorists. Liberal and structuralist economists have, on the other hand, focused on the impact of external factors such as the decline in industrial country growth and changing terms of trade. In this view, Latin American policies may have needed correction, but the required adjustment varied in different countries, while the crisis has been global in nature.

Left explanations of the crisis have differed with these accounts in a number of ways. First, many reject the mainstream treatment of the capital account as a passive adjuster to a current account battered by poor internal policies or negative external events. . . . Radical economists instead view the capital account as more a constraint than an equilibrating residue. In this perspective, the dominant feature of the 1970s was a dramatic increase in Latin America's access to international capital markets—in essence, a relaxation of the constraint imposed upon the current account. But then in the early 1980s there was a cutoff of new loans to Latin America; as a result, even countries adopting orthodox programs have found it difficult to obtain significant net capital flows.

While the importance of this dramatic shift in the pattern of international finance has been noted by a variety of structuralist economists, the emphasis on the changing nature of international capital flows and the constraints such flows place on domestic policy has been a consistent feature of many radical or neo-Marxian analyses of the crisis. Moreover, radical economists and some others have tended to stress the cyclical nature of these shifts in capital availability. The pattern, in brief, is initiated by a phase of "overlending" in which banks aggressively seek new clients in order to protect market share; then, because of either a shock-effect (such as the turn toward tight money in 1979) or general market instability, banks collectively retreat from the market in a sort of "panic." For the current period, this overall analysis of finance and capital availability suggests (1) that international bankers had a large role in the crisis and should bear a far larger share of what is now termed the "adjustment burden," and (2) that renewed growth in Latin America relies in the short and medium run on again relaxing the constraints on the current account. Given the unwillingness of private banks to extend new credit in the midst of a "panic," the latter will necessitate default or debt forgiveness.

Left analyses also differ from other accounts in stressing *both* external and internal factors. My own regression analysis of the determinants of the current account in a set of 19 Latin American countries over the period 1973-1982 suggests that (1) external variables such as U.S. growth, real interest rates, the terms of trade, and capital availability played a role, and (2) when the effects of these external variables are accounted for, exchange rate management was a significant determinant but fiscal policy was generally not.

Disentangling the relative contribution of external and internal factors is certainly important for both analysis and debt policy. However, the importance of both sets of factors suggests that neither a sole focus on the North-South dynamic nor exclusive attention to Latin American restructuring will be sufficient for resolving the problem.

What is, however, most distinctive about left analyses is their attempt to go beyond the *proximate* causes of Latin America's debt problems and instead to link together the various external and internal factors in a general theory of capitalist crisis. On the external side, for example, left analyses usually place Latin America's debt accumulation within the context of a crisis of capitalism in the core, particularly in the United States. This crisis in core countries, it is noted, had a negative "external" impact on Latin America, partly because the resulting secular decline in growth in the United States and other advanced capitalist countries through the 1970s had had both direct and indirect (via the terms of trade) effects on Latin deficits in the 1970s. The rising deficits, which might have required severe trade adjustments in an earlier period, instead found available financing from Western banks with relatively abundant capital and lagging loan demand from core customers. Debt accumulation was the result.

Explaining this change in capital availability is, as indicated above, a special concern of radical scholars. Some . . . argue that the "deregulation" of the international monetary system brought about by the breakdown of the Bretton Woods system led profit-hungary banks to seek new customers in the Third World. Others locate the process earlier, suggesting that it was the "dollar overhang" of the 1960s—when the United States, with the dollar as the key currency, could run persistent payments deficits and so expand worldwide liquidity—that allowed the creation of the unregulated Eurodollar market so key to future loans to Latin America. In both views, Organization of Petroleum Exporting Countries (OPEC) surpluses and petrodollar recycling exacerbated the lending phenomenon, but they did not cause it. For one thing, the two major waves of liquidity expansion occurred prior to the oil price increases of 1973 and 1979; for another, the OPEC surpluses "are best explained as a symptom of the decline and breakup of U.S. hegemony". Here again, the external changes so often treated as *exogenous* "shocks" in mainstream liberal treatments are developed by radicals into a larger theory of capitalist crisis in the core and/or international system.

As for the internal factors causing debt accumulation, left scholars chide the IMF and its orthodox officials for not offering any real analysis of *why* Latin America engaged in the "overborrowing" and "policy mistakes" that the Fund now criticizes. In contrast, left accounts of the crisis locate the "errors" within structurally oriented explanations. Frieden, for example, has located "overborrowing" in the context of an exhaustion in import substitution in the late 1960s; seeking to maintain accumulation in the 1970s while simultaneously avoiding *direct* foreign investment, local capitalist classes and governments turned to a strategy of debt-dependent development. I have suggested that, in the Southern Cone at least, the so-called "policy mistakes" of overvaluation and fiscal "excess" were deeply embedded in the monetarist/authoritarian models of accumulation adopted there. Overvalued exchange rates, for example, reflected an attempt to maintain cheap consumer imports, easy borrowing abroad, and capital flight in order to shore up the thin social basis for authoritarian regimes among middle and upper classes. Similarly, the refusal of these regimes to reduce domestic absorption during the 1979-1982 period can be linked to the need to maintain authoritarian regimes' fragile claims to legitimacy—economic success. Naturally enough, the analysis of the "internal" reasons for deficits and debt differs substantially between countries and is the object of intense research and debate; what unites the left analysis is an attempt to go beyond "policy errors" and understand the "underlying structural and institutional forces" that produced rapid debt accumulation.

Despite differences in the various structural explanations of the crisis, there is general agreement that the shift to restrictive monetary policy in the United States turned these structural difficulties into conjunctural crisis. This policy shift in the U.S. was, in part, a response to various symptoms of the U.S. crisis: high inflation and a falling dollar. The monetary restriction did reduce inflation and increase the value of the dollar by raising U.S. interest rates, but at the cost of a dramatic recession in the United States. The resulting world slowdown led to declining export volume and falling prices for Latin America's products; in 1982, the worst year of world recession, export revenues for the region fell by 10 percent. At the same time, high interest rates swelled interest payments on the region's previous debt (most of which had been contracted with variable interest rates) and "pulled" flight capital north. With out payments rising and revenues falling, international reserves dwindled: between 1979 and 1982, Latin America's official reserves and reserves as a proportion of imports both fell by over 30 and 50 percent, respectively. Meanwhile, the real interest rate burden from Latin America's perspective—the nominal rate minus the change in its export prices—rose dramatically, reaching nearly 20 percent in the years 1981-1983.

When oil-rich Mexico announced its inability to make debt payments in late 1982, the problem became painfully clear. Banks responded by raising "spreads" (the interest charge above a standard loan rate such as the U.S. prime or the London Interbank Offer Rate [LIBOR]) and reducing the availability of new credit to the entire region; given the previous debt financing of interest payments noted above, this reduction in new capital aggravated payments problems. Countries sought to adjust for falling exports and reduced credit by restricting imports; between 1981 and 1983, regional imports fell by around 40 percent. Since 65 to 80 percent of Latin American imports are intermediates used in production, growth slowed; indeed, one estimate suggests that Latin American output loss during the years of U.S. monetary restriction between 1980-1983 was approximately $361 billion (in 1987 dollars)—almost enough to pay off the entire regional debt. This growth slowdown and the concurrent payments problems lowered capitalist confidence, leading to reduced foreign investment inflows as well as giving an additional "push" to capital flight and making local elites reluctant to repatriate earnings from previously acquired foreign assets. In short, the balance of payments was pressed from every side. Led by Mexico, Latin America began turning to the official purveyor of bridge financing and advice: the IMF.

THE POWER OF THE IMF

In one sense, the turn to the Fund was quite normal; throughout the postwar period, the IMF has played the role of "lender of last resort," providing short-term finance and harsh adjustment programs to countries in balance of payments difficulties. Yet the shift toward Fund control was quite a turn from the late 1970s. Between 1979 and 1981, for example, even as many observers worried about underlying debt problems in Latin America, less than a third of the countries in the region were operating under Fund arrangements and IMF officials were complaining that Fund resources were being "underutilized." In addition, program countries' observance of performance clauses had deteriorated substantially, seeming to signal a relative reduction in the Fund's power to enforce its arrangements.

Why was there such a decline in the Fund's control over Latin America (and the rest of the Third World as well) in the 1970s? And what were the factors that restored the Fund's power in the early 1980s? In this section, I begin by examining the reasons behind Latin America's desire and ability to avoid Fund conditionality through much of the 1970s; in brief, I suggest that Latin America's new independent access to private credit eroded the institutional power of the Fund and forced it to make certain policy changes. In the 1980s, however, the IMF's power was ascendant in a capital-scarce world. As a result, almost all of Latin America fell under IMF-sponsored stabilization programs and the policy shifts of the previous decade were put to one side in favor of old-fashioned austerity remedies.

The 1970s

While it is easy to overstate the impact of an ideological challenge, it is clear that the Fund and its policies were under significant attack throughout most of the previous decade. Much of this challenge arose from a "Third Worldist" argument that was essentially concerned with the effects of IMF programs on economic growth and political independence. Sustained politically by Third World leaders such as Julius Nyerere in Tanzania and Michael Manley in Jamaica, and nurtured intellectually by a variety of dependency and structuralist economists, this critique suggested that IMF programs were recessionary and punished deficit countries for trade problems that were both endemic to the development process and the result of external and uncontrollable factors. While the stress on the IMF's negative impact on output and development had its theoretical roots in a long-standing debate between monetarists and structuralists, the focus on growth was also important on a political level; it united both Third World dictators and democrats, capitalists and socialists, around a call for a New International Economic Order in general and looser IMF policies in particular.

Throughout the 1970s, the IMF seemed to respond to this political and ideological challenge in a variety of ways. On the one hand, it expanded resources by developing new credit facilities (including some, such as the Oil Financing Facility, designed especially to deal with the external shocks noted by its critics) and loosened the conditionality of access to both these new facilities and some old ones. In addition, it developed the Extended Fund Facility, a credit program under which countries could borrow for time periods exceeding the one-year limit typical of

Stand-by Arrangements; this it was argued, would allow countries time to overcome any of the structural rigidities impeding adjustment. At the same time, Fund economists issued the results of cross-country studies, showing that Fund programs had no consistently negative impact on the rate of growth. These results on growth were later confirmed by researchers outside the Fund.

Despite the attempt to both placate the growth critics and prove them wrong, Third World countries continued—and were able—to avoid the Fund. For Latin America at least, the reason lay largely in its new independent access to international finance. While Latin American governments had been able to borrow to tap into the Eurodollar market and other private sources in the 1960s, the volume of loans and the percentage of debt owed to private sources remained relatively small. In the 1970s, however, with a world awash in dollars because of the breakdown of Bretton Woods and the recycling of OPEC's dollar-denominated trade surpluses, commercial banks returned aggressively to Third World borrowers.

This shift toward Third World borrowers reflected in part an attempt to avoid the lower returns on loans that were the result of the ongoing crisis in the industrialized countries. For U.S. banks, for example, the inflationary problems of the 1970s meant that the real interest rate that might be earned from U.S. loans—the so-called "prime rate" minus the change in a U.S. price index—was quite low (though usually positive) throughout the 1970s. Lending to Latin America with an extra charge or "spread" was sufficient to return the real rate of return to the real rate that had been obtained from U.S. customers in the 1960s; meanwhile, the general rise in the prices of Latin America's commodities meant that the real interest rate from the borrowers' view—the nominal interest rate minus the inflation in export prices—was mostly negative. It was a situation that could make even prudent governments eager to borrow; given the confluence of this financial situation with the exhaustion of old accumulation models in Latin America and the need and desire to maintain development, rapid debt accumulation became common.

Through the 1970s, then, increased access to external credit essentially relaxed the previous constraints on current account deficits; as a result, the regional deficit more than tripled between 1973 and 1980. Such growing deficits would normally have frightened private lenders away, forcing deficit countries to adopt a regime of IMF conditionality. But with profit rates weakening in the industrial world, international banks discovering the growing loan market in the Third World, and Latin American countries eager to take advantage of their new access to credit, the previous restraints against lending to deficit countries had been put to one side. Given the availability of independent financing, fewer countries adopted Fund programs precisely because fewer countries *had to.*

Thus the percentage of Latin American countries operating under IMF programs fell from around two-thirds between 1966-1970 to around one-third by 1979-1981. Indeed, in the late 1970s, some countries in serious balance of payments difficulties, like Jamaica and Peru, tried to bypass the Fund altogether and obtain payments financing from private creditors directly. While these efforts were ultimately unsuccessful, the fact that countries even attempted to reject the Fund's financing and advice in favor of private credit and stabilization programs of their own design indicated a general weakening of the Fund's institutional power.

By the late 1970s, then, much of Latin America could use private credit to avoid both adjustment in general and IMF conditionality in particular. Seeking to reassert its influence, the IMF generally lowered the conditionality of its programs, responded directly to its critics with the studies mentioned earlier, and began to evidence a new awareness of the political difficulties of implementing IMF plans. In Bolivia, for example, the Fund backed away from harsh adjustment demands in the 1978-1980 period of democratization in order to avoid straining fragile interim regimes; after the military coup in 1980, however, the Fund's usual harshness returned. However limited the change, the Fund's enhanced responsiveness to Third World demands was quite significant, was generally noted positively by its critics, and was, I would argue, a sign of the Fund's relative weaknesses. Like the dollar-based Bretton Woods system itself, the Fund's power had been eroded by the vast expansion of world liquidity.

The 1980s

The decline in Fund influence was dramatically reversed with the emergence of the debt crisis in 1982. Cut off from new private credit due to ongoing "panic," Latin America found that the "lender of last resort" was now the negotiator of first resort. With countries seeking both short-term relief and the IMF's aid in renegotiation of long-term loans, the 1970s resistance to IMF-sponsored stabilization programs was rapidly overcome. By 1983, three-quarters of the Latin American countries were operating under either a Stand-by Arrangement or the Extended Fund Facility; moreover, *all* of the programs in this period were so-called "upper credit tranche" arrangements involving a high degree of conditionality. As the decade proceeded, most of the remaining one-quarter of Latin America also fell under IMF control and the few countries that escaped direct IMF intervention were often under indirect IMF supervision.

This control over the region was reinforced by a subtle but significant transformation of the IMF's relationship with private bankers. Throughout the 1960s and 1970s, banks had often withheld new credit until a country agreed to an IMF-sponsored stabilization program; the banks took this as a "seal of approval" and *followed* the IMF, pouring new loans onto a fire presumably already dampened by Fund advice. In the debt crisis, however, bankers were reluctant to extend credit to even those countries agreeing to Fund stabilization programs and instead sought to reduce their own exposure. This posed a classic collective action problem; while it was profitable for each *individual* bank to insist on prompt repayment and refuse new credit, the simultaneous pursuit of such self-interest would leave debtors with no resources to refinance and every incentive to default.

In short, the banks needed the Fund to organize a "creditors cartel" that would both dictate macroeconomic policy to debtors *and* force individual banks to continue the "involuntary lending" that was necessary for the system as a whole. Beginning with the Mexican case, IMF officials approached international creditors directly and indicated that Fund credit to problem debtors would be withheld unless there was a fresh inflow of capital from the bankers as well. This in effect expanded the IMF's command over resources beyond the stock of currencies already in its possession. At the same time, IMF control over Latin America was enhanced by the Fund's virtual monopoly over credit lines; after all, an agreement with the Fund was necessary to obtain even "involuntary" lending.

In a capital-scarce world, then, the IMF became a sort of global capitalist planner. By this I mean that the Fund (1) tried to solve the collective action problem and enforce the collective self-interest of the banks, and (2) used its new leverage to determine the macroeconomic policy of almost all of Latin America. Even as it took on these global tasks, the Fund carefully maintained a case-by-case approach that blamed the crisis on various domestic "mistakes"; this helped to ensure that the creditor's unity of interest would not be mirrored by the organization of a debtor's cartel. With its power expanded, the Fund promptly reversed the changes of the late 1970s, tightening conditionality and imposing austerity with little concern for political constraints. What were the policies the Fund promoted and what were the effects?

LATIN AMERICA UNDER THE IMF

The IMF Approach in Theory

As noted above, the IMF's orthodox framework ignored the global aspects of the crisis and instead stressed domestic mismanagement as the primary cause of Latin America's payments problems. Despite this notion that the Latin American crisis had emerged as the result of separate and unrelated inadequate policies in individual countries, the IMF recommended virtually the same policy package to all of Latin America: devaluation, reduction of fiscal deficits (with the presumption that monetary contraction would follow), and decreases in real wages (usually by freezing nominal public sector wages—and therefore indirectly private sector wages—in the context of ongoing inflation). In addition, the Fund argued for the relaxation of controls on trade and capital flows in the international sphere and the elimination of subsidies and other government interferences; indeed, the only price the IMF wished host governments to regulate was the price of labor.

While this policy package of devaluation, fiscal restriction, and wage repression is problematic under any circumstances, it is particularly inappropriate in the context of a global economic slowdown. Devaluation, for example, is unlikely to improve the trade balance through export growth when core country growth is stagnant. Moreover, simultaneous devaluation by a large number of countries is unlikely to have the benefits expected when such a policy is pursued by an individual country. While devaluation might be expected to slow capital flight (by raising the price of foreign assets), it is also likely that rapid devaluation shakes capitalist confidence and so spurs capital flight. Meanwhile, a deliberate attempt to reduce fiscal deficits in the midst of global slowdown is a reckless procyclical policy. In addition, excessive attention to fiscal measures may be misplaced since econometric tests for Latin America do not demonstrate a statistically significant association between government deficits and current account problems when account is taken of other external and internal factors.

Wage repression, while it serves to unite the various factions of local capitalist classes that have to carry out the program, is also problematic from a macroeconomic viewpoint. In the sort of global conditions ruling in the early 1980s, lowering wages for export advantage faces the same problems as devaluation: stagnant Northern markets and reduced benefits if other countries follow the same policy. Meanwhile, wage cuts hardly seem necessary to relieve excess demand when domestic consumption is already curtailed by the multiplier effects of collapsing export demand, attempts to restrain government spending, and an output decline resulting from the curtailment of intermediate imports. And slack demand and excess capacity mean that lowering wages to improve cost conditions will not necessarily attract new local or foreign investment.

What about the Fund's penchant for removing controls on the economy in general and trade and capital flows in particular? . . . The problem with the IMF is its insistence that devaluation and inflation reduction will be sufficient to attract capital "back home," while any attempt to impose capital controls will only shake capitalist confidence and result in more flight. Such reliance on the "magic of the marketplace" is misplaced in the midst of a generalized economic and social crisis and does not readily follow from the low levels of flight evidenced by those developing countries with capital controls. In addition, my own econometric work on the flight problem seems to indicate that while controls do not allow the reckless pursuit of misguided policy, they do "muffle" the effects of policy changes or external shocks on outward capital flows: in short, they slow flight.

The IMF has thus stressed a set of domestic adjustments that fit poorly into the global conditions. The reason is partly ideological—after all, despite disasters like Chile, the orthodox economists of the Fund retain their deep belief in the benefits of liberalization and global monetarism. But the focus on domestic adjustment has also been dictated by the perceived need to keep debtors disorganized while keeping the "creditors cartel" functioning: this could only be accomplished by arguing that the problem in Latin America was the result of "policy mistakes" in individual countries and that therefore a case-by-case approach was required. Moreover, core domination of Fund resources—and the fact that the Fund can generally dictate policy only to deficit and not surplus countries—meant that the IMF was unable and unwilling to force changes in the continuing negative external factors emerging from the core countries: declining terms of trade, slow growth in industrial countries, high interest rates, and what has amounted to a credit embargo.

Unfortunately for the Fund's prescriptions for domestic adjustment, the deficits and debt accumulation of the 1970s had important external determinants and the current crisis was largely triggered by a shift in U.S. macropolicy and a curtailment in new credit. Requiring individual country adjustment in this context is a bit like telling the Depression-era unemployed to retrain—it simply doesn't address the global causes of the problem. What were the results?

The IMF Approach in Practice

Economic Performance ... Latin America was able to turn a trade deficit of $3.2 billion in 1981 into a trade surplus of over $32.7 billion in 1985. This, however, was accomplished mostly through import restraint; exports had actually fallen by $3.4 billion between 1981 and 1985 while imports were slashed by over $40 billion. This painfully achieved trade surplus was the real counterpart to what has been termed the "basic transfer" due to the debt: net inflows of capital minus interest payments. . . . [U]ntil 1982 this measure was positive, indicating a transfer of financial resources from North to South. As new loans became difficult to obtain after 1982 ... the "basic transfer" turned negative, sinking from a peak inflow of $24.6 billion in 1981 to an astounding outflow of $34.7 billion in 1985. Instead of the beneficent orthodox vision of capital flows from the advanced capitalist countries financing Third World development, the pattern had been directly reversed: Latin America was now exporting capital in order to finance Northern economic growth.

The growth cost of maintaining this international redistribution was . . . the dramatic decline of the region's annual growth rate from its 5.8 percent average between 1968 and 1980.

. . . By the mid-1980s, fiscal deficits had eased from their extraordinary 1982 levels, but the performance here does not seem that impressive and could worsen if growth again slows. Meanwhile, the years of crisis have been marked by a significant drop in gross capital formation as a percentage of GDP. The latter effect is likely due to the curtailment of new loans, the collapse of domestic markets, and cuts in government investment in order to bring fiscal deficits in line. In order to maintain the capital export implied by the negative "basic transfer," Latin America has sacrificed needed investment for future growth. Even if an alternative accumulation model is developed, much of the surplus that could finance its implementation and development has been drained by the legacy of the previous debt-dependent growth strategy.

Equally foreboding for the future is the behavior of the debt-related variables. . . . Between 1982 and 1986 real external debt ... was essentially unchanged; for 1987, the IMF estimates an increase that is far below historic rates. Given the behavior of the macroeconomies, however, external debt as a percentage of GDP has actually worsened since 1982 and 1983. The debt service ratio—amortization and interest payments as a percentage of exports—has improved slightly, falling from over 50 percent in 1982 to around 45 percent in 1986 and 1987. The percentage of debt service devoted to just interest payments has also dropped slightly from its 1983 high (an extraordinary 72 percent). Yet there has been a distinct lack of fresh funds (in real terms) and none of the debt-related variables has shown significant improvement. If Latin America is to grow again, it must reverse the "basic transfer"; that is, it must both reduce the surplus drain implied by debt service and obtain "fresh" capital. Given the curtailment of credit by international capital, this will only come by relieving old obligations through default or debt forgiveness. Until then, the region remains firmly mired in the debt crisis, with over 6 percent of each year's production surrendered to foreign creditors.

Distribution and Class This international redistribution of resources in the recent era has been accompanied by a regressive redistribution on the domestic level. This should come as no surprise given the general redistributive logic of Fund austerity programs; while Fund economists have argued that income is merely shifted from nontradable to tradable sectors, my own research has suggested that the most consistent and statistically significant impact of Fund programs in Latin America in the precrisis period (1965-1981) was the reduction in labor share of income. Evidence from the crisis period suggests that IMF programs continue to be associated with significant declines in both the real wage and labor share.

Besides this generally regressive character of IMF programs, there have been several specific ways in which IMF policy in the crisis has helped prompt a redistribution toward local elites. For example, the existence of capital flight and the Fund's attitude toward it have had profound but little noted consequences. . . . [T]he magnitude of such flight is large. Indeed, some major borrowers would have their debt drastically reduced or eliminated if the private assets abroad could be "mobilized." Instead, a significant portion of the interest payments to international banks is "returned" to local elites as interest on the stock of previous capital flight; according to one estimate, for example, interest earnings on previous capital flight amount to about 40 percent of debt payments in Argentina and Mexico and about 70 percent in Venezuela (again, Brazil, with its history of capital controls and a buoyant economy, is the exception at around 10 percent).

While the IMF has insisted that a dose of its orthodox medicine would be enough to stimulate a return of such capital, this has not occurred. With local elites remaining unwilling to repatriate either the capital or interest payments, Latin nations incapable of taxing such foreign earnings, and the IMF insisting on "liberalization" of trade *and* capital accounts, the existence of these substantial assets have done little to relieve the liquidity problems confronting Latin America. In this sense, popular classes in Latin America have been forced to undergo the rigors of trade adjustment not simply to pay the international banks but also to fund their own upper classes.

Another source of redistribution has to do with the treatment of private external debt. Early in the debt crisis, Western banks and local elites pressured Latin American governments to "consolidate debt"—that is, to absorb what had been privately contracted external loans. The banks, of course, wanted assurances of repayment and held the rescheduling of publicly contracted loans "hostage" to a government agreement to take over these private sector liabilities. Elites had equally strong incentives: given their inability to service debt, bankruptcy was threatening. While the procedure differed slightly by country, the essential logic involved the conversion of private sector dollar loans into local currency obligations payable to the state, often utilizing special exchange rates that reduced the real obligations and thus constituted a subsidy to private borrowers. The government, in turn, took on the burdensome foreign currency obligations and reduced government services to the poor in order to finance both debt service and these private subsidies. Accompanying these redistributive effects has been a profound ideological contradiction: while the IMF insists that a careful pursuit of market principles (i.e., limited government "interference" in the economy) will eventually encourage locals to reverse capital flight and bring their assets home, such principles have been rapidly abandoned when international creditors and local rulers stood to lose in the market they espouse. . . .

[I]t is clear that the debt crisis is more than a confrontation of core and periphery; it also involves a confrontation of classes within Latin America itself.

It is further clear to almost all concerned on which side of this international and class conflict the Fund stands. In steering Latin America through the crisis, the Fund has focused on keeping debts serviced and international bankers solvent. In doing this, it has advised Latin America into economic stagnation. The reward for pliant Latin elites is a regressive redistribution that punishes the sectors that did not borrow while rewarding those that did with the socialization of their private liabilities even as their substantial private foreign assets remain untouched. The contradictions and inequities of this approach are, however, increasingly recognized. As I suggest below, Latin America may be preparing to move beyond the IMF.

CONCLUSION

In the years of the debt crisis, the Fund's power and command over Latin America has risen dramatically. With a virtual monopoly over access to private capital flows and with almost all of Latin America operating under its programs, the IMF has presided over an era marked by continuing debt tribute coupled with stagnant growth and regressive redistribution. It is a performance that has hurt the vast majority of Latin Americans while delivering benefits to a thin strand of elites in North and South.

Excusing itself for the poor economic performance, the Fund has sometimes suggested that there have been a number of negative external factors (such as declining terms of trade) that are beyond its control. Yet if the Fund should receive no blame for negative external factors, then neither should the program countries; in short, this sort of self-defense really argues for a less restrictive conditionality than the Fund has applied. Moreover, the Fund's inability to alter the external environment—to force some Northern adjustment—is part of the problem. For despite the clear importance of external factors in the debt build-up and debt crisis, the IMF has stressed individual and purely domestic adjustment. These domestic policies have been particularly ineffective in the context of slowed core country growth, high real interest rates, falling terms of trade, and a credit embargo. Unable to force the requisite Northern adjustments, the IMF has instead ignored the *linked nature* of the crisis, a strategy that does not, however, cause the links to disappear.

Nor has the IMF evidenced any ability to steer Latin America toward a new development model that would be characterized by anything except perpetual crisis. Its project of austerity in the short-run impedes the investment necessary for long-run growth even as it deepens class conflict. Its recommendation to further develop export production, particularly of raw materials and foodstuffs, seems a recipe for future problems of market glut, particularly since the Fund has demonstrated little ability to prevent core country slowdown or protectionist pressures. As for the Fund's typical insistence on domestic "liberalization," the experience of the "successful" developing countries would seem to indicate that planning and not liberalization is the key even to a strategy geared toward external markets. In short, the IMF's restructuring project—short-run austerity, reorientation toward exports, and domestic liberalization—may have little future.

Of course, one cannot blame the dismal regional performance, the regressive redistribution, or the failure successfully to restructure entirely on the Fund. The crisis, as I noted earlier, has deep roots in the instability of the international monetary system, the slowdown in core country growth, and the exhausted structure of Latin American development models. But at the same time, the last few years did see a resurgence in the Fund's control over international capital flows to developing countries as well as the expansion of Fund influence over Latin American domestic macropolicy. So while it may be difficult to distinguish theoretically the "IMF effect" from the generalized crisis, the Fund cannot escape blame for the disaster of the last five years—particularly since the Fund has been unwilling and unable to deal with the key pressing issues: the need for both Northern adjustment and a new development alternative for Latin America. As a result, the IMF has become irrevocably associated in Latin America with austerity, stagnation, regressive redistribution, and often popular protest.

This close association of the IMF with low economic benefits and high political costs may be rendering the Fund increasingly exhausted as a vehicle for resolving the debt crisis. As a result, both South and North have begun to search for an alternative to the IMF and its policies. . . .

Whether such displacement of the Fund actually happens, of course, depends partly upon the desires of international finance capital. Certain actions—such as the recent moves by money center banks like CitiCorp setting aside reserves for loan write-downs while aggressively "swapping" debt for direct ownership of assets in Latin America—signal an attempt to go beyond the previous phase of IMF-coordinated "involuntary" lending. Yet banks are likely to continue pushing for the Fund to play a role in determining "responsible" macroeconomic policy in Latin America and may make short-term trade credit and debt "swapping" contingent upon IMF programs.

The future role of the Fund is also quite dependent on the internal politics and class structure of Latin America. I suggested above that the debt crisis involves a confrontation of classes as well as conflict between North and South. This is not simply because of the distributional patterns noted above but also because the new accumulation models that must be created in order for Latin America to exit this crisis will necessarily have a class character and basis.

In this sense, the Fund and its policies may also be analyzed as having a class character. In the 1970s, for example, IMF programs in Latin America were associated with wage repression coupled with increased access of national elites to foreign credit; this pattern both secured the allegiance of local ruling classes and cemented their relationship with international finance. . . . The IMF, in short, is not simply acting in the North's interest with policies designed to "deindustrialize" Latin America and maintain its adverse position in the international division of labor. The Fund and its policies are also benefiting various factions of local elites and maintaining their position of social and economic domination.

This implies that for the IMF and its policies to be rejected, it is not enough to argue that Latin America should stand up to the international bankers. Despite the current broad appeals for Latin unity against Western banks, none of the more radical proposals—full or partial repudiation, debt service limits, or mobilizing the foreign wealth of local elites—will be adopted without a redistribution of political power in Latin America. In the 1960s and 1970s, the Latin bourgeoisie resolved the difficulties of import-substitution industrialization by abandoning the nationalist project and reasserting their links with international capitalism. The result was a debt-dependent accumulation model, the inequities of which were often enforced by political authoritarianism. . . . If Latin America is to move truly beyond the IMF, internal factors—the social and class realities of the debtor nations—will play a crucial role.

D. Trade

The international trade regime constructed under American leadership after World War II and embodied in the General Agreement on Tariffs and Trade (GATT) has facilitated the emergence of the most open international economy in modern history. After World War II, political leaders in the United States and many other advanced industrialized countries believed, on the basis of their experience during the Great Depression of the 1930s, that protectionism contributes to depressions, depressions magnify political instability, and protectionism therefore leads to war. Drawing upon these beliefs, the United States led the postwar fight for a new trade regime to be based upon the liberal principle of comparative advantage. Tariffs were to be lowered, and each country would specialize in those goods that it produced best, trading for the products of other countries as necessary. To the extent that this goal was achieved, American decision makers and others believed that all countries would be better off and prosperity would be reinforced.

The American vision for the postwar trade regime was embodied in a plan for an International Trade Organization (ITO) to complement the International Monetary Fund. As originally presented in 1945, the American plan offered rules for all aspects of international trade relations. The Havana Charter creating the ITO was finally completed in 1947. A product of many international compromises, the Havana Charter was the subject of considerable domestic opposition within the United States. Republican protectionists opposed the treaty because it went too far. Free-trade groups failed to support it because it did not go far enough. President Harry Truman, knowing that it faced almost certain defeat, never submitted the Havana Charter to Congress for ratification. In the absence of American support, the nascent ITO died a quick and quiet death. The GATT was drawn up in 1947 to provide a basis for the trade negotiations then under way in Geneva. Intended merely as a temporary agreement to last only until the Havana Charter was fully implemented, the GATT became the principal basis for the international trade regime with the failure of the ITO

Despite its supposedly temporary status, the GATT has emerged as the most important international institution in the trade area. It is based upon four norms. First, all members of the GATT agree to extend unconditional most-favored-nation (MFN) status to one another. Under this agreement, no country will receive any preferential treatment not accorded to all other MFN countries. Additionally, any benefits acquired by one country are *automatically* extended to all MFN partners. The only exceptions to this rule are customs unions, such as the European Community.

Second, the GATT is based upon the norm of reciprocity, or the concept that any country that benefits from another's tariff reduction should reciprocate to an equivalent extent. This norm ensures "fair" and equitable tariff reductions by all countries. In conjunction with the MFN or nondiscrimination norm, it also serves to reinforce the downward spiral of tariffs initiated by the actions of any one country.

Third, "safeguards" or loopholes and exceptions to other norms are recognized as acceptable if they are temporary and imposed for short-term balance-of-payments reasons. Exceptions are also allowed for countries experiencing severe market disruptions from increased imports.

Fourth, in 1965, a development norm was added to the GATT that allowed (1) generalized systems of preferences (or unilateral and unreciprocated tariff reductions by developed countries on imports from their developing counterparts), (2) additional safeguards for "development" purposes, and (3) export subsidies by developing countries.

The GATT has been extremely successful in obtaining its declared goal of freer trade and lower tariffs. By the end of the Kennedy Round of GATT negotiations in 1967, which was initiated by President John F. Kennedy in 1962, tariffs on dutiable nonagricultural items had declined to approximately 10 percent in the advanced industrialized countries. In the Tokyo Round, concluded in 1979, tariffs in these same countries were reduced to approximately 5 percent. By the late 1970s, tariffs were only a relatively minor impediment to trade. These significant reductions initiated an era of unprecedented growth in international trade, the two most rapidly increasing areas of which are the overlapping ones of trade between advanced industrialized countries and intrafirm trade (the exchange of goods within, rather than between, corporations).

The GATT continues to be an active force for liberalization. In the late 1980s, the Uruguay Round began to focus on the thorny issues of services and agricultural trade, two areas of increasing interest to the United States and other countries which had been excluded from earlier negotiations. Governments have long regulated many of their domestic service industries—insurance, banking, and financial services for example. Often differing dramatically from country to country, these regulations have become one of the most politically contentious barriers to trade. Likewise, governments in most developed countries subsidize their agricultural sectors, leading to reduced imports and increasing surpluses which can only be managed through substantial sales abroad. Nearly all analysts agree that national and global welfare could be enhanced by reducing agricultural subsidies and returning to trade based upon the principle of comparative advantage; yet, politicians have found it difficult to resist demands from farmers for continued government intervention. Here, as in other areas, the tension between national wealth and the self-seeking demands of domestic interest groups have created a difficult diplomatic issue, but one which, after years of comparative neglect, is now on the GATT agenda.

At the same time that tariffs have been declining and trade increasing, however, new threats have emerged to the free-trade regime. With the success of the GATT, more and more industries have been exposed to increased international competition. Industry demands for some form of protection have multiplied in nearly all countries. Increasingly, governments seek to satisfy these demands for protection through nontariff barriers to trade (NTBs). The most important of these NTBs are voluntary export restraints (VERs), in which exporters agree to restrain or limit their sales in the importer's market. Current estimates suggest that almost one-half of all manufactured goods imported into the United States enter under a VER or other NTB. Nor is the United States alone. Nearly half of the non-Communist world's trade is subject to some form of nonmarket control. While the GATT regime has not been destroyed, it has certainly become weaker and more fragile.

The readings in this section address two broad issues. The first concerns the causes and implications of the recent trend toward increased protection in the United States. Three different theoretical perspectives are presented—all of which can be applied to other countries as well. Edward Ray summarizes recent trends and suggests that domestic interest groups are important determinants of the emerging pattern of protection (Reading 21). Robert Baldwin, on the other hand, relates the rise in protection to the decline of American hegemony. Both are relatively pessimistic on the future of the liberal international trade regime. Gerald Helleiner takes a different approach to explaining the current trade regime (Reading 22). Free trade, Helleiner argues in Reading 23, has generally been supported by the large multinational corporations, which require open international markets to take full advantage of their worldwide production capabilities. As capital has become internationalized, however, labor has increasingly turned toward protection in an effort to save jobs at home. Thus, trade politics have become increasingly divided along class lines. Helleiner, nonetheless, remains more sanguine on the likely future of free trade.

The second issue concerns the role of trade in the development strategies of the so-called Third World—countries which generally have, for a variety of reasons, either been excluded from or chosen not to participate in the GATT-based trade regime. Joan Robinson (Reading 24) examines the effects of trade in primary commodities on the possibilities for economic progress in developing countries, and finds that this strategy is generally not a formula for rapid growth. John Macomber (Reading 25) and Robin Broad and John Cavanagh (Reading 26) present contrasting views on the potential for export-led industrialization in the Third World. In recent years, considerable attention has been devoted to the East Asian Newly Industrializing Countries (South Korea, Taiwan, Hong Kong, and Singapore, also known as the NICs), rapidly growing economies which have adopted market-conforming, export-oriented industrial policies. For Macomber, a Liberal, the East Asian NICs provide a model which can and should be emulated by countries in Latin America. For Broad and Cavanagh, however, market saturation and, more important, the increasing protectionism of the developed economies limit the number of countries that can successfully pursue such strategies. This article, written from a dependency theory perspective, suggests how the actions and policies of the core capitalist countries can constrain the development opportunities available to states in the periphery.

21

Changing Patterns of Protectionism: The Fall in Tariffs and the Rise in Non-Tariff Barriers

EDWARD JOHN RAY

In this essay, Edward Ray seeks to explain the pattern of trade protection in the United States, both over time and across industries, and the recent rise of nontariff barriers to trade. He argues that trade policy is determined by both the general beliefs and policy positions of the government—in this case, that free trade is the socially optimal policy—and interest group pressures. At present, he concludes, the government of the United States continues to believe in the general efficacy of free trade, while interest groups have turned increasingly protectionist, resulting in an ambiguous policy of gradually expanding nontariff restrictions on trade.

I. INTRODUCTION

Repeating the current litany of concerns about an apparent rise in protectionist rhetoric in the United States and abroad is not the aim of this Article. Rather, its focus is on describing and explaining changes in the pattern of protectionism that have emerged in the United States and other industrialized nations since World War II through use of a simple analytical framework. With generous reference to the

---

21 "Changing Patterns of Protectionism: The Fall in Tariffs and the Rise in Non-Tariff Barriers" by Edward John Ray. Reprinted by special permission of Northwestern University, School of Law, 8, *Northwestern Journal of International Law and Business*, 285, (1988).

abundant literature on the political economy of trade restrictions, this Article also attempts to explain the shift in protectionism from tariff to non-tariff barriers over the last two decades. It also describes how the changing pattern of protectionism is likely to influence future trade policy in both the United States and abroad.

The model constructed in this Article explains how the efforts of special interest groups within a nation interact with its domestic political and foreign policy objectives to influence the nation's overall structure of trade regulations. Section II of the Article, therefore, begins by providing a simple analytical framework which can help to explain the evolution of both the pattern and the level of protectionism in the United States and other countries. Section III of the Article reviews the history of United States trade policy and summarizes the current economic and political climate for protectionist legislation in the United States. The Article will then expand its analysis in Section IV by attempting to explain historical events more fully in terms of the framework set out in Section II. Section V describes the reasons behind the growth in non-tariff barriers ("NTBs") over the past several decades.

II. AN ANALYTICAL FRAMEWORK

A. The Micro and Macro Views of Policy Decisionmaking

Historically, there have been two generally accepted explanations of how trade policy is determined. The first—the micro view—is that trade policy is the aggregate outcome of industry battles over protection; government policy simply mirrors the preferences of industrial constituents. The second—the macro view—is that the international policy of a given government may be difficult to trace back to individual industry interests. The central government acts as an independent agent reflecting aggregate or collective interests. In this view, national objectives are the primary determinants of domestic and international policies. National governments interact to determine international trade policies. In this context, protectionist positions are heavily influenced by the means available to nations for adjudicating trade disputes between countries.

Studies stressing the macro perspective have attempted to demonstrate how the mechanisms for adjudicating trade disputes between countries might be changed to move the United States and the rest of the world back toward a more consistent trade liberalization stance. Implicit in many of these papers is the notion that government trade policies are constrained by domestic concerns, such as full employment, price stability, and economic growth, that are not necessarily related to the wants of any particular interest group, but are of great concern to the populace as a whole. In this view, trade policy is an integral part of both national domestic policy and foreign policy.

The micro perspective presumes that special interest groups shape the pattern of protection within a given country. This perspective often leaves the impression that government policy is either a weighted sum of the preferences of special interest groups adopted in a passive fashion or the end product of a sinister calculation by a group of frightened politicians who are committed to nothing but keeping themselves in office.

While there are times when governments appear to behave in a way that is consistent with one or the other of these views, there is little evidence to suggest that either is superior to the other as a general model for predicting government behavior. Within the context of the Stigler-Peltzman-Becker framework, one can argue that in conjunction with the equilibrium distribution of rents established in a regulated market, there is in fact also a political equilibrium that is the product of both self-interest (the micro view) and shared values (the macro approach). This Article argues that contemporary trade policy is best understood in this light. That is, trade policy actually results from the interaction of self-promoting economic interest groups with national economic and political policies. These latter "national" policies represent shared or consensus values which are slow to change and thus are quite durable. This Article describes these values and their effectiveness in checking protectionist demands over the last decade.

B. A Combined Framework

What follows is a simple attempt to define an analytical framework with which one can analyze the post-war pattern of protectionism generally described in Section IV. The debate over trade policy in Congress in the last decade has resulted in the kind of policy drift consistent only with a genuine clash between long-held national principles and the pressures that are generated by special interest groups. The model proposed here is that United States trade policy is the joint product of these two clashing forces. This framework combines elements of both the micro and macro perspectives within it; both national political objectives and economic special interest groups play a significant role in defining trade policy.

The first step in demonstrating the model's efficacy is to show that shared national values actually exist. There is a great deal of evidence supporting this proposition, as seen in the hypothesis that governments in industrialized countries are committed to the shared value of providing a trade restriction safety net for weak industries. Two researchers have demonstrated empirically that declining industries not only were favored by minimal Kennedy Round tariff cuts, but were also given enhanced protection in the form of NTBs. In addition, it has been argued that shifts in United States trade policy, including the adoption of the Generalized System of Preferences ("GSP") and the Caribbean Basin Initiative ("CBI"), resulted from a national foreign policy commitment to aid developing nations trying to compete effectively for exports of manufactured goods. These programs are clearly inconsistent with the long-standing United States policy of adhering to the most favored nation ("MFN") principle. This inconsistency suggests an activist government that is not simply responding to special interests or voters.

Although the aforementioned policies suggest that shared values play an important role in decisionmaking, one must be aware that special interests are also a contributing factor. For example, there is evidence that special interest groups influenced the content of the GSP and effectively undermined its goal of opening up United States markets for key exports from developing countries. One might therefore be led to believe that United States policy is merely the servant of economic special interest groups, and that policies like the GSP and CBI are part of a cruel charade. A brief discussion of the "pure" special interest group model of trade policy decisionmaking is thus in order.

The special interest group model cannot be understood unless one is quite specific about the makeup of the various special interest groups which try to influence trade policy and which groups constitute the winners and losers. One important group is consumers, who always have an interest in freer trade for access to a variety of products at the least possible cost. In addition, highly competitive export-oriented firms and their workers will favor free trade because domestic trade restrictions may lead to retaliation from abroad and reduce foreign market access. In contrast, producers and workers in less competitive or import sensitive sectors of the economy will always favor protection. Trade restrictions can preserve jobs and protect profits that would otherwise be lost to foreign competitors.

Four modest extensions complete a summary of the key elements of all of the special interest models and aid in the construction of a paradigm. First, assume that consumers are a diverse group who cannot form an effective coalition to promote free trade, and the price of producing an effective lobby for protection increases with the size of the interested group. One may conclude that concentrated industries with a handful of dominant firms will be more effective in obtaining protection than industries with many small firms. Second, firms that purchase capital equipment or other intermediate goods abroad will surely favor freer trade for those goods. Third, these importing industries are likely to be more concentrated than consumers, creating a presumption that protection will be biased toward final consumer goods and away from intermediate inputs. Fourth, the government serves simply as the agent for all of these interests while pursuing a trade policy consistent with its own survival or electability.

The pure special interest model clearly presents an incomplete picture of how trade policy is formed, however. Most plainly, it ignores foreign policy. The United States-Israel and United States-Canada free trade agreements, and attempts to provide preferential access to United States markets for manufactured imports from developing countries through the GSP and the CBI, suggest that as a nation we have staked out international political positions which do not easily follow from the pure special interest model. The current battle between the executive branch and Congress over trade policy shows that at a time when special interest groups are quite outspoken in their demands for government trade relief, the government is working hard to maintain the nation's long-standing commitment to continued trade liberalization. This type of conflict cannot be explained by a model in which the government proceeds to make policy decisions based solely on its appraisal of the wishes of special interest groups.

In light of the foregoing, it becomes clear that the federal government, as a distinct, separate entity, is itself a key player in the trade policymaking process. Particular government actions are guided by established national policies subject to feedback from special interest groups. When both national preferences and special interest group preferences favor trade liberalization (as this Article will argue they did in the early post-World War II period), national policy will be unambiguously in favor of freer trade. When national preferences are for freer trade and competition, but special interest preferences are on balance protectionist (as this Article will argue they have been in recent years), United States policy on international trade will reflect the kind of ambiguity we are now observing. The presumption is that national policy can be turned away from the current pro-trade stance if a special interest group bias continues to remain strong for a number of years.

The primary distinction between the model proposed here and the normal special interest group models is that the government is explicitly included as an active player with a long-term agenda of its own. The government is sensitive to special interest group pressures but is not their captive. At the same time government policy is not unrelated to the concerns of special interest groups. If special interest group preferences persist in favoring a particular stand on trade issues, the national agenda may shift to adopt that position. This model highlights the dynamic interaction between individual and collective interests which is so important to an understanding of current United States policy. As this Article proceeds, the value of this model as an analytical tool will become increasingly apparent.

III. THE PATTERN OF PROTECTION IN THE UNITED STATES

The value of providing some historical perspective to any study of trade policy or protectionism is suggested by the now common caution that history does indeed repeat, but never in exactly the same way. Drawing simpleminded historical parallels can thus be as foolhardy as ignoring history altogether. If analyzed properly, however, history can provide useful insights. For example, in the late nineteenth century the United States built a world class navy in order to assume the role of a major player in international political affairs. Coincidentally, that same period say the emergence of major manufacturing sectors such as steel and textiles as serious competitors in world markets. That combination of national ambitions and private economic interests played a critical role in shifting United States trade policy away from highly protective tariffs toward freer trade at the turn of the last century.

In the late twentieth century the United States faces changed political and economic fortunes that threaten to end four decades of commitment to trade liberalization. The framework outlined above can explain these changes, if considered in the historical context of the last 100 years. The shift in political support toward protectionist legislation in the United States in the last decade, for example, is not without precedent. Political support for trade liberalization within the United States during the 1950s and 1960s is also not without precedent. A brief review of

United States history demonstrates how economic interest groups can and have reinforced or undermined federal government trade policies.

A recent study of trade policy in the United States during the last half of the nineteenth century identified a number of important relationships behind the trade policy of the time. First, contrary to the general thrust of United States trade policy throughout most of the post-World War II period, the United States pursued a policy of high tariffs throughout its period of rapid industrialization between 1870 and 1914. Based on a sample of 97 manufacturing industries (including every industry that proved to be significant in 1914), the average United States tariff rate was 45.8% in 1870, 40.6% in 1910 and 26.3% in 1914 following the substantial tariff cuts associated with the Underwood-Simmons Tariff Act of October 1913.

Second, . . . United States tariff policy appears to have been systematically geared to accommodate rapid industrialization. Specifically, the study found that tariff protection was concentrated on finished manufactured goods rather that intermediate goods. That same general strategy has been used by developing countries in this century to promote import substitution in manufacturing. While the results of contemporary cases are somewhat mixed, the historical evidence suggests that throughout the period from 1870 to 1914, those manufacturing sectors which were highly protected by the tariff structure in 1870 emerged as the most rapidly expanding industries in the United States. Finally, the study noted that tariffs were systematically higher on liquor, tobacco products, and other price inelastic commodities which one would expect to be reliable sources of federal government revenue at a time when tariffs funded well over half of the federal budget.

The point to emphasize is that during its industrialization period the United States was highly protectionist, used tariff policy to promote the growth of its manufacturing sector, and relied heavily on tariffs to fund central government programs. Those policies can be seen in many developing countries today and present a sharp contrast to the trade liberalization stance that the United States has professed for the last fifty years.

Except for the brief interval of time associated with the Smoot-Hawley Tariff of 1930, (resulting in tariffs reaching an all time high average of 59% in 1932), tariffs have declined steadily in the United States from 1914 to 1986 (when the General Agreement on Tariffs and Trade ("GATT") Tokyo Round tariff cuts were scheduled to be fully implemented). The rapid decline in United States tariffs from 59% in 1932, to a little over 7% after the implementation of the Kennedy Round tariff cuts by the early 1970s, paralleled changes in other industrialized nations and contributed to a genuine sense of progress toward free international trade. The model set forth in Section II should be able to explain how these changes came about.

Another important aspect of the pattern of protectionism in the past several decades is the growth in NTBs. Even before the Kennedy Round concluded, a number of authors noted either that: 1) the multilateral agreements were not providing substantial access to industrial country markets for the manufactured exports of developing countries; or 2) remaining NTBs might affect trade differently than would tariffs. Unfortunately, NTBs have yet to be successfully addressed in any of the GATT negotiating rounds. The negotiators at the Kennedy Round meetings abandoned their efforts to deal with NTBs when it became clear that their work on tariff cuts would warrant their full attention. The negotiators at the Tokyo Round did succeed in hammering out codes of conduct for the use of NTBs, but actual agreements to reduce them in line with tariff cuts remained for later rounds of multilateral negotiations.

The fact that international negotiations have not dealt effectively with NTBs is a crucial element in any explanation of the shifting pattern of protectionism in the last twenty-five years. If trade policy is determined by the impact of economic special interests within a country on the national political agenda through the political process, the outcome at any point will surely be influenced by underlying political and economic circumstances. Which positions ultimately prevail, however, will also depend upon the means available for controlling trade flows. This Article argues that as NTBs have become more effective and more prevalent protectionist devices, they have also increased the likelihood that protectionist interests will be successful in any given set of political and economic circumstances.

IV. EXPLAINING THE HISTORY OF PROTECTIONISM IN THE UNITED STATES

The changing pattern of protectionism in the United States over the course of the last century is not difficult to explain if one keeps the model set forth in Section II in mind. This model suggests that trade policies are ultimately defined by governments which act in accordance with shared social values subject to special interest group pressures. Changes in political and economic conditions and innovations in methods of protection contribute to changes in the protectionist regime within any given country. Applying the model to historical trends provides worthwhile examples of the changing nature of protectionism.

A. Partisan Politics and the Model

After the end of the Civil War, Congress was dominated by eastern economic interests which strongly supported rapid industrialization. This support produced a consensus that the United States should promote industrialization. The rapid industrialization that subsequently occurred undercut arguments that further protection was needed. Consequently, export interests became more important over time and, on balance, special interest groups favored free trade. This shift from protectionism to substantial trade liberalization took nearly twenty years. The sixteenth amendment to the United States Constitution, passed in 1913 and authorizing the collection of income taxes, resolved a conflict between the general consensus to liberalize trade and the need to finance rapidly expanding federal programs.

A striking paradox in United States trade policy that the proposed analytical framework must explain are the positions on trade policy which have historically been taken by the two primary political parties. Throughout the late nineteenth century, Democrats opposed the high tariffs adopted by Congress and fought to reduce them. Republicans were equally staunch in their support for high tariffs. By contrast, in the post-World War II era Democrats have systematically championed protectionist legislation over the objections of the Republicans. This apparent reversal of the major parties with respect to trade restrictions is explained by reference to the proposed model.

What has changed since World War II is not the respective parties' constituencies but rather the economic interests of those constituencies. Even before the depression of the 1930s solidified labor support for the Democrats, the basic division between Democrats and Republicans put farmers and industrial workers in the Democrat camp and business in the Republican camp. During the 1950s and early 1960s both Democrats and Republicans supported trade liberalization because United States agricultural and manufactured products dominated competition in world markets. Democrats, however, became divided on the trade issue during the late 1960s and early 1970s. It then became clear that despite continued United States competitiveness in agricultural products and capital equipment, some industries (like textiles, footwear, steel, and automobiles) were beginning to lose sales to foreign competitors. Democrats pushed programs to provide unemployment assistance to steel and auto workers, and they also supported trigger prices and quotas in steel and textiles. Although most of the push for protectionism has come from the Democrats, by the late 1970s Republicans from "rust belt" states (like Michigan, Ohio, Indiana, and Illinois) which were particularly affected by the decline in United States steel and auto sales, also supported relief from import competition. The positions of the two major political parties on trade issues have thus changed in response to the changing preferences of their constituent special interest groups; this shift lends credence to the model proposed above.

B. Historical Data and the Model

An examination of historical data highlights the long-term relationship between tariffs in the United States and key economic variables related to our model for the period 1913 to 1980. This relationship helps illustrate the direct and predictable link between changes in domestic and international economic conditions and United States trade policy over the course of the last century. Specifically, analysis shows that when special interests and national policies coincided to support or oppose trade restrictions, United States trade policies were unambiguous. When the net impact of special interest groups is poised in opposition to declared national policy on trade issues, as seems to be the case today, actual trade policy appears contradictory, ambiguous, or both.

It is clear that tariffs have declined substantially between 1913 and 1980, while per capita income has increased. A more careful look at the data makes it clear that rising incomes in the period from 1913 to 1920 were accompanied by tariff cuts from 17.4% to 6%. As income fluctuated during the 1920s and plummeted during the early 1930s, tariffs rose quickly to almost 12% in 1921 and a high of 24% in 1932. In 1933, average income reached a low point in the United States and, as incomes recovered throughout the post-World War II period, tariff rates generally declined. That inverse relationship between tariffs and incomes is consistent with the assumption that rising incomes are associated with increasing consumer preferences for product variety which consequently leads to pressure for liberalization in international trade.

Data from 1913 to 1980 illustrate the relationship between tariff protection and business cycles, as indicated by the occurrence of recessions in the United States economy in that period. Based on the model discussed in Section II, one would expect special interest groups to be most united against free trade when economic conditions are depressed and most solidly in favor of free trade during relatively prosperous times and the data bear out this expectation. Tariffs increased with the recession of 1921 and 1922 and with the beginning of the depression in 1930. Until 1939, the average tariff rate on imports did not fall below the pre-Depression 1929 level of 13.5%. The consequent steady decline in tariffs ended during the recession in 1950, and tariffs rose slightly in 1951. Similarly, tariffs increased slightly during the recessions of 1958 and 1974-75 and following the recession in 1961.

Economic declines, and the job losses and business failures that they inevitably bring, have served to rally support for restrictions on international trade. It is therefore not surprising that pressures to restrict trade were less during the 1950s and 1960s, when recessions were less frequent and severe, than during the 1970s and early 1980s, when the United States experienced its most severe recessions since World War II.

An interesting relationship also exists between tariff protection and the relative commodity export strength of the United States in international trade. This relationship once again highlights the association between special interest group demands for protection from import competition and the ability of United States firms to compete. One expects support for trade liberalization to increase and fall in concert with the success or failure of United States companies in selling more goods and services abroad than foreigners sell in the United States. This expectation, too, is supported by the data. For every year from 1936 to 1970, net merchandise exports from the United States were positive and often quite high relative to the sum of imports and exports. The relative net export figure averaged 37.7% during the 1940s, 10.7% during the 1950s, and 9.8% during the 1960s. During the early postwar period, the United States took the lead in promoting trade liberalization, not only because of its advantage in international competitiveness, but also because this stance helped achieve the foreign policy goals of re-industrializing war-torn Europe and Japan and including developing nations as trading partners in the world economy. In the context of the framework set forth above, it is worth noting that throughout the 1950s and the 1960s these foreign policy goals reinforced the international economic interests of the highly competitive United States business community.

Tariff movements and changes in the relative size of the trade sector in the United States since 1913 also bear out the usefulness of the model. Over this period, the larger the trade sector was (compared to the overall economy), the stronger the special interest group concern, and the more likely it was that domestic economic conditions would be linked to trade policies.

These observations follow directly from the argument in Section II that trade policy is the result of government enforced consensus policies tempered by the influence of special interest groups. This argument is further supported by recent trends in the relative net export figures of the United States. In contrast to prosperous post-World War II years, the United States relative net exports dropped to -4.2% during the 1970s, and was -16.0% from 1981 through 1986. Moreover, the net merchandise export position for the United States has been negative for each of the last ten years. It is therefore no accident that the United States commitment to liberalization has seemed less certain over this period. In fact, based on the framework set forth in Section II and earlier in this section, one would have expected the recent deterioration in the net merchandise export position of the United States to have generated special interest group efforts to undermine commitment to trade liberalization. This is exactly what happened.

The rapid deterioration in the merchandise export position of the United States since the mid-1970s has created a collision of interests between trade sensitive industries and government. That conflict is evident in the current disagreement between the Congress and the executive branch over trade policy. In addition, it is worth noting that the rapid expansion in the relative size of the trade sector over the past twenty years represents a return to pre-World War II proportions. During that period tariffs averaged well over 10%, and domestic economic problems were closely identified with international economic conditions. This rapid growth of the trade sector—accompanied by a deterioration in the United States trade balance and the two worst recessions since World War II—has fueled the protectionist argument that our domestic economic problems are somehow the fault of our trading partners. Because tariff increases are prohibited by the GATT agreements, protectionism has had to take the form of NTBs since the 1970s.

By the mid-1970s it was clear that while tariffs were declining in the United States and other industrial countries, there remained systematic differences in protection across industries. However, there was no consensus that NTBs were a serious threat to further trade liberalization. Further, there was no particular concern that NTBs might disguise the extent of protectionism and thereby foster a false perception among policy makers that gains in international economic cooperation were actually being achieved. It was not until the emergence of national and international economic crises in the late 1970s that the power of special interest groups in setting trade policies and the effectiveness of NTB protectionism was recognized.

V. THE SHIFT FROM TARIFFS TO NON-TARIFF BARRIERS

A. The Growth in Non-Tariff Barriers

The rise of NTBs as trade restriction devices over the past several decades is a development inextricably linked to governmental preferences as to the form of protection for import sensitive industries. While protection in general was diminishing among industrial countries in the early post-World War II period, the trade restrictions known as NTBs were expanding in several specific areas. For example, in 1956 the United States persuaded Japan to adopt one type of NTB, a voluntary export restraint ("VER"), on exports of cotton textiles to the United States; the United Kingdom concluded a similar agreement with Hong Kong.

There are numerous other examples of NTBs in the post-World War II era. A number of factors help explain this shift in trade policy. The first is that the existence of effective income tax systems in the industrialized countries makes them less dependent on the use of tariffs to finance central government operations than is the case for most developing nations. Second, as explained below, special interest groups that are too large to win tariff protection (because of public resentment) may be able to secure NTBs. These demands for protection, along with the relatively greater number of trade restrictions that are available to industrial country governments, make the industrialized nations likely candidates for the adoption of innovations in NTBs. Finally, there is always some domestic and international political advantage to being able to assist special interests in a less publicizable way. NTBs have the advantage of being more difficult to assess in terms of winners and losers and their general welfare effects. For these reasons, industrial countries that are not required to use tariffs for revenue purposes and prefer the political advantages of NTBs in masking government support for special interest groups are likely to prefer NTBs to tariffs.

The first factor in the industrialized nations' shift to NTBs is the fact that these countries no longer require tariff-related income. Historically, the development of nation-states meant that central governments needed funding. Tariff revenues were one fairly easy way to get that funding. It was not until the early twentieth century that tariffs ceased to provide the majority of federal government revenue in the United States. In many developing countries, tariffs continue to play a major role in financing national government expenditures. It is therefore not surprising that developing countries still rely more heavily on tariffs than do the industrialized nations. Nor is it surprising that, once freed of the need for tariff-generated revenues, the industrialized nations would lead the way in developing NTB innovations for regulating international trade.

A number of historical examples illustrate the link between the need for revenues and the existence of tariffs. First, trade liberalization in England in the 1840s occurred only after the central government instituted an income tax system. A second example is found in the United States. One of the most hotly contested domestic political issues during the 1890s was whether the expanding economic role of the central government should be financed primarily with tariff revenues or through the adoption of an income tax system. The ratification of the sixteenth amendment in 1913 was a critical factor in the first dramatic tariff cuts in the United States in over fifty years.

The second advantage of NTBs is that while GATT is equally outspoken in its condemnation of tariff and NTB restrictions on trade, it has been much easier to ascertain the quantitative effects of tariffs than it has been to gauge the effect of NTBs like product standardization requirements, government procurement practices, and others. Therefore, as successive GATT rounds achieved further reductions in tariff rates, NTBs were used either to support already weak industries, or compensate industries that were adversely affected by tariff cuts. That shift is evidenced by multifiber agreements beginning in the early 1960s and in the NTB protection given to the footwear, steel, and auto industries.

A third explanation for the rise in NTBs is that they can be used effectively by special interest groups incapable of getting government support for tariff protection. One study provides empirical support for the notion that, other things being equal, NTBs are found predominantly among less concentrated industries. The importance of this finding derives from this Article's earlier assumption that concentrated industries with a small number of dominant firms have been most successful in gaining government trade protection, and that less concentrated multifirm industries are notably less successful. The study's findings suggest, however, that where NTBs are at issue rather than tariffs, effective coalitions with even large numbers of participants are quite possible, and more likely to be successful.

There is at least one other plausible explanation for the rise in NTB's. Consider an industry composed of fifty firms that are each losing domestic sales to foreign firms and therefore have a collective interest in getting the government to restrict imports with a tariff on foreign goods. One problem which the group faces is a firm's electing not to help in the lobbying effort, thereby benefiting from the reduction in foreign competition along with the other forty-nine which worked for that outcome. The one firm is therefore a free rider because it benefits from the collective effort of the other producers without bearing any of the costs. The more firms there are in an industry, the more likely it is that the free rider problem will prevent an effective coalition from being formed because each of the fifty firms has an incentive to try to get others to do the work and be a free rider.

If, however, the same group of fifty firms could get the government to restrict imports of competitive goods and distribute import licenses among those producers that participated in the coalition to limit imports, the group would have a means by which it could reward participants and exclude free riders. In this case, each participant in the coalition gains not only the benefits of reduced foreign competition but also part of the economic rent which would have gone to the government with a tariff (in this case, excess price) associated with the domestic sale of foreign goods. Firms which try to free ride will still benefit from the increased price of foreign goods but can be prevented from importing and selling foreign goods at the higher domestic price. They will not capture any of the tariff equivalent rents generated by the quota. This reduces the free rider problem substantially and enhances the prospects for a successful coalition.

Another example of an NTB would be "buy American" government purchase plans which provide government contracts to domestic firms that lobbied for the program while excluding free riders from access to those government contracts. Large coalitions which could not get tariff protection might succeed in getting "buy American" status associated with their products. What is disturbing is that the relatively greater effectiveness of NTBs as means of regarding participants and excluding free riders may increase the overall extent to which protection is granted to domestic industries.

B. Empirical Evidence for the Rise in Non-Tariff Barriers

The GATT Kennedy Round failed to deal with the problem of NTBs and focused instead on tariff reduction. The Tokyo Round developed codes with respect to the *use* of NTBs, but left the issue of how to dismantle them for later GATT rounds. In effect, then, these Rounds left countries free to develop NTBs as a response to domestic political economic interests.

A pair of studies found clear evidence of this, demonstrating first that NTBs had been used in the United States and abroad to substitute for lost tariff protection resulting from the Kennedy Round, and second, that NTBs were systematically used to complement tariff protection in industries which were already receiving relatively high tariff protection. These studies indicated that industries which had the highest tariff rates before the Kennedy Round still had the highest tariff rates after the round was implemented. Furthermore, NTBs introduced during the late 1960s and 1970s did not go to industries with low tariff rates after the Kennedy Round; rather, NTB protection was given to those industries which benefited most from tariff protection before and after the Kennedy Round.

Another study provided a more precise test of the substitution and complementary protective effects of NTBs which were implemented in response to the Kennedy Round tariff cuts. The study demonstrated that industries (like steel, textiles, processed foods, and consumer durables) which experienced small if any tariff cuts during the Kennedy Round were precisely the industries which gained NTB protection. In short, NTBs were not used only to substitute for the general loss of tariff protection but also to increase protection for industries least affected by Kennedy Round tariff cuts. One can conclude, therefore, that the Kennedy Round was more effective in changing the *form* of protectionism than in changing the *relative level* of protectionism.

C. Voluntary Export Restraints

There is one NTB innovation particularly worth mentioning in the current context. The VER poses a particular problem for international trade negotiations. Although GATT explicitly condemns the use of quantitative trade restrictions (and allows for retaliatory sanctions by injured parties), it is difficult to imagine a means of policing self-imposed export restrictions negotiated bilaterally. VERs effectively bribe foreign governments and producers with tariff-equivalent revenue if they agree to limit exports. This system avoids open confrontations that ordinary quotas invite, and, as in the case of Japanese restrictions on automobile exports to the United States, can be worth billions of dollars to exporters and to the government of the exporting country. Since VERs produce transfers of wealth to the exporting country, these exporters are unlikely to complain to the GATT Council. This in turns suggests that VERs are likely to become the trade restriction of choice for all but the poorest nations.

Moreover, in contrast to tariffs and multilateral quotas, VERs are extremely well suited to the needs of special interest groups seeking protection. First, they are bilateral agreements worked out by consenting rather than competing nations. They can be structured to provide protection to import sensitive industries and to provide rents to both governments and producers in the exporting countries. This means that producers in both the importing and exporting countries can collude with their governments in restraining competition and capturing monopoly rents at the expense of the consuming public. VERs present no incentive for retaliation and GATT has no effective means for preventing such collusive agreements. Multilateral tariffs and quotas, on the other hand, are likely to generate retaliation; this possibility reduces the likelihood that special interest groups within a country will succeed in having them adopted.

United States trade policy has become clouded by the conflict between protectionist groups and the free trade oriented government. Despite the vacillations, however, the severity of the protectionist threat is easily underestimated. NTBs are an especially dangerous weapon in the protectionist arsenal. The fact that NTBs can reduce the free rider problem and increase the likelihood that special interest groups will be successful in their quest for protection means that NTBs markedly enhance the protectionist threat.

This point is important and bears repetition. Imposing tariffs is a hostile economic action, multilateral in effect and easily observed. Given the common desire of developed nations to liberalize trade after World War II, the GATT member states had no trouble rejecting unilateral impositions of tariffs without just cause. So effective was this commitment that tariffs declined dramatically throughout the period. Special interest groups seeking added tariff protection for their industries generally failed in their efforts because of the obvious international economic and political harm. Multilateral quotas have many of the same characteristics as tariffs and are not a likely vehicle for successful protection. VERs, on the contrary, are not multilateral in effect and are not likely to draw complaints from the participating countries. They are therefore likely to become an increasingly popular protectionist vehicle and deserve close observation. . . .

VII. CONCLUSION

In conclusion, it seems clear that the period of United States dominance in international economic competition is over, and with it the unanimity with which United States politicians pushed for trade liberalization in the early post-World War

II period. It is also clear that NTB innovations to restrict trade have had the net effect of strengthening protectionist interests. On balance, however, the continued growth within the United States and the accompanying decline in the unemployment rate to 6% by August 1987 has reduced the pressure to use protectionist measures to provide a safety net for industries and workers. The decline in the dollar has already begun to reduce the commodity trade deficit and moderate the impact of special interest groups. Thus, the United States has not abandoned its commitment to further trade liberalization, although the commitment does remain somewhat shaky.

The world seems poised for a long struggle over international economic cooperation, however. Without greater growth rates in industrial and developing countries, the drive to liberalize world trade will be thwarted by special interest groups. Yet without further—and genuine—liberalization in world trade, the prospects for accelerated real growth rates are not good. It is hoped that this article has identified some of the factors that determine the nature of the ongoing struggle between free trade and protectionist interests, and shown the importance of NTBs as hindrances to further world economic growth. While this work may not provide the answers, it may provide conceptual tools with which to face the problem.

22

Transnational Enterprises and the New Political Economy of U.S. Trade Policy

G. K. HELLEINER

In this reading, G. K. Helleiner develops an interest-group-based explanation of recent American trade policy. He notes a number of changes in the contemporary political lineup within the United States on trade issues—labor has, for example, abandoned its traditional free-trade orientation—and proposes an explanation based on the rise of the multinational corporation. Multinational enterprises, Helleiner points out, have an interest in the freest possible movement of their goods, services and capital across borders; they thus support economic openness both in their sectors and more generally. American labor, on the other hand, has been weakened by the rise of the multinational corporation and is attempting to protect itself with trade barriers. The two crucial interests in American trade policy disputes, then, are labor and multinational corporations; Helleiner generally regards the corporations as more likely to predominate in the conflict.

1. INTRODUCTION

Little of the orthodox literature of the theory of international trade addresses the question of the political sources of trade policies. The various arguments for the use of trade barriers are typically considered from the standpoint of 'the national interest' and, on the basis of conventional assumptions, the conclusion is reached

---

22 "Transnational Enterprises and the New Political Economy of U.S. Trade Policy" by G.K. Helleiner. © Oxford University Press, 1977. Reprinted from *Oxford Economic Papers*, Vol. 29, No. 1 (1977), pp. 102-116, by permission of Oxford University Press.

that in all instances other than those where the terms of trade can be favourably altered, trade barriers are harmful to 'the nation' or are second-best means of attaining the stipulated 'national' objectives. The state is perceived as the representative of the collectivity of individuals and firms within the nation, for whom it (somehow) acts to maximize their collective welfare. There exists some discussion in this theoretical literature of the effects of trade barriers upon the distribution of the national income, but it is typically based upon crude two-factor assumptions which are not too illuminating for the understanding of empirically observable phenomena.

Among the few 'modern' trade economists who attempted, fairly early on, to explore the behaviour of the state with respect to international trade was Charles Kindleberger who, some 25 years ago, wrote a stimulating paper on group behaviour and trade policies in the late nineteenth century in such countries as Germany, Denmark, and the U.K. The state, he argued, was not 'neutral' and it, in effect, pursued the interests of powerful groups.[1] In recent years, these issues have been further explored in both theoretical and empirical terms with particular reference to the American context. This paper attempts to explore some of the roots of recent U.S. commercial policies and, in particular, to consider the implications of the rise of the U.S.-based multinational corporation for them. Implicit in the analysis which follows is a theory of the U.S. state which assumes that directly involved interests, of varying power and influence, bring pressure to bear upon the various institutions of government which form trade policy. The policy which results reflects the divergent strengths of these interests rather than the 'social welfare', however defined, of the United States.

2. THE STRUCTURE OF TRADE BARRIERS IN THE U.S.

. . . One observes, first of all, some major recent shifts in traditional U.S. political attitudes towards international trade and trade barriers:

1. U.S. organized labour (represented by the AFL-CIO) has shifted its over-all position from one of liberalism to one of protectionism.
2. The traditional trade policy stances of the major political parties have been reversed; the Democratic Party has become more protectionist than the Republican Party.
3. Such representations as are made by business interests on the subjects of trade policy have become much more focused and industry-specific; pressures both for liberal trading policies and for protection are now more frequently offered by *particular* industry representatives rather than by broad-based cross-industry associations.
4. Labour and industry positions on trade policy *within the same industry* are now frequently at odds whereas traditionally they have typically been congruent.

Traditional studies of the politics of U.S. trade policies have concentrated on the functioning of lobbies, the attitudes of businessmen and politicians, the regional and/or sectional roots of the political parties and their consequent positions, and so forth. There have as yet been none which specifically take full account of the growing influence of the U.S.-based transnational enterprise. Yet, so far as an understanding of postwar U.S. international economic policy is concerned, the most significant new factor has been its rapid emergence, which has profoundly altered the structure of international exchange. The political changes described above can all be explained in terms of the rise of the U.S.-based transnational enterprise and the response of the U.S. labour movement to it. The next two sections outline the interests of these enterprises and of labour, respectively, in order to provide the background to such an explanation.

3. TRANSNATIONAL ENTERPRISES AND U.S. TRADE POLICY

There has recently been very rapid growth of 'international production' under the auspices of multinational firms; whereas in 1939 the value of international production made up only one-third of that of international trade, by 1970 the former exceeded the latter. A remarkably high proportion of international trade now takes place on an intrafirm basis in oligopolistically organized markets. The intrafirm trade is additional to the intra-industry trade which has also been widely remarked upon in recent years. The latter is the consequence primarily of differentiation in the final product and of inadequately detailed commodity classification systems. The intrafirm trade is, instead, associated with trade in intermediate products, technology gaps, and oligopoly. Intrafirm trade in intermediate goods and services stems from the fact that the markets for them are typically highly imperfect. In order to reduce search and transactions costs and to ensure their own maximum share of available quasi-rents, in these various imperfect markets, firms have every incentive to internalize transactions in them.

A detailed census for 1966 and a sample survey of 298 major U.S.-owned multinational firms (and their 5,237 majority-owned foreign affiliates) in 1970 have provided the first major compilation of data with respect to the dimensions and composition of U.S. international intrafirm trade.[2] These data indicate that in 1966, 66 per cent of total U.S. exports and 46 per cent of total U.S. imports were associated with U.S.-based transnational enterprises; these figures include transactions between U.S. residents who were not majority owners of overseas affiliates and U.S.-owned affiliates, and those between U.S. firms and foreigners who were not majority-owned affiliates. It seems reasonable to assume, however, that a considerable proportion of these latter transactions are, in fact, between enterprises with some form of link, e.g. minority ownership, licensing agreements, etc. An absolute lower bound on the relative dimensions of U.S. intrafirm trade is given by the proportions of total trade accounted for by trade between U.S. transnational enterprises and their own majority-owned affiliates: 21 per cent for exports and 16 per cent for imports in 1970.

Between 1966 and 1970, the trade associated with 298 multinational corporations (MNCs) which responded to the survey (and which accounted for over 70 per cent of total MNC-associated trade in 1966) rose more quickly than total U.S. trade—both in terms of export and import values. The trade between majority-owned foreign affiliates and U.S. parent firms grew most quickly of all. Between 1966 and 1970, while total U.S. imports grew by 56.3 per cent, imports by U.S. multinational firms from their own affiliates grew by 92.2 per cent in the manufacturing sector and by 81.9 per cent over all. (On the export side, the corresponding figures were: 43.3 per cent for total exports, 68.2 per cent for intrafirm manufacturing, and 71.2 per cent for intrafirm over all.) This relative increase in the importance of intrafirm and MNC associated trade is found in both exports and imports. This suggests that intrafirm trade and the role of the transnational enterprise in trade is growing as part of a structural alteration in the mode of organizing the world's industry and not because of some chance correlation with industries experiencing particular characteristics.

Although transnational enterprises can be extremely adaptive and quick to respond to governmental policy shifts, they are none the less not without preferences of their own with respect to official policies. As powerful pressure groups they can be expected to seek to influence governmental policy in all the countries in which they operate, either through direct lobbying or through less direct means. U.S.-based multinational firms are sure to exert powerful influence upon the formation of U.S. commercial policy (as well as a wide range of other foreign economic and political policies). What, then, are these firms likely to want?

In their efforts to rationalize their world-wide activities and so maximize their long-run profits, national boundaries are decided nuisances to them. They involve the payment of customs duties, the meeting of various administrative requirements (particularly those relating to currency controls), frequent prohibitions or regulatory mechanisms, and the complications introduced by differential (and sometimes conflicting) tax and other legal stipulations. All of these impediments to the free flow of intrafirm resources can be regarded as analogous to transport costs for the purpose of optimizing a firm's world-wide operations. Like transport costs, these international barriers are less troublesome (and costly) when they are lower. One cannot therefore be surprised to find multinational firms acting as strong general advocates of freedom in international exchange and payments. Openness with respect to financial and human capital flows and technology trade is obviously no less important to them than free trade in goods and services. (As the U.S. shifts to the export of services, freedom in these respects will increasingly be in the U.S. national interest as well.) Indeed, the links between factor flows and goods flows are so close, in the context of a particular multinational firm's operations, as to be inseparable; the firm's decision as to whether to service a foreign market by exporting or producing abroad, for example, is largely a function of the barriers to goods, technology, and investment flows between the countries in question.

Still at the general level, firms with international interests have a further reason for opposing barriers to international flows imposed by the government of their own home country. Not only may these barriers impede their activities directly but, even where they do not, they may also stimulate foreign countries in which they are active to retaliatory action against either their exporting or investing activities (which may be in sectors unrelated to those in which the original action was taken). The survey already mentioned, of 298 of the biggest U.S.-based transnational manufacturing enterprises, found that on average, in 1970, they serviced foreign markets through overseas production to a (sales) value which was 2-3 times as large as that of their exports to these countries.[3] Thus their concerns with respect to retaliation are likely to be less focused upon trade than upon investment.

At a more specific level, what sort of trade policies should a particular transnational enterprise be most interested in? Above all, it seeks to avoid paying taxes or encountering other obstacles to intrafirm transactions.... One must therefore know what are the goods and services which are internationally traded by the firm in question. In general, it seems safe to say, primary inputs and intermediate products dominate intrafirm international trade. There is also evidence that products traded internationally within U.S.-based firms are relatively capital intensive and research-intensive.

4. LABOUR AND U.S. TRADE POLICY

Were skilled and semi-skilled labour homogeneous and sold on perfect markets, it would always have made perfect sense for U.S. trade unions to seek to protect their members' income by restricting international exchange. They would gain both from the restriction of imports (and of labour itself) from countries in which labour is relatively more abundant, and from the restriction of outflows of capital and technology from the U.S. to such countries. This is because unskilled and semi-skilled labour is the relatively scarce factor in the U.S., or, in the context of a world of mobile capital and technology, because it is paid at very high rates by international standards. Their behaviour in recent years is thus fully in accord with the tenets of orthodox factor endowment theory, even though its assumptions are not, on the face of it, even approximately matched by the reality of either factor or product markets. It is not necessary to demonstrate . . . that the AFL-CIO is not representative of U.S. labour to explain its actions. What rather seems to require explanation is why the U.S. labour movement was previously so liberal in its approach to international trade.

One could postulate that U.S. labour was impressed by the exponents of the view that trade barriers caused or rendered more serious the depression of the 1930s, a repetition of which they wanted at all costs to avoid. An equally good explanation for earlier liberal positions could run in terms of the existence of non-competing groups—differentiated by skills, by industries, and by regions—which would render important the question of the representativeness of labour spokesmen.

Bergsten's data show convincingly that a majority of the membership of the AFL-CIO is *not* in industries directly affected by international trade; 56 per cent of the membership is not even in manufacturing.[4] This fact alone could account for organized labour's prior opposition to protectionism.

If the latter explanation is correct, the recent alteration in position must derive from some *change* in the international environment since the composition of the membership has not recently altered significantly. Such a change is the emergence of the transnational enterprise, which has significantly weakened the position of the scarce factor labour, in every U.S. industry.... Labour is obviously particularly concerned with the implications of international trade in those firms and sectors in which there is little prospect of expanded intra-industry trade (notably where competing imports originate in less developed countries) and therefore employment gains to offset the possible job losses from imports.

5. THE NEW POLITICAL ECONOMY OF U.S. TRADE POLICY

The revised line-up of the two traditional political parties reflects the new elements of the political and economic scene. As the party of labour, the Democrats—despite their liberal traditions—have followed labour's shift toward protectionism. The business-oriented Republican party, now responsive to the needs of U.S.-based transnational enterprises, has become the party of liberalization in trade.... Both are highly receptive to the special cases made by particular industries; wherever labour and capital are still allied in seeking protection (wherever, that is, the firms in question have few international connections), both favour protection. Where in a particular industry, however, unions face a transnational enterprise, the conflict generally is resolved in favour of the latter.

U.S. trade policy is thus now being determined with reference to two main contributing thrusts: (1) that of organized labour which presses most vigorously for the maintenance or increase of protection in those industries in which labour is most vulnerable; (2) that of U.S.-based transnational enterprises, which press most vigorously for trade barrier reductions in those commodity classifications in which they themselves trade, and show no particular interest in those relatively labour-intensive and declining industries in which they are not directly involved. The result of these twin pressures, of which the latter is more powerful, is that particular combination of liberalization and protectionism which has, in fact, emerged.

This interpretation is supported by several pieces of suggestive evidence.

1. It is well known that import duties upon primary and intermediate products are typically lower than average duties on final products. Whether such products dominate intrafirm international trade because import duties on these products are typically lower or whether the duties are lower precisely because of the pressure from the producing firms to this effect cannot be firmly proven, but the presumption is usually that the causation runs in the latter direction. Only where there are already local producers of the inputs can there be any political pressure for duties or other

protection on them; once they are imposed, the transnational enterprises are among those thereby stimulated to produce inputs locally rather than continuing to import or buying at arm's length from local suppliers, and if this local production is subsequently taken over by internationally-oriented firms, pressure for continued protection can be expected to decline.

2. This escalation in the tariff as one moves from primary to processing activities could also be interpreted more simply—as a reflection of the frequent total absence of U.S. production of certain raw materials and the consequent absence of protectionist pressures. But if the latter simpler explanation is accepted, one still requires an explanation for the usual continued escalation from semi-processed to processed and more manufactured goods, for the semi-processed product can be, and frequently is, made locally with imported (tariff-free) materials. One would expect, other things being equal, political pressure from these local producers to generate just as much protection as that achieved for local raw materials or local final products. The fact that this is not, in fact, typically found suggests that the pressures from the users are relatively more effective than those from these particular producers. Presumably, this is at least partially explained by the fact that these local producers, particularly in the case of new products, are themselves often vertically integrated with the eventual (often transnational) users, to whom the duty on the input is of no protective significance. (In political terms, one might also note the likelihood that using firms will be considerably more geographically dispersed within the country, and thereby able to influence more Congressional voters, than the original semi-processing firm itself.) One can, then, explain this particular escalation in terms of the political power of transnational enterprises the bulk of whose intrafirm trade is in such intermediate products.

3. Since capital-intensity and research-intensity characterize the products which are traded across international borders within U.S.-based firms, the facts that U.S. trade barriers are lower and Kennedy Round reductions were greater in such products also support the view that transnational enterprises have been influential in the determination of the structure of U.S. trade barriers. U.S. production of labour-intensive products in which these firms do not trade has clearly been relatively well protected in consequence of unopposed labour pressure.

4. The creation of value added tariffs in the U.S. (duties levied upon the difference between the gross value of the products concerned and the value of inputs originating in the U.S., permitted under items 806.30 and 807.00 of the tariff schedule) reflects the same political pressures. The only firms capable of employing such provisions are the transnationally oriented ones, although in this case these include trading firms as well as manufacturers. There has been a remarkably rapid rate of growth in the use of the 807.00 provision, since its introduction in the second half of the 1960s. Imports under the terms of item 807.00 have risen fivefold from 1966 to 1974.[5] Even in the recession year 1974, dutiable value under this item rose by 26 per cent. In 1974, fully 94 per cent of this total dutiable value was found in the multinational-firm dominated metal products group (notably, motor vehicles, engines, office machines, radio and television apparatus, semiconductors, aircraft,

electronic memories, sewing machines, etc.). It is noteworthy that despite vigorous opposition to these provisions in the U.S. tariff on the part of the AFL-CIO they remain firmly in place. The presumption is that they do so because they generate substantial gains for politically powerful interests, the transnational enterprises, which more than offset these pressures from labour. At the industry level, where labour and capital are at odds in their approaches to the policymakers, so far, the preferences of the latter prevail.

5. A further striking example of the political strength of the transnational enterprise in the formation of U.S. (actually of North American) trade policy is the U.S.-Canadian auto agreement. While its origins lay in the desire of the Canadian Government to increase Canada's share of North American automobile production, the agreement reached was one peculiarly favourable to the transnational automobile industry. It provided for free trade in automobiles and automobile parts but, in the Canadian case, it was available *only to the producing firms* and not to Canadian consumers. (In the U.S. case, the deal actually required a special waiver from the provisions of the GATT because of its specific exclusion of third-country firms.) The agreement permitted a substantial rationalization of the North American automobile industry while offering significant continued price support for automobiles in Canada. Potential opposition from the labour movement in the U.S. (the UAW) was, in this case, bought off by a fairly liberal adjustment assistance programme, considerably more liberal in its effects than that developed for the Kennedy Round.

6. To some extent, the bias in trade barriers against products which are not traded by transnational enterprises extends to the trade in IOUs as well, that is, to capital markets. While the U.S. Government offers investment guarantees and insurance, and tax deferrals, for direct investors overseas, there are no corresponding encouragements to the importation by arm's-length U.S. investors of foreign bonds. (IBRD bonds seem to be the exception proving the rule.) To the contrary, there exists legislation in many states limiting or prohibiting the holding of foreign securities in the portfolios of banks, insurance companies, and pension funds. The effect is to discriminate in favour of capital flows which are intermediated by the transnational enterprise. . . .

CONCLUSION

This paper has been concerned to develop a pressure group approach to the understanding of recent U.S. trade policy. It has argued that the shift in the attitudes towards trade of the traditional political parties and the labour movement, and the increased differentiation of business attitudes thereto, are best interpreted as responses to the development of U.S.-based transnational enterprises in the postwar period. U.S. trade policy is now the product primarily of the political pressures from transnational enterprises on the one hand and organized labour on the other. Where these interests are in conflict in particular industries, the evidence suggests that the former will usually win out, and liberal trade policies will be pursued. Where U.S. firms are not internationally oriented, however, they are likely to ally with labour and to achieve some success in generating protection from competitive imports. Since the new political forces operative in the U.S. are likely to be replicated in other industrialized countries, the 'model' presented here may be of wider relevance.

NOTES

1. C. P. Kindleberger, "Group behaviour and international trade", *Journal of Political Economy,* vol. 59, no. 1, Feb. 1951.

2. Betty L. Barker, "U.S. foreign trade associated with U.S. multinational companies" *Survey of Current Business,* Dec. 1972. The data which follow are all taken from this source.

3. Ibid.

4. C. Fred Bergsten, "The cost of import restrictions to American consumers", in Robert Baldwin and J. D. Ricardson (eds.), *International Trade and Finance* (Boston: Little, Brown 1974), pp. 136-7.

5. These data were supplied by the U.S. International Trade Commission.

23

The New Protectionism: A Response to Shifts in National Economic Power

ROBERT BALDWIN

This economist argues that the post-war liberal order was a function of U.S. economic and political hegemony. Because freer trade was beneficial to the United States, the U.S. led the world toward this goal. In recent years, however, there have been a number of structural changes in the world economy, especially the decline in U.S. competitiveness and in the role of the U.S. dollar, and the growing economic importance of other countries. Under these conditions, there has been increased recourse to protectionist measures both abroad and in the United States. Trade restrictions will grow and there is the potential for creeping protectionism, although it is not inevitable that the world will descend into generalized protection.

INTRODUCTION

The international trading economy is in the anomalous condition of diminishing tariff protection but increasing use of non-tariff trade-distorting measures. The former trend is the result of the staged tariff cuts agreed on in the GATT-sponsored Tokyo Round of multilateral negotiations concluded in 1979. The latter trend is taking place largely outside the framework of GATT and threatens to undermine the liberal international trading regime established after World War II.

---

23 "The New Protectionism: A Response to Shifts in National Economic Power" by Robert Baldwin. Reprinted by permission of the publisher from "The New Protectionism: A Response to Shifts in National Economic Power," by Robert E. Baldwin. Originally appeared in O. Salvatore, ed., *The New Protectionist Threat to World Welfare*.

This paper relates the new non-tariff protectionism to significant structural changes in world industrial production that have brought about a decline in the dominant economic position of the United States, the concomitant rise to international economic prominence of the European Economic Community and Japan, and the emergence of a group of newly industrializing countries (NICs). The first two sections describe the rise of the United States to a dominant position in international economic affairs in the immediate postwar period and indicate the types of 'hegemonic' actions it took. 'Shifts in international economic power' explains how changes in trade, finance, and the energy situation have led to modifications in national trade policy behaviour, particularly on the part of the United States. We then speculate about the nature of the international regime that is evolving under the present pattern of economic power among nations. The paper's final section is a summary and conclusion.

THE RISE IN US HEGEMONY

The role of the United States in the evolution of the modern trading system has been central. Although this country became an important trader on the world scene after World War I, it gave little indication at the time of a willingness to assume a major international leadership role. The American share of the exports of the industrial countries rose from 22.1 per cent in 1913 to 27.8 per cent by 1928, but during this period the United States chose political and economic isolation, rejecting membership in the League of Nations and erecting in 1930 the highest set of tariff barriers in its peacetime history. The failure of the London Economic Conference of 1933 due to the inward-looking economic position of the United States marks the low point of US internationalism in the interwar period.

A major policy reorientation toward participation in international affairs began to occur in the United States during the late 1930s and especially in World War II. More political leaders and the electorate generally began to accept the view of key policy officials in the Roosevelt administration that continued isolationism would bring not only renewed economic stagnation and unemployment to the American economy but also the likely prospect of disastrous new worldwide military conflicts. Consequently, active participation in the United Nations was accepted by the American public, as were the proposals to establish international economic agencies to provide for an orderly balance-of-payments adjustment mechanism for individual nations and to promote reconstruction and development. International trade had long been a much more politicized subject, however, and all that was salvaged (and then only by executive action) from the proposal for a comprehensive international trade organization was the GATT.

The economic proposals initiated by the United States were not, it should be emphasized, aimed at giving this country a hegemonic role. They envisioned the United States as one of a small group of nations that would cooperate to provide the leadership necessary to avoid the disastrous nationalistic policies of the 1930s. The envisioned leadership group included the United Kingdom, France, China and, it was hoped, the Soviet Union.

Hegemony was thrust upon the United States by a set of unexpected circumstances. First, the failure of the United Kingdom to return to anything like its prewar position as a world economic power was unforeseen. US officials thought, for example, that the US loan of $3.75 billion to the United Kingdom in 1946 would enable that country to restore sterling convertibility and to return to its earlier prominent international role, but the funds were quickly exhausted and it was necessary to restore exchange control. The 1949 devaluation of the pound was equally disappointing in its failure to revitalize the country. Economic reconstruction in Europe also proved much more costly than envisioned. The resources of the International Bank for Reconstruction and Development proved much too small to handle this task and massive foreign aid by the United States became necessary. Meanwhile the US economy grew vigorously after the war rather than, as many expected, returning to stagnant conditions.

The failure of either China or the USSR to participate in the market-oriented international economy placed an added leadership burden on the United States. But perhaps the most important factor leading to US hegemony was the effort by the Soviet Union to expand its political influence into Western Europe and elsewhere. American officials believed they had little choice from a national viewpoint but to assume an active political, economic and military leadership role to counter this expansionist policy, an action that most non-communist countries welcomed.

HEGEMONIC BEHAVIOUR

The significant expansion of productive facilities in the United States during the war, coupled with the widespread destruction of industrial capacity in Germany and Japan, gave American producers an enormous advantage in meeting the worldwide pent-up demands of the 1940s and 1950s. The US share of industrial-country exports rose from 25.6 per cent in 1938 to 35.2 per cent in 1952. (The combined share of Germany and Japan fell from 24.0 per cent to 11.4 per cent between these years.) Even in a traditional net import category like textiles, the United States maintained a net export position until 1958.

Static trade theory suggests that a hegemonic power will take advantage of its monopolistic position by imposing trade restrictions to raise domestic welfare through an improvement in its terms of trade. However, like the United Kingdom when it was a hegemonic nation in the nineteenth century, the United States reacted by promoting trade liberalization rather than trade restrictionism. A restrictionist reaction might have been possible for a highly controlled, planned economy that could redistribute income fairly readily and did not need to rely on the trade sector as a major source of employment generation or growth, but the growth goals of free-market firms, together with the nature of the political decision-making process, rule out such a response in modern industrial democracies.

Industrial organization theory emphasizes that firms in oligopolistically organized industries take a long-run view of profitability and strive to increase their market share. By doing so, they try both to prevent new competitors from entering the market, possibly causing losses to existing firms, and old competitors from increasing their shares to the point where others might suffer progressive and irreversible market losses. US firms organized in this manner seized the postwar competitive opportunities associated with American dominance to expand overseas market shares through both increased exports and direct foreign investment. The desire of US political leaders to strengthen non-communist nations by opening up American markets and providing foreign aid complemented these goals of US business, and business leaders actively supported the government's foreign policy aims. Even most producers in more competitively organized and less high-technology sectors such as agriculture, textiles and miscellaneous manufactures favoured an outward-oriented hegemonic policy at this time, since they too were able to export abroad and were not faced with any significant import competition.

The United States behaved in a hegemonic manner on many occasions in the 1950s and early 1960s. . . . [I]n doing so, it did not coerce other states into accepting policies of little benefit to them. Instead, the United States usually proposed joint policy efforts in areas of mutual economic interest and provided strong incentives for hegemonic cooperation. In the trade field, for example, US officials regularly pressed for trade-liberalizing multilateral negotiations and six such negotiations were initiated between 1947 and 1962. But the United States traded short-term concessions for possible long-run gains, since the concessions by most other countries were not very meaningful in trade terms due to the exchange controls they maintained until the late 1950s. The US goal was to penetrate successfully the markets of Europe and Japan as their controls were eased and finally eliminated.

One instance in which the United States did put considerable pressure on its trading partners to accept the American viewpoint was in the Kennedy Round of multilateral trade negotiations. At the initial ministerial meeting in 1963, US trade officials—with President Kennedy's approval—threatened to call off the negotiations unless the EC accepted the American proposal for a substantial, across-the-board tariff-cutting rule. Members of the Community had regained much of their economic vitality and the United States wanted economic payment for its earlier unreciprocated concessions and its willingness to support a customs-union arrangement that discriminated against the United States.

In the financial area the $3.75 billion loan to the United Kingdom in 1946, the large grants of foreign aid after 1948 under the Marshall Plan, and the provision of funds to establish the European Payments Union in 1948 are examples of hegemonic leadership by the United States. American leaders envisioned the postwar international monetary regime to be one with fixed and convertible exchange rates in which orderly adjustments of balance-of-payments problems would take place. When the IMF proved inadequate to cope with the magnitude of postwar payments problems, the United States provided financial aid until the affected countries were strong enough economically for the IMF to assume its intended role. A US hegemonic role was also exercised in the energy field, as American companies, with the assistance of the US government, gained control over Arab oil during the 1940s and 1950s.

SHIFTS IN INTERNATIONAL ECONOMIC POWER

Trade Competitiveness

The hegemonic actions of the United States, aimed at maintaining the liberal international economic framework established largely through its efforts and at turning back the Soviet Union's expansionism, succeeded very well. By 1960 the export market shares of France, Germany, Italy and Japan had either exceeded or come close to their prewar levels. Among the industrial countries only the United Kingdom failed to regain its prewar position by this time. The restoration of peacetime productive capabilities in these countries meant that the exceptionally high market shares of the United States in the early postwar years declined correspondingly. The 35.2 per cent US export share of 1952 had dropped to 29.9 per cent by 1960, a figure that was, however, still higher than its 1938 share of 25.6 per cent.

For manufactured products alone, the picture is much the same. The US world export share decreased from 29.4 per cent in 1953 to 18.7 per cent in 1959, while the shares of Western Europe and Japan rose from 49.0 per cent to 53.7 per cent and from 2.8 per cent to 4.2 per cent respectively. The export market share of Western Europe remained unchanged in the 1960s, but the Japanese share continued to rise and reached 10.0 per cent in 1971. At the same time the US share of world exports of manufactures fell to 13.4 per cent by 1971.

While aid from the US government played an important part in restoring the trade competitiveness of the European countries and Japan, the governments of these nations themselves were the prime driving force for revitalization. The French government, for example, formulated an industrial modernization plan after the war and two-thirds of all new investment between 1947 and 1950 was financed from public funds. Similarly, the British government under the Labour Party created an Economic Planning Board and exercised close control over the direction of postwar investment, while even the relatively free-market-oriented German government channelled capital into key industries in the 1950s. Government investment aid to the steel, shipbuilding and aircraft industries and the use of preferential governmental policies to promote the computer sector are other examples of the use of trade-oriented industrial policies in Europe during this period.

Japan is perhaps the best-known example of the use of government policies to improve international competitiveness. During the 1950s and 1960s the Japanese government guided the country's industrial expansion by providing tax incentives and investment funds to favoured industries. Funding for research and development in high-technology areas also became an important part of the government's trade policy in the 1970s. Governments of newly industrializing developing countries use industry-specific investment and production subsidies to an even greater extent than any of the developed nations in their import-substitution and export-promotion activities.

Not only had the prewar export position of the United States been restored by the late 1960s, but the period without significant import pressures in major industries with political clout had come to an end. Stiff competition from the Japanese in the cotton textiles industry was evident by the late 1950s, and the United States initiated the formation of a trade-restricting international cotton textile agreement in 1962. A broad group of other industries also began to face significant import competition in the late 1960s. The products affected included footwear, radios and television sets, motor vehicles and trucks, tires and inner tubes, semiconductors, hand tools, earthenware table and kitchen articles, jewelry and some steel items.

Trade-pattern changes in the 1970s and early 1980s were dominated by the price-increasing actions of the Organization of Petroleum Exporting Countries (OPEC). This group's share of world exports rose from 18.2 per cent in 1970 to 27.3 per cent in 1980. By 1984 OPEC's share, however, had fallen to 23.5 per cent as the power of the cartel declined. During this period the US export share fell from 13.7 per cent to 10.9 per cent, while that of the EC dropped from 36.1 per cent to 30.7 per cent. Japan, however, managed to increase its share from 6.1 per cent to 8.4 per cent. The latter figures reflect Japan's continued strong performance in manufacturing; its share of industrial countries' manufacturing exports rose from 9.9 per cent in 1971 to 15.3 per cent in early 1984.

The 1970s and early 1980s were a time of relative stability in the US manufacturing export share, with this figure rising slightly—from 19.6 per cent in 1971 to 20.1 per cent in 1984. In contrast, the EC's manufacturing export share declined from 59.9 per cent in 1971 to 54.6 per cent in 1984. Another major development of this period was the increase in the manufacturing export share of the developing countries from 7.1 per cent in 1971 to 11.0 per cent in 1980.

An important feature of the shifts in trading patterns of industrial countries in the 1970s and 1980s has been that not only have labour-intensive sectors like textiles, apparel and footwear continued to face severe import competition but that large-scale oligopolistically organized industries such as steel, automobiles and ship-building have had to contend with such competition. Machine tools and consumer electronic goods have also come under increasing import pressure.

The decline in the dominance of the United States in trade policy matters became apparent in the Tokyo Round of multilateral trade negotiations as well as when the United States proposed a new negotiating round in 1982. As it had in the Kennedy Round, the United States proposed an across-the-board linear tariff-cutting rule at the outset of the Tokyo Round, whereas the EC again proposed a formula that cut high tariff rates by a greater percentage than low duties. This time the United States did not prevail. The other industrial nations treated both the United States and the Community as major trading blocs whose negotiating objectives must be satisfied. The result was a compromise duty-cutting rule that met the US desire for a deep average cut and at the same time produced the significant degree of tariff harmonization sought by the EC. At the 1982 GATT ministerial meeting the United States again called for a new multilateral exercise that included as major agenda items negotiations aimed at reducing export subsidies in agriculture and barriers to trade in services. The Community and the developing countries both rejected the US proposals, and it has become clear that the United States can no longer determine the pace at which such negotiations will be held.

International Financial and other Economic Changes

As a decline in the dominant trade-competitive position of the United States became increasingly evident in the 1960s, both the United States and many other countries became dissatisfied with the US role in international monetary affairs. Since the supply of gold in the world increases only slowly, the demand for additional international liquidity that accompanied the rapid growth in world trade had to be met by greater holdings of dollars, the other official form of international reserves. As these holdings grew, a number of countries became concerned about the freedom from monetary and fiscal discipline that such an arrangement gave the United States and they resented the seigniorage privileges it granted. The United States also became increasingly dissatisfied with its inability to change the exchange rate of the dollar as a balance-of-payments adjustment means. Another indication of the decline in US hegemony was the creation in 1969 of a new form of international liquidity in the IMF: Special Drawing Rights (SDRs), designed to reduce the dependence of the international economy on the dollar.

The shift to a flexible exchange-rate system in 1971, however, was the clearest manifestation of the decline in US dominance in the monetary field. Although the results of this action have not given countries the expected degree of freedom from US financial influence, the role of the dollar as a reserve and vehicle currency has declined. Another institutional change directed at reducing the monetary influence of the United States was the formation of the European Monetary System in 1979.

The difficulties faced by the industrial nations in the energy field as a consequence of the success of OPEC have already been mentioned, but the importance of this shift in economic power is hard to exaggerate. This development was an especially devastating blow to the international economic prestige of the United States.

TRADE POLICY RESPONSES TO THE REDISTRIBUTION OF NATIONAL ECONOMIC POWER

The non-hegemonic members of the international trading regime (i.e., countries other than the United States) responded to the inevitable industry disruption caused by the shifts in comparative cost patterns in a manner consistent with their earlier reconstruction and development policies. With the greater postwar emphasis on the role of the state in maintaining full employment and providing basic social welfare needs, these governments intervened to prevent increased imports and export market losses from causing what they considered to be undue injury to domestic industries. Assistance to industries such as steel and shipbuilding injured by foreign competition in third markets took the form of subsidies. These included loans at below-market rates, accelerated depreciation allowances and other special tax benefits, purchases of equity capital, wage subsidies and the payment of worker social benefits. Not only had such activities been an integral part of the reconstruction and development efforts of the 1940s and 1950s, but the provisions of the GATT dealing with subsidies other than direct export subsidies also did not rule out such measures.

Because of the difficulties of modifying the tariff-reducing commitments made in earlier multilateral trade negotiations, import-protecting measures generally did not take the form of higher tariffs. By requiring compensating duty cuts in other products or the acceptance of retaliatory increases in foreign tariffs, increases in tariffs could have led to bitter disputes and the unravelling of the results of the previous negotiations. Therefore, to avoid such a possibility, governments negotiated discriminatory quantitative agreements outside the GATT framework with suppliers who were the main source of the market disruption. For example, quantitative import restrictions were introduced by France, Italy, the United Kingdom and West Germany on Japanese automobiles as well on radios, television sets and communications equipment from Japan, South Korea and Taiwan. Flatware, motorcycles and videotape recorders from Japan and the NICs of Asia were also covered by such import restrictions of various European countries. In the agricultural area, which had been excluded from most of the rules of the GATT, governments did not hesitate to tighten quantitative import restrictions (or restrictions like those under the EC's Common Agricultural Policy that have the same effect) or provide subsidies to handle surpluses produced by high domestic price-support programmes.

In the United States the disrupting effects of the postwar industry shifts in competitiveness throughout the world produced basic policy disputes that continue today. Except for the politically powerful oil and textile industries, until the late 1960s import-injured industries were forced to follow the administrative track provided for import relief under the escape-clause provision of the GATT. Moreover, many of the industry determinations by the ITC were rejected at the presidential level on foreign policy grounds—the need for the hegemonic power to maintain an open trade policy. Industry subsidies provided by foreign governments, though subject to US countervailing duty laws, were largely ignored by the executive branch for the same reason.

The official position of the United States began to change under the strong import pressures of the late 1960s. As their constituents described the competitive problems they were facing, fewer members of Congress accepted the standard argument that a liberal US trade policy was essential to strengthen the free world against communism. The intensity of congressional views on trade issues is indicated by their rejection of President Lyndon Johnson's 1968 request for new trade authority and by the near-approval in 1970 of protectionist legislation. The growing unwillingness of US allies to accept the unquestioned leadership of the United States in international political, military and economic affairs also caused officials in the executive branch to question the traditional American position on trade policies.

The view that gradually gained the support of the major public and private interests concerned with trade matters was that much of the increased competitive pressure on the United States was due to unfair foreign policies such as government subsidization, dumping by private and public firms, preferential government purchasing procedures, and discriminatory foreign administrative rules and practices relating to importation. This argument had appeal for several reasons. No new legislation was required to provide import relief; stricter enforcement of long-existing domestic legislation seemed to be all that was necessary. After a material-injury clause was introduced into the US countervailing duty law in 1979, these laws also were consistent with the provisions of the GATT dealing with unfair trade practices. Consequently, stricter enforcement of US unfair trade laws was unlikely to lead to bitter trade disputes with other countries. By placing the blame for their decline in competitiveness on unfair foreign actions, US managers and workers could avoid the implication that the decline might be due to a lack of efficiency on their part. Finally, government officials could maintain that the United States was still supporting the rules of the liberal international regime that the country had done so much to fashion.

The emphasis on the greater need for fair trade is evident in the 1974 legislation authorizing US participation in the Tokyo Round of multilateral negotiations. In reshaping the proposal of the president, the Congress stressed that the president should seek 'to harmonize, reduce, or eliminate' NTBs and tighten GATT rules with respect to fair-trading practices. Officials in the executive branch supported these directives not only on their merits but also because they deflected attention from more patently protectionist policies. . . .

The unfair trade argument has been used in support of most other trade-restricting or trade-promoting actions taken by the United States in recent years. The textile and apparel sectors have been described by government officials as 'beleaguered' by disruptive import surges, justifying more restrictive import controls. Similarly, when temporary orderly marketing agreements (OMAs) were negotiated in the 1970s with selected East and South east Asian countries, the implication conveyed was that these were responses to unfair export activities of these nations. Even the Japanese voluntary export restraints on automobiles were sometimes justified by American industry and government officials on the grounds that industry's competitive problem was in part due to the unfair targeting practices of the Japanese government. On the export promoting side, it is routinely claimed that subsidized export credits through the Export-Import Bank and special tax privileges to exporters establishing foreign sales corporations are necessary to counter unfair foreign practices in these areas. In short, fair-trade arguments using such phrases as the need for 'a level playing field' or 'to make foreign markets as open as US markets' have become the basic justification for the greater use of trade-distorting measures by the United States.

THE FUTURE OF THE INTERNATIONAL TRADING REGIME

The United States fared well economically in its hegemonic role; American exporters and investors established substantial foreign market positions from which they are still benefiting greatly. The open trade policy that US officials were able to maintain for so long also promoted growth and resource-use efficiency and thus extended the period of US economic dominance. But the postwar recovery of Europe and Japan and the emergence of the NICs brought an inevitable relative decline in US economic and political power. The comparative economic position of Western Europe also receded from its postwar recovery level as Japan and the NICs grew more rapidly. The outcome has been an increase in industrial-country protection that takes the form of non-tariff trade-distorting measures.

No country or country group is likely to assume a dominant role in the world economy during the rest of the century. Japan would seem to be the most likely candidate for this leadership role with its highly competitive industrial sector, but it appears to be too small economically to be a hegemonic power. Moreover, like the United States in the 1920s, Japan is still quite isolationist. Government officials and business people are conditioned by the disastrous outcome of the country's expansionist efforts in the 1930s and 1940s and by its past history of inwardness. Furthermore, when a potential hegemonic nation first demonstrates its competitive strengths over a wide range of products, certain traditional sectors (such as agriculture) that are faced with difficult adjustment problems tend to be able to prevent the national commitment to trade openness required of a dominant economic power. This occurred in the early stages of both the British and the American rise to economic dominance and is now keeping Japan from making a commitment to openness commensurate with its competitive abilities. In addition, Japanese consumers have not yet developed the taste for product variety needed to make Japan an important market for foreign-manufactured goods. The EC possesses the size and resources to be the dominant economic power, but the economic diversity among its members and the severe structural adjustment problems faced by almost all of them preclude a hegemonic role for this economic bloc.

The United States remains the country most able to identify its trading interests with the collective interests of all. However, a number of the industries that were the most competitive internationally during the rise of US hegemony have become victims of their success. The high profits these oligopolistically organized industries were able to maintain provided the investment funds needed to take advantage of the expanding market opportunities at home and abroad. But their economic structures were also favourable to the development of powerful labour unions that wished to share these profits through higher wages. The outcome was wage increases in these industries that far exceeded wage increases in manufacturing in general. As other countries developed their productive capabilities, these American industries found themselves penalized by above-average labour costs and an institutional framework that made it very difficult to adjust to the new realities of international competition. Also, management in some of these industries failed to keep up with the most advanced practices. Another important feature of these industries is their ability to obtain protection by exerting political pressure at the congressional and presidential levels, if they fail to gain it through administrative routes involving the import-injury, antidumping and countervailing duty laws.

As a consequence of these developments, protectionism has gradually spread in the United States as such industries as steel and automobiles have come under severe international competitive pressures. European governments are faced with even stronger protectionist pressures for similar reasons and have also moved toward more restrictive import policies. . . .

There seems to be no reason why the recent trend in non-tariff protectionism at the industry-specific level will not continue in the United States and Europe and become more important in Japan. But one should not conclude from this that the present international trading regime will turn into one where protectionism is rampant. There are—and will continue to be—dynamic, export-oriented industries in the older industrial countries that will seek access to foreign markets and see the relation between this goal and open markets in their own country. Moreover, such industries will have considerable political influence, as US high technology and export-oriented service industries have demonstrated. These sectors will continue to provide the United States, Western Europe and Japan with the economic power that makes international openness a desirable trade policy objective, and none of these trading blocs is likely to adopt a policy of general protection.

But will not creeping protection at the industry level eventually bring a *de facto* state of general protection? This is, of course, a real possibility, but this conclusion need not follow because protection usually does not stop the decrease in employment in declining industries. Even politically powerful industries usually have only enough political clout to slow down the absolute fall in employment. Furthermore, while employment tends to increase due to the fall in imports from the countries against which the controls are directed, offsetting forces are also set in motion. These include a decrease in expenditures on the product as its domestic price tends to rise; a shift in expenditures to non-controlled varieties of the product, to either less or more processed forms of the good and to substitute products; a redirection of exports by foreign suppliers to more expensive forms of the item; and, if the import controls are country-specific, an increase in exports by non-controlled suppliers. Also, the larger industry profits associated with the increased protection are likely to be used to introduce labour-saving equipment at a more rapid pace than previously.

The continued decline in employment after increased protection is well documented from histories of protection in particular industries. In the European Community and the United States, even such politically powerful industries as textiles and apparel and steel have been unable to prevent employment from falling despite increased import protection.

There are many factors that determine an industry's effectiveness in protection seeking. Its size in employment terms is one important factor. With declining employment, an industry faces diminution of its political power because of the fall in its voting strength and attendant decrease in its ability to raise funds for lobbying purposes. The decline in the political power of the US agricultural sector as the farm population has declined is an example that supports this hypothesis. It seems likely that highly protected industries such as textiles and apparel will gradually lose their ability to maintain a high degree of import protection. Consequently, in older industrial nations the spread of protection to sectors in which NICs gradually acquire international competitiveness may be offset by a decrease in protection in currently protected sectors. Counter-protectionist pressures also build up as industry-specific protection spreads. The stagnating effect of this policy becomes more obvious, as do the budgetary and economic-efficiency costs. A state of affairs may thus be reached in which protectionism will not increase on balance in the current group of industrial countries, or only at a very slow rate. Meanwhile, export-oriented high-technology and service sectors will encourage continued international cooperation to maintain an open trading regime.

Even if this sanguine scenario takes place, the international trading regime is likely to operate quite differently than it did in the years of US dominance. Industrial countries will seek short-run economic reciprocity in their dealings with each other. In particular, the United States will no longer be willing to trade access to its markets for acquiescence to US political goals and the prospect of long-term penetration of foreign economic markets. The developing countries and nations with special political relationships with particular major trading powers will probably continue to be waived from the full-reciprocity requirement but their trade benefits from this waiver will be closely controlled. Greater emphasis will be placed on bilateral negotiations to reduce non-tariff trade distortions, though the negotiations may still take place at general meetings of GATT members. The articles and codes of the GATT will provide the broad framework for the negotiations, but the variety and discriminatory nature of non-tariff measures make true multilateral negotiations too cumbersome. Bilateral negotiations will also be used to a greater extent in handling trade disputes. The GATT dispute-resolution mechanism will be utilized by smaller countries in their dealings with the larger trading nations and by the larger nations to call attention to actions by one of their members that are outside of generally accepted standards of good behaviour. These means of settling disputes do not differ essentially from the practices followed throughout the history of the GATT.

Greater discrimination in the application of trade restrictions and in the granting of trade benefits is another feature of the emerging international trading regime. The safeguard provisions of the GATT, for example, will probably be modified to permit the selective imposition of quantitative import controls on a temporary basis. It will be justified, at least implicitly, on the grounds that injury-causing import surges from particular suppliers represent a form of unfair competition and thus can be countered with discriminatory restrictions under GATT rules. More state assistance for the development and maintenance of high-technology and basic industries will be another characteristic of the international trading order likely to evolve during the rest of the century. The governments of both industrial and developing nations will continue to insist on domestic subsidies to develop a certain minimum set of high-technology industries and to maintain a number of basic industries on the grounds that these are needed for a country to become or remain a significant economic power.

The international trading regime described above is not one that will gain favour with economists. It will not yield the degree of economic efficiency or economic growth that economists believe is achievable in an open, non-discriminatory trading order. But this is an essay on the probable nature of the future international trading order, not the one economists would most like to see evolve. Free trade is not a politically stable policy in an economic world of continuing significant structural shifts involving severe adjustment problems for some politically important sectors and the demands of infant industries for special treatment. But neither is general import protectionism a politically stable state of affairs in modern industrial democracies with dynamic export sectors. Stable conditions in this type of world economy involve openness in some industries and protection in others, with the industries in each category changing over time. The particular mix of openness and import protection can vary significantly, depending on such factors as the country distribution of economic power and the pace of structural change. The present situation, in which there are three major industrial trading powers and a rapid rate of new technology development and international transfer of old technologys suggests that the currently evolving trading regime will be characterized by more government control and private cartelization than has existed throughout most of the postwar period.

SUMMARY AND CONCLUSION

The new protectionism threatening the international trading regime is related to significant structural changes in world production that have brought about a decline in the dominant economic position of the United States, a concomitant rise of the EC and Japan to international prominence and the emergence of a highly competitive group of newly industrializing countries.

The trading regime expected to develop after World War II involved the major economic powers' sharing responsibility for maintaining open and stable trading conditions. But the unexpected magnitude of the immediate postwar economic and political problems thrust the United States into a hegemonic role. US economic dominance manifested itself in the trade, finance and energy fields and enabled American producers to establish strong export and investment positions abroad. Yet, by facilitating the reconstruction and development of Western Europe and Japan as well as the industrialization of certain developing countries, US hegemonic activities led eventually to a marked decline in the American share of world exports and a significant rise of import competition in both labour-intensive sectors and certain oligopolistically organized industries. These developments significantly diminished the leadership authority of the United States.

Most industrial countries responded to the inevitable market disruptions associated with these shifts in comparative advantage by providing extensive government assistance to injured industries in the form of subsidies and higher import barriers. Such behaviour was consistent with the extensive role the governments of these countries played in promoting reconstruction and development. For the hegemonic power, the United States, the policy adjustment has been more difficult. Government and business leaders have gradually adopted the view that unfair foreign trading practices are the main cause of the country's competitive problems. By focusing on more vigorous enforcement of US statutes and GATT rules on fair trade, they are able to press for import protection and still maintain their support for the type of open trading regime the United States did so much to establish after World War II. Attention has been diverted from the role that high labour costs and inefficient managerial practices in certain industries play in explaining these problems.

No other trading bloc seems able or prepared to become a hegemonic power, but free trade is not a politically stable policy in a dynamic economic world in the absence of such leadership. Without the foreign policy concerns of the dominant power, domestic sectors injured by import competition and the loss of export markets are able to secure protection or other forms of government assistance through the political process in industrial democracies. Nevertheless, these industries are unlikely to be able to stop market forces from preventing the decline in employment in the industries and thus an erosion of their political influence. General protectionism is also not a politically stable policy in a rapidly changing economic environment. Politically important export industries that can compete successfully abroad will press for the opening of foreign markets and they realize the need to open domestic markets to achieve this result.

While it is possible that particular instances of protectionism will continue to spread and bring about an essentially closed international trading order, a more sanguine outcome, involving the support of the three major trading powers (the United States, the EC and Japan) seems possible. This is the emergence of a regime characterized by more trade-distorting government interventions than at the height of American hegemony and by the existence of a significant group of government-assisted industries. But while new industries will be added to this group, assistance will be withdrawn from others as they lose political influence so that, on balance, the list does not increase over time or does so only very slowly. Such a regime will not yield the growth and efficiency benefits of an open-trading system, but at least it will not lead to the disastrous economic and political consequences brought about by the type of trading order that prevailed in the 1930s.

24
Trade in Primary Commodities

JOAN ROBINSON

Well-known Marxist economist Joan Robinson explores here the constraints that developing countries face in a world market they have little control over. She asserts that a variety of economic and noneconomic factors place the developing nations in a subordinate position in the international trading system. For Robinson, unlike for Liberals, foreign trade has a very mixed impact on the development process, and may indeed serve to disrupt Third World economies. Robinson's view is representative of that of Marxists and others who believe that international capitalism, and world trade in particular, is structured to ensure the maintenance of the Third World in economic and political subordination to the developed countries.

The Third World countries of today were drawn into the capitalist world market, under regimes of formal and informal colonialism, as appendages of the metropolitan nations to supply raw materials and exotic commodities to the industrial centre. These may be divided into broad types, though there are important variations within each type. Minerals had to be produced where the deposits were found. Animal products required vacant land for ranching. The tropical belt around the world provided facilities for vegetable products, some, such as rubber, transplanted from west to east; some, such as coffee, from east to west. These provide the basis for consumption-goods industries, especially some fruits, tea, coffee and chocolate, and for some industrial raw materials including rubber and natural fibres. They now provide the basis for export earnings which are potentially valuable for develop-

24 "Trade in Primary Commodities" by Joan Robinson. From "Trade in Commodities" by Joan Robinson in *Aspects of Development and Underdevelopment*. Copyright © 1979 (Cambridge University Press). Reprinted with permission.

ment, but their distribution amongst the territories of modern states is completely arbitrary, depending upon accidents of economic geography and of their history in colonial and neo-colonial times.

This raises once more the question of what constitutes a national economic entity. The sources of raw materials which were developed by investment from the metropolitan countries are largely still owned and controlled by capitalist corporations. Mining companies in Africa, for instance, employ local labour and have been induced to train local personnel for the lower rungs of management but policy is still in the hands of the overseas headquarters and is administered on the spot by expatriates whose loyalty is to the corporation rather than to the country where they are working. The policy is directed towards making profits for the corporation as a whole. When a single corporation operates in many countries and in many activities—for instance fabricating metal as well as mining ore—the amount of profit attributable to any one activity can be manipulated, by the prices at which products are transferred from one branch to another, to suit the convenience of the corporation, not the needs of the country where the activity is carried out.

The share in proceeds that the local government obtains as royalties and taxes depends upon the relative economic power and negotiating ability of the parties when an agreement between the corporation and a newly-independent government was drawn up. . . .

There is nothing in economic theory to say what is a fair return on natural resources. A corporation can claim that a country within whose boundaries ore happens to have been discovered had neither the finance nor the know-how to develop for itself. Only investment and management by the corporation have turned it into economic wealth. The spokesman for the country can reply that without access to its soil no wealth could have been created. Here there is a sharp clash of interests which cannot be settled by appeal to any accepted rules.

To keep up supplies to the industrialised countries will require new investments, and the Third World countries may be able to demand stiffer terms in the future. Then the interests of the industrial nations will be involved and the outcome will depend upon the balance of power in the world market, not upon any economic principle. . . .

TERMS OF TRADE

There has been much discussion of the overall terms of trade between primary and manufactured products and much complaint from spokesmen for the Third World that the world market system operates unfavourably for them. . . .

In the Third World countries, the level of wages on plantations and mines is kept low by a massive reserve of unemployed labour and the absence of strong trade unions. Where comparable commodities are produced in the West as well as in the Third World (say, sugar in Australia) output per head is generally much lower in the Third World (because of the high investment that has taken place in the West) but wage rates are lower in a greater proportion, so that the Third World countries are low-cost producers. Does this give them an advantage in trade?

Where there is direct competition between natural commodities and synthetics performing the same function—for instance fibres and rubber—low wages have proved an advantage in a defensive sense, for if costs had been higher those products might have been wiped out altogether. In many lines, however, while it is true that the lowest-cost producer has a competitive advantage, this is only an advantage over other producers of the same commodity. For all of them together, demand at any moment is rigid and does not vary much with prices. One can take the market away from another and so appear to gain from being able to sell at a lower price, but the total demand for the commodity as a whole is not increased.

Competition between rival producers, say of tea or oil seeds, may shift demand from one to another but it does not bring about an increase in total receipts for all the competitors taken together. Indeed, when demand is 'inelastic' to price, a reduction in selling price increases the amount bought, if at all, less than in proportion to the fall in price, so that total receipts for all the sellers of the commodity taken together are reduced. This situation is sadly common in the market for primary commodities.

For this reason, the favourite remedy of the IMF for a trade deficit— depreciation of the exchange rate—is often disastrous. Devaluation by a country which is an important source for a commodity precipitates a fall in its price and reduces export earnings all round.

Many countries, each anxious for exports, can produce the same or closely similar commodities; they keep prices low for each other by causing supply to run ahead of demand. Thus, the entry of East Africa into the production of tea and coffee has been a disadvantage to India and Brazil. All three southern continents compete with each other in many tropical specialities. Each can gain an advantage in competition with the others but the result is to keep down the gains from trade for the Third World as a whole. . . .

MONOPSONY

Unfavourable terms of trade emerge in a more or less competitive world market; they are also influenced by the inequality of the commercial and financial power of the parties concerned.

Even in competitive conditions, there is a large gap between the sales value of a raw material at the point of export and at its final destination, which covers transport and handling costs and the profits of dealers. Freight rates are kept at a level that makes shipping profitable. For the workers employed in transport and commerce, wage rates are generally much higher than those in the producing country, and dealers' profits have to be high enough to cover the risks (from their point of view) created by fluctuating prices. Furthermore, nowadays the world market is far from competitive. For most raw materials, the fabricators have open or tacit cartel arrangements to limit competition amongst themselves, while they are buying from weak, scattered and competitive sellers.

The trade in tropical foodstuffs has been to a large extent taken over by a few large transnational corporations who evidently do not compete keenly with each other but agree in keeping down purchase prices.

This phenomenon is strikingly illustrated by the trade in bananas. Two corporations, with another smaller one, dominate sales in USA, West Europe and Japan, and dominate purchasing in the producing countries, particularly in Central America. The formation of a union of banana exporting countries (UBEC) precipitated a trade war in 1974 in which the buyers penalised countries which tried to impose an export tax by refusing to buy, stopping production on their plantations, and physically destroying boxes of bananas at the ports. The buyers won, and the taxes were withdrawn.

The break-down of the final price in 1971 was such that the gross return to growers was 11.5 per cent of proceeds. The retailers' gross margin was 31.9 per cent. The rest was costs and profits on transport and handling. Formerly shipping and ripening were provided by separate companies. Now the great corporations are integrating these stages of the business, presumably saving costs and increasing their own profit margins.

Technical changes, such as disease resistant breeds, irrigation and improvements in packing and transport have lowered costs. The benefit was partially passed on to consumers but not at all to the primary producers.

The inability of countries competing with each other for exports to restrict supply has led to a continuous deterioration of the terms of trade for the sellers of bananas.

The corporations pass a part of the surplus that they extract from the Third World to the rich countries in taxation (though they are experts at evasion), to rentiers, and in the salaries of their personnel (some of whom may be nationals of poor countries by origin); the rest they amass as finance to increase their own operations.

The consumers in the rich countries have the advantage of secure supplies and guaranteed quality, as well as of the low cost at point of origin (though this makes only a small difference to the final price). It is in this sense that workers in the rich countries, as well as capitalists, are benefiting from the exploitation of the poor countries.

This story is typical of many food products supplied to Western consumers by the great monopsonistic buyers from the Third World.

INSTABILITY

The greatest drawback of depending upon primary commodities for export earnings is the unpredictability of the market. The agricultural sector within an industrial economy usually has enough political leverage to see that it is sheltered in one way or another from the worst effects of instability, while strong capitalist firms in extractive industries can form protective rings for themselves. The Third World countries which import such commodities must pay the protected prices, while their own products, for the most part, are left to the mercy of the laws of supply and demand.

Instability is at three levels. For particular commodities, changes in technology, in consumers' habits or in prices of complementary or substitutable commodities, from time to time cause unforeseeable long-run changes in conditions of demand. These may go either way; for instance, the demand for natural fibres was first devastated by synthetics and then revived by the rise in price of oil that made them expensive. As the rich countries grow, demand sometimes runs ahead of potential supply, so that one commodity or another enjoys a seller's market for a time. This very fact encourages both substitution and a search for new sources of supply so that the advantage of scarcity is soon lost. There is likely to be a general long-run tendency to check the growth of demand relatively to supply; the great versatility of modern technology and the malleability of consumption at a high standard of life mean that no individual natural commodities are indispensable. In spite of all the anxiety nowadays about exhaustible resources, it seems likely that the central buyer will continue to have the whip hand over the peripheral seller for a long time still.

Changes on the side of production also create instability. Crop failure in one region gives a sudden bonus to rival producers in others, or the opening up of a new source of supply is a disaster for the old ones.

Such accidents affect particular commodities. General and chronic instability is transmitted to the market as a whole from the instability of the industrial capitalist economy. The rise and fall of activity in booms and slumps at the centre affects all the countries of the periphery, and the ebb and flow of military expenditure affects very many.

On top of the large swings in demand are superimposed continuous day-to-day oscillations in prices. Direct purchase by the great corporations bypasses the organised produce exchanges, but they still have an important sphere of operation in the trade in many commodities. The business of dealers is to bridge the gap both in time and space between producers and purchasers. They invest finance in buying commodities from the original producers and pass them on to the buyers as required.

The opportunity to make profits by this use of finance arises from the shortage of finance that usually besets the sellers, particularly of seasonal crops. The working capital of a producer is absorbed in a season's output and he needs to sell in order to replenish it and start the next cycle of production. The dealer can buy when price is at its lowest, hold stocks and feed supplies out to the market as prices rise. The inability of the producers to hold back sales to wait for a rise of price is most pronounced for small peasants, but even institutions such as a marketing board may be pressed for cash. Moreover, to hold stocks is to take a risk. Apart from more or less predictable seasonal swings, movements in commodity prices are continually being brought about by changes in the relations of supply and demand. The dealers have to be better informed about market conditions than the producers and, indeed, part of their business is to make profits out of superior knowledge and successful guess-work.

This business is necessarily speculative in the sense that it depends upon taking a view of what will happen next. According to textbook theory, dealers perform a service to the economy by buying in stocks when prices are tending to fall and selling out when prices are tending to rise, thus stabilising prices through time. But guess-work is not always stabilising. Since each watches the others to try to divine how their guesses are going, there is a natural tendency for movements of opinion to set up perverse reactions. A rise in price, instead of restraining demand, as in the textbook theory, increases buying in expectation of a further rise and a fall in price increases sales. Thus, the dealers may themselves bring about the fluctuations that it is supposed to be their function to mitigate.

In popular language 'speculation' is a bad word, and certainly vicious manipulations of the market do occur, but in the general way this kind of speculation cannot be regarded as vicious for it is a normal and inevitable result of playing the game according to the rules of the free market system.

These three layers of instability—long-run shifts in demand, cyclical swings and speculative oscillations—interact with each other, and for countries which depend on the world market for their export earnings, make coherent economic policy difficult and turn long-range planning into a dubious gamble.

STABILISATION SCHEMES

The unsatisfactory operation of the market for commodities has long been recognised and spokesmen for the Third World are now urgently demanding reform. They hope to find means, within the world market system, to improve their terms of trade, and to mitigate the nuisance of instability, which works against their interests far more than in their favour.

In principle, the price of a commodity can be kept within a certain range by holding supplies off the market when demand is falling and releasing them when it is rising. This can be done through the operation of a buffer stock, buying and selling the commodity, or by an agreement among producers to restrict output when price has reached a lower limit and to permit sales to expand when price reaches an upper limit; or by some combination of these two principles.

There has been a great deal of talk about the advantages of schemes to stabilise prices but in practice very little has been done. . . . This arises from the fact that the main advantage of stabilisation is to the sellers, who are weak and disorganised, while finance and economic power belong to the buyers—traders and manufacturers in the industrial countries.

The instability of primary product prices is a nuisance for buyers as well as for sellers, but the problem is much more urgent for the sellers than for the buyers. The cost of materials plays a small part in the total trade of the industrialised economies and a still smaller part in their total income, while for many Third World countries receipts from sales of a single commodity, or two or three, dominate their export earnings, and export earnings have a strong influence over the prosperity of their whole economy. From a national point of view, the rise of prices is far less damaging to the buyers than a fall to the sellers, while from the point of view of the traders and manufacturers concerned, in the industrial country, most of a rise in costs is passed on in prices to their own customers. The buyers, therefore, have much less at stake than the sellers. Moreover, the ideology of a capitalist democracy permits government interference with the free play of market forces to favour interests in the home country (for instance by support prices or protection) but is extremely reluctant to admit any responsibility for the effects of home policies upon interests abroad.

If the problem were merely fluctuations of prices about a predictable trend, the operation of a buffer stock would clearly be profitable and capitalist finance would be devoted to stabilisation. But a trend is something that statisticians can perceive over a run of years in the past. It cannot be perceived in advance, particularly in the present age of drastic political and technological discontinuities in the evolution of patterns of supply and demand.

The buyers have generally found that a period of scarcity and high prices for a particular raw material leads before long to a shift in demand (say, the substitution of a synthetic for a natural product) and calls into being fresh sources of supply, so that a brief seller's market is followed by a prolonged buyer's market. (This is just what the spokesmen for the sellers complain of.) The free market system hitherto has suited the interests of the buyers on the whole and they do not encourage plans to interfere with it.

On the side of the sellers, there is a general interest in stabilisation and improvement in their terms of trade, but there are conflicts of interest amongst themselves. The basic mechanism of stabilisation is to withhold supplies from a falling market, but for any one seller it is better to get something than nothing. There is always a temptation to sell, although at the expense of another supplier's market, and the temptation is all the stronger when a scheme to raise prices is getting under way. Restriction requires the imposition of discipline over individual interests in a common cause. This means that there must be an authority in each country where the commodity is produced to regulate output, for instance by a system of central procurement or by the allocation of quotas; there must be an agreement amongst the countries on the distribution of the burden amongst them and there must be mutual confidence that it is being fairly carried out.

Furthermore, there are great technical difficulties in arriving at an agreed formula for dealing, for instance, with the relative prices of varieties and grades, for what goes under the name of any single commodity is by no means homogeneous, either technically or commercially. A scheme which has to cover a number of sources of supply involves conflicts of interest amongst them; there is a general conflict between new entrants to the market who want to be allowed to expand their share in output and the old producers who want to restrict it; and there are innumerable minor conflicts over details in any scheme, which make it hard to find a formula which all parties will, first, agree to accept and, second, abide by in face of change. When the buyers are not particularly keen on supporting an agreement, they have ample opportunity to play upon the conflicts within the group of sellers. Over and above all these difficulties, the sellers lack the finance required to set a scheme afloat . . . .

MONOPOLY POWER

There is one notable case in which a group of sellers were able to use the laws of the market in their own favour—that is the rise in the price of oil in 1973. The Organisation of the Petroleum Exporting Countries was founded in 1960. It arose out of conversations between Venezuela and Iran with the Arab League about the possibility of defending the oil exporters against reductions in the price being imposed upon them by the international oil companies. A secretariat was set up, and all the exporters made gains from their improved bargaining position.

For the Arab League, oil had always had a strategic and political importance. In support of the October War with Israel in 1973, a boycott was instituted against Israel, the USA and Holland. (The distributing companies went through the motions of implementing it while seeing that none of their customers were effectively deprived of supplies.)

This experience made the Arabs realise the potential monopoly power of the oil producers and OPEC imposed a quadrupled price of oil. This was implemented by the distributors, who made enormous profits for themselves.

The success of OPEC has inspired the idea that other groups—for instance, the sellers of bauxite—might also exercise monopoly power to improve their proceeds from sales, but it is unlikely that any general solution to the problem of the weakness of Third World exports could be reached by this means.

There were certain unique features about the case of oil. First, the whole pattern of development in industry had grown round cheap oil from the Middle East, so that demand was inelastic and could not quickly be shifted; secondly, the main producers were bound together by a political motive and had no difficulty in carrying the smaller ones with them; thirdly, the largest producers were in the unusual position of having a sparse population (as well as preserving a highly unequal distribution of income) so that the only imports they required were luxury goods, prestigious buildings and armaments. They had no urgent need for any more export earnings than they were receiving already, and so they did not have the usual reluctance to restrict output in order to maintain the level of prices for the group as a whole. Finally, the distributors were ready to play along with the producers, and, indeed, made huge profits for themselves in the process. This concatenation of circumstances in unlikely to be repeated.

The spokesmen for the industrialised nations appeared to be deeply shocked by the whole affair, but, though OPEC states regard themselves, formally, as part of the Third World, it is only natural that their sudden wealth should incline them towards playing the financial game according to the rich countries' rules.

WORLD INFLATION

One of the complaints made by spokesmen for the Third World is that the purchasing power of their exports is constantly being eroded by inflation in the industrial countries raising the prices of the products that they want to buy.

In the capitalist world today, there are two separate systems of price formation, which can be broadly distinguished, though there is some overlap between them.

For primary products, as we have seen, prices oscillate with the relations of demand to supply; for manufactures, a system of cost-plus prevails; that is to say that the business concerned form selling prices by adding a gross margin to direct running costs (wages, materials and power) calculated to cover overhead costs at some normal level of operation, plus an allowance for net profit.

There are great differences in the power of different types of business to control the prices at which they sell, but monopoly does not necessarily mean restricting output to keep profits high, for the great corporations compete with each other, continually expanding into new markets. The general rule that movements of prices are governed by movements of costs applies to them as much as to small competitive producers.

The main element in costs in industry as a whole is the cost of labour. The price level for manufactures in general is therefore governed by the relation of money-wage rates to productivity. The level of wage rates, in turn, is determined by the fortunes of the class war, that is the struggle of organised labour to maintain its share in the proceeds of industry.

During the long run of expansion and prosperity (interrupted only by minor recessions) for a quarter of a century after the end of the second world war, real-wage rates were rising in all the Western countries, though, as we have seen, their fortunes were not all alike. The continuous rise of money wage rates, necessary to keep the share of real wages from falling, had a tendency to overshoot, so that money wages rose faster than productivity, bringing about a rise in the level of prices; thus, what now seems a mild degree of inflation became chronic.

During this period, various commodities experienced different movements but, on the whole, growth of supply kept ahead of demand and the terms of trade, overall, moved in favour of manufactures. This contributed to the rise of real-wage rates and to some extent to allay inflation in the Western countries. But foodgrains were an exception. The growth of prosperity, particularly in the Soviet sphere, was increasing the consumption of meat and deflecting grain into feeding livestock.

In the 1970s a strong boom developed, particularly in the United States, and the prices of materials shot up. The rise in the price of oil in 1973 exaggerated a movement that was already taking place. In industry, a rise in the cost of materials raises prices relatively to money-wage rates, and therefore generates a demand for a compensating rise in money wages.

Thus the Western world experienced an alarming increase in the rate of inflation, which coincided with a serious slump in activity; the slump brought a fall in the prices of industrial materials (except for oil) but inflation in the West continued and, with rising unemployment, the class struggle became all the more embittered. This experience has brought about a new phase in capitalist development. Western governments are now more anxious to check inflation than to preserve employment. (The neo-neoclassical economists have obligingly come forward with a new theory that inflation is due to a decline in unemployment below its 'natural level'.)

Now as soon as an upswing in industrial activity causes material prices to begin to rise, fear of inflation puts a brake on revival. The new international economic order which is evolving in this situation does not seem to be propitious to meeting the demands of the Third World to an improvement in their share in the benefits of international trade. . . .

25

East Asia's Lessons for Latin American Resurgence

JOHN D. MACOMBER

John Macomber contrasts East Asia's startling economic performance during the past 30 years with the rather dismal growth record of Latin America. While recognizing that state intervention in the economy is a fact of life in both regions, Macomber draws a single central lesson: when intervention is undertaken with the clear intent of strengthening the ability of the economy to take advantage of market forces, as in East Asia, it can work well; when it is undertaken in contravention of market forces, as in Latin America, it appears to work poorly. Thus, like most Liberals, Macomber sees the market as a progressive and beneficial force for economic growth and development; countries do best, he concludes, when they follow its dictates.

Latin America has become so symbolic of the problems of Third World economies that it is difficult to believe that only 25 years ago the region rivalled many West European and most East Asian economies for wealth and prosperity. Yet during a period when much of the free world has grown, Latin America's economies have stagnated. What happened to change so dramatically the region's prospects—and make it one of the most troubled parts of the world economy?

The Pacific Basin is a natural region to examine in seeking explanations for Latin America's problem because most East Asian economies have boomed when Latin American ones have declined. Between 1960 and 1985 the gross domestic product (GDP) per capita of the Republic of Korea, Singapore and Taiwan increased more than fourfold. In the major Latin American countries,with the exception of Brazil, it increased less than twofold. Even Brazil, whose per-capita GDP increased slightly

25 "East Asia's Lessons for Latin American Resurgence" by John D. Macomber. From *The World Economy*, Vol. 10, No. 4 (December 1987). Reprinted by permission of Basil Blackwell Publisher Ltd.

more than twofold, did not do well in comparison with such West European countries as Austria, Finland, Italy, Spain, Greece and Portugal. Even Turkey, low man on the Mediterranean totem pole, matched Brazil's performance.

East Asia's success is viewed by some as proof that a system dedicated to private enterprise and open markets guarantees economic success. Yet, while it is true that many Latin American governments have a statist orientation, the governments of East Asia are active market interventionists as well. Others argue that cultural differences between Latin America and East Asia explain the latter's economic success. This is too facile an explanation because economic success has been achieved in many different countries with varied cultural heritages. Thirty years ago the conventional wisdom said that cultural differences would preclude development in countries like Taiwan and South Korea. Since Latin America was making meaningful economic progress 25 years ago, there is no compelling reason why its cultural heritage should keep it from doing so once again.

WHY HAS LATIN AMERICA FALLEN BEHIND?

What factors have spurred East Asia's remarkable economic performance over the last twenty to thirty years? Perhaps there are lessons for revitalizing Latin American economies.

Over the past six years, the differences have accelerated, even though the two regions have faced an almost identical external environment. GDP grew by 5.8 per cent in East Asia between 1981 and 1984, while in Latin America growth was a negative 0.4 per cent. Inflation averaged only 6.5 per cent in East Asia, but averaged 137.9 per cent in Latin America. The external debt of almost every Latin American country was rescheduled at least once. By contrast, in East Asia, only the Philippines,in many ways more Latin than Asian in policy terms, has had to reschedule.

Perhaps Latin America, because of its greater dependence on commodities as exports, suffered more severe external shocks than did the East Asian countries, thus compounding the debt problem. Yet this conclusion does not withstand close analysis. There were both Latin American and East Asian countries that were negatively affected by external shocks caused by changes in the commodity terms of trade. And several countries in Latin America, particularly Mexico and Venezuela, were positively affected. One significant factor in distinguishing between those countries able to adjust without recourse to rescheduling and those which were not is the size of the debt burden relative to exports. Those countries that had by then been successful in developing a strong export base were better able to weather the debt crisis than those that had not.

A review of the economic policies pursued by East Asian and Latin American countries confirms that the approaches have been fundamentally different. East Asia has emphasized export-driven development while Latin America has opted for the more 'independent' approach of inward orientation. East Asia has maintained realistic exchange rates while Latin American currencies have generally been overvalued. While both have large state-enterprise sectors, the goals for these sectors and the ways in which they have been managed differ. And, while both have made efforts to target specific industries for special treatment, the East Asians have successfully implemented policies that have eluded Latin America. But the contrast in policies between Latin America and East Asia is not as stark and obvious as some think. It is not a question of state intervention versus the free market. Rather it is a much more subtle issue of the goals to which state intervention is directed and how that intervention is managed.

IMPORT SUBSTITUTION VERSUS EXPORT ORIENTATION

The essence of inward orientation is import substitution, which was widely adopted by the developing countries, as a basis for economic development, in the years following World War II. It was believed that developing countries would remain forever providers of basic commodities on deteriorating terms of trade with the industrial countries unless they created manufacturing industries to produce the industrial products they were importing. Latin America's commitment to import substitution was strengthened by nationalist desires to reduce dependency and by a concern to create employment.

In Latin America high tariffs were established to protect 'infant industries'. Theoretically they would remain in place only until the industries grew large and efficient enough to compete. But this seldom happened. Protection often became a requirement for survival. High capital-investment and technology costs combined with the lack of a local market large enough to achieve economies of scale raised production costs well beyond those of competitive products. As Santiago Macario, the research director of the Economic Commission for Latin America (ECLA), which was a major and early proponent of import substitution, has remarked, it became a policy of 'import substitution at any cost'.[1]

In addition to highly protective tariff walls, Latin America has generally allowed its currencies to become grossly over-valued. This supports import substitution by keeping the prices of imported components lower than they would be with realistic exchange rates. But it also over-prices exports, thereby reducing their competitiveness. Over-valuation, in fact, has been the undoing of efforts to liberalize and rationalize import protection. The Southern Cone countries of Argentina and Chile, along with Mexico, are good examples. By contrast, it was a devaluation of exchange rates in Brazil in the mid-1960s that enabled the country to pursue a substantial reduction in import protection. The impact of those policies, along with other export-promotion incentives, can be seen in Brazil's position today as the leading exporter of manufactured products in Latin America.

In several East Asian countries the pattern has been different. After World War II, Taiwan pursued common developing-country policies, namely high tariffs on imports and an over-valued currency. But in the late 1950s the policy was radically changed. Devaluation was coupled with trade liberalization. In South Korea, export-oriented policies generally stem from 1965, when fiscal and financial incentives to export were introduced. Since then, South Korea and Taiwan have shared several similar policies, ones that are crucially different from those pursued in Latin America.

In exchange-rate policy, Taiwan moved to set a single exchange rate and keep it as close to the clearing rate as possible. South Korea, on the other hand, has moved back and forth between floating rates and an established rate with discontinuous devaluation. But devaluation has not been put off until the currency was grossly over-valued and local producers have lost faith in the predictability of exchange rates.

Latin America has followed almost precisely opposite policies: multiple exchange rates, over-valued currencies and unpredictable devaluations. While inflation has been continuous, devaluations have been resorted to only intermittently. As a result, the prices of export products have fluctuated radically—hardly a situation that would encourage investing for export.

Latin American countries all too often appear to have used their exchange rates for social and political goals rather than to achieve balance-of-payments equilibrium and international competitiveness. They have been used to try to control inflation, to maintain the standard of living or to promote national prestige and confidence. This has not worked and ultimately the currency has had to be devalued with an ensuing loss of confidence in policy stability and in the government's ability to manage the economy.

Beyond maintaining realistic exchange rates, South Korea and Taiwan adopted a similar set of export incentives. They provided tax incentives for, and remitted indirect taxes on, imported inputs for export production, granted exemption from income taxes on part of export earnings, established export-processing zones and provided inexpensive quality-control programmes to help upgrade and ensure the quality of their export products.

Meanwhile, in Latin America, producers not only lacked such incentives to get into exporting. They also faced absolute obstacles to doing so, such as payment of full duties on inputs for products to be exported, taxes on exports and a multiplicity of bureaucratic steps—147 in one country—just to export a product. In addition, most incentives, such as inexpensive credit, were directed to import-substitution rather than export-oriented industries.

Finally, the overall environment for business in Latin America must not be overlooked. Unlike East Asia, there is a deep-rooted suspicion of business and capitalism. This translates into a milieu of suffocating regulations, taxes, labour laws and restrictions on foreign investment. This is set forth clearly in an excellent study of economic growth in Latin America, commissioned by the Americas Society in New York and carried out under the auspices of the Institute for International Economics, in Washington, the Colegio de Mexico, in Mexico City, and the Fundacao Getúlio Vargas, in Rio de Janeiro.[2] This study is a major source for this article. It concludes that most of the larger Latin American countries are among the most regulated market economies in the world. The Latin American businessman is likely to face price controls, high corporate profit tax rates, heavy mandated fringe benefits and limitations on the ability to reduce employment. Thus, even if exchange rates were competitive and the bias against imports was eliminated, the cost structure faced by Latin American industry would make questionable its ability to compete successfully in export markets.

The issue is not one of state intervention versus the free market. The governments of East Asia intervened continuously. The difference lies in the nature of the policies and the way in which they are implemented. The East Asians know how to harness market forces in their economic policies and achieve impressive rates of growth. Latin Americans, on the other hand, seem to make an almost conscious effort to move against market forces.

STATE ENTERPRISES AND INDUSTRIAL POLICIES

Many have assumed that the deep involvement of the state in business ownership in Latin America is one of the sources of its problems. Yet the fact of ownership does not, itself, appear to be the problem. A comparison of the share of gross domestic investment in state enterprises between Latin America and South Korea does not indicate significant differences in the extent of state ownership. Instead, the differences appear to lie in the reasons for which the state became involved and, as a logical consequence, the way in which the enterprises are managed.

In Latin America, the state most often becomes involved in business for political reasons. While some enterprises were originally established by the state because the size of the investment seemed to be beyond private means, many others are the result of takeovers of privately-owned companies, either through nationalization, as with the banks in Mexico, or through bail-outs of firms about to declare bankruptcy. In the latter case, the objective is almost always to preserve jobs. By contrast, in countries like South Korea, the primary motivation seems to be the national interest, but defined in economic rather than political terms. Public-sector investments are carefully analyzed for viability. Before the government decides to participate, it must be convinced that a competitive advantage is achievable and that there is potentially a large domestic or international market.

The differences in reasons for the involvement of the state lead directly to the differences in management. Where involvement is essentially for political reason, efficiency is not the paramount criterion for managers. Thus, while Latin American governments will talk about efficiency, they will often impose price controls on output, reduce managerial compensation, raise wages and impose a myriad of operating restrictions. The clear message to the public-enterprise manager is that he is being judged not on efficiency but on the extent to which he meets the political criteria set by the government.

As pointed out in the Americas Society report, in Mexico all expenditures by public enterprises, including current expenditures, are subject to government approval. State enterprises are given very little room to manoeuvre within their monthly allotments. Evaluations by supervising agencies focus on compliance with the budget rather than on efficiency. By contrast, public-enterprise managers in Brazil have 'considerable freedom of action' from governmental intervention in managing their enterprises, which may help to explain their relative efficiency. But unlike East Asian state enterprises and more like those in the rest of Latin America, they have few constraints placed on their investment (until the debt crisis did so).

A useful illustration of the differences can be found in comparing the steel industries of South Korea and Mexico. In each instance, the government controls the largest plants in the country. Government involvement in the South Korean steel industry is motivated by recognition of the importance of steel to the plans for the economy. The Government studied the steel industry and decided not only that South Korea could compete but also that becoming a world producer was a high-priority economic goal. It concluded, however, that the size of the project required direct government participation.

In 1973, the Government established the Pohang Iron and Steel Company, which *Iron Age* magazine named the most efficient producer of steel in the world in 1983. In 1984, South Korea's steel industry exported some 40 per cent of total production, about $2 billion worth of steel. While plans for a new plant are condemned by some as an unwelcome addition to an industry already plagued by worldwide over-capacity, the Koreans reply that 'the problem is not an oversupply of "efficient" steel capacity'.[3]

Contrast this with Las Truchas, Mexico's newest and most modern steel-making facility, which became operational in 1975. As an astute observer of Mexico has pointed out: 'it became . . . a monument to the perils of government involvement in the economy . . . Equipment came from numerous countries, with the accompanying problems of maintenance and spare parts; it produced steel wire when the country's main need was for flat products; nearby iron ore reserves were smaller than anticipated; numerous illicit fortunes were made; and because there was no railroad link to the rest of the country, coal had to be imported from Colombia and initial steel production was exported.'[4] The accumulated losses of Las Truchas 'probably exceed the original investment of $800 million. The plant's production costs are reportedly twice those of Korean plants.'[5]

East Asian encouragement of efficient solutions rather than inefficient protection is in sharp contrast to what has been done in most Latin American countries. There, industry after industry has been maintained at significant cost to the state, and in the face of great inefficiencies, because the basic criteria have been political rather than economic. Change is occurring, but often under the pressure of debt crisis and ensuing severe restriction of financial resources. For example, Mexico recently closed a steel plant, the Fundidora de Monterrey, which had been taken over by the state years before. This step related to the International Monetary Fund's demand for a decrease in public-sector spending as part of the debt-refinancing negotiations. All the countries that have rescheduled debt repayments are under heavy pressure to reduce expenditures on state enterprises. Doing so, however, generally implies a reduction in wages and/or employment, thereby raising difficult political problems.

A further area of difference is industrial policy. Both East Asian and Latin American countries have selected industries they wish to promote. But the East Asian countries have gone much further in terms of effective implementation of policies to meet their goals—and of promptly acting to retrench when problems occur. In this sense, they are much more interventionist than the Latin American countries. The problems of Brazil, a country which has probably gone further than most other Latin American countries in promoting specific industries, illustrates the problems with industrial policy in Latin America. A recent analysis of national industrial policies in Brazil describes what has happened: '[The] multiplicity of institutions involved in industrial development objectives permits contradictory or inconsistent moves to occur, undercutting any embryonic effort toward policy.'[6]

The East Asians, on the other hand, are able to focus attention on a national objective and change direction when the policy is not working. For example, South Korea's rush into heavy industry in the 1970s was not nearly as successful as her venture into steel. In heavy machinery and also in petro-chemicals, she went too far and is having to retrench. But she was able to pursue both policies—promotion of new industries and then retrenchment—without conflicting objectives diverting the implementation of policies.

In a similar way, the Japanese Government often aids its troubled industries in restructuring. Recently, the Ministry of International Trade and Industry (MITI) has extended its help to two declining industries, namely aluminium and petro-chemicals. This help is not in the form of import protection or subsidies, because the Government refuses to waste valuable resources in support of industries without sufficient growth prospects. Instead, help has come in the form of encouraging an orderly decline of surplus capacity, particularly in the aluminium industry. There have also been government efforts to form cartels during economic recessions so that costs might be cut through joint marketing efforts. In addition, the removal of tariffs and taxes on essential inputs has been used as a restructuring tool.

But the fact that retrenchment takes place at all is a telling point. Given that the goal of moving into these industries was to provide growth and strength to the national economy, scaling back when problems arose clearly was the only sensible move to make. Since the state of the economy is first on the minds of government planners, there is little inclination to dawdle in reshaping industries. Yet, in Latin America, although the goal is ostensibly the same, to strengthen the national economy, the management of the policy is completely different, beginning with the involvement of numerous institutions, each with their own objective. The centralized governmental structures of the East Asian countries enable them to change course as required to meet market forces in ways that the more independent bureaucracies of Latin America cannot do.

The lesson seems clear. If a country is going to be interventionist, then it needs to be able to manage the implementation of the policy, as well as take the initial decision to intervene.

THE RESULT AND THE EXCEPTION

The record suggests that Latin American countries have paid a substantial price for their inward-oriented policies. Raúl Prebisch, who is generally accredited with being the primary architect of the policy, recognized the shortcomings of the import-substitution approach:

> As is well known, the proliferation of industries of every kind in a closed market has deprived the Latin American countries of the advantages of specialization and economies of scale, and owing to the protection afforded by excessive tariff duties and restrictions, a healthy form of internal competition has failed to develop, to the detriment of efficient production.[7]

Thus much of Latin America is left with a base of inefficient industries, in both the public and the private sectors, ill-prepared to compete in highly competitive world markets. Ironically, import substitution, which was intended to guarantee independence, has left Latin America more dependent on the developed countries for both foreign aid and bankers' concessions than East Asia, which has pursued a policy based on integration into world markets.

The impact which these different policies have had on the economic structures of the two regions is dramatic. East Asian economies are dominated by export industries. On average, one third of GDP results from exports, twice that of Latin America.

The growth of Latin American exports has remained relatively flat, less than one sixth of GDP between 1960 and 1980. During the same period, East Asian countries expanded their export base from less than one sixth of GDP in 1960 to more than one third in 1980. Because exports as a percentage of GDP did not grow as rapidly in Latin America, and foreign investment was discouraged, borrowing became the only means to attract scarce capital.

Market forces have now caught up with Latin America. As Jeffrey Sachs, of Harvard University, has observed in his comparison of Latin America and East Asia, capital-scarce developing countries can profitably borrow over the long term 'only if the borrowed resources are invested sufficiently in the tradeable goods that ultimately will be used to service the accumulated foreign debt . . . Moreover, investment in tradeables should be in sectors that are profitable when outputs and inputs are evaluated at world prices, rather than tariff-distorted prices.'[8] It is not surprising that Latin American countries now face a debt crisis because their economies have consistently failed to meet either of these criteria.

The Latin American approach to state enterprises has only served to make the situation worse. Between 1970 and 1982, public-sector outlays for state enterprises, as a percentage of GDP, actually declined in South Korea while they increased significantly in almost all of Latin America. In fact, in the seven largest economies of Latin America, one quarter of the public-sector deficit in the mid-1970s was accounted for by the deficit of state enterprises. By 1980-82, this had doubled, accounting for three quarters of the deterioration in their public-sector finances.

Brazil is somewhat of an exception to these generalizations about Latin America. She is a tantalizing suggestion that not only are the policies being discussed here correct, but they are feasible in Latin America. In the mid-1960s, Brazil adopted far-reaching economic reforms, including export incentives and maintenance of fairly realistic exchange rates. Between 1966 and 1973 she increased the value of her per-capita manufactured exports tenfold. In 1973, Brazil made exchange-rate adjustments that compensated for domestic inflation and allowed the real effective exchange rate to depreciate. Over the next ten years her per-capita exports of manufactured goods increased more than five fold. Chile and Uruguay had similar experiences when, after 1973, they turned outward and adopted realistic exchange rates.

After 1973, however, Brazil maintained her exchange rate through large borrowing. And, while Brazil's public enterprises are generally known for being more efficient than most ones in Latin America, as noted above, there have been few constraints placed on their investment. So although Brazil did incur massive real debts and had to have them rescheduled, she demonstrated a better growth rate (positive rather than negative) than the other major Latin American debtors between 1981 and 1984 and, in general, has been faster to recover. Indeed, Brazil achieved a greater increase in per-capita GDP than the other Latin American countries between 1960 and 1985.

CONCLUSION

State intervention in the economy is a fact of life in both East Asia and Latin America. There are two issues: What are the criteria for intervention? And how are the intervention policies managed? When intervention is undertaken with the clear intent of strengthening the ability of the economy to take advantage of market forces, it can work well. When it is undertaken in contravention of market forces, it appears to work poorly. Thus, when the East Asian countries moved to establish and maintain competitive exchange rates and to provide incentives for export, they strengthened the ability of their economies to respond to the market. When they moved to promote new industries, requiring special assistance, such as the Korean steel or petro-chemical industries, the state did not hesitate to intervene. But it intervened to make the industries competitive and, if they did not become so, as in the case of petro-chemicals, the state retrenched. In Latin America, on the other hand, state intervention in most cases served to create non-competitive industries, in both the public and the private sectors, and then to maintain them in the face of market forces to the contrary.

The four policy areas discussed here, namely export orientation, competitive exchange rates, state enterprises and industrial policies, provide a good basis for beginning to re-evaluate the Latin American economies, not in terms of state intervention versus capitalism, but in terms of the steps which the state can take to assist the economy in taking advantage of market forces.

It will take a long time to effect real change in Latin America. It will require extraordinary political will and persuasive abilities on the part of Latin American leaders to run counter to the powerful interest groups that support the present system. Businesses dependent on protection, state enterprises, organized labour, bureaucracies and political parties all tend to favour the *status quo*. They must be convinced that basic changes in the system will benefit them, if not in the short term then in the medium and long term.

Crucial support for the process is required from abroad. The most important thing the developed countries can provide is markets. None of the proposed policies will work if markets are not open and available to respond to more competitively priced products. The willingness of the United States, Japan and the European Community to provide markets is crucial to Latin America's ability to implement and sustain more market-based policies. Nor is this a one-way street. Only when Latin American purchasing power has increased will the United States be able to recoup the significant loss in export sales to Latin America that it has suffered since the debt crisis began.

NOTES

1. Quoted in Bela Balassa, Gerardo M. Bueno, Pedro-Pablo Kuczynski, and Mario Henrique Simonsen, *Toward Renewed Economic Growth in Latin America* (Washington: Institute for International Economics, 1986), p. 58.

2. Ibid.

3. John Burgess, "South Korea Forges Ahead with Steel Industry: Construction of New Plant Draws Fire," *Washington Post*, Washington, 22 May 1985, p. D12.

4. Alan Riding, *Distant Neighbors: A Portrait of the Mexicans* (New York: Vintage Books, 1986), p. 206.

5. Balassa et al., op. cit., p. 141.

6. Jack N. Behrman, *Industrial Policies: International Restructuring and Transnationals* (Lexington, Massachusetts: D.C. Heath, 1984), p. 37.

7. Balassa et al., op. cit., p. 139.

8. Jeffrey D. Sachs, "External Debt and Macroeconomic Performance in Latin America and East Asia," *Brookings Papers on Economic Activity*, Washington, No. 2, 1985, pp. 535 and 536.

26
No More NICs

ROBIN BROAD and JOHN CAVANAGH

The authors, following a general dependency view, challenge the position of such analysts as Macomber (Reading 25) that export-oriented industrialization leads to developmental success. They believe that the space for new export-led growth is very limited because world demand is stagnant, protectionism against LDC products is rising, and competition among LDCs for markets is increasing. Broad and Cavanagh advise LDCs not to bind their future to the international economy, but rather to look inward to domestic reform and development of the domestic market.

For more than a decade the most common policy advice to developing countries the world over has been a simple formula: Copy the export-oriented path of the newly industrializing countries, the celebrated NICs. These economies—Brazil, Hong Kong, Mexico, Singapore, South Korea, and Taiwan—burst onto world manufactures markets in the late 1960s and the 1970s. By 1978 these six economies plus India accounted for fully 70 per cent of the developing world's manufactured exports. Their growth rates for gross national product (GNP) and exports were unequaled.

No wonder the call was sounded for others to follow. Dozens have tried. But with the possible exceptions of Malaysia and Thailand, no country has come close. Why not? The answer lies in far-reaching changes in the global economy—from synthetic substitutes for commodity exports to unsustainable levels of external debt—that have created a glut economy offering little room for new entrants.

Despite these shifts the foremost international development institutions, the World Bank and the International Monetary Fund (IMF), continue to promote the

---

26 "No More NICs" by Robin Broad and John Cavanagh. Reprinted with permission from *Foreign Policy 72* (Fall 1988).

NIC path as the way for heavily indebted developing countries to escape the debt crisis. Yet in 1988, 8 years into a period of reduced growth in world markets, the bankruptcy of this approach should be all too apparent. By the end of the 1970s the World Bank had singled out the four Asian NICs as models to be studied by a second rung of developing countries. Having mastered the production of textiles, clothing, shoes, simple consumer electronics, and other light-manufactured wares, the four NICs were moving into more sophisticated products like automobiles and video cassette recorders. Therefore, the Bank argued, as the NICs' level of industrial development advanced, they would abandon the more basic industries to other countries. . . .

But the World Bank did more than offer the intellectual underpinnings for this development theory. In the late 1970s it positioned itself as a central actor in pushing the would-be NICs up the ladder to the NIC rung. In May 1979 then World Bank President Robert McNamara, in an address to a United Nations Conference on Trade and Development (UNCTAD) meeting in Manilla, called for developing countries to "upgrade their export structure to take advantage of the export markets being vacated by more advanced developing countries." McNamara added that the Bank would move to the forefront of this new "program of action." To do so, however, the Bank needed to move beyond its more traditional microlevel project lending with a new instrument that would maximize its leverage with developing countries. Loans for hydroelectric dams, highways, and urban renewal, among other projects, had made the Bank the key international development player; but they did not confer on the Bank adequate leverage for the proposed global restructuring.

Consequently, the Bank turned to a new set of policy prescriptions, dubbed "structural adjustment," the key ingredient of which was structural adjustment loans (SALs). These large balance-of-payments loans—targeted toward broad sectors and heavily conditioned on a recipient's economic reforms—sought to hasten the new international division of labor whereby the would-be NICs would mimic the established NICs' light-manufactures export successes. The SALs were "the World Bank's best weapon yet," as a close aide of McNamara said in 1981.

SALs carried a broad set of policy prescriptions that focused on trade-related economic sectors; they were designed to enhance efficiency and export orientation. . . .

Who are these would-be NICs that the World Bank and the IMF hoped to push up the development ladder? According to various classification systems, including those of the World Bank, this group comprises up to 30 second-tier less developed countries (LDCs) across Africa, Asia, and Latin America.

These would-be NICs largely received the big loans and amplified attention from the Bank during the later 1970s and early 1980s. Of the 9 LDCs rewarded with a structural adjustment loan of more than $50 million as of mid-1982, 7 were would-be NICs and 1 was a NIC. Moreover, the IMF's attention largely complemented the Bank's. Of the 20 LDCs that by mid-1982 had received one of the IMF's extended fund facilities—highly conditioned loans with a 10-year repayment period—of more than $50 million, 12 fell into the would-be NICs grouping and 2 were NICs.

More insight into the Bank's role in the would-be NICs can be gained by looking at one illuminating case, the Philippines. By the end of Ferdinand Marcos's administration in February 1986, the Philippines had borrowed more than $4.5 billion from the World Bank in more than 100 project and program loans. The country was, in the words of Gregario Licaros, one of Marcos's Central Bank governors, the "guinea pig" for structural adjustment. Indeed, one of the Bank's first SALs was a $200 million loan geared specifically toward restructuring the Philippine industrial sector. Its final approval by the Bank in September 1980 capped 2 years of intense policy-related dialogue between the Bank and Philippine government officials. Aided by its benevolent image as a bestower of funds for long-term development projects, the World Bank was able to take on the short-term stabilization role traditionally played by the IMF.

After a record Philippine balance-of-payments deficit of $570 million in 1979, the Bank put together the 1980 SAL package, which was attached not to a specific project but to a group of policies stipulating an export-oriented course for Philippine industry. Former high-ranking Philippine officials, including both proponents and opponents of the reforms, agree that the negotiations marked a critical juncture in the Philippine development path. Tariffs were slashed. Protective import restrictions were lifted. The exchange rate began a steady and steep devaluation, while export–and investment-promotion policies diverted resources from domestically oriented output. New free-trade tax havens, using generous incentives for transnational corporations (TNCs) to exploit low-cost Filipino labor, were established across the archipelago. Individual light-manufacturing industries, such as textiles, cement, food processing, furniture, and footwear, were slated for restructuring according to World Bank specifications.

During this period, similar policies were pushed in other would-be NICs. World Bank SALs to the Ivory Coast, Kenya, Pakistan, Senegal, and Turkey—like the Philippine SAL—all concentrated on improving export incentives and performance. In Thailand, where a Central Bank official vowed in mid-1979 that the World Bank's policies would "never be listened to or followed by top people here," the government implemented economic policy changes almost identical to those of the Philippines a few years and a SAL later. In other cases, notably Chile and Indonesia, would-be NICs followed the Bank's blueprint for development without a formal SAL.

NIC RIVALRY

In effect the World Bank was helping to create a group of countries that would compete against each other to become NICs. The result was two vicious battles—one to offer cheaper, more docile labor forces and more attractive financial incentives to lure TNC assembly lines away from the other countries, and the other to win scarce export markets.

This competition soon became clear to each would-be NIC. As a deputy governor to the Philippine Central Bank remarked in a 1980 interview: "We've got to always be careful now, always watching, on the lookout for other [developing] nations' next moves. . . . And then we've got to make sure we meet their offer and better it." Sri Lanka's advertisement in the October 16, 1981, issue of the *Far Eastern Economic Review* said it well: "Sri Lanka challenges you to match the advantages of its Free Trade Zone, against those being offered elsewhere. . . . Sri Lanka has the lowest labor rates in Asia." Variations on that appeal were issued by one would-be NIC after another, putting TNCs in a choice position from which to bargain the most lucrative investment or subcontracting deals.

The competition encouraged labor repression and exploitation. One Manila-based TNC executive explained in a 1981 interview: "We tell the [Philippine] government: you've got to clamp down [on labor]. . . . Or we threaten to move elsewhere. And we'll do just that. There's Sri Lanka [and] now China too."

Most of the Bank's public documents sought to play down the problems associated with rivalry among the would-be NICs. But the Bank was not unaware of the potential zero-sum game. In a January 1979 working paper assessing the LDC's manufacturing export potential, two leading Bank economists, Hollis Chenery and Donald Keesing, forecast that "the increasing number of successful competitors may make it increasingly difficult for newcomers to get established" and that the success of a "few" could leave " too little" opportunity for the rest. . . .

Yet who had set in motion this chain of competition? An October 1979 World Bank report had counseled the Philippines to take advantage of the fact that its wages had "declined significantly relative to those in competing . . . countries," notably Hong Kong and South Korea. Almost simultaneously, as reported in the *Southeast Asia Chronicle* in December 1981, the Bank helped steer Indonesia onto a parallel course, advising that "incentives for firms to locate there rather that in some other Southeast Asian country . . . must be provided." Meanwhile, Sri Lanka received a $20 million World Bank loan to establish a new export platform for apparel subcontracting, and the Bank pushed the People's Republic of China (PRC), Thailand, and some of the Caribbean Basin countries into the light-manufactures arena as well.

The competition among would-be NICs was further exacerbated by the exporters of an earlier era, the Asian NICs of Hong Kong, Singapore, South Korea, and Taiwan. World Bank theory to the contrary, these countries were not abandoning textiles, apparel, and electronics assemble as they moved into higher stages of industrialization. Indeed, since the 1960s the Asian NICs had been spreading throughout the entire range of industry—from light to heavy, from unsophisticated to sophisticated—leaving little space for would-be NICs.

The export performance of the Asian NICs between 1979 and 1985 illustrates this point. Their combined exports leaped from $60.5 billion to $113.9 billion, a stunning 88 per cent increase during years of slow global economic growth. More sophisticated "strategic" industries like telecommunications, complex electronic equipment, and motor vehicles were encouraged by NIC governments through various tax holidays and subsidized loans. Over this period South Korean motor vehicle exports rose from $300 million to close to $1 billion and Hong Kong telecommunications and sound equipment rose from less than $1 billion to more than $2 billion.

On a regular basis export surges in these high value-added industries captured newspaper headlines. Little attention was paid, however, to the continuing rapid NIC export growth in traditional light manufactures. Through a combination of innovation, cost-cutting measures, upgrading capital equipment, and state and private-sector cooperation these countries held on to and expanded their markets. Textile and clothing exports from the four grew from $14.6 billion to $23.4 billion over the 6 years, a 60 per cent rise. The Asian NICs enjoyed a rising global market share in the textile and clothing industries. The same rapid growth was noticeable in other light-manufacturing sectors. For example, Hong Kong's exports of footwear doubled, from $125 million to $250 million. And South Korea's exports of toys grew from $300 million to $670 million.

Another factor also was inhibiting the would-be NICs' economic ascension—new technologies. The more than a decade that separated the NICs' debut from that of the would-be NICs witnessed technological advances in several sectors that changed the very definition of Third World industrialization.

By the late 1970s technological innovations, led by the microprocessor revolution, made the global fragmentation of production highly profitable and desirable. Whereas the original NICs had received complete industrial processes such as shipbuilding and machinery, the would-be NICs won marginal segments of scattered assembly lines for semiconductors and consumer electronics, textiles, and apparel. In Sri Lanka, for example, workers in export-processing zones used basic sewing machines to stitch together garments from imported fabric. In the Philippines, female workers in 1980 were performing only 1 or the 10 major operations of electronic production, attaching hairlike gold wires to silicon chips.

As a result, these new global assembly lines left gaping disparities between the gross value of the would-be NICs' industrial export earnings and the actual value added to the product in the developing country. Consider again the Philippine case. When proclaiming the non-traditional-export strategy's supposed triumphs, the Philippine government naturally focused on the higher of the two figures, the gross value of exports. Yet when stripped of import components' costs, the "value added" by the domestic side of production was but a fraction of the export earnings.

With the Philippines importing cartons for its banana exports, cans for some food exports, and a wide assortment of machinery and component parts for its limited apparel and electronic assembly lines, value added in most Philippine industries was quite low. Although a public version of a 1979 World Bank document admitted that the aggregate value added for Philippine nontraditional exports was "at best only 40 percent," a confidential report revealed the precise Bank calculation to be 25 per cent. In other words, for every dollar of nontraditional-export earnings, only 25 cents stayed in the Philippines; the rest was siphoned off by import payments. Low value added was a fact of life in the Philippines' part in the new international division of labor.

According to one of the bast analyses of electronics subcontracting, the long-term outlook for increasing the amount of value added in developing countries in the industry was bleak. As this December 1981 United Nations Industrial Development Organization report, *Restructuring World Industry in a Period of Crisis,* detailed, the per cent of value added attributable to new LDC microprocessor production lines rose until 1973. By 1977, however, value added in the newest LDC factories already had begun to fall. This downward turn came even as the gross value of semiconductors re-exported to the United States soared tenfold from 1970 to 1978. Of the seven LDCs studied, the Philippines was the last to start silicon chip assembly. Entering on the downswing of the curve, value added in its factories was the lowest of all.

Since 1977 a growing share of the value was being held in the electronics companies' home countries. The U.N. report emphasized that, "as complexity of circuitry increases, more value added is produced in the early wafer-fabrication stage, i.e., in the United States, in Japan, or in some locations in Western Europe. Furthermore, the more complex, computerized final testing, which again is usually done in OECD [Organization for Economic Cooperation and Development] locations, particularly in the United States and Japan."

If the production side of the would-be NIC experience offered less than what was advertised, the marketing side was even grimmer. For light-manufactured exports to be the engine of growth for the would-be NICs, world trade—that is, global demand for these products—had to grow each year. There was no way to escape this logic in the aggregate.

But in the late 1970s and early 1980s, at precisely the time when would-be NICs were induced to embark on a nontraditional-export path, these necessary conditions were decidedly absent. Over the decade from 1963 to 1973 the volume of world exports rose at a rapid average annual rate of 8.5 per cent. Beginning in 1973, however, an economic deceleration slowed the average annual expansion to 4 per cent. By 1980 exports were crawling ahead at only 1 per cent per year, and in 1981 they showed no growth. Moreover, 1981 had the dubious distinction of being the first year since 1958 to experience an actual decrease in world trade in current dollar terms, a shrinkage of 1 per cent.

Behind these global trade statistics lurked the domestic stagnation of the industrialized economies. According to IMF figures, from 1976 to 1979 the real GNP of industrialized countries grew at a tolerable average yearly rate of 4 per cent. By 1980, OECD growth was limping ahead at only 1.25 per cent; the next year it increased again by only 1.25 per cent. These 2 years presaged a decade of vastly reduced growth. From 1981 to 1985 world output slowed to an average of 1.7 per cent per year and trade to 2.8 per cent. These aggregate statistics become even more dismal if Eastern Europe and the PRC are excluded: Output over the first half of the 1980s grew at an average annual rate of only 1.4 per cent in developing countries and 2.3 per cent in developed countries.

As more countries battled for the same tepid export markets, prices plunged. Between 1981 and 1985, world prices of food commodities fell at an average annual rate of 15 per cent; agricultural raw materials dropped at an average annual rate of

7 per cent; and minerals and metals fell 6 per cent. The year 1986 proved even dimmer, when a 30 per cent decline in the developing countries' terms of trade (the ratio of prices of developing-country exports to prices of their imports) translated into a staggering $94 billion to the developed world.

Another pitfall facing the LDCs' export-oriented industrialization was the panoply of quantitative restrictions that had spread to cover fully one-half of global trade. Despite official encomiums to "free trade," the OECD countries increasingly were barricading themselves behind what even President Ronald Reagan's Council of Economic Advisers admitted were "neomercantile" policies.

These defensive machinations to moderate the recessionary bite at home were baptized the "new protectionism"—a proliferation of American, European Economic Community, and Japanese trade barriers, notably quotas on LDC-manufactured exports. "New" referred to the dazzling array of nontariff barriers not regulated by the General Agreement on Tariffs and Trade. Voluntary export restraints and orderly marketing arrangements flourished. As the World Bank and the IMF encouraged free-trade policies on LDCs, the major voting blocs within those institutions retreated from any semblance of free trade at home. The retreat of free trade became inextricably meshed with the recession: As OECD growth slackened, quotas were tightened. The more successful a particular LDC export category was, the more restrictive the quota became.

By the calculations of the World Bank's own economists in 1979, the most dangerous of the new protectionist barriers was centered in the apparel, textile, and footwear sectors. Yet it was precisely these sectors—along with furniture, wood products, electronics, and other light-manufactured exports—that the Bank had pinpointed as the engine of growth for the would-be NICs. The restrictive allotments of the Multi-Fiber Arrangement made textiles and apparel perhaps the most heavily controlled sectors in international trade. As a result, the LDCs' share of textile and apparel exports began to shrink in the early 1980s.

Did the Bank adequately address the impact of slow global economic growth and rising protectionism on its policy directives? As early as 1974 the Bank understood certain pitfalls that the 1970s and 1980s might hold for export-oriented industrialization. That year McNamara, in an address to the Board of Governors, noted: "The adverse effect on the developing countries . . . a reduction in economic growth in their major markets would be great. There is a strong—almost one-to-one—relationship between changes in the growth of OECD countries and that of oil importing nations." The Philippines was especially vulnerable, the Bank acknowledged in a country program paper 2 years later, "with international trade the equivalent of almost half of GNP." And in his May 1979 address to the UNCTAD conference in Manila, McNamara noted that the World Bank had perceived the onset of the new protectionism as early as 1976.

Yet in the late 1970s and early 1980s Bank officials who were planning Third World development strategies continually made assumptions that ignored slow growth and rising protectionism. Their model, grounded in theories of free trade and comparative advantage, posited the absence of such conditions. They opted instead for what was termed "one set of reasonable assumptions" without explaining their legitimacy. The set of "reasonable" assumptions about trade and protectionism that underpinned the Bank's structural adjustment reports and advice to would-be NICs was some permutation of the following: Industrial countries were to grow 4 per cent annually in the 1980s; "worldwide economic recovery" stood on the horizon; and "no major set-backs" would occur in major markets.

Did Bank economists really believe this? In the Philippine example a wide chasm between these assumptions and the private assessments of Bank officials was revealed time and again during interviews conducted by one of the authors in the early 1980s. One World Bank consultant and member of the Bank's appraisal mission for its first Philippine SAL, John Power, privately admitted his doubts about a successful outcome of Philippine export-oriented industrialization given the gravity of the "world situation." Yet a 1979 book he coauthored as background for the Philippine SAL, *Industrial Promotion Policies in the Philippines*, refused to give credence to any such misgivings. In a similar case of conflicting assessments, a January 1979 study by the Bank economists Chenery and Keesing acknowledged existing "severe import restrictions" imposed by key developed countries and increasingly smaller quotas for up-and-coming LDC manufactures exporters. But in another working paper, published about 2 years later, the Bank economist Barend de Vries argued that "considerable opportunities" existed for Philippine nontraditional exports.

The potential effects of this unsubstantiated optimism about the Philippines and other would-be NICs were never seriously considered by Bank officials. The development prescriptions of Bank officials were transformed into a kind of dogma: "The more hostile the external environment, the more urgent" the need for restructuring, an August 1980 *Report and Recommendation* urged. In one instance, a Bank director took the floor at the executive board's final meeting on the Philippine SAL to question the management's scenario of Philippine "dynamic" export-led growth in light of "an adverse environment [including] lower than projected growth rates in industrial countries and increased protectionism." The board chairman's response epitomized the Bank's unquestioning attitude: "If the environment turned out to be more adverse than projected, then the ultimate benefits under the adjustment program would be reduced, but the nature of the adjustment needed would not be changed." But such a response was no more than conjecture. No hard evidence and no computer runs were offered to answer what should have been a basic question: If world trade did not grow, and if key markets became increasingly protected, would export-oriented industrialization be the optimal route to growth?

The Bank's 1981 *World Development Report*, in fact, did present formally a quantitative global model incorporating "slower industrial [country] growth" and "increased protectionism." But the exercise was at best questionable; at worst, it was deceptive. Although lower than either the accompanying bast-case scenario or previous *World Development Report* estimates, the low-case scenario for 1980-

1985 still promised growth rates higher than what transpired. Indeed, over the past 9 years the Bank consistently has projected average developing-country export growth rates of more than 5 per cent per year; between 1981 and 1986 the actual annual growth rates averaged instead a negative 4 per cent. . . .

In any event, the low-case projections were largely ignored in the plans and projections for specific countries. When incorporating global growth estimates in aggregate economic work for various LDCs, the Bank used figures closer to high-case yields. This was done without any caveat mentioning that the Bank also had somewhat less optimistic forecasts.

It was becoming increasingly clear that the World Bank had no vision of development in a world economy of curtailed growth. To a large extend Bank officials had equated growth with development. To them, development did not primarily mean providing adequate food, clean water, clothing, and housing—in short, offering a standard of living consistent with human dignity. Those had become secondary concerns to be met through growth. In the Bank's view, no growth meant no development and therefore could not be considered seriously. . . .

In recent public Bank documents, slow growth in the world economy is still viewed as a short-term or cyclical aberration that does not undermine the basic soundness of the Bank's structural adjustment advice. Indeed, as late as its 1987 *World Development Report,* the Bank was still stressing that the world economy was continuing to "expand," albeit at a "modest and uneven" rate. That outlook enabled the Bank to continue unabashedly to counsel "the outward-oriented trade policies which have proved so successful for the NICs in recent years."

A NEW WORLD ECONOMY

World Bank forecasts notwithstanding, global stagnation is likely to prove harder to shake than most would like to believe. Aside from protectionism pressures, a series of corporate developments has stunted demand globally, leaving increasing numbers of people at the margins of market activity. Prominent among these developments are the commercial banks' handling of the Third World debt crisis, corporate substitution for Third World raw materials, and labor-saving technological innovations in the developed world.

The debt crisis arose inevitably from the export-oriented development strategies, which depended on heavy borrowing for infrastructure and in many countries fed corruption and capital flight. In the early 1980s, as oil prices and interest rates rose and primary commodity prices fell, country after country announced its inability to service debts owed to banks in the developed world. In rapid succession the creditor banks sent these countries through IMF austerity programs, which prescribed a kind of shock treatment to bring countries' balance of payments out of deficit. Wage freezes, currency devaluations, and government spending cuts reduced imports into the Third World; indeed, many countries wiped out trade and national budget deficits within a few years. But the lowered wages and imports also dampened global economic growth.

Technological breakthroughs in substitutes for Third World raw materials also hurt growth performance in the developing world. A single anecdote typifies the impact of longer-term corporate development on commodity markets. Until 1981 the largest consumer of the world's sugar was Coca-Cola. That year, in a move rapidly emulated by other soft drink giants, Coca-Cola began to shift its sweetener from sugar to corn syrup. Western consumers might not have viewed the change as significant to them, but it displaced millions of Third World sugar workers for a product produced within industrial countries.

Advances in plastics, synthetic fibers, food chemistry, and biotechnology are bringing similar far-reaching changes to other raw material and commodity markets. Cumulatively these substitutions have pushed tens of millions of Third World workers into the margins of the marketplace, further curbing global demand.

Likewise, new corporate technologies are transforming developed-country economies. The computer revolution, the major technological breakthrough of the last two decades, is strikingly dissimilar from earlier technological breakthroughs. The advent of electricity and the automobile, for example, generated millions of jobs in related industries and sparked economic booms in the leading countries. The microprocessor revolution has also created millions of jobs. However, applications of microprocessors have spread through almost every manufacturing and service sector in uses that are labor saving. Bank tellers, supermarket check-out clerks, assembly-line workers, and others are all joining the ranks of the unemployed. This phenomenon is reflected in Western Europe, where for 17 straight years the unemployment rate has risen.

The result of these three changes is that all over the world industry is turning out more than consumers can buy. The new global glut economy coexists with billions of people with enormous needs and wants but with little ability to buy.

As world economic growth has slowed, so have the Third World activities of its central private institutions: TNCs and banks.Much of the growth of the 1960s and 1970s was based on a rapid expansion of production around the world by subsidiaries of such TNCs as Ford, John Deers, and Texas Instruments. Western banks followed to provide financing. Then, after 1973, they became major economic actors in the developing world in their own right as recyclers of billions of petrodollars.

This is no longer the case. Banks and corporations go where there is growth and hence profit. Since the early 1980s the Third World basically has stopped growing; many countries have even slipped backward. Consequently, U.S. banks have returned home for new short-term rewards—consumer credit, corporate mergers, and the get-rich-quick gimmicks of financial speculation.

Again, the statistics are stark. In 1983 international bank lending to developing countries, excluding offshore bank centers, totaled $35 billion. By 1985 a mere $3 billion in new lending had trickled in. . . .

Yet the changing world economy has created a desperate need to rethink the kinds of adjustments that will produce growth and development. At the very least, the adjustment strategies must be built on realistic assumptions. The NICs were the product of a radically different world economy. That they cannot be replicated in the 1980s is an indication of how much that world economy has changed.

Rather than increasing their reliance on a hostile world environment, developing countries should try to reduce this dependence and to diversify trading partners and products. This approach implies a careful restructuring of trade and financial linkages to conform with a development logic that is driven by internal economic forces.

If economies can no longer be pulled along primarily by external growth, stronger internal buying power must be generated. The great challenge is to transform crushing social needs into effective demand and then to meet that demand by turning first to domestically produced goods and services, next to the region, and only after that to the wider world market. In most developing countries this development framework implies vast internal adjustment quite different from the World Bank's brand of structural adjustment. Most of the Third World's people cannot afford to purchase many goods and services. Wages are locked into rock-bottom subsistence rates; wealth and income are heavily skewed toward a relatively small, wealthy elite. As a result, spreading income more evenly requires, for a start, extensive land reform, progressive taxation policies, and guarantees of worker rights.

To offer more specifics on internal demand-driven development strategies is risky. Vastly different resource bases and social strata among countries suggest that a country-specific approach is essential. Indeed, the sin of universality in development strategies was perhaps the central weakness of IMF and World Bank adjustment programs. Further, the successful implementation of any development strategy depends on its acceptance by entrenched interests in that country. However desirable comprehensive agrarian reform may be in the Philippines, for example, a powerful landowning group has substantial influence in the government and is likely to block serious reform efforts.

These caveats noted, a few general principles for development in a hostile world economy can be sketched out. Most would-be NICs remain predominantly agricultural societies; hence the starting point of internal demand-led development must be in farming. Two undertakings are central to increasing buying power in the countryside: redistributing wealth and raising productivity.

Agrarian reform remains the major means of redistributing wealth and income and thereby increasing the effective purchasing power of the rural population. The people in Third World rural areas are largely either poor tenants or agricultural workers who earn only subsistence wages. They have meager resources to consume in the marketplace. Only through agrarian reform can this population begin to produce a surplus that can be translated into consumption. In economic terms, small farmers have a higher "marginal propensity" to consume than larger ones, and much of their consumption could be satisfied by locally produced products.

Raising productivity depends in large part on upgrading infrastructure—from irrigation and roads to credit institutions and marketing channels. In this area, as in efforts to upgrade social infrastructure through health, education, and nutrition loans, the World Bank could play a positive role by providing loans and technical assistance. In many respects, this emphasis would return the Bank to its original purpose as a development bank. In all loans, the Bank would do well to work closely with producer and neighborhood associations and cooperatives and other non-governmental organizations that have proliferated in developing countries of late.

From this starting point, industrialization based on maximizing industrial linkages with agriculture makes great sense. In particular, three strands of industry could be encouraged:

Agricultural inputs. An agricultural sector with rising productivity will need locally produced fertilizer, pesticides, water pumps, and a wide range of tools, from plows to tractors.

Processing farm products. From cocoa and coffee to sugar and cotton, increased domestic processing offers more foodstuffs for local consumption and increases the value added of exports.

Consumer goods. As purchasing power grows in the countryside, so does the market for locally produced textiles, clothing, shoes, bicycles, refrigerators, and other consumer goods. Here, too, World Bank loans could help by improving the technology of small and medium-sized industries.

The cycle of agriculture-linked industrialization does not stop there. As industry grows, the increased buying power of industrial workers provides an expanding market for farm goods from rural areas. Agriculture and industry would grow in tandem. It is worth pointing out that, popular myths not withstanding, South Korea pursued this basic strategy in its earliest phase of industrialization. . . .

This agriculture-linked industrialization strategy should not be confused with import-substitution policies for industrialization. Those were decidedly different—more capital–and import-intensive, often dependent on protecting inefficiencies, and less sensitive to creating markets for new production. Nor does agriculture-linked industrialization shun exports. Rather, it focuses on exporting products offering higher values added.

In a highly interdependent world, such demand-centered development does not and cannot imply autarky. What cannot be produced locally is produced nationally. What cannot be produced nationally is purchased from regional partners—which suggests the importance of revitalizing regional integration institutions. Only for those products for which regional producers cannot satisfy demand is trade necessary with countries on the other side of the globe. Domestic needs should shape trade patterns rather than vice versa. . . .

Beyond domestic market policies in agriculture and industry, development strategies should seek to curtail the wasteful economic activities that are rampant in some countries. These range from large, unproductive land-holdings and capital flight to production and export monopolies and cronyism. Rooting out these practices is a monumental political task, threatening as it does entrenched groups of speculators, moneylenders, and landlords and bloated militaries. Development strategies also must pay closer attention to the pressing need to maintain fragile natural resource bases around the world. The disappearance of rain forests, plant and animal species, clean rivers, and clean air has become the dominant trend in too many countries. . . .

Most observers continue to view the Asian NICs as role models. And they offer glowing imagery in support of their views: Asian NICs have "already taken off," and the rest of the noncommunist Southeast Asian countries are "on the runway revving" up to follow, as former Japanese Foreign Minister Saburo Okita has described it.

The would-be NICs have fallen for such prophecies for nearly a decade. Now is the time to demand not imagery but a realistic assessment of options. The debate on adjustment and development should be reopened; strategies that proclaim that the only option is greater dependence on an increasingly hostile and turbulent world economy need to be challenged. It is time to ask whether any more developing countries can really hope to become the South Korea of the late 1980s or the Hong Kong of the early 1990s.

IV

CURRENT PROBLEMS IN INTERNATIONAL POLITICAL ECONOMY

The 1990s will be important years in the international political economy. Among the complex economic and political issues of the decade, five broad problems stand out: the changing international role of the United States, the associated rise of Japan, the growing integration of the European economies, economic reform in the Soviet Union and Eastern Europe, and the decaying environment. The readings in Part IV address these topics.

Since the 1970s, the United States has gone from a position of unchallenged dominance of the world economy to a position of first among major economic powers. Indeed, a number of economic problems faced by the United States have, in the opinion of many, driven the rest of the world economy perilously close to instability. By the same token, many Americans feel that the international economy has come to threaten their well-being. In Reading 29, Barry Bosworth and Robert Lawrence address this set of issues, arguing that most of the concern on the part of Americans is misinformed or misplaced.

Closely related to widespread perception of a decline in the international position of the United States has been the rise of Japan as a global economic power. Japan is now the world's largest investor, and its banks and corporations have come to dominate many markets. Both the Japanese and others have considered the implications of Japan's impressive growth in wealth and power. In Reading 27, Takashi Inoguchi presents a Japanese view of how the world might evolve as we move toward the twenty-first century.

If America's changing position and the rise of Japan have unsettled the world's political economy, so too has the accelerated pace of European economic integration. The member nations of the European Community (the Common Market) have moved rapidly toward eliminating all barriers to trade and investment among themselves, and have even talked of establishing a common central bank and a common currency. As Western Europe becomes a more cohesive economic unit, some in the United States and Japan have expressed concern that it might turn away from the rest of the world economy. Fiat chairman Giovanni Agnelli argues in Reading 28 that European economic integration is a natural outgrowth of long-standing economic trends, and that it poses no real threat to other members of the international economic community.

As the nations of Western Europe have brought their economies closer together, the countries of Eastern Europe have shifted rapidly away from their past policies of semi-autarky and planning. In different ways, all are dismantling elements of their previous economic models and moving toward greater reliance on international and domestic market forces. The most important of these experiences, of course, is that of the Soviet Union. Richard E. Ericson, in Reading 30, explains the reasons for the new economic thinking in the USSR, and evaluates some of its implications for the Soviet Union and the rest of the world.

The fifth problem likely to occupy the attention of political leaders during the 1990s will be managing the environment. The air we breathe, the water we drink, are all part of the global "commons." To the extent that it is costly to use air and water without polluting these resources, it is always in the interest of an individual, firm, or country to get a "free ride"—to use the resource and pass the environmental cost onto others. In the past, providing such public goods has been an important rationale for government intervention in the economy (see the Introduction). Accordingly, Richard Ablin (Reading 31) suggests that private enterprise cannot solve the problem of environmental pollution by itself. The difficulties of managing the environment at the international level, however, are even more acute given the absence of a central authority capable of providing public goods by itself or enforcing agreements among countries. Solving the problem of global pollution may require that countries accept unprecedented constraints on their national sovereignty.

27

Four Japanese Scenarios for the Future

TAKASHI INOGUCHI

In this speculative essay, Takashi Inoguchi, a political scientist at the University of Tokyo, examines four scenarios for the future currently under discussion in Japan and elsewhere. The first scenario envisions a resurgent American hegemony, the second, a "bigemony" based on Japan and the United States, the third, a world of many powers and economic blocs, and the fourth, a "Pax Nipponica." Given the continuing importance of nuclear weapons, the likely pace and origin of scientific and technological innovation, and the legacy of World War II, Inoguchi posits that a soft landing proceeding from the first to the third scenarios is most likely—if mildly optimistic. In developing this argument, Inoguchi recognizes both the growing economic clout of Japan and the country's reluctance to assume a greater leadership role in international political and security affairs.

Japan is in an era of transition. Behind a facade of confidence in their country's future, many Japanese feel adrift in the world of the late twentieth century. The Japanese energy that is currently directed overseas is no longer based, as it was in the 1960s, on a nationally orchestrated strategy. Governments are no longer sure how to guide society, or with what goals. And Japanese society itself displays its loss of faith in the belief-system so dominant in the 1960s. Today the almost blind belief of that period in the loyalty to big business firms has lost its appeal. It is not an exaggeration to say that in the 1980s Japan has been improvising its responses to the

---

27 "Four Japanese Scenarios for the Future" by Takashi Inoguchi. Reproduced in abridged form by permission from "Four Japanese scenarios for the future," *International Affairs*, Vol. 65, No. 1 (Winter 1989). Takashi Inoguchi, professor of political science at the Institute of Oriental Culture, University of Tokyo, specialises in international relations, international political economy, and Japanese politics. He has published numerous works in Japanese and in English, including *The Political Economy of Japan*, Vol. 2: *The Changing International Context* (Stanford, CA; Stanford University Press, 1988, co-edited with Daniel Okimoto) and *The State and Society*, Vol. 1 of The Contemporary Political Science Library (Tokyo: University of Tokyo Press, 1988).

unfamiliar challenges from within and without on an *ad hoc* basis, tenaciously adhering to time-honored ways of doing things.

Bereft of a sense of direction, and uncertain about the future, Japan has been haunted by a vague angst about its future which has led it sometimes to hedge, and at least to limit, its commitment to the demands, requests and suggestions coming from overseas that Japan, now a global economic power, should take on more global responsibility. . . .

One of the salient themes which has emerged in the directionless Japanese society of the 1980s is an emphasis on traditional values: values such as perseverance, frugality, diligence, effort, family, community, sacrifice, humility, the spirit of harmony, and deference for the elderly. This fact is instructive. The problem is that these traditional values cannot be the basis for Japanese principles in guiding Japanese global policy. Prime Minister Noboru Takeshita's favourite saying, "when you do something, sweat by yourself and give credit to others", may be the epitome of humility, generosity and altruism, but it cannot be the sole organizing principle of Japanese diplomacy. The same can be said about economic efficiency and profitability. They cannot dominate other considerations when the dollar's volatility could shake down the world economy or when the United States makes it imperative for its allies to implement tighter measures on technological transfer to communist countries.

Apart from these traditional values and economic criteria, which are too vague to allow one to fathom how the Japanese would like to see the world evolve, what are Japan's conceptions of its global position and its global roles? In other words, how is the country shaping its scenarios of the future worlds in which Japan will occupy a not unimportant position? This article addresses these and related questions, especially in relation to burden-sharing and power-sharing with the United States in the management of the world economy and international relations.

I will present below four Japanese scenarios of the world system in 25-50 years' time, making a clear distinction between the economic and the political and security arrangements envisaged in each scenario. In each scenario, Japan's role and the degree of burden-sharing/power-sharing with the United States will also be indicated. Next, the feasibility of the four scenarios will be discussed in terms of three major conditions, assessing the relative feasibility and desirability of each scenario. The United States and Japan will be the primary focus, though other major actors, no less important to Japan than the United States, will be touched on as much as possible. Lastly, I will reflect on my findings in the light of the dominant aspirations and apprehensions of the Japanese. . . .

THE FOUR SCENARIOS

The following four scenarios of the world in the next 25-50 years are seen by the Japanese as "visions of the future". Although in some respects they overlap, they represent differing views on the future of global development, the distribution of economic and military power, and institutions for peace and development. It should also be mentioned that these scenarios have not been sketched out by the Japanese alone; both Japanese and non-Japanese have articulated their preferences, given a future in which Japan will play an enhanced role.

1. Pax Americana, Phase II

This image of the future was first articulated by the Americans. It is the image of an America retaining its leading position in the world and making full use of its advantage in having created the institutions of post-Second World War order and security. This scenario depicts an America experienced in forging the "balanced" or globalist view of the Western alliance and deftly prodding and cajoling its allies into enlightened joint action. The outline of this scenario was first made during the latter half of the 1970s, when the post-Vietnam trauma was still strong and when Soviet global influence was somewhat exaggeratedly felt in the United States. In the parlance of American political scientists, the key word was "regimes"—rules and practices in international interest adjustment—whereby the United States would retain its enlightened hegemony and control the direction of world development. . . .

In Japan, this image of America's future has been a consistent favourite. Naohiro Amaya, a former vice-minister in the Ministry of International Trade and Industry, was fond of talking about "Ko-Bei" ("later United States"), as if the United States prior to Vietnam was called "Zen-Bei" ("earlier United States"). This is an analogy with the later Han dynasty of ancient China, which was restored after 17 years of disappearance and survived for another two centuries. Similarly, Yasusuke Murakami, a well-known economist, has argued that the hegemonic cycle that has been observed for the last few centuries has ceased to repeat itself largely because the world economy has been transformed from something based on individual national economies to a much more integrated structure. His scenario delineates an America which is an enlightened and experienced *primus inter pares* in an increasingly multipolar world.

This image has been a favourite one, not least because it encourages the basic retention of Japan's traditional concentration on an economic role with no drastic increase in its security role, which is largely delegated to the United States. Although Japan's profile in the world has changed a great deal in the 1980s, the Japanese preference for limiting the country's commitment to military matters, many of which are generally deemed to have dubious utility, has not been altered.

Japan's roles in Pax Americana phase II are not significantly different from its present ones. Essentially, these are primarily of an economic nature, with the bulk of global security shouldered by the United States. Even if Japan-US security cooperation is accelerated, this basic division of labour is unlikely to change. Even if Japan were to enhance its out-of-area security cooperation by sending warships to the Persian Gulf to shoulder the costs of oil imports, it would be bolstering the US dominated world rather than becoming a main security-provider in the region.

Even if Japan were to increase its security-related assistance to some Third World countries like Pakistan, Turkey, Papua New Guinea, and Honduras, the security leadership of the United States would remain strong. Needless to say, there are those who argue that Japan will start in due course to exert influence by accumulating credit in the United States and other countries. But in this scenario Japanese self-assertiveness will be restrained by various domestic and international factors.

Japan's regional roles in this scenario will be heavily economic. More concretely, Japan will become the vital core of the Pacific growth crescent, encompassing three areas: (1) northern Mexico, the Pacific United States and Canada, (2) Japan, and (3) the Pacific—the Asian newly industrializing countries, coastal China, the Association of South-East Asian (ASEAN) countries and Oceania. The incorporation of the second and the third economic groups into the extended US economic zone will be a vital factor in a US revival. In short, Japan's role in this scenario will be to link the US economy with the Asian Pacific economies in a more balanced manner than today. In this scenario, the current US efforts to liberalize the Pacific Asian markets, revalue local currency-dollar exchange rates and promote burden-sharing in development aid and finance and international security will be given further momentum. At the same time, Pacific Asian nationalistic anti-Americanism will be considerably restrained. Perhaps it is important to note that Pax Americana phase II will need a no less vigorous Western Europe. An enlarged and enhanced European Community (EC) will remain a pillar of this scenario. But if it degenerates into regional protectionism of the sort that can be glimpsed in the tougher EC anti-dumping policy on printing machines, through arrogance derived from an expected enlarged size and power, then it will elicit a negative reaction from the United States and Japan.

2. "Bigemony"

This second scenario for the future has been propagated by economists and businessmen, fascinated by the rapid development and integration of what Robert Gilpin, a Princeton political scientist, calls the "*nichibei* [Japan-US] economy". That is to say, the economies of Japan and the United States have become one integrated economy of a sort. C. Fred Bergsten, an economist who worked as a senior bureaucrat under the Carter administration and is now director of the Institute for International Economics coined the word "bigemony", which denotes the primordial importance of the United States and Japan in managing the world economy. Zbigniew Brzezinski, National Security Advisor to President Jimmy Carter, coined the expresion "Amerippon" to describe the close integration of the American and Japanese manufacturing, financial and commercial sectors and indeed the two economies as a whole. This image of the future has been enhanced by the steady rise in the yen's value compared to the US dollar, and the concomitant rise in Japanese GNP, now registering 20 per cent of world GNP.

In Japan this image has been put forward most forcefully by former Prime Minister Yasuhiro Nakasone. In one of his meetings with President Reagan, he suggested that the two countries should forge a single community of the same destiny, although what he envisaged focused on security rather than on economic aspects of the bilateral relationship. It must be noted that Japanese images of the future have tended to focus on Japan-US relations, to the dismay of Europeans and Asians, let alone other Third World countries. This tendency itself shows the strength of this second scenario.

Japan's roles in the "bigemony" scenario may appear to some to be very similar to those envisaged in Pax Americana phase II. However, economic power becomes military power almost inevitably, and Japan does not constitute the historic exception to this rule. But the form in which Japan's economic power will be translated into military power needs close attention. Under "bigemony" the technical/economic/strategic cooperation-integration between the United States and Japan will become formidable, and of the largest scale in history. It is therefore not difficult to foresee, for instance, advanced fighter aircraft being developed jointly and manufactured primarily for Japanese use, with Japanese finance, though with American know-how, and also sold to third countries under the label, "Made in the United States". The large-scale strategic integration between these two countries as developed in the Pacific in the 1980s will come to be seen as a good testimony of the bigemonic roles Japan can play in security areas.

Japan's regional role in"bigemony" is an acceleration of the features presented in Pax Americana phase II. A gigantic Pacific economic community will be forged, with Japan's role reminiscent of the role played by the corridor stretching from northern Italy through north-eastern France, the Rhineland and the Low Countries to southern Britain in modern European economic development. Under this scenario, the potentially heated contest between the United States and Japan over the structural framework of Pacific Asia's economic relationship with the United States will be largely dissipated. Currently, Pacific Asia faces increasingly clear alternatives as to its economic framework: either a US-led free-trade regime established through a bilateral agreement with the United States, or a regional community with *de facto* Japanese initiatives, which would try to retain a free-trade zone even if North America and Western Europe fell into the temptation of protectionism and regionalism of a malign kind. Furthermore, the strategic integration of many countries in the region may make it hard to accommodate the Soviet Union within an invigorated bigemonic structure, thus relegating it to a far less important status than it currently occupies, unless some other countervailing moves are continuously taken. In this scenario Western Europe, though large in size and high in income level, will be increasingly localized within Europe and its immediate vicinity. . . .

3. Pax Consortis

Japan's third scenario portrays a world of many consortia in which the major actors proceed by busily forging coalitions to make policy adjustments and agreements among themselves—a world in which no single actor can dominate the rest. This scenario resembles Pax Americana II in its crude skeleton with its "regimes" and "cooperation under anarchy". However, the major difference is that the thrust of the third scenario rests on the pluralistic nature of policy adjustment among the major actors, whereas that of the first conveys the desirability or necessity (or even the hoped-for inevitability) of "administrative guidance" or "moral leadership" by the state that is *primus inter pares*—the United States. This third image is favoured by many Japanese, not least because Japan is averse to shouldering large security burdens. It is also favoured because Japan is not completely happy about America ordering everyone around, especially when it only grudgingly admits its relative decline.

Kuniko Inoguchi, a Sophia University political scientist, articulates this scenario most eloquently and forcefully in the context of the American debate on post-hegemonic stability of the international system. The image has also been put forward by former Vice-Minister Shinji Fukukawa of the Ministry of International Trade and Industry (MITI), which favours minimizing the role of military power. Recently MITI and the Ministry of Foreign Affairs, conscious of the increasing intrusion by other ministries into foreign affairs, trying to use national security and the Western alliance as a stick to discipline other ministries which might otherwise move in an "irresponsible" direction (as in the Toshiba machine case, when it came to light in 1987 that the Toshiba company had sold equipment to the Soviet Union which the United States claimed was in breach of the COCOM agreement on technology transfer). The image of Pax Consortis accords on the whole with the pacifist sentiments of most Japanese.

Japan's role in the Pax Consortis scenario is twofold. First, with the superpowers' strategic nuclear arsenals increasingly neutralized either by the *de facto* US-Soviet detente process or by technological breakthroughs, Japan's primary role is that of quiet economic diplomacy in forging coalitions and shaping policy adjustments among peers, no one of which is predominant. Secondly, Japan's role is that of helping to create a world free from military solutions. That would include, if possible, the diffusion of anti-nuclear defensive systems to all countries and the extension of massive economic aid tied to cease fire or peace agreements between belligerent parties. Japan's primary regional role in this scenario would be that of coordinator or promoter of the interests of the Asian Pacific countries which have not been fully represented either in the UN system or in the economic institutions of the industrialized countries, such as OECD. Japan's secondary regional role is that of moderator, especially in security areas. This might include acting as an intermediary and attempting to achieve reconciliation between North and South Korea, or the provision of neutral peacekeeping forces in Cambodia and/or Afghanistan in order to facilitate reconstruction through massive aid flows from such multilateral institutions as the Asian Development Bank. Western Europe will loom larger in this scenario that in the other three. In line with its role in such forums as the Western seven-power summits, Western Europe will continue to play an even larger role, having been traditionally quite adept in those situations where multiple actors adjust conflicting interests. The increasing economic ties between Western Europe and Pacific Asia will also encourage thinking along the lines of this scenario.

4. Pax Nipponica

A fourth image of the future "Pax Nipponica", was first put forward by Ezra Vogel, a Harvard sociologist, who in 1979 published a book entitled *Japan as number one*. It is a world in which Japanese economic power reigns supreme. This scenario has been propagated by those Americans who are concerned about the visible contrast between the United States' relative loss of technological and manufacturing competitiveness and Japan's concomitant gain. Most recently, Ronald Morse of the US Library of Congress has published an article entitled "Japan's drive to pre-eminence". This view has also been gaining power in Japan, reflecting both the noticeable rise in the value of the Japanese yen compared to the US dollar and other currencies and Japan's leading position as a creditor country. The steady rise of Japanese nationalism, in tandem with what the Japanese call the internationalization of Japan, is contributing to the strength of this scenario, because the intrusion of external economic and social forces into Japanese society stimulates nationalistic reactions against internationalization.

Japan's role in this scenario is best compared to that of Britain during the nineteenth century, when it played the role of balancer among the continental powers, its global commercial interests presumably helping it to fulfill this role. As for Pax Consortis in its fullest version, a prerequisite for the advent of Pax Nipponica is either the removal of the superpower's strategic nuclear arsenals or the development of an anti-nuclear defense system.Without the neutralization of nuclear weapons, Japan's leading role in the security area would be minimized, and Pax Nipponica in its fullest form would not be realized. In this scenario, Japan's regional role will coincide with its global role, as its pre-eminent position will enable it to play the leading role in the Asian Pacific region as well.

These scenarios offer substantially different visions of Japan's future. I will now consider what conditions must prevail if they are to be realized.

REQUIREMENTS FOR FOUR SCENARIOS

To what extent are these scenarios feasible? Under what conditions will the scenarios come into being? In attempting to answer these questions, I will first identify three factors which seem to distinguish these scenarios from each other, and secondly, speculate on the feasibility of each scenario in the next 50 years.

There appear to be three major factors which are crucial in distinguishing these scenarios from each other—(1) the effective neutralization of strategic nuclear arsenals, (2) scientific and technological dynamism, and (3) the debt of history.

1. Neutralizing the Nuclear Arsenals

It is the arsenals of strategic nuclear forces that have allowed the United States and the Soviet Union to retain their superpower status and global influence. Whether these weapons will become obsolete—in other words, whether they cease to be a crucial factor determining global development—remain to be seen. Whether the

United States or the Soviet Union or any other country will be able to arm itself with a defensive weapon system which makes it immune to nuclear attack is another question which needs to be answered, and the American SDI and its Soviet counterpart are directly related to this factor. The Conventional Defence Initiative (CDI) which the United States has recently proposed that Japan be jointly involved in may be included as a miniature version of a less ambitious yet more solid kind of effort. Ronald Reagan's fascination with the SDI and Japan's quiet effort to build the CDI may simply reflect what might be called a "Maginot complex" surfacing again years after its failure.

If such a revolutionary weapons system is realized, strategic nuclear arsenals will be neutralized. Unless this happens, the fourth scenario, Pax Nipponica, will have difficulty in emerging because while superpower status is based on ownership of strategic nuclear weapons, both the United States and the Soviet Union will remain superpowers despite all their economic difficulties. In a similar vein, the third scenario, Pax Consortis, will not materialize into a system comprising both economic and security regimes without a similar neutralization of strategic nuclear forces. With the disarmament process between the United States and the Soviet Union slowly making progress, strategic nuclear forces may not make much difference in determining global developments. There are those who, arguing in favour of Pax Consortis, maintain that nuclear weapons and even military power in general have already ceased to be a major factor in international politics and that economic interdependence has deepened sufficiently to make war an obsolete instrument for resolving conflicts of interests, at least among OECD countries and in direct East-West relations. Even granting that military power has become less important, I would argue that what is sometimes called the "Europeanization of superpowers", in Christoph Bertram's phrase, will progress so slowly as to make it hard to envisage the fully fledged scenarios of Pax Consortis or Pax Nipponica inside the twentieth century. Needless to say, those who argue for Pax Consortis talk about it in a somewhat nebulous future most of the time.

2. Scientific and Technological Dynamism

Factor two concerns the innovative and inventive capacity of nations—how vigorous they are in making scientific and technological progress and in translating it to economic development. Needless to say, forecasting technological development is not easy. However, even a cursory examination of the social propensity to innovate seems to tell us that the Americans have been the most innovative nation, with the Japanese following on steadily behind. Such conditions as open competition, abundant opportunities, a strong spirit of individualism and freedom and high social mobility, which are observed in the United States compare very favourably to conditions in Japan.

There is another argument, however, which completely opposes this: that is to say, that Japanese technological innovation has been making steady progress. The following evidence is adduced for the argument:

1. The number of licences obtained by Japanese companies and individuals in the United States has come very close to that of the United States itself. In 1987 the top three companies were all Japanese firms—Canon, Hitachi and Toshiba (in that order).
2. More articles by Japan-based authors have appeared in *Chemical Abstracts* than by authors from any other country for several years.
3. The United States in the first 30 years of this century produced as few as five Nobel prizewinners, which is about on a level with Japan's seven winners for the 40 year period since 1945.

Yet as far as general innovativeness is concerned, the United States seems likely to enjoy its dominant position at least until the end of the twentieth century. If this argument is sufficiently strong, then the first scenario gains force.

3. The Legacy of History

Factor three is related to the memory of the peoples of the nations occupied in the Second World War of their treatment, primarily at the hands of the Germans and the Japanese. As the former Secretary-General of the Chinese Communist Party, Hu Yaobang, once said to Toyoko Yamakazi, a Japanese novelist, the memory of people who have suffered from war disappears only 80 years after the event. His evidence for this is the Boxer intervention in China in 1900, which has virtually been forgotten, whereas he argues that the memory of the second Sino-Japanese war of 1937-45 will not disappear from the memory of the Chinese for another 40 years. With the question of their wartime atrocities still a politically controversial issue, as shown by international reaction to Japanese official visits to the Yakasuni shrine in Tokyo (which contained the remains of Japanese war criminals) and President Reagan's 1985 conciliatory visit to Bitburg cemetery (which contained the graves of Waffe-SS men), Japan or West Germany cannot play a leading global role without facing many barriers. Pax Nipponica is inherently difficult because of this factor.

THE FOUR SCENARIOS RECONSIDERED

Let me now examine the four scenarios in the light of these three factors.

Pax Americana II

Whether Pax Americana II is realized or not will critically depend on factor two—scientific/technical dynamism. The argument for this scenario tends to be based on the free spirit, open competition and dynamic character of American society, which it is thought will help the United States to reinvigorate its innovative and inventive capacity.

In my view this scenario has a fairly high feasibility if the present predicament is managed well. For that purpose two policies are essential: first, close Japan-US macroeconomic policy cooperation, and, secondly, the full-scale interlinking of the US economy with the Asian Pacific economies under US leadership. Whether the United States can achieve this without igniting Asian nationalism against it remains to be seen.

"Bigemony"

The feasibility of "bigemony" depends critically on factor three—the debt of history. In other words, whether Japanese pacifist feeling can be overcome and whether the East Asian neighbours can be at ease with Japanese leadership in regional and global security matters, even a leadership based on cooperation with the Americans, remains to be seen. To be feasible, therefore, this scenario requires very close friendship between the United States and Japan as a precondition for overcoming the debt of history problem. The argument against this scenario is that the steady progress of Japan-US economic integration and defence cooperation has been accompanied by recurrent and at times almost explosive friction between the two countries, which augurs ill for the future.

In my view, the "bigemony" scenario can only progress slowly and steadily, in a moderate manner, as technological progress and economic dynamism push Japan and the United States closer together.

Pax Consortis

The feasibility of Pax Consortis depends critically on factor one—nuclear neutralization. This is conceivable in the distant future, but certainly not in the foreseeable future. For the two superpowers to relinquish superpower status and revert to less important roles will take time, even assuming that their decline has already begun. One may recall Edward Gibbon's remark that it took another 300 years for the Roman empire to disappear after its inevitable decline and demise were declared by Tacitus. It is utterly beyond speculation whether, and how, an unknown perfect anti-nuclear defensive weapon system might be developed and deployed. The weaker form of Pax Consortis, one could argue, is more feasible. One may cite the inability of the superpowers to have much influence on the course of events in Nicaragua and Afghanistan, for example; the increasing importance of monetary and economic policy coordination and consultation among major powers; increasing international collaboration in research and development; and the very frequent formation of consortia in manufacturing and financial activities. Needless to say, conventional forces will become more important when nuclear weapons are neutralized. Thus arms control—a kind of consortium—in conventional forces will become an important focus under Pax Consortis.

Pax Nipponica

The feasibility of Pax Nipponica depends critically on factors one and two—neutralization of nuclear weapons and scientific and technological dynamism. If both factors are realized together, the historical factor may become less important. But the difficulty of neutralizing nuclear weapons has already been mentioned. It must also be emphasized that the obstacles to Japan taking security leadership will not be easy to surmount. First, it will not be easy to persuade the overwhelmingly pacifist Japanese public. Secondly, it is not easy to see Japan shouldering the burden of the level of overseas armed forces the United States currently possesses for a prolonged period of time. It could easily lead Japan to suffer the kind of inefficiency that the Soviet Union has been so painfully experiencing. Thus estimates of Japan's likely scientific and technological dynamism will also affect the likelihood of Pax Nipponica.

In my view, Japan's innovative and inventive capacity for the next 10-20 years should not be underestimated. But beyond that period the expected fall in demographic dynamism and associated social malaises that are bound to arise, such as the overburdening of the small productive working population for extensive social welfare expenditure and for Japan's increased contributions for international public goods, seem to augur ill for this scenario.

To sum up. It seems to me that scenarios one and two—Pax Americana II and bigemony—are more likely than scenarios three and four in the intermediate term of 25 years, while in the longer term of 50 years a mixture of Pax Americana II and Pax Consortis seems more feasible. Of the two scenarios feasible in the medium term, Pax Americana II is the more desirable because it entails fewer risks to the United States as well as to the rest of the world. The effort necessary to sustain the US hegemonic position in its fullest form whether alone or jointly with Japan or other allies, may cause more stresses than benefits. In the larger term, a soft landing on a Pax Consortis seems desirable.

CONCLUSION

These four scenarios are, admittedly, incomplete. Yet their delineation is useful in order to know better what kind of futures the Japanese have in mind in their assiduous yet uncertain search for their place in the world. Some readers may be struck by the fact that these scenarios reflect peculiarly Japanese aspirations and apprehensions. The weight of the past not only lingers on, but fundamentally constrains the Japanese conception of the world. Any drastic restructuring of Japan's foreign relations away from the ties with the United States seems virtually impossible to the majority of Japanese. It is instructive to learn that in Japan only

7.2 per cent of the population are neutralists, who want to abrogate the country's security treaty with the United States, while in West Germany as many as 44 per cent are neutralists.

The same thing can be said of the three major factors. First, the debt of history to the Pacific Asian neighbours has been deeply felt as a major constraining factor in our scenarios. It is as if an anti-Japanese alliance in Pacific Asia were always ready to be forged, despite the near half-century since the war, just because Japan once crossed a certain threshold of misconduct. Secondly, the neutralization of nuclear weapons has been the dream of most Japanese since 1945, when two nuclear bombs were dropped on two Japanese cities. Thirdly, the innovative and inventive capacity of nations is one of those things many Japanese have long felt lacking within themselves. Perhaps reflecting that, they waver between unnaturally timid and exceedingly bold estimates of their own scientific and technological capacity.

Some may argue that my overall scenario—a soft-landing scenario proceeding from Pax Americana II to the Pax Consortis—is more than mildly optimistic. This may be true. It is arguable that this optimism is somewhat unfounded when the United States, the architect of the postwar order, is beset by severe problems. The point is that a large majority of responsible Japanese leaders have found it virtually impossible to think beyond a world where the United States is of primary importance to Japan and where the Japan—US friendship is a major pillar of global stability. My delineation of four scenarios, including the Pax Nipponica and bigemony, should not be understood as a disclosure of non-existent plans for Japan to become a world supremo, or co-supremo. Rather, it should be interpreted as a manifestation of the kind of independent impulse long suppressed, yet only recently allowed to appear on a very small scale in tandem with Japan's rise as a global economic power. The Japanese are perplexed as they continue to rise in influence. Under what combination of the four scenarios Japan will stand up on the world stage remains a matter for our common interest.

28
The Europe of 1992

GIOVANNI AGNELLI

The chairman of Fiat, one of Europe's largest private firms, takes an optimistic view of the impending unification of the markets of the 12 members of the European Community (Common Market). Agnelli sees the greater integration of these nations as an economic necessity, and believes that global economic and political realities demand the continuation of such efforts to break down national borders.

In my frequent visits to the United States these days, I am asked most insistently two questions about Europe: "What will happen in 1992?" and "Can a united European market work?" Many Americans are either skeptical about the future of Europe or nervous about it. Some predict that when put to the test a united Europe will quickly splinter under national and local political pressures. Others fear that Europeans will drop their internal trade barriers only to erect a higher new external wall, creating a kind of "Fortress Europe."

I have reason to believe that neither of these doomsday scenarios will come to pass. My hope is not mere irrational optimism, but is rooted firmly in the history of the last forty years. Who would have believed that the very same nations that twice in this century nearly destroyed each other would be as closely united as they are now? If we are able to travel a similar distance in the next forty years, a truly united Europe is well within our grasp. . . .

---

28 "The Europe of 1992" by Giovanni Agnelli. Reprinted by permission of *Foreign Affairs* (Fall 1989).

II

The current unity of Western Europe is not so much the result of a utopian dream as it is the political recognition of economic reality: the reality of global markets, the reality of economic interdependence and the reality of competitive pressures—all of which make cooperation essential.

Since the act creating a single European market was signed in 1986, progress has exceeded expectations. . . . The reason that the project has continued to progress and defy the odds against it is that it does not depend entirely on political goodwill; 1992 was born for sound economic reasons and those forces continue to be its engine. Ironically, it was politicians who in 1957 first conceived the idea of a common market—often over objections from the business community. Now the situation has been reversed: it is the entrepreneurs and corporations who are keeping the pressure on politicians to transcend considerations of local and national interest. We believe that European unity is our best hope for stimulating growth and technological innovation, and for remaining an influential presence in the world.

Only a few years ago, Europe passed through a deeply pessimistic period, a time of gloomy soul-searching during which many believed that it was facing an inevitable decline as a world force. Looking at the future it seemed impossible for individual French, British or Italian companies to survive on their own, against much larger American or Japanese competitors. In order to make the kind of massive capital investment needed to keep up in the high-technology race, many European businesses looked to pool their resources with new partners from across the continent. The increased cooperation of recent years—among both private companies and nations—seemed to point the only way out of Europe's crisis. Now, with the prospect of creating an entity of 322 million people with a combined gross national product of $4.2 trillion, Europe has a legitimate hope of competing in the world market with resources roughly equal to those of the United States.

Because 1992 has grown out of a recognition of the advantages of a free market, I believe that its success will depend on strengthening Europe's traditional economic and political alliances, rather than excluding the rest of the world. In seeking to accomplish this goal, a host of problems great and small await resolution—from such major issues as the elimination of national border controls to seemingly minor ones such as the standardization of electrical plugs. Some countries are concerned that doing away with border checks will complicate efforts to combat terrorism. Unless every country is convinced that entry points throughout Europe are equally secure, their resistance on this issue will continue. Ironically, however, resolving this problem may prove easier than solving the mundane problem of adopting a standard electrical plug; standardization in this area alone would cost European countries an estimated $80 billion. For now the European Community (EC) has prudently decided to keep three different kinds of plugs. But in many other technical areas—the standardization of safety and pollution control devices, for example—considerable progress has already been made.

One of the toughest, and I believe most important questions remaining, is that of establishing a single currency. The Single European Act of 1986 makes no mention of a European currency. While resolution of this debate will certainly have to wait until after 1992, I believe it is an inevitable development. All of the 12 member nations, except Britain, have keyed their domestic currencies to a new European currency, the ECU, and this system has produced promising results. For example, during the last two years, Fiat has begun to calculate its balance sheet in terms of the ECU as well as in the currency of the various countries in which it operates.

The fact that 25 percent of Europe's combined total income comes from inter-Community trade should make it obvious that there is a limit to independent national monetary policies. Ultimately a truly continental market will demand a standard currency. And all member states—including Britain—officially gave their commitment to this idea at the EC leaders' meeting in Madrid last June.

The idea of defending national currencies seems inconsistent with a borderless Europe. The uncertainty of costs due to fluctuating currencies is a barrier to truly free trade. Imagine a California company worrying about the shifting value of different currencies when shipping to each of the other 49 states! The motivation to standardize is likely to come from within the business community; only a year and a half ago a handful of industrialists formed the Association for the Monetary Unification of Europe; since then membership has grown to 150 major corporations.

Europe's internal market cannot do for long without the power represented by a single currency. A European currency would represent a valid alternative to the dollar as a currency of reserve and of international payment, acting also as a stabilizing influence in the world monetary system. This is not a change that can occur immediately, but there are some interim steps that would help smooth the way. Italy, for example, must limit the range of oscillation of the lira with respect to the ECU, and Britain must enter the European Monetary System. We must overcome the pride that continues to see the defense of national currency as the defense of sovereignty. I think it is reasonable to expect the gradual establishment of a federal system of central banks in order to regulate the coordination between the various national currencies and the ECU.

Reforms of the EC's political system have made it much easier to tackle problems of this magnitude. For many years, the political process was made exceedingly cumbersome by the veto any single member of the EC could exercise. The Single European Act changed the rules of the European Parliament, making it impossible for one or even two countries to block changes voted by a large majority.

III

In the first years after 1992, there will be an intense period of competition and restructuring. Businesses that are now in a favorable position may not necessarily be so in the future. In the long run this competition will be a boon to both European business and consumers, but in the short term it is indeed possible that some businesses will lose out when national protection is removed. At the moment,

European corporations are far from constituting the critical mass necessary to survive international competition on an equal footing.

The process of mergers and acquisitions that has already started in Europe in recent years will continue. When certain companies that have become national symbols become the object of mergers there will be strong protectionist reflexes on the part of local governments. (The battle for control of Belgium's Société Général is a case in point.) The EC has already begun modifying some anti-merger legislation in countries such as West Germany and Britain. It is inevitable, however, that mergers and hostile takeovers will remain under some type of regulation, provided this regulation does not hamper the growth of European businesses.

Mergers in the automobile industry present especially delicate political problems. Many of the major European automakers are their country's largest industry, their single largest employer and a source of national pride. But as out market opens up more to foreign competition, a greater degree of consolidation and cooperation is almost inevitable. While the U.S. auto industry is divided among three main manufacturers, in Europe there are more than a dozen, with the largest single automaker, Fiat, holding only 15 percent of all European sales. Cooperation, joint ventures, research consortia and various kinds of strategic alliances will be necessary for European car manufacturers to compete effectively with our larger American and Japanese rivals. . . .

The transition to a truly free market—in the automobile industry and others—will not be instantaneous. At the moment, some nations, such as France and Italy, have import quotas on Japanese cars, while Germany, for example, does not. Because of the importance of various industries, there will clearly be an interim period in which such restrictions are lifted gradually and in a coordinated fashion. Along with strengthening our own position in this period, the EC, acting in unison, must guarantee true reciprocity from the Japanese.

This does not, however, imply the creation of a "Fortress Europe." Europe is today—and I believe will remain—the freest economic region in the world. Let us not forget that 45 percent of American capital currently invested overseas is in equity ownership within Europe. It is a very strange fortress indeed that welcomes its "enemies" to buy parts of its fortifications. The creation of a united Europe was inspired by a faith in the benefits of a free market. To close it off would defeat our main purpose: remaining in the vanguard of industry and technological innovation.

A united Europe with its 320 million consumers represents a great potential market for Japan and the United States. The United States should regard such a Europe as an opportunity rather than a problem, an opportunity to create new synergies in the areas of industrial production and technology. This can happen, assuming that free trade works both ways. Europeans are concerned, for example, that anti-dumping legislation pending in the U.S. Congress may camouflage a new wave of protectionism.

The strengthening of Europe as a united economic and political entity inevitably changes the current world equilibrium. A united European economy has not come about in a vacuum. It is, above all, the result of what is perhaps the chief political development of the twentieth century: the failure of state-controlled communism to fulfill man's hopes and the vindication of the free market system as the surest guarantee of both freedom and prosperity. The current plan for 1992 represents an extraordinarily broad consensus, supported by Socialist, Conservative and Christian Democratic governments. Even some West European Communist parties support the idea of European unity. Such a consensus would have been unthinkable even ten years ago when ideological conflicts polarized the continent.

In North America, the recent trade agreement between Canada and the United States reflects a similar view that both sides will be winners in an open market. And in the Soviet Union, the bastion of the Marxist-Leninist ideal, the Communist Party is abandoning the disastrous collectivization of agriculture (and other forms of state control) in order to restore some measure of private enterprise. It is hardly accidental that the momentum toward 1992 came just as Mikhail Gorbachev was attempting to institute his policy of perestroika.

IV

Some in the United States fear that the drive for European unity will widen the differences between the United States and Europe and weaken the NATO alliance. In some ways, the United States and Europe do appear to be growing apart. Ever since Europe recovered from the ravages of World War II and began to create its dream of unity, it has been pushing for a position of greater autonomy. As ideological tensions lessen, West Europeans have a new interest in normalizing relations with Eastern Europe.

The United States, for its part, is looking increasingly toward the Pacific and Latin America. As first Japan, and now Korea and Taiwan, have developed into formidable economic powers, many have begun to see America's future in the Pacific. California has replaced New York as the most populous and powerful state; Los Angeles has grown into an economic capital rivaling Wall Street. While for over 300 years the great bulk of the immigrants to North America came from Europe, the latest waves of immigrants have come principally from Mexico, Central America and Asia. This, too, has changed the country's orientation.

At the same time, there are tensions within NATO that flare up from time to time. The Europeans are alternately grateful for and resentful of American help; they are resistant to spending more on defense and yet become nervous when the United States talks of reducing its commitment to the alliance. The United States is tired of having to twist arms every time it wants to modernize a weapons system and resents having to pay such a high portion of the common defense of the West. Some Americans are concerned that a united Europe will drift away from the United States as it falls victim to Gorbachev's seductive charm.

. . . I believe, however, that while NATO will have to undergo major changes, its basic strength and validity have been underscored in recent years. Europeans should not forget that the NATO alliance is the foundation on which we have built one of the most durable periods of peace and prosperity in our history, and we must be careful not to risk that for the intriguing but still hazy prospects of glasnost and perestroika.

Similarly, I do not believe that the United States will quickly erase its 400-year historical connection to Europe and 40-year military alliance with its friends there. As alluring as the markets of Asia look, Americans may find themselves more at home in a so-called Fortress Europe than in what are, in truth, the comparatively closed markets of Asia.

In many ways, the Europeans have their American allies to thank for their current unity. 1992 is the child of the Marshall Plan, and the cooperation fostered by a joint military alliance undoubtedly facilitated European political and economic cooperation. The farsighted American administrations of the postwar period understood that a strong, autonomous Europe was in the best long-term interests of the United States. That remains true today. . . .

29

America in the World Economy

BARRY P. BOSWORTH and ROBERT Z. LAWRENCE

These two Liberal economists focus on popular concern with America's apparent economic decline. They assert that blaming the country's economic position on international factors is misguided; the American trade deficit is largely the result of trends within the United States. The decline in the relative size of the U.S. economy is, more generally, the result of natural developments in the international political economy, and is not a cause for alarm. Government policy can help best if it reduces the budget deficit, avoids restrictions on international trade, and resists attempts to manage exchange rates.

For much of the post World War II period, the United States was the colossus of the world economy. American living standards were the world's highest, and the United States was often the only source of the products based on the technologies that emerged after the war. Sure of their economic advantage, U.S. business and labor leaders agreed that free trade was in the nation's interest and that prosperity abroad was good for America. The nation's international economic policies were based on the principle of multilateralism: the notion that international economic policies should be used not only to increase American power, but also to open markets for all.

While America was important to the world economy, events in the world economy had little effect on the United States. The greatest threat to America was perceived to be a political one from the Soviet Union. American policy therefore

29 "America in the World Economy" by Barry P. Bosworth and Robert Z. Lawrence. From *The Brookings Review*, Vol. 7, No. 1 (Winter 1988/89), pp. 39-48. Reprinted with permission.

focused on political rather than economic goals—often trading economic advantage, such as access to U.S. markets or technology, for political gains.

Today, America finds itself in a new situation. The postwar economic recovery in other industrial countries has brought their standards of living much closer to those of the United States. The United States offers little that is unique on the production side: American workers do not always have the best skills or work with the most modern equipment. Increasingly, American management has failed to maintain quality, motivate its work force, and make decisions for the long term.

Instead, the importance of the United States rests on the sheer size of its markets and the defense umbrella it provides. It continues to support a large research base, but new technologies are often introduced faster and better in other countries. This change in the relative position of the United States has been gradual, and in many cases it simply reflects an expected return to a more normal international economy.

A second change is of more recent origin and is the result of decisions made at home. In the 1980s the United States has been on a consumption binge, selling assets and borrowing heavily both domestically and abroad. Since 1980 the growth of consumption has far outstripped that of production. In the short run, the experience for many Americans has been a pleasurable one. Tax cuts have bolstered their spending power, cheap imported goods have cut the rate of inflation, and unemployment has fallen to levels last reached in the early 1970s.

The spending spree, however, has been at the cost of a sharp decline in national saving. The net national saving rate averaged only 2 percent of net national product in 1986-87 compared with 6-7 percent in prior decades. The country has been spending more than it produces, importing more than it exports, at an annual rate of $150 billion. The resulting trade deficit caused a wrenching realignment of American industry as many companies found themselves priced out of world markets by the sharp rise in the exchange rate of the dollar during the first half of the decade. Increasingly, the pleasures of the spending binge are being tempered by a recognition of its costs: a loss of world markets and the burden of debt placed on future generations.

These changes have damaged U.S. confidence both in the open international trading system and in itself. With the United States no longer in control of the world economy, its politicians often seek to blame trade practices abroad for the costs of the domestic policy changes. U.S. foreign economic policy can no longer be used solely to achieve political goals: it has become crucial to domestic economic well-being. The nation's freedom to control its own destiny is constrained by its position as a debtor country, forced to dance to the tune of its creditors.

During the next decade the United States will face continued pressures from the world economy. It will ultimately be forced to end its reliance on foreign borrowing, accepting reduced growth of domestic spending and further depreciation of the dollar. It will become even more concerned about foreign industrial and trade practices as it struggles to recover lost export markets. Even if it chooses to delay adjustment, it will have to respond to the concerns of foreign investors by offering higher interest rates on U.S. securities or by borrowing in foreign currencies. As foreign debt and interest payments grow, it will have to borrow more or reduce the deficit in the trade account. Delay also places pressure on monetary policy in the short run and ensures that when adjustment does occur, the required shifts in economic structure and spending patterns will be even greater.

As convenient as it is to blame the rest of the world for problems of the U.S. economy, those problems primarily reflect two failings in U.S. domestic policies: excessive consumption and faltering productivity. The growth of the international economy alters the symptoms of those policy failings and complicates the adjustment process but does not change the prescription for recovery: increase national saving and productivity growth. To repeat,the international economy is not the source of U.S. problems. The United States is not disadvantaged by economic growth abroad, it is not the innocent victim of unfair trade practices by others, and its tradable-goods industries do not suffer from a fundamental inability to compete.

THE ISSUE OF COMPETITIVENESS

Many believe that American policies toward the global economy must be radically altered. These concerns have reached a fever pitch in the national debate over competitiveness. Some advocate reducing the links between the United States and the rest of the world; others suggest that industrial and trade policies need to be restructured. A common theme is that the United States must abandon its multilateral approach to international economic issues and pursue its own national advantage. Some even suggest a system of managed trade in which the United States uses the lure of access to its large market to extract larger reciprocal concessions from major trading partners.

The discussion is often confusing, however, because the term competitiveness is not well defined. It is important to distinguish between arguments about how well the United States performs in world markets (particularly, the argument that the trade deficit of the 1980s is a symptom of America's inability to compete) and the issues that arise out of the changed relative position of the United States in the world economy.

Trade Performance

Much of the current concern about trade competitiveness springs from the large trade deficit in the 1980s. However, a trade deficit is a result of a nation's saving and investment, not a measure of its ability to compete in world markets. Even if it is highly innovative and productive and its goods are attractive in world markets, a country whose domestic saving is lower than its domestic investment opportunities must borrow from abroad and run a trade deficit. In 1987, for example,Americans spent 98 percent of their income on consumption, and the remaining 2 percent of income—national saving—was insufficient to finance its investment needs. Thus it was forced to borrow abroad.

The trade balance tells little about competitiveness because any country can achieve balanced trade if it is willing to lower the price of its products sufficiently. Thus a nation's terms of trade, the price of its exports relative to its imports, are a better indicator of competitiveness. The higher the terms of trade associated with a given trade balance, the better off the country will be.

Adjusted for variations in the trade balance, the terms of trade do show a long-run tendency to move against the United States, but the magnitude of the decline appears to be small—about half a percent annually. Since 12 percent of U.S. income is spent on imports, this decline reduces U.S. living standards by about one-twentieth of a percent annually. The terms of trade were roughly constant in the 1960s, but fell sharply after 1971. That decline can be traced largely to the rise in the price of oil: the price of exports had to fall to earn the foreign exchange to pay for oil imports. By 1980 the United States actually had a surplus of $57 billion in non-oil trade. Since 1980 the terms of trade have improved slightly—but against the backdrop of a large trade deficit. If the United States were to have a trade balance today, the price of its exports would have to be reduced substantially in world markets and the terms of trade would be below the level of 1980.

Those who believe that U.S. competitiveness has suffered advance two major arguments. The first is that American workers cannot compete against workers in low-wage countries. Given the international mobility of capital and technology, they reason, production will go where labor is cheapest. Economists argue that the spread of technology will bring about a convergence of world living standards as wage rates in other countries rise to the U.S. level. American workers, however, fear that the convergence process is for them one of regression.

The second argument is that the multilateral world that has defined past American trade policy is a myth. The real world is dominated by nationalistic policies that systematically discriminate against imports (through trade protection and selective procurement policies) and target major markets in the United States. The United States should act like other countries and manage trade to its advantage.

The first argument has little empirical support. Imports into the United States are not coming more and more from low-wage countries In 1960 two-thirds of American imports came from countries with wages less than half the U.S. level. By 1986 their share had fallen to less than one-third. Nor does the emergence of a trade deficit in the 1980s support the argument; the United States lost ground with every major trading area of the world, not just with low-wage countries. Furthermore, the argument ignores the fact that growth in low-income countries expands the market for American exports. In 1987 less developed countries accounted for 34 percent of American exports and 37 percent of imports.

Those who believe that low-wage countries are hurting U.S. competitiveness assume that high American wages can be maintained only be preventing the flow of technology abroad. In fact, American workers are paid high wages not because they have a monopoly on technology but because of their own high productivity, which in turn is based on their education, skills, capital, and technical knowledge. American productivity and living standards are not diminished by improvements abroad. Only about 10 percent of U.S. production, on which those living standards are based, is traded with other nations. Future improvements in American living standards will depend, as they have in the past, on productivity improvements in the American economy. The welfare of Americans does not depend on the maintenance of poverty abroad.

Could the trade deficit be the result of the sudden introduction of trade restrictions by other countries? If so, the effort was well coordinated and worldwide. The United States now has a deficit with every major region of the world, and the increase in the deficit between 1980 and 1987 is roughly proportionate to the volume of trade with each region. Furthermore, in recent years the United States has increased restrictions on imports more than other countries have.

Such a sudden deterioration of the trade balance with every region of the globe suggests not worldwide conspiracy but change here at home. That leads back to the collapse of domestic saving. The trade deficit is simply a symptom of a nation living beyond its means: domestic spending exceeds domestic production capacity.

Relative Economic Performance

The relative economic decline of the United States is clear. Its share of world Gross Domestic Produce (GDP) has fallen from 27 percent in 1950 to 18 percent in 1984. During that period all six of the other leading industrial countries posted GDP gains relative to the United States. Japan's GDP grew from only 9 percent of U.S. GDP in 1950 to 36 percent in 1987. Output per worker in Japan expanded from only 15 percent of that of the United States to 71 percent. The change in relative size, however, does not reflect a failure on the part of the United States, but its success in rebuilding the world economy after World War II. The United States has been joined by many nations with similar technologies, productivity, and standards of living—a return to the situation that existed before World War I. The period after World War II has seen an unparalleled expansion of the world economy, due in part to the opening of world trade and economic relations. Americans shared in the prosperity through a large gain in their standard of living.

Because reconstruction of the world economy was the avowed objective of U.S. policy, its success should hardly be taken as a sign of American failure. U.S. foreign policy failed only if its goal was to maintain American superiority. If the goal was to maximize the welfare of Americans, which is enhanced by rapid foreign growth, relative decline is neither unexpected nor undesirable.

The relative decline of the United States has differing implications for American "power" and for American living standards. One base for the power of a nation is its relative economic capacity—the economic performance of the United States compared with that of other nations, particularly its adversaries. In this sense the power of the United States declines in a richer world economy. Conversely, the welfare of a nation's citizens is largely a function of its absolute economic capacity: living standards are primarily based on the nation's productivity, which is increased, not reduced, by trade. Productivity is also raised when increased innovation abroad provides U.S. manufacturers more opportunities to emulate foreign products and processes. When the relative economic performance of the United States is evaluated, the perspective matters greatly: the United States is made less powerful when others do well, but the welfare of its citizens is improved.

Relative Income and Productivity Growth. Concern about the relative decline of the economic power of the United States has surfaced at a strange time. The U.S. share of total income of the large industrial countries fell far more before the 1980s than during the 1980s. It dropped from 59 percent in 1950 to 49 percent in 1970. In the 1980s, by contrast, GDP grew as rapidly in the United States as in the rest of the world. U.S. industrial production rose 5 percent faster than the average of all market economies, and the U.S. share of GDP in the seven largest industrialized countries actually increased.

Relative economic growth, however, offers no insight into the more important measure of economic performance—the absolute gain in American living standards. Most of the recent U.S. economic growth is simply the result of rapid growth in the labor force. Except for Canada, labor force growth is much lower in other industrial countries. Growth in the total economy may be relevant to measures of economic power, but it has little relation to improvements in standards of living.

The comparison with other countries is less favorable if the focus is on the growth in productivity, which is most closely related to living standards. Since 1950 growth in GDP per worker in the United States has been consistently below that of other countries, and the rate of improvement has been especially low since 1973.

A comparison of productivity growth rates, however, is distorted by the low starting point in other countries. The difference in levels of output per worker calculated using purchasing power parity exchange rates between the United States and other countries remains surprisingly large in America's favor. In 1987 the average French, German, and Japanese worker produced 14.7 percent, 18.9 percent, and 29.3 percent less than the average American worker.

It is far easier to copy than to innovate. In the past foreigners were able to increase productivity by adopting U.S. technologies, while productivity gains in the United States came from pushing out the frontiers of knowledge. As other countries have moved closer to the United States, their rates of productivity growth have tended to decline. The difference between productivity growth in the United States and in the Organization for Economic Cooperation and Development has narrowed since 1973. The difference for total factor productivity growth (output per unit of capital plus labor) declined from 1.4 percent annually before 1973 to 0.5 percent during 1979-85. The differential with Japan narrowed in the same way.

Not all of the difference in productivity growth between the United States and other major industrial countries reflects catch-up. Although U.S. productivity in total manufacturing remains the world's highest, productivity levels in Japan have surpassed those in the United States in industries such as automobiles and steel. In part, that is because foreign economies have been accumulating capital per worker at a more rapid pace than the United States has.

Foreigners are also shifting from copying to innovating. The share of sales spent on research and development by German and Japanese manufacturers is now similar to that of American companies. In the past the product cycle originated in the United States and moved abroad. Now innovations cross the Atlantic and Pacific in both directions. According to the National Science Foundation, in 1970 the United States granted 18 and 11 patents to Americans for every 1 granted to Japanese and German nationals, respectively. By 1985, the ratios had declined to 3 and 6.

Relative Productivity Growth and Trade Performance. Since 1973 the growth of U.S. productivity (output per hour of labor) has slowed significantly, and the real earnings of American workers have stagnated. Over the same period, the United States suffered numerous shocks from the world economy, including the emergence of a large trade deficit after 1981.

Given the current infatuation with "competitiveness," it is tempting to see causal links between these problems. Many blame the sluggish growth in U.S productivity and earnings on the changed international environment, particularly unfair trade practices of other countries. Others use what they call a decline in U.S. trade competitiveness to justify greater efforts to raise productivity growth. The apparent link between trade performance and productivity, however, is misleading for two reasons. First, U.S. productivity growth has slumped mainly in sectors that do not engage in international trade. Although individual sectors are difficult to measure, productivity growth in U.S. manufacturing seems to have accelerated in the 1980s. Second, relatively faster productivity growth abroad does not diminish U.S. terms of trade or living standards. During the period before 1973, when foreign economic growth exceeded that of the United States by a wide margin, American living standards grew faster than at almost any time in U.S. history. Furthermore, if higher productivity growth abroad is absorbed by higher wages and profits in these countries, prices will not change, and U.S. devaluation will not be necessary. And if higher productivity abroad results in a lower rate of foreign price increases, reduction in the *nominal* exchange rate might be required to maintain relative prices and trade balance. The decrease, though, would not raise import prices relative to domestic prices in the United States and would thus leave absolute U.S. living standards unaffected.

International Buying Power. Differences in the prices of the goods and services produced in different countries make it difficult to compare real productivity and living standards between nations. Our earlier comparisons of relative GDP, adjusted for differences in expenditure patterns and prices between the United States and other countries, suggest that American standards of living are still substantially higher than those of other industrial countries. Yet simple comparisons based on 1987 market exchange rates imply that GDP per employed worker was 11.1 percent, 5.2 percent, and 4.3 percent higher in Germany, France, and Japan, respectively.

These comparisons highlight an important difference between the United States and its trading partners: other major industrial countries have matched or exceeded American performance in tradable goods industries, but they lag far behind the United States in their ability to provide nontradables, primarily in the distribution, food, and services sectors. Their standards of living would be much higher if they could buy nontradable goods from the United States, rather than at home. Because of the high cost of domestic nontradables, these nations, particularly Japan, have much lower overall living standards than their efficiency in producing tradable goods would suggest.

Critics of American economic performance often focus on the manufacturing sector—a proxy for tradable goods. But an improvement in productivity in the tradable goods industries is not necessarily better than one in nontradables. Ninety percent of the goods and services consumed by American's future living standards will depend on the gains in the economy as a whole.

POLICY OPTIONS

Although the United States no longer dominates all areas of the global economy, its ability to raise the living standards of its citizens is not thereby diminished. There may be less scope for the United States to exercise its will at the expense of others, but economic growth abroad brings with it important benefits to the United States, including a productivity boost from the technological innovations of others, access to larger markets as a producer,and greater variety as a consumer. In the near future, moveover, no other country is likely to approach the importance of the United States to the world economy. The United States remains the pivot of the global trading system; its trade flows with both Europe and Asia far exceed those between Asia and Europe.

Over the next decade, the foremost challenge for U.S. economic policy at home is to boost living standards by raising national saving and productivity. The task of U.S. economic policy abroad is to provide an international environment supportive of the adjustments in spending patterns required to achieve these goals.

Productivity Growth

As we argued earlier, the growth in American living standards has slowed because U.S. productivity growth has fallen. One key to future growth in living standards is to restore productivity. Although improvements in productivity will likely improve competitiveness and U.S. trade performance, their primary importance is as a source of gains in the overall standard of living. They are beneficial regardless of whether the nation engages in trade. Moreover, productivity improvements are of approximately equal value in industries that do and do not engage in trade.

Although much of the post-1973 slowdown in U.S. productivity growth remains a puzzle, experts agree on a set of actions that the government could take to reverse the trend. It could encourage a higher rate of private capital formation; it could increase its own investments in the social infrastructure (for example, transportation); it could expand research and development outlays; and it could improve the quantity and quality of education. Government has traditionally played a role in all these areas, but that role costs money. Americans must be willing to reduce their current level of public or private consumption to pay for the steps the experts recommend. In a country already faced with large deficits on its government budget and heavy overseas borrowing, greater spending in these areas will be very difficult to achieve.

None of the actions, moreover, will have large immediate effects on economic growth. They do not, as is sometimes suggested, provide a means for the United States to grow out of the budget deficit.

In the immediate future, the dominant issue for American economic policy is how to cut the growth of consumption, both to eliminate the need to borrow abroad and to provide the investment resources to improve U.S. living standards in the future. From a political perspective slower consumption growth is a dismal prospect, and the extent to which political debate seeks to redirect public attention to the international arena and to blame the policies of other countries should not be a surprise. If the United States lowers its budget deficit, however, it will increase the national rate of saving, and market forces, supported by an easier monetary policy, will translate that saving into a lower trade deficit and a higher rate of domestic investment. Once it has reestablished a balance between its current government programs and the taxes to finance them, the country will be able to engage in a rational debate over the merits of spending more money to promote productivity growth.

A balanced budget would change U.S. policies toward the international economy in two ways. First, the United States would discover a strong interest in promoting a more open trading system—a turn away from protectionism—as it sought to recover its export markets. Second, it would cease its cooperation in international government efforts to fix exchange rates.

Trade Policy

Trade policy has three primary dimensions: ensuring that foreign markets are open to American exports; ensuring that other nations' trade policies do not harm U.S. interests; and helping domestic companies and workers adjust to international competition. In the near term, given the improved price competitiveness of U.S. exports that followed from a lower exchange rate, U.S. policy should concentrate on the first.

There is a growing view that U.S. trade policy goals and objectives should shift to reflect the country's decline in global preeminence. In the 1950s and 1960s, advocates of such a shift suggest, it was appropriate for the United States to fashion its trade policies primarily for the benefit of others and to keep its market open while turning a blind eye to protectionist policies abroad. At that time, they argue, the United States was correct to aim for a system with liberal rules and norms achieved through application of the most-favored-nation principle, under which concessions granted to one country were extended to all. But today the striving for an open international trading system under the General Agreement on Tariffs and Trade (GATT) rules represents the triumph of ideology over the national interest. Instead, it is contended, the United States should aim for a system of managed international trade, which best serves American national interests by exploiting U.S. leverage to obtain reciprocal advantage.

Advocates of this view stress that the weaknesses of U.S. policies have become most apparent in trade relations with Japan. The Japanese allegedly take advantage of the openness of the U.S. market while reserving local markets for domestic companies. The U.S. response has been to pressure Japan to remove trade barriers in a series of piecemeal negotiations. That policy has engendered much friction between the two nations, and many find the results disappointing. After tough negotiations, Americans often obtain concessions only to find that other barriers remain.

Because interpretations differ so radically over the meaning of the rules, the solution, according to come commentators, is to bargain over results. Essentially that solution implies a regime in which the emphasis shifts toward more managed trade.

Several concrete suggestions about how to implement this new approach have been made. The United States, for example, could determine the largest trade deficit it could afford to run with Japan and then auction off, each quarter, import licenses in the appropriate amount. Alternatively U.S. trade in particular sectors could be allocated along the lines of the international airline cartel. Just as airlines from different nations divide up the traffic between them, so companies from the United States and other nations could divide up the business in any sector.

In fact, the United States already engages in some managed trade. Examples include the voluntary restraint arrangements with the Japanese in textiles, steel, and automobiles, the multifiber agreement, and the Japan-U.S. cartel arrangement embodied in the 1986 semiconductor agreement. But would the widespread application of these principles actually improve the system for the United States?

A managed trade system will afford the greatest benefits to those governments best able to control trade and industrial development—activities to which the U.S. political system is not well suited. Aside from the inefficiencies inherent in such a system, it will not necessarily lead to improved trading conditions for the United States. Managed trade generally involves setting quotas. By limiting the quantity or dollar value of the products or services that a nation can sell in the United States,the United States encourages that nation to charge as high a price as possible. If foreign governments can limit competition for quotas among their companies, they can act like monopolists, maximizing the benefits to their nation.

Japan, in particular, would reap great benefits under such a system. Given a particular dollar value for its U.S. sales, Japan would undoubtedly select products in which it enjoyed either the greatest current benefits (because profit margins were highest) or future benefits (because the products were perceived as high-tech or strategic). Given the ability of the Japanese Ministry of Trade and Industry (MITI) to guide its companies, Japanese strategies would be effectively implemented. Facing similar restrictions, the United States would be much more likely to allocate its products on political, rather than strategic, grounds. Many advocates of a managed trading system believe it would reconcile the differences in national economic systems. In fact it would expose their contradictions.

A managed trade system reinforces precisely the differences between the United States and other nations that exacerbate trade tensions. When the United States persuades Japan to "volunteer" to limit its sales of automobiles, it vastly increases the power to the MITI to influence the Japanese automobile industry. Indeed, it is the United States rather than Japan that becomes the proponent of Japanese industrial policy.

A managed trade system could be disastrous for some nations, especially smaller and poorer nations with limited bargaining power. These nations now reap the greatest relative benefits from the economies of scale that trade provides. Bilateral negotiations based on power would severely restrict their ability to raise their incomes through specialization. The result would be a more sluggish global economy—a result scarcely in the U.S. economic or political interest.

In a pluralistic world economy the clash of different systems will always produce tension, but that does not imply that trade between nations needs to be managed. A better way to ease tensions is to define practices that are generally recognized as unjustifiable and then to eliminate them. It would be especially inappropriate for the United States to legitimate a system of controls now that market forces are shifting trade trends in its favor. Following the sharp change of the dollar-yen exchange rate in 1986-87, American exports have expanded at a 25-30 percent annual rate; and the Japanese trade surplus, on both a global and a bilateral U.S. basis, has declined dramatically. Trade negotiators, understandably, get caught up in sectoral particulars, but it is macroeconomic conditions, not trade in specific industries, that determine overall trade balances.

It is important to distinguish between the objectives of the trading system—an open system of international trade—and the negotiating techniques for bringing this system about. Traditionally the United States has relied on the GATT and multilateral negotiations. It should continue to do so. At the same time, the GATT itself acknowledges that broad free-trade areas negotiated bilaterally can encourage the long-term trend toward multilateral free trade. The European Community has proceeded in this direction, and recently the United States negotiated a major arrangement with Canada. These measures should continue. Indeed the European initiative to achieve a high degree of economic integration by 1992 should benefit the United States. First, integration should stimulate European growth, which will in turn raise U.S. exports. Second, it should provide the United States and other exporters with a more unified market with common standards. Third, it should undermine nationalistic commitments to protection in individual European countries and thus promote liberalization. Other countries should be alert to the possibility that the initiative could divert trade from countries outside the EC, but the volume is likely to be small.

Despite all the focus on market shares, it should be realized that a rapid expansion of the total world market is the most important determinant of U.S. export growth. Developing countries have always been an important outlet for U.S. capital goods exports. A resolution of their debt problems and a resumption of their investment-led growth would therefore be of great benefit to U.S. exporters. Thus it is a mistake for the United States to view the debt crisis solely from the perspective of its banks. It has become evident that some debt relief will be required, and speedy resolution of this issue is in the interest of American industry.

Exchange Rate Policy

In recent years, the United States has acceded to the demands of other countries that it cooperate in government efforts to control exchange rates. Pressure is increasing to return to an international monetary system where governments fix exchange rates. The interest of other countries is understandable because they wish to maintain their export surplus with the United States. Although the policy is attractive to American consumers, who have no desire to pay higher prices, it could be dangerous to American workers.

If the United States should adopt a tighter fiscal policy, it will risk higher unemployment. One way to counter that risk would be to reduce the trade deficit, so that jobs would shift from industries that do not engage in trade to industries that do. But for the trade deficit to shrink, U.S. incomes must fall (reducing the demand for imports), or foreign growth must expand (raising the demand for American exports), or the prices of American goods must decline in world markets. The first option is highly undesirable, and the second is beyond American control. The third is the strongest balancing force.

Because the U.S. current-account deficit is so large, economists are unable to project the precise change in the exchange rate needed to balance it. The rate will depend on what other countries do to stimulate their domestic demand and on the policies they follow on trade. The United States cannot afford to commit itself, at a time of imbalance, to an exchange rate that may be inconsistent with a future current-account balance and high employment. Without the possibility of a recovery of trade, policies to reduce the budget deficit are likely to translate into higher unemployment.

If the United States does not reduce the budget deficit, the exchange rate may, in fact, rise in the short run. Improved export performance at the current lower level of the dollar, combined with strong domestic spending, may strain the economy's resources and threaten to increase inflation. If the Federal Reserve reacts by tightening credit, U.S. interest rates would rise relative to those of other countries, capital inflows would increase, the exchange rate would go back up, and the improvement in the trade balance would be choked off.

Although the wide fluctuations in the value of the dollar were highly disruptive to the world economy in the 1980s, they should be seen as a symptom of the extreme imbalance in U.S. fiscal-monetary policies, not as a cause of the problems. A return to a system of fixed exchange rates would make deficit countries turn to domestic deflation as the primary means of strengthening their trade performance. Since surplus nations are unwilling to cooperate by accepting higher inflation rates, the system is biased against growth. A fixed-rate exchange system is even more impractical in view of the greatly increased mobility of private financial capital, which necessitates that countries undertake the adjustments quickly.

FIRST AMONG EQUALS

In the 1950s, as a dominant and independent economy, the United States could use its international economic influence to achieve political and security objectives. Today, the United States is merely the first among equals in an interdependent world economy. Economic developments abroad, once matters of interest only to foreign policy specialists, are now vitally important to economic performance at home. The emergence of large trade and budget deficits and the transformation of the United States to a large net-debtor country have heightened that dependence. Strong foreign growth not only makes the world less susceptible to Soviet influence, it is critical for sustaining U.S. employment as these deficits are reduced.

While American policies must shift with the changing environment, new policies must be based on a realistic perception of that environment. It is wrong to see foreign growth as damaging to U.S. welfare, to emphasize improving competitiveness over improving productivity, and to abandon the goal of a liberal trading order for a system of managed trade. The future of American living standards overwhelmingly depends, as it always has, on domestic productivity and saving. Given the need to change our policies to achieve these goals, we need an international economy capable of accepting far more American exports and a reduction in the U.S. trade deficit. An exchange rate that makes American products competitive in open and rapidly growing foreign markets will be key elements.

U.S. foreign policy will have to be more creative in an era in which the United States has limited material means. The political battle to restrain spending at home will limit U.S. ability to project influence abroad. Yet U.S. dependence on the international economy has never been greater. The challenge for America is therefore to join in partnership with its allies to build a liberal international system supportive of our mutual interests. While American power may have diminished, the American interest in U.S. leadership has rarely been greater.

30

Soviet Economic Reforms: The Motivation and Content of *Perestroika*

RICHARD E. ERICSON

Perestroika, Ericson argues, is driven in large part by the Soviet Union's deteriorating economic position relative to the advanced capitalist world. Accordingly, the Soviets seek to improve aggregate economic performance, modernize their economy, and resuscitate the now widely discredited Soviet Economic Model. After reviewing the specific objectives and policies of the reform movement, Ericson finds that the actual results so far have been quite poor. Increasingly, the Soviet Union is turning toward greater trade and economic interaction with other countries to stimulate further growth. This requires, however, that the Soviets alter longstanding foreign policies, reduce international tension, and dramatically cutback military spending. Thus, not only is perestroika motivated by economic competition with the West, but its success depends upon improving relations with the United States, Europe, and Japan. This demonstrates that even—or especially—in nonmarket economies, international politics and economics are intimately related.

Ekonomicheskaia perestroika, the sweeping economic reform introduced by Mikhail S. Gorbachev at the party plenums of January and June 1987, is primarily a Soviet domestic phenomenon. It arose largely from a growing perception of the massive failure of the traditional Stalinist economic system to achieve the levels of development desired by the Soviet leadership and, in particular, to maintain its

---

30 "Soviet Economic Reforms: The Motivation and Content of *Perestroika*" by Richard E. Ericson. Published by permission of the *Journal of International Affairs* and the Trustees of Columbia University in the City of New York.

economic position relative to the developed "capitalist" economies. This failure is seen as a correctable defect arising out of the distortions of "true socialism" imposed during the period of the "cult of personality." Thus, the primary objective and focus of *perestroika* has been to renew Soviet socialism, to breath new life into shared ideals by developing new, and returning to old, Leninist forms of economic organization and interaction. The lion's share of this effort is thus naturally far removed from, and in a sense prior to, foreign policy concerns and issues.

Despite the inherent and overwhelmingly domestic focus of *ekonomicheskaia perestroika,* one can discern a natural linkage between its objectives and Soviet foreign policy. This essay will try to develop some ideas about that linkage, pointing to a particular direction of linkage that may help explain some of the policies pursued to implement the economic objectives of perestroika. That direction runs from long-term foreign policy considerations that will affect economic objectives and their subsequent policies, to short-term political aspirations for the future. The short-term goals will create an imperative to economic reform which in turn requires a relaxation of international tensions and an opening to greater international interaction, at least in the interim. In this manner, foreign policy can in part be seen as an instrument for furthering economic reform and modernization; indeed, an impetus that has perhaps the greatest chance of helping in the near term (within five to 10 years). This is of critical importance because, as many others have emphasized, *ekonomicheskaia perestroika* is a process that will only bear fruit, if at all, in the next century. This can be seen in the broad sweep of the proclaimed economic objectives of *perestroika.*

ECONOMIC OBJECTIVES

The objectives of *ekonomicheskaia perestroika* arise from the economic, social and moral stagnation, and the gathering sense of loss of control and direction that results from them, of the last 15 to 20 years of Soviet history. Ultimately, the goal is to improve aggregate economic performance, particularly relative to the developed economies, thereby enhancing Soviet economic stature in the world. This would resuscitate the now widely discredited and ignored Soviet Economic Model by openly exploiting the "advantages of Socialism" in a way, and with results, clearly deserving of emulation.

To do so, we can discern six intermediate objectives, revolving around the concept of "modernization" that are currently being pursued. The first and most obvious has been the emphasis on technological modernization. This means raising the level of technology in use to developed world standards in all sectors of the economy, but most particularly in the engineering and machine tool sectors. Second, a modernization of organizational structures and management methods is sought, together with new forms of economic interaction and centralized control, to replace the existing "command-administrative (*kommandno-administrativnaia*) system." Third, a major proclaimed objective is to eliminate the inherently wasteful nature of Soviet production and distribution activity *(zatratnyi mekhanism)* associated with traditional Stalinist methods. Fourth, the Soviet leadership seeks to modernize the sectoral structure of the economy, the share of different sectors in volume of economic activity and the relationship between production, distribution, investment and consumption. Fifth, they see a need to modernize the structure of consumption in order to raise the standard of living of the Soviet people and improve the quality of life (e.g., longevity, mortality, disease incidence, etc.). This entails bringing consumption patterns into line with those of developed economies, particularly with regard to consumer, housing and medical services. Finally, they hope to bring the Soviet Union into the mainstream of the world economy in the direct sense of participation commensurate with its size and importance. Trade and international financial interaction, as well as technology, productivity, consumption and quality of life levels, would be brought up to par with those of developed Western economies. The thrust of *ekonomicheskaia perestroika,* therefore, is to prevent the continued obsolescence and eventual irrelevance of the Soviet system, to maintain the economic basis for its world power and international influence, and thereby to hold its own, and indeed prevail, in competition with the capitalist West.

These economic objectives can all be seen as intimately related to the position of the Soviet Union in the world polity. They are ultimately directed toward the maintenance and expansion of Soviet power and influence in the world, and are rooted in a realization that one cannot maintain a first-rate military power on the basis of a third-rate economy. We see in the rhetoric of the leadership greater emphasis on international economic opportunities and threats. The long-term objective of becoming a predominant player in all spheres of international activity, of maintaining and expanding the influence of socialism (and eventually communism), are seen to require a significant restructuring of all aspects of the economy. This, in turn carries significant implications for short-term foreign policy. In particular, the emphasis seems to have become threefold: (i) to buy time, (ii) to gain political support for the reformist leadership and (iii) to release and/or acquire resources for *perestroika*.

First, there is a need for a breathing space, a period during which the full attention of the central authorities might be focused on addressing economic problems and the challenge of *perestroika*. This would also be a period during which pressure on the economy could be reduced by *lessening the burdens of empire and superpower status*, thereby allowing the slack necessary for successful economic reform. Second, the reduction of international tensions, and the diminishing of the perceived threat of war, lends the stature of successful statesmanship to the reformist leadership, in particular Gorbachev, enhancing their ability to achieve and maintain political and popular support for the necessary changes. Finally, we see a number of policies that enhance the resource base for *ekonomicheskaia perestroika*. The new thinking on defense policy allows the burden of defense to be reduced as fewer resources are needed to maintain reasonable sufficiency. Furthermore, the new thinking places greater stress on *economic threats* to national well-being through stiff competition, thereby legitimizing a shift of resources. The increased emphasis on arms control further reduces the military threat and allows the avoidance of new resource commitment to defense. It also implies less support for world revolutionary movements and a greater emphasis on socialist integration into the world economy. Economic support of client states can be reduced, saving resources for perestroika as they turn instead to the world economy for trade and finance.

ECONOMIC POLICIES

As noted above, the overall objective is a wide-ranging economic modernization with its attendant payoff in terms of power, respect and participation in the world. Though modernization always has been a Soviet economic objective, it is now understood somewhat differently. Rather than viewing economic development on the basis of material output levels, modernization today is seen as a process that includes the creation of a modern social structure, much like that of advanced Western economies. Consequently there has been a growing emphasis on *reform* in policy discussions, and a diminishing emphasis on the acceleration in rates of growth that dominated Gorbachev's first two years. Acceleration of growth and physical restructuring, the old standby of previous reforms, remain a critical part of the program nonetheless.

A central policy change has been the restructuring of investment, with an emphasis on renovation and reequipment of existing capacities and capital rather than on new construction. It includes introducing modem technologies and altering the sectoral structure of capital, with particular emphasis on the machine tool, engineering, and high technology branches. A new priority has been assigned to housing construction.

Another key aspect of Gorbachev's restructuring effort is the hardy perennial of administrative reorganization. A number of new central coordinating organs have been created to administer six major economic complexes. A new form of "socialist corporation," the state association (*gosob"edinenie*), was temporarily created, while old forms are now marked for abolition. The ministerial structure is being streamlined together with the staffs of most central planning and economic administrative organs.

Beyond this, however, ideas of true economic reform are becoming increasingly central to *perestroika*. They are increasingly radical in formulation, yet still subject to significant watering-down during implementation. Thus far, there have been two waves of radical reform. The first, the reform of the state productive sector in June 1987, was followed by a period of bureaucratic retrenchment from July 1987 to February 1988, reflected in its implementing decrees. The second, a more radical and privatizing reform of June 1988 is still unfolding. Both of these waves of radicalization followed an initial period of more traditional measures, extending the reforms and economic experiments of preceding periods. It must be emphasized that all of these aspects of *ekonomicheskaia perestroika* are highly conducive to economic disruption, require time to implement and work out, and require new resource inputs if they are to be implemented smoothly. Here is where the foreign policy changes, in particular a striving for greater interaction with the world economy, become critically important.

This development of radical economic reform as the core of the new economic policies can be seen in the specifics of the major thrust of Gorbachev's economic policies as they have evolved since mid-1985. The first major direction, beyond physical restructuring, was a crackdown on antisocial behavior, in particular drinking, absenteeism, sloth on the job and unearned incomes. This comprised the first step in the major campaign to mobilize the "human factor," stressing discipline, individual responsibility and reward only for final results.

The second major direction, also associated with mobilizing the human factor, involved administrative decentralization and a massive shakeup of the economic bureaucracy. It consisted of ongoing reorganizations and dismissals, some democratization of decision-making processes, and their opening up to greater public scrutiny and criticism *(glasnost')*. It also included the introduction of financial accountability for decisions, and a significant reallocation of economic rights and responsibilities that accompanied the first wave of radical reform revolving around the Law on the State Enterprise, including the replacement of bureaucratic procedures with economic criteria. Furthermore central economic organs were to relinquish operational responsibility for economic outcomes to production organizations (enterprises and associations) and local governments were to assume greater rights and responsibilities for economic activity in their regions.

The third major direction of emphasis, again associated with mobilizing the human factor, revolved around improving individual, as opposed to organizational, incentives for proper economic performance. This was also enshrined in the Law on the State Enterprise and its supporting documents and discussion. Henceforth monetary reward and income were to be tied to the measured *value* of economic outcomes, individually where possible and collectively where not. In addition, social and communal services were now to be far more dependent on the economic success of enterprises in the area, thus tying the welfare of workers more closely to economic performance. To make the reward for economic activity more meaningful, central emphasis was placed on increasing the output and quality of consumer goods and services, especially quality of food and housing availability. To improve the availability of consumer services, traditionally the weakest sector of the Soviet economy, a new stress was placed on for-payment services and the revival of a mass cooperative movement in that area. In addition, very small-scale private enterprise was legalized with a law on individual labor activity that allowed individual pursuit of economic activity for profit after work, or by those legally exempt from work in the state sector. Finally, an emphasis was placed on using enterprise and personal savings to support the production of goods and services to meet consumers' needs. Taken together, these measures might be described as Soviet "supply side economics": administrative decentralization coupled with a broad mobilization of individual, and even private, initiative (i.e., the human factor).

Part two of Soviet supply side economics, *à la* Gorbachev, comprised a radical reform of the state economic mechanism. It represents a conscious effort to replace the Stalinist "mechanism of waste" *(zatratnyi mekhanism)* with a more flexible, economically motivated way of organizing and controlling economic activity. The primary objective of this reform was to increase enterprise autonomy in both planning and plan implementation, and to increase enterprise responsibility, both financial and legal, for final results—that is, for the value, usefulness and quality of its product or service. To that end, five basic principles were proclaimed: (i) self-management, (ii) self-planning, (iii) self-financing, (iv) contractual pricing and (v) wholesale trade of producers' goods. The first three were to guarantee the independence and responsibility of the enterprise for its own results. The latter two were to make true exercise of that independence and responsibility possible. They provide the foundation for the creation of genuine socialist markets by replacing the detailed coordination of the preceding administrative allocation of resources. Socialist enterprises are to maneuver within these markets in the pursuit of customer satisfaction, new opportunities, quality and innovation, and setting prices through mutually beneficial contractual agreements. Further these principles are extended to international economic interaction, allowing enterprises, in principle, to develop their own foreign markets, thereby somewhat decentralizing foreign economic policy.

The success of such enterprise autonomy is supposed to reduce the need for detailed central planning and controls. Thus ministries are conceived under the reform as staffs, rather than the command centers, of their respective branches of the economy, and the number and scope of central planning instruments and directives are to be strictly limited. Indeed, all operational plans are to be drawn up by the enterprises themselves, subject to only four types of central economic instruments: state orders, ceilings, control figures and economic normatives (*ekonomicheskie normativy*). Only state orders and limits resemble the preceding command plans, and their role is to shrink until they cover less than a third of the value of economic output in the 1990s. Control figures are shifted from mandatory planning guidelines and constraints to indicative guidelines and measures of efficiency against which performance can be judged. Finally, economic normatives form the heart of the new, more flexible mechanism of central guidance and control. They essentially comprise tax, financial allocation and pricing/valuation parameters that can be used to steer profit-maximizing socialist state enterprises toward socially desirable decisions. They are intended to replace the need to command administratively particular economic performances: enterprises should now find socially desirable activity profitable. Through manipulating these instruments the central authorities hope to maintain control over the overall direction and aggregate structure of economic activity and development. In priority areas, direct physical control will be maintained through state orders and limits, but most of the details of planning and carrying out economic activity are to be devolved to more autonomous state enterprises interacting in the pursuit of profit largely within socialist markets.

Finally, this stage of the reform brought with it the need for massive reform of the monetary, banking and credit systems aimed at placing financial decisions on a solid economic basis, rather than on highly politicized criteria of plan implementation. The most crucial step in this process is the creation of a true money, both necessary and sufficient for any transaction, that would then allow financial measurement, verification and control of the value of any economic activity. The development of such necessary preliminary commodity convertibility of money is a precursor to the eventual foreign currency convertibility that is required as a foundation for significant foreign economic interaction. Once a stable, real currency is established, then the way is open to true price reform, a topic much discussed but far from decided at this stage of the reform. Yet, as many have argued, without true, far-reaching price reform, this attempt at radical reform of the state economic mechanism faces insurmountable obstacles.

The key idea behind this first wave of truly radical reform was to give operational economic organizations, especially enterprises, the authority, information, incentives and access to material means to act properly in the central (i.e., social and economic) interests. That is, they should be able to act autonomously without jeopardizing central control over important actions and changes. In particular, the reform foresaw the unification, through appropriate economic measures, of the incentives of economic agents with those of society as represented by the central authorities. This was to achieve a combination of efficiency, innovation and quality of performance, while still pursuing centrally planned general objectives.

The third wave of Gorbachev's economic reforms took a further significant step in the direction of radicalization. Building on the incentive-enhancing measures of the first stage, it opens the door to the possibility of a significant, if still minority, *privatization* of Soviet economic activity in the form of producer and seller cooperatives. The legitimate scope of non-state economic activity was dramatically expanded by the Law on Cooperation which took effect in July 1988 after the 19th Party Conference, the crest of the second wave of radicalization of Gorbachev's reforms. This law allows the organization of producer and seller cooperatives with the same formal rights as state enterprises yet significantly greater autonomy. They can own productive property, engage in any form of legal economic activity, and must be accepted as legitimate and treated as equals by state authorities. They are to operate entirely on markets largely of their own creation, without the support of the state planning and allocation systems. They can, however, accept work from and for state organizations on a contractual basis, essentially accepting a subcontract to implement part of that organization's plan.

The third stage of supply-side reforms provides a natural complement to and extension of the first two. First, it is a bold step to rescue *perestroika* for consumers, who have watched their situation deteriorate in the last several years. It dramatically extends the scope and scale of cooperatives and individual entrepreneurs to provide consumer goods and services, and hence promises to improve incentives to earn income. Further, it is hoped that the extension of cooperative activity will increase competition in consumer markets, increasing supplies and thereby holding down prices and giving workers some economic reason to support reform and to work harder and more creatively. The second potential contribution of enhanced cooperative activity is to allow the socialist markets created in the second stage to become truly operational. For any kind of market to begin to function properly there must be some alternatives for both suppliers and demanders. Soviet industry, like that of the other socialist economies, is far more monopolized than that of any real market economy. Thus, granting socialist enterprises autonomy within the current Soviet industrial structure naturally leads to dramatic price increases, and assortment and quality restrictions. The creation of industrial cooperatives might counteract this by introducing some real competition, and substituting market discipline for traditional administrative discipline. It should stimulate lower prices, innovation and the maintenance of quality by providing an alternative source of supply at the margin. Furthermore, this competition can provide a basis for the price reform so essential to the proper functioning of the State Enterprise Law, thus allowing the devolution of planning and allocation to enterprises operating on markets. This would finally allow the central authorities to concentrate on strategic tasks, without worrying about the micromanagement of production and trade activity.

Parallel to these increasingly radical internal reforms has been an equally dramatic policy of turning to the outside world. Despite early reservations about dependence on the rest of the world to solve Soviet economic problems, this has become an essential and growing part of Gorbachev's strategy of *perestroika*. It has involved an emphasis on greater trade, together with a thorough restructuring of foreign trade organizations and access rights, export promotion and participation with foreign firms in joint ventures. In addition, there is growing discussion of participation in international economic organizations, with some exploratory steps already taken, and of borrowing from Western sources to finance the investment and capital restructuring plans of *perestroika*. All of these represent a departure from previous attitudes and practice, but none more so than the increasingly liberal joint venture legislation. For the first time since the 1920s, capitalist firms are allowed to own and manage productive capital and directly sell for a profit within the Soviet Union. Moreover, in order to encourage the initially hesitant Western response, the joint venture law has been steadily modified, now even allowing majority ownership by the capitalist partner.

All of these foreign economic measures are aimed at providing critical support for *ekonomicheskaia perestroika*. First, they open the world economy as a source for technology, managerial know-how and capital. But perhaps more important is the role that expanded trade and joint ventures can play in meeting consumer needs and providing the competition needed to set domestic markets in operation. Turning to the world economy is an extension of, or perhaps a substitution for, the third stage of domestic reform—the introduction of an active non-state (i.e., cooperative and private) production sector. It is a further source of private initiative, production and capital. Finally, this attempt to increase interaction with the world economy is perceived as desirable in its own right. It allows the Soviet Union to seek the role that the Soviet leadership believes it deserves to play in the international economic arena—a role commensurate with its importance and potential economic strength.

These policies and reforms have been implemented, more or less consistently, in a flurry of laws, decrees and documents beginning with the 27th Party Congress in February 1986. They reached an early peak of radicalization at the June 1987 party plenum, and then became noticeably more conservative during almost a year of retrenchment. Indeed, following the passage of 11 rather conservative implementing decrees in July 1987, the primary focus of *perestroika* seemed to shift from the economic to the political and social spheres. As the State Enterprise Law began to be implemented, the main emphasis shifted to *glasnost'* and democratization, resulting in the significant political changes of the June 1988 19th Party Conference and the succeeding party plenums and Supreme Soviet sessions. However, the third stage of radical economic reform was under discussion, bursting forth in late May as the Law on Cooperation. What has been the impact of all this? How is restructuring faring to date?

ECONOMIC PERFORMANCE

With respect to the results of reform, as opposed to the development of the reform process, *ekonomicheskaia perestroika* has been doing quite poorly. Indeed this was the overwhelming message Gorbachev received during his postvacation visit to the Krasnoiarsk region in September 1988. Consumers have systematically suffered, and changes introduced in the economic mechanisms have systematically disrupted regular channels and the flow of economic activity; the changes have also created confusion about rights and responsibilities. This has stymied initiative and reinforced bureaucratic conservatism, leading to a broad general deterioration in aggregate economic performance. This is clearly seen in the growth statistics calculated by the CIA. . . .

Further, there has been no improvement in quality, despite the strong central priority it has been given, which is reflected in the introduction of a government bureau of State Acceptance (*Gospriemka*) of industrial products (i.e., quality control by outside inspectors). The assortment and supply of industrial inputs has also shown no improvement, though there is a growing degree of fulfillment of contract specifications. That, however, has been achieved in good part due to reducing the detail and requirements specified in contracts. In addition, the economy has shown an inability to absorb the ambitious investments planned for this period, leading to delays in capacity renovation and expansion, and a continuing rapid rise in unfinished construction. In particular, the modernization of the key machine-building sectors is seriously lagging. There has been virtually no change in the actual structure of investment and capital construction, and hence no prospect of change in the productive structure of the economy as envisioned by Gorbachev's program. Finally, signs of the diminishing impact of the "human factor" campaign (i.e., incentives and discipline) are beginning to appear in both slowing productivity growth and in the complaints of consumers and workers.

Even more disappointing than this lack of physical progress, however, has been the lack of progress in implementing the measures that constitute radical economic reform. The reform is still largely on paper, supported in words but not by actions, even where it has supposedly been fully introduced. Though it is still too early to talk about the impact of the second, privatizing wave of radical reform, the State Enterprise Law has been largely stillborn. Detailed plans were still imposed from above in 1988 through the new "economic levers," in particular state orders and limits. Self-financing remains an accident, arbitrarily determined by capricious decisions of superiors about normatives (*ekonomieheskie normativy*) and the totally irrational pricing and valuation systems. Further, the same normative, price and valuation systems provide perverse incentives with respect to quality, efficiency and innovation. Indeed, they force a return to administrative measures and detailed centralized planning, in order to counteract the force of this *zatratnyi mekhanism.* As a result, wholesale trade has remained administrative allocation, or rationing by another name. And finally, cooperatives and individual labor activities have been strangled by excessive taxation and bureaucratic opposition. Their failure to develop into instruments furthering and enhancing *perestroika* was an important factor in the further radicalization of the reforms through the Law on Cooperation.

This situation naturally raises the question as to why economic performance under *perestroika* should be so poor. On one level, however, it should not surprise us at all. This is just the beginning of what promises to be an extended period of major economic change, and "aller Anfang ist schwer!" Any economic changes, in any system or society, take time before they begin to have the intended impact. Some disruption is inevitable in any major operative change in an economy. Therefore, we should not be surprised by an initial deterioration in performance; indeed it may just signal that real change is taking place. However, such a conclusion here may be too facile, as there seem to be two deeper problems affecting performance.

First, it is now clear even to Soviet economists, and increasingly, it seems, to Gorbachev, that the Soviets are attempting too much at once. As Gorbachev's advisor Leonid Abalkin noted in his speech before the 19th Party Conference, a choice must be made between acceleration and restructuring, between short-term growth and long-term modernization of the economic mechanism. An economy cannot increase the growth of output while totally rearranging the nature and structure of its economic activities. Indeed it must find a way to save or borrow resources both to maintain the standard of living during the inevitable disruption of restructuring and to invest in that restructuring of organizational and productive capital. Here is where foreign policy becomes important, perhaps critical, to the success of *ekonomicheskaia perestroika*. It is a crucial potential source of capital, technology, and organizational and economic knowhow (i.e. of additional resources for restructuring and modernization).

An even deeper problem, and one that we can only touch on in passing here, is that the reform itself is inconsistent, both internally and with economic logic, and hence is unlikely to improve the situation, at least as it is currently conceived. It must become much more radical in conception, much more willing to accommodate diversity, experimentation, and change, in order to provide a consistent framework within which economic agents can pursue social welfare through the pursuit of their own financial benefit. For agents to face the uncertainties associated with innovation, the potential benefits must compensate for the expected costs, despite the fact that a lion's share of innovation must inevitably fail as an undesirable change. To make even approximately rational economic decisions, the prices faced (including those of capital and productive operations) must truly reflect value, and this requires real, living competition with free choice of activity and pricing.

Thus, the reform will have to go much further in stimulating effective competition, in liberalizing price setting, choice of activity or business, and, indeed, privatization and property rights. A first step in this direction must include much more severe restrictions on the rights and responsibilities of central authorities. Only such radicalization of *perestroika* can begin to yield the flexibility, innovativeness and efficiency, characteristic of modern market economies, that is the proclaimed goal of *ekonomicheskaia perestroika.*

THE FOREIGN POLICY TRUMP

Though the task of reforming the Soviet economic system in the pursuit of long-term political and social goals is extremely difficult, it is by no means hopeless. Recent developments have already indicated a growing radicalization of *perestroika*, including its economic component. Indeed the Law on Cooperation and the lowering of taxes on individual labor as well as cooperative activity amounts to a first step toward the kind of liberalization and privatization that seems to be required. In addition, the kinds of foreign economic policies evolving under Gorbachev can help in both of the problem areas noted above.

Increased trade and international economic interaction can provide useful support for the process of reform proper. First, importing consumer goods can both resolve critical shortages and absorb excess liquidity, allowing a stabilization of the currency and proper price reform. Somewhat more slowly, but perhaps more fundamentally, the same result can be achieved by importing consumer goods capital and technology from the West, generating a rapid expansion of consumer goods production and quality internally. The latter seems to be the preferred approach, though the former has some support among Soviet economists. International trade can also place useful competitive pressure on Soviet enterprises, giving teeth to self-financing, stimulating innovation and the improvement of both quality and assortment. In doing so, it also provides useful signals for proper pricing and valuation of activities and outputs. Finally, interaction with foreign firms, and in particular participation in joint ventures, can impart useful information, both directly and by example, on modern management and business techniques and on how to survive and thrive in markets. This is particularly important for preparing Soviet managers to operate in the intended new economic system.

The foreign policy arena is also important for generating resources to support the physical side of restructuring and modernization. The pursuit of arms control, the reduction of tensions and increased international cooperation permit the release of high-quality resources from the defense/military sectors. These sectors have always had a first priority claim to the best of labor, machines and materials, resources that might now be turned to the urgent tasks of modernizing the bulk of the economy. The policies of stepping back from the pursuit of empire building and maintenance, the reduction of the subsidies to client states, the lessening of support for national liberation movements and the withdrawal from the Afghan adventure, all further release resources that might be profitably applied to *perestroika*.

In addition, the Soviet Union has begun to ask more of Eastern Europe and other closely-tied clients in return for subsidies and political support. In particular, they are being asked to raise the quality of machinery, equipment and technology that they supply to the Soviet Union within the Council for Mutual Economic Assistance (COMECON) framework. Last, but far from least, Soviet foreign policy initiatives have been aimed at attracting resources and technology from the developed West. Such resources will come from opening Western product markets to Soviet exports, tapping Western credit markets and perhaps international economic organizations, and drawing in resources through joint ventures. Efforts in this last area are accelerating because the pace of the alternatives (i.e., internal change, arms negotiations and the Afghan withdrawal) is so slow, delaying internally generated resource augmentation. Indeed, those efforts were crowned with some substantial success by the end of September 1988.

It is these possibilities, some of which are beginning to be realized, that provide substantial motivation for some of the changes we see in Soviet foreign policy under Gorbachev's new thinking. While they clearly do not come near to a full explanation of those changes, they do indicate a natural connection between *ekonomicheskaia perestroika* and the developments in Soviet foreign policy. They provide an economic rationale for some of the short-term maneuvering that we see on the international arena in the pursuit of basic Soviet long-term policy objectives.

31

Saving the Environment: The Shrinking Realm of *Laissez-Faire*

RICHARD ABLIN

This reading presents a Liberal economist's justification of government intervention to alleviate environmental problems. While markets are appropriate mechanisms to allocate resources in general, resources whose pricing is difficult or impossible must be allocated in some other way. Clean air and a healthy environment, are, Ablin argues, goods that cannot easily be priced (and thus traded) by private entrepreneurs. Therefore, Ablin believes that only government action can counteract the trend toward destruction of the natural environment.

The range of relevance of the classic liberal prescription of *laissez-faire* economics introduced by Adam Smith, and powerfully revived in the last generation by Milton Friedman (and the Chicago school), has been shrinking at a growing rate in recent years.

The idea that private interest, operating within unfettered markets, will tend to produce a close approximation of the socially optimal allocation of resources, was close to the truth when output (population, too) was so much smaller. The social costs involved in the private use of collective unpriced resources (e.g., air, water, highways) were smaller too.

Such costs, however, are an inherently rising proportion of conventionally measured GDP. Social costs *seem* to rise exponentially, and within a very few years various components jump from the barely noticeable to the hardly bearable. Basically, this expresses the law of diminishing returns (i.e., as more and more of

---

31 "Saving the Environment: The Shrinking Realm of *Laissez-Faire*" by Richard Ablin. Reprinted with permission of publisher, M. E. Sharpe, Inc., 80 Business Park Drive, Armonk, N.Y. 10504 USA, from the March/April 1989 issue of *Challenge*.

a variable factor is added to a "fixed" factor of production, the net addition to output becomes smaller and smaller).

In economic theory, agricultural land was the model of a fixed factor. But land was at least divisible into parcels, and therefore easily "priced" by the market according to the value of its alternative uses. The fixed capacities of air and water (rivers, lakes, seas) for waste absorption play a similar role. For a long time after growth begins, these are so large that their growing exploitation, even with zero pricing, hardly creates a cost in the degradation of alternative uses.

At a certain point, however, these resources cease to be "free goods." Pricing is then called for to economize their use properly, but, for several reasons— mainly the indivisibility of inputs or outputs—pricing cannot spring up naturally under laissez faire. The result is an accelerating degradation of alternative uses, essentially those which—like drinking, swimming, and breathable air—do not inflict external costs.

Roads and city streets present such a problem. Starting with few cars and a small population, a city's congestion costs are minimal. But, eventually congestion leaps up, with vehicle proliferation and excessive building density, into a massive blight to the quality of urban life.

The items mentioned so far have received greatly increased attention in the last several years. This is all to the good, but it will not be widely disputed if we say that, so far, little more has been done than to slow down the rise of external costs relative to measured income and GDP.

Thus, while a few advanced cities have actually cut congestion by means of massive investment in highways and railways, as well as in some degree of decentralization, dozens of formerly pleasant—even charming—other cities are rapidly suffocating themselves in the course of a development process, as devoid of effective collective control of external costs as were those of their predecessors. "Learn nothing from the experience of others" seems to be the motto of most cities worldwide.

Until perhaps the past decade, pollution and congestion were still, at least to our comprehension, mainly local problems, and extreme "marketeers" could still point to the possibility of long-term correction of such problems by means of geographic shifts (decentralization and the like).

A NEW AWARENESS

In the past decade, however, we have become more and more aware of the environmental sickness spreading over national or even continental borders: acid rain and the deterioration of forests and lakes, the pollution of the sea, and the ominous international effects of deforestation in Africa, Asia, and South America.

Finally, during the record hot summer of 1988, we began to consider seriously the warning, long murmured, but certainly not shouted, that the recent uptrend in average world temperature probably reflects a growing "greenhouse effect" from the ever-rising proportion of carbon dioxide ($C0_2$) in the earth's atmosphere. It was always a rather simple scientific problem to calculate the effect of rising levels of $C0_2$ per se, but scientists had not reached unanimity on the net heating likely to occur, due to uncertainty about possible side effects (e.g., a reduction of cloud cover would tend to offset rising $C0_2$).

The easy-going attitude of governments to the need for research to clear up uncertainties about a danger of such vast proportions (as well as virtually every official plan for future energy development) clearly reveals that—until 1988—the mild warnings had not penetrated.

Let us assume here that the diagnosis of a rising net greenhouse effect is certain (rather than probable), and consider the implications for a moment. They are not small.

Our entire industrial civilization has been supported by nonhuman, nonanimal energy produced overwhelmingly through the burning of fossil fuels. Apparently such a civilization, getting under way in a single country (England) about 200 years ago, could go on growing and spreading for upwards of 175 years, continuously dumping more and more $C0_2$ into the world's fixed stock of air, without producing a very noticeable cost with respect to this effect.

But it now appears quite possible that, in the past 10 to 20 years, this effect already contributed greatly to the horrendous problem of increasingly chronic droughts in the Sahal. Deforestation practiced in these regions and elsewhere also may have contributed. (Moreover, there is an interaction; deforestation has directly increased the greenhouse effect worldwide, since $C0_2$ levels are the net outcome of emissions from combustion and absorption in the photosynthesis of green plants.)

The absurdity of a civilization proliferating on this basis indefinitely is fairly obvious upon reflection. Consider that the presently advanced industrial world contains about 730 million inhabitants, with a per capita GDP of about $15,000. But this seemingly huge population constitutes only about one-seventh of the world's present population of 5 billion! On average, the other six-sevenths enjoy a per capita GDP of not much more than one-tenth of the industrial world.

Almost all of them, with strong encouragement from the rich nations and international organizations, are striving to emulate the advanced countries. But even if we project a continuing downtrend in energy use/GDP (a characteristic of the years since the 1973 oil crisis), it is obvious that their successful achievement of this objective would (using present energy sources) increase annual $C0_2$ emissions fivefold—and this in addition to the constant rise of $C0_2$ from current levels of emission. Global hot house indeed!

NO TIME TO LOSE

It becomes obvious therefore that we must not only prevent an acceleration of the greenhouse effect, but must virtually halt its present rise. Moreover, there is no time to lose, certainly not until scientific imprecision has been reduced to insignificance. This follows from the ominous warning of scientists that "the thermal inertia of the seas delays the warming itself by several decades," which means that if we could stop the rise in the proportion of ''greenhouse gases'' in the atmosphere today, average world temperature would still go on rising (at a slowing rate) for 20 to 30 years.

To actually stabilize world temperature before then we must do even better than this! Such a project must involve the following: (a) a drastic revision of energy production, with solar and nuclear power the most acceptable candidates for support (provided we can solve the problem of nuclear waste); (b) a vast reforestation campaign worldwide, including payments by the rich countries to rapidly reverse the ongoing destruction of tropical forests. The alternative is a drastic slowdown, or even reversal, of worldwide GDP growth.

It appears then that we may be confronting the ultimate social cost, one from which there is no geographical escape. Governments, and concerned citizens, should urgently begin to concentrate minds on how to implement (a) and (b); the rapid phasing out of fossil fuels, and reforestation.

INDEX

F

N

O

Q

R